D0908159

OXFORD STUDIES IN
SOCIAL AND LEGAL HISTORY

OXFORD STUDIES IN SOCIAL AND LEGAL HISTORY

EDITED BY

SIR PAUL VINOGRADOFF

M.A., D.C.L., LL.D., Dr. Hist., Dr. Jur., F.B.A.

CORPUS PROFESSOR OF JURISPRUDENCE IN THE UNIVERSITY OF OXFORD

VOL. VI

XI. STUDIES IN THE HUNDRED ROLLS
SOME ASPECTS OF THIRTEENTH-CENTURY
ADMINISTRATION

By HELEN M. CAM, M.A.

XII. PROCEEDINGS AGAINST THE CROWN (1216-1377)

By LUDWIK EHRLICH, B.Litt., D.Jur.

OCTAGON BOOKS

A DIVISION OF FARRAR, STRAUS AND GIROUX

New York   1974

Originally published in 1921 by the Clarendon Press

Reprinted 1974
by special arrangement with Oxford University Press, Inc.

OCTAGON BOOKS
A DIVISION OF FARRAR, STRAUS & GIROUX, INC.
19 Union Square West
New York, N. Y. 10003

Library of Congress Cataloging in Publication Data

Cam, Helen Maud, 1885-1968.
   Studies in the hundred rolls some aspects of thirteenth-century
   administration.

   Reprint of the 1921 editions published by the Clarendon Press,
   Oxford, which were issued as v. 6, no. 11-12 of Oxford studies in
   social and legal history.

      1. The Hundred rolls.   2. Great Britain—Politics and govern-
   ment.   3. Prerogative, Royal—Great Britain.   4. Great Britain
   —Kings and rulers.   I. Ehrlich, Ludwik, 1889-   Proceedings
   against the crown (1216-1377) 1974.   II. Title.   III. Title: Proceedings against the crown (1216-1377)   IV. Series: Oxford
   studies in social and legal history, v. 6, no. 11-12.
JS3041.C32   1974   320.9′42′03   73-22295
ISBN 0-374-96165-4

Printed in USA by
Thomson-Shore, Inc.
Dexter, Michigan

PREFACE

THE two monographs of the present volume are closely connected : they illustrate the two aspects of the Constitutional development of England in the thirteenth and fourteenth centuries. The inquests as to misdoings of officers and encroachments on public rights show the insistence of the Crown in its efforts to keep order and to suppress administrative abuses. But this very insistence was a source of hardship and gave rise to constant grievances, because the King and his ministers were apt to brush away established customs and to exert arbitrary despotism on the pretext of enforcing discipline and serving the interests of the Community. A strong opposition to such high-handed acts was manifested on many occasions, and found an appropriate basis in the juridical conceptions and traditions of feudal society—a society which looked upon convention and custom as the ruling principles of the law. Dr. Ehrlich traces the influence of this peculiar legalism in the early history of Proceedings against the Crown, and shows that the contradictory statements of Bracton's treatise are connected with different tendencies in the actual practice of the law.

I have had occasion to express the opinion [1] that it is impossible to reconstruct the course of legal evolution in the thirteenth and fourteenth centuries on the line of a gradual development of a single principle—either that of Royal authority or that

[1] In my article on Magna Carta, cl. 39.

of civic rights. We witness in those days a constant struggle between various currents of political thought. In a sense the Crown was indeed the agent of great judicial reforms and the centre of a progress in the direction of a unified State. But the feudal elements —the Barons, the Knights, the Church, the towns— cannot be regarded as striving only for selfish interests and reactionary privileges. In so far as their claims were directed towards the maintenance of legal and customary rights, they presented a powerful counterpoise to the arbitrary propensities of Royal power. Altogether the notion that appeals to feudal ideas were necessarily *reactionary* [1] seems to be misleading in so far as it introduces modern terms and standards into mediaeval controversies.

I should like to illustrate my meaning by one or two examples.

The report of the great trial of the King *v.* the Earls of Gloucester and Hereford (Rot. Parl. 20 Ed. I, n. 1, pp. 70 ff.) contains emphatic assertions of the superior authority of the Crown in cases when the welfare of the Community is concerned. The Commissioners appointed to investigate the facts of the private war between the two earls tried to obtain statements on oath from John of Hastings, Roger Mortimer, and a number of other Barons holding estates in the March of Wales, but these magnates refused on the ground that it was not the custom to exact oaths from them and that no judicial Commission of this kind had ever been known in that part of the country. The Commissioners tried to

---

[1] See, for example, Prof. Tait's review of the Magna Carta commemoration volume in *The Eng. Hist. Rev.* xxxiii (1918), pp. 262 f.

explain that ' when the Commonwealth is concerned (*pro utilitate communi*) the King in virtue of his prerogative stands in many cases above the law and the customs used in his Realm '. But the Barons refused to swear on the Gospel proffered to them, and declared that they would not do anything of the kind without the award of their peers (*sine consideratione parium suorum*). The conjunction between the appeal to customary law and the pronouncement of peers is characteristic of the period which follows in the track of the Great Charter. The complaint of *voluntas* — arbitrary treatment — is one of the standing grievances in the reigns of Henry III and Edward I. The Abbot of Westminster complained of *voluntas*, because Royal Justices had cited him to their Court without any formal writ, and as a Baron of the King he challenged their jurisdiction. The Court which eventually decided the case in favour of the Abbot was the King in Council, seemingly in a full Parliament Session afforced by Magnates.[1] In 1290 Margery [2] the wife of Thomas of Weyland, the Chief Justice, who had been found guilty of felony by the inquest of 1289, petitioned the King for redress because a manor in which Thomas had only a life interest had been seized by the King ' for year and waste'. This was a case of *voluntas* if Margery's contention that the fee was in her and her son Richard was right. The intricate questions of law arising from this petition were discussed in a Parliamentary Session of the Council in which all the Justices participated. In the records of Henry III's time we find several instances in which the King

---

[1] Rot. Parl. I, 41.   Ibid., p. 66.

admits that he has acted *per voluntatem* and against the law. In the case concerning the seizure of the manor of Cottingham the tenant, Eustace d'Estuteville, is reinstated in possession in order to be impleaded *secundum legem terrae*.[1] The outlawry of Hubert de Burgh and his release by the Earl Marshal gave rise to several cases in which the arbitrary measures of Henry were reversed. In one of these cases mentioned in the *Notebook of Bracton* the refusal to the adherents of the Earl of a trial by their peers is mentioned conspicuously among the illegalities committed by the King during Peter des Roches' ascendancy.[2]

The combination between trial by peers and process according to the law of the land was not an absolute one, in so far as the trial by peers could be pleaded as a privilege in contrast with the ordinary course of justice before the King's Court. Only the most powerful people could insist on such a claim, and even they did not always succeed in enforcing it in such an extreme form. But compromises were possible by introducing feudal or popular elements as integral parts of the Royal tribunals. In the case of the higher tenants this was effected by the afforcement of the Court mentioned in many complicated trials. In the litigation about the succession to the Earldom of Chester it is expressly stated on two occasions that the claims of the parties were brought before meetings of the Magnates. The latter were not able to come to any decision in the first case.[3] On a later occasion they refused to make an award, because they considered that there were too few

---

[1] *Notebook*, 1106.   [2] Ibid., 857.   [3] Ibid., 1227.

assessors present.[1] These two examples show that there was no necessary opposition between the demand to be judged by the ' law of the land ' and the demand for a trial by peers : the two claims were usually combined. From the point of view of the representatives of the military aristocracy the best way to ascertain and to maintain the law of the land was to entrust the decisions to the peers of the parties. Maitland's view that the *vel* in cl. 39 of the Great Charter was used conjunctively[2] as well as disjunctively is sufficient to explain the tendency of the enactment as regards the higher tenants. In practice the King's Bench was commonly enlarged in such a way as to represent a curia of great vassals.

In the case of the lower freemen, who were also included in the provision of cl. 39 by the expression *nullus liber homo*, the principle was not so definitely put into practice. But in their case the element of trial by one's own peers was traced to the dooms of the County Courts and to the verdicts of juries.[3]

The monarchical and the aristocratic elements of mediaeval life were engaged in a constant struggle for supremacy, and their conflicts have given rise to many a dramatic incident. But it would be impossible to account for the development of the English Constitution and of Common Law without taking stock of their co-operation.

It would be impossible to summarize in a few pages the particular results of the monographs we are submitting to the readers. I should like, however, to point at least to one characteristic example

[1] *Notebook*, 1273.   [2] *Hist. of Eng. Law*, I. 173.
[3] Cf. Magna Carta Commemoration Essays, p. 92.

of Miss Cam's investigations. Students of English
legal institutions have been much puzzled by the
use and the meaning of records termed *Rotuli de
Ragemannis* or *Rotuli Ragemannorum,* and the like.
At the same time the collection of Statutes contains
an ordinance or act entered under the year 1276
which is commonly styled Statute of Ragman, but
whose title in the manuscript runs—*de iusticiis
assignatis.* What places do these documents refer
to, and what is the connexion between the Rolls and
the Ordinance ? Miss Cam proves conclusively, as
it seems to me, that the Ragman Records in question
were the so-called Hundred Rolls of 1274–9, and
that the Statute of Ragman was an instruction issued
to justices in eyre empowering them to try cases on
the strength of the presentments contained in the
Hundred Rolls. Copies of these Ragman records
were delivered to them for this purpose. A plausible
explanation of the term itself is derived from the
fact that the presentments collected in the Hundred
Rolls were drawn up on membranes sealed with the
seal of the jurors. These seals were attached by
bands of parchment cut out at the foot of the Roll
which became in consequence ragged. It is for
philologists to make out how the word 'ragman' or
'ragment' could arise with such a connotation, but
Miss Cam's suggestion will probably recommend
itself to record students. In any case the peculiar
position of the so-called Hundred Rolls in the midst
of records of Special Inquisitions is at last established
by her inquiry.

Dr. L. Ehrlich's essay traces the beginnings of
what is termed *Crown practice* nowadays. It supplies

the famous statements of Bracton on the relation between King and Law with a background in the course of actual administration.

The rule of law as understood in the thirteenth and fourteenth centuries proves to be by no means a dead letter, although it comes often into conflict with the Royal prerogative and there is a good deal of fluctuation in the apportionment of right to individuals as against the Crown. I should like to draw special attention to a number of cases—many of them unpublished—which throw light on the methods of asserting claims, e.g. the Hautboys case (pp. 110 f.), the Frannceys case (pp. 121 ff.), Kent v. Molyns (pp. 156 ff.), the Clifton case (pp. 124 ff.). A particularly interesting instance is presented by the proceedings in the case of the Men of St. Albans (pp. 113 f., cf. 146, App. 243 ff.). Henry III had granted by charter to the vill of St. Albans, that they should not implead or be impleaded by a writ of attaint, and this privilege was confirmed by Edward II and Edward III. However, in 1359 a case arose in which the plaintiff obtained a writ of attaint against an Assize which had pronounced a verdict against him. When the Charter of Henry III was produced in bar of the action, the question as to the legality of the privilege was raised and the Chancery called up the men of the vill to show cause why the charter should not be declared null and void. It was contended on behalf of the King that his predecessor had no power to grant a privilege in infringement of Common Law. Eventually the case was decided by the King's Council with the participation of judges. The decision is highly significant in form and substance. ' Et quia (manifeste) apparet quod carta predicta est legi communi contraria et si huiusmodi carte concederentur et in suo valore starent conquerentes a remedio iuris excluderentur, quod in exheredationem totius communitatis regni cederet, videtur iusticiis et aliis peritis de consilio Regis quod carta predicta est omnino revocanda et adnullanda, per quod consideratum est quod carta illa revocetur et adnulletur. (Et in) Cancellario cancelletur et dampnetur et perdat vim et rigorem imperpetuum ' (pp. 245, 246). Perhaps the most interesting feature of the process consists in the fact that the quashing of the Charter is demanded by a representative of the King and in the King's name. It is emphatically an appeal from Caesar to Caesar better informed. The case is conducted on judicial lines before the King's Council, while the Chancery is instrumental in introducing it and in carrying out the decision. Royal authority appears in this case as the champion of Common Law. In most of the other cases we have to deal with rights asserted against arbitrary acts of the King or of his officers.

PAUL VINOGRADOFF.

ERRATA

Page 4 (Contents).

Transfer sub-headings i, ii, of Chapter II, § 2, to Chapter III, § 2, and pages 143, 144 respectively.

page 19, l. 24. *for* Statute of Exeter *read* Statute of York.

page 20, n. 3 (corr. *et*) instead of *ut*.

page 36. *per potestatem* instead of *potestato*.

page 46, n. 7. *nomine* instead of *homine*.

page 62, ll. 5-3 from bottom. *Delete* unless . . . Westminster, *and read* although this is the first dated occurrence of the article *de advocaria habenda*.

page 92, n. 10. *denarios* instead of *denariis*.

page 98, n. 35. *pro minore pretio* instead of *minori*.

page 119. *comitatu predicto* instead of *predicta*.

page 173, l. 16. *for* Barons Gifford *read* Bowers Gifford.

XI

STUDIES IN THE HUNDRED ROLLS: SOME ASPECTS OF THIRTEENTH-CENTURY ADMINISTRATION

BY

HELEN M. CAM, M.A., F.R.Hist.S.

STAFF LECTURER IN HISTORY, THE ROYAL HOLLOWAY
COLLEGE, UNIVERSITY OF LONDON

CONTENTS

CONTENTS

ABBREVIATIONS

A. R.	=	Assize Rolls. [P. R. O.]
C. R. C.	=	Calendars of Close Rolls.
C. S.	=	Camden Society's publications.
E. H. S.	=	English Historical Society.
Ex. R.	=	Extract Hundred Rolls. [P. R. O.]
H. R.	=	Hundred Rolls. [P. R. O.]
[Hundred Rolls] C. H.	=	Chapter House Series. [P. R. O.]
[„] T.	=	Tower Series. [P. R. O.]
Mem. R. K. R.	=	Memoranda Rolls, King's Remembrancer Series. [P. R. O.]
„ L. T. R.	=	Memoranda Rolls, Lord Treasurer's Remembrancer Series. [P. R. O.]
P. R. C.	=	Calendars of Patent Rolls.
P. R. O.	=	Public Record Office.
R. H.	=	Rotuli Hundredorum (Record Commission Ed.).
Rot. Pat.	=	Patent Rolls. [P. R. O.]
R. S.	=	Rolls Series.
Rot. Cl.	=	Close Rolls. [P. R. O.]
S. R.	=	Statutes of the Realm.
S. S.	=	Selden Society's publications.

INTRODUCTION

THE following studies have, as it were, two foci of interest : the one an aspect of history, the other a set of records. The so-called Hundred Rolls of 1274–5 have in the past been regarded mainly from the standpoint of feudal history. To Stubbs and to most of those who followed him [1] their importance lay in the fact that they recorded the usurpations of feudal magnates—the growth of unwarranted franchises in the latter years of the reign of Henry III. The Inquest of 1274–5 was to these writers an early exemplification of the ' national ' policy of Edward I, the first campaign in his war on political feudalism. The Statute of Gloucester and the Quo Warranto proceedings were not only the natural consequences of the Inquest but the only consequences worth noting. The Hundred Rolls as a field of research have thus been practically monopolized by the students of feudal custom, of topography, and of genealogy.

But there are other aspects of the Inquest of 1274–5 and of its records. In the history of administration in England, which has yet to find its Stubbs and its Maitland, it takes a very different colour. On the one hand, it ceases to stand out as a unique act of royal policy. It falls into line with a long series of administrative inquests, stretching from the time of Henry II onwards, and its close kinship with the general eyre, that most effective instrument of the supervision exercised by the central over the local administration, becomes evident. On the other hand, the double aspect of the inquest as a vindication of royal rights not only against the king's vassals but against his own servants becomes clear ; the Statutes of Westminster I, of the Exchequer and of Rageman are seen to be no less closely related to it than the Statute of Gloucester, and the evidence of the Hundred Rolls with regard to non-feudal local administration is seen

[1] Sir J. Ramsay (The Dawn of the Constitution, p. 327) must be excepted.

to be as worthy of investigation as that which they afford on franchises.

The following pages are to be regarded as merely the beginnings of such an investigation. In the first chapter an attempt is made to set the inquest of 1274–5 in its true perspective against the background of English administrative history by an examination of the evolution of the articles of the eyre, the history of which is so closely connected with that of the articles of 1274 that neither can be understood in isolation. It will be found that this exposition does not depart, to any marked extent, from the accepted view of the history of the eyre, with the exception of the significance attributed to the Statute of Rageman, in connexion with which, it is believed, some new facts of importance have been brought to light. In the second chapter the procedure and the records of the inquests are analysed ; a necessary preliminary to their use for statistical purposes. In the third chapter an attempt is made to analyse the returns for one county with a view to discovering the evidence they afford as to the character of local government in the third quarter of the thirteenth century. As will be seen, the evidence is incomplete and one-sided, and it would not be safe to assume that the conditions revealed in one eastern shire are typical of the whole of England. Similar inquiries into the evidence for other shires will, it may be hoped, reveal important local variations, both in the normal and the abnormal conditions of county administration. This preliminary essay does little more than indicate the wealth of material afforded by the returns of 1274–5 for the researches of the student of administrative history.

CHAPTER I

CAPITULA ITINERIS : THE ARTICLES OF THE EYRE

§ 1. The Importance of the Articles of the Eyre

The general eyre of the thirteenth century, from whichever standpoint we consider it, was an imposing and mighty engine of government. To the needy king a never-failing source of revenue, to the good folk of the country an incubus, to be dreaded, and if possible postponed or evaded, to the lawyer a visible embodiment of the royal majesty, it is to the student of administration one of the main links in that mighty chain forged by the Angevin kings whereby the frame of government was held together and the local institutions of England were made to contribute their share to the centralized polity of the Norman. By means of the eyre the whole machinery of local government was drastically supervised, and the losses, pecuniary and political, which the crown was liable to suffer, not only at the hands of spiritual and temporal lords of franchises, but also at the hands of its own servants, from the, escheator of half England to the bailiff's clerk, were, to some extent at least, made good. Moreover, the unofficial police of the township and hundred knew to their cost that at the general eyre every failure to report, to catch, or to keep the criminal would be brought home to them, and a corresponding penalty exacted. The control exercised by the central government through the sheriff's annual account at the Exchequer was capricious and slight as compared with their comprehensive inquiry, to which all men must lend their aid, into the doings of sheriffs, coroners, escheators, bailiffs, and sub-bailiffs since last the justices came into the shire for all pleas.

Visits of justices itinerant were not as a rule of this character. The commissions, issued under Henry III to the number of 2,000 a year, to the justices of assize, whose visitations Magna Carta demands four times in the year, had a far more limited scope. The records of the general eyres show the justices exercising jurisdiction in all the matters which could occupy the justices of assize ; they hold pleas of assizes and of gaol delivery, and they receive bills and determine plaints.[1]

In all this the functions of the justices for all pleas are not different from those of their fellows ; they are merely more comprehensive. To find the distinctive quality of the general eyre we have to turn to the *placita coronae*, the pleas arising out of the articles of the eyre : they are its hall-mark. In the articles of the eyre, the *Capitula Itineris*, the series of questions put by the justices to the jurors of the hundreds, is to be found the essence of the eyre. They indicate the ideal of administration which the crown set before its servants, and though facts do not warrant us in regarding it as more than an ideal, they show its practical significance, in the long roll of fines and amercements with which the typical eyre roll concludes. If not to the honour of the crown, it was to its pecuniary advantage, at times, that juries should fail to present and that felons should escape.

The articles of the eyre are then worthy of study, and in their changes may be followed the development alike of the machinery and of the ideals of the government. In the following pages their growth will be traced from the stage recorded by Hoveden in 1190 to that recorded in the *Liber Custumarum* in 1321, and an attempt will be made to show their relation to the special inquests of this period, of which the inquests of 1274–6 had the most marked influence upon their form.

§ 2. The Relation of the Articles to Special Inquests, 1170–1341

As the *raison d'être* of the articles is rather administrative than judicial,[2] it is not surprising to find that they bear

---

[1] See Bolland, Select Bills in Eyre (S. S.), for examples of this procedure ; and see below, Chap. II, § 7.

[2] With regard to the many articles which deal with the abuses of officials, Britton says : ' Let such presentments as shall be made concerning these officials be enrolled and transmitted to the Exchequer and there determined ' (I. xxii, ed. Nichols, p. 86). The Memoranda Rolls give the latter stages of such proceedings.

a close relationship to the series of special inquisitions,[1] political or statutory, whose frequency, from 1085 onwards, attests the efficacy of the new Norman inquest procedure. These special inquests are sometimes strictly occasional ; the Inquest of Sheriffs of 1170, the Inquest of grievances under the Provisions of Oxford in 1258, Kirkby's Quest of 1284–5, the Commissions of 1341,[2] were none of them repeated in the same form, yet in their subject-matter they are nearly akin to some one or more of the manifold inquiries of the articles of the eyre. In some other cases, notably in that of the inquest of 1274–5, the articles were directly and permanently modified as a result of the inquest. Again, special inquests are to be found, as that for the two Welsh shires in 1242,[3] the formulas for which are largely borrowed from the articles, supplemented by special questions relative to local needs.

Maitland, following Britton, has grouped the articles of the eyre into four main sections, according as they inquire into felonies, the proprietary rights of the crown, the assumption or abuse of franchises, and the official misdoings of royal officers.[4] The first of these special inquests deals mainly with this last class. The Inquest of Sheriffs of 1170 was in the first place an inquiry into the conduct of the sheriffs, bailiffs, and foresters,[5] as to how they had oppressed men, what they had taken by the judgement of the shire or hundred, and what without judgement, and the like, but it is also concerned with crown proprietary rights [6]—the exacting of the aid *pur fille marier* and the rendering of homage, and also with the amercements,[7] and the whole inquest is stamped with the fiscal character of the eyre. In wording there is no connexion with the *Capitula Itineris* ; in subject-matter and in purpose the relationship is close.

With regard to the inquests of which the Exchequer records give evidence in such documents as the *Rotuli de Dominabus*,

---

[1] For typical examples of such inquisitions see Hall, Formula Book of Legal Records, pp. 126–78, and Hall, Studies in English Official Historical Documents, pp. 297 ff.

[2] French Chronicle of London (C. S.), p. 88 ; Rot. Pat. 14 Ed. III, pt. iii, m. 40 d. (P. R. C., p. 111).   [3] Rot. Pat. 26 Hen. III, m. 9 d.

[4] Pollock and Maitland, ii, p. 521.   [5] cc. 1, 3, 4, 7, 9.

[6] cc. 6, 11.   [7] cc. 5, 10.

and the Fees and Serjeanties Returns in the King's Remembrancer's department,[1] from 1124 onwards, it is not clear in every case whether these are to be taken as records of special inquests or as lists compiled from the returns of general eyres. In several cases they are undoubtedly of this character, for instance, the *Rotuli de Dominabus* are based on an eyre of 1185, and the lists based on the eyres of 1198, 1219, and 1227 are extant.[2] In other cases returns of a similar character are introduced by writs directing the holding of special inquests, such as the famous inquest into serjeanties of 1212,[3] and the inquests into lands and fees of 1237, 1243, and 1244.[4] These inquests were held throughout the country, but the series is of a miscellaneous character, and in some cases the inquest is not only local but individual in its scope. As to subject-matter, on the other hand, they are included in the earliest versions of the articles that we possess,[5] under the inquiries—*De custodiis puerorum, de maritagiis, de escaetis, and de serieantiis,* and throughout the history of the eyre, these are the articles to which the largest number of returns are made by the jurors.

Again, in the earliest versions of the *capitula* we find articles which are of ephemeral importance and drop out of the list as it becomes stereotyped. It is the inclusion of such articles as that concerning the chattels of John, the king's brother, or that on the ransom of Richard in 1194, or those on the thirteenth and on the export of corn in 1208, or that on John's debts in 1244, or that on the Assize of Arms in 1254, or, we might almost add, that on the export of wool to Flanders in 1274, that explains the statement of Bracton, ' quandoque augentur, quandoque minuuntur '.[6] For, apart from a few local additions, such as are found in London and in the Cinque Ports, the *capitula* are stereotyped from 1254 onwards, and the slavish repetition of queries that must have been out of date, such as the allusion to the ' Assize made

---

[1] A number of these are printed in the Record Commission volume of Testa de Nevill.
[2] Exch. K. R. Serjeanties and Fees, 2/1, 2/9, 2/11.
[3] Printed, Testa de Nevill, p. 54.   [4] Ibid., pp. 63, 198, 352.
[5] 1194, Hoveden (R. S.), iii, p. 263.   [6] Bracton (R. S.), iii, p. 240.

last year' (1253) which is retained right down to 1321, and the retention of queries to which apparently no returns were ever made, certainly does not accord with his statement, ' Variantur secundum varietatem temporum et locorum '.

It will be well to consider more particularly the relation to the articles of those three special inquests of 1255, 1274-6, and 1279, returns to all of which are printed together in the Record Commission edition of the Hundred Rolls, and also of the inquest of 1258, whose returns, once carefully preserved,[1] are now for the most part lost.

The articles of the inquest of 1255 are given in full in the Burton Annals.[2] They fall into the series of inquests dealing with the proprietary rights of the crown, containing the customary inquiries of the eyre as to wardships, marriages, serjeanties, escheats, and advowsons, as well as the more recent articles on purprestures and suits withdrawn, but the inquest adds to these not only a special set of questions as to the condition of the royal demesnes and the tenants upon them,[3] but also articles on the assumption or abuses of franchises,[4] of which cap. 11 is a good example : *De hiis qui clamant habere libertates sine charta Regis, et quales.* There is also a comprehensive inquiry into the conduct of sheriffs, bailiffs, and hundredors for the last twenty-one years.[5]

None of these articles were incorporated in form in the *Capitula Itineris*, but in their scope and range they are the direct forerunners of the articles of 1274. In the chapter just quoted is the germ of all those elaborate Quo Warranto inquiries,[6] the answers to which filled the Hundred Rolls of 1274-5 and led to the passing of the Statute of Gloucester and to the series of pleas which extend throughout the reign of Edward I. Again, in the questions on demesne lands and tenants the first three of the 1274 articles are anticipated.

---

[1] Palgrave, Kalendars of the Exchequer, i, p. 97.

[2] Annales Monastici (R. S.), i, p. 337. The editor of the Gloucester Cartulary (R. S.), ii, p. 276, describes them wrongly as articles of the Staffordshire eyre.

[3] cc. 3, 7.   [4] cc. 1, 10, 11, 21.   [5] c. 22.

[6] This statement is not intended to imply that Quo Warranto proceedings are new in the reign of Edward I. Quo Warranto pleas are found on an Essex eyre roll for 1229 (A. R. 229, m. 18).

The inquest of 1255 then, in so far as it covers new ground, is a first sketch for the articles of nineteen years later, but at the time it exercises no direct influence on the articles of the eyre.

The inquest of 1258 was a general inquiry into administrative abuses, held in pursuance of the Provisions of Oxford.[1] The articles are given in Matthew Paris, ' Liber Additamentorum ',[2] and one return, for the hundred of Lose in Suffolk, is preserved in the Record Office among the so-called Fragments of Hundred Rolls.[3] The articles are twenty-three in number, and provide for minute investigation of the conduct of royal and other officials—sheriffs, bailiffs, beadles, coroners, and escheators. As in the case of the inquest of 1255, the articles do not influence the form or phraseology of the chapters of the eyre, but on the other hand they anticipate in scope and contents the latter part of the articles of 1274, as the inquest of 1255 had anticipated the former part. Though the influence of the 1258 articles on the chapters of the eyre is indirect, it is none the less significant.[4]

The articles for the inquests of 1274–5 are to be found in a truncated form on the Patent Roll.[5] A complete copy is to be found in a semi-official collection of statutes preserved in the Exchequer,[6] which shows that the inquest of 1274, like that of 1255, was intended to cover a long period. The justices were to take cognizance of all matters done or committed within twenty-five years past, in the course of which many general eyres had been held.

Whereas only a very few returns to the inquests of 1255 are extant, those for 1274–5 are voluminous, though imperfect. The printed rolls fill the greater part of the two folio volumes of the Hundred Rolls, and may be supplemented by some

---

[1] Annales Monastici (R. S.), i, p. 446.
[2] Paris, Chronica Maiora (R. S.), vi, p. 397.
[3] Fragments of Hundred Rolls, no. 9. Cf. P. R. C., p. 655 (1258).
[4] Compare also the terms of the sheriff's oath (P. R. C., pp. 695–6, 1258) administered on this inquest. The restrictions on the sheriff's rights of lodging may be compared with the opening chapters of the articles upon the statutes, vide Appendix II.
[5] See below (§ 4, i), p. 30.
[6] Exch. K. R. Miscellaneous Books, vol. ix (P. R. O.).

unprinted ones. Of the value of these returns much has been written, though generally with a somewhat limited appreciation of their scope.[1] It is probably their volume and importance which has obscured the fact that the inquest of 1274–6, far from being unique, was repeated as a part of the regular machinery of administration, at intervals of varying length, throughout the reign of Edward I into those of his son and grandson. For the articles of 1274 became the *Nova Capitula* of the eyre, and were repeated as often as a general eyre was held, with practically no modification, the clause *de omnibus infra xxv annos commissis* being included with the others.

The articles for the inquest of 1279 are possibly condensed in the writ on the Patent Roll.[2] The returns, unlike those of 1274–5, do not recite the article which they answer ; they have been thrown into list form by the inquisitors. But from the writ and the returns the nature of the inquest is clear. It deals with the feudal proprietary rights of the crown and of others, and is in effect an expansion of the first ten of the *Nova Capitula*, seeking as it does for information as to the lands of the king and those upon them, and as to the franchises and privileges possessed both by the king and by others. Its interest is feudal and economic rather than administrative, and it is distinctly a side-issue in the history of the articles of the eyre. It cannot be said to have exercised any influence upon their development.

After 1274 it is rather to the statute than to the special inquest that we shall look for an explanation of the changes in the articles of the eyre. Special inquests are still held ; some of them inquests which, like those of the eyre, are repeated and standardized, notably those under the statute of Winchester and the Commissions of Trailbaston,[3] but the articles of the eyre, as far as our documents take us, remain

---

[1] The only contemporary reference to the inquest in the chronicles treats it as primarily an administrative inquiry, ' Dominus rex . . . misit inquisitores ubique ad inquirendum qualiter vicecomites et alii ballivi se habuissent ; sed nullum commodum inde venit ' : Ann. Dunstapl., p. 263 (Annales Monastici, R. S., vol. iii).

[2] Rot. Pat. 7 Ed. I, m. 21 d. Printed R. H., ii, p. ix. For the returns, see ii, pp. 237–887.

[3] See below, pp. 75–6.

unaffected by them. The fact is at once evidence and explanation of their obsolescence. On the one hand, the stereotyping of the chapters made them increasingly inadequate, as their multiplication had made any new additions a serious matter ; on the other hand, rival machinery was being developed. The Statute of Winchester and the Commissions of Trailbaston, if they had no direct influence on the eyre, yet played their part in developing the functions on the one hand of the Justice of the Peace, on the other of the Justice of Assize. To the special commissions of 1289 and 1304 succeeded other special commissions of Oyer and Terminer. And on the fiscal side, as on the administrative, the general eyre was being superannuated. Young as parliament was, it offered more hopeful prospects for the augmentation of the king's revenues. Unwieldy and inadaptable, the eyre was being beaten along both lines. The change of government in 1307, as it seems, dealt the decisive blow ; with the reign of Edward I, its effective period ended.

§ 3. The Evolution of the Vetera Capitula, 1166–1276

The development of the old chapters of the eyre, so far as it can be shown diagrammatically, is shown in Appendix II. The explanation of these changes, in so far as it can be given by known facts, will be attempted in the following sections. At the time of their greatest extent, the articles are approximately 143 in number, and fall into two sections : the *Vetera Capitula* and the *Nova Capitula*, a division recognized by all the versions. In three manuscripts [1] the *Nova Capitula* are subdivided after the 41st article, whilst in four [2] they end at this point; but this division, though of historical significance, is recognized neither in the working lists of the jurors nor in the semi-official list in the Exchequer Book.

The *Vetera Capitula*, about seventy in number, are those which have undergone most variation. The gradually lengthening lists of Henry III's reign give varying combinations and permutations of them, and the British Museum lists, all of

[1] MS. Rawlinson, c. 160 ; Liber Custumarum, f. 136 b ; MS. Harl. 395.
[2] MS. Harl. 1120, 1033, 673 ; Add. MS. 6061.

a later date, are so different from each other in details of wording and order as to defy all scientific classification. But as the official lists for the same year and the same county present similar, though less marked variations, it may be inferred that the precise order of the articles is not of great importance, as the general type of arrangement is constant enough to give a standard.

The *Nova Capitula* are less eccentric : with a few minor variations, their order is constant, and such additions as are made are tacked on to the end, without disturbing the arrangement of the previous clauses. It is mainly with the *Vetera Capitula* that we shall have to deal in the following sections.

i. *The Assize of Northampton,* 1176

Though the existence of eyres in the reign of Henry I is generally accepted, and the inquisitorial procedure of the eyre is sketched in the Assize of Clarendon, it is only with the Assize of Northampton that we approach a definite statement of the questions put to the jurors. In the directions to the justices in 1176 [1] are to be found the articles of the eyre in their embryonic form. ' Item Iustitiae inquirant de excaetis, de ecclesiis, de terris, de feminis quae sunt de donatione domini regis. Item Iustitiae inquirant de custodiis castellorum, et qui et quantum et ubi eas debeant.' It was from the returns to an eyre of 1185 that the *Rotuli de dominabus* were compiled. [2]

ii. *The Articles of* 1194 *and* 1198

Roger of Hoveden's list for 1194 [3] is, however, the first distinct enrolment of the articles. Under the heading of *Capitula Placitorum Regis* he gives nineteen articles to be submitted to the jurors, beginning with what was to be the standard opening : *De placitis coronae novis et veteribus . . . quae nondum sunt finita coram iusticiariis domini regis.* Of

---

[1] Stubbs, Select Charters (8th ed.), p. 152, cc. 9, 11.
[2] Rotuli de dominabus et pueris et puellis. Edited by J. H. Round for the Pipe Roll Society, 1913, pp. xviii–xx.
[3] Hoveden (R. S.), iii, p. 263.

these nineteen articles, cc. 3–6, dealing with the king's
proprietary rights, escheats, wardships, and so forth; cc. 7
and 8, with felonies, and c. 16, dealing with the Assize of
Wines and of Measures, became permanently incorporated in
the articles. Cc. 9, 15, and 17 deal with the chattels of Jews,
usurers, and Crusaders, and the first two also become permanent.[1] The last chapter, *de defaltis*, under which absentees
from the eyre were presented, is also found in all lists henceforth, generally with the addition of 1198, *Si omnes venerunt
ad summonitiones iustitiarum domini regis, sicut venire debent.*
On the other hand, cc. 2 and 18, dealing with the territorial
assizes, were omitted as the *iuratae et assisae* were separated
from the *placita coronae* in the business of the eyre, whilst
cc. 10 to 14, dealing with the king's ransom and the conduct
of the government under his brother, were in their nature
occasional and transitory, and do not recur after this year.
It should be noted, moreover, that the list of articles is
followed by directions for the holding of one special inquest,
by special juries, into the condition of the royal demesnes,[2]
including escheats and lands and wardships, and for the
postponement of another[3] into the takings of the royal
officials, from justices to foresters, which was again postponed
in 1196.[4]

The articles of 1198,[5] while omitting the occasional articles
of 1194, enlarge the scope of the permanent ones. The section
on the proprietary rights of the crown now includes seven
articles,[6] dealing as it does with serjeanties, advowsons,
marriages of widows, and treasure-trove. The chapter on
measures is enlarged; inquiry is made into purprestures and
roads blocked up. The purprestures article becomes permanent, and later returns show that it was taken to cover
encroachments on the king's highway. The section on
felonies and offences is supplemented by c. 13, on amercements not yet collected, and by c. 18 on returned runaways;
both of these articles have come to stay. The questions on

---

[1] Returns to the article on Crusaders' chattels are found on a Shropshire
roll of 1204 (A. R. 732, m. 2).   [2] c. 23.   [3] c. 23.
[4] Hoveden, iv, p. 5.   [5] Ibid., p. 61.
[6] cc. 6–11, 16.

the territorial assizes are repeated and enlarged,[1] but for the last time. Only two articles are peculiar to this list: an inquiry into the collection of the carucage and hidage of 1198, and as to the keeping of the ports.[2] In these we may see the practical fulfilment of the attempts of 1194 and 1196, and the first appearance of Maitland's fourth group, the misdoings of royal officers.

In these two earliest versions of the *capitula*, then, three of Maitland's four classes of topic are traceable. The section on the king's proprietary rights far outweighs all the others, and it is clear that the pecuniary point of view predominates ; the eyre, born in the Exchequer, is true to its origin. But the section on felonies and lesser offences is growing ; an inquiry into the abuses of government officials is conducted by the ordinary machinery of the eyre, and with the question on purprestures we are approaching the conception of encroachments upon royal rights, in other words, the usurpation of franchises.

Another characteristic of the articles, which becomes more marked as time goes on, is illustrated in these versions : their close relation to legislation. The eyre is the instrument for enforcing legislation, and as the latest version of the articles inquires into the keeping of Edward II's Statute of Exeter, so the earliest refers to the Assize of Wines [3] and the second to the Assize of Measures of 1197 [4] and the *custodes mensurarum* appointed by it.[5]

iii. *The Articles of* 1208

The articles for an eyre of 1208 are to be found in two MSS., both formerly belonging to the Guildhall archives, the British Museum Additional MS. 14252, which was written before 1216, and the fourteenth-century parts of the Liber Albus.[6] They can be dated both by the names of the justices

---

[1] cc. 2, 3, 4, 5.   [2] c. 20.
[3] This assize seems to be lost.   [4] Hoveden, iv, p. 33.
[5] ' Si iv homines, qui sunt atornati ad haec . . . in unaquaque villa, fecerint quod inde statutum est, et si attachiaverunt transgressores illius assisae.'
[6] Printed in Munimenta Gildhallae (R. S.), i, p. 117.

and by the allusion to the Thirteenth of 1207.[1] They are twenty-four in number, and are headed *Capitula domini Regis per cursum errantium iusticiarum*. Seventeen of these are not new,[2] but correspond more or less closely with those of 1194 or 1198, though some of them have grown larger and split into two. Of the seven new articles two, dealing with the chattels of alien enemies,[3] and the export of corn to enemy countries,[4] arise out of the French wars of John; it may be noted, however, that the first of them becomes an integral part of the list, presumably because wars with France, if not with Flanders, were chronic throughout the duration of the general eyre. Of the other new articles, two are permanently added to the list,[5] c. 21 on malefactors in parks and stews, and c. 23 on prises by sheriffs and constables; whilst the others are, like c. 18, temporary and, it would seem, local in their application—cc. 19 and 20, which inquire into the collection of the Thirteenth of 1207, and c. 16, which deals with the tenants of the Honour of Peverel.

Whilst this last query appears to touch the proprietary rights of the crown, the new articles are for the most part concerned either with felonies (cc. 17, 21) or with administrative abuses, whether contrary to the interests of the crown, as in cc. 18 and 20, or to those of the subject, as in c. 23.

iv. *The Articles of* 1227

These articles were issued on September 28, 1227, for an eyre for the Cinque Ports, to which the men of Yarmouth and Dunwich were also summoned. It is one of the versions quoted by Bracton,[6] who gives some slight variations in order and wording, but as Bracton's latest editor[7] has shown that

---

[1] c. 19.   [2] cc. 1–13, 15, 17, 22, 24.

[3] c. 14 ' De catallis francorum ut flandrensium ut inimicorum regis quae arestata fuerunt, quae catalla sint arestata et quis illa habeat.'

[4] c. 18 ' De portubus maris, si bene seruati fuerint et si quis blada adduxit vel alia uenalia in terra inimicorum regis.'

[5] c. 17 is enlarged by the query as to outlaws and burglars, which becomes permanent.

[6] Lib. iii, tr. 2, c. 2 (R. S. Ed., ii, p. 252). Mr. Bolland (Eyre of Kent, I. xxxix) duplicates this reference as Bracton, f. 117b.

[7] G. E. Woodbine (1915).

none of our Bracton MSS. are contemporary, and all are corrupt, his version may be safely abandoned in favour of the contemporary and official record on the Close Roll.

There are twenty-five articles; ten [1] are new and bear witness alike to the development of administrative and judicial machinery in the preceding twenty-four years, and to the influence of Magna Carta upon that development. Three deal with criminal jurisdiction; c. 11 is on the holding of pleas of the crown by sheriffs,[2] c. 22 on gaol delivery without warrant, and c. 8 on robbery. Four deal with the regulation of industry and trade, a royal privilege and a source of amercements; c. 7 on the enforcement of the Assize of Cloths supplements the earlier articles on the Assizes of Wines and Measures,[3] c. 15 concerns the change of market-days,[4] c. 16 the exchange of money, and c. 23 prises from foreigners in time of peace, that is, customs. Chapter 18 deals with an administrative abuse, the taking of bribes by royal officials to remit prises of corn, and the opposite abuse of unjust purveyance.[5] Chapter 20, *de novis consuetudinibus*, deals with the assumption of franchises,[6] and takes us another step towards the *quo warranto* articles. All these articles, c. 8 alone excepted, become integral parts of the *capitula*, and only the last two articles of 1227 are transitory; c. 24 which inquires concerning the ships captured by W. de Wrotheham,[7] and c. 25, on the sale of timber or ships to the enemy. These, it may be supposed, were local as well as transitory in their incidence, for they apply only to coast towns.

Thus the new articles are still concerned with the fiscal if not proprietary rights of the crown more than with any

---

[1] cc. 7, 8, 11, 15–16, 20–5.   [2] Cf. Magna Carta (1225), c. 17.

[3] Cf. Magna Carta, c. 25. A return to this article is to be found as far back as 1204. See A. R. 732, m. 2 (Shropshire).

[4] This article is apparently not new in 1227; returns to it are found on an eyre roll of 4 John (1203). See Select Pleas of the Crown (S. S.), p. 23.

[5] Cf. Magna Carta, c. 19.

[6] Mr. Bolland (Eyre of Kent, p. 30) translates this ' customs levied ', but the returns on the eyre rolls show that the assumption of any franchise may be taken to come under this head in the reign of Henry III. It occurs as early as 1221 on the eyre rolls. See A. R. 733 a.

[7] W. de Wrotham, according to Sir T. Twiss, Bracton, ii, p. 254, was keeper of the king's ports, and died 1218 or 1219.

other matter, though the sections on felonies and on maladministration are both enlarged, and the usurped franchise
is beginning to appear.

v. *The Articles of* 1244

These articles belong to a London eyre, and are preserved
in the Liber Albus.[1] They are thirty in number, and of these
twenty-two are already familiar. A comparison with the
final and stereotyped form of the *Vetera Capitula* shows that
they are arranged for the most part in the order which was
to become the standard ; an order which can be explained
neither on logical nor on chronological grounds, but which,
in spite of constant minor variations, is broadly observed in
all the working copies of the *capitula* that we possess, though
Fleta and Britton, making them the text for discourses on
the pleas of the crown, regroup them drastically.

Of the seven new articles, c. 4 deals with the debts owing
to King John, c. 10 with the escheats and tenements of Jews,
c. 29 with living Christian usurers. These are concerned with
the fiscal rights of the crown, in debts and forfeitures.
Chapter 27 deals with an administrative abuse : the arbitrary
arrest and release of men by bailiffs. None of these articles
are permanently annexed to the *Capitula Itineris* in the precise
form they bear in 1244, but questions practically identical in
scope, though different in wording, take their place. Article 28,
on wreck, is alone incorporated with the chapters of the eyre
in the form here given. Lastly there are two articles, cc. 5
and 6, which inquire concerning the malicious destruction of
houses in London, and are both transitory and local.

The articles of 1244, then, do not seriously modify the
form or proportion of the *Capitula Itineris*.

vi. *The Articles of* 1254

The articles of 1254 mark an important stage in the evolution of the *capitula*, not only by their approximation in order,
though not in number, to the conventional form of the *Vetera*

---

[1] Printed Munimenta Gildhallae (R. S.), i, p. 79. The original records
of the eyre, from which the account in the Liber Albus was abridged, are
also preserved in the Guildhall Records Office.

Capitula, but by the great increase in number upon those of ten years previous.[1] Moreover, of the undated versions of the articles, four end at the point where the list of 1254 ends,[2] and Bracton's latest list appears to be based upon one of this date.[3]

There are two versions for 1254, varying only in detail. They both appear to derive from the eyre held in 1254 in Staffordshire and Gloucestershire.[4] They are to be found in the Gloucester Cartulary[5] and the Burton Annals.[6] The former contains fifty-seven articles, the latter fifty-three, and of the thirty articles that are new, twenty-four are common to both versions. The variations are thus of little importance for our purpose, and the Gloucester version will be used for reference as being slightly the fuller.

The new articles are of great interest. Four deal with felonies and forfeitures ; cc. 17, 22, and 48 with the chattels of Jews, outlaws, and strangers, and c. 29 with poachers. Another group concerns the evasion of duties and the unwarranted assumption of franchises ; the refusal to follow hue and cry (c. 15),[7] or to detain outlaws found on the lands of the offenders (c. 23), refusal to admit the king's officers (c. 31), the tenure of foreigners' lands without licence (c. 36), the withdrawal of suit from shire or hundred (c. 37), the evasion of knight-service by those holding full knight's fees,[8] the erection of warrens (c. 51), or of weirs (c. 52) without licence.

In some of these articles there are traces of recent acts of

---

[1] Of the articles added since 1244, three are to be traced on an eyre roll of 1253 (A. R. 615) ; article 38 on m. 2 ; article 47 on m. 4 d ; article 50 on m. 6 (Numbering of the Statutes of the Realm).

[2] Brit. Mus. MSS. Harl. 395, 1033 ; Lansd. 467, 652.

[3] MSS. Digby 222 (Bodleian Library), Bodley 170, and Bodley 344, include most of the 1254 articles, and none of a later date. These were selected for collation as representative of Mr. Woodbine's three classes, and are practically identical. See Appendix II.

[4] P. R. C., p. 392.   [5] Annales Monastici (R. S.), i, p. 330.

[6] Cartularium monasterii S. Petri Glouc. (R. S.), ii, p. 276.

[7] In the later versions this article is run into the preceding one, thus becoming an inquiry into the holding of inquests *de hutesio levato et non secuto*, as well as *de morte hominis*, by the sheriff. On the other hand, returns are made to it as to a separate article in 1281 (A. R. 486, m. 10).

[8] Article 36 in the Annales de Burton.

the government. The question concerning the lands of Normans probably owes its origin to the special inquests of 1236[1] and 1244.[2] Similarly the article on knight-service may be connected with the special inquest of 1243,[3] and possibly also with the Assize of Arms of 1252, which prescribed the possession of horse and armour for men holding fifteen librates,[4] a regulation interpreted by Matthew Paris[5] as distraint of knighthood. Again the writ of watch and ward of 1253[6] has recently reinforced that of 1233[7] in insisting on the suit of hue and cry.

But the most important of the new articles are those which deal with administrative abuses. If the inquiries as to the assumption of franchises foreshadow the special inquest of 1255,[8] the inquest of 1258[9] is anticipated by the investigation here instituted into the conduct of officials. Have bailiffs been taking bribes to exempt men from jury-service (c. 34) or from knight-service (c. 39)? Have the sheriffs been summoning extraordinary meetings of the hundred court (c. 14[10])? Have they been exceeding their judicial powers (cc. 38, 41), abusing their judicial position (c. 42), taking bribes from both parties to a suit (c. 43), letting out hundreds to farm for their own profit (c. 44), abusing their rights of purveyance (c. 45), brewing scot-ales[11] or commandeering corn (cc. 46, 47), taking excessive fines for non-attendance at the shire (c. 50),[12] conniving at the escape of indicted felons (c. 53), exacting the same amercement twice over (c. 55), or forcing men to pay more than was due (c. 56), distraining two men for one payment,[13] failing to produce men before the justices in eyre (c. 57), selling the king's writs (c. 58)? In this series of ques-

---

[1] Hall, Formula Book of Legal Documents, p. 159.
[2] Testa de Nevill, p. 352.   [3] Ibid., p. 63.
[4] Select Charters (8th ed.), p. 370.
[5] Hist. Ang. (R. S.), iii. 134. Quicunque XV libratas terre haberet miles fieret. Cf. Abbreviatio Chronicorum, p. 325 of same volume, which adds ' Praeterea ', suggesting that there were two distinct enactments.
[6] Select Charters, p. 374.   [7] Ibid., p. 362.
[8] See above, p. 13.   [9] See above, p. 14.   [10] Cf. Prov. West., c. 21.
[11] This article, or one like it, had been found in an earlier set, if we may judge from the returns to an eyre of 1221. See Select Pleas of the Crown (S. S.), p. 110.
[12] Cf. Prov. West., c. 4 (= Statute of Marlborough, x).
[13] Article 49, in the Burton Annals.

tions, whilst there is evident the traditional policy of safe-guarding the interests of the crown against the malversation of its servants, we seem also to feel the momentum of that critical and reforming impulse which had found expression in the debates of the parliament of 1254,[1] and was to accomplish not merely the transitory revolution of which the Provisions of Oxford are the record, but also the permanent and prosaic reforms embodied in the Provisions of Westminster and the Statute of Marlborough.

Of all the new articles, only one was not permanently attached to the *Capitula Itineris* : c. 49 of the Gloucester list, which supplements the other inquiries into the observance of the Assize of Arms by a definite reference to the ' precept ' of Archbishop Walter of York concerning swearing to arms.[2]

vii. *The Eyres of 1276, and the Final Version of the Vetera Capitula*

The maximum number of the *Vetera Capitula* is, we may say, seventy.[3] Of these, some sixty have become stereotyped by 1254, and are found, approximately in the standard order, in the versions which we have just been examining. There is, however, no clear evidence as to the provenance of nine of the ten other articles which are found in the complete versions.[4] There is no dated list of the old chapters including these articles and excluding the new chapters. On the other hand, many undated lists in fourteenth-century law books [5] omit most of the ten articles, whilst including the new chapters which were added to the articles of the eyre in 1278. Again, one of the ten is found at the end of the new chapters as well

---

[1] M. Paris, Chronica Maiora (R. S.), v, p. 440.

[2] This is the writ of 1252, printed on pp. 370–3 of the Select Charters (8th ed.). It is curious that another article which appears to refer to the assize of 1253, and which becomes one of the conventional series, should be missing from these versions : *De hiis qui capiunt denarios ab hiis qui hospitati sunt extraneos contra assisam factam anno preterito.* It is given in Bracton's latest version. See Appendix II.

[3] This number can only be approximate, as different versions split one article into two, or fuse two into one, by adding or omitting a paragraph or rubric.

[4] Nos. 57–61, 64, 66–9 in the Pucklechurch Roll. See Appendix II.

[5] Add to the manuscripts cited under vi, MS. Harl. 489.

as at the end of the old, and can be definitely assigned to the year 1279.[1]

To what date then are the other nine articles to be assigned? The eyre rolls of 1255–72 have been searched in vain for evidence of their existence, but this negative result is inconclusive. Throughout the history of the eyre the majority of the articles evoked no presentments. Where, as in the case of Wiltshire in 1281, of Gloucestershire in 1287 or of Surrey in 1294, we possess the verdicts of the hundreds in the original, *Nihil sciunt* is by far the commonest return. We always find the bulk of the information given under the oldest of the headings—*de ecclesiis, de serieantiis, de valettis, de purpresturis, de novis placitis coronae.*[2]

The records of 1272–8 are not quite so barren. One of the nine missing *capitula* is to be found on the Bedfordshire eyre roll of 1276.[3] This eyre was a continuation of that begun in the last year of Henry III, and cut short by his death,[4] and the roll contains some memoranda of its earlier sessions.[5] It is possible that the occurrence of this article,[6] fifth of the ten, is evidence that the others also had been added to the list which the justices of 1272 gave to the Bedfordshire jurors.

Again the records of the London eyre of 1276 afford evidence, extremely interesting but fragmentary. The official eyre roll has found its way into the British Museum, where it is catalogued as Additional Charters 5153. It includes a list of the articles, both those to which returns are made and those of which *iuratores nihil sciunt.* This list differs in many respects from the standard type with which the preceding

---

[1] *De mutuis sacramentis.* See below, pp. 58–9.

[2] One heading that occurs with great regularity upon the eyre rolls is never found among the *Capitula Itineris.* It deals with indicted felons, who have as a rule escaped from justice : *De indictatis.* It is most probably the record of the presentments made *in secretis* on the second day of the eyre. See below, § 4, vi. The returns are occasionally voluminous, and always considerable.

[3] A. R. 7, m. 35 d.

[4] Rot. Pat. 95, m. 21 ; Annales Monastici (R. S.), iii, p. 269.

[5] m. 39.

[6] *De hiis qui currunt in alienis warennis.* No. 61 on the Pucklechurch Roll.

fifty years have familiarized us. In the first place, the order of the articles is unusually irregular; the questions on escheats and purprestures are placed at the end instead of in their usual position at the beginning with those on churches and serjeanties; and throughout, although there is a general conformity to the standard order, stray articles are found in unfamiliar positions. In the second place, a good many of the articles are omitted; only thirty-eight of the ordinary seventy *Vetera Capitula* are to be found. It is possible that the returns do not fairly represent the lists given to the jurors, but it appears on the face of it to be as complete a record as that of the Surrey and Gloucestershire eyres of a later date. In the third place, there are a great number of special and local questions, as we should expect in view of the unique constitutional position of the city of London and the recent upheavals within its walls.[1]

Of these thirteen articles peculiar to London, one is repeated from the London eyre of 1244,[2] namely that on the malicious destruction of houses.[3] Some of the others are amplifications of the ordinary articles; thus there are two additional questions on the Assizes of Wines and of Measures,[4] and that on the sheltering of fugitives is amplified by a special inquiry as to runaway poachers,[5] whilst the ordinary question on churches is supplemented by one on abbeys and priories.[6] There is an article on the goods of Jews[7] which may be compared with that on the escheats of Jews in 1244, and there is a special inquiry into the cruelty of Jews to Christian boys.[8] The remaining articles peculiar to this list are of more general interest: one on purveyance of goods which have not reached the king;[9] one on the murage and other municipal dues of London;[10] one on the assessment of

---

[1] See Liber de Antiquis Legibus (C. S.) for municipal disturbances during the Barons' Wars.

[2] The records of the intervening eyre of 1251 are not extant. The next after 1276 was in 1321.

[3] Second on m. 15 d.

[4] Seventh and eighth on m. 15 d.

[5] Twenty-first on m. 15 d.

[6] Fourth on m. 15 d.

[7] Thirteenth on m. 15 d.

[8] Fourteenth on m. 15 d.

[9] Third on m. 16.

[10] Fifth on m. 16.

tallage,[1] and one on the enforcement of the regulations laid
down by the justices on their last eyre.[2]

These interesting and perplexing local variations do not,
however, affect the history of the articles. It is more to our
purpose to note that among the thirty-eight normal articles
included in this list, three more of our missing nine *capitula*
are to be found.[3] Taking this fact in conjunction with the
other evidence, remembering that neither the Bedford nor
the London record is comprehensive in character, the presumption is strong that these nine articles formed an integral
part of the *Vetera Capitula* before 1278; in view of the general
cessation of eyres, 1272–8, we might say, before 1272. The
year 1267, in which a general iter throughout England was
commanded,[4] might well have been the occasion. Some of
the articles are very similar in scope to those of the inquest
of 1258,[5] and might well go back to the eyres of 1261–2.
Unfortunately only two eyre rolls of 1261–2 and comparatively few of 1268–72 are extant,[6] and they do not
help us.

On the other hand, the fact that these articles are mainly
concerned with police matters might link them to another
document of a later date. Two (61, 67) deal with poaching,
two (59, 64) with the arrest, detention, or release of felons,
two (57, 60) with the chattels of felons, one (58) with the
highways, one (66) with the watch, and one (68) with fraudulent evasion of jury-service on the eyre.[7] Should we connect
these with the *officium coronatoris* of 1275–6?[8] or, bearing
in mind the fact that two of these articles, that on stopping

---

[1] Sixth on m. 16.   [2] Fourth on m. 16.

[3] Sixteenth, seventeenth, and eighteenth on m. 16 ; viz. *De hiis qui
capiunt denarios ab excommunicatis, De pontibus et calcetis, De felonibus
dampnatis.*

[4] 'Provisum fuit per Dominum Regem et consilium suum quod iustitiae itinerantes missi sint per totam Angliam ' (Liber de Antiquis Legibus
(C. S.), p. 100). See also Rot. Pat., December 7, 1267, where justices
are assigned to thirty-seven counties. Of these some thirty-two were
probably visited before the cessation of eyres in 1272–3, not counting
Bedfordshire. See Appendix III.

[5] See above, p. 14.

[6] There are records for twelve shires only.

[7] The numbers are those on the Pucklechurch Roll. See Appendix II.

[8] Statutes of the Realm, i, p. 40.

up ways and bridges, and that on robbing dovecots, are found in the articles of the Tourn, as given in the *Statutum Walliae*,[1] are we to postulate some measure for the regulation of the Sheriffs' Tourn, more comprehensive than the clause in the Statute of Marlborough,[2] but following up that measure, and first enforced in the eyres of 1271 to 1276 ?

§ 4. THE HISTORY OF THE NOVA CAPITULA

i. *The Inquests of* 1274–5

In the hundred years from 1176 to 1276 the articles of the eyre had multiplied from the five headings of the Assize of Northampton to the seventy searching questions of the completed *Vetera Capitula*, and with the corresponding extension of activity on the part of the justices *ad omnia placita* had grown the unpopularity of the eyre. By 1261 counties are successfully demanding the observance of a minimum seven years interval between one eyre and the next,[3] and Matthew Paris does not scruple to affirm that the administration of justice is merely a pretext, and that the real object of the eyre is the collection of ' infinite sums of money ' for the king's use.[4]

Thus on the accession of Edward I in November 1272, the suspension of all general eyres was a judicious bid for popularity.[5] A comprehensive *iter* had been announced in 1267, to begin in January 1268,[6] and a good many eyres were still proceeding in the earlier months of 1272 ;[7] of these, the Bedfordshire eyre was, as we have seen, arrested in full course. No eyres were held until Edward's return in August

---

[1] Statutes of the Realm, i, p. 57.
[2] Stat. of Marlb. x ; Statutes of the Realm, i, p. 22 (Provisions of Westminster, 4). Cf. also Mem. R. L. T. R. 36, m. 1 d. *Provisio de turno vicecomitis* ; Rot. Cl. 75, m. 17 d.
[3] Annales Monastici (R. S.), iv, p. 446. See below, Note on the Frequency of General Eyres.
[4] Chronica Maiora (R. S.), iv, p. 34.
[5] Annales Monastici, ii, p. 113 ; iv, p. 462.
[6] Liber de Antiquis Legibus, p. 100 ; and see above, p. 28.
[7] Eyres were held in Bedford, Bucks., Cambridge, Essex, Salop, Southants., Stafford, and Surrey ; probably also in Herefordshire, Hunts., and Lancashire. See Appendix III.

1274, and with the exception of the Worcester eyre of 1275, the Middlesex eyre of 1274–5, and the London eyres of 1276, no eyres were held till the end of 1278.

This long cessation is explained by the fact that the years 1274–5 were occupied by the holding of a special inquest more comprehensive in scope and more effective in its results than any other of which the records are extant since 1086. As will be shown later, two and possibly three distinct inquests were held in the years 1274–5, and though they appear to have been completed before the summer of 1275, the proceedings initiated by them were spread over many years ; the annotations upon the records go as late as 1284, and the official abstract was not begun till after 1280.

The Hundred Rolls inquest was not reckoned as a general eyre, but its procedure must have resembled that of the *placita corone* at the eyre fairly closely.[1] There are traces in some shires at least of a jury of twelve knights of the shire alongside of the jurors of the hundred, and in some cases the vills and burghs had the jury of six, not twelve, as on the ordinary eyre. But the process stopped short at the eliciting of information ; and the judicial proceedings based upon the evidence thus collected took place at a later date.

Most of the articles of the inquest of 1274 are to be found upon the Patent Roll of 2 Edw. I, and are printed in the Record Commission edition of the Hundred Rolls. A·cursory comparison with the returns, however, reveals the fact that the list is incomplete ; there are numerous returns to six more articles than it includes.[2] The list of the new articles of the eyre, as recorded in the semi-official collection in the Exchequer[3] and in all good versions, includes five of these six articles, and ends with a direction to the justices which rounds off the articles and makes a formal instrument of what on the Patent Roll seems a shapeless and incomplete document. The condition of the Patent Roll itself strengthens this inference. The list of articles comes to an end at the

---

[1] See below, Chap. II, § 6.
[2] e.g. see R. H. i, pp. 411 b, 169 a, 172 a ; for other articles of apparently local incidence see below, p. 33.
[3] Exch. K. R. Miscellaneous Books, vol. ix, f. 42 d.

bottom of a membrane, so that it is quite possible that the carelessness of the clerk, whether in losing a membrane or in failing to complete the list after taking a new membrane, accounts for the truncated form of our one official list.

Of these forty-one or more articles for inquisition, several cover old ground. Question 5 on the farms of hundreds, question 6 on suits withdrawn, question 10 on the raising of warrens, question 12 on purprestures, question 16 on releasing men from jury-service, question 24 on granting respite from knighthood, and question 28 on refusing bail are all practically identical with existing *Vetera Capitula*,[1] as the jurors who had to reply to both at a later date recognized.[2]

The articles which are new in substance as well as in name are much fuller and more minute in scope than the *Vetera Capitula*. Each chapter has as many sub-headings as the examination question designed to help the weakling : *Que maneria, et qui ea tenent, quo waranto, et a quo tempore, per quem et quomodo fuerunt alienata*. But these complex questions have often in fact been evolved from the bald questions of the old chapters. The questions on capital fees and manors[3] are expanded from the questions of the special inquest of 1255 and 1259,[4] and yet descend also from the old articles on escheats and serjeanties. The origin of the series of elaborate questions on claims of franchises goes back beyond those inquests to their embryonic form *de novis consuetudinibus levatis*, the returns to which, as we have seen, prove its bearing and scope. The long section on the misdoings of sheriffs and bailiffs (cc. 14–31) is a fuller expansion of that part of the *Vetera Capitula* which, as we have seen, had been steadily growing in size since the early days of the chapters of the eyre, and provides the most comprehensive list of the sins fiscal, administrative, and judicial, of local officials in the thirteenth century that we possess.

[1] According to the numbering in the Statutes of the Realm (i, p. 233) cc. 43, 37, 46, 8, 35, 38, and 49 respectively in the *Vetera Capitula*.

[2] A. R. 895, m. 4 'De purpresturis factis super Dominum Regem responsum est in veteribus capitulis.'

[3] cc. 1, 2, 3.

[4] Provisions of Westminster, as given on Rot. Cl. 44 Hen. III, m. 18 d, and MS. Cotton Nero D. 1, f. 138 d.

The section on the escheators (cc. 32–9) corresponds to the earlier articles on wardships, marriages, and escheats.

The stamp of the baronial struggle, as permanently recorded in the Provisions of Westminster and Statute of Marlborough, is clearly traceable on these articles, whether it is to be seen in the later additions to the *Vetera Capitula* or no.[1] The eleventh article refers to the Statute of Marlborough, being the first article of the eyre explicitly to refer to a dated enactment, though by no means the first to be based upon legislation. Chapter 18, on the sheriff's tourn, deals with one of the abuses touched upon in the Provisions. The thirteenth article, on knights' fees given to ecclesiastics, recalls the famous clause of the Provisions which forbids religious men to enter into any man's fee without the consent of the chief lord.[2]

These forty-one[3] articles are permanently annexed to the chapters of the eyre as they stand, preserving as a rule the order they have on the Patent Roll, but generally accompanied by those directions to the justices,[4] which, as the records stand, we know not whether to assign to 1274, 1276, or 1278.[5] But from the returns to the Inquest we learn that

[1] See above, § 3, vii.

[2] S. R. i, 10 ; Annales de Burton, p. 482.

[3] The article, *qui ceperint munera a quibuscunque pro officio suo exequendo vel non exequendo*, which is found both on the Patent Roll and in the Exchequer Book next after article 33 (S. R.) in the section on the escheators, and is printed as a foot-note in S. R., is not as a rule included in the later lists, whether on the Assize Rolls or in the law books. It appears to be identical in scope with article 29 (S. R.), *qui dona vel lucra receperint pro officiis suis exercendis vel non exercendis*, and this probably accounts for its disappearance, though the latter was not originally designed to cover the doings of escheators.

[4] ' Et de omnibus predictis factis vel commissis infra xxv annos proxime preteritos predicti iustitiarii se intromittant. Et omnes illi qui sentiunt se super hiis gravatos et inde conqueri voluerint, audiantur, et fiat eis iustitia et ipsi iustitiarii sequantur pro hiis que ad dominum Regem contingunt ' (S. R. i, p. 236. Cf. below, § 4, iv).

[5] At the foot of one of the unprinted Cambridgeshire Rolls, dated December 15, 1275 (Hundred Rolls, Cambridge, No. 3), there is written ' Audiantur conquerentes qui conqueri voluerint ', a phrase taken from the directions to the justices. This would settle the question as to date, were it not possible that the phrase had been added, like many other notes on the roll, by the justices of the Cambridgeshire eyre in 1287. The character of the ink and handwriting leaves the question open. It should be noted also that the returns of 1274–5 are often accompanied by *querele*, e.g. i, 68,

there were at least eleven other questions [1] which formed part of the inquests of 1274–5, though not permanently incorporated with the *Nova Capitula*. In Gloucestershire and Worcestershire, returns are made *de retonsoribus et falsonariis*.[2] One question occurs apparently only in Yorkshire,[3] and, it may be noted in passing, is found also on the Yorkshire eyre rolls for 1280 ;[4] this is the article *de iudicibus ecclesiasticis*, and appears to deal with usurpations of secular jurisdiction by the spiritual courts. Other questions which appear to be peculiar to Yorkshire are *de tolnetis antiquis, qui ea augmentaverunt ;*[5] *de muragio et pontagio*,[6] *de mensuris et ponderibus*,[7] and *de civitatibus et burgis et dominicis domini Regis dimissis ad firmam*.[8] These articles are of the ordinary type of eyre chapter, dealing, as they do, with the fiscal rights of the crown. As none but the Extract Rolls are extant for Yorkshire, they are only found in a curtailed form. For Lincolnshire, Rutland, and Northants, however, original returns survive, unusually complete in the case of Lincolnshire, and these furnish seven more articles, some of which are found in other counties also. They are given in fairly constant order, at the end of the other articles, and on one return are carefully capitalized.[9] The first of them is *De collectoribus vicesimi denarii vel de communiis amerciamentis et tallagiis*.[10] Returns *de vicesima* are found also in Bucks, Devon, Essex, Herts, Kent, Norfolk, and Suffolk.[11] These refer to the Twentieth granted in 1269, the collection of which, deferred

137 a, the presence of which may be explained by the same clause. On the whole, then, it seems probable that the directions to the justices date from 1274.

[1] The returns to the article *De talliis* for Bedfordshire (R. H., i, pp. 4 b to 8) and for Devonshire (R. H., i, pp. 84–6) belong to ' Kirkby's Quest ', of 1284–5, and have only been included with the Hundred Rolls by an oversight.

[2] R. H., i, pp. 176 a, &c. ; ii, p. 282 b. See below, § 4, vi.

[3] R. H., i, pp. 105 a, 106 b, *et passim*.

[4] A. R. 1078, m. 6 d, m. 36 d.

[5] R. H., i, p. 108 a.   [6] R. H., i, p. 130 a.

[7] R. H., i, p. 108 b. *De pannis* on p. 106 b is probably the same article.

[8] R. H., i, p. 108 a.

[9] R. H., i, p. 248 a. For Rutland see ii, pp. 51–2 ; for Northants, ii, pp. 4–5.

[10] R. H., i, p. 267 a.

[11] R. H., i, pp. 45 a, 70 a, 137–9, 194 a, 200 b, 449 a ; ii, p. 160 b.

until 1270,[1] dragged on for several years, so that the payment of arrears is still being recorded in the Memoranda Rolls of 1273 and 1275.[2] The other articles are : *Qui levaverunt paagia pro defectu pontis vel calceti contra consuetudinem regni ;*[3] *De vicecomitibus seu dominis et ballivis qui ceperunt redemptionem de hominibus pro veredictis coram iusticiis ;*[4] *De custodibus operacionum ut muragiorum et similium ubicunque factarum per preceptum domini Regis qui magis computaverunt in eisdem quam rationabiliter apposuerunt;*[5] *De magnatibus et eorum ballivis quibuscumque qui fecerunt districtiones extra feoda sua ;*[6] *Qui fecerunt recussum et impedimentum ballivis domini Regis in districtionibus faciendis ;*[7] *De viris religiosis vel aliis qui appropriaverunt sibi advocationes ecclesiarum qui solent esse in advocatione domini Regis, et a quo tempore.*[8] Why these six articles should have been administered in the Eastern Midlands [9] and nowhere else is hard to say. Mr. Hall would connect them with the *De Ministris* roll,[10] but, as will be shown hereafter, no *De Ministris* records exist for these counties, nor is there any reason to think that such ever did exist. The articles have no obvious correspondence with any special local characteristics. For the most part they deal with matters already covered by the articles of October 11, 1274, if not by the old chapters of the eyre, and this probably accounts for their failure to be added to the articles of the eyre, since they lack the temporary character which explains the disappearance of *de vicesima* and *de lanis ductis*. This last article seems to have been administered in every county. It runs as follows : *Qui*

---

[1] See Chron. Wykes, Annales Monastici (R. S.), iv, pp. 227–8 ; Cotton (R. S.), p. 143 ; Royal Letters (R. S.), ii, pp. 336–8 ; Liber de Ant. Leg. (C. S.), pp. 122, 125 ; Pipe Roll 1 Ed. I, m. 6.

[2] Mem. R. K. R. 48, m. 2 d ; 50, mm. 3, 4.

[3] R. H., i, pp. 249 b, 267 a.

[4] R. H., i, p. 322 a. Cf. Vetus Cap. 35 (S. R.).

[5] R. H., i, pp. 249 b, 322 a. This article bears a close resemblance to Novum Cap. 30 (S. R.) but does not replace it.

[6] R. H., i, p. 267 a. Cf. Cap. in statutis 15 (S. R.).

[7] R. H., i, p. 282 a ; ii, p. 52 b. Cf. Vetus Cap. 34, Novum Cap. 11 (S. R.).

[8] R. H., i, p. 315 b.

[9] Lincolnshire, Northants, and Rutland formed a district for one pair of commissioners. See Appendix IV.

[10] Hall, Formula Book of Legal Records, p. 128.

durante discordia inter dominum et comitissam de Flandr'
contra inhibicionem et defencionem Regis defuncti vel nunc
duxerint vel ducere fecerint lanas aliquas ultra mare, quantum
vel ad quem portum.[1] The history of the commercial restrictions imposed upon the wool trade by Henry III and Edward I
in their quarrel with the Countess of Flanders, 1270–3, is
told very fully in the *Liber de Antiquis Legibus*,[2] and fully
explains this article and the returns to it upon the Hundred
Rolls. Included, as it doubtless was, in the lists given to
the jurors in 1274, it is yet another example of those temporary additions to the chapters which characterize their
history throughout.[3]

ii. *The First Statute of Westminster,* 1275

The impress of the inquests initiated in 1274 is seen upon
the legislation of the next few years. In a series of enactments the parliaments of 1275–8 dealt in turn with the
different abuses revealed by the jurors' verdicts. Edward's
first parliament of April 1275 passed the Statute of Westminster I, designed to check the misconduct of local government officials ; the October parliament supplemented it with
the Statutes of the Exchequer, which regulated the taking
of distraints ;[4] the October parliament of 1276 or some later
assembly passed the Statute or ordinance *de iustitiis assignatis*,[5]
which provided for the speedy punishment of the offenders
revealed by the Hundred Rolls ; and the August parliament
at Gloucester passed the Statute of Gloucester providing for
the curtailment or regularization of the usurped liberties
recorded in the Hundred Rolls by empowering the justices
in eyre to deal with such cases, and by defining the procedure
to be used. The same parliament, according to Heming-

---

[1] R.H., i, pp. 167 b, 415 a, and 411 b, where it is numbered with the
others.
[2] Liber de Antiquis Legibus (C. S.), pp. 126, 127, 135–7, 140–2, 144,
159–61. Note also the series of commissions on the Patent Roll for inquiry
into the export of wool, from June 1274 to January 1275 (P. R. C., pp. 68,
69, 71, 115). It is to the last commission that reference is made in the notes
on the Lincolnshire rolls, R. H., i, pp. 259, 276, 293, 308, 343.
[3] It is, however, included in the list of articles used on the Wiltshire
eyre of 1281. See below, § 4, v.
[4] See below, p. 37.   [5] See below, pp. 41–56.

burgh,[1] dealt with the abuses of money clipping of which the Gloucestershire Hundred Rolls, to go no further, had given evidence.

The first Statute of Westminster occupies a unique position in the history of the articles of the eyre. It is, to a large extent, based upon the results of the inquests held upon the articles of 1274, and it is itself the source of the last main section of the *capitula*, which is in most versions found inseparably annexed to those of 1274, but is distinguished from them alike by internal evidence, and by the headings of some few copies.[2] It is, as Stubbs has said, rather a code than a statute; the official description on the Patent Roll speaks of *provisiones et statuta*,[3] and the singular form of title appears to be modern. A thorough inquiry into its importance and significance would thus involve us in intricate legal details, and only the clauses relevant to our subject will be considered here.[4]

Clauses 7–11, 15–20, 24–28 deal with local administration, and mainly with that of the sheriff. Of these clause 9, concerning the pursuit of felons and concealment of felonies, bears a close relation to cc. 14 and 27[5] of the *Nova Capitula* of 1274. Clause 10, regulating the election of coroners, provides a remedy for the misdoings reported in answer to the whole section 14–29, which deals with erring coroners as well as other bailiffs and sheriffs. Clauses 24–28 are clearly based upon the returns to the question *qui per potestate officii sui aliquos maliciose occasionaverint*, which had elicited a wealth of information as to the various abuses and extortions of the local official. Clause 32 deals with the sharp

---

[1] Walter of Hemingburgh, ii, p. 5 (E. H. S.) ' Tractatum est de moneta retonsa per Iudaeos '. Cf. R. H., p. 176 a, *et passim*. ' Dicunt quod Iudei Bristoll' sunt falsonarii et retonsores sed ignorant qui.'

[2] MS. Rawlinson, c. 160 ' Capitula tangentia Prima Statuta Westmonasterii in anno R. R. E. filii R. H. tercio.' MS. Harl. 395 ' Articuli qui contingunt statuta D. R.' Liber Custumarum ' Expliciunt capitula prima Statuta R. E. contingentia.' Of the sixteen versions examined at the British Museum four include the 1274 articles, but omit the articles upon the statutes, two contain them intermixed with the others, five give them with no separate heading, but separated from those of 1274 by the instructions to the justices, and one only gives the separate heading.

[3] Rot. Pat. 3 Ed. I, m. 10.   [4] S. R., I, pp. 28 ff.

[5] The numbering is that of the Statutes of the Realm.

practices over royal debts into which article 22 had inquired. In short, the Statutes of Westminster carry yet further the process of definition which we have noted in the articles of 1274 ; the searchlights of the central machinery were turned upon every nook and cranny of local administration, and the provision for proclaiming the statutes every month in the county court[1] was meant to secure the co-operation of the injured parties with the government in bringing offenders to justice.

But in addition to this monthly publication commanded by the letters patent of May 28, 1275, a new series of articles was drawn up, to be added, along with those of 1274, to the chapters of the eyre, when next the justices should go round the shires to hold general pleas. These *articuli qui contingunt statuta* follow the wording of the statutes sentence by sentence in those portions which they touch.[2] One lawyer's copy, printed by Mr. Bolland in his edition of the Eyre of Kent for the Selden Society, gives the references clause by clause,[3] so that it is not necessary here to elaborate this point. It has not, however, been pointed out that articles 26–28 refer explicitly [4] to a statute or ordinance made in the October parliament of 1275 concerning the taking of distresses, supplementary to clause 17 of the first statute of Westminster, to which article 16 corresponds. This statute can be identified with the Statutes of the Exchequer, printed amongst those of uncertain date in the Statutes of the Realm. Clause 13 has the subheading ' Districciones de Scaccario ', and refers to the abuses of the royal officials, forbids the sale of a distress within fifteen days of the taking, and forbids distraint by ploughing cattle or by sheep.[5] The Statutes of

---

[1] Rot. Pat. 3 Ed. I, m. 10 ; printed S. R., i, p. 39.

[2] Stat. c. 1 = Art. 1–6 ; S. 3–7 = A. 7–9 ; S. 9 = A. 11, 12 ; S. 13 = A. 13 ; S. 15–17 = A. 14–16 ; S. 19–20 = A. 17–18 ; S. 23 = A. 19 ; S. 25–7 = A. 20–1 ; S. 31 = A. 22–3 ; S. 32 = A. *note* 6, 24 ; S. 35 = A. 25.

[3] Lincoln's Inn MS. Hale 141. Eyre of Kent, pp. 40–6.

[4] Article 26 ' Hoc intelligendum est post Parliamentum de termino Sancti Michaelis, anno r.r.E. nunc tertio.' 27 ' De districcionibus factis postquam Rex inhibuit in dicto Parliamento per animalia ad Wannagium terrarum deputata . . .' (MS. Harl. 489, f. 59.)

[5] Ke les avers . . . ne seient venduz dedenz les quinze jurs de la prise. Nul houme . . . ne seit distreint par ces bestes ke gaignent sa terre, ne par ces berbiz. (S. R., i, p. 197 b.)

the Exchequer thus bear the same relation to the chapters of the eyre as does the First Statute of Westminster, for they are partly based on the returns of 1274–5, and they originate two of the articles upon the statutes.

One more point remains to be noted in connexion with these articles. They, like those of 1274, conclude with instructions to the justices, which, like those of 1274, are repeated as a rule in all subsequent working lists, and, like them again, set a term to the period from which offences are punishable. ' Et hec omnia que contingunt dicta statuta distincte et aperte inquirantur ita quod cuilibet adquerenti fiat Iusticia et quod pene in eisdem statutis contente cuilibet offendenti adiudicantur sive ad sectam Regis sive aliorum secundum quod in eisdem statutis continetur. Pene autem in eisdem statutis contentis adiudicande sint de commissis post festum Sancti Michaelis anno r.r.E. secundo [1] et non ante. Tamen de transgressionibus et offensis prius factis adiudicetur pena qualis ante predicta statuta adiudicari consueuerit in casibus consimilibus.'

Michaelmas, 1274, is approximately the date of the Hundred Rolls Commission, but in spite of the concurrence of three good manuscripts in setting this date as the term we are probably right in preferring 1275, the date given by MS. Harl. 867 ; the date of the statute based on the first Hundred Roll returns. The *capitula* of 1274 having been used to inquire into all offences for twenty-five years before that date, they are now supplemented by the new articles designed to enforce the legislation of 1275 and to inflict the new penalties created in that year on those who continue the abuses revealed by the inquests, and the two together form the *Nova Capitula* of the eyre.

Thus the articles of the eyre, old and new chapters together, include in themselves the vestiges of the three several stages

---

[1] So Exch. K. R. Miscellaneous Books, vol. ix ; Rawlinson MS. c. 160 and MS. Harl. 489, from which the above is taken. MS. Harl. 867 gives *anno tercio*. The other versions follow Liber Custumarum in omitting the date, except MS. Harl. 1214, a late fourteenth-century manuscript, which assigns the Statute of Westminster to 4 Ed. I (article 26, f. 11). This can only be a slip.

of their evolution. Upon the shoulders of clerks and jurors is laid the appalling burden of some hundred and forty chapters, in which the whole field of offence is crossed and recrossed by a network of paths ancient and modern. There is little wonder that the articles upon the statutes include an inquiry into the fees taken by the justices' clerks for delivering the articles of the eyre to the jurors.[1]

Recurring to our original classification, we note that the section on administrative abuses, originally so slight, and of very little significance before 1254, has now grown to vast proportions. More than half of the articles of 1274 have to do with official sins ; and more than three-quarters of the articles upon the statutes. The section on the king's proprietary rights is overshadowed ; even the usurpation of liberties by magnates seems a secondary matter. It seems hardly fanciful to say that the *Nova Capitula* are an embodiment of that ideal of the rule of law which was coming to oust the Norman conception of government as a private affair conducted for the king's behoof, by his activities and at his will.

iii. *The Statute of Gloucester*, 1278

The first Statute of Westminster had taken up the question of administrative abuses, and the new articles based upon it were soon to be delivered to the jurors in the series of eyres that began in 1278. But these justices had a twofold commission ; the same parliament which ordered the eyre on August 16 [2] had just completed and published the Statute of Gloucester,[3] which reflects the other aspect of the Hundred Roll inquiry, namely the usurpation of franchises.

Like the legislation of the Easter Parliament of 1275, the Statutes of Gloucester form rather a series of acts than one act. There is first a long section giving directions to the justices,[4] parallel to the statute *de iustitiis assignatis*, which

---

[1] Articles 21, 22.

[2] Rot. Cl. 6 Ed. I, m. 6 d (C. R. C., p. 503) ; P. R. C., p. 277.

[3] August 7. See S. R., i, p. 50. The entries on the Close Rolls show that both Walter of Hemingburgh and the older printed copies of the statutes give impossible dates.

[4] S. R., i, pp. 45–6.

we shall have to consider shortly; and then a series of numbered clauses[1] dealing with various points of legal procedure,
of no general political significance. A supplementary explanation of these legal points then follows, bearing the same date
as the introductory passage.[2] The account of the statute
given by Walter of Hemingburgh[3] would lead us to suppose
that the first section, dealing with inquiries into franchises,
was known separately as the statute *de quo warranto*, and
a Latin version of it is actually found so entitled in many
of the law books and printed in the statutes at large.[4]

It is with this introductory section alone that we are
concerned. This provides for the interim enjoyment of
franchises; orders the inquiry into claims to franchises
before the justices next in eyre in the county in question;
and lays down the procedure by which such inquiry shall be
held, including a pattern writ. The *quo warranto* pleas,
based upon the information secured in the inquests of 1274-5,
are to be held in the ordinary eyre, and the chapters, as
newly augmented, will be adequate to supplement the information already at the justice's disposal. Thenceforward *placita
de quo warranto* are found on the rolls of most eyres.

The directions to the justices conclude with a brief reference to some previous ordinance. 'Concerning complaints
made and to be made of the King's bailiffs and of other
bailiffs; it shall be done according to the ordinance before
made thereof, and according to the inquests before had
thereupon. And the justices in eyre shall do therein according to what the king hath enjoined them and according to
the articles which the king hath given them in charge.'[5]
The ordinance in question may be the Statute of Westminster I, but is more probably *de iustitiis assignatis*. The
inquests, however, are clearly those of 1274-5, and the
articles are those *Nova Capitula* of the eyre whose genesis we

---

[1] S. R., i, pp. 46–50.   [2] S. R., i, p. 50.
[3] ii, p. 5 ' Fecit statuta quae dicuntur Statuta Gloucestriae, continentia
XV capitula, et . . . statutum quo Warranto.'
[4] Statutes at Large (1786), i, p. 70. This is not a close translation, and
contains two writs which are not included in the French version.
[5] S. R., i, p. 46.

have just been considering. The Latin version of the statute quotes a writ to the sheriff [1] bidding him summon all complainants against royal and other officials before the royal justices, a writ which corresponds verbally to the justices' commission as entered upon the Patent Roll,[2] and which forms yet another link between the inquests of 1274-5 and the eyre of 1279-81.

Before turning to the records of that eyre, however, we must consider the bearing of the last and the least readily explicable of the statutes of 1275-8, the *Statutum de iustitiis assignatis, quod vocatur Rageman.*

iv. *The Statute of Rageman and the Placita de Ragemannis*

The statute *de iustitiis assignatis* or Rageman is a good example both of the laxity of the term statute, as used in the reign of Edward I, and also of the haphazard way in which, to all appearance, these instruments were enrolled and preserved. It is not to be found in any of the official records ; the Statutes of the Realm print it from compilations of a later date.[3] There is, however, a copy under the heading ' Les estatuz a enquere de trespassurs ' in a collection of writs and statutes preserved among the Miscellanea of the Exchequer.[4] Though neither contemporary nor official,[5] it would appear to be the earliest version extant, and it is interesting to note that it immediately precedes a list of the *Nova Capitula*, including those upon the statutes. Here as elsewhere the ' statute ' is undated, and its position among the other statutes included in the collection gives no help in placing it. In the printed collections it is assigned to the

Uncertainty of date.

---

[1] Statutes at Large, i, p. 71.　　　[2] Rot. Pat. 7 Ed. I, m. 19.
[3] MS. Harl. 395, f. 73 d ; 667, f. 347 ; MS. Cott. Vesp. B. vii, f. 89. Other copies are to be found in Royal MSS. 9 A. vii, f. 107 d, and 10 A. v, f. 66 d.
[4] Exch. K. R. Miscellaneous Books, vol. ix, f. 42 (38).
[5] The compilation appears to have been made about 22 Ed. I, possibly for the use of Hugh of Cressingham, justice in eyre in Lancashire in that year. The writing differs widely from the court-hand of the Chancery or Exchequer clerk, and is monastic rather than official in character.

year 1276, but the only evidence for this date is the mention, in the statute itself, of Michaelmas 1276 as the term from which the twenty-five years of the justices' inquiry was to be reckoned.[1]

In the assize rolls of 1292 [2] reference is made to a statute which at first sight appears to be this. Four foresters of H. de Lacey are indicted ' in le Rageman ' for the imprisonment of a man, and the case is adjourned because the jurors testify that they claim that the deed was done before the time of the statute. But the statute in question turns out to be that of Westminster I, ' ubi statuit contra huiusmodi transgressiones ' ; there is no reference to the term of twenty-five years.[3] Again, the ' ordinance ' mentioned in the Statute of Gloucester [4] may well be *de iustitiis assignatis*, and this would narrow the possible date to between Michaelmas 1276 and August 1278, but closer than that it does not seem possible to go.

Uncertainty as to purpose of Statute. Turning to the statute itself [5] we find that it is in fact rather an administrative order than an act of legislation. It orders justices to be sent throughout the land to hear and determine complaints against the king's officials and others for offences committed within the last fifteen or twenty-five years.[6] Sir J. Ramsay describes it as ' the first step towards taking action on the reports of the Commissioners of 1274, now sent in and embodied in the Hundred Rolls ', and considers that it was designed to obtain special powers for the ordinary itinerant justices.[7] If so, these powers were not used for two years after 1276 ; the next eyre was sent out in the autumn of 1278, when the justices' powers were further enhanced by the terms of the Statute of Gloucester, and the ground was further cleared for them by a wholesale renewal

---

[1] ' Iustices ailent parmi la terre a enquere e oier e terminer les plaintes e les quereles de trepas feez dedenz ses xxv aunz passez avaunt la Seint Michel Lan du Regne le Rei Edward quart.'

[2] A. R. 408, m. 13. Printed in Quo Warranto Rolls (R. C.), p. 387 b.

[3] Cf. A. R. 667, m. 11 (Notts. 1280), where a return to a *vetus capitulum* (49) relates how three sheriffs, whose terms of office range from 1271 to 1274, ' ceperunt huiusmodi redemptionem post statutum '.

[4] See above, p. 40.   [5] S. R., i, p. 44.

[6] The manuscripts vary.

[7] The Dawn of the Constitution, p. 327.

of the sheriffs.[1] Mr. Scargill-Bird, on the other hand, says that the Extract Hundred Roll entitled *Veredicta de Ministris*,[2] which is endorsed 4 E. I., contains pleas on the Statute of Rageman,[3] a theory which would involve the journey of justices in at least six, and those scattered, counties of England, between Michaelmas and November 20, 1276, when the fifth year of Edward's reign began. Again, the statute not only gives the justices power to determine cases arising out of the inquests heretofore found by the king's command, but also to punish offences committed since, ' especially trespasses since committed by any bailiffs whomsoever against the good men by whose oaths those inquests were made ' ;[4] and specifically refers to the articles delivered to the justices for this purpose. Are we to see here yet another special inquest, occurring between the summer of 1275, when the Hundred Rolls were complete, and the autumn of 1278, when the general eyre began whose justices, as the Close Rolls show,[5] bore with them copies of the Hundred Roll returns ?

Both external and internal evidence as to the character of the statute is thus ambiguous. Possibly some additional light may be thrown on the question by a consideration of its alternative name—The statute called Rageman. It may be noted that this name is not used in the body of the statute, nor, as I have shown, is the instrument quoted by this name in any official record. On the face of it, it looks like a popular nickname, possibly of a later date than that of its promulgation. Of the derivation and root meaning of this word the

Meaning of name Rageman.

---

[1] In October 1278 the sheriffs of twenty-four of the counties were changed. Most of the outgoing men had held office since October 1274. P. R. O. Lists and Indexes, no. ix.

[2] Ex. R. 4. (Unprinted.)

[3] Guide to the Public Records, p. 271. For the true character of Extract Hundred Roll 4 (De Ministris) see below, c. ii, § 2. It may be noted at once, however, that it records merely verdicts or presentments, not pleadings, and that there is no warrant for dating it 4 Ed. I.

[4] An entry on one of the Lincolnshire Hundred Rolls illustrates this clause. ' Et isti predicti iurati de istis suprascriptis inquisitionibus factis monstramus domino Regi quod ballivi sui et etiam ballivi aliorum in dicto wappentakio de Kirketon causa istius veredicti nostri minantur nobis gravare et ea occasione iniustis districtionibus et gravioribus extorsionibus plus nobis modo gravantur quam unquam antea fecerunt ' (R. H., i, p. 308 b).

[5] R. H., i, p. (11), and see below.

literary authorities are in doubt ;[1] its earliest dated occurrence is in a legal record. In a general sense it seems to have
been used of a charter or deed to which many seals were
attached by strips of the parchment itself. Any document
with many signatories might present the ragged appearance
which the nickname would connote. Apart from the mediaeval
game there are three historical instances : the Ragman Roll
of 1291,[2] in which the Scots acknowledged the supremacy of
Edward I, the *indenturae ragmannicae*, by which the con-
spirators against David II of Scotland bound themselves,[3]
and the blank charters or Ragmans in which the counties,
cities, and boroughs of Richard II sought to propitiate the
king by confessions of all sorts of treasons.[4] In both cases
the charters described would end in a fringe of parchment
strips with seals attached.

Earliest
occur-
rence :
placita de
Rageman-
nis.

If we turn to the earliest occurrence of the word, we find
it in the records of the eyre of 1280. Both for Yorkshire,
Notts, and Derbyshire (1281) there are rolls of *placita de
ragemannis*.[5] In the case of Notts and Derbyshire they are
coupled with the *placita de quo warranto*, in that of Yorkshire

[1] See Halliwell's Dictionary (ii, 663) ; the New English Dictionary ;
' Instrumenta publica sive processus super fidelitatibus et homagiis
Scotorum ', 1291–6 (Bannatyne Club, 1834, p. xx).
' A Scottis, propter multa sigilla dependentia, Ragman vocabatur '
(Chron. Lanercost, p. 261).
[3] Fordun, Scotichronicon, Lib. xiv, c. 25 ' Indenturae (sive literae)
ragmannicae sigillis firmiter roboratae.'
[4] Rot. Cl. 1 Hen. IV, pt. i, m. 13. Printed Rymer, Foedera, viii, p. 109
' Scripta, Cartas sive Literas Patentes vocata Raggemans sive Blank
Chartres, sigillis eorundem subditorum separatim consignata.'
[5] A. R. 670 ' Placita de Ragemannis et de Quo Warranto coram J. de
Vall' et sociis suis iustic' itin' in com' Notingham in crastino Animarum
a. R. R. E. octavo incipiente nono.' A. R. 1078, m. 54 ' Placita Corone
de residuo com' Ebor' et de Rageman.' A. R. 152, m. 11 ' Rotulus de
Rageman et de Quo Warranto.' The nineteen Assize Rolls which contain
Placita de Ragemannis, eo nomine, are as follows :
For 1280 : A. R. 670 (Notts), 1078 (Yorkshire).
For 1281 : A. R. 152, 154 (Derbyshire).
For 1287 : A. R. 17 (Beds.), 279 (Gloucestershire).
For 1292 : A. R. 134 (Cumberland), 408 (Lancashire), 985, 987 (West-
moreland).
For 1293 : A. R. 650, 651, 652, 653, 655 (Northumberland).
For 1330 : A. R. 683, 686 (Notts).
For 1331 : A. R. 166, 169 (Derbyshire).
Note also A. R. 543, m. 69 (Middlesex, 1294) *De diversis presentationibus
super Ragemannis.*

with the *placita corone* of the shire. The cases recorded under this heading deal with liberties usurped, with purprestures, warrens, capital fees, and administration abuses. They cover, that is, precisely the ground covered by the *Nova Capitula*, and in the Yorkshire roll they are grouped under the headings of the *Nova Capitula*.

The name is next found in the Close Rolls of 1281. Walter de Wymburn delivers to William de Giselham and to Gilbert de Thornton respectively, the *Rageman* of Wilts and the *Rotulos Ragemann'* of Lincolnshire.[1] Walter de Wymburn, the king's chief justice, had been appointed in June 1275 custodian of all the rolls of the justices and of all the inquisitions of the Treasury,[2] and during the years 1278–81 there are several records of the delivery by him of rolls to the justices in eyre and others. Thus on October 24, 1278,[3] he delivers certain inquisitions of the counties of Cumberland, Northumberland, and Westmoreland to Metingham, justice of the eyre which began on November 3 at Carlisle. On April 18, 1279,[4] he delivers the inquisitions made in the counties of York, Notts, and Derby, concerning the liberties withdrawn from the king's manors and fees to W. de Saham in order to plead the inquisitions in the aforesaid counties. On July 8, 1279, he delivers the records of the last eyre in Kent and Sussex to P. de Perhanz, to be carried to J. de Reygate and his fellows, then justices in eyre in the county of Surrey.[5] On November 14, 1280,[6] he delivers to S. de Roffa the rolls of the last eyre in Southants and to W. de Saham, his fellow justice in eyre, the inquisitions lately made in Southants concerning the king's rights withdrawn. On November 10, 1281,[7] he delivers to William of Giselham, the inquisitions made in the county of Devon concerning the king's liberties and the withdrawals from the king, for him to plead the same inquisitions before the justices next in eyre in the county of Devon.

It was at Whitsuntide 1281 that the Rageman Rolls of

Margin notes:
Rotuli Ragemannorum.

Connexion with Quo Warranto pleadings of 1281.

---

[1] Rot. Cl. 98, m. 6 d (C. R. C., p. 123).
[2] C. R. C., p. 185 (1275).
[3] C. R. C., p. 509 (1278).
[4] C. R. C., p. 558 (1279).
[5] C. R. C., p. 568 (1279).
[6] C. R. C., p. 67 (1280).
[7] C. R. C., p. 139 (1281).

Wilts and Lincolnshire were delivered to William of Giselham and Gilbert of Thornton. The eyre of Wiltshire was then in full swing, for it continued from Easter to Michaelmas of this year, first at Wilton and then at Marlborough.[1] The eyre of Lincolnshire began at Trinity of this year.[2] On turning up the Wiltshire rolls we find that ' Willelmus de Giselham sequitur pro Rege ' in a series of cases which are in fact Quo Warranto pleadings, though they are headed *Placita domini Regis.*[3] William of Giselham is in fact the king's serjeant, and the rolls show him suing for the king in other counties besides Wilts.[4] Gilbert of Thornton is described as the king's advocate or *narrator*, and we find him obtaining from the Chancery copies of charters concerning the manor of Doncaster, which was claimed by the king from its holder, as if he too were suing in *placita de quo warranto.*[5] The rolls of the Lincolnshire eyre confirm this impression ; Gilbert sues for the king in a series of pleas which are headed *Placita de Libertatibus et de Quo Warranto.*[6] But the Lincolnshire rolls throw yet more light on the Close Roll entry ; they include a writ to the justices in eyre which enjoins them to render all assistance in their power to John de Metyngham, whom the king has specially assigned to examine and determine the king's pleas and the verdicts of the inquisitions as to lands and fees alienated, *which inquisitions have been delivered to the king's attornies.*[7] If we accept ' attorney ' as an adequate description of Gilbert de Thornton, it becomes impossible to avoid the conclusion that the ' Rotuli de Ragemannis ' are identical with those inquisitions concerning liberties and

---

[1] A. R. 1001, m. 1, m. 90.   [2] A. R. 486.   [3] A. R. 1001, m. 47.

[4] In Surrey 1279, C. R. C., p. 546 ; in Devon 1281, A. R. 185 ; in Norfolk 1283, C. R. C., p. 225 ; in Norfolk 1286, C. R. C., p. 397 ; in Suffolk 1286, A. R. 828.

[5] C. R. C., p. 124 (1281). Gilbert sues for the king in Rutland 1286 (A. R. 722), and in Gloucestershire 1287 (A. R. 279).

[6] A. R. 498, m. 1 d, &c.

[7] A. R. 498, m. 2 ' ... Volumus quod dilectus et fidelis noster Iohannes de Metyngham placitis nostris que sunt coram vobis in itinere vestro predicto per brevia nostra homine nostro specialiter intendat ad placita nostra perplacitanda et ad veredicta inquisitionum de terris et feodis nostris alienatis quas quidem inquisitiones attornatis nostris coram vobis liberari precepimus examinanda et terminanda secundum legem et consuetudinem regni nostri.'

rights withdrawn which, as far back as 1812, were identified with the Hundred Rolls.[1] This view is reinforced by a closer inspection of the Assize Rolls. They enable us to go further, and assert that the inquest of 1274–5 was popularly, if sporadically,[2] known as ' The Rageman '.

The pleadings under the Statute of Gloucester are recorded in the Eyre Rolls of 1278–87 under various headings : *Placita domini Regis, Placita de Quo Warranto, Placita de Ragemannis, Placita de Libertatibus.* A comparison of the subject-matter in the procedure of the cases so recorded suggests that the meaning of these headings was not as yet clearly differentiated. Quo Warranto claims are made under the other three headings, and though in all the records, Quo Warranto cases far outnumber any others, cases which cannot be so described are found under the Quo Warranto heading.[3] Where these cases are introduced by present-ments, at least two sets of presentments are in question. Besides the verdicts of the hundreds in the current eyre, the counsels and the justices have before them the record of previous presentments. Thus the Sussex roll of 1279, to take the earliest of many, uses the phrase, ' Iuratores alias presentaverunt quod . . . '.[4] The Yorkshire Roll of 1280 has ' Presentatum fuit alias coram inquisitoribus '.[5] The Hants Roll of 1280–1 has ' Iuratores de inquisitione alias pre-sentaverunt quod . . . '.[6] Collation with the Hundred Rolls always produces the required reference, if the returns are complete and unabridged, but in many cases there are only Extract Rolls, and in others the returns for the hundred in

The Rotuli de Rage-mannis are the returns of 1274–5.

[1] R. H., i, p. (11).

[2] It will be noted that the heading *Placita de Ragemannis* of the Assize Rolls appears to be confined to the Northern Circuit, the Gloucestershire Roll of 1287 being the one exception, and that in spite of the Close Roll mention of the Rageman of Wilts, the name is not used in the records of the Wiltshire eyre. In Kent (A. R. 369) and Surrey (A. R. 877) reference is made to the Inquisitions of Bryanzun, one of the commissioners of 1274 for Kent, Surrey, and some other counties. E.g. in A. R. 369, m. 59, the township of Malling returns *De inquisitionibus de Bryanzun nichil sciunt sicut patet in inquisitione eiusdem.* In Somerset (A. R. 759, m. 4) refer-ence is made to the Inquisitions of Bartholomew le Jevene, commissioner for that county.

[3] e.g. A. R. 722, 804.   [4] A. R. 915, m. 4.

[5] A. R. 1078, m. 54.   [6] A. R. 784, m. 35.

question are lost. The 'Inquisition' in question is undoubtedly that of 1274–5.[1]

In several of the eyre rolls, however, another more definite form is used. 'Iurati de Rageman' presentaverunt'[2] or 'Presentatum est in Rageman''.[3] This phrase has been interpreted by Mr. Hall[4] to mean 'indicted under the statute of Rageman', presumably by a special jury to which special articles were administered, but a closer examination of these Rageman presentments shows clearly that the inquest of 1274–5 is meant. The Derbyshire Roll of 1281 proves that presentments are not contemporary. 'Presentatum est in Rageman . . . quod R. de Reresby tenuit manerium de Pleseley . . . Et modo predictum manerium est in manu magistri T. Beck Episcopi Menenens' ex alienatione R. de Wilughby cui predictus R. de Reresby dimisit. . .'.[5] The Yorkshire Roll has 'Compertum est in Ragemannis quod . . . ',[6] indicating reference to some record of the past. The most unmistakable evidence, however, is that of the Gloucestershire Roll of 1287.[7] Sometimes, as on membrane 12, the general phrase 'Presentatum fuit alias coram inquisitoribus' is used, but more often we find expressions like 'Presentatum fuit alias coram inquisitoribus de Ragemannis' (m. 9), or 'Presentatum fuit per xij iuratores de Rageman' de hundredo de Derhurst' (m. 14). The passage which dates the inquisition occurs on m. 16, where an entry is taken almost verbatim from the Hundred Rolls, with the period of twenty years altered to that of thirty-three, the thirteen years difference representing the interval between 1274 and 1287.[8]

The Northumberland Roll of 1293 is even more precise. Under the heading,[9] *De presentationibus de Rageman apud*

---

[1] It was so identified in the introduction to the Record Commission edition of the Rotuli Hundredorum, p. (11), which is, however, concerned only with Quo Warranto proceedings.

[2] A. R. 408, m. 6.   [3] A. R. 152, m. 11.

[4] English Official Historical Documents, p. 320, note 5.

[5] A. R. 152, m. 11 d.   [6] A. R. 1064, m. 68.   [7] A. R. 279.

[8] 'Presentatum fuit alias coram inquisitoribus per xii de Duddeston . . . quod W. de Valentin sectas subtraxit . . . iam triginta tribus annis elapsis.' Cf. H. R., i, p. 181 'viginti annis elapsis.'

[9] A. R. 655, m. 2.

Novum Castrum we read, 'Presentatum fuit alias coram Galfrido Aguillon et Philippo de Wylughby assignatis ad inquirendum super quibusdam articlis ex parte domini Regis quod ...'. The returns which follow can in most cases be traced, exact in substance and detail, in the printed Extract Rolls and the unprinted roll *De ministris*,[1] though these are of course incomplete. Unfortunately the names of the commissioners for Northumberland are not given on the Patent Roll, but there can be no doubt that the inquest of 1274–5 is meant. The relation of that inquest to the eyre is indicated in the entry on murage on membrane 3 : ' Et quia iusticie itinerantes hic tam ratione presentationis predicte quam articlorum itineris sui volebant ad plenum super hiis certiorari preceperunt vicecomitem quod venire faceret coram eis omnes collectores muragii.'

The Nottingham roll blends the two uses of the word in a characteristically mediaeval fashion ; *Rageman* is at once the inquiry and the record of the inquiry. Under the *Placita de Ragemannis et de Quo Warranto* we read first that Gerard de Hedon ' super quo nichil presentatur in Ragemannis ' comes and shows his charter of free warren,[2] as holders of liberties had been invited to do by the Statute of Gloucester. Then follows the entry ' Presentatum est per omnes wapentakios totius comitatus Notingham, prout plenius patet in omnibus Ragemannis eiusdem comitatus quod . . .' a certain coroner has committed certain offences.[3] Indeed, the word appears to designate the jurors themselves in a third passage, ' Compertum est per presentationem Ragemannorum '.[4]

The evidence adduced warrants the statement that the inquest of 1274–5 was popularly known, at least in some quarters, as the Rageman Inquisition ; that its jurors were the 'iuratores de Rageman', and its returns, the Hundred Rolls as we now call them, were the 'Rotuli de Rageman' or Rageman Rolls.

The inquest of 1274-5 was called the Rageman.

The few facts known of the history of the records themselves support this view.

---

[1] See R. H., ii, pp. 19, 20, 24 : Ex. R. 4, m. 11.
[2] A. R. 670, m. 1 d.   [3] Ibid., m. 1 d.   [4] Ibid., m. 4.

Tradition-
al use of
the name
in the Ex-
chequer.

The origin of the official designation, ' The Hundred Rolls ', is not clear, but it is certainly not contemporary. The Deputy Keeper of the Public Records, writing in 1841,[1] refers to a ' bag called the Ragman, in which there are many inquisitions in divers shires touching liberties withholden from the King in Edward I's time '. The contents of this bag are described in detail in the Ninth Report,[2] and amongst a heterogeneous mass of documents, ranging from Henry III to Henry VIII, there are the *Extracte Inquisitionum* 3 *and* 4 *Edward I*, which the Record Commission had printed under the title of the Extract Hundred Rolls, as well as the unprinted Extract Roll, *De Ministris*. There is also a small mutilated roll of membranes [3] endorsed, but probably not in a contemporary hand, ' Articuli de quibus inquirendum scilicet Rageman '. This contains portions of several lists of Articles of the Eyre, both Old and New, differing in no way, where they are legible, from the standard versions, and throws no further light on the question, except as reinforcing the presumption that no independent Rageman Records exist.[4] Lastly, one of the Herefordshire Hundred Rolls bears the endorsement ' Ragman ' in an Elizabethan hand.[5]

Two exter-
nal refer-
ences.

Two instances of the use of the term come from the early years of the seventeenth century. In the pleadings on the case of Dowell *v.* Saunders in the Hilary Term of 15 James I it was declared that ' le erecting dun pigeon house serra enquirable come sewee pur le Roy pur ceo que ceo est come un franchise et pur ceo Ragman Rowle in le Exchequer '.[6] This might well be an allusion to those of the New Chapters

---

[1] Second Report, Appendix I, p. 10.

[2] Ninth Report, Appendix II, p. 243.

[3] Now catalogued Miscellanea of the Exchequer 2/31.

[4] Mr. Hall's reference, p. 302, to ' distinct records ' in this connexion is misleading : neither separate articles nor separate verdicts are traceable in connexion with the Statute de Rageman.

[5] H. R., Hereford 3 (C. H. Series). R. H., i, p. 186 (Hundred of Welbetre) does not print the endorsement.

[6] In an unprinted manuscript, quoted Notes and Queries, 8th Series, xii, p. 244. Of the two references cited by Mr. Neilson, ' Vet. Magna Carta Cap. Itineris, fo. 123 ', corresponds to the paging of Tottel's Magna Carta, edition of 1556, but I have been unable to trace ' lestatute de Rageman ibidem ' (sc. in the Exchequer), fo. 28, unless it is a mistake for fo. 38 of the Exchequer Book ix, where a copy of the statute is given. See above, p. 41.

which deal with franchises usurped or abused, or to the returns made to them. A less equivocal reference is to be found in the works of the Gloucestershire antiquary, John Smyth, steward to three generations of Berkeleys. In his ' Lives of the Berkeleys ', written between 1618 and 1628, he makes careful and copious use of national no less than manorial records. Writing of Joan, wife of Thomas of Berkeley, he says, ' Shee held also a Manor in Aure in the hundred of Bledislowe in the County of Gloc: ', and gives as his reference, ' Rot: Ragem: in rec: Scii: 4 Ed. I '.[1] The Extract Hundred Rolls for Gloucester, which are endorsed 4 Ed. I, give under the heading *de purpresturis* for the hundred of Blideslawe, ' Item Iohanna de Berkel' in manerio de Aure '.[2] Again, in writing of Maurice II of Berkeley, Smyth says, ' The grand jury that served for the hundred of Berkeley before the justices itinerant at Gloucester in the 4th year of King Edward I . . . presented, That this Lord claimed to have returne of writtes throughout his said hundred, the rating of the Assize of bread and ale, gallows for the execution of thieves, tumbrell and the like . . . And that he had distrained Ancelme de Gurney . . . And like complaint against this lord did the jury in Somersetshire make touching his hundred of Portbury, who presented that he used to take wrecks of sea, but not knowne by what title.' [3] All these details correspond, sometimes word for word, with the entries in the Extract Hundred Rolls for Gloucestershire and Somerset ; [4] and the reference given by Smyth is ' Rot: Rageman: 4 Ed. I in recept: Scii '. These facts finally establish the identity of the ' Rageman Rolls ' of James I's reign with the ' Hundred Roll ' of to-day.

The explanation of this popular nickname for the Hundred Roll Inquisitions may be found in the form of the original returns, where these are preserved. The records printed in the Record Commission volumes are of varying character, and require a closer analysis than they have yet received

Origin of the term.

---

[1] Smyth, Lives of the Berkeleys, i, p. 117.　　[2] R. H., i, p. 181 b.
[3] Smyth, Lives of the Berkeleys, i, pp. 131–2.
[4] R. H., i, p. 181 b, Hundredum de Berkel' ; p. 181 a, Hundredum de Burnetr'. R. H., ii, p. 130 b, Hundredum de Portbury.

before their exact relation to the inquest can be established,[1] but in some instances the original returns are undoubtedly extant. As in the ordinary eyre,[2] the jury of each hundred presented a written verdict, but unlike those few verdicts of the eyre which we possess, the returns to the inquest of 1274–5 are sealed as well as signed by the jurors, thus resembling the returns to special inquests, many examples of which are preserved at the Record Office.[3] In the case of the Nottinghamshire rolls,[4] for instance, the return of each hundred is made on a separate membrane, the foot of which is split up into twelve or twenty-four strips, which originally bore the seals of the jurors whose names are appended to the record.[5] The rolls are emphatically ' ragged ' in aspect, and belong to the class of record to which the name ' rageman ' or ' ragment ' was later held to be appropriate.

Connexion with the Statute.   How then are we to explain the transfer of this name from the Inquisitions of 1274–5 to the ' statute ' *de iustitiis assignatis* ?

Notwithstanding the ambiguity and incompleteness of the records it is possible to show that from the inquisitions of 1274–5 one or more compilations were made, and either these extracts or the original inquisitions were given to the justices sent on the general eyres of 1278–87.[6] Till the matter has

---

[1] A close inspection of the returns for Essex shows that the three records, in the *Inquisitiones*, the *Extracta Inquisitionum*, and the *Veredicta de Ministris*, whilst covering the same ground geographically, and very frequently giving the same information, each contain material lacking in the other two, and each refer to another record. See below, Chap. II, § 2.

[2] See below, p. 62.

[3] See, for instance, Sheriff's Accounts, Bundle 3, No. 1, Inquest on debts of late Sheriff: ' Inquisitionem . . . sub sigillo tuo et sigillo inquisitorum.' Bundle 13, No. 1, Inquest on adherents of the Scots : ' In cuius rei testimonium sigilla sunt presente apposita.' Bundle 14, No. 4, Inquest on goods of a collector of a Twelfth; includes mandate and return with seals attached. Bundle 22, No. 7, Inquest into unlicensed sale of leather. The return ends, ' in cuius rei testimonium predicti iuratores huic inquisitioni sigilla sua apposuerunt '.

[4] Hundred Roll Nottingham, Tower Series. Printed R. H., ii, pp. 300–20. E.g. p. 309 a ' Et in omnium premissorum testimonium omnes supra dicti iurati presenti inquisitioni sigilla apposuerunt.'

[5] The verdict of the Hundred of Tiverton (H. R. Devon, No. 40) still retains one seal intact.

[6] Probably the original inquisitions ; the Extract Rolls for Yorkshire at least are of later date than 1280. See note on R. H., i, p. 135 b, which

been further investigated, it must remain uncertain whether any judicial proceedings were taken upon those returns before November 1278.[1] It seems probable, on the whole, that if peccant officials were brought to book, it was rather in the Exchequer or in the King's Bench than before 'Justices of Rageman' or any others specially assigned; and if the government used the information collected 1274–5, it does not appear on the records to have been put in evidence formally.[2] The proceedings of 1278 appear to mark a new departure.

explains the incompleteness of the extracts by the failure of the justices in eyre to return all the *Veredicta*. Cf. C. R. C. (1280), p. 67.

[1] Mr. Hall (Eng. Off. Hist. Docts., p. 320, note 2) suggests that Assize Roll 1233 (Easter 1277) contains pleadings under the 'Statute of Rageman', and prints parallel passages from the Extract Roll *De ministris* in support of his theory (Formula Book of Legal Records, pp. 145–7 ; note that the two page references on p. 145 should be exchanged). The Assize Roll has been collated with the Extract Roll, with the result that no case has been found recorded upon both save that of John de Gymmingham, which Mr. Hall cites, whilst there is no sign that the proceedings in his case were originated by the presentments of 1274–5, as the *placita de Ragemannis* upon the eyre rolls from 1278 onwards are, on their own showing. The Assize Roll records the accusations brought, in some nineteen cases, against some twenty-seven officials, mostly of the county of Norfolk ; the Extract Roll records the misdeeds of some 350 officials of that county, and though a few names are found on both rolls, no offences are common to the two records save those of John de Gymmingham's oppressors. Moreover, the pleas in question are not held before justices assigned or Justices of Assize ; they are held *coram Rege*, when Edward I and his Bench were at Norwich and Ipswich at Eastertide 1277 (see T. Craib, An Attempted Itinerary of Edward I, P. R. O., in typescript), and their adjournments are taken in the King's Bench at Westminster and Shrewsbury (Coram Rege Rolls 31, 33). The Assize Rolls proper of 1275–8 have been searched in vain for ' De Ministris ' proceedings based upon the Hundred Rolls presentments.

Some notes upon one of the Lincolnshire Hundred Rolls seem at first sight to refer to some independent ' Rageman ' proceedings. They seem to have been made by the justices of the Lincolnshire Eyre of 1281, and concern a certain Walter Clerk, R. H., i, p. 247 a ' Nichil de eo hic nec alibi quia coram R. de Loveday fecit finem pro omnibus transgressionibus'; R. H. i, p. 256 b ' Walterus fecit finem pro omnibus transgressionibus in Ragem'.' Loveday, however, was one of the justices of this eyre, and on turning up the eyre roll head with his name was found the entry (A. R. 488, m. 4), ' De Waltero clerico de fine pro transgressione in Ragemann' xxs.'. The transaction noted upon the Hundred Roll took place in the eyre of 1281 ; the note is either a memorandum by one of Loveday's fellows, probably indicating a division of labour amongst the justices which necessitated occasional notes to prevent overlapping, or else one added later than 1281, at another eyre, or in some other court.

[2] It may be noted that a large proportion of the sheriffs appointed in October 1274 held their offices till October 1278, when a wholesale renewal took place. See P. R. O. Lists and Indexes, ix, under several shires.

The 'statute' *de iustitiis assignatis*, together with the Statute of Gloucester, which, as we have seen, appears to refer to it, instruct the justices to proceed upon the inquests recently made, both as to franchises claimed and as to administrative abuses. It is possible that these proceedings might have taken place sooner, but for the Welsh campaign of 1277,[1] and that the statute *de iustitiis assignatis* really belongs to 1276; on the other hand, the very close resemblance of its terms to those of the instructions which conclude the first section of the new articles delivered to the justices in 1278,[2] which, as we have seen, immediately follow it in the semi-official Exchequer Book, may indicate that it should be assigned to the late summer of 1278. We need not postulate a parliament of three estates, for it is drawn up by the king and his council.[3] In any case, comparison with the Statute of Gloucester and the new writ of the eyre [4] makes it almost certain that the justices assigned are justices in eyre, and not justices of some special commission of Oyer and Terminer,[5] and sets the Statute of Rageman in its true perspective as the complement of the Statute of Gloucester. On this showing, then, the popular nickname of Rageman picked up and appropriated by the justices of the northern circuit [6] or their

---

[1] Cf. P. R. C. (1277), p. 239, where command is given that certain pleas be suspended on account of the Welsh war.

[2] 'Item de omnibus predictis factis vel commissis in terra xxv annos proxime preteritos predicti iustitii se intromittant, et omnes illi qui sentiunt se grauatos super hiis et super hiis se conqueri voluerint audiantur, et fiat eis super hoc iustitia, et ipsi iustitii sequantur super hiis que dominum Regem tangunt' (K. R. Misc. Books, vol. ix, printed S. R., i, p. 236). Cf. Dorset Roll for 1280, *De querelis citra xxv annos* (A. R. 204, m. 14).

[3] 'Accorde est pur nostre seygnur le Roy et sun counsayl' (MS. Harl. 667, f. 247). [4] See below, v, p. 57.

[5] 'Constituimus etiam eosdem iusticiarios nostros ad audiendum et terminandum placita de libertatibus . . . et transgressiones . . . et querelos . . . de ministris. . . .' Cf. 'Justices ailent parmi la tere a enquere e oier e terminer les plaintes e les quereles de trepas. . . .' The wording of the writ has led the compiler of the Patent Roll calendar to describe the commission of an eyre of 1292, identical in form with that of 1278, as 'a commission of eyre together with a commission of oyer and terminer'. See P. R. C., p. 485.

[6] It may be noted that William de Saham, who pleaded the king's pleas on the Yorks, Notts, and Derbyshire eyres, was justice at the Gloucestershire eyre of 1287, which furnishes the only example of the use of the name in the south.

clerks, came into general use as designating the inquests of 1274-5, and was transferred, either at the time or later, to the instrument which authorized the justices to follow up the inquiry. The justices who went their rounds in the years 1278-87 under this commission carried with them the rolls, upon some of which their notes are still to be read. The connexion between their activities and the Hundred Roll Inquest was obvious; it was as natural that the statute which gave them power to act upon the presentments of 1274-5 should come to bear the same name as that its fellow should come to be called the statute *de Quo Warranto*.

None of the records that we have been considering suggests Scope of the *placita de Rage-mannis.* that the *placita de Ragemannis* were confined to the mis-doings of officials. Most often the heading *Placita de Quo Warranto et de Ragemannis* leaves it uncertain which are Rageman pleas, but when there is a single heading, the pleadings are very miscellaneous in character. As in the rolls of 1281 we find returns ' in Ragman ' to a large pro-portion of the *Nova Capitula,*[1] so, as late as 1331, we find the *placita de Ragemannis* including returns not merely to the new but also to the old chapters of the eyre,[2] and touching on matters like the breaking down of bridges, the sale of wines, failure to attend the eyre, and conspiracy to defeat justice. It would seem that in the last days of the eyre the heading ' Rageman ' covers all except the coroner's returns and the Quo Warranto pleadings, which are quite distinct in the eyre.[3]

The Statute of Rageman, then, and the Rageman proceed-ings arise out of the inquests of 1274-5, and, so far as can be seen, are concerned only with the articles of the eyre, and mainly with the New Articles. Throughout they are closely associated with the Statute of Gloucester. As we have seen, the records of the Quo Warranto and Rageman proceedings are hardly distinguishable at first, though it would seem that by the reign of Edward III the Quo Warranto cases form a distinct class, and the *placita de Ragemannis* appear to cover all other kinds of proceedings arising out of the *Nova*

---

[1] A. R. 152, m. 11.   [2] A. R. 166, m. 51.   [3] A. R. 164.

Capitula, and as the statute says, ' as well all manner of trespasses, quarrels and offences . . . touched in the inquests heretofore found as trespasses committed since, whether by the King's bailiffs or by others '.

v. *The Eyres of* 1278–81

On August 16, 1278,[1] the king and others of his council at Gloucester appointed justices in eyre for the north, namely for Cumberland, Westmoreland, and Northumberland, and for the south, namely for Hertford and Kent. Thus was initiated that series of general eyres which continued throughout the next three or four years, for whereas Henry III had appointed six or eight circuits,[2] and so accomplished a comprehensive *iter* in one or two years, Edward, throughout his reign, preferred to appoint a smaller number of judges, and thus to spread the *iter* over many years. With the help of the Assize Rolls we can follow the steps of the two sets of justices on the northern and southern circuits, from county to county,[3] and can even trace the different idiosyncrasies, whether of the judges or of their clerks, in the varying form of the records, some examples of which have already been given.

The commissions of the justices bear the stamp of recent legislation, and point to innovations both in the form and in the proceedings of the eyre. Comparison with the announcement of the Middlesex eyre of 1274 will be useful. This runs :

' De itinere Iustitiarum in com. Midd. Rex constituit

---

[1] C. R. C., p. 503 ; P. R. C., p. 277.

[2] e.g. in 1234, P.R.C., pp. 76–8.

[3] In the south : November 3, 1278, Hertford ; January 21, 1279, Canterbury ; June 25, Chichester ; October 2, Guildford ; January 21, 1280, Sherborne ; May 31, Somerton ; November 18, Winchester ; April 21, 1281, Wilton ; September, Marlborough ; November, Exeter.

In the north : November 3, 1278, Carlisle ; 1279, Appleby and Newcastle, the justices going back and forth from January to May ; October 7, 1279, York ; November 3, 1280, Nottingham ; January 13, 1281, York ; Easter, 1281, Derby ; Trinity, 1281, Lincoln. Lancashire was almost certainly omitted. The Yorkshire eyre, extending from Michaelmas 1279 to Michaelmas 1280, and from Hilarytide to Easter of 1281, beats the ten months Eyre of Kent in 1313, which Mr. Bolland suggests as a possible record for duration (Eyre of Kent, S. S., p. li).

magistrum R. de S., J. de C., W. de H., et S. de R. Iustitiarios suos ad itinerandum ad communia placita hac vice in com. Midd. Et mandatum est Archiepiscopo . . . et omnibus aliis de comitatu predicto quod eisdem . . . tanquam Iustitiariis Regis itinerantibus in omnibus que ad placita illa pertinent intendentes sint et respondentes sic alias in aliis itineribus facere consuerunt.'[1]

The commission of 1278 runs as follows :

' De itinere iusticiarum. Rex archiepiscopo (etc.) de com. Cumberl' Westmorl' et Northumberl' salutem. Sciatis quod constituimus dilectos et fideles nostros abbatem Westm., I. de V., W. de S., G. de L., I. de M., et T. de S., Iusticiarios nostros ad itinerandum ad communia placita hac vice in comitatibus predictis. Constituimus etiam eosdem Iusticiarios nostros ad audienda et terminanda placita de libertatibus iuxta provisionem et ordinacionem inde factas et ad transgressiones et querelas omnium conquerentium seu conqueri volentium tam de ministris et ballivis nostris quibuscumque quam de ministris et ballivis aliorum et aliis quibuscumque et ad quascunque querimonias audiendas et competentes emendas inde faciendas secundum legem et consuetudinem regni nostri et iuxta ordinationem per nos inde factam et iuxta tenorem statutorum nostrorum et iuxta articulos eis inde traditos et iniunctos. Et ideo vobis mandamus quod eisdem . . . tanquam Iusticiis nostris itinerantibus in omnibus que ad placita illa pertinent intendentes sitis et respondentes sicut predictum est.'[2]

The twofold character of the inquests is still reflected ; franchises and administrative abuses are alike to be the subject-matter of the eyre ; the recent ordinance (*de iustitiis assignatis*) and statutes (of Westminster and Gloucester) and the new articles (of the eyre) are all expressly mentioned.[3] It may be noted also that the procedure of *querimonium*, the seeking of justice by *querele* or bills, which would seem to be an innovation in the proceedings of the eyre, is apparently taken over from the inquests of 1274-5.[4]

[1] Rot. Pat. 2 Ed. I, m. 3.
[2] Rot. Pat. 6 Ed. I, m. 6 (August 16, 1278). Cf. writ to sheriff printed Statutes at Large, i, p. 71 ; and see also writ for eyres of Kent, Surrey, and Sussex, Rot. Pat. 7 Ed. I, m. 19.
[3] This becomes the model writ of the eyre, and is unchanged in form as late as 1321.
[4] See below, Chap. II, § 7.

The term *Nova Capitula*, later to become stereotyped in many law books and records, is thus of real significance in the eyre rolls of 1279–81, and the method of administering the new articles clearly varied locally. In Cumberland the *Vetera Capitula* are presented hundred by hundred, and then comes the heading: *Placita corone de corpore comitatus secundum Nova statuta et additiones capitulorum.*[1] The Hertford Roll gives the heading *De novis capitulis* under each hundred.[2] The Kent and Surrey Rolls do the same, adding, as we have seen, the heading *De inquisitionibus de Brianzun.*[3] The Nottingham and Derby Rolls make no reference *eo nomine* to the new articles, but, as we have seen, returns are made to the *Nova Capitula* under the headings *de quo warranto et de Ragemannis.*[4] We should gather from these facts that the justices of the northern circuit used a different procedure in administering the old and the new chapters, whereas the southern justices gave the old and new together to the jurors of the hundreds.

Before the *iter* had proceeded far one more article had been added to those concerning which inquiry was to be made. On January 13, 1279,[5] the king issued to his justices in eyre letters close, instructing them to inquire into conspiracies to defeat justice. This writ, which anticipates to some extent the statute or ordinance *de Conspiratoribus* issued in 1305 in connexion with the Trailbaston inquiries,[6] is worth quoting in full.

'Dominus Rex mandavit Iusticiariis suis itinerantibus in diversis comitatibus breve suum in hoc verba. Edwardus dei gratia etc. Iusticiariis suis itinerantibus in com' Kant' salutem. Quia datum est nobis intellegi quod quidam maliciosi homines de pluribus comitatibus regni nostri propter incrementum utilitatis proprie proniores ad malum quam ad bonum quasdam detestabiles confederationes et malas cogitationes, prestitis mutuo sacramentis, ad amicorum et benivo-

---

[1] A. R. 132, m. 32. [2] A. R. 323, m. 40 et seq.
[3] A. R. 369, 877.
[4] A. R. 152, 664, 670. Some of the cases under this heading appear to arise out of 1275 presentments, but some are undoubtedly new.
[5] A. R. 789, m. 4 d, and Rot. Cl. 7 Ed. I, m. 10.
[6] S. R., i, p. 145 ; and see below, § 5, i.

lorum suorum partes in placitis et loquelis ipsos contingentibus in comitatibus illis utpote in assisis, iuratis et recognitionibus fallaciter manutenendas et defendendas, et ad inimicos suos fraudulenter grauandos, et in quantum in ipsis est plerumque exheredendos, inter se facere presumpserunt, et nos considerantes grauibus periculis et dampnis innumeris que tam nobis quam ceteris de regno nostro ex huiusmodi hominum malicia provenire possent, in futurum eorundem insolentiam congruis remediis reprimere volentes, vobis mandamus quod in singulis comitatibus in quibus vos itinerare contigerit ista vice de huiusmodi confederatoribus et conspiratoribus quanto diligentius poteritis inquiratur. Et si quos inde culpabiles inveneritis sine dilatione capi et in prisona nostra salvos custodiri faciatis, donec aliud inde preceperimus ; et hoc nullatenus omittatis. Teste meipso apud Wyndelesore xiij die Ianuarii a.r.n. septimo.'

Upon this writ was based the article *De mutuis sacramentis*, which, added to the chapters of the eyre in 1279, is thenceforth known immutably as *Novum capitulum per breve Regis*,[1] and is found in all complete lists, sometimes annexed to the *Vetera Capitula* and sometimes to the *Nova*. The searching inquisitions of the government were doubtless beginning to defeat their own end, and the ingenuity of the guilty was devising both evasion and exploitation of royal justice, as the returns to this article on the Somersetshire Roll of 1280 prove.[2] The ' new chapter ' was to be one of the first of a long series of measures directed against the practice of maintenance.[3]

Besides the traces of this eyre on the Assize and Chancery Rolls, it is the origin of four of our law-book versions. The Harleian MS. 489 heads its list of articles *Capitula placitanda coram iusticiis de Itinere anno r. r. E. filii r. H. viii*, prefaces it with a writ to the sheriff of Somerset and by extracts from the French form of the ' Statute de Quo Warranto '.[4] It derives undoubtedly from a copy of the articles belonging to some clerk or judge who took part in the proceedings of the Somersetshire eyre of 1280. After the concluding section of instructions to the justices with regard to the enforcement

---

[1] A. R. 903, m. 5.
[3] See also Stat. West. I, cc. 28, 33.
[2] A. R. 759, m. 9 d.
[4] MS. Harl. 489, § 53.

of the Statute of Westminster I there are added two isolated chapters, neither of which are to be found in the Exchequer Book, the article *de mutuis sacramentis*, and this : *de hiis qui ceperunt mercedem de aliquibus pro advocaria*[1] *habenda cum non sint eorum tenentes nec residentes in eorum terris.* Both the Statute of Westminster I[2] and the Statute of Gloucester[3] legislate upon vouching to warranty, but this article has a closer connexion with the Statute de Bigamis (1276),[4] and is probably designed to check a fraudulent use of the provisions securing a lord's voucher to his tenant. It would appear that the article was added during the eyres of 1278–81, since wherever it occurs it is found before the article *de mutuis sacramentis*, which belongs to 1279, and a return to it is found on a Devonshire eyre roll of 1281.[5] The fact that it does not appear in the version of Harl. MS. 1214, which purports to belong to the Lincolnshire eyre of 1281, suggests that its use may at first have been confined to the western counties, but this manuscript is so carelessly written that its evidence has little weight.

Three versions[6] of the articles open with the writ addressed to the Lincolnshire justices,[7] which possibly justifies us in assigning their origin to the eyre of 1281. Only one of them, however, MS. Harl. 1214, includes the articles upon the statutes, and these are intermixed with the articles of 1274, owing to the shifting of a page in the book from which they were copied.[8] It is a late and unintelligent copy, and adds

---

[1] The reading *advocaria* is preferable to *advocatione*, which is given in S. R. and some manuscripts. See Bolland, Eyre of Kent, p. 46, and compare return quoted below, which clearly refers to vouching to warranty and not to advowson.

[2] c. xl.   [3] c. xii.   [4] c. vi : S. R., i, p. 43.

[5] A. R. 189, m. 39, Hundred of Tuuertone : ' De hiis qui capiunt denarios sibi aliquibus pro advocaria habenda. Dicunt quod J. Savage magister hospitalis Sancti Iohannis de Bothemescul capit quolibet anno unam libram cere de R. Coleman de Tyverton et de R. Scadde dimidiam libram cere pro huiusmodi advocaria habenda ut sint sicut ceteri tenentes hospitalis quieti de sectis et aliis.'

[6] MS. Harl. 1214 ; MS. Harl. 1120 ; Add. MS. 6061.

[7] ' Edwardus Dei gratia (etc.). Iusticiariis suis Itinerantibus in Com' Lincoln' salutem. Scire facias nobis diligenter in fide quam nobis tenemini de articulis subscriptis qualiter et quomodo servantur et sub qua forma.'

[8] Article 14 of the 1274 articles (f. 9 d) is followed by article 5 of the articles upon the statutes, which are given in their true order up to article

little to our information. But the three versions have much in common in small textual variations, and the fact that the first two of the *Vetera Capitula* are omitted in all of them, suggests a close relation to the list of articles as it appears on the typical *Veredictum Hundredi*, where the coroner's returns to Article 2 are always so bulky as to isolate the first two articles from the remainder. Why the articles on the statutes are omitted from two of the lists it is impossible to say ; we have conclusive proof that they were delivered to the jurors upon this eyre.[1]

There is in existence a *Veredictum Hundredi*—one of the original returns made in the Wiltshire eyre of 1281. It is ill written, incomplete, and very much contracted ; far inferior to the similar records for 1287 and 1294, which we shall have to examine shortly. On the other hand, it forms the first official version of the articles since the list upon the Patent Roll of 1227, unless that in the Exchequer Book is to be so considered, and it has various points of unique interest. It has not hitherto been identified as an eyre record, but is catalogued among the Chapter House Hundred Rolls as Wiltshire, Roll 36, while a modern endorsement attributes it to 39 H. III and 3 E. I. The heading and the coroner's returns are missing, but internal evidence and a comparison with the Assize Rolls prove it to be the verdict of the Hundred of Chippenham for the eyre of 1281.

A detailed comparison with earlier versions will be found in Appendix II, but certain points of general interest may be noted here. The main block of the *Vetera Capitula* terminate approximately where the versions of 1254 ended. The *Nova Capitula* include all the articles of 1274, though in some cases the order is unusually disturbed, and, in addition, the article *qui durante discordia*,[2] which, but for this record, we should have supposed confined to 1274–5. The inquiries as to the illicit export of wool were apparently not completed by 1281, as the note on the Lincolnshire Rolls also would suggest.[3]

28 (f. 11), when the 1274 articles begin again at No. 16, and are given in their normal order, followed by the remainder of the articles upon the statutes.   [1] e.g. A. R. 133, m. 30 ; 323, m. 45.
    [2] See above, § 4, i.   [3] See above, note on p. 35.

The directions to the justices are omitted. The articles upon the statutes are given fully and in their normal order ; but the article *de advocaria habenda* is omitted, though that of 1279 is given. Then follow three of the *Vetera Capitula*, all of them later than 1254 in origin. Of the ten articles added to the *Vetera Capitula* after 1254, six are found in this list, two in the first block of articles, four at the end of the third block. It is the first dated occurrence of four of them. The remaining four may be covered by the phrase ' De ceteris capitulis tactis nichil quam quod supra dicitur ', with which the record concludes, and which accounts for the other omissions in the list.

vi. *The Articles of* 1287, 1288, *and* 1294

For 1287 we possess a far more satisfactory list of the articles. Catalogued among the Hundred Rolls of the Chapter House Series there is a small roll which belongs to the Gloucestershire eyre of 1287.[1] It is headed : ' Hic est veredictum de Pukelechirche per vj juratos (names follow) coram domino Willelmo de Saham '—the rest being obliterated. The dates of the *nova placita* extend from 55 H. III to 15 E. I, and it was in that year that William de Saham and his fellows held the first Gloucestershire eyre of Edward's reign.[2] The roll is in fact the verdict of the jurors of the half-hundred of Pucklechurch in that eyre, and it is parallel to the Wilts verdict of 1281 which has just been described and to the Surrey series for 1294 preserved among the Assize Rolls.[3] Together they give a final confirmation of Maitland's conjecture that the jurors' verdicts were made in writing.[4]

The list does not provide any new articles, unless, as we suggested above, the article *de advocaria habenda* is subsequent to the second Statute of Westminster. On the other hand it appears, on collation with other versions, to be the most careful and complete of any that we have yet considered,

---

[1] H. R., C. H. Series, Gloucester 6.   [2] A. R. 278–84.
[3] A. R. 892–906.
[4] Select Pleas of the Crown (S. S.), p. 28 : ' This seems to show that, at least occasionally, the jurors put in writing their answers to the Articles of the Eyre.' See also Pollock and Maitland, ii, p. 646.

being a much better version than that printed in the Statutes of the Realm from the *Liber Custumarum*. Only one of the articles is omitted,[1] and none are duplicated, with the exception of that *de mutuis sacramentis*, which is appended to both the Old and New Chapters. The fullness of the returns, due to the long period since the last eyre, and the fact that the *capitula* are not abbreviated, make this an even more valuable record than those of the Surrey eyre of 1294.

Another working list of the articles is preserved among the Assize Rolls. Fastened up with a stray Trailbaston return and three bills in French, there is preserved the verdict of the borough of Midhurst in the Sussex eyre of 1288.[2] This version, very clearly written on four membranes, presents some interesting and unique features. It corresponds closely to the Pucklechurch Roll, affording an almost complete list of the articles; unlike the Pucklechurch Roll it contains very few returns, only four presentments being made in response to the 138 articles enrolled. Of these 138 articles, three, so far as I know, are peculiar to this record. After chapter 31 of the articles of 1274 occur the following : *De catallis Iudaeorum dampnatorum pro tonsura et falsonaria monete concelatis ; De hiis qui falsas platas et conflatas vendiderunt vel eschambiaverunt.*[3] Here, it may be, is the full text of the article *de retonsoribus*, so many returns to which occur upon the Hundred Rolls.[4] Again, at the end of the articles upon the statutes, after the article *de advocaria* is written, *De excessibus forestiarorum, woduuardorum et aliorum ministrorum de forestis, parcis et aliis boscis qui grauant populum maliciose per extorsiones suas.*[5] Whilst conforming to the general type of the *Nova Capitula*, the article, appropriate as it is to localities like the Sussex Weald, is an instance of that ' variation according to the variety of places ' of which Bracton spoke.[6]

[1] The article *de feodis militaribus datis religiosis* (Novum cap. 13 in S. R.) is either omitted or obliterated ; it is missing also in the three later versions. See Appendix II.

[2] A. R. 935, mm. 3–6. There are no dates, but a collation with A. R. 924, m. 68 (Burgus de Midhurst) shows that the verdict belongs to the eyre of 1288, the same presentments being recorded in both rolls.

[3] m. 6 d.   [4] See above, p. 33.   [5] m. 5 d.
[6] See above, p. 13.

The Assize Rolls 892–906 have long been noted as a useful record of the articles of the eyre. Roll 894, on which, unlike its fellows, the articles are unabridged, has been endorsed, ' An excellent good Recorde for the charge of the Justices for the Crown ' ; and Roll 892 has been printed, in slightly abridged form, in Mr. Hall's Formula Book of Legal Records.[1] The verdicts of fifteen Surrey hundreds are given, in the same form as that of the Pucklechurch Roll, but as the last eyre had been comparatively recent, the returns are scantier, and there is much reiteration of *nihil sciunt*. A comparison of the fifteen different lists reveals slight variations in order, and omissions of articles through carelessness, but the list resulting from a combination of these variants is practically a duplicate of the Pucklechurch one. The *Novum Capitulum per breve regis* is given twice over, the direction to the justices occupies the same position, the article *de advocaria habenda* is found in the same place. The only well-marked difference is that the article on trapping doves is placed in the Pucklechurch Roll third from the end of the *Vetera Capitula*, and in the Surrey Rolls twelfth from the end. This chapter varies almost equally between these two positions in the different versions of the articles that we possess, and the editors of the Statutes of the Realm go so far as to make two chapters of it, but it is never duplicated in the same list.

A remark in one of these verdicts may throw some light on the question raised by Mr. Bolland[2] in connexion with the jurors' presentments. He quotes from the Cornwall eyre of 1302 the case of a juror who made a presentment *in secreto suo sine assensu sociorum et consensu*, and, translating *secretum suum* ' his list of private presentments ', concludes that each juror made a separate series of presentments in writing. On Assize Roll 901 we read, *De burgatoribus responsum est in secretis. De utlagatis nihil. De fugitivis responsum est in secretis. In secretis* here clearly refers to the ' return of such matters as were private '[3] that had to be made on the second day of the eyre, with a view to the immediate arrest of those

---

[1] pp. 196–202.   [2] Eyre of Kent (S. S.), i, p. xlvi.
[3] Ibid., i, pp. 13, 20, 28.

indicted, before the complete returns to the chapters were made on the third day. Such returns were probably made in writing,[1] and are represented upon the eyre rolls by the lists of names under the heading *de indictatis*.[2] It is possible that the separate jurors may have made individual presentments *in secretis*, but neither the Gloucestershire nor Surrey rolls give any evidence to suggest that the ordinary verdicts were compiled from the separate lists of individual jurors which Mr. Bolland postulates.

vii. *The Articles of* 1313, 1321, *and* 1330

There remain two dated versions of the articles to consider —those from the Year Books of the eyre of Kent in 1313,[3] and those of the eyre of London in 1321. Each of them adds one new article to the list of 1294.

The first of these presents some problems. It runs as follows : *De terris et tenementis que devenerunt in manum mortuam post statutum Gloucestrie anno regis Edwardi vi.* MS. Harl. 867[4] and MS. Cott. Vesp. B. VII[5] also include this article, but without dating the Statute of Gloucester. Three of the manuscripts of the Year Books also omit the date, whilst one adds *filii regis Edwardi*, thus attributing the

---

[1] Bracton, Lib. III, Tr. 2, c. 2 (R. S., ii, p. 240) ' Si sit aliquis in hundredo vel Wapentakio suo qui malecreditus sit de maleficio aliquo, illum statim capiant si possint, si autem non, tunc secreto habere faciant iustitiariis nomina talium et omnium illorum qui malecrediti sunt in quadam schedula, et praecipietur vicecomiti quod illos statim capiat.' Eyre of Kent, i, p. 28 : ' Comanderent qil meissent touz lor priuetes en bille.' It may further be noted that similar ' secret ' presentments were made in the sheriff's tourn, and made in writing there also. A. R. 1233, m. 4, records that Hamo of Tatersete, serjeant itinerant in the county of Norfolk under the sheriff William Giffard, ' fecit se clericum xij militum ad turnum . . . et sine assensu predictorum militum irrotulavit in eorum secretis quod . . .' See also the evidence cited by Pollock and Maitland, History of English Law, ii, p. 646, notes 2 and 3.

[2] See above, p. 26. We have here undoubtedly the origin of those *Bagae de secretis* or lists of indictments the later history of which has been traced by Mr. Vernon Harcourt (E. H. R. xxiii, pp. 508–29). He derives ' the employment of privy bags . . . from the practice in eyre ' (p. 510), and shows that the series of *bagae de secretis* begins at the time when the eyres are becoming extinct (p. 511) ; but does not appear to have noticed Bracton's account of ' secret presentments '.

[3] Printed Eyre of Kent (S. S.), i, pp. 28–46.

[4] This manuscript is certainly later than 1392.

[5] Later than 1349.

statute to the year of the eyre itself. This is probably to be discounted as a pure error, but the connexion between the Statutes of Gloucester and Mortmain is rather mysterious, since the Statute of Gloucester contains no reference to mortmain tenure, and the statute *De viris religiosis* was passed at Westminster.

The Statute of Mortmain opens with a reference to a recent provision against the entry of religious men into a fee without licence of the chief lord. This has been taken [1] to refer to the clause to that effect in the Provisions of Westminster, which was not re-enacted in the Statute of Marlborough. On the other hand, it may be noted that Trevet [2] speaks of a mortmain statute passed at London in 1275, whilst the Gloucester Cartulary attributes it to 1278,[3] without stating the place of promulgation.

Whether there was another act on mortmain tenure passed at Gloucester, either before or after 1279, or whether the allusion is simply to the new duties with which the justices in eyre had been charged at the Gloucester Parliament of 1278, must remain as uncertain as is the date when the new article was added to the *Capitula Itineris*. It is not found on the lists of 1294, and it is upon the list of 1313. No returns to the article have been noted on the eyre rolls between these dates, but they are so few that this evidence goes for little ; on the other hand, the eyre rolls of 1330 give returns to it.[4]

It is noteworthy that the article is only found in four versions, which, on internal evidence, derive from the reign of Edward II. MS. Harl. 867, MS. Cott. Vesp. B. VII, and the *Liber Custumarum*, f. 241, alike refer to the Parliament of 1275 as held in the third year of the reign of King Edward's father. Is it possible that the Year Books refer to a lost statute of the reign of Edward II ?

---

[1] Pollock and Maitland, i, p. 334.

[2] Trevet, Annales (E. H. S.), p. 293 ' Inter alia multa inhibitum est ne de cetero possessiones terrarum et redituum sine speciali Regis licentia ad manum mortuam devolvantur.'

[3] (R. S.) i, p. 33 ' A.D. 1278 et E. I. post Conq. VI, rex Edwardus cum proceribus edidit statuta contra mortuam manum . . .'

[4] A. R. 24, mm. 6, 28.

Apart from the appearance of this article, there is nothing remarkable about the list given in the Year Books. It approximates closely to the standard type; the variations in order and the occasional omissions revealed by a comparison of the different manuscripts are no greater than those of the working lists used by the Surrey Hundreds in 1294. We have already noted the references to the Statute of Westminster I added by the writer of the Lincoln's Inn MS.

The list of articles for the London eyre of 1321 is given in the *Liber Custumarum*.[1] In a few minor details, where it differs from other versions, it approximates to the list of 1313,[2] but its variations are normal and present no new problems. It may be noted that in this it differs from all the London lists we have had to note; in 1207, in 1244, and in 1276 there were articles of special and local interest. It may be indicative of the obsolescence of the eyre that this is not the case in 1321. The list closes with one new article, to which returns are made in the Notts Eyre Roll of 1330,[3] though it is not to be found in any complete list but this. It is in French, and inquires into trading by municipal officials since the Statute of York in 12 Edward II. The reference here is clear,[4] and our last complete list of articles thus conforms strictly to type, illustrating afresh the function of the *capitula* in linking up legislation and administration.

From the eyre rolls of 1330 we gather traces of other articles which never appear on the complete lists; an article *de malefactoribus*,[5] which deals not with poachers or fugitives but with men who beat and wound, and an article *de taxatoribus*.[6] Both of these classes of offender were inquired into under the Commissions of Trailbaston and of the Peace, and it may be that after the Statute of Northampton[7] some or all of these new articles were added to the chapters of the eyre for those few eyres which were held under Edward III.

---

[1] Printed, Munimenta Gildhallae (R. S.), ii, pp. 347 ff.
[2] e.g. with regard to position of article *de Wrecco maris*.
[3] A. R. 683, m. 94 d.   [4] S. R. i, p. 178; Stat. Ebor., c. 6.
[5] A. R. 24, m. 5.   [6] A. R. 24, m. 13 d.
[7] 1328. See below, pp. 73 ff.

But from the fact that they are included in none of the lists of the law books, most of which are of the fourteenth century, it may be inferred that, if used at all in this connexion, it was too seldom for the association to become stereotyped. The list in the *Liber Custumarum* represents the latest stage in the evolution of the *Capitula Itineris* as an official instrument.

viii. *Fleta and Britton*

The successive versions of the articles considered hitherto have all been either working lists, or copies of such lists preserved by chroniclers or clerks. They bear the traces of their growth in their multiplicity and lack of logical arrangement ; few examples of condensation or of assortment have been noted. This matters little if the history of the articles is being viewed from the administrative rather than from the legal standpoint. It is worth while, however, to glance at the versions given by the two legal writers who attempted an analysis of the completed articles according to subject-matter. They have been cited as authorities on the form of the articles, and their different method of approach may throw new light on the history of the articles. Both of these writers belong to the late thirteenth or early fourteenth century ; they are known traditionally as Fleta and Britton.

Bracton had treated of the chapters of the eyre some half a century before. In the one manuscript of Bracton [1] which contains a complete version of the articles, distinguishing their three main sections by separate headings, they are, of course, a later interpolation. The stage at which they had arrived in Bracton's day is represented by the list as it appears in the other manuscripts, [2] a list corresponding to those

---

[1] Rawlinson MS. C, 160, printed R. S., ii, pp. 584 ff. Assigned by Mr. Woodbine (p. 6) to the fourteenth century and described by him as a good text with much extraneous matter incorporated.

[2] Three other Bracton MSS., Digby 222, Bodley 170, 344, have been examined, as representative of Mr. Woodbine's three classes, and these correspond very closely to the text printed in the Rolls Series edition (ii, pp. 240 ff.), ending, however, at *de thesauris inventis*. The three articles following, from whatever text they are derived, belong, as we saw above, to the period 1255–76.

in the Burton Annals and the Gloucester Cartulary for 1254,[1] for though the order of the articles is slightly shifted and a few comments are inserted among them, the textual resemblance is very close. Bracton was clearly with this, as with the 1227 articles,[2] working from official copies.

In the case of Fleta and Britton, however, the treatment of the articles is very different. Neither the wording nor the arrangement of the articles is preserved in many cases. As we have seen, the order of the articles is so haphazard, and they overlap in scope to such an extent, that any legal discussion of them is bound to ignore their order. Both Fleta and Britton, however, not only rearrange but paraphrase and condense, and, moreover, supplement the chapters of the eyre with articles entirely alien to the eyre, and intersperse them with legal comment and discussion without indicating in any way where text and comment are divided.

The information to be gleaned from them is thus of no great importance in a history of the evolution of the *Capitula Itineris*. They have helped to spread the idea that the chapters are to be found in a great diversity of forms and variety of orders, but, ambiguous as their origin is, their authority is not sufficient to outweigh the evidence we have already reviewed. They are generally assigned to the period 1290–3, and there is nothing in their treatment of the articles inconsistent with this date, though there are indications that Fleta wrote before Britton.

A short analysis of the composition of Fleta's twentieth chapter,[3] *De capitulis Corone et Itineris*, is given below, from which his method of treatment is fairly clear.

In this table the numbering of Fleta's *Capitula* is that of Selden's edition. Under *Capitula Itineris*, I = Vetera Capitula, II = Articles of 1274, III = Articles upon the Statutes; and the numbers are those of the Statutes of the Realm version.

---

[1] See above, § 3, vi.   [2] See above, § 3, iv.
[3] Ed. Selden, 1647, p. 24.

Analysis of Fleta.

cc. 1–4. A summary of crimes, from high treason to man-
slaughter.

5–9. A further summary of crimes, owing a little to
I. 19, and possibly to the Articles of Trailbaston.

Fleta.	*Capitula Itineris.*	*Fleta.*	*Capitula Itineris.*
10	I 21–3	80	III 13
11, 12	I 23	81–91	III 20–30
13	I 1	92	I 34
14–18	I 4–8	93	I 16
19–22	I 10	94	I 38
23	I 12	95	I 40
24	—	96	I 41
25	I 9	97	I 48
26	—	98	II 28
27	I 40	99–101	I 50–2
28	I 15	102–3	I note 1, 2, p. 234
29	I 24	104	II 14, 15
30	I 28	105–7	II 17–19
31	I 26	108	II 21
32	I 27	109	II 26
33–5	I 29–31	110–11	II 27
36	I 55	112–13	II 29
37	I 36	114	II 30, 31, 17
38	I 37	115	II 25
39–40	I 46–7	116	III 6
41	I 54, 56	117	III 12
42–4	I 57–9	118–20	III 15–17
45–56	II 1–11	121	III 19
57	II 13	122–38	Articles on clipping and
58–9	II 22–3		forging money, related possibly
60–7	II 32–9		to the legislation of 1275 or the
68, 74	III 1–5		trials of 1279.
75–9	III 7–11		

The attempt of Fleta to group the articles logically breaks
down completely ; the arrangement is utterly confused, and
fully justifies Maitland's condemnation of the author.[1] We
may note by way of negative evidence that he does not
include the article on mortmain.

Britton,[2] like his prototype Bracton, prefaces the list of
chapters with the statement that they vary in number.
' Car ausi com les malices de gentz cresent, si covent de
acrestre chapitres et autres remedies.' He departs much

---

[1] Pollock and Maitland, i, p. 210.
[2] Ed. Nichols, i, cc. ii–xxvi, pp. 18–134.

further than Fleta from the wording of the articles, para-
phrasing freely, and regrouping under headings which clearly
indicate their scope.[1]   In fact he digests the chapters into
a code, but his paraphrase is so free and his comment so
ubiquitous that he throws no more light than Fleta upon
their evolution.

Britton's chapters iv–viii deal with various crimes, corresponding to some eight of the *Vetera Capitula* and one of the
articles upon the statutes.   Chapter xviii, *De droit le Roi*,
covers Vetera Capitula 4–8, and 1–6 of the Articles of 1274,
but their order is rearranged.   Chapter xix, *De Franchises*,
covers 7 and 9 of the 1274 Articles; chapter xx, *De plusieurs
Tortz*, covers a varied assortment of articles from all three
sections; chapter xxi, *De ministres*, begins with a large
block (32–38) of the 1274 Articles, and then follows with
a selection from all three sections intermixed, freely para-
phrased and amplified.

Britton thus draws out for us that classification of the
articles which is becoming more clear throughout their history,
the classification under the headings royal rights, torts and
crimes, franchises and administrative abuses.   But as he looks
at the matter from the legal rather than the administrative
standpoint, all that we have to note is that he, like Fleta,
does not include the mortmain chapter, and, unlike Fleta,
includes the article *de mutuis sacramentis*.[2]   That both these
legal writers are working from typical if not official lists is
clear from the fact that blocks of articles in their normal
order occur in the midst of completely disordered ones, but
neither of them is concerned to give us a practical working
juror's list.

The history of the chapters of the eyre has now been traced
from the twelfth to the fourteenth century.   We have seen
the five headings of the Assize of Northampton develop, eyre
by eyre, into the sixty-nine *Vetera Capitula* of the standard
versions.   We have seen the machinery of the eyre employed

---

[1] It may be noted that his order and arrangement are quite different
from Fleta's, though in one or two passages he seems to follow Fleta.
See p. 69, *de eglises* = Fleta, no. 15 ; p. 70, *de eschates* = Fleta, no. 17.

[2] p. 95.

by Edward I to drive home the results of the inquest of 1274–5, and the articles of the eyre permanently augmented by the addition of some seventy-two *Nova Capitula* in the eyres of 1278 and the following years. The ample records of Edward's reign have enabled us to trace the work of the justices *ad omnia placita* from shire to shire throughout its greater part, to see the old and new chapters fulfilling their functions of restraining the irresponsibility of the local official and increasing the royal revenues. And we have also noted the cessation of growth, the crystallization of the articles in the pattern of 1278, the trifling nature of the additions that can be detected after that date. Between 1244 and 1278 some hundred and five articles were added to the list ; between 1278 and 1330 some eight at most. The period of growth had ceased. We have now to examine the causes of this phenomenon, and the accompanying phenomenon of the sudden dwindling in the flow of eyre records in the reign of Edward II.

§ 5. The Decline and Disappearance of the General Eyre

All the evidence that we possess goes to indicate that the decline of the eyre was sudden and rapid. The reign of Edward I had seen fewer eyres than that of Henry III, but this was apparently due to Edward's deliberate policy of sending the same justices to as many counties as possible, and thus spreading the proceedings over so many years that all the eyres were bound to come at longer intervals. But in the reign of Edward II the eyres became almost non-existent. Unless a catastrophic fate has overtaken the Assize Rolls of this period, there cannot have been more than some six or eight eyres in all the shires of England put together in the whole reign. There is a revival in the opening years of Edward III,[1] but the day of the eyre is clearly over by 1307.

Some of this change may be attributable to the general ' lack of government ' of Edward II's reign, but more is

---

[1] It is noteworthy how constantly Edward III's early statutes hark back to the days of ' le Roi Edward ael nostre seignur le Roi qore est '.

probably due to the supplanting force of new institutions. On the one hand, the fiscal importance of the eyre was diminishing with the development of non-feudal taxation ; on the other, new machinery was being devised for the enforcement of local order and the supervision of local officials. The conservators and justices of the peace stole the thunder not only of the sheriffs, but also of the justices *ad omnia placita*.

i. *The Commissions of Trailbaston and the Statute of Northampton*

Of the new devices which contributed to the supersession of the eyre, one deserves special consideration—the Trailbaston inquiry. Whether the justices of Trailbaston are to be regarded as forming a connecting link between the justices in eyre and the justices of the peace, or whether the commissions of Trailbaston and of the peace are parallel developments from a common origin cannot at present be determined, but an attempt may be made here to indicate a relation which seems not to have been recognized.[1]

Stephen, in his History of Criminal Law, says of the articles of Trailbaston : ' They look as if they were meant to define the duties of the justices. They read like a short abridgement of the articles of the Eyre.'[2] The Trailbaston Inquisitions have indeed something in common with those of the eyre ; the machinery is similar, the scope, though limited, is similar, the object is frankly fiscal, as well as political,[3] and the special inquests of 1304–5, like those of 1274–5, are stereotyped and

---

[1] Miss Putnam, to whose suggestions and criticism I am greatly indebted, formerly identified A. R. 891 as an early record of Justices of the Peace (E. H. R. xxviii, p. 321, note 4).   Mr. Hall prints a part of it in his Formula Book of Legal Records, p. 204, where he apparently assigns the inquest to 1300, though from internal evidence it can be assigned to 1307 ; see m. 1 d.   In his Studies of English Official Historical Documents, p. 305, he restricts the name of Trailbaston to the proceedings of 1305, and appears to describe A. R. 891 as an eyre record. Mr. Bolland describes it correctly as a series of Trailbaston returns (Eyre of Kent, i, p. xl, note).

[2] History of Criminal Law, i, p. 110.

[3] French Chronicle of London (C. S.), p. 28 : ' Mesme l'an . . . pur restorer ses grauntz despence fait par xx aunz devant, fist justice fer sur maufesours, et fust apellé Traylebastoun, et par ceo le roy gaygna graunt tresor.'

repeated, so that the justices of Trailbaston became associated with those of the eyre, both in law and in the popular mind.[1]

The history of the Trailbaston proceedings is well documented and has been given by various writers.[2] On November 23, 1304,[3] the first writ was issued for the holding of a special inquiry into various transgressions, mainly of robbery and battery, and into their fraudulent concealment. It was to be held in Lincolnshire, Notts, and Derbyshire,[4] and was extended in the following spring to Norfolk, Suffolk, and Lancashire, and in April 1305 to the whole of England.[5] A similar commission, for the whole of England, was issued in 1307.[6] It is the inquiry of 1305 that evoked the notoriety and the nickname ; the poets and chroniclers speak of the writ Trailbaston as originating in 1305.[7] For our purpose the official returns are more important. The Assize Rolls of 1305–7 [8] contain records of a series of judicial inquiries which,

[1] See Pike, Year Books of Edward III, 14–15 (R. S.), p. xxxviii ; and see below, p. 80.

[2] There is a full account in Foss, History of the Judges, iii, pp. 28, 29, 204. See also Maitland, Memoranda de Parliamento de 1305 (R. S.), p. liii. Coke (4th Inst., c. 34) is of course wrong in identifying the Statute of Rageman with the ordinance of Trailbaston, but he appears to have misled Mr. Holdsworth (H. E. L., i, p. 118) and Mr. Pike (op. cit., pp. xxxvi ff.). Chronicles, Patent, Statute, and Assize Rolls alike combine to put the origin of the Trailbaston proceedings in 1304–5, whilst proceedings under the Statute of Rageman, as we have seen, had been taking place from 1278 on. The fact, however, that these three legal historians find the authority for the Trailbaston commissions in the instrument which did in fact remould the commissions of the eyre, illustrates further the close relations between the justices of Trailbaston and those *ad omnia placita*.

[3] Fine Roll 33 Ed. I, m. 20 (in Schedule), printed Parliamentary Writs, i, p. 407. This writ, accompanied by a version of the Articles of Trailbaston in French, will be found on f. 229 d of the MS. Royal 9 A. vii (B. M.). [4] Parl. Writs, i, 407.

[5] Rot. Pat. 33 Ed. I, pt. i, m. 8 d (P. R. C., p. 354), printed, Parl. Writs, i, p. 408 : *De transgressionibus nominatis Trailbaston audiendis et terminandis.* [6] Rot. Pat. 35 Ed. I, m. 31 d.

[7] Political Songs (C. S.), pp. 231, 319 ; Liber de Ant. Leg. (C. S.), p. 250 ; Trivet (E. H. S.), p. 404 ; Hemingburgh (E. H. S.), p. 208 ; Rishanger (R. S.), p. 224 ; Chron. of Edward I and Edward II (R. S.), i, p. 135 ; Flores Hist. (R. S.), iii, pp. 122, 328 ; Ann. Wig. (R. S.), pp. 224, 557. Note also that the jurors of Brixton in 1307 declare that they have no further returns to make to the first article, because these matters were terminated before the justices of Trailbaston, i.e. in 1305 (A. R. 891, m. 4).

[8] For 1305, A. R. 508, 676, 744, &c. ; for 1306, A. R. 159, 466, &c. ; for 1307, A. R. 422, &c.

by a comparison of the names of the justices with those on the Patent Roll, can safely be identified as those held by the Trailbaston commissioners. These are happily supplemented by a series of original verdicts of the jurors, from which other lists of the articles of Trailbaston can be recovered [1] to check that upon the Fine Roll. The versions vary slightly. That upon the Fine Roll has some six articles ; the Kent Roll of 1305 has ten, the Surrey Roll of 1307 has nine, supplemented by eight articles on the Statute of Winchester,[2] and two special articles on Thames fishing rights. The version of the Kent Roll is given below.[3]

The main purpose of the inquiries is, as might be gathered from the nickname, to seek out and put down open and violent breaches of the peace. The articles cover not only

[1] A. R. 396, (Kent) 1305. A. R. 935, m. 7 ; 946, (Sussex) 1305 ? A. R. 394, (Kent) 1307. A. R. 891, (Surrey) 1307.

[2] See S. R., i, p. 245, for another version of these articles, which were used in special inquiries held in 1287 (Rot. Pat. 15, m. 13, Cal., p. 451), in 1300 (Rot. Pat. 28 Ed. I, m. 14, Cal., p. 515) and 1310 (Rot. Cl. 3 Ed. II, m. 7, Cal., p. 204), as well as in 1307 ; probably at other dates also.

[3] The following version is compiled from the fragmentary quotations given on the returns for the different hundreds of Kent. There are no numbers in the originals.

I. De malefactoribus et pacis domini Regis perturbatoribus et depredatoribus et de homicidiis et incendiatoribus et alia dampna quamplurima perpetrantibus.

II. De eorum scienter receptatoribus et eis consentientibus vim et auxilium prebentibus seu dictas transgressiones fieri procurantibus et percipientibus.

III. De illis qui pro muneribus pactum fecerunt et faciunt cum pacis Regis perturbatoribus et eos conduxerunt et conducunt ad verberandum vulnerandum et maletractandum etc., et etiam pro eo quod in assisis iuratis recognitionibus et inquisitionibus pro muneribus vel minis etc.

IV. De illis qui huiusmodi munera dederunt et dant, quantum et quibus et qui huiusmodi munera ceperunt et recipiunt.

V. De illis qui ratione potestatis domini sui aliquo in protexionem et advocationem suam pro suo dando receperunt et susipiunt (sic).

VI. De illis qui pecuniam tenementa vel aliud quodcunque ab aliquo per graves minas iis factas maliciose extorserunt.

VII. De illis qui manutenent placita pro pecunia vel pro parte rei implacitate habendo false et maliciose etc. et etiam de conspirationibus et confederatis etc.

VIII. De malefactionibus in parcis et vivariis et ubi et quando et eorum receptatoribus.

IX. De hiis qui ministros domini Regis per se vel per alios perturbaverunt, perturbant, seu perturbare procurant ne officia sua . . .

X. De vicecomitibus ballivis et subballivis vel aliis ministris domini Regis qui prece vel precio omittunt exequi officia sua ita quod malefactores et felones per concilium . . . discurrunt non attachiati.

the old offence of poaching, but also homicide, robbery, arson, assault and battery, the hiring of assailants, the extortion of money or tenements by threats, the reception, concealment, or protection of offenders, by their lords and others, the intimidation of jurors or royal officials, and the maintenance of pleas. Besides these inquiries into conspiracy and breach of the peace there is a question concerning bailiffs and other ministers of the king who for fear or favour fail to fulfil their office and suffer felons to wander at large. The affinities with the articles of the eyre are obvious. The questions on peace-breakers are in effect an amplification of the old chapter *De burgatoribus et malefactoribus et eorum receptatoribus*; that on administrative abuses is an abridgement of the latter part of the articles of 1274, whilst those on conspiracy and maintenance are akin to the *novum capitulum per breve Regis* [1] of 1279.

A French version preserved in a lawyer's note-book at the British Museum [2] contains fifteen articles, differing in format and arrangement from those of 1305. It appears to represent a later development of the articles,[3] for, in addition to the offences covered by the first inquests, it inquires concerning the disturbance of constables at their duty, the hiring of men to make forcible entry for taking seisin, armed resistance to the levy of the king's debts, housebreaking, and other offences not included in the formulae of 1305–7. The list corroborates the other evidence for the later activities of justices of Trailbaston. Commissions of Trailbaston did not cease in 1307. They were issued from time to time, and though they may have been exercised along with commissions of the eyre, they remained distinct from them.[4] They appear

---

[1] See above, p. 59.

[2] MS. Royal, 9 A. vii, f. 229 d.

[3] The collection appears to have been made 1305–15, the Statute of Lincoln (1315), which has been inserted in the fly-leaf in another hand, being the latest document included.

[4] For commissions under Edward II see Foss, iii, p. 204. There is also some local evidence. In 1318, Lord Berkeley bribes the jury of Portbury Hundred, Somerset, ' pro favore habendo coram Iusticiariis de Trailbaston in negotiis suis ' (Smyth, Lives of the Berkeleys, i, p. 242). In the Merton College Bailiffs' Accounts there is an allusion to a Trailbaston session at Cambridge, lasting three weeks, in 1336 (T. Rogers, History of Agriculture

to have been exploited for political purposes, as in 1321, when the Flores Historiarum ascribe the outbreak of civil war to the unjust issuing of one such commission,[1] and again in 1340–1. Moreover, apart from these extraordinary commissions of Trailbaston so called, a number of more normal commissions closely related to it are to be found upon the Assize Rolls of Edward III's reign [2] of 1329 onwards. These commissions have evidently a close connexion with the Statute of Northampton (1328), the sixth and seventh chapters of which provide that justices assigned shall have authority to punish breaches of the peace, and that commissions shall be granted to certain persons to hear and determine offences before committed. The wording of the statute is reminiscent of that of the ' Statute of Rageman ' ; the offences that the commissioners are empowered to hear and determine are those of the new chapters of the eyre, and at the same time, those of the Trailbaston articles. The exact place of these commissions, however, in the history of judicial evolution is not easy to define, nor can a satisfactory technical description readily be found for them. Whenever the early history of the justice of the peace comes to be written, they will have to be examined carefully. Some of them are undoubtedly commissions of Oyer and Terminer,[3] but the exact characteristics of a commission of Oyer and Terminer have not as yet been adequately defined. As we have seen, the phrase *ad audiendum et terminandum* is found in the commission of the eyre from 1278 onwards, and it occurs also in the commissions of Trailbaston and of the Peace. Mr. Pike has said that the commission of Trailbaston is a special form of the

and Prices, ii, p. 613). For 1340–1 see French Chron. of London (C. S.), p. 88. Cf. Mr. Lapsley in E. H. R., xxx, pp. 10–14 ; Pike, *op. cit.*, pp. xl ff. Note also Eyre of Kent (S. S.), i, p. 53 : ' Those who have been attainted in Trailbastonry and convicted . . . may afterwards be indicted in Eyre upon the same facts.' The Trailbaston proceedings mentioned on p. 6 are those of 1305. Note also Year Books 2 Ed. III, Trin., No. 15, p. 27 : ' Justices de T. sont en lour case come Justices en Eire.'

[1] Flores Hist. (R. S.), iii, p. 345 ; cf. Rot. Parl., i, p. 371.

[2] e.g. 1329, A. R. 516 ; 1330, A. R. 548 ; 1333, A. R. 520 ; 1339, A. R. 769 ; 1356, A. R. 525 ; 1365, A. R. 527 ; and see Miss Putnam's list of rolls, E. H. R., xxviii, p. 322.

[3] e.g. A. R. 525 (1356), 527 (1365).

commission of Oyer and Terminer.[1] Again, in some instances the same persons exercise powers simultaneously under more than one commission.[2] But, by whatever name they should be called, the terms of many of these commissions, on a most superficial investigation, show a close relation to those of the commissions of 1305–7, and are, on the other hand, akin also to those of the later commissions of the peace. The fact that the commissions are based upon the Statute of Northampton only puts the problem a step farther back ; for the wording of the statute itself, as we have seen, owes something to earlier commissions. Again, as the statute is concerned both with keepers of the peace and justices assigned to hear and determine felonies, so in the commissions, alongside of justices of Oyer and Terminer, we find *custodes pacis*, the nature of whose judicial functions is not clear,[3] but who appear to be holding inquests which link their activities alike with those of the justices of Trailbaston in the past and those of the justices of the peace in the future. At the same time the connexion with the old eyre procedure is not altogether lost; in a commission of 1356 we learn that the composition of the court was to be that of the old ' full county ', and that inquiry was to be made as of old by articles.[4]

Local disorder, local administrative abuses form the subject-matter of these new commissions of Trailbaston, Oyer and Terminer, and of the Peace, as they had of the old articles of the eyre. The significant fact is that neither the articles of Trailbaston, nor those on the Statute of Winchester, are incorporated with the *Capitula Itineris*. Special means are

---

[1] Pike, *op. cit.*, p. xxxvi.

[2] e.g. A. R. 525 (1356) ' coram vobis, custodes pacis nostri et iusticiariis nostris ad huiusmodi felonias et transgressiones . . . audiendas et terminandas assignatis '.

[3] A. R. 520 (1333) and A. R. 769 (1339) appear to recognize judicial powers in the *custodes*. But these were not conferred on them by statute till 1344, according to the received theory.

[4] A. R. 525 (Commission of February 19, 1356) ' Preceptum fuit vicecomiti quod venire faceret coram iusticiariis prefatis de quolibet hundredo et Wappentachio . . . et de qualibet villata comitatus predicti que per duodecim responderunt in itinere decem et octo probos et legales homines . . . ad faciendum et inquirendum super premissis omnibus et singulis et aliis articulis ea tangentibus.'

devised for their administration, and though they are used again and again the existing machinery of the eyre is not employed. The fact attests the unpopularity and unwieldiness of the eyre ; it both arose from and accelerated its obsolescence. With the growth in scope and efficiency of the new commissions of the peace the old procedure of the eyre was finally abandoned. The last stages of its dissolution must now be considered.

ii. *The Eyres of Edward III and the later Tradition*

We have seen that the silence of the records, not of itself conclusive, but supported by other indications, goes to show that the reign of Edward II saw a sudden falling-off in the issuing of commissions of the eyre. Though the opening years of Edward III were marked by an apparent revival, no general eyre seems to have taken place after 1337.[1] Mr. Scargill-Bird is incorrect in stating that no such commissions were issued after that date,[2] but though an eyre was proclaimed at the Tower of London in 1341, its course was arrested half-way and never completed.

The events of 1341 are narrated in Letter-Book F of the Guildhall Records.[3] The citizens of London refused to allow the special inquest into the conduct of the royal officials initiated by Edward III to be held within their liberty,[4] and in consequence the king ordered an eyre *ad omnia placita* to be held at the Tower in the second week of Lent,[5] thus securing, presumably, plenary powers for the justices. The eyre opened on March 5, and pleadings continued till March 17, when it was adjourned to April 16. Having been again adjourned to May 17, it was then terminated, and the citizens were released from it by letters patent of June 3, 1341.[6]

---

[1] The latest eyre roll that I have examined is A. R. 389 for an eyre of Kent in 1334, but it is incomplete, containing neither list of sheriffs nor pleas of the Crown, though it is headed by a writ of the eyre in French. For Commission (October 30, 1333) see P. R. C., pp. 475–6.

[2] Guide to the Public Records (3rd ed.), p. 269.

[3] Calendar of Letter-Book F, ed. Sharpe. See also Mr. Lapsley's article, E. H. R., vol. xxx.

[4] Letter-Book F, p. 59.

[5] Ibid., p. 60.   [6] Ibid., p. 61 ; P. R. C., p. 224.

The preliminaries of this eyre were entirely regular. The writ is identical with that of 1278,[1] and the truncated records on the Assize Roll[2] show that the proceedings were being conducted on the traditional lines; though as the stage of pleading the *placita corone* (apart from gaol delivery) was not reached, there are no articles or returns to articles traceable.

The events of 1341, so far as we can see, close the history of the eyre as a working institution. But that the tradition of the eyre was alive, that the kings still held it as a weapon in reserve, and that their subjects feared it as of old, is attested by a series of allusions throughout the fourteenth century.

The writ which terminated the eyre of 1341 promised the citizens that no eyre should be held in London for seven years from the date of the Letters Patent.[3] The Commons in the Parliament of 1348 state as a condition of their grant ' qe Eyres de Justices, si bien de Foreste come des Communes Pleez et generals Enquerrez, per tote la terre cessent '.[4] In 1371 the king consents to a petition ' q'il ne grante en nulle partie du Roialme Eire ne Trailbaston durante la guerre, par queux les communes purront estre troblez ne empoveres, fors qe en horrible cas '.[5] In 1377 a similar petition for the remission of eyres for the next five years was refused.[6] In 1382 a similar petition is granted, in so far that the king undertakes to send no justices of Trailbaston for the next year, and no justices in eyre for the next two years.[7]

In view of the fact that no general eyre had been held for some forty-five years, this bargaining is so strange that one doubts whether these petitions are not directed against the lesser commissions of Oyer and Terminer rather than the commission *ad omnia placita*. But there is nothing ambiguous in the petition of 1362,[8] which goes into details as to the

---

[1] A. R. 549, 552.   [2] A. R. 549, m. 1.
[3] See below, Note on the frequency of the eyre.
[4] Rot. Parl., ii, p. 200.
[5] Rot. Parl., ii, p. 305. Mr. Bolland interprets these last words to mean urgent financial necessity; it is more probable that they refer to some outrageous crime, conspiracy, or riot, for which a commission of Trailbaston might be issued (Eyre of Kent, p. xxxviii, note).
[6] Rot. Parl., iii, p. 24.   [7] Rot. Parl., iii, p. 138 b.
[8] Rot. Parl., ii, p. 272.

scope of the eyre. The Commons have prayed to be discharged of all the articles of the eyre, save pleas of land and *quo warranto*, and treasons, robberies, and felonies, whereby a man may lose life or limb, and the council considers that this would be prejudicial to the crown if it were generally granted ; so the Commons renew their petition, explaining that they do not wish to ask anything that shall bring loss to the crown, as in the matter of escheats, wardships, purprestures, serjeanties, mortmain, usurped franchises, and the like, but they pray for remission of the articles of the eyre which deal with long-past crimes, and which lead to fines and amercements of towns and vills, or of officials' heirs who have not themselves offended. Wherefore they ask a general pardon for all such ancient offences. They also ask that the articles of the eyre be delivered to the justices of the peace in every county, that they may publish them to the community and let them know the contents of the said articles, that they may govern themselves better, and eschew the perils and punishments of the said articles. The king grants the petition, in so far as time past is concerned, but saves to himself and his heirs all his rights for time to come.

This petition is of interest not only as showing the attitude of king and people towards the eyre at this date, but also as accounting for the careful preservation of the articles in so many law books of the fourteenth century. The inclusion of a series of articles, the use of which was superseded and the meaning, as the manuscripts themselves show, half forgotten, in the working handbook of a lawyer would be difficult to explain without this injunction to the justices of the peace to have copies of the *Capitula Itineris*, and to make them generally known.

The last reference to the eyres upon the parliamentary roll is in 1397,[1] when Richard II, to induce the Commons to make him a grant of the customs for his life, gives a general pardon to all his subjects for all escapes, negligences, misprisions, ignorances, and all other articles of the eyre, the punishment of which would take the form of fines or amercements, whether of communities or of individuals.

[1] Rot. Parl., iii, p. 369.

The tradition of the eyre might still be utilized by king or parliament as a means to some desired end, but as an effective arm of government the eyre itself had ceased to exist. To some extent this was doubtless due to its cumbersome and conservative forms ; more to the development of new and more efficient substitutes. We have seen how the justices of Trailbaston, of Oyer and Terminer, and of the peace came to exercise jurisdiction in cases which would formerly have gone before the justices in eyre. For purposes of clearing up arrears of legal business, the justices of assize, whose activities had been extended by the Statute of Westminster II, c. 30, and yet further by the statute of 1293,[1] were performing the work that had formerly been done by justices in eyre, whilst the statute 20 Edw. III, c. 6,[2] by giving them power to inquire into the misdeeds of sheriffs, escheators, and bailiffs of franchises, yet further diminished the *raison d'être* of the eyre, and is, perhaps, mainly responsible for its final disappearance. To quote Coke [3] : ' As the power of the Justices of Assises by many Acts of Parliament, and other Commissions increased, so these Justices Itinerant by little and little vanished away.'

Yet, in spite of Coke's further assertion that ' the Authority of Justices of Assises Itinerant through the whole realm, and the Institution of Justices of the Peace in every county being duly performed, are the most excellent means for the preservation of the King's peace, and quiet of the Realm, of any other in the Christian World ', it may be doubted whether these more recent authorities were efficient substitutes for the justices in eyre as checks upon local lawlessness.[4] It is true that the sheriff was no longer the mighty official that he had been in the thirteenth century, but as the supremacy in local government passed from him to the justices of the peace, whose powers tended steadily to become despotic in

---

[1] S. R., i, p. 112 : ' Because as well the Justices of the Bench as the Justices in Eyre . . . could not come at the days and places which they had appointed . . .' eight justices are assigned to take assizes and juries throughout the realm.

[2] S. R., i, p. 305. See Holdsworth, History of English Law, i, p. 116.

[3] First Inst., sect. 514.   [4] Cf. Holdsworth, iii, p. 312.

theory as well as in practice, the control of the central government over the county officials slackened. The unwarranted
franchises of the thirteenth century were less dangerous to
the order of the realm than the unwarrantable maintenances
of the fifteenth, and that special commissions of Oyer and
Terminer could be exploited for the benefit of local factions
in a way that the elaborate machinery of the eyre would
have made very difficult is amply proved by the Paston
Letters. To the disappearance of the eyre, amongst many
other factors in the breakdown of the central control, we may
attribute the necessity for the jurisdiction of the Star Chamber.

NOTE

On the Frequency of General Eyres

The statement is sometimes made that general eyres were
held at intervals of seven years.[1] All those who have examined
the facts at all closely know that this was not always the
case, and from Foss[2] and Stubbs,[3] and the various editors
of eyre rolls[4] come a series of qualifications and exceptions
to the supposed general rule. On investigation the ' rule '
appears to have very ancient authority. Selden[5] quotes
Scrope as an authority for it in the early part of Edward III's
reign, and the most dogmatic of all statements is to be
found in Britton,[6] who, in the mythical statute or proclamation of Edward I with which he begins his treatise, has the
words : ' Further we will that Justices Itinerant be assigned
to hear and determine the same articles in every county and
franchise every seven years.' If Nichols is right in assigning Britton's work to the period 1291–2,[7] the rule was currently

[1] e.g. Coke, Inst., iv, c. 33 : ' They road from seven years to seven
years.'
[2] History of the Judges, ii, p. 191.
[3] Const. Hist. ii, § 234. Stubbs does not distinguish between eyres
ad omnia placita and others ; the annals he quotes do not furnish ' abundant
evidence ' that the general eyres were much more frequent. See table.
[4] Bolland, Eyre of Kent (S. S.), i, xix ; Parker, Lancashire Assize Rolls,
pt. i, p. ix.
[5] Notes upon Hengham (1616 Ed.), p. 143 : ' So seies Scrope in Temps
Edw. 3, fol. 143 a.' I have been unable to trace this reference.
[6] Ed. Nichols, p. 3.
[7] Nichols, p. xxvi. See also Holdsworth, History of English Law, ii, p. 268.

accepted while the eyre was still a living and effective organ of the government. Yet neither then nor at an earlier date is there traceable any promise or undertaking that an eyre shall take place in each county every seven years ; neither then nor at any date did eyres take place automatically or even regularly. The facts, as far as they can be ascertained, may be seen from the subjoined table,[1] and though the records are not complete, there is sufficient evidence to show that London and Northumberland and Kent were not alone in escaping the visitation of justices *ad omnia placita* for ten, fifteen, or twenty years together.

Whence, then, does this persistent ' seven years ' theory come ? It is impossible to give a definite and final answer to the question, but this at least is clear ; there was a working rule in 1261 that an eyre should not be held in any one county oftener than every seven years. It seems fairly certain that the fictitious rule that eyres must be held every seven years has been evolved, whether by lawyers or by laymen, from the rule that they may not be held oftener, somewhat in the same way that the competence of the shire court became limited to 40s. pleas.[2]

The facts in 1261 are as follows. According to the Close and Patent Rolls,[3] something very like a general *iter* over all England was ordered by the king. Two at least [4] of the counties successfully resisted the opening of the eyre by the justices. In the case of Worcester,[5] the justices on their arrival from Gloucester on July 1 found neither litigants nor criminals awaiting them. The county put forth the twofold claim, that according to the provision of the realm, the justices might not exercise their jurisdiction there, as seven years had not elapsed since the last eyre, and that reasonable notice, in accordance with ancient custom and the law of England, had not been given. The story, as told in the

---

[1] Appendix III, pp. 103 ff.   [2] Pollock and Maitland, i, p. 553.

[3] Rot. Cl. 77, m. 13 d, m. 26 d ; P. R. C., pp. 157–8.

[4] Pollock and Maitland, i, p. 202, refer to the cancelling of a Norfolk eyre, but I have been unable to trace any reference either to its summons or to its revocation. The Assize Rolls prove that none was held. See Appendix III.

[5] Flores Historiarum (R. S.), ii, p. 472 ; Ann. Wig., p. 446 (Annales Monastici, iv (R. S.)).

Annals of Worcester and the Flores Historiarum, ends there : possibly the justices were aware of the precedent of May, and made no fight.

Two months before another county had obtained an authoritative recognition of this right. On May 2 the justices attempted to set up their court at Hertford,[1] and certain of the party of the baronage resisted them, alleging both the short notice (forty days being the customary period from the summons) and the short interval since the last eyre. The justices appealed to the king, and his letter, dated May 12, is on the Close Roll.[2] 'Since we learn for a certainty that six years have not yet elapsed since our justices last came into this county, we command you to supersede this eyre, and pass on to Northampton.' And this the justices did, at their best speed, according to the Flores Historiarum.

The king then recognizes some obligation, and the pressure to which he yields is exerted by the baronial party. These indications, together with the significant use of the word ' provision ', and the distinction made in the case of Worcestershire between the *lex Anglicana* which is the source of the right to forty days' notice, and the *provisio regni* on which the seven years claim is based, prepare one for the statement of Trivet[3] that ' the justices had come contrary to the form of the Provisions of Oxford '.

Unfortunately, however, as Stubbs[4] has already pointed out, the Provisions of Oxford, as we have them, do not mention the eyre. Is the reference an error on the part of Trivet, who is not a strictly contemporary authority, and appears to have followed the misreading of the later manuscripts of the Flores Historiarum, or are we rather to see some political manœuvring here on the part of the barons ;

[1] Flores Hist. ii, p. 468. *Hereforde* is undoubtedly an error for Hertforde, as on p. 427 of the same volume, where the editor has corrected it. Comparison with the Close Roll shows that, as might be expected, the eyre which included Northampton was for Hertford, not Hereford.

[2] Rot. Cl. 77, m. 12, *De itinere in comitatu Hertford revocando.*

[3] Triveti Annales (E. H. S.), p. 248 ' Iustitiarii regis Angliae qui dicuntur Itineris missi Herefordiam pro suo exsequendo officio repelluntur, allegantibus his qui regi adversabantur, ipsos contra formam Provisionum Oxonie nuper factarum venisse.'

[4] Const. Hist. ii, § 234.

an attempt, like that of their seventeenth-century successors with the Petition of Right, to make the Provisions of Oxford an all-embracing document, to be interpreted so as to check any and every constitutional vagary of the king?

Possibly both considerations ought to be weighed. Most probably Trivet includes under the title *Provisiones Oxonie* the Provisions of Westminster of the following year. The St. Albans chronicler of the Flores Historiarum, who had access to an official copy of the administrative clause of the Provisions,[1] speaks of them as a revision of the earlier articles,[2] and clearly looks upon the two sets of regulations as forming one code. It is very much to the point, then,, to consider what conditions are prescribed in the Provisions of Westminster for the eyre.

Both in the official Latin version of the Close Roll and the semi-official French version of the Flores Historiarum and the Annales de Burton,[3] the septennial period recurs in connexion with an eyre, but seemingly it is the special *iter* or inquest of 1259. Thus in the second of the Provisions on the Close Roll it is said that the justices itinerant are to hear complaints of transgressions done within the last seven years, and in the sixth, that all bailiffs, royal or seignorial, who have held office during the last seven years are summoned to be present before them. The French version comes nearer to the point: 'Where justices itinerant have lately been on circuit let there be appointed wise men to hear and inquire into all the complaints which can be terminated without writ of seven years therefrom, so that if any one has not made plaint before the seven years and has not had his right, that he recover so as to have his writ.' [4]

---

[1] The copy in the Liber Additamentorum of Matthew Paris and the Flores (Brit. Mus. MS. Nero D. 1, f. 138 d) is a fairly close transcript of that on the Close Roll, 75, m. 13 d.

[2] Flores Hist. ii, p. 437 'Provisum est . . . de i(ustitiariis) itineraturis . . . ad eorundem provisiones (*sc.* Oxonie) publicandas . . . ita quod . . . de omnibus articulis iam renovatis plenum fiat scrutinium.'

[3] Nero D. i, ff. 138 d–140 d ; Annales de Burton, pp. 471–84 (Annales Monastici (R. S.), vol. i). The different elements in and versions of the Provisions of Westminster deserve more detailed examination than they seem, as yet, to have received.

[4] Annales de Burton, p. 476, translated, p. 508.

No one can make out of these passages a definite regulation
as to the eyre. The circuits prescribed and outlined in the
Provisions of Westminster were not those of an ordinary
general eyre. From the regulations one might gather that
the ordinary chapters of the eyre would be laid before the
jurors, supplemented by special articles,[1] and the procedure
sketched undoubtedly was based upon that of the general
eyre. But the commission and writs lay more stress on the
clearing up of judicial arrears than on the overhauling of
local administration, and from the few records that remain,[2]
we can see that it was a special inquest, like those of 1255
and of 1258 to which its articles refer. Moreover, the scheme
outlined by the barons was postponed by the king on his
return from France;[3] Bigod and others of the justices
specially appointed were too busy to do their part,[4] and if
there had been any such general eyre in prospect, it is to
1261, not 1259, that we must look for its fulfilment.

The regulations of 1259 cannot be taken as marking an
epoch in the history of the eyre ; either in prescribing its
procedure or in limiting its frequency. And yet it seems
more than a coincidence that they are so soon followed by
a successful protest against the exploitation of the eyre
system, and are quoted as the warrant of popular privilege
in this matter. Two theories are tenable : either our versions
of the Provisions of Westminster, diverse and inchoate as
they are, are incomplete, and the negotiations included a
definite undertaking on Henry's part as to the preservation
of a seven years' interval, which has been lost ; or else the
references to a seven years' period, barely intelligible as they
are to us, were unambiguous to contemporaries, and were

---

[1] Rot. Cl. 75, m. 18 d ' Inquirant de transgressionibus factis secundum
articlos quos habent ordinatos per consilium et placitent brevia de dote . . .
et de ultima presentatione (etc.). Venire faciant coram eis xij tam milites
quam alios liberos et legales homines de quolibet hundredo quibus dicti
Iustitiarii liberent primo die articlos de quibus est inquirendum, et
assignent eis alium diem . . . quo redeant coram eis et reddant suum veredictum cum predictis articlis.' Cf. also writ to Audley and Erdington on
same membrane. [2] A. R. 456, 1189.

[3] Rot. Cl. 75, m. 14 d : *De prohibitione Itineris Iusticiarum* (June ?).

[4] Rot. Cl. 75, m. 14 d : *De assisis et placitis tenendis in Com' Sussex*
(June 11). Cf. Rot. Cl. 77, m. 18 d, m. 8 d, for revised lists of justices.

taken by both parties as the official recognition and sanction of a custom which had long been growing up but had not as yet been accepted by the crown.

APPENDIX I
LIST OF VERSIONS OF THE CAPITULA ITINERIS [1]
A. Dated

(1) 1194. Chronicle of Roger of Hoveden (R. S.), iii, p. 263.

(2) 1198. Ibid., iv, p. 61.

(3) 1208. British Museum, Add. MS. 14252, f. 117 d.

(4) „ Guildhall Records Office, Liber Albus, f. 36 b. *Printed, Munimenta Gildhallae* (R. S.), i, p. 117.
[(3) and (4) are practically duplicates.]

(5) 1227. Rot. Cl. 11 Hen. III, m. 4 d. *Printed*, Rotuli Litterarum Clausarum, ii, p. 213 (Public Record Commission, 1844).

(6) „ Bracton, lib. iii, tr. 3, c. 2. *Printed*, R. S. edition, ii, p. 252.

(7) 1244. Guildhall Records Office, (a) Misc. Rolls, A. A., (b) Liber Albus, f. 28 b. *Printed*, Munimenta Gildhallae (R. S.), i, p. 79.

(8) 1254. Annales de Burton (Annales Monastici, R. S., vol. i), p. 330.

(9) „ Historia et Cartularium Monasterii S. Petri Gloucestriae (R. S.), ii, p. 276.

(10) 1276. British Museum Additional Charters 5153.

(11) 1280. British Museum MS. Harl. 489, f. 54 : *Capitula placitanda coram Iusticiis de Itinere anno regni regis Edwardi filii regis Henrici viii.*

(12) 1281. Hundred Rolls, Chapter House Series, Wilts, No. 36 (P. R. O.).

(13) 1287. Ibid., Gloucester, No. 6 (P. R. O.).

(14) 1288. A. R. 935, mm. 3–6 (P. R. O.).

(15) 1294. A. R. 892–906 (P. R. O.).

---

[1] The starting-point of this list has been those given in Pollock and Maitland, ii, p. 521, note, and Bolland, Eyre of Kent, i, pp. xxxix–xl, but neither the references nor the descriptions given by Mr. Bolland are correct in all cases. Bracton, f. 1176, should be f. 117 b, and duplicates Bracton, R. S., ii, p. 252 ; Add. MS. 5761, f. 121, should be f. 126 ; nor is there any evidence for assigning the Exchequer Book version to 4 Ed. I, or Add. MS. 5761 to 8 Ed. I, whilst MSS. Harl. 1214, Harl. 1120, and Add. 6061 are not ' contemporary '.

(16) 1313. Year Books of the Eyre of Kent. *Printed,* Eyre of Kent (S. S.), pp. 28 ff. For list of manuscripts see p. xvi.

(17) 1321. Guildhall Records Office, Liber Custumarum, f. 241 a. *Printed,* Munimenta Gildhallae (R. S.), ii, p. 347.

B. UNDATED

(18) Bracton, lib. iii, tr. 2, c. 1. Vetera Capitula only. 1254 ?

> [Three manuscripts have been examined, one out of each of Mr. Woodbine's three groups, viz. Digby 222, f. 60, Bodley 344, f. 134 d, and Bodley 170, f. 122, all in the Bodleian Library These are practically identical, and appear to belong to 1254. The version in MS. Rawlinson, c. 160, which is printed R. S., ii, pp. 240 ff., 584 ff., is a later interpolation.]

(19) Exch. K. R. Miscellaneous Books, vol. ix, f. 42 d (38), *Articli de inquisitionibus faciendis.* Nova Capitula only. Readings from this are printed, S. R., i, pp. 235 ff. (1275–8 ?).

(20) Liber Custumarum, f. 136 b. *Printed,* S. R., i, pp. 233 ff. (1278 1313 ?).

(21) Bodleian MS. Rawlinson, c. 160, f. 63, *Capitula de quibus duodecim respondere debent. Nova Capitula de tempore Regis Edwardi filii Regis Henrici tertii.* f. 64, *Item Capitula Tangentia Prima Statuta Westmonasterii in anno regni Regis Edwardi filii Regis Henrici tercio. Printed,* Bracton, R. S., ii, pp. 240 ff., 584 ff. (1278–1313).

> [(20) and (21) appear to have a close affinity.]

British Museum MSS. :

(22) MS. Harl. 1214, f. 7. Includes writ of Lincoln Eyre (of 1281 ?). The Articles of 1274 and those upon the Statutes are intermixed.

Collection later than 1382.

(23) MS. Harl. 1120, f. 63. Includes Lincoln writ ; ends with Articles of 1274.

Collection later than 1337.

(24) Add. MS. 6061, f. 135. Includes Lincoln writ ; ends with Articles of 1274.

> [(22), (23), and (24) have well-marked affinities in textual variations.]

(25) MS. Harl. 395 (1280 ?).

> ff. 95–7. *Capitula corone* (Vetera Capitula).
>
> ff. 103–6. *Articuli novi inquirendi per iusticias itinerantes.*
>
> f. 106. *Articuli qui contingunt statuta Domini Regis.*
>
> [A good version, with some affinities with (11).]

(26) MS. Harl. 1033, f. 112. Ends with Articles of 1274.
Collection later than 1290.

(27) MS. Landsowne 652, f. 181. Vetera Capitula only.
Collection later than 1292.

> [(25), (26), and (27) have affinities in textual variations, as far as the Vetera Capitula are concerned.]

(28) MS. Harl. 667, f. 236 d. Includes all three groups of articles, but omits the instructions to the justices.
Collection later than 1300.

(29) MS. Cott. Vesp. B. vii, f. 71 d. Includes all three groups of Articles, and the Mortmain Article.
Collection later than 1341.

(30) MS. Harl. 867, f. 59 d. Includes the Mortmain Article.
Collection later than 1392.

> [(29) and (30) are very closely related to each other and to (17).]

(31) Add. MS. 5761, f. 126. A very confused copy ; a few of the Articles upon the Statutes are tacked on to the Vetera Capitula, and some on to those of 1274, which are incomplete.

> [(28), (29), (30), and (31) have some textual affinities.]

(32) MS. Harl. 673, f. 60 d. *Articuli de Itinere.* The Articles of 1274 only, without the instructions to the justices.

(33) MS. Harl. 1208, f. 81 d. Vetera Capitula only.
Collection later than 1292.

(34) MS. Harl. 1690.

> f. 14. *Incipiunt Capitula in Itinere.* Annotated in later hand, ' Stat. xj '.
> f. 15 d. *Expliciunt Capitula Vetera in Itinere Iusticiarum.*
> f. 18 d. *Incipiunt Novi articuli in Itinere iusticiarum.* Annotated in later hand, ' Stat. xviij '.

Includes Articles upon the Statutes, but they are incomplete, because the page following f. 20 has been lost.
Collection later than 1290.

(35) MS. Lansdowne 467, f. 128. Vetera Capitula only.
Collection later than 1292.

(36) MS. Egerton 656, f. 210. Vetera Capitula only, and too fragmentary to have any value.

APPENDIX II

TABULAR COMPARISON OF DIFFERENT VERSIONS, SHOWING THEIR CHRONO-LOGICAL DEVELOPMENT

NOTE

1. The Pucklechurch Roll (1287) is taken as the standard, as being the most complete. The numbering of the version in the Statutes of the Realm is given for purposes of reference, but no manuscript version numbers the articles.
2. For the sake of simplicity, no articles are included which do not become incorporated permanently in the Chapters of the Eyre. The symbol = means that the article in the version in question is only broadly equivalent. Minute textual differences are ignored.
3. The three main sections of the Vetera Capitula, the Articles of 1274, and the Articles upon the Statutes are numbered separately under the headings I, II, and III.
4. The numbering of the versions corresponds with that of Appendix I, in which details of the manuscripts are given.

(13) *Pucklechurch Roll: H. R. Gloucestershire*, No. 6. (1287)	S. R., i, 233 ff.	(1) 1194	(2) 1198
I 1. De veteribus placitis corone . . . que non fuerunt terminata.	1	} = { I	} = I
2. De nouis placitis corone que postea emerserunt . . .	2	II	
3. De hiis qui sunt in misericordia d. R. et non sunt amerciati.	3	..	= XIII
4. De valettis et puellis qui sunt . . . in custodia d. R. . . .	4	} = { V	} = IX
5. De dominabus que sunt in donatione d. R. . . .	Note 1	VI	
6. De ecclesiis que sunt in donatione d. R. . . .	5	IV	= VII
7. De eschaetis d. R. que sunt et qui illas tenent . . .	6	= III	= VIII
8. De serviantiis d. R. que sunt et qui illas tenent . . .	7	..	= XI
9. De purpresturis factis super d. R. . . .	8	..	= XIV
10. De hiis qui ceperunt denariis ab hiis qui hospitati sunt extraneos contra assisam . . .	9	..	..
11. De mensuris . . . et si custodes mensurarum ceperunt mercedem . . . et si assisa latitudinis pannorum . . .	10	} = { XVI·	} = XIX
12. De vinis venditis contra assisam . . .	12		
13. De tessauris inventis.	11	..	= XVI
14. De vic' . . . qui convenire fecerunt wappentakia . . . pro inquisitione facienda de morte hominis vel pro hutesio . . . non secuto . . .	13	..	..
15. De vic' . . . qui tenerunt placita corone . . .	..	..	..
16. De usurariis christianis mortuis . . .	15	= XV	= XII
17. De catallis francorum . . . et aliorum inimicorum d. R. . . .	16	..	..
18. De catallis Iudaeorum occisorum . . .	Note 9	= IX	..
19. De falsonnariis et retonsoribus denariorum . . .	17	= VIII	..
20. De moneta et excambio d. R. . . .	18	..	..
21. De burgatoribus et malefactoribus et eorum receptatoribus tempore pacis.	19	VII	= XVII
22. De utlagatis et fugitivis et si quis redierit . . . sine waranto.	= 20, 21, 22	..	= XVIII
23. De hiis per quorum terras utlagati . . . transierunt et non fecerunt sectam . . .	23	..	·..
24. De mercatis remotis ab uno die ad alium. . . . Si quod mercatum de novo levatum sit . . .	24, 25	..	·..
25. } De hiis qui ceperunt mercedem pro blado et catallis . . . ne capiantur . . .	26	..	..
26. } Et similiter de prisis factis per vicecomites . . . contra voluntatem . . .	27	..	..
27. De novis consuetudinibus leuatis . . .	28	..	..
28. De hiis qui sumoniti fuerunt . . . coram iusticiis . . .	29	= XIX	= XX
29. } De gaolis deliberatis sine warranto . . .	30	..	..
30. } Et similiter de hiis qui tenent placita de probatoribus sine warranto.	14	..	..
31. De malefactoribus in parcis viuariis . . .	31	..	..
32. De evasione latronum.	} 33	..	..
33. De wrecco maris.		..	..
34. De rapinis factis et prisis extraneis. . . .	32	..	..
35. De hiis qui non permittunt balliuos Regis intrare in terras suas . . .	34	..	..
36. De balliuis qui ceperunt denarios pro recognitoribus ammouendis de iuratis . . .	35	..	..
37. De hiis qui tenent terras Normannorum . . .	36	..	..
38. De hiis qui subtraxerunt sectas schirarum . . . post guerram . . .	37	..	..
39. De hiis qui tenent placita de Namio Vetito . . .	..	..	..
40. De vicecomitibus . . . qui ceperunt redempcionem de valettis . . . ne milites furent . . .	38	..	..

(3) 1208	(5) 1227	(7) 1244	(8) 1254	(9) 1254	(18) 1254?	(10) 1276	(11) 1280	(12) 1281	(14) 1288	(15) 1294	(16) 1313	(17) 1321
{3	1	1	1	1	1	1	1	[missing 1]	1	1	1	1
{4	=2	2	2	2	2	2	2	[missing 2]	2	2	3	2
2	3	3	3	3	3	3	3	3	3	3	2	3
5	..	7	4	4	4	{5	{4	4	4	4	4	4
7	..	..	5	5	5	{5	{5	5	5	{5	5	5
8	4	9	6	6	6	7	7	6	{6	6	6	6
6	5	..	7	7	7	47	6	7	{6	7	7	7
..	..	8	8	8	8	8	11	8	7	8	8	8
9	6	11	9	9	9	48	8	9	8	9	9	9
..	..	..	..	..	12	9	9	{10 11	9	10	10	10
10	7	12	10	10	10	50	10	{12 13	10	11	11	11
11	9	13	=11	11	11	..	12	14	11	12	12	12
12	10	14	12	12	54	12	13	15	12	13	13	13
..	..	..	{14 15	{14 15	14	..	15	16	13	14	15	15
..	11	15	13	13	13	=13	14	..	14	15	17	16
13	..	16	16	18	15	=14	16	17	15	16	16	17
14	12	=17	..	35	..	..	..	18	16	17	..	..
=15	..	..	17	17	16	42	17	..	17	18	..	..
24	13	18	18	19	17	17	..	19	18	19	18	18
..	16	19	19	16	18	18	18	..	19	20	19	19
}={17	14	20	20	20	19	}19	20	20	20	21	20	20
{22	17	21	{21 23	{21 22	=20 =21		={19 50	21	21	{22 23	21	21
..	..	..	22	23	22	..	21	22	22	24	22	22
..	15	..	24	24	23	..	=22	23	23	25	23	23
..	18	22	..	{25	{25	20	23	24	{24	{26	{24	24
23	19	23	..			..	24	25	{25			25
..	20	24	25	26	24	21	25	26	26	27	25	..
=1	21	25	26	27	26	46	26	27	27	28	26	26
..	22	26	27	{28	27	24	27	28	28	29	{27	{27
..	..	..	..		28	..	28	..	..	30		{28
=21	..	..	28	29	31	..	29	29	29	31	28	29
..	..	..	30	32	30	..	33	{31	{31 30	32	14	14
..	..	28	29	33	29	23	32			33	29	30
..	23	30	..	30	33	25	30	30	32	34	30	31
..	..	..	31	31	34	43	31	32	33	35	31	32
..	..	..	32	34	35	44	34	33	34	36	32	33
..	..	..	33	36	..	..	37	34	35	37	33	34
..	..	..	=34	37	..	..	38	35	36	38	34	35
..	..	..	..	38	..	..	..	36	37	39	35	36
..	..	..	=35	=39	36	..	39	37	38	40	36	37

(13) Pucklechurch Roll : H. R. Gloucestershire, No. 6. (1287)

	S. R.	(1) 1194	(2) 1198
41. De valettis integrum feodum militis tenentibus . . .	39	..	..
42. De vicecomitibus qui . . . placita terminatur (*sic*) per sacramentum xij cum nullam habeant . . . potestatem.	40	..	..
43. De excessibus vicecomitum . . . si aliquam litem fouerunt . . . per quod iustitia . . . suffocantur.	41	..	..
44. De vicecomitibus . . . qui capiunt ex una parte et altera	42	..	..
45. De wappentakiis et truthingiis positis ad firmam . . .	43	..	..
46. De prisis d. R. . . .	44	..	..
47. De parvis ballivis . . . qui faciunt seruisiam que vocatur scottale . . .	Note 1	..	..
48. De hiis qui non facunt (*sic*) servisum garbas in Autumpno extorquentibus . . .			
49. De catallis extraneorum . . . captis dum Rex fuit in Wasconia . . .	45		
50. De hiis qui leuauerunt warennam . . . sine waranto.	46	..	..
51. De hiis qui piscantur cum kydellis et starkellis.	47	..	..
52. De vicecomitibus qui ceperunt denarios ab hiis qui retectati (*sic*) fuerunt ut dimitterentur per plevinam.	48	..	..
53. De vic' qui imprisonauerunt illos . . . et detinuerunt . . . quousque redemptionem ceperint.	49		
54. De vic' . . . qui bis . . . ceperunt . . . denarios . . . pro uno amerciamento . . .	50		
55. De hiis qui manuceperunt habere aliquem . . . coram iusticiis . . .	53	..	..
56. De hiis qui subtraxerunt brevia d. R. . . . et vendiderunt			
57. De coronatoribus qui denarios . . . ceperunt pro officio suo exequendo et si catalla felonum concelaverunt . . .	54	..	..
58. De pontibus et calceis fractis . . .	56	..	..
59. De captibus et incarceratis . . . qualiter deliberati fuerint . . .	57	..	..
60. De felonibus dampnatis . . . alibi quam coram iusticiis ad communia placita . . .	58	..	..
61. De hiis qui currunt in alienis warrennis . . .	59	..	..
62. De hiis qui distrinxerunt aliquem ad pacandum plus quam ad quod fuerit amerciatus.	52	..	..
63. De hiis qui distrinxerunt plures habentes unum nomen . . .	51	..	.
64. De vic' qui ceperunt denarios ab . . . excommunicatis . . . ne caperentur.	Note 12 a (p. 234 a)	..	..
65. De denariis captis de non venientibus ad sumonitionem vicecomitis . . .	Note 12	..	..
66. De vic' . . . qui ceperunt denarios pro vigiliis constitutis in regno non obseruatis.	Note 12 c	..	..
67. De hiis qui in hyeme columbas aereas . . . per retia . . . capiunt . . .	Note 12 d = 55	..	..
68. De hiis qui . . . terras et tenementa sua alienant contra adventum iusticiarum . . .	Note 12 e	..	..
69. De hiis qui mutuis sacramentis . . . se adinvicem astringunt . . . per quod veritas et iustitia suffocantur.	Note 12 f	..	..
II 1. Quot et que maneria dominica D. R. habet . . .	1	..	..
2. Que etiam maneria esse solent in manibus regum . . .	2	..	..
3. De feudis etiam d. R. et tenentibus suis et qui ea modo tenent . . .	3	..	..
4. De terris et tenentibus de antiquo dominico corone . . .	Note 2 (p. 235)	..	..
5. Simili modo inquiratur de firmis hundredorum . . .	4	..	..
6. Quot etiam Hundredi Truthingii . . . sunt in manu d. R. . . . et quot in manibus aliorum . .	5	..	..

(3) 1208	(5) 1227	(7) 1244	(8) 1254	(9) 1254	(18) 1254 ?	(10) 1276	(11) 1280	(12) 1281	(14) 1288	(15) 1294	(16) 1313	(17) 1321
..	..	..	36	40	..	..	40	..	39	41	37	38
..	..	..	37	41	37	..	51	38	40	42	38	39
..	..	..	38	42	38	..	52	39	41	43	39	40
..	..	..	39	43	39	31	41	40	42	44	40	41
..	..	..	40	44	40	..	42	41	43	45	41	43
..	..	..	41	45	41	..	43	42	44	46	42	44
..	..	..	42 {	46	47	..	..	..	45	47	43	45
..	..	..		47	48	..	..	..	46	48	44	46
..	..	..	43	48	49	..	..	43	47	49	45	47
..	..	..	44	51	51	..	..	44	48	50	46	48
..	..	..	45	52	..	45	35	45	49	51	47	49
..	..	..	47	53	42	30	36	46	50	52	48	50
..	..	..	50	54	43	32	45	47	51	53	49	51
..	..	..	48	55	44	33	46	48	52	54	50	52
..	..	..	52	57	52	36	48	..	53 }	55 {	51	53
..	..	..	53	58	53	37	49	51	54 }		52	54
..	..	..	..	..	..	..	..	52	55	56	53	55
..	..	..	..	..	..	40	..	III 36	56	58	..	57
..	..	..	..	..	..	..	54	III 37	57	59	55	58
..	..	..	..	..	..	41	53	..	58	60	56	59
..	..	..	..	..	..	..	44	..	59	61	58	60
..	..	..	51	56	46	34	..	50	60	62	59	61
..	..	..	49	..	45	35	47	49	61	63	60	62
..	..	..	..	..	..	39	..	..	62	64	57	42
..	..	..	46	50	50	38	..	..	63	65	61	..
..	..	..	..	..	..	..	..	..	64	66	62	63
..	..	..	..	..	= 32	..	..	53	65	= 57	= 54	= 56
..	..	..	..	..	..	..	..	III 35	66	67	63	64
..	..	..	..	..	..	..	..	•III 34	67	68	64	65
..	..	..	..	..	..	..	1 }	1	1	1	1	1
..	..	..	..	..	..	..	2		2	2	2	2
..	..	..	..	..	..	..	3	2	3	3	3	3
..	..	..	..	..	..	..	4	3	4	4	4	4
..	..	..	..	..	..	..	5	4	5	5	5	5
..	..	..	..	..	..	..	6	5	6	6	6	6

(13) *Pucklechurch Roll : H. R. Gloucestershire,* No. 6. (1287)

	S. R.	(1) 1194	(2) 1198
7. De sectis antiquis ... et aliis rebus subtractis ... et qui huius modi sectas ... sibi ... appropriauerunt.	6	..	..
8. Qui etiam ... clamant habere returnum breuium ... wreccam ... et alias libertates ...	7	..	..
9. De hiis ... qui libertates regias ... concessas ... aliter usi fuerunt ... quam debuissent ...	8	..	..
10. De libertatibus concessis que impediunt communem iustitiam ...	9	..	..
11. Qui etiam de novo appropriauerunt sibi nouas chacias vel warrennas ...	10	..	..
12. Qui ... non sustinuerunt execussionem mandatorum d. R. a tempore constitutionum ... apud Marleberche.	11	..	..
13. De omnibus purpresturis factis super d. R. vel regalem dignitatem ...	12	..	..
[14. De feodis militaribus ... et terris ... datis vel venditis religiosis ... *(Omitted or obliterated in Puck. Roll.)*]	13	..	..
15. De vic' capientibus munera ... ad concelandum felonias ...	14	..	..
16. Simili modo de clericis et aliis balliuis ... qui ita fecerunt tempore d. Regis. H. ...	15	..	..
17. De vic' ... capientibus munera pro recognitoribus amovendis de iuratis ...	16	..	..
18. De vic' qui amerciauerunt illos qui sumoniti fuerunt ad inquisitiones ... pro defalta ...	17	..	..
19. De vic' qui tradiderunt balliuis extorsoribus ... hundreda ... ad alias firmas ...	21	..	..
20. Cum vic' non debeat facere turnum suum nisi bis per annum ...	18	..	..
21. Cum fines de redisseisina ... factis ... qui perceperunt fines huiusmodi ...	19	..	..
22. Qui per potestatem officii sui aliquos occasionaverint ...	Note 3	..	..
23. Qui ceperint mandatum d. R. ut debita sua solverent et a creditoribus ... porcionem ceperint. ...	22	..	..
24. Qui ceperint debita Regis ... et debitores ... non inde aquietaverunt ...	23	..	..
25. Qui summonaverunt aliquos ut fierent milites et pro respectu habendo ... lucra ceperunt ...	24	..	..
26. Si vic' ... fecerint non debito modo sumoniciones ... vel minus sufficienter executi fuerunt precepta D. R.	25	..	..
27. Qui habuerunt felones imprisonatos et pro pecunia eos abire ... permiserunt ... impunes ...	{ 27 { 28	..	..
28. De hiis qui habuerunt probatores ... et fecerunt eos appellare ... innocentes causa ... lucri ...	26	..	..
29. Qui dona ... ceperunt pro officiis ... exercendis ... vel non exercendis ...	29	..	..
30. Qui ... de operationibus d. R. ... magis computaverunt ... quam rationabiliter apposuerunt ...	30	..	..
31. Et similiter qui petram vel maeremium ... ad huiusmodi operaciones ... ad opus suum detinuerunt.[1]	31	..	..
32. De eschaetoribus ... facientibus vastum ... infra custodias sibi commissas per d. R. ...	32	..	..
33. De eisdem qui ... ceperint bona defunctorum ... in manu d. R. iniuste donec redimerentur.	33	..	..

[1] Here follows in the Midhurst Roll: (30) De catallis Iudaeorum dampnatorum pro tonsura et falsonaria monete concelatis; (31) De hiis qui falsas platas et conflatas vendiderunt vel eschambiaverunt.

(3) 1208	(5) 1227	(7) 1244	(8) 1254	(9) 1254	(18) 1254?	(10) 1276	(11) 1280	(12) 1281	(14) 1288	(15) 1294	(16) 1313	(17) 1321
..	..	..	..	..	..	..	7	6	7	7	7	7
..	..	..	..	..	..	..	8	7	8	8	8	8
..	..	..	..	..	..	..	9	8	9	9	9	9
..	..	..	..	..	..	..	10	9	10	10	10	10
..	..	..	..	..	..	..	11	10	11	11	11	11
..	..	..	..	..	..	..	12	11	12	12	12	12
..	..	..	..	..	..	..	13	12	13	13	13	13
..	..	..	..	..	..	..	16	13	..	..	..	..
..	..	..	..	..	..	..	14	} 14	14	14	14	14
..	..	..	..	..	..	..	15	}	15	15	15	15
..	..	..	..	..	..	..	17	15	16	16	16	16
..	..	..	..	..	..	..	18	16	17	17	17	17
..	..	..	..	..	..	..	19	18	18	18	18	18
..	..	..	..	..	..	..	20	19	19	19	19	19
..	..	..	..	..	..	..	21	20	20	20	20	20
..	..	..	..	..	..	..	22	21	21	21	21	21
..	..	..	..	..	..	..	23	22	22	22	22	22
..	..	..	..	..	..	..	24	17	23	23	23	23
..	..	..	..	..	..	..	25	23	24	24	24	24
..	..	..	..	..	..	..	26	24	25	..	26	25
..	..	..	..	..	..	..	{28 29}	26	26	25	{25 27}	{26 27}
..	..	..	..	..	..	..	27	25	27	26	28	28
..	..	..	..	..	..	..	30	27	..	27	29	29
..	..	..	..	..	..	..	31	} 28	28	28	30	30
..	..	..	..	..	..	..	32	}	29[1]	29	31	31
..	..	..	..	..	..	..	33	29	32	30	32	32
..	..	..	..	..	..	..	34	30	33	31	33	33

(13) *Pucklechurch Roll : H. R. Gloucestershire*, No. 6.   (1287)   S. R.   (1)   (2)
                                                                                 1194   1198

34. De eisdem qui minus sufficienter [extenderint] terras   34   ..   ..
    alicuius in fauorem eiusdem.

35. De eisdem qui prece, precio, vel favore consenserint . . .   35   ..   ..
    custodias d. R. vendere pro minori precio quam . . .
    debuerint . . .

36. De eisdem qui procurauerint . . . quod iuratores in-   36   ..   ..
    quisitionum . . . de etate heredum dicerent heredes
    fuisse plene etatis cum non fuerint.

37. De hiis qui reservaverunt ad opus suum custodias . . .   37   ..   ..
    per concelamentum . . .

38. Cuiusmodi seisierunt terras et per quantum tempus   38   ..   ..
    eas in manu d. R. tenuerunt.

39. De terris captis in manu d. R. que capi non deberent[1] . . . 39   ..   ..
    De omnibus predictis et commissis infra xxv annos
    proximos preteritos predicti iustitiarii se intro-
    mittant . . .

III 1. De magnatibus . . . venientibus . . . ad domos religio-   ⎫   ..   ..
        sorum . . .   ⎬ 1
     2. De hiis qui occasione . . . affinitatis . . . fugaverunt in⎭   ..   ..
        parcis . . . sine licentia . . .

     3. Et similiter de hiis qui . . . fenestra fregerunt . . . et   2   ..   ..
        victualia . . . ceperunt sub colore empcionis.

     4. De hiis qui triturari vel capi fecerunt blada . . . reli-   3   ..   ..
        giosorum . . . contra voluntatem eorum . . .

     5. De hiis qui ceperunt boves . . . ad cariagium faciendum Note 2   ..   ..
        . . . sine voluntate . . .

     6. De hiis qui vindictam fecerunt quibuscunque quod . . .   4   ..   ..
        ospicium . . . eis negaverunt . . .

     7. De hiis qui miserunt . . . ad domos religiosorum homines   5   ..   ..
        . . . vel canes . . . ad perendinandum . . .

     8. De vic' venientibus ad hospitandum cum pluribus   6   ..   ..
        quam v. vel vj equis . . .

     9. De hiis qui leuauerunt eschapea latronum . . . antequam   7   ..   ..
        adiudicata fuerunt per iustitiarios.

    10. De hiis qui sub colore de wreko maris bona quorum-   8   ..   ..
        cumque sibi appropriaverunt . . .

    11. De hiis qui amerciati sint sine rationabili occasione . . . 9   ..   ..
        et non per pares suos . . .

    12. De prisis constabulorum castrorum . . . exceptis antiquis   10   ..   ..
        prisis debitis . . .

    13. De hiis qui . . . sequi vel arestare non fecerint felones . . . 11   ..   ..
    14. De vic' . . . vel aliis qui prece vel precio vel . . . affinitate 12 ..   ..
        concelaverunt . . . felonias factas.

    15. De hiis qui rapuerunt damycellas . . .   13   ..   ..
    16. De vic' . . . qui replegiaverunt personas cum non essent   14   ..   ..
        replegiabiles. . . .

    17. De hiis qui ceperunt averia . . . in uno comitatu et ea   15   ..   ..
        fugaverunt extra comitatum . . .

    18. De hiis qui fugaverunt averia ad castra . . . et ibi   16   ..   ..
        detinuerunt . . .

    19. De vic' . . . qui ceperunt debita . . . d. R. . . . et debi- 17   ..   ..
        torem non inde acquietaverunt . . .

    20. De malefactoribus parcorum . . . et de hiis qui . . .   18   ..   ..
        roberiam fecerint . . .

---

[1] Here follows in the Wiltshire Roll : (37) Item qui durante discordia etc.

(3) 1208	(5) 1227	(7) 1244	(8) 1254	(9) 1254	(18) 1254?	(10) 1276	(11) 1280	(12) 1281	(14) 1288	(15) 1294	(16) 1313	(17) 1321
..	..	..	..	..	..	..	} 35	3^1	34	3^2	34	34
..	..	..	..	..	..	..		3^2	35	33	35	35
..	..	..	..	..	..	..	36	33	36	34	36	36
..	..	..	..	..	..	..	37	34	37	35	37	37
..	..	..	..	..	..	..	38	35	38	36	38	38
..	..	..	..	..	..	..	39	36^1	39	37	39	39
..	..	..	..	..	..	..	1	1	1	1	1	1
..	..	..	..	..	..	..	2	2	2	2	2	2
..	..	..	..	..	..	..	3	3	3	3	3	3
..	..	..	..	..	..	..	4	4	4	4	4	4
..	..	..	..	..	..	..	..	5	{ 4 5	5	5	5
..	..	..	..	..	..	..	5	6	6	6	6	6
..	..	..	..	..	..	..	6	7	7	7	7	7
..	..	..	..	..	..	..	7	8	8	8	8	8
..	..	..	..	..	..	..	8	9	9	9	9	9
..	..	..	..	..	..	..	9	10	10	10	10	10
..	..	..	..	..	..	..	10	11	11	11	11	11
..	..	..	..	..	..	..	11	12	12	12	12	12
..	..	..	..	..	..	..	12	13	13	13	13	13
..	..	..	..	..	..	..	13	14	..	14	14	14
..	..	..	..	..	..	..	14	15	14	15	15	15
..	..	..	..	..	..	..	15	16	15	16	16	16
..	..	..	..	..	..	..	16	17	16	17	17	17
..	..	..	..	..	..	..	17	18	17	18	18	18
..	..	..	..	..	..	..	18	19	18	19	19	19
..	..	..	..	..	..	..	19	20	19	20	20	20

H 2

(13) *Pucklechurch Roll: H. R. Gloucestershire,* No. 6. (1287)	S. R.	(1) 1194	(2) 1198
21. De hiis qui fecerint destricciones in civitatibus . . . super homines forinsecos . . .	19	..	..
22. De ministris Regis qui manutenuerint . . . loquelas . . . ut habeant . . . proficuum.	} 20	..	..
23. De vic' . . . capientibus munera . . . pro officiis suis exercendis.		..	..
24. De clericis iusticiarum . . . capientibus denarios pro capitulis liberandis . . .	21	..	..
25. De hiis qui ceperunt superflua vel indebita theolonea.	22	..	..
26. De civibus . . . capientibus muragium . . . plus quam facere debent . . .	23	..	..
27. De hiis qui ceperunt . . . necessaria ad opus Regis . . . et . . . detinuerint creditoribus.	Note 6	..	..
28. De hiis qui ceperunt plures equos ad cariagium d. R. quam necessarie fuerint . . .	24	..	..
29. De magnatibus . . . quo . . . atthathiaverint quoscumque . . . de transgressionibus factis extra posse . . .	25	..	..
30. De vic' . . . qui non permiserunt quoscunque pascere de suo . . . averia sua . . . imparcata . . .	26	..	..
31. De averiis captis . . . et venditis infra xv dies . . .	28	..	..
32. De districcionibus factis . . . per animalia ad waynagium . . . vel et per bidentes.	} 27	..	..
33. De superfluis districcionibus factis tam post idem parliamentum quam ante.		..	..
Et hec omnia que contingunt dicta statuta distingte et aperte inquirantur . . . Pene autem in eisdem statutis contente adiudicande sint de commissis post festam sancte Michaelis anno r. r. E. tertio et non ante[1] . . .			
34. De hiis qui capiunt mercedem de aliquibus pro advocaria habenda[2] . . .	29	..	..
35. De hiis mutuis sacramentis qui iniuste se astringunt . . . per quod rei veritas non potest convinci.	Note 5	..	..
[1313. De terris et tenementis quae devenerunt ad manum mortuam . . .]		..	..
[1321. De ministres le Roi en citez . . . queux sunt merchaundes des vyns et des vitailles . . .]		..	..

[1] Those versions which include these directions are marked *.

[2] Here follows in the Midhurst Roll : (32) De excessibus forestiarorum wodewardorum et aliorum ministrorum de prestis parcis et aliis boscis qui grauant populum maliciose per extorsiones suas.

(3) 1208	(5) 1227	(7) 1244	(8) 1254	(9) 1254	(18) 1254?	(10) 1276	(11) 1280	(12) 1281	(14) 1288	(15) 1294	(16) 1313	(17) 1321
..	..	..	..	..	..	..	20	21	20	21	21	21
..	..	..	..	..	..	..	21	22	21	22	22	22
..	..	..	..	..	..	..	22	23	..	23	23	23
..	..	..	..	..	..	..	23	24	22	24	24	24
..	..	..	..	..	..	..	24	25	23	25	25	25
..	..	..	..	..	..	..	25	26	24	26	26	26
..	..	..	..	..	..	..	26	27	25	27	27	27
..	..	..	..	..	..	..	27	28	26	28	28	28
..	..	..	..	..	..	..	28	29	27	29	29	29
..	..	..	..	..	..	..	29	30	28	30	30	30
..	..	..	..	..	..	..	30	31	29	31	31	33
..	..	..	..	..	..	..	} 31	32	} 30	32	32	31
..	..	..	..	..	..	..		33		33	33	32
							*			*	*	*
..	..	..	..	..	..	..	32	..	31 [2]	34	34	34
..	..	..	..	..	..	..	33	34	..	35	35	..
..	..	..	..	..	..	..	..	..	..	..	36	35
..	..	..	..	..	..	..	..	..	..	..	..	36

APPENDIX III

A PROVISIONAL LIST OF THE GENERAL EYRES 1194–1341, TRACEABLE FROM THE PUBLIC AND OTHER RECORDS

KEY TO THE SYMBOLS USED IN THE FOLLOWING TABLE

The evidence for the occurrence of a general eyre may be :

I. A notice, generally on the Close or Patent Rolls, that such an eyre
    (1) is intended to be held : this is indicated by the symbol →.
    (2) is in process of being held : this is indicated by the symbol ↓ .
    (3) has been held : this is indicated by the symbol ←.

II. The records of the eyre itself on the Assize or Curia Regis Rolls.
    If the reference is followed by a ?, this implies that no records
    of pleas of the Crown exist, though there is reason to think
    they were held.

III. The list, on the rolls of the next following eyre, of the sheriffs who have
    held office in the interval. By comparison with the P. R. O.
    List of Sheriffs (Lists and Indexes, No. ix), it is generally
    possible to fix the dates of the sheriffs' terms of office. The
    dates between which an eyre must have occurred, according
    to these data, are indicated by a ? The years during which
    no eyre can have occurred are indicated by —.

The columns are left blank if there is no evidence for or against the
occurrence of an eyre. If columns are omitted, there is no evidence of
any eyres having been held in the years omitted, and any negative evidence
is noted at the foot of the page.

KEY TO ABBREVIATIONS OF AUTHORITY FOR EYRE

A. R.   = Assize Roll. Referred to by No. in P. R. O. List (Lists and
            Indexes, No. iv).
C. R.   = Close Roll. Referred to by membrane.
C. R. C.   = Close Roll Calendar. Referred to by page.
C. R. R.   = Curia Regis Roll.
Misc. Exch. = Miscellanea of the Exchequer.
P. R.   = Patent Roll.
P. R. C.   = Patent Roll Calendar. Referred to by page.
Pp. R.   = Pipe Roll.

Annals and Chronicles are referred to by page in R. S. edition.

	1194	1195	1198	1202	1204	1208-1209	1211	1218
Bedford	—	C.R.R.4		A.R.1				P.R.C.207→
Berks	Pp.R.							P.R.C.207→
Bucks	—	C.R.R.4						P.R.C.208→
Cambridge	Pp.R.					Add.MS.14252		P.R.C.207→
Cornwall	Pp.R.			A.R.1171				P.R.C.207→
Cumberland	Pp.R.					Add.MS.14252		P.R.C.208→
Derbyshire	Pp.R.					Add.MS.14252		P.R.C.208→ ?Misc.Exch.2/9
Devon	Pp.R.							P.R.C.207→
Dorset	Pp.R.			A.R.1171				P.R.C.207→
Essex	Pp.R.		C.R.R.9					P.R.C.208→
Gloucester	Pp.R.						?Maitland [1] Glouc.Pleas.XX	
Hereford	Pp.R.							P.R.C.209→
Herts	Pp.R.		C.R.R.9					P.R.C.208→
Hunts	Pp.R.					Add.MS.14252		P.R.C.207→
Kent	Pp.R.							P.R.C.208→
Lancashire	Pp.R.					Add.MS.14252		P.R.C.208→ ?Misc.Exch.2/9
Leicester	Pp.R.							P.R.C.209→
Lincoln	Pp.R.					(Add.MS.14252 A.R.479-80?		P.R.C.208→ ?Misc.Exch.2/9
Middlesex	Pp.R.		C.R.R.9					P.R.C.208→
London	Pp.R.							
Norfolk	Pp.R.					Add.MS.14252		P.R.C.208→
Northants	Pp.R.							P.R.C.207→
Northumberland	Pp.R.					Add.MS.14252		P.R.C.207→
Nottingham	Pp.R.					Add.MS.14252		P.R.C.208→ ?Misc.Exch.2/9
Oxford	Pp.R.							P.R.C.207→ ?Misc.Exch.2/9
Rutland	Pp.R.							P.R.C.207→
Salop	Pp.R.				A.R.732	Add.MS.14252		P.R.C.209→
Somerset	Pp.R.			A.R.1171				P.R.C.207→
Southants	Pp.R.							P.R.C.207→
Stafford	Pp.R.				A.R. 799-800	Add.MS.14252		P.R.C.209→
Suffolk	Pp.R.					Add.MS.14252		P.R.C.208→
Surrey	Pp.R.							P.R.C.208→
Sussex	Pp.R.							P.R.C.208→
Warwick	Pp.R.					Add.MS.14252		P.R.C.209→
Westmoreland	—					Add.MS.14252		P.R.C.208→ ?Misc.Exch.2/9
Wilts	C.R.R.3							P.R.C.207→
Worcester	Pp.R.							
York	Pp.R.					Add.MS.14252		P.R.C.207→

[1] No general eyre was held in Gloucestershire between 1211 and 1221. See Maitland, Pleas for the County of Gloucester, p. xx; C. R., 5 Hen. III, m. 11 d.

1219	1220	1221	1222	1223	1224	1225	1226	1227	1228
Ann.Dunst. ←55								C.R.m. 5d.→[2]	·A.R.2·
								...*...	
								...*...	C.R.C.35 ↓
		C.R.m.11d→							
							P.R.C. 83→	...*...	C.R.C.23←
							P.R.C. 83→	?Misc.Exch.11[2]←	
							C.R.m.15d→	*P.R.C.207→	—
								?Misc.Exch.11[2]←	
								...*...	
—	—	A.R.271-2					C.R.m.15d→	?Misc.Exch.11[2]←	
		C.R.m.11d→						...*...	
	P.R.C. 271→							...*...	
								...*...	
								*·A.R. 358	
							P.R.C. 83→		
		C.R.m.11d→					P.R.C. 83→	?Misc.Exch.11[2]←	←C.R.C.16
							P.R.C. 83→		←C.R.C.14
	Lib.de Ant. Leg.5 · M.Gildh. I62 }	—	—	—	—	—	Lib.de Ant. Leg.M.G.I81	—	—
								...*...	
								...*...	
							P.R.C. 83→	?Misc.Exch.11[2]←	←C.R.C.23
							P.R.C. 83→	?Misc.Exch. 11[2]←	
								*P.R.C. 142→	
		C.R.m.11d→	A.R.733a					...*...	
								?Misc.Exch. 11[2]	
								P.R.C.207→ *	
		C.R.m.11d→						...*...	
								...*...	
						A.R.863			
	A.R.950						P.R.C. 83→	?Misc.Exch.11[2]	
							P.R.C. 83→		←C.R.C.23
		C.R.m.11d→						?Misc.Exch.11[2]←	
		A.R.1021					P.R.C. 83→	?Misc.Exch.11[2]←	
A.R.1040							P.R.C. 83→	...*...	←C.R.C.23

[2] A general eyre was ordered for the counties marked * ; see C. R., m. 5 d.

	1229	1230	1231	1232	1233	1234	1235	1236
Bedford								C.R.C. 348→ / Ann.Dunst.?145
Berks							C.R.C.146↓	C.R.C.348↓
Bucks	A R.54							Grossteste Ep.77
Cambridge						P.R.C.78→	C.R.C.104↓	
Cornwall					Ann.Dunst. 135			
Cumberland						P.R.C.77→	C.R.C.174→	
Derbyshire								C.R.C.349→
Devon	—	—	—	—	—	—	—	
Dorset							P.R.C.128→	C.R.C.250↓
Essex	A.R.229					P.R.C.78→	A.R.230	
Gloucester								Ann.Theok.99 / C.R.C.261↓
Hereford								C.R.C.349→
Herts						P.R.C.78→		
Hunts	A.R.341					P.R.C.78→ ←C.R.C.184		
Kent							P.R.C.128→	C.R.C.349↓
Lancashire						P.R.C.78→	?	?
Leicester								C.R.C.348→ / ←C.R.C.320
Lincoln						P.R.C.77→		
Middlesex						P.R.C.78→	A.R.536	
London		—	—	—	—	—	—	
Norfolk	C.R.C.80?↓					P.R.C.77→		
Northants				A.R.614a?				?
Northumberland						P.R.C.77→		
Nottingham								C.R.C.319↓
Oxford							C.R.C.110↓	—
Rutland						P.R.C.77→		
Salop								C.R.C.349→
Somerset							P.R.C.128→	C.R.C.348↓
Southants							P.R.C.128→	A.R.775
Stafford	A.R.801							C.R.C.367↓
Suffolk	C.R.C.80?↓					C.R.C.12↓		
Surrey	C.R.C.229→						A.R.864-6	—
Sussex	C.R.C.266↓						C.R.C.205↓	
Warwick				A.R.951				C.R.C.348→
Westmoreland								
Wilts							P.R.C.128→	C.R.C.333↓
Worcester								C.R.C.349→
York			A.R.1043			C.R.C.12↓		

1237	1238	1239	1240	1241	1242	1243	1244	1245
?	?	?	?	—	—	—	—	—
—	—	—	—	A.R.87	?	?	—	—
				A.R.55	—	—	—	—
			←C.R.C.344 M.Paris·IV52					
	C.R.C.125→ Ann.Theok. ?107						C.R.C.156→	
							←C.R.C.280	
								C.R.C.323→
								C.R.C.356→
—	A.R.174	—	—	—	—	—	A.R.175	—
—		—	—	—	—	—	A.R.201	
			C.R.C.238→					
	?	?	?	C.R.C.350→	—	—	—	—
				C.R.C.350→				
			M.Paris IV51?	—	—			
—	—	—	—	A.R.360				
?	?	?	?	?	—	—	—	—
?	?	?	?	—	—	—	—	—
			Grosseteste Ep.84					C.R.C.351→
—	—	—	—	—	—	Lib.de Ant.Leg. M.Gild.177		
←C.R.C.494					?	?	?	?
?	?	?	?					
								C.R.C.356→
—	—	—	—	A.R.696	—	—		—
←C.R.C.494								
				C.R.C.350→		A.R.756		
		?	?	?	—	—	—	
			A.R.818					
—	—	—	—	A.R.867-9				
				C.R.C.352→				
			C.R.C.238→	?	?	?	?	?
				C.R.C.350→				
				C.R.C.350→	?	?	?	?
			C.R.C.238?↓					

	1246	1247	1248	1249	1250	1251	1252
Bedford	—	A.R.4					
Berks	—	—	A.R.38		?	?	?
Bucks	—	A.R.56					
Cambridge							
Cornwall							
Cumberland							
Derbyshire							
Devon	—	—	—	A.R.176			
Dorset		C.R.C.544→					
Essex			A.R.232	—	—	—	—
Gloucester	—	—	A.R.274				
Hereford		C.R.C.544→	?	?		—	—
Herts	—	—	A.R.318	—	—	—	—
Hunts							
Kent				?	—	—	—
Lancashire	A.R.404						
Leicester	—	A.R.454-5					
Lincoln					P.R.C.62→		
Middlesex							
London						Lib. de Ant. Leg. 18	—
Norfolk	?	?	?	—	A.R.562-5	—	
Northants	—	A.R.614b.	—	—	—	—	
Northumberland	←C.R.C.468						
Nottingham							Ann. Dunst. ? 184
Oxford	—	A.R.700					
Rutland		C.R.C.544→					
Salop		C.R.C.544→	?	A.R.733b?	—	—	—
Somerset		C.R.C.544→					
Southants	—	—	A.R.776		—	—	—
Stafford		C.R.C.544→					
Suffolk							
Surrey	?	?	?	?	—	—	—
Sussex				A.R.909			
Warwick	—	A.R.952					
Westmoreland							
Wilts				A.R.996			
Worcester	?	C.R.C.544→	?		—	—	—
York					—	—	—

1253	1254	1255	1256	1257	1258	1259	1260	1261
	P.R.C. 373→ Ann.Dunst.193							P.R.C.178→
?	?	—	—	—	—	—	—	A.R.40
	Ann.Dunst.192 P.R.C. 373→	—	—	—	—	—	—	—
								C.R.m. 26d→ ←P.R.C.182
			P.R.C.511→					
			P.R.C.511→	—	—	—	—	—
				P.R.C. 659→ Ann. Dunst.206				
			P.R.C.511→					
			P.R.C. 511→	?	—	—	—	
—	A.R.233-6							C.R.m.13d→
	P.R.C.392→	P.R.C.436→						C.R.m.26d→ ←P.R.C.157
—	—	A.R.300c						C.R.m.26d→
—	—	A.R.320	—	—	—	—	—	
?	?	—	—	—	—	—	—	A.R.343
—	—	A.R.361						
			P.R.C.511→					
			P.R.C.523→					
—	—	—	—		—	—	—	—
—	—	—	—	A.R.568	—	—	—	—
A.R.615								C.R.m.13d→
			A.R.642					
				P.R.C.602→				
	?	—	—		—	—	—	A.R.701
—	—	—	A.R.734					
			P.R.C.511→					
	—	—	A.R.778					
	Ann.Burt.329 P.R.C. 392→		—					
				P.R.C. 602→				
—	—	A.R.872						
			?	?	—	—	—	—
?	?		—		—	—	—	—
		—	A.R.979	—	—	—	—	—
			P.R.C.511→	?	—	—	—	
—	—	A.R.1022						C.R.m.26d→ [3]
—	—	—	P.R.C.535→	A.R.1109 ? A.R 1053 ?				

[3] This eyre was never held. See Ann. Wig. 446.

	1262	1263	1264	1265	1266	1267	1268	1269	1270
Bedford	Ann. Dunst. 217	—	—	—	—	*—[4]	—	...	—
Berks......						*—	←P.R.C.244 A.R.41?	—	—
Bucks......	A.R.58					*—	—	—	—
Cambridge ...	—		—	—	—	*—	—	—	—
Cornwall ...	P.R.C.227→	:				*—	P.R.C.244→ ?	?	?
Cumberland ..	—				—	*—	—	—	—
Derbyshire ..						*—	—	P.R.C.314→ A.R.144?	P.R.C.314→
Devon	P.R.C.227→					*—	—	P.R.C.364→	—
Dorset	—	—	—	—		*—	A.R.202	—	—
Essex	P.R.C.223↓	—	—	—	—	*—	—		—
Gloucester ..						*—	—	P.R.C.307→ ←P.R.C.384 A.R.275?	—
Hereford ...						*—	—	—	—
Herts......	A.R.321	—	—	—	—	*—	—		—
Hunts......						*—	—	—	—
Kent	P.R.C.227→					*—	—	—	—
Lancashire...						*—	—	—	—
Leicester ...	P.R.C.200→ ←P.R.C.247					*—	—	—	—
Lincoln		P.R.C.277←				*—	—	—	—
Middlesex ..						*—	—	—	—
London.....	—	—	—	—	—	*—	—	—	—
Norfolk	—	—	—	—	—	*—	A.R.569	—	—
Northants						*—	—	P.R.C.307→ ←P.R.C.579	—
Northumberland						*—	—	C.R.C.479 A.R.643?	—
Nottingham ..						*—	—	P.R.C.314→	—
Oxford	—	—	—	—	—	*—	A.R.703	—	—
Rutland		A.R.721	—	—	—	*—	—	—	—
Salop	—		—	—	—	*—	—	—	—
Somerset ...						*—	←P.R.C.206	—	—
Southants ..		P.R.C.257→				*—	—		—
Stafford	—		—	—	—	*—	—	—	—
Suffolk						*—	?	?	—
Surrey	P.R.C.227→	Lib.Ant.Leg 32				*—	—	—	—
Sussex ...	—	A.R.912				*—	—	—	—
Warwick ..	A.R.954					*—	—	—	?
Westmoreland	—		—	—	—	*—	—	—	—
Wilts	—	—	—	—	—	*—	A.R.998	—	—
Worcester ..						*—	—	—	—
York						*—	A.R.1051	—	—

[4] A general eyre was ordered for all counties marked * ; see P. R. C., p. 172.

1271	1272	1273	1274-5	1276	1277	1278	1279	1280	1281
—	A.R.7 m.39[5]	—		A.R.7,9	—	—	—	—	—
—	—	—	—	—	—	—	—	—	—
—	A.R.60	—	—	—	—	—	—	—	—
—	A.R.85	—	—	—	—	—	—	—	—
?	?	—	—	—	—	—	—	—	—
—	—	—	—	—	—	—	A.R.131-3	—	—
—	—	—	—	—	—	—	—	—	A.R.147-52
—	—	—	—	—	—	—	—	—	A.R.181-6
—	—	—	—	—	—	—	—	A.R.204-8	—
—	A.R.235	—	—	—	—	—	—	—	—
—	—	—	—	—	—	—	—	—	—
—	P.R.C.641→	—	—	—	—	—	—	—	—
—	—	—	—	—	—	A.R.323-4	—	—	—
—	C.R.C.567→	—	—	—	—	—	—	—	—
A.R.364-6	—	—	—	—	—	—	A.R.369-71	—	—
—	P.R.C.614→[6]	—	—	—	—	—	?	?	?
P.R.C.498→	?	—	—	—	—	—	—	—	—
P.R.C.569→ A.R.483?	—	—	—	—	—	—	—	—	A.R.486-97
—	—	—	A.R.538-40	—	—	—	—	—	—
—	—	—	—	P.R.C.131→ Add.Charters 5153	—	—	—	—	—
—	—	—	—	—	—	—	—	—	—
—	—	—	—	—	—	—	A.R.645-8	—	—
—	—	—	—	—	—	—	A.R.664-70	—	—
—	—	—	—	—	—	—	—	—	—
—	—	—	—	—	—	—	—	—	—
—	A.R.736	—	—	—	—	—	—	—	—
—	—	—	—	—	—	—	—	A.R.758-63	—
—	A.R.780	—	—	—	—	—	—	A.R.783-89	—
—	A.R.802-3	—	—	—	—	—	—	—	—
—	—	—	—	—	—	—	—	—	—
—	C.R.C.567→ A.R.875?	—	—	—	—	—	A.R.876-9	—	—
P.R.C.582→ A.R.913?	—	—	—	—	—	—	A.R.914-23	—	—
?	—	—	—	—	—	—	—	—	—
—	—	—	—	—	—	A.R.980-3	—	—	—
—	—	—	—	—	—	—	—	—	A.R.1000-5
—	—	—	— A.R.1025-8	—	—	—	—	—	—
—	—	—	—	—	—	—	A.R.1057-1078	—	—

[5] All general eyres were prohibited on the death of Henry III (November 16, 1272). See Ann. Wig. 462; Ann Winton. 113. The Bedford eyre was suspended, and resumed in 1276.

[6] For evidence that this eyre was held, see P. R. C. for 1279, p. 328.

	1282	1283	1284	1285	1286	1287	1288	1289	1290	1291
Bedford	—	⊤	—	—	—	A.R.11-18				
Berks	—	—	A.R. 43-8							
Bucks	—	—	—	—	A.R.63-8					
Cambridge	—	—	—	—	A.R. 86-92	—	—	—	—	—
Cornwall	—	—	A.R. 111-15							
Cumberland	—	—	—	—	—	—	—	—	—	—
Derbyshire	—	—	—	—	—	—	—	—	—	—
Devon										
Dorset	—	—	—	—	—	—	A.R.210-15			7
Essex	—	—		—	A.R. 242-9	—	—	—	—	—
Gloucester	—	—		—	—	A.R. 271-84				
Hereford	—	—			—	—	—			—
Herts	—	—		—	—	A.R. 325-9				
Hunts	—	—		—	A.R. 345-51					
Kent	—	—		—	—	—	—	—	—	—
Lancashire	?	?	—	—	—	—	—	—	—	—
Leicester	—	—	A.R. 457-63							
Lincoln										
Middlesex	—	—	—	—	—	—		—		—
London	—	—	—	—	—	—		—	—	—
Norfolk	—	—	—	—	A.R. 572-81					
Northants	—	—	—	A.R. 619-23	—	—	—	—	—	
Northumberland	—	—	—	—	—	—				
Nottingham	—	—	—	—	—	—				
Oxford	—	—	—	A.R. 704-10						
Rutland	—	—	—	—	A.R. 722-5					
Salop	—	—	—	—	—	—	—		—	—
Somerset										
Southants										
Stafford	—	—	—	—	—	—	—	—	—	—
Suffolk	—	—	—		A.R. 826-35b					
Surrey	—	—	—	—	—	—	—	—	—	—
Sussex	—	—	—	—	—	—	A.R.924-32 A.R.935			
Warwick	—	—	—	A.R. 956-62						
Westmoreland	—	—		—	—	—	—		—	—
Wilts	—	—	—	—	—	—	—	A.R.1006-13		
Worcester										
York	—	—	—	—	—	—	—	—	—	—

⁷ No general eyre was held in Essex between 128⁵ and 1291 ; see C. R. C., p. 168.

1292	1293	1294	1295	1296	1297	1298	1299	1313	1321	1330	1334-5	1341
. . . .	. . . .	. . .	. .	. .	. .	. .	. . .	. . .	. . . . .	*A.R.* 23-6	. . . .	. . . .
. . . .	. . . .	. . .	. .	. .	. .	. .	. . .	. . .	. . . . .	. . .		
. . . .	. . . .	. . .	. .	. .	. .	. .	. . .	. . .				
— .	. — .	. — .	. — .	. — .	. — .	— .	. —	*A.R.* 95-6	. . .	. . . . .	. . .	. . .
A.R. 134-7	. .									. . .		
. — .	. — .	. — .	. — .	. — .	— .	. — .	. — .	. — .	. —	*A.R.* 168-8 [10]		
. . . .	. . . .		. .	. .	. .	. .	. . .	. . .		. .		
. . . .	. . . .	. . .	.	. .	. .	. .	. . .	. . .				
A.R. 302-3	. . .											
C.R.C. 309→	. . .											
. — .	*A.R.* 373-7	— .	. — .	. — .	. — .	. — .	. —	*A.R.* 383 [8]		. .	*A.R.389 P.R.C.475* →	. . .
A.R. 408-16	. . .						. .	. . .				
C.R.C. 309→							. .	. . .				
. — .	. —	*A.R.* 543-4								. .		
. — .	. — .	. — .	. — .	. — .	. — .	. — .	. —	*A.R.547* [9] *Liber Cust. M.G.H.II.347*		. . .	*A.R.* 549-52
C.R.C. 309→	. . .	. . .					. .	. . .		. .	
. — .	. — .	. . .	. — .	. — .	. — .	. — .	. —	. .	. —	*A.R.* 629 [11]	. .
. — .	*A.R.* 650-6	. . .								. .	
. — .	. — .	. . .	. — .	. — .	. — .	. — .	. —	. .	. —	*A.R.* 683-6 [12]	
. . . .	. . . .	. . .					. .	. . .		. .	
A.R. 739-41	. . . .										
. . .	. . . .										
. — .	*A.R.* 804-6	. . .								. .	
. — .	. —	*A.R.883 893-906*									
C.R.C. 309→	. . .	. . .									
. . .	. . . .	. . .									
A.R. 985-8	. . . .	. . .									
. . .	. . . .										
. — .	*A.R.* 1084-1101	. .									

[8] First Kentish eyre since 1293 ; see A. R. 383.
[9] First London eyre since 1276 ; see A. R. 547.
[10] First Derbyshire eyre since 1281 ; see A. R. 166.
[11] First Northants eyre since 1285 ; see A. R. 632.
[12] First Notts eyre since 1280 ; see A. R. 683.

CHAPTER II

THE INQUESTS OF 1274-5

§ 1. INTRODUCTION

BEFORE any conclusions can be drawn from the Hundred Rolls as to the history of administration in the thirteenth century it is necessary to make a closer analysis of the documents themselves than has yet been undertaken. The Record Commission edition of 1812–18, invaluable as it has been to the genealogical and topographical historian, gives little guidance as to the comparative value of the various kinds of document which it prints. Endorsements of a later date are printed as if contemporary with the record on which they are found ; there is no note where, as often occurs, information is duplicated ; though the character of the Extract Rolls is indicated in the introduction, it is unlikely to be appreciated by the casual reader, whilst their date is left undetermined, though the casual reader, again, would draw the quite unjustifiable conclusion that they belonged to 1274–6. Nor are the imperfections, any more than the duplications of the records, pointed out. The table at the end of this chapter indicates to some extent the amount of the material preserved, but a closer analysis of the character of the documents, together with an investigation of the procedure of which they are the record, is a necessary preliminary to any attempt to base statistics upon them.

§ 2. THE RECORDS

The rolls which record the proceedings of the inquest of 1274–5 fall into two classes : those catalogued at the Public Record Office as Hundred Rolls, and those catalogued as Extract Hundred Rolls. The greater part of both series is printed in the Record Commission edition, in which the Extract Rolls are generally [1] so designated in the table of

---

[1] The following corrections are needed in the table of contents : Volume i, pp. 58, 104, 175, 190, 237, *add* (Extract) ; p. 425 is described in the text as Extract, but is catalogued in the P.R.O. as Hundred Roll. Volume ii,

contents, and the Hundred Rolls proper are, as a rule, correctly dated and numbered in the margin.

The documents catalogued as Hundred Rolls are somewhat miscellaneous. The returns to the inquests of 1255 and 1277 are distinguished in the printed edition; there are some unprinted returns of these dates, which are readily identifiable by their form. With these we are not here concerned. But amongst the other documents preserved as Hundred Rolls are to be found a return to the inquest of 1258,[1] stray membranes from Plea Rolls,[2] verdicts returned by crown juries in general eyres,[3] an Extract Roll and a portion of one,[4] articles for some special inquest, as yet unidentified,[5] and returns to the inquest of 1284-5, generally known as Kirby's Quest.[6] In the records which clearly belong to 1274-5 there are three distinct types. The first is the verdict of the hundred jury, recorded on a separate membrane,[7] which is of no uniform size or shape; headed, frequently, by the names of the commissioners (*inquisitores*), less often by the place and date of the inquest;[8] generally signed with the names of the jurors, sometimes cut for the appending of their seals.[9] On this type of return the answers are grouped

p. 1, *delete* (Extract); p. 6, *add* (Extract); p. 201 is correctly described as Extract but is catalogued as Hundred Roll.

[1] Fragments of Hundred Rolls, No. 9.

[2] H. R. [C. H.] Dorset 1, m. 4 (unprinted); [C. H.] Hereford 2 (unprinted; [C. H.] Northants 2 (1330) (unprinted); [C. H.] Sussex 1, m. 8 (1278) (unprinted).

[3] H. R. [C. H.] Wilts. 36 (1281) (unprinted).; [C. H.] Gloucester 6 (1287) (unprinted).

[4] H. R. [C. H.] Sussex 1, mm. 1-7 (printed R. H., ii, pp. 201-20); [C. H.] Dorset 1, m. 3 (unprinted).

[5] See Fragments of Hundred Rolls, No. 10: *Articuli Inquirendum.*

[6] [C. H.] Bedford, 3 (printed R. H., i, pp. 4 b to 8); [C. H.] Devon, 42, 43 (printed R. H., i, pp. 84-6); [T.] Huntingdon 6 (unprinted). See Inquisitions and Assessments relating to Feudal Aids, i, p. xi.

[7] This is not the case in Kent, where the verdicts of several hundreds are recorded on one membrane, and the last appears to be the unit.

[8] e.g. Nottingham, R. H. ii, p. 300 'Inquisitio facta apud Notingham in octavis Sancti Hillarii anno regni regis domini Eadwardi iij° coram domino Ricardo de Crepinges et Thoma de Leukenouer Inquisitoribus domini Regis in comitatu Notingham per (18 names) iuratores de wapentagio de Berteselaw ad inquirendum per sacramentum suum super articulis subscriptis'.

[9] e.g. Devon, R. H. i, p. 63 'In cuius rei testimonium iuratores presenti veredicto sigilla sua apposuerunt.'

according to the articles of the inquest, which are quoted either in full or by their opening words. The second type is found in several of the eastern shires.[1] Returns are made by groups of hundreds ; the jurors are belted knights ;[2] and in some cases the articles of the inquest are entirely omitted, and the returns given under the headings of the names of vills.[3] Thirdly, in the case of Somerset and Southants there are short returns, more limited in scope than the *veredicta* of the first class, in which neither vill nor article headings are used. These are quite complete in form, being dated and sealed, and will receive separate consideration.[4] The London returns seem to form a class by themselves ; the *veredicta* which belong to the first class are followed by so-called Extract Rolls,[5] which appear to have been made by the London municipal authorities and not by the Exchequer, as they are peculiar in form and type.

The rolls catalogued as *Extract Hundred Rolls* are four in number, and the contents of three of them are printed in the Record Commission edition under the different counties, as a rule after the Hundred Rolls proper. Each of these Extract Rolls deals with a number of counties ; between them they cover twenty-six of the thirty-nine counties in which we have reason to believe inquests were held, reckoning London as a county.[6] They are endorsed *Extracte Inquisitionum* (Rolls 1, 2) or *De inquisitionibus* (Roll 3) ; *anno regis Edwardi filii regis Henrici iii* (Roll 1) or *iiij Edwardi primi* (Rolls 2, 3). The script, however, shows that none of these endorsements are contemporary. The endorsement on Roll 3, ' Anno iiijto E. Primi coram Willelmo de Saham et sociis suis iusticiis ', which is also obviously not contemporary, is probably traceable to a misunderstanding of the entry at the foot of m. 10, which will be discussed below.[7] Roll 4 has

---

[1] Essex, R. H., i, pp. 136–49 ; Herts., i, p. 188 ; Norfolk, i, pp. 434–95 and 504–14 ; Suffolk, ii, pp. 150–60, 174 b–178 a.

[2] e.g. R. H. i, p. 189 'Veredictum xiicim militum gladio cinctorum de comitatu Herteford '.

[3] e.g. i, p. 136 ; ii, pp. 174 b ff.   [4] See below, § 3 of this chapter.

[5] R. H., i, pp. 425–33. The endorsement *Rotuli Extracti de veredictis civitatis Londonie*, printed R. H., i, p. 433, seems contemporaneous, though the date 3 Ed. I is not.   [6] See Appendix IV.   [7] See p. 118.

no endorsement, but is headed *De Ministris*. In handwriting and general make-up the four rolls correspond closely ; they appear to have been written at one time and in one hand. A stray membrane among the Dorset Hundred Rolls [1] and one of the Sussex Rolls [2] conform to the same type and may unquestionably be assigned to this series ; the London ' Extract Rolls ' are quite different in writing and form.

An examination of the contents of the Extract Rolls shows clearly that they are official compilations from a series of original returns to the inquests. They contain frequent references to the original returns : *sicut patet in inquisitione*,[3] *sicut patet in veredictis*,[4] *de aliis minutis patet in inquisitione*.[5] In one case there is what looks like a reference to the Extract Roll added in a later hand to the original return.[6] It is possible in many cases to lay the corresponding entries in the Hundred Rolls and Extract Rolls side by side and note the various methods of abridgement whereby the exchequer clerk saved time and parchment and the careless and sometimes comical errors that he made, above all, in copying proper names. In many other cases the originals from which the extracts were made are not preserved. Before considering the object of the compilation an inquiry into its date will be useful. It may be noted that the grouping of counties in the Extract Rolls does not correspond with the grouping in the commissions issued for the inquest in October 1274 ;[7] for instance, the same commissioners were sent to Cornwall and to Dorset, but the Cornwall returns are on Extract Roll 4, and the Dorset returns on Extract Roll 3. The dates endorsed upon the two records are not identical ; the Essex Hundred Rolls bear the date 1274, and the Extract Roll which contains the Essex returns is endorsed 1275 ; the Bucks Hundred Roll is dated 1275, and the Extract Roll containing the Bucks

[1] H. R. [C. H.] Dorset 1, m. 3 (printed R. H., i, pp. 98 b–99).
[2] H. R. [C. H.] Sussex 1, mm. 1–7 (printed R. H., ii, pp. 201–19).
[3] R. H., i, p. 104 a (Yorkshire) ; p. 164 a (Essex) ; p. 192 b (Hants) ; p. 539 a (Norfolk).
[4] R. H., i, p. 114 a (Yorkshire).
[5] R. H., i, p. 135 a (Yorkshire). Note also R. H., i, p. 543 b (Norfolk). 'Prout patet in inquisitione in capitulo, De hiis qui habent libertates ' etc.
[6] H. R. [T.] Lincoln 18. See below, p. 133.   [7] See Appendix IV.

returns is endorsed 1276. It might be inferred that the dates upon the Extract Rolls represent the time of making the compilation, which might have extended from 1275 to 1276, and this, I think, has been generally assumed, in spite of the fact that the grouping has no relation to the chronological order of the inquests. There is, however, an important indication of date which seems to have been overlooked on membrane 10 of Extract Roll 3, at the end of the Yorkshire extracts.[1] 'Et sciendum quod de veredictis Hammelack, Luffeld et capituli Beati Petri Eboracensis nichil invenitur . . .[2] veredicta simul cum aliis veredictis de comitatu Eboracense liberantur Willelmo de Saham et sociis suis . . .[2] praedicto.' From the Close Roll for 1280 we learn that the inquisitions for Yorkshire—being the returns or *veredicta* of the hundreds to the inquests of 1274-5—were delivered to William of Saham on April 18, 1279, when he was about to open the general eyre in Yorkshire.[3] He, like the other justices for all pleas who were sent out 1278-87, carried with him the records of the great inquest for purposes of reference, and he, possibly again like others of his colleagues, failed to return the full tale to the custody of the chief justice, so that the compilation based on those records was defective. This fixes the date of the compilation of the Yorkshire Extracts as later than 1279, and, as the other extracts are uniform with them, proves that the endorsements of the third and fourth of Edward I cannot refer to the period of writing. It seems probable that these dates are a rough approximation, made at some distance of time, to the date of the inquest, which, as we shall see, extended from November 1274 to March 1275.

Extract Roll No. 4 differs from the other three in character, and, for this reason probably, has not been printed. In handwriting and gauge of parchment it is uniform with the other three, and it covers the same group of counties as Roll 1. It is headed *De Ministris,* and is a selection of those returns which bear directly upon the conduct of officials.

[1] R. H., i, p. 135.   [2] The corner of the roll is torn off.
[3] C. R. C., p. 558.

The fragments of articles quoted are those of the inquests of 1274-5, that which occurs most frequently being ' Qui per potestatem officii sui . . .' A close comparison with Roll No. 1 has been made of the returns for Herts and Norfolk, which proves that the two compilations were made at the same time and from the same original. On m. 9 of Roll 4 (under Herts) occurs a passage which is found *verbatim* on m. 38 of Roll 1,[1] but is there cancelled, with the note ' Vacat quia alibi inter ministros de comitatu predicta '. In the case of Norfolk it is possible to refer to the original returns, and here we find that the extracts in Rolls 1 and 4 are both taken, often verbatim, from the original Hundred Roll, but that the same entry is never reproduced on both Extract Rolls. This will be made clear by a comparison of the passages from the Norfolk Rolls on the following page.

Rolls 1 and 4 are complementary ; between them they contain the greater part of the contents of the original Hundred Roll. That they were intended so to be is clear from the cross-references, which are frequent. The extracts for the Hundred of Brotherscross, Co. Norfolk, for instance, end ' De ceteris articulis nichil nisi quod dicitur in rotulo de Ministris'.[2] From this collection we also learn that the compiler of Roll 4 often threw together under one heading entries which in the Hundred Roll were given under two or three. For instance, returns made to the articles ' qui et domini . . . ' and ' De omnibus purpresturis . . . ' on the Norfolk Hundred Roll 8[3] are grouped on Extract Roll 4 under the one article ' qui per potestatem officii sui . . .' The collation leaves no room for doubt ; the two Extract Rolls were made at the same time by the same clerks, from the same originals.[4]

---

[1] Printed R. H. i, p. 195 ' Articuli de Ministris in comitatu Herteford.'
[2] R. H., i, p. 536 a.   [4] R. H., i, pp. 496, 497.
[3] It will be seen that Mr. Hall's account of the *De Ministris* roll in his Studies in English Official Historial Documents is misleading. There was no ' separate inquisition ' (p. 302), nor were there ' special articles ' (p. 320), in 1274-5 ; there is no sort of evidence that the articles mentioned in Bishop Stapleton's calendar (quoted Hall, p. 302, note) belong to this period rather than to any other at which inquiries were held into the conduct of royal officials ; Miscellanea of the Exchequer 2/31 (p. 302, note 6, p. 321, note 1) is a list of the ordinary articles of the eyre, as are the articles printed in Bracton, vol. ii, appendix ii ; the ' form of the

ORIGINAL RETURNS

Hundred Rolls Norfolk 9, m. 1 [C. H.]. (Printed, R. H. i, 499 a.)

Item de hiis qui per potestatem officii sui etc.

Dicunt (*illegible*) hundredi de Mitford capiunt ad letas suas tenendas certam porcionem de villis ne occ (*illegible*) nunc vero petunt illam porcionem pro certo reddendo ad opus episcopi et nunc nichilomi (*illegible*) capiunt (. . .) alios fines maiores ut possent respondere sine occasione. Item dicunt quod Willelmus de

EXTRACT ROLL 1

Extract Roll 1, m. 14. (Printed, R. H. i, 515 a.)

De hiis qui per potestatem officii etc.

Dicunt quod ballivi de Mitford quando tenent letas suas capiunt quamdam certam porcionem de singulis villis ne occasionentur et hoc de antiquo et illam porcionem nunc petunt ad opus episcopi Eliensis tanquam arentatum et nichilominus capiunt de eisdem villis fines maiores ut possint respondere sine occasione.

EXTRACT ROLL 4

De Ministris, m. 1. (Unprinted.)

De hiis qui potestate officii etc.

Dicunt quod Willelmus de Goldingham senescallus comitis Warenni et ministri eius per potestatem officii sui iniuste distringunt homines infra libertatem hundredi predicti et pecuniam ab eis extorquent ita quod non possunt habere communem iusticiam sicut solent in preiudicium episcopi Eliensis et domini Regis si idem episcopatus vacaret et esset in manu sua. Et Alexander de Acra minister dicti senescalli cepit de Ranulpho del Hil cumbam frumenti pro averiis suis replegiandis. Et Adam ad ecclesiam de Gymmingham ballivus dicti comitis cepit averia Iohannis Wolmer et ea retinuit quo usque finem fecisset cum eo per ii marcas. Et idem Adam cepit de Ricardo Warin ij solidos eodem modo et de Radulpho de la Hefe xij denarios Et Robertus de Ausing' minister ballivi hundredi predicti cepit de Iohanne de Angulo v solidos per extorsionem. Et Ricardus le Bavant extorsit de Radulpho de Aula x solidos.

Goldingham senescallus comitis Wareni et ministri eius per potestatem officii sui impediunt homines infra libertatem hundredi de Mitford et eos iniuste distringunt et pecuniam ab eis extorquent ita quod non possunt habere communem iusticiam in hundredo sicut solent in preiudicium episcopi Eliensis et domini Regis tempore vacationis episcopatus et hic fecerunt iam per iiij annos vel amplius. Item dicunt quod Alexander de Acre minister dicti senescalli cepit de Radulpho del Hyl unam cumbam frumenti pro replegiando averiorum suorum. Dicunt etiam quod Adam ad ecclesiam de Gymmingham ballivus dicti comitis cepit averia Iohannis Wulmer de Lectun et retinuit ea donec finem fecisset cum eo pro ij solidis. Idem Adam cepit de Ricardo Warini de Lectun eodem modo ii solidos. Item dicunt quod Robertus de Aveing' minister tunc ballivi hundredi predicti cepit de Iohanne de Angulo v solidos per extortionem.

Hundred Rolls Norfolk 9, m. 2. (Printed, R. H. i, p. 499 b.)

Item de hiis qui habuerunt probatores . . . etc. . . . Item dicunt quod dictus Ricardus le Bavant extorsit de Radulpho de Aula de Reymerston x solidos quos Thomas de Ludinglond dedit dicto Radulpho.

The question next arises, with what object were these Extracts made? The original returns were made on parchment of very different shapes and sizes; they were often encumbered with seals, though most of these have been cut or torn off by now; there was much waste of space in the recording of articles to which no returns were made. The compact and uniform Extract Roll, even in its printed form, conveys far more information than a Hundred Roll in the same space. But there are omissions, as well as condensations, in the Extract Roll, and no principle appears to explain them, unless it be that proceedings had already been taken upon the original presentment when the summary was made. Again, the Extracts appear in some cases to have been taken round by the justices in eyre; there are notes, similar to those which occur on the original returns, on the Extracts for Yorkshire, Somersetshire, Worcestershire, and indeed all the counties in Extract Roll 3. But the Extracts, as we have seen, contain references to the unabridged original returns, so that it would seem as if the justices carried both series of records round with them after the first eyres of Edward I's reign. It does not seem possible to arrive at a definite conclusion as to the object of the compilation. The existence of Roll 4, again, is not easy to explain. There is no indication that similar parallel rolls existed formerly for the other groups of counties; no references to a *Rotulus de Ministris* are to be found on Rolls 2 and 3. As we shall see, a different procedure seems to have been employed in taking the inquests in several of the eastern counties, and one allusion seems to suggest that the inquests were held twice. It may be that the officials of the eastern counties were more grasping and

articles ' (p. 321) is clearly traceable from the existing records and is identical with that of the articles of 1274-5. No references occur 'in the body of the returns' (p. 302) to a separate inquisition *de Ministris* (see also p. 321, note), but the Extract Roll 1, from which Mr. Hall quotes (p. 302, note), gives many references to a *Rotulus de Ministris,* namely Extract Roll 4, its fellow, derived like itself from the original returns or Hundred Rolls proper, and both Extract Rolls contain references to that record as the *Inquisitiones.* The passages printed on pp. 145 and 146 of Mr. Hall's Formula Book of Legal Records are taken from Extract Rolls 1 and 4 respectively; the proceedings recorded in the Assize Roll printed on p. 147 are initiated by private suit, not by presentment, and deal with different offences from those presented in 1275.

corrupt than those elsewhere, and that the returns necessitated special proceedings, for which a separate roll was compiled ; or again it may be that the terrorization of the jurors to which the Statute of Rageman refers was practised on so large a scale in the eastern counties that a supplementary inquest was ordered, and the returns were so bulky as to render further classification desirable.[1] On the other hand, the isolated Extract Roll for Sussex has traces of the same classification of returns. At the end of the extracts for the Rape of Hastings [2] occurs the heading *De Ministris*, under which returns similar to those on Extract Roll 4 are summarized for three of the five rapes for which extracts have already been given. There is no separate roll ; the extracts *De Ministris* are made on the same membrane as the previous extracts, but we have here, it would seem, a *Rotulus de Ministris* in embryonic form ; an entry made, possibly like the Hertfordshire one, before it had been decided to have a separate roll for this class of extract. It may be that a similar classification was pursued in making the Extracts—now lost, if they ever existed—for the other southern counties, Surrey, Kent, Middlesex, Southants, and Wilts, as it was for Dorset.

The nature of the records of the inquest of 1274–5 having been examined, we are now in a position to attempt to reconstruct its circumstances. In so doing we shall depend mainly upon the original returns or Hundred Rolls proper, though it will be necessary to supplement the information which they supply by occasional reference to the rolls of the eyre next after 1275, and to the originating commission on the Patent Roll.

§ 3. The Inquests of March–July, 1274

In the case of twenty counties there are indications of the date of holding the inquests, direct or indirect. These are

---

[1] As Mr. Hall points out (Formula Book of Legal Records, p. 128), a number of additional articles, mostly dealing with the conduct of ministers, are recorded upon the Lincolnshire returns ; but it is noteworthy that there are no traces of the existence of a *De Ministris* Extract Roll for Lincolnshire.   [2] R. H., ii, p. 218 b.

obscured for us to-day by our unfamiliarity alike with the church calendar and with the regnal method of dating, and it has apparently never been remarked that in two counties inquests were held before the issuing of the commission of October 11, 1274. The third type of return noted above belongs to a series of inquests held in Somerset at Ivelchester, Bruton, Montacute, Langport, Wells, and Bath, at different dates in March, April, and July, whilst for Southants there are two similar returns of inquests held at Basingstoke and W . . .[1] extra Suwyk in the middle of June.[2] Articles for these inquests are not quoted in the returns, but their scope is indicated in the opening formula : ' Inquisitio facta per preceptum domini Regis . . . de iuribus et dominicis terris sive redditis domini Regis alienatis et subtractis '; that is to say, it concerns itself only with the king's territorial rights and with seignorial usurpations, and does not raise the question of ministerial abuses. The inquisitors' names, Bartholomew de Yatingeden and Guy de Taunton, are the same for the two counties ; they must have gone to Hampshire in May or June, and returned to Somerset in July. In the October Commission, Southants and Somerset are assigned to different inquisitors,[3] and though Guy de Taunton is named for Southants, he was superseded on February 7 by William of Gerberd,[4] who held the inquests in Southants and in Wilts in his place.[5] Yatingeden's name does not occur at all on the commission of October 11, or on any of the autumn and winter returns.

The explanation of these divergent data is found in an entry on the Patent Roll under the date January 28, 1274, where is enrolled a commission to these two men for holding an inquest into the withdrawal and alienation of royal demesne liberties and rights in the counties of Kent, Surrey, Southants, Wilts, Dorset, Somerset, Gloucester, Worcester, Northants, Sussex, and Cambridge.[6] It is impossible to say

---

[1] Illegible.   [2] R. H., ii, pp. 118–24, 220, 223–4.
[3] See Appendix IV.   [4] Rot. Pat. 3 Ed. I, m. 31 d (P. R. C., p. 116).
[5] R. H., ii, pp. 220 b, 242 a.
[6] Rot. Pat. 2 Ed. I, m. 24 d (P. R. C., p. 65) ' De inquisitionibus faciendis.   Rex Bartholomeo de Yatingdene et Guidoni de Taunton

whether the inquests were carried farther than Southants and Somerset. The negative evidence afforded by the Extract Rolls is against any general fulfilment of the commission. Extract Rolls are extant for seven of the eleven counties, and whilst the Somersetshire extracts contain material based on the spring returns, given in a different form and arranged under a separate heading,[1] such double entries are found for none of the other counties. No Extract Rolls exist for Southants, nor for Kent, Surrey, and Wilts, so that the chances are even as regards those counties; but with regard to the six others, the presumption is, on the whole, against the holding of the inquests ordered in January.

The inquest of the spring of 1274 was then quite distinct from that initiated in October. It was far more limited in scope; dealing with only one class of the abuses which disturbed the realm, it was never intended to cover the whole of England, and, in all probability, was held only in one or two counties. It forms another of those special and local inquests of which so many examples have been noted; that of 1242 for the counties of Carmarthen and Cardigan probably offers the closest analogy.[2] Its political significance is less easy to determine. Are we to view it as a timid and tentative venture on the part of the lords justices to remedy a notorious evil, a venture soon overshadowed by the drastic measures taken by the king himself on his return in August? Or, again, did the experience of March–July reveal the inadequacy of the scope of the inquest, and lead to its abandonment half way, and to the more thoroughgoing terms of the October

salutem. Quia accepimus plures libertates et iura ad dominica nostra in comitatibus Kant' Surr' Suthampt' Wiltes' Dors' Somers' Glouc' Wigorn Northampt' Essex et Cantebr' pertinentia temporibus domini Henrici Regis patris nostri et aliorum predecessorum nostrorum in preiudicium iuris nostri et ad deteriorationem eorundem maneriorum sunt subtracta (sic) assignavimus vos ad inquisitiones super dictis subtractionibus et alienationibus diligenter faciendas. Et ideo nobis mandamus ' (etc.).

[1] Compare Extracts on R. H., ii, pp. 125–35, with Extracts beginning p. 135, under the heading *Supplēc Inquisitionum de comitatu Sumerset.* (I have not succeeded in expanding this contraction.) The second set of extracts are derived from the returns printed R. H., ii, pp. 118–24; there are no originals extant for the first set.

[2] Rot. Pat. 26 Hen. III, pt. i, m. 9 d 'Quantum terre teneat unusquisque qui tenet de nobis in capite; que terre alienate fuerunt de dominicis nostris; qui libertates ad se alienant;' etc.

commission ? In view of the expression of policy in the January commission it seems, on the whole, unlikely that the two inquests are entirely unconnected.

§ 4. Date and Duration of the Hundred Roll Inquests

We have now to consider the date and duration of the Hundred Roll inquests proper. From the table in Appendix IV it will be seen at once that we have no exact knowledge of the date at which the inquests were held in about half the counties. We have also to discount several obvious errors in the dates affixed to the records ; by slips in referring to the regnal year some of the returns are dated a year out.[1] Ignoring these palpable errors and assuming that the inquests were held approximately at the same time in all the districts, we should conclude that the inquest began before the end of the second year of Edward's reign, that is, before November 20, 1274, and was over by the end of March 1275.[2] The subdivision of the country into many separate districts was clearly intended to secure dispatch, and forms a strong contrast with the allocation of eleven counties to the commissioners of January 1274, and the division of England into two circuits only for the eyres initiated in 1278. Considering the wide scope of the articles, the commissioners seem to have made short stay in each shire. According to the Shropshire returns, which are unusually full, the taking of the inquests was completed in six days in that county, whilst in Wiltshire, where they were held at four different centres, they lasted less than a fortnight. In Norfolk there is a complaint over the scant time allowed to the jurors. ' Dicunt et quod multe transgressiones ... facte sunt ... de quibus ad presens non bene certi sunt ... nec possunt inquirere propter brevitatem temporis.' [3]

§ 5. The Commissioners

The commission on the Patent Roll includes the names of six pairs of commissioners, assigned to twenty counties.

---

[1] e.g. R. H., ii, p. 89, the inquest for the hundred of Chirbury is dated November 26, 1273 (should be November 27, 1274) ; R. H., i, p. 35, the inquest for the hundred of Brehull is dated November 18, 1275 (should be November 18, 1274).

[2] See Appendix IV.　　　　　　　[3] R. H., i, p. 483 a.

From the returns, from the Patent Roll, and from the Assize Rolls the names of four more pairs of commissioners and of two substitute commissioners [1] have been recovered, assigned to eight or probably nine more counties. This leaves eleven counties, in which there is reason to think that inquests were held,[2] with no commissioners assigned to them. The names we possess are for the most part those of men already in the service of the government, many of them in high positions, such as Philip of Wilughby, escheator north of Trent in 1274,[3] Robert of Ufford, justice of Chester and later of Ireland.[4] Some held posts of especial trust, such as Ralf of Sandwich, steward of the king's demesne lands in the south,[5] Guy of Taunton, bailiff of the king's manor of Gillingham,[6] William of Pereton, clerk of the king's works,[7] and Bartholomew le Jevene, later a king's serjeant.[8] Many of them were to be collectors of the Fifteenth of 1275.[9] Of those who held important local positions, Edmund de Caldecote was keeper of the town of Dunwich,[10] Bartholomew le Jevene was constable of Bristol Castle,[11] and Roger l'Estrange keeper of the Forest of the Peak.[12] Several are found acting later as justices of Oyer and Terminer,[13] and three of them—Richard de Creppinges, Geoffrey de Aguillon, and Sampson Foliot—were commissioners in the inquest of 1279.[14] In some cases at least the principle of sending a man to the district which he knew best seems to have been followed ; whilst Warin de Chalcumb, judging by his name, came from Northants, William de

---

[1] See Appendix IV.

[2] In the case of Cumberland, Lancashire, and Westmoreland the holding of the inquests is presumed from the references found in Assize Rolls of a later date to the Rageman returns for these counties, *Rageman*, as has been shown above, being the contemporary name for the inquests of 1274–5.

[3] C. R. C. (1274), p. 138.

[4] C. R. C. (1276), p. 314 ; P. R. C. (1276), p. 149.

[5] C. R. C. (1276), p. 268 ; P. R. C. (1275), p. 127.

[6] C. R. C. (1275), p. 262.

[7] C. R. C. (1279), p. 539 ; P. R. C. (1277), p. 213.

[8] P. R. C. (1275), p. 99.   [9] C. R. C. (1275), pp. 250–1.

[10] P. R. C. (1275), p. 89.   [11] C. R. C. (1275), p. 202.

[12] C. R. C. (1275), p. 172.

[13] Bartholomew de Bryancon, P. R. C. (1275), p. 244 ; (1277), p. 285 ; William de Brayboef, P. R. C. (1277), p. 244.

[14] P. R. C. (1279), p. 342.

Gereberd held lands in Berks and Wilts[1] and Robert de Ufford in Norfolk and Suffolk,[2] in which shires they were respectively appointed inquisitors.

The commissioners were, then, judging from those of whom we have further information, men of substance and standing, possessing, in some cases, local knowledge of the districts to which they were assigned.

§ 6. THE PROCEDURE OF THE INQUESTS : LOCAL VARIATIONS

The procedure employed by the commissioners appears to have varied locally. The returns for some counties—notably Devon, Lincoln, Norfolk, Salop, and Wilts—are so full that it is possible to reconstruct the proceedings with some certainty. At one or more centres in the shire the juries of the several hundreds, wappentakes, boroughs, liberties, and in some instances manors and vills[3] were assembled ; the articles of the inquest were delivered to each jury, on one day or several successive days ; and the verdicts were returned by the jurors to the inquisitors, subscribed with their names and often sealed with their seals. In one instance we can see that the verdict has been read out to the jurors, and supplemented before sealing. The return for Ekerdon hundred in Dorset ends with directions for 'interlining' two notes to the answers already given.[4] The number of jurors is usually twelve; occasionally six,[5] or eighteen,[6] or twenty-four[7] are found.

As we have seen, the proceedings generally took no more than a week in each shire, but it is possible that the articles had been sent to the sheriffs in advance. The following entry on the Memoranda Roll may refer to some such arrangement : ' *Baronibus pro Rege.* Rex eisdem mandat quod omnia

---

[1] C. R. C. (1275), p. 228.   [2] C. R. C. (1275), p. 239.

[3] For verdicts of boroughs see R. H., i, pp. 63, 68 (Devon) ; ii, p. 98 (Salop), &c. ; of liberties, R. H., ii, pp. 97, 98 ,101 (Salop) ; of manors, R. H., i, p. 65 (Devon), p. 265 (Lincoln) ; ii, p. 87 (Salop), &c. ; of vills, R. H., i, p. 63 (Devon) ; pp. 288–90 (Lincoln), &c.

[4] R. H. i, p. 98 b 'Item est interlineare " per mortem Radulphi de gorges ", " Et quod tunc liberatum fuit manerium domine Matildae Walerond quae nunc tenet ad voluntatem domini Regis ".' The notes have been added as directed (H. R. (C. H.), Dorset, 3).   [5] R. H., i, p. 184 a.

[6] R. H., ii, p. 300.   [7] City of Exeter, R. H., i, p. 69 b.

capitula comitatuum regis per Angliam contingentia que vicecomites eorundem comitatuum ad idem scaccarium liberaverunt vel liberabunt super diversis iuribus et libertatibus Regis alienatis fidelibus Regis quos ad diversas inquisitiones in dictis comitatibus faciendas assignavit sub sigillo predicti scaccarii ad citius quod fieri potuerit transmittant. Ut ipsi fideles Regis super premissis una cum aliis per regem sibi iniunctis reddere valeant ad plenum certiores' etc.[1] This entry is somewhat perplexing, and no further light on it has been found in the Memoranda Rolls or elsewhere. Three interpretations are possible. The passage may mean that the sheriffs have received copies of the *capitula* of October 11, 1274, and are to return them to the Exchequer that the barons may deliver them to the commissioners assigned to take the inquests. On the other hand, it may mean that the sheriffs are to deliver the *returns* of the inquests of March–July 1274, to the commissioners of the October inquests to check the returns for the counties in which the first inquests had been held. Lastly, it may command the sheriffs to deliver the *returns* of the 1274–5 inquests to the Exchequer, as the inquests are completed, so that action may be taken upon them by justices assigned. If the last is the correct interpretation, the returns would have remained in the custody of the Exchequer until June 1275, when the chief justice, Walter de Wymburn, took charge of them.[2]

The description so far given is incomplete as regards the eastern group of counties assigned to Robert of Ufford and Ralph of Sandwich—Essex, Herts, Norfolk, and Suffolk. Here the returns of the hundred juries seem to have been supplemented by inquests made by the knights of the shire. We have here, apparently, a parallel with the procedure of the general eyre, in which the knights of the shire make their returns in addition to the jurors of the hundreds, though the exact purpose of this duplication of presentments has never yet been elucidated.[3] It will be as well to examine the returns

---

[1] Mem. R. L. T. R. 48, m. 3 'Communia de termino Sancti Michaelis' (before December 10).

[2] C. R. C., p. 185 ; see above, p. 45.

[3] See Bolland, Eyre of Kent, i, pp. xlix-l.

of these four counties more closely. For Herts there is only
one Hundred Roll, which differs in no respect from the verdict
of a hundred jury as to form, but covers the whole shire, and
is endorsed, *Veredictum xii militum gladio cinctorum de
comitatu Herteford*.[1] The Essex returns are exceedingly confused and ill-written,[2] and raise a series of problems peculiar
to themselves, though there is sufficient similarity in character
to the returns of the other three counties to make it probable [3]
that Essex was assigned to the same commissioners with
them. The verdicts are presented by knights—the twelve
knights of the county of Essex.[4] But the knights have
obtained them from the vills; as the heading to membrane 6
runs : ' Hoc est veredictum presentatum coram militibus
iuratis de hiis que possunt fideliter inquiri per omnes villatas
comitatus.' [5] The verdicts of these vills are not like those
already noted, in Devon and Lincolnshire ; verdicts written
each on its own membrane, verdicts which cite the articles
at due length, which are parallel in form to those of the
hundred. These vills appear, like some manors and liberties,
to have had extra-hundredal status for the purposes of the
inquest. But in Essex we have to do with short returns
arranged under the heading of each vill, returns which
generally do not cite the articles,[6] and in which a great
number of vills are grouped together on one membrane.
More than this, returns for the vills of several hundreds, one
after another, occur on the same membrane and in the same
hand.[7]

From these fragmentary and confused returns we should
infer that returns were made by the vills, grouped according
to hundreds, under the direction of the knights. The names

---

[1] R. H., i, p. 189 b.

[2] At one point (R. H., i, p. 143 a), for no obvious reason, the Latin changes
to French, and later back again, with no break in the handwriting or the
subject-matter. See Chap. III, § 2.

[3] No names of inquisitors are attached to the Essex returns.

[4] R. H., i, p. 144 a.

[5] R. H., i, p. 148.

[6] There are enough citations to make it clear that the articles of October 11,
1274, are being administered. See, e.g., p. 140 a.

[7] See H. R. (C. H.), Essex 1, 2, and note heading printed p. 148 a, where
five hundreds are grouped together.

of two knights are endorsed upon one return,[1] as if the knights had divided the shire amongst themselves for the purposes of the inquest ; this would account for several hundreds' returns being recorded together.[2]

There are indications, however, that these returns were merely supplementary to some other inquest. The Chafford verdict concludes, ' Dicunt quod ultra predictam magis nequeunt inquirere de omnibus articulis praeter ea que continentur in principali rotulo '.[3] Further light is thrown upon the existence of another record by a comparison of these returns with the Extract Rolls 1 and 4. These contain material which is not to be found in the extant Hundred Rolls already described. If the three existing records are laid side by side and compared in detail, it becomes evident that each contains matter peculiar to itself. Some facts are common to two of the records, but both the Extract Rolls contain names and facts which are not to be found in the ' verdicts of the knights of Essex '. The presumption is that the Extracts were based on verdicts, now lost, made by the ordinary procedure, by the hundred juries, and forming, perhaps, that ' principal roll ' [4] to which the knights' verdicts refer. As will be seen, verdicts of that type are preserved for Norfolk and Suffolk alongside of the knights' verdicts.

There is, however, one further complication for Essex. There are several indications that the inquests had to be taken twice over.[5] Possibly a second inquest may have been necessitated by the sending round of some extra articles, though only one is traceable in Essex—that on the twentieth.[6] On the whole it seems most probable that the inquests were repeated because of some technical defect, due, it may be, to the corruption or intimidation of the juries by local officials.[7]

---

[1] Hundred of Berdestaple : a Sir Peres Talworthe et Sir Nicole de Bret (R. H., i, p. 139 a).

[2] Compare the procedure for Norfolk described below.

[3] R. H., i, p. 149 b.   [4] pp. 149 b, 150 a, 151 b.

[5] See below, Chap. III, § 2.

[6] R. H., i, pp. 136–9, give many returns on this subject.

[7] Note R. H., i, p. 137 b ' In cedula. Sciatis quod non potuimus officium nostrum totum perimplere quia hundredus de Wenstre noluit conperire coram nobis nec villani nec libere tenentes per impedimentum balivi qui nunc est et qui ante erant.' Cf. Lincolnshire entry, R. H., i, p. 308 b. See p. 43.

The second inquests were held at an early date, to judge by the endorsement of the Barstable return, which is assigned to December 21, 1273, an obvious error for 1274.[1] The returns for Norfolk are more orderly and very full,[2] and the procedure employed can be more easily traced. The assignment of groups of hundreds to one or two knights, which seemed probable in Essex, is here undoubted. The returns are endorsed with the names of the knights and of the hundreds assigned to them. The twenty-four knights of the shire were divided into six groups,[3] and each of these groups held inquests in a number of hundreds, varying from two to nine.[4] In these districts verdicts were presented by twelve men of each hundred and six of each vill.[5] In one case it is specifically stated that villeins participated in the presentments.[6] In some cases a separate verdict is given for each hundred ; in others the knights' verdict covers the whole district, the hundreds being thrown together.[7] In Norfolk, as in Essex, we find that these knights' verdicts, though far more full and careful than in Essex, have not been used as the basis for the Extracts. For Norfolk, however, unlike Essex, some verdicts of the ordinary type have survived.[8] These are parallel with those contained in the knights' verdicts, and cover the same ground to some extent, as is to be expected, but on comparison with the Extracts they

[1] R. H. i, p. 137 a ' Inquisitio facta apud Hornindon die Sancti Thome apostoli anno regni R. E. filii R. H. secundo (*rectius* tertio).'

[2] Of the thirty-two hundreds whose names are given in the *Nomina Villarum* (1316) not one is missing from the knights' verdicts.

[3] R. H. i, p. 443 b ' Inquisitio per Willelmum de Gyney, Ricardum de Bellehus et Willelmum de Merkehale, milites iuratos de xxiiij de comitatu Norfolk.' See also pp. 434 a, 452 b, 466 a, 491 b, 504 a, and note the refusal of one knight to serve, p. 443 b.

[4] R. H. i, p. 466 a ' Veredictum militum gladio cinctorum in parte comitatus Norhtffolch hundredi de Clakelose Frethebrige Smethesden Galehoge et Brotherecros.'

[5] R. H. i, p. 436 a ' Inquisitio facta per milites . . . super certis articulis per dominum Regem et hoc per (xii) liberos et legales homines iuratos et per v homines cum preposito de qualibet villa similiter cum aliis per quos melius veritas sciri poterit quorum nomina . . .'

[6] ' Inquisitio facta . . . tam de liberis quam de willanis ' (R. H. i, p. 466 a).

[7] e.g. R. H. i, pp. 466–83, where the verdicts of eight hundreds are blended in one.

[8] R. H. i, pp. 495–503 ; Hundreds of North Erpingham, Mitford, Hensted, and Diss.

prove to be the source of that official summary. A passage from one of these verdicts has been printed above ; any one of the four hundreds in question would afford as good examples.

The Suffolk returns are very incomplete, but provide instances of both types of verdict. Of the nine Suffolk rolls extant,[1] two are presentments of knights,[2] and the remaining seven are the ordinary verdicts of the hundred jury. There are not enough returns to set the procedure beyond doubt, but the presentments under vill headings,[3] without citation of articles, suggests that the same routine was followed here as in Norfolk and Essex.

The only other district that demands special mention is that assigned to Warin de Chalcombe and William of St. Omer —the counties of Lincoln, Northampton, and Rutland. There are thirty-five Hundred Rolls extant for Lincolnshire, and they are unusually rich in annotations, which afford valuable evidence of the relation of the inquest to later inquests and eyres.[4] Only one Hundred Roll has survived for each of the other two counties, but these are full enough to show that the three are alike in containing returns to six articles, which, as has been seen,[5] are peculiar to the district. Finally, there are indications of what looks like a peculiar local procedure in the towns of Stamford and Northampton and the city of Lincoln. This is the presentment of parallel verdicts, not by knights and hundredmen, but by ' greater ' and ' lesser ' men of the town. For Lincoln there are three verdicts,[6] *de magnis, de secundariis hominibus, de minoribus hominibus.* They are very full, and have supplementary schedules of fees and tenements attached ; there is some duplication in the matter returned, but the verdicts are clearly independent, and each contains facts peculiar to itself. For Stamford there is the verdict *de superioribus in comitatu*

---

[1] H. R. Suffolk 9 (Hundred of Carleford) is unprinted.
[2] R. H., ii, pp. 150 a–160 b, 174 b–178 a.
[3] R. H., ii, pp. 174 b–178 a. Contrast form of return of *Villata de Subyry*, pp. 178 a–179 b.
[4] Note especially the references to the inquest of wool of 1275 (P. R. C., p. 115), R. H., i, pp. 276 a, 293 b, 308 b, 343 b ; and the references to the *placita ragemannorum* and *placita corone* of the eyre of 1281, R. H., i, pp. 247 a, 256 b (see A. R., 488, 498), and the adjournment noted on p. 242 b.
[5] See above, Chap. I, § 4, 1.   [6] R. H., i, pp. 309, 315, 322.

Lincolnie in Kecstevene, per xij iuratos de villa Stanford scilicet de maioribus eiusdem ville, and also the verdict *minorum xij iuratorum Staunford.*[1] For Northampton there is only one verdict, but it is endorsed *Villata de Northampton de minoribus.*[2] An inquiry into the local institutions of these towns might explain the phraseology, but cannot be attempted here. The *veredicta de minoribus* may have some analogy with the verdicts of the vills in Norfolk and Essex, which, as we have seen, were made with the co-operation ' tam de willanis quam de liberis ',[3] but the form of the returns is quite different. It is remarkable that the returns of the city of London offer no examples of local divergences, beyond the fact that the ward jury takes the place of the hundred jury elsewhere. One other allusion on the Lincoln Rolls is worth noting. On the unprinted roll for the wapentake of Coringham [4] it is noted under the return, *de sectis subtractis,* ' iste articulus patet in magno rotulo '. It might seem at first sight that some parallel return, like that of the knights of the shire in the eastern counties, was here intended. A careful collation, however, shows that the entries on the Extract Rolls [5] tally almost verbatim with those of the verdict. The note, moreover, seems on inspection to have been added later, and the most obvious inference is that the ' Great Roll ' is simply the contemporary name for the Extracts, which no doubt bulked largely in comparison with the single membrane of the Coringham verdict. It should be noted also that a cancelling line runs from top to bottom of the original return ; the note probably indicates that the contents of the roll have been so fully transferred to the Extracts that it is not worth preserving. No other reference to the ' magnus rotulus ' has been traced in the Lincolnshire verdicts.

§ 7. The Procedure : Querele

There are traces in the records of the inquests of another method of procedure besides that of presentment by juries. Here and there among the verdicts we find *querele*, or plaints

---

[1] R. H., i, pp. 351, 354. [2] R. H., ii, p. 5 b.
[3] R. H., i, p. 466 a ; R. H., i, p. 137 b *(in cedula).*
[4] H. R. Lincoln [T.], No. 18. [5] R. H., i, p. 381 b.

of the injured parties themselves. These are endorsed upon or incorporated in the verdicts of the juries, and may thus have formed a part of their presentment,[1] but their form bears evidence to their different origin. One of the shortest of them may be quoted from the Essex Rolls. Under the vill of Paching Picot, in the hundred of Chelmsford, we read ' Willem le fitz Water se pleint a chevalers ke Richard le Brun le lundi procheyn devant jur Saint Thomas le Apostle en la vile de Chelm'ford li tolit sun cheval en la haut chemin le Rey a tort et sauns acheson '.[2]

These *querele* are not very numerous.[3] It is possible that in many cases the complaints of the injured parties had been made to the jurors, and had been absorbed into the verdict so completely that no trace of their *provenance* is left.[4] The relation of the verdict and the *querele* is well illustrated in the case of Petronilla of Assildeham, also on the Essex Rolls. The *querela* itself, beginning ' Petronilla de Assildeham queritur de Ricardo le Brun et Ricardo le Bel de Haniggefeld ', is endorsed upon the return for the hundred of Dengie.[5] It gives a full and picturesque account of the injuries suffered by Petronilla and her husband at the hands of the bailiff who entered her house, beat and bound her and her husband, and carried off goods to the value of £4, a full inventory of which is given. The date is carefully specified—Martinmas

---

[1] Cf. State Trials of Edward I (C. S.), p. 69, cited by Mr. Bolland, Eyre of Kent, ii, p. xxii. Mr. Bolland's distinction of these bills from the ordinary bills in eyre seems unnecessary, and the acceptance of this passage as a description of the customary procedure would obviate some of the difficulties raised by him, pp. xxviii ff.

[2] R. H., i, p. 144 a.

[3] The returns have not been exhaustively ransacked, and the following list of *querele* is therefore only provisional : R. H., i, p. 68 a, Ricardus Bysothewimpel (Devon) ; i, p. 136 b, Sarra Uxor Ade Coker ; i, p. 137 a, Petronilla de Assildeham ; i, p. 138 b, William de Maunsde ; i, p. 141 b, William Picot ; i, p. 144 a, William fitz Walter ; (Essex) Cambridge H. R. 1, m. 1 d (unprinted), Isabella Pancefot, Robertus de Vera ; Cambridge H. R. 3 (unprinted), Alexander Swan, Gilbert de Barun, Eustachius de Barun, Thomas de Harle, Homines de Harleton, Gilbertus de Dotesham, Alicia de Insula.

[4] An instance of this is perhaps to be found in a presentment on the Essex Rolls, where a presentment is made by the jurors of the injuries done by William of Creppinge to six men, ' et hoc omnes intendunt probare contra eum coram quibuscunque iudicibus debeant ' (R. H., i, p. 142 a, Brumleye).

[5] R. H., i, p. 137 a. The bill is printed in full below, Chap. III, p. 185.

1271. The juries of the vills of Bradwell, Little Woodham, Norton, and Dengie each present that 'Richard le Brun came by night to the house of Petronilla and bound her, and carried off all her goods '.[1] The trespass is brought before the commissioners both by the inquests and by the injured party herself, the presentments of the vills giving the outline, the *querela* the detailed facts.

Two points of interest arise in connexion with these *querele* : their connexion with the commission of October 20, 1274, and their relation to the Bills in Eyre, the origin and significance of which have recently been discussed by Mr. Bolland.

On one of the unprinted Cambridge Hundred Rolls which contains several *querele* occurs the note 'Audiantur conquerentes qui conqueri voluerunt ', etc.[2] This appears to be a quotation from the instructions which wind up the first section of the *Nova Capitula* of the eyre, as given in all complete versions, including that of the Exchequer Book.[3] ' Et de omnibus predictis factis vel commissis infra xxv annos proxime preteritos predicti iustitiarii se intromittent. Et omnes illi qui sentiunt se super hiis gravatos et inde conqueri voluerint audiantur, et fiat eis super hoc iustitia, et ipsi iustitiarii sequantur pro hiis que dominum Regem contingunt.' We have before noted the difficulty of dating these instructions. It is obvious that the commission of October 11, 1274, is truncated in the form in which it now appears upon the Patent Roll,[4] and the directions would form a natural and consistent conclusion to the list of articles, but for the fact that all the evidence goes to show that the commissioners of 1274-5 merely collected facts and exercised no judicial functions. The note upon the Cambridgeshire return may belong to the Cambridge eyre of 1286, and not to the inquest itself ; the evidence of the handwriting is not clear. There is no doubt that the justices of the eyres of 1278-87 were empowered to hear and determine plaints,[5] and the directions may belong to 1278, and may have been inserted

---

[1] R. H., i, p. 136 a. See also i, p. 142 b, under Assildeham, where Petronilla's surname is given.

[2] H. R. Cambridge (C. H.) 3.   [3] See above, p. 32.

[4] See above, p. 30.   [5] For terms of writ, see above, p. 57.

to distinguish the time-limit for offences under the articles of 1274 from that for offences under the articles upon the Statutes. But the fact that *querele*, of the very nature that the direction invite, are found upon the returns of 1274–5 suggests forcibly that some such invitation to the injured party to complain in person to the commissioners or to the juries formed part of the instructions issued to the inquisitors, and sent in advance of them, in all probability, to the sheriffs of the counties where the inquests were to be held.

The relation of the *querele* to the bills in eyre is a matter of more general interest. In his edition of the Eyre of Kent Mr. Bolland discusses the nature of the bills in eyre, examples of which are printed in a later volume of the Selden Society's publications. He points out that these bills range in date from the reign of Edward I to that of Edward III,[1] but can find no statutory authority for them.[2] Mr. Bolland notes that the commission for the justices in eyre of 1278, which for some reason he considers 'less comprehensive' than others,[3] gave the justices power to hear complaints and make fitting amends therefor, but he does not appear to recognize the importance of that year in the history of the general eyre. As has been shown above, it forms an epoch in its development. The new and extensive powers assigned to the justices by the Statutes of Gloucester and Rageman were then first put in force ; the New Chapters, comprising both the articles of 1274 and the articles based on the statutes of Easter and Michaelmas 1275, were then first administered to the jurors of the eyre, and the writ of the eyre then for the first time instructed the justices to hear and determine plaints, in the form which it preserved henceforth so long as the eyre endured—' Ad querelas omnium conquerentium seu conqueri volentium audiendas.' If statutory authority be sought for the terms of the writ, that of the statute of Rageman may be quoted. ' E veut le Rei qe par le allegaunce del poeple et per haster dreit qe les pleintes de chacun seint oyz devant les avantdiz justices e terminez ausi bien par bref

---

[1] Eyre of Kent (S. S.), ii, p. xxii. In Select Bills in Eyre, p. xv, Mr. Bolland states that no bills have been found earlier than 14 Ed. I.

[2] Eyre of Kent, ii, p. xxvi. [3] Ibid., p. xxiii.

com saunz bref solum les articles bailez a meme ceux justices.
. . . Ensement veut le Rey qe mesmes ceus justices enquergent,
oient et terminent ces pleints de ceus qe pleindre se vodrent.'
Here is the very authorization for dispensing with procedure
by writ that Mr. Bolland desiderates. It is true that neither
the statutes, the writ, nor the directions to the justices pre-
scribe the details of procedure by bill, but it seems a warrant-
able inference that this procedure was in fact followed. The
changes in the character of the eyre in 1278 and the following
years have been shown to be closely related to the inquest
of 1274-5, and the *querele* presented during those inquests
may well have influenced the procedure of the eyre. In the
Assize Rolls from 1278 onward,[1] cases are recorded under the
heading of *Placita de querelis*, which, in the few instances
when the original bills in eyre are extant, can be shown to
correspond with the cases initiated by bill. Mr. Bolland
considers it likely that only a small proportion of the bills
presented have been preserved.[2] All the evidence appears
to indicate that this procedure was employed in the general
eyres from 1278 onwards, and that the heading *Placita de
querelis* covers records of cases initiated by bill, from that
year onwards.[3]

It is possible that further investigations might reveal earlier
instances of *querele* in connexion with special inquests, similar
to those of 1285-6 and 1289-91,[4] so that the origin of the

[1] One membrane of *placita de querelis de transgressionibus* occurs in an
eyre roll for 1261 (A. R. 343, m. 10 (Hunts.)). If these are based upon the
procedure by bill, they would seem to show that the ' Statute of Rageman '
merely legalized an existent practice.

[2] Select Bills in Eyre, p. xv. Three bills in French are preserved with some
odd *veredicta* in A. R. 935 ; they appear to belong to the Sussex Eyre of 1288.

[3] The bills themselves are catalogued as Assize Rolls 1552-8. Some
of them were undoubtedly presented to justices other than those *ad omnia
placita*. Those presented at Lincoln in 1286 (Select Bills in Eyre, pp. 79 ff.)
belong apparently to the special inquisition known by the popular name of
Kirkby's Quest, and the corresponding judicial records are to be found in
A. R. 502 C, 502 B. No general eyre was held at Lincoln in that year. For
an account of ' Kirkby's Quest ' see Inquisitions and Assessments relating
to Feudal Aids (Record Publications), i, pp. viii–xxii. Note especially c. 12 :
' Quod omnes qui querelam facere velint de vicecomitibus vel ballivis quod
sint ibidem coram Thesaurario et eam proponant ' (p. xiii). The bills in
A. R. 1556-8 are described in the P. R. O. list of plea rolls as petitions to
justices of Trailbaston.

[4] State Trials of Edward I (C. S.), vol. ix, 3rd series.

procedure could be carried back beyond 1274, but on the evidence already shown the connexion between the inquests of 1274–5 and the use of bills in eyre seems fairly established.

§ 8. Conclusion

From the foregoing analysis it will be seen that the material preserved and printed as ' Hundred Rolls ' is of various degrees of value. In the past this has been very generally ignored. The fact that the ground is often most inadequately covered, and often covered twice or three times ; the fact that the Extract Rolls are neither contemporary nor always intelligently compiled, and that they are, as they profess to be, merely extracts ; and the fact that the original returns are the product of different local procedures, hardly appear to be matters of common knowledge. When one so familiar with the records as Mr. Hall has not thought it essential to discriminate between the Extracts and the original returns as authorities ;[1] when Mr. Morris has argued from the silence of the Hundred Rolls as to the distribution of the frankpledge system,[2] and has drawn up tables to show the frequency of the allusions to view of frankpledge in the Hundred Rolls ;[3] and when the parallel between the *querele* and the bills in eyre has escaped the attention of Mr. Bolland, it seems clear that such an analysis is not superfluous on general grounds. To the inquirer who seeks to elicit new facts as to the local administrative system under Henry III and Edward I, it is indispensable.

[1] Hall, English Official Historical Documents, p. 302 ; Formula Book of Legal Records, p. 145.
[2] Morris, Frankpledge System, p. 46.   [3] Ibid., p. 66.

APPENDIX IV

THE INQUESTS OF 1274-5

TABLE OF DATE, DURATION, RECORDS AND COMMISSIONERS

Commissioners,[1]	County		Date of Inquest	Place of Inquest	Reference for Date and Place	No. of Veredicta Extant	Extract Roll	Other Evidence of Inquest
Ricardus de Fukeram } Osbertus de Bereford }	C.R. {	Salop	Nov. 24–9, 1273[2]	Shrewsbury	R.H.,ii,89,106	22	—	Rot. Pat. 3 Ed. I, m. 31 d (P.R.C., p. 116).
	C.R. {	Stafford	?	?		1 (unpr.)	3	
Roger Extraneus } Osbertus de Bereford }	C. {	Cheshire	After Feb. 7, 1275	?	P.R.C., p. 116	—		
	Rot. Pat.							
Bartholomeus de Bryauncon	C.R.	London	Jan. 23, 1275	St. Martin le Grand	R. H., i, 420, 421	16	Special roll	
	C.	Sussex	After Oct. 26, 1274	?	R. H., ii, 207	1 (unpr.)	Special roll	
Jacobus de Sancto Vigore {	C. } (A. R. 877)	Surrey	?	?		—	—	
	C. } (A. R. 369)	Kent	?	?		72	—	
	C.	Middlesex	?	?		—	—	A. R. 543.[3]
Willielmus de Brayboef } Guydo de Tantone }	C.R.	Oxford	Before Nov. 20, 1274	Oxford	R. H., ii, 46	1	2	
Willielmus de Brayboef } Willielmus Gerberd } Guydo de Tantone }	C.R.	Southants.	Feb. 15, 1275	Winchester	R. H., ii, 220	3	—	
	R. } C. }	Wilts.	March 5–21, 1275	Wilton / Sarum / Marlborough / Malmesbury	R. H., ii, 252, 249	35	—	
	C.	Berks.	?	?		—	2	
Bartholomeus le Juvene } Rogerus de Chenne }	C.R.	Devon	Jan. 16–13, 1275	Exeter	R.H., i, 64, 88	44	2	1.
	C. }	Cornwall	?	?		—	2	
	C. } (A. R. 759)	Somerset	?	?		—	3	
	C.	Dorset	?	?		2	1, 4	
Willielmus de Sancto Omero	C.R.	Lincoln	2 & 3 Ed. I. Begins before Nov. 20, 1275; ends before Feb. 25, 1275 ?	Stamford, Lincoln	R. H., i, 332, 308	33	2	
Warinus de Chalcumbe	C.R.	Northants	3 Ed. I.	Northampton	R. H., ii, 1	1	3	
	C.R.	Rutland	?	?		1	3	

Name	C./R.	County	Date	Place	R. H. reference			A. R. reference
Thomas de Boulton } Willelmus de Pereton }	C.	York				—	3	
Robertus de Ufford	R.	{Herts.	Dec. 12, 1274	Hertford	R. H., i, 188	1	1, 4	
		[Essex ?]	Dec. 21, 1273 [2]	Hornindon	R. H., i, 137	15	1, 4	
Radulfus de Sanwyco	R.	{Suffolk	Jan. 9, 1275	Bury St. Edmunds	R. H., ii, 171	9	1, 4	
	R.	Norfolk	3 Ed. I.	?		21	1, 4	
Ricardus de Creppinges	R.	{Derby	Jan. 10–13, 1275	Derby	R. H., ii, 287, 289	4	3	
Thomas de Leuknor	R.	{Notts.	Jan. 14–20, 1275	Nottingham	R. H., ii, 300, 309	4	3	
Sampson Foliot	R.	{Bucks.	Nov. 18, 1275 [4]	Aylesbury	R. H., i, 35	3	2	
Edmund de Caldecote	R.	{Cambridge	Dec. 13–17, 1274	Cambridge	H. R., Camb., 1–4 (unpr.)	4	2	
Galfridus Aguillon Philippus de Wilughby A. R. 655, m. 2 [5]		Northumberland	?	?		—	1, 4	A. R. 655.
?		Gloucester	2 Ed. I.	?	R. H., i, 166	5	3	
?		Hereford	3 Ed. I.	?		3	—	
?		Bedford				—	2	
?		Hunts.				—	2	
?		Leicester				—	3	
?		Warwick				—	3	
?		Worcester				—	3	
?		Cumberland				—	—	A. R. 134.[3]
?		Lancashire				—	—	A. R. 408.[3]
?		Westmoreland				—	—	A. R. 985.[3]

[1] C.=named on the Commission of Oct. 1274; R.=named on the Return. [2] Probably a mistake for 1274; the roll is dated 2 Ed. I, and the 3rd of Edward I began on Nov. 20, 1274. [3] This Assize Roll refers to the 'Ragemannis', the contemporary name for the Hundred Rolls of 1274–5. [4] Probably a mistake for 1274; the rolls dated 3 Ed. I. [5] This roll refers to an inquest held before these men, quoting presentments which can be identified on the Extract Roll.

CHAPTER III

THE EVIDENCE OF THE HUNDRED ROLLS AS TO ADMINISTRATIVE ABUSES IN THE COUNTY OF ESSEX

§ 1. The One-sided Nature of the Evidence

It would be unjust to the local official of the thirteenth century, whether in Essex or elsewhere, to take the evidence of the returns of 1274–5 as typical of the normal workings of local government. Not only was the period over which the inquiry extended unusually disturbed, both by actual civil war, a wave of which touched Essex itself in 1267,[1] and by the dislocation of the central administration resulting from the alternating control of different factions, but the nature of the inquiry itself was such as to make the maladministrator conspicuous and throw the conscientious and loyal official into the shade. The returns, moreover, as the following section will show, are incomplete, and bound, from their origin, to be one-sided. The remarks made by the editors of the State Trials of 1289–93 [2] as to the unsatisfactory nature of statistics based on this class of record, hold good here also. The information is both vague and defective. The issue of the cases, the justice or injustice of the charges remain a mystery. The central administration, to which we owe the records, is concerned at least as much with ' the monetary profit to be got from the business ' as with ' the demands of abstract justice '. Yet, for all this, the attempt to analyse the returns is worth making, and the presentments of the jurors, biassed though they may be, throw a vivid light on the ordinary routine of the government of the shire and on the idiosyncrasies of one type, if not the dominant type of bureaucrat of the thirteenth century.

---

[1] See below, p. 175.
[2] State Trials, ed. by H. Johnstone and T. F. Tout (C. S.), pp. xxxv–xlii.

§ 2. The Records

i. *The Different Rolls*

Three parallel records are extant for Essex : the *Inquisitiones*, consisting of three rolls covering seventeen hundreds or half-hundreds ;[1] the Extracts on Extract Roll 1, which cover twenty hundreds, four vills, and one borough ;[2] and the Extracts on Extract Roll 4, ' De Ministris ', which cover fourteen hundreds and four vills.[3]   Between them these records cover the whole area of Essex.[4]   They cannot, however, be regarded as complete.   A comparison of the Extracts with the *Inquisitiones* soon makes it clear that these are not the only original returns from which the Extracts were compiled, if they were used at all in the process of compilation. Again and again information is found in the Extracts which is lacking in the *Inquisitiones*.   For instance, there is no common fact in the administrative returns of the two records for the hundred of Dunmow.[5]   In the records for Hinckford hundred the *Inquisitiones* recount the misdeeds of twenty-five officials ; Extract Roll 1 mentions eight of these and eleven others, and Extract Roll 4, in a list of fifteen names, gives four which are to be found in neither of the other records.[6] Again, the Extract Rolls give returns for the two hundreds of East and West Uttlesford, where the *Inquisitiones* include the same area under the one heading of the hundred of Uttlesford.   To the reference ' sicut patet in inquisitione ' of the Extracts for Hinckford Hundred, there is no corresponding entry in the *Inquisitiones*.[7]   The Extracts are evidently based upon some returns which are now lost.   The relation of the two Extract Rolls to each other has already been shown ;

[1] Rolls 1 and 2 are printed R. H., i, pp. 136–51 ; roll 3, covering Thurstaple and Rochford hundreds, and largely illegible, has not been printed.
[2] Printed R. H., i, pp. 152–65.   [3] Ex. R. 4, m. 8.
[4] Returns for Ongar and Winstree hundreds are lacking from the *Inquisitiones* ; for Ongar, Becontree, Chelmsford, Dunmow, Harlow, and Witham, from Ex. R. 4.
[5] R. H., i, pp. 144 f., 157 f.
[6] See R. H., i, pp. 146–7, 158–9, and Ex. R. 4, m. 8.
[7] Cf. pp. 147 a, 159 a.   Note also on Ex. R. 4, for Dengie H., ' Sicut patet in inquisitione in articulo de vicecomitibus qui tradiderunt . . .'   This article is not quoted in the *Inquisitiones* for Dengie.

they are contemporary, similar in format, and complementary, the same fact being rarely, if ever, repeated in both records. The ' De Ministris ' Extract is concerned almost exclusively with ministerial abuses, and is at times little more than a list of the names of peccant officials. The other Extract Roll is correspondingly scanty on administrative abuses as compared with seignorial usurpations. The three records for Essex, then, have, as they stand, independent authority.

The *Inquisitiones* are confused and perplexing in their form. They do not conform to the general type of hundred roll, in which each membrane contains the verdict of a separate hundred, with the jurors' names and often their seals appended, and the date and place duly recorded. Nor do they follow the Norfolk rolls in their orderly grouping in units of three, four, or five hundreds. One such group of hundreds is found in Roll 2,[1] but elsewhere both neatness and uniformity is lacking. The records of Tendring and Lexden hundreds are intermixed, stray vills from Thurstable hundred are found among the Dengie returns, Dunmow and Freshwell hundreds share one membrane, as do Uttlesford and Clavering. Twice, in the records of Chelmsford and of Chafford hundreds,[2] the return suddenly changes from Latin to French, without any alteration in the handwriting or scope of the record.

ii. *Form of Procedure*

The inquests recorded in these returns are not presented by jurors of hundreds. Wherever indications of procedure can be traced, the juries are those of vills. In many cases the articles of the inquest are not quoted at all, and the only headings are the names of the vills.[3] In some cases presentments are made to the articles intermixed with presentments from the vills.[4] The superscription to the Chafford returns describes the inquests as being made before sworn knights

---

[1] Roll 2, mm. 6–9, printed R. H., i, pp. 148–51. ' Veredicta Hundredorum de Chafford, Bekentr', Dimidii Hundredi de Herlawe, Dimidii Hundredi de Watham, Dimidii Hundredi de Witham.'

[2] pp. 143 a, 149 a. (In this and subsequent citations, the reference is to R. H., vol. i, unless otherwise specified.)

[3] e.g. Dengie Hundred, p. 136 ; Barstable Hundred, p. 137.

[4] e.g. Tendring, p. 140 ; cf. Chelmsford, p. 142.

by all the vills of the shire,[1] and later on in the same roll
reference is made to the jurors of the vills of the hundred of
Chafford.[2]   From the unprinted roll for Thurstable and
Rochford we learn that these juries conformed to the usual
type.   ' Quatuor homines et prepositus de Estwode dicunt
quod ' . . .[3]   The schedule to the Barstable roll, which explains
the absence of a return for Winstree, shows that villeins as
well as free tenants took part in the presentments.[4]   On the
other hand, there are references to juries of twelve, to the
twelve jurors of the manor of Writtle,[5] to the ' twelve first
sworn ' of the hundred of Witham,[6] which suggest a double
procedure of juries for both vill and hundred, similar to that
which is traceable in Suffolk.   Though the Essex records are
far less orderly and symmetrical than those for Suffolk and
Norfolk, it seems probable that they belong to that group of
returns for the eastern counties which have, as has been
shown,[7] certain well-marked characteristics of their own—
the grouping of hundreds, and the use of sworn knights as
inquisitors below the royal commissioners.   The endorsement
of the Barstable roll, ' A Sir Peres de Talworthe et Sir Nicole
le Bret ',[8] appears to give the names of two of the knights to
whom reference is made on the Chelmsford and Chafford
rolls.[9]

On the other hand, there are special features in these Essex
returns which, as has been said, suggest not merely parallel
but successive inquests.   Several vills in Barstable hundred
return that they have nothing to add to what they have said
before the twelve knights.[10]   The group of hundreds that go
with Chafford return answer ' tam de articulis ultimo liberatis
quam de primis oblitis et omissis ',[11] and several of them refer
separately to the returns ' que continentur in principali
rotulo qui presentatus est per xii primo iuratos'.[12]   It would

---

[1] p. 148 a.   [2] p. 149 a.   [3] H. R. Essex 3, m. 2.
[4] ' Hundredus de Wenstre noluit comperire coram nobis nec villani nec
libere tenentes per impedimentum balivi qui nunc est et qui ante erant '
(p. 137 b).   [5] p. 142 a.   [6] p. 151 b.
[7] See above, Chap. II, § 6.   [8] p. 139 a.
[9] ' Veredictum xii militum de Essex . . .' (p. 144 a).   ' Veredictum presentatum coram militibus iuratis ' (p. 148 a).
[10] p. 137 b, Dundingeherste, Coringeham ; p. 138 a, Parva Troke, Bur-
gestede Magna.   [11] p. 148 a.   [12] pp. 150 a, 151 b.

seem that the inquest has had to be repeated, for what reason can only be surmised. Possibly the inquiry into the collection of the twentieth [1] may have been an afterthought which necessitated a second inquisition. Possibly the inquest by vills was held to check and supplement the inquests by hundreds, which were considered unsatisfactory, though, on the other hand, the reference to a previous return made *coram militibus* in Barstable hundred suggests that the procedure of the former and latter inquests was identical. It is highly probable that the conduct of officials like the bailiffs of Winstree who would not suffer men to appear to make their presentments [2] had something to do with it. The Statute of Rageman alludes to the vindictiveness of the local official towards those men who had exposed his offences,[3] and the jurors of a Lincolnshire hundred add to their verdict the statement that the bailiffs within that hundred threaten them with more grievous distraints and extortions than before on account of their presentments.[4] The extent to which ministerial abuses outweigh every other element in the Essex returns lends some colour to this theory. If the Essex officials do not equal those of Norfolk in the extent of their misdoings,[5] they afford ample material, alike to the unfortunate juror of the thirteenth and to the investigator of the twentieth century for a tale of maladministration on a grand scale.

Whether the different inquests to which the *Inquisitiones* refer were held side by side or in succession to one another, we shall probably be right in assuming that the Extract Rolls were based upon a series of verdicts found by the juries of the Essex hundreds, but now lost, like most of those for Suffolk and Norfolk. There is nothing in the form of the Essex Extracts to suggest that the returns from which they were compiled differed from those for the western and southern counties of England.

[1] See below, § 4, iii (*b*).   [2] See above, note 7, p. 130.
[3] ' E nomement de trespas fetz puis par baillifs quel qe il seit a les bones gens par qui serement les enquestes furent fetes ' (S. R., i, p. 44).
[4] p. 276 b. (Quoted in full, note 4, p. 43, of Chap. I.)
[5] The ' De Ministris ' Extracts for Norfolk cover both sides of four membranes and one of a fifth, and recount the misdeeds of 343 officials.

§ 3. THE OFFICIALS

The Essex Hundred Rolls supply a conspectus of the ordinary staff of local officials for a county where few great honours or franchises broke up the system of royal administration. A list based on these returns contains the names of 188 officials, 166 royal and 22, apparently, seignorial, who exercised and abused their powers between the years 1254–74. The scope of the inquiries had not been generally limited, but in two of the articles the Statute of Marlborough and the battle of Evesham had been named as dates beyond which information was not sought, and the *tempus guerre* is clearly looked upon as the landmark on the hither side of which the field of investigation lay. The offences described are seldom assigned to any given date, but with the help of the Pipe Rolls and the Assize Rolls,[1] the period of office of all the sheriffs and of many of the bailiffs and coroners can be safely defined. Thus it is possible to say that, although charges are made which go back to the sheriffdom of Ralph of Arden, who was appointed in 1254, by far the greater number are of quite recent date. Walter of Essex, who easily heads the list with some 130 offences laid to his account, has held office for a few months in 1269 and then again from Michaelmas 1270 to October 1274. John Barun, bailiff of Hinckford, against whom 53 charges are brought, was appointed by Walter of Essex, and held office from 1272 to the time of the inquest—probably December 1274. Richard le Brun, bailiff of Dengie and Thurstable, who is accused of 57 abuses of power, belongs roughly to the same period. Every indication goes to show that the greater part of these little tyrants were exercising power contemporaneously. Essex may not have complained like Norfolk and Nottingham in the same year, ' Quod supraonerata est de ballivis ',[2] but it affords an excellent illustration of the truth of Maitland's statement that the England of those days was a much governed England.[3]

---

[1] A. R. 238, the record of the Essex Eyre of 1272, contains (m. 50) a list or ' calendar ' of the bailiffs of the Essex hundreds in that year.

[2] Ex. R. 4, m. 3. Hundred de Fourhowe (R. H., ii, p. 307 a).

[3] Pollock and Maitland, i, p. 688.

The officials fall into two classes : those whose activities extend throughout the county, and those who exercise their function in one or two hundreds only. In the first class come the sheriffs—Ralph of Arden, Matthew de la Mare, Richard of Suthecherche, Richard of Harlow, John de Kaumvil, William de Blumvil, Walter of Essex, and Ralph of Sandwich ; then the coroners, of whom three are mentioned ; then the escheators—Hubert de Boucingham, William Clay, Roger de Fering, Geoffrey de Mores, Robert de Pereres, Ralph de Poley, Robert de Ros, and Ralph de Winterfled. Below these come a hierarchy of officials dependent upon them, under-sheriffs, sub-escheators, sheriff's clerks, bailiffs, and sub-bailiffs. The sheriff's underlings may be considered first. Roger of Kelvedon, under-sheriff to Walter of Essex, is charged with offences in nine different hundreds ; he is also spoken of as the sheriff's clerk. William de la Mare, another under-sheriff, is less notorious. A series of sheriff's clerks, ' ministri ' and sergeants, such as William de Bradeleye, charged with offences in five hundreds, Peter Bude, Richard Clerk, Digun or Dike, Roger de Derneford, Walter Picard, Thomas Sporun, and Robert de Wode, exercise functions, it would seem, of varying importance, but all co-extensive with the sheriff's own activities. There are also a body of officials connected with the castle of Colchester, the custody of which seems to have been in the sheriff's control during the last part of Henry III's reign.[1] Three constables, presumably dependent upon the sheriff, are mentioned by name—John Flinchart, Hugh Parker, and William de Roinges. These, and their subordinates, a body of some seven or eight clerks and bailiffs,[2] appear to exercise their authority at large in the county.

These facts point to the existence of a county staff of officials, attached to the sheriff's person, described by varying titles, not very precisely defined. The term *ballivus*

---

[1] 1261, M. de Mare, P. R. C., p. 164 ; 1264, N. Le Espigornel, P. R. C., p. 334 ; 1268, R. de Herlawe, P. R. C., p. 218 ; 1271, W. de Essex, P. R. C., p. 509.

[2] Roger Clerk, William de Creppinge, Roger de Gasebek, Motin, Roger Redhed, Walter de Tillingham, Richard Munde le Warrener, Bartholomew de Wynesham.

would seem to be the most comprehensive, covering *serviens,* *minister, subballivus,* and *clericus.* The distinction which Cowell makes at a later date between the localized and errant bailiff [1] is traceable in the phraseology of the Norfolk Hundred Rolls. Here we read of errant or itinerant bailiffs,[2] of bailiffs of the county of Norfolk,[3] and of the 'clerks and other bailiffs' of the sheriff.[4] It is quite likely that the sheriff transferred individuals from his personal staff—'gentes suos', as the Norfolk Roll calls them[5]—to the bailiwick of some hundred, and vice versa, as he undoubtedly shifted them from hundred to hundred, but it is impossible to prove this in any one case, for the offences recorded are so rarely dated that the career of an official below the rank of sheriff can seldom be traced in detail.

All the officials mentioned so far are dependent directly or indirectly upon the sheriff, and their activities are geographically co-extensive with his own. The position of the sub-escheators is not so clear. At this period there was only one escheator for all the counties south of Trent, and it may be supposed that all county officials who had the charge of escheats were, strictly speaking, only sub-escheators. The sheriffs had been ordered by a writ of 1268 to be 'intendant to the escheator',[6] and presumably their functions were technically parallel with those of the county escheator and sub-escheators rather than superior to them. In one case at least, that of Robert Ledet, a sheriff had exercised the functions of sub-escheator in Essex.[7] As we have seen, eight escheators are mentioned in Essex, none of whom can be identified with the 'escheator south of Trent', and of these two are also described as sub-escheators. Nine other sub-escheators or escheators' officials are named.[8] The records suggest that their activities were confined to a smaller area

---

[1] Cowell, Law Dictionary, *s.v.*: 'Ballivi itinerantes be those which the sheriff maketh and appointeth to go hither and thither in the county, to serve writs, to summon the county sessions, assizes, etc.'

[2] R. H., i, pp. 465 b, 477 a.   [3] R. H., i, p. 452 b.
[4] R. H., i, p. 465 a.   [5] R. H., i, p. 481 a.
[6] P. R. C., p. 306.   [7] P. R. C. (1267), pp. 68, 75.
[8] William Arthur, Thomas de Basing, Robert de Chigwell, Adam Clerk, Thomas de Clay, Thurstan de Colchester, Robert de Derby, Robert Ledet, Wychard Ledet.

than were those of the sheriff's ' ministri ', but it is possible
that the evidence is less widely distributed simply because the
more specialized functions of an escheator limited his power
to do evil.   In the case of one sub-escheator at least, Robert
Chigwell,   there   are   tales   of   his   misdemeanours   in   three
hundreds.

With the exception of the notorious Walter of Essex the
chief offenders, however, are the bailiffs of the hundreds.
Many, if not all of them, are the nominees of the sheriff ; in
fact, his appointment of extortionate bailiffs is one of the
charges made against him.   Some of them are described both
as his bailiffs and as bailiffs of hundreds, but as a rule their
powers are limited to their own hundreds.   The Eyre Rolls
give   frequent   instances   of   one   bailiff   administering   two
hundreds at once ; in 1272, for instance, Elyas Poley was
bailiff of the two Uttlesford hundreds together with the half
hundred of Freshwell, all these being adjacent.   The Extract
Rolls show that he had also been bailiff of Hinckford at one
time.[1]   Similarly in the Hundred Rolls we find Richard le
Brun bailiff of Dengie, Thurstable, and Chelmsford ;[2] Gilbert
de la Dune bailiff of Thurstable, Dengie, and Dunmow ;[3] John
Barun   bailiff   of   Hinckford   and   Chelmsford ;[4]   Henry of
Codinton bailiff of Chafford and Dunmow.[5]   Still, on the
whole it is more usual for one bailiff to administer no more
than one hundred at a time.[6]

The sum total of the charges brought against these bailiffs
of hundreds is very high.   Reference is made to some forty
of them by name, and though a good many are only mentioned once, the average number of complaints is six or seven
per head.   From the Hundred Rolls alone one would gain
the impression that the upright bailiff did not exist.   But the
list from the Eyre Roll of 1272 supplies the names of several

[1] A. R. 238, m. 50 ; R. H., i, p. 159 a.   [2] pp. 136 a, 141 b, 153 b.
[3] pp. 136 a, 162 a ; Ex. R. m. 8.   [4] pp. 153 b, 158 b.
[5] A. R. 238, m. 50 ; R. H., i, p. 148 a.
[6] The Eyre Rolls, in their ' calendars ', appear to distinguish between
a ' capitalis ballivus ' and other bailiffs of hundreds, and it has been suggested that the ' subballivus ' is the official who administers a hundred for
a chief bailiff who holds several.   There might, however, be two sub-bailiffs
of one hundred (p. 140 b, Wythermundeford).· Cf. E. H. R. xxxiii, p. 356.

against whom no offence is alleged. Some bailiffs and some
hundreds are pre-eminent for lawlessness; John Barun of
Hinckford and Richard le Brun of Dengie are easily first,
but Roger of Chaudeford of Witham, Gilbert de la Dune of
Dunmow, and William of Haningefeld of Chelmsford are also
conspicuous with fifteen, eighteen, and seventeen charges
against them respectively. It is possible that longer tenure
of office is one explanation of this prominence; John Barun
was bailiff of Hinckford in 1272, and was still holding office
there at the end of 1274.[1] Hinckford, Chelmsford, and
Lexden are the hundreds with the worst records. Thirty to
thirty-two different officials are accused in each of them, and
five to eight bailiffs in each.[2] Rochford appears to have been
especially unlucky in its bailiffs; of the eight offenders
mentioned in this hundred, six seem to have been bailiffs.
As we have seen, there are indications that the same man
held the position of bailiff in different hundreds successively.
Besides the bailiffs of the hundreds, nine sub-bailiffs are
mentioned, alternatively described in some cases as bailiffs'
clerks; and a number of persons of unspecified functions,
who seem to be the bailiffs' underlings.

   With the seignorial officials the tale is complete. The chief
lords in the county employing officials who have abused their
powers are Robert de Brus, five of whose seneschals or bailiffs
are mentioned, the prior of Canterbury, the abbot of St.
Osyth's, Philip Basset, Maurice of Berkeley, and Richard of
Cornwall. The bulk of their abuses of power is, however,
trifling as compared with those of the king's officials. On
the showing of the Hundred Rolls, the chief blame for the
conditions of local government in Essex would seem to rest
ultimately on the shoulders of the king himself. Either
Edward himself, as heir to the throne, or his attorneys had
given the county into the custody of Walter of Essex,[3] who
not only heads the list of offenders, but was in the main

---

[1] A. R. 238, m. 50; R. H., i, p. 159 a.
[2] R. H., i, p. 159 a, gives the names of eight different extortionate
bailiffs of Hinckford hundred.
[3] P. R. O. Lists and Indexes, ix, p. 43. Walter of Essex held office
July–November 1269, January 1271–October 1274. Edward sailed for
the Holy Land August 20, 1270.

responsible for the appointment of the 'extortionate bailiffs, oppressing the people with immoderate burdens ',[1] whose misdeeds the jurors of 1274–5, in spite of intimidation and coercion, exhibited in detail to the royal commissioners.

§ 4. The Offences

We have now to consider the nature of the offences charged against these Essex officials. An analysis of the charges on the scale employed by the editors of the State Trials of 1289–93 would bulk far too largely for the size of this volume, and could, moreover, only be imperfect, in view of the fact that the complainants were more concerned with the harm they suffered than with the colour of the pretext under which the wrong was inflicted. The wrongful seizure of beasts, of corn, of land is alleged again and again without any indication of the sheriff's or bailiff's ostensible warrant for the proceedings. Statistics based, however, merely upon the victim's sufferings, would be both more monotonous and less illuminating than those which take the official standpoint, whether it be that of the king, defrauded and discredited by his servant's misdoings, or that of the sheriff or bailiff, using or abusing the functions of his office. An attempt will be made, therefore, to group the charges according to the duties and powers of the shire officials, whether sheriffs, bailiffs, escheators, or coroners, but it must be recognized that this classification can only be rough, and that scientific precision is impossible.

i. *The Police Functions of the Officials of the Shire*

(a) The sheriff's tourn and the view of frank-pledge.

One article of the inquest was especially directed against the too frequent holding of the tourn, which, according to the Magna Carta of 1217, 1224, and 1251, ought to be held only twice a year: ' Cum vicecomites non debent facere turnum suum nisi bis in anno qui pluries fecerint in anno turnum suum.' None of the Essex returns gives a direct answer to this, and though the Finchingfield jurors allude to

---

[1] H. R. Essex 3, m. 1 'De vicecomitibus qui tradiderunt ballivis extorsoribus etc. Dicunt quod W. de' Essex tradidit R. le Brun hundredum de Turstaple qui supra modum gravabat populum,' etc. See also pp. 153 b (Chelmsford), 159 b (Dengie), p. 165 a (Westodelesford).

the four tourns of Walter of Essex,[1] there is nothing to show whether local custom was not on his side. On the other hand, there are complaints of enforced attendance. The vill of West Horndon has been compelled to make suit to the sheriff's tourn by sixteen when it ought not to do so.[2] Again, suitors have been compelled to make payments at the tourn in excess of the customary dues. This complaint is very frequent ; in Dengie the villagers of Norton have been forced to pay three or four shillings in excess,[3] in Barstable the villagers of Langdon have paid half a mark,[4] and in Chelmsford,[5] Freshwell,[6] and Hinckford[7] hundreds sums varying in amount beyond the usual dues for two, four, or even six years. No regular scale of increase is traceable, nor is it possible to make out any standard rate for the amount lawfully due. In Chelmsford hundred four shillings are paid when two are owing.[8] One man at Pentloe has been forced to pay sixteen shillings for the last four years when he should only pay three.[9] Walter of Essex has taken half a mark from the vill of Middleton when it ought only to pay two shillings, eight shillings from Bulmer, which only owes three, and two shillings from Twinstead, which only owes sixpence.[10]

It may be noted that the customary payment due at the sheriff's tourn and at the bailiff's view of frankpledge is in these returns generally called the *certum*. 'Walterus vicecomes Essexie cepit ad quemlibet turnum suum per quinque annos xxs. iniuste ultra certum suum.'[11] *Certum*, no doubt, meant originally no more than ' the fixed amount ', and it is found occasionally in connexion with other payments also in

---

[1] R. H., i, p. 146 b.
[2] p. 137 b. Compare the complaint of Tendring hundred in 1272, that Richard de Suthchirche enforced attendance at his tourn without the king's command (A. R. 438, m. 46).
[3] p. 136 a.   [4] p. 138 b.   [5] p. 143 a, Widfer.
[6] p. 145 b, Hamborden (6s. 6d.). This is probably the same abuse, though the exaction is called an amercement.
[7] p. 146 a, Brudon et Balidon (18s.), Pentelawe (13s.) ; p. 146 b, Midelton (4s. 8d.), Panfield (2s.), Gosfeld (16s.), Finchincfeld (17s.) ; p. 147 a, Beuchamp de Waus (8s.), Hengham Sibil (16s.), Bolemere (5s.), Stevynsted (1s. 6d.), Bumsted (3s.) ; p. 147 b, Maplederested Magna (4s. 8d.), Henye Mangna (2s.).
[8] R. H., i, p. 143 a, Widfer.   [9] p. 146 a.   [10] p. 147 a.
[11] p. 146 a, Parva Reynes.

the Hundred Rolls, but its special use for the customary payments for view-making, with which the sheriff, by Magna Carta, was enjoined to be content, may be compared with the expression *cert-money*, used in the fifteenth century as the technical term for the payments made for frankpledge.[1] Probably the Extracts refer to the same due in their statement that the same Walter ' solitus erat amerciare villam ad turnum suum extra communem finem '.[2] The same customary payment is mentioned in the rolls for other counties, for instance Gloucestershire and Kent ; but the term *certum* appears to be peculiar to Essex.

At the sheriff's tourn other extortions are made besides that of the *certum* ; extortions such as that of the fine for fair pleading[3] or the collection of arrears of the Twentieth,[4] which will have to be considered under the head of the sheriff's judicial or fiscal duties. It is at the tourn, again, that men are accused of reception of thieves or neglect of hue and cry, and forced to redeem themselves by fines or amercements.[5] Only a few charges are made in connexion with the sheriff's duty of supervising the police organization of the vill. Two men imprisoned for not raising the hue and cry are unjustly detained in prison till they buy their release of the sheriff with 16s. 8d.[6] A vill is fined for allowing a criminal to escape from ward, when the man in question had been given into the sheriff's own keeping and had escaped owing to his neglect.[7] Two men are fined by William of Crepping, the constable's clerk, on the false pretext that they were pledges for a certain Godwin Leverer until the delivery of Colchester gaol.[8] Richard le Brun commits the chattels of a prisoner to the custody of Robert Smith of Great Tolleshunt, and then amerces him 2s. for delivering them up in

---

[1] Hone, The Manor and Manorial Records, pp. 154 ff.   [2] p. 153 b.

[3] p. 139 b, Wyvenho : ' Vicecomes cepit ab eis ad quemlibet turnum xii*d*. pro pulchro placitando.'

[4] p. 147 b, Stebing : ' W. de E. cepit ad turnos suos pro visesyma dimidiam marcam.' Cf. p. 146 a, Lyston.

[5] p. 144 b, Lyndesel : ' W. de E. ubi tenebat turnum suum apud Dunmawe retinuit R. de B. et dicebat eo quod fuit receptator latronum . . . et finebat cum dicto vicecomite xxs. antequam potuit deliberari.' Cf. p. 136 b, Tolleshunte Creppinge ; p. 136 a, Danseie ; p. 144 a, Taxsted.

[6] p. 144 a, Taxsted.   [7] Ibid.   [8] p. 142 a, Brumleye.

spite of the fact that the bailiff's own letters had authorized
Robert to do so.[1]

The sheriff's extortions at his tourn are matched by the
extortions of the hundredors at the view of frankpledge.
John Barun, Robert de Belencumbre, Geoffrey de Merey,
Robert Derby, and Roger of Kelvedon take sums varying
from 2s. to 5s. beyond what is customary.[2] Walter of Tillingham unjustly fines the vills of Frinton and Great Holland
a mark on pretext of making default at the view of frankpledge.[3] John Barun fines a man unjustly ' quia non fecit
responsum ad voluntatem suam ad visum franci plegii '.[4]
Gilbert de la Dune amerces a man for being out of frankpledge, and at the same time amerces another man as his
capital pledge.[5] Robert de Belencumbre fines Peter de Alton
3s. for attempting to prevent Robert from holding the view
in Peter's house, contrary to right and custom.[6]

The apprehension and custody of felons indicted in the (b) Arrest
tourn or elsewhere formed a large part of the duty of the and custody of
sheriff and his subordinates, and the Hundred Rolls represent felons.
their offences in this connexion as manifold. They can be
grouped roughly in four classes : failure to arrest, the accusation and arrest of the innocent, the release of the guilty, and
the extortion of payment for replevin. It is not always easy
to determine from the bald outline of facts given by the
jurors whether the official is accused of accepting bribes for
the release of the guilty or with extorting bribes from the
innocent, but it is clear that most officials are charged alike
with exceeding and abusing their powers, and neglecting
their duties, in this connexion. Many of the proceedings
recorded doubtless passed at the tourn, but the place is not
as a rule stated, and the sheriffs and bailiffs in question were
not men to stand upon ceremony.

[1] p. 136 b, Toleshunte Tregos.
[2] p. 146 a, Brudon et Balidon : ' Iohannes Barun capit de eadem
villata ad visum franci plegii ultra certum ijs. iniuste per sex annos.'
p. 147 a, Gestinthorp : ' Galfridus de Merey et Robertus Derbi ceperunt
de eadem villata xs. ad visum franci plegii ubi non solebant dare nisi xl*d*.'
See also p. 146 b, Gelham Mangna, Gosfeld ; p. 147 b, Bumsted ; p. 146 a,
Mangna Salyng.   [3] p. 139 a. See also p. 138 b, Horindon.
[4] p. 146 a, Mangna Salyng.   [5] p. 136 b, Toleshunte Tregos.
[6] p. 147 a, Beucham de Waus.

(1) Failure to arrest.

De vicecomitibus capientibus munera ad concelandas felonias factas in ballivis suis vel qui negligentes extiterint ad felones huiusmodi attachiandos.

To this article there are some thirty-four returns, of which the following are typical. Richard le Brun takes one cow of two stolen by certain thieves, allowing them to keep the other.[1] William of Haningfeld takes 20s. from an indicted felon to let him go free.[2] Ralph la Wayte, clerk of the bailiff of Lexden, takes various small fees to conceal the felonies done in his bailiwick, presumably by falsifying the records.[3] Robert of Smalebregge, sub-bailiff of Lexden, extends his hospitality and his personal protection to a man indicated at the sheriff's tourn and generally of evil reputation in the country, eventually conniving at his escape on a stolen horse, ' sed nescitur quo pacto '.[4] The constable of Colchester takes a bribe of 20s. not to arrest another man indicted of theft at the tourn.[5] In Hinckford hundred we hear of men indicted over and over again at the sheriff's tourns, who are neither attached nor imprisoned, or, if arrested, are let free again.[6] The sheriff himself, Walter of Essex, is one of those implicated; he takes 40s. from one suspect,[7] but the bailiffs, Richard le Brun, John Barun, and Roger of Kelvedon are the chief offenders. In the hundred of West Uttlesford, John of Essex takes five marks from a woman, and two oxen, two bullocks, one cow, and three pigs from two men for concealing their felonies.[8] Walter of Essex even consents for half a mark not to arrest Gilbert of Foxerth, indicted of robbery before the justices in eyre,[9] and a horse worth 100s. is a sufficient bribe for him to release a man suspected of homicide.[10] Perhaps the most flagrant case is that of Thomas Lovel, who, having been indicted of homicide, flees the country. Walter of Essex confiscates his goods, extends them at 53s., and

---

[1] p. 136 b, Toleshunte Tregos.   [2] p. 137 b, Tundresle.   [3] p. 139 b.
[4] p. 140 b, Wythermundeforde.   [5] p. 141 b (=p. 164 a, Ex. R.).
[6] R. H., i, pp. 146–7. Note especially Stevynsted : ' E. clericus et G. Attewyche indictati sunt semper per patriam et nunquam capti et habent suspiccionem quod ballivi capiunt mercedem ad dimittendos eos esse in pace.'
[7] p. 146 a, Parva Reynes.
[8] p. 165 a [Ex. R.].   [9] p. 158 b, Hengford [Ex. R.].
[10] p. 156 a, Chafforde [Ex. R.].

then, on the return of the fugitive, sells them to him once more and allows him to go free ' sine aliqua occasione '.[1]

The fact that guilt and innocence are all one to Walter of Essex is well illustrated in an entry on the Extracts for East Uttlesford Hundred. Whilst Thomas Lovel goes free in the country for a fee of four marks to the sheriff, G. Skarie, who has been indicted and acquitted by the country has likewise to pay his fee of half a mark to go free.[2] But the officials are suspected of a worse offence yet, of causing approvers, prisoners who have turned king's evidence, to appeal the innocent and loyal for the sake of gain.[3] Thus W. of Haingden, probably an approver, accuses S. Voidin of being a thief when the men of the vill have declared him honest.[4] The worst story of this nature is one told of two sub-bailiffs of Lexden, who, meeting an unknown man upon the highway, accuse him of theft and order him to denounce his accomplices. On his refusal, with protestations of honesty, they attack him fiercely, bind him, beat him till he is senseless, and then extort 2s. from the neighbourhood of Warmingford to hire a prison for him in Colchester, in which he dies eight days later.[5] The clerk of the bailiff of Barstable attaches a certain clerk, who can get no peace till he pays down 6s.[6] One of the charges against Richard of Suthchirche is worth quoting as expressing forcibly the views of the countryside. ' Uncor dient ke le avant dit Richard de Sutcherche per le pouer de sa office demeyne fist prendre un mestre Auvre le Ku et le mist sur ke il out freit la pes le Rey ke unkes taunt ne trespasa encuntre la pes le Rey en tote sa vie cum le avant dit Richard fit en un jur, et ce fist il par heyne.'[7] Short of arrest, fines are inflicted on the innocent. Roger of Chaudeford, bailiff of Witham, is said to have extorted 40s. from Hugh le Goite by false accusation.[8] W. of Boliton, the seneschal of Robert Brus, takes linen cloth to the value of 20s. from a man accused by him of felony but declared honest by the whole countryside, and 10s. from another man

(2) Arrest of the innocent.

---

[1] p. 145 a, Stansted.   [2] p. 155 a.
[3] See Article 28 of the Inquest, and cf. Matt. Paris, Chron. Maj. V, pp. 577–80.
[4] p. 138 b, Horindon.   [5] p. 140 b, Wythermundeforde.
[6] p. 138 b, Barlinge.   [7] p. 149 b.   [8] p. 150 b.

as receiver of the felon.[1]   John Barun takes half a mark from a man on the pretext that he has been indicted, when he has not been indicted.[2]   Richard le Brun, meeting a shepherd with a flock of sheep, accuses him of having stolen some of them, imprisons him and keeps the sheep himself.[3]

More often we hear of arrest without formal pretext. Richard of Harlow, sheriff 1267–8, imprisons a man unjustly in Colchester Castle, exacting 60s. from him to be released.[4] Oliver, seneschal of Robert de Brus, keeps one man two days and another six days in prison unjustly.[5]   Richard le Brun arrests an innocent man of Dengie hundred, and ties his hands behind him and detains him as a thief till he makes fine with half a mark.[6]   Two of the Lexden sub-bailiffs arrest a certain law-abiding citizen called Stephen Smith at Aldham church, compel him to pay a fine of half a mark and to find pledges of half a mark, and plunder him of his axe, his girdle, and knives to the value of 8d.[7]   Richard of Suthcherche attaches Nicholas Engayne and takes 20 marks from him unjustly; 'propter quam causam eum attachiavit nesciunt nisi propter pecuniam suam habendam.'[8]   In the 'De Ministris' roll a general charge is brought against the bailiff of the Abbot of St. Osyth's of imprisoning some men maliciously and of accusing others and thus extorting money from them 'sicut plenius patet in inquisitione'.[9]   The above are typical instances of the charges brought against the sheriffs, the hundredors, and the seignorial officials of arresting and imprisoning 'loyal' men, women, foreigners, and priests on false charges or without cause shown, and releasing them on their own authority.[10]

(3) Release of the guilty.   *Qui habuerint felones imprisonatos et eos pro pecunia abire et a prisona evadere permiserunt liberos et impune.*

[1] p. 150 a, Macchinge.   [2] p. 147 b, Halsted.
[3] p. 141 b, Assildeham.   [4] p. 150 b.
[5] Ex. R. 4, m. 8, V. de Hatfeld Regis. See also under V. de Writel.
[6] p. 137 a, Parochia Sancti Laurentii.   [7] p. 139 b.
[8] p. 148 a, Chafford.   [9] Ex. R. 4, m. 8, H. de Chafforde.
[10] e.g. p. 143 b, Ginge Joyberd and Laundry : 'Roger de Reddelege emprisona un lel homme e une lele femme, E pus delivera la femme . . . par sa propre autorite . . . Jon Barun prist de Thomas le prestre de Botulvespiri ijs. et vid. e li mit sur ke il eut herberge le felun le Rey e ne ont pas.' See also p. 151 a, Jordanus filius Stephani.

The returns to this article charge the sheriffs and bailiffs at best with exceeding their authority, at worst with connivance at felony.   William of Haningfeld keeps a man indicted of homicide in prison for six weeks, and then releases him on his own authority without view of the hundred.[1]   Walter of Essex replevies a man from Colchester Castle on his own authority, in consideration of two marks, without waiting for the king's [2] writ.   In another instance he grants replevin for 40s., but refuses to show the writ.   He allows Richard Pot to go free for a fine of 20s., although guilty.[3]   He takes 20s. from W. de Afford, appealed of the murder of a man.[4]   Lesser officials take lesser fees for the same service.   Gilbert de la Dune takes from a woman the clothes she has stolen to let her go quit.[5]   The serjeants of Brentwood manor take various articles of clothing from one felon, and two bushels of barley from another, to release them ' propria auctoritate '.[6]   Roger of Chaudeford takes four cows from a man indicted of theft, and varying fees from men imprisoned for murder to release them.[7]   Stephen Bukerel takes the land of Martin of Chingford to release him from prison.[8]   The Extracts give a long list of the payments made to bailiffs and sub-bailiffs on this score.[9]

At the same time, men imprisoned for replevisable offences are forced to pay fees for replevin, contrary to law.   Walter of Essex and Richard of Suthchirche are both accused of taking sums, ranging from a mark to 100s., on this pretext.[10]

(4) Payment for replevin.

ii. *The Judicial Functions of the Shire Officials*

The extension of royal justice in the twelfth and thirteenth centuries brought about a shrinkage in the strictly judicial powers of the sheriff, but it may be doubted whether his

---

[1] p. 138 b, Horindon.
[2] p. 140 b, Lexden.
[3] p. 114 b, Dunmauwe Magna.
[4] p. 146 a, Bockynges.
[5] p. 158 a, H. Dunmauwe.
[6] p. 149 a, H. Chafford.
[7] p. 150 b, H. Witham.
[8] p. 165 b, H. Westodelesford (Ex. R.).
[9] e.g. p. 157 a, to Roger Prick 2s., two sheep worth 3s.; p. 162 b, to Jacobus de Camera 40s., 20s., 20s., 1 mark, 9s., half a mark. One man pays a mark to the bailiff, 2s. to the bailiff's clerk, and a lamb worth 6d. to the sub-bailiff, to get his release. Compare also the case noted below (p. 163) of the irregular release of a felon from sanctuary.
[10] p. 140 a, H. Lexden.

power to influence judicial proceedings had diminished in proportion, whilst his activities had undoubtedly been much increased by the development of the judicial writ and the inquest procedure. It is on these ancillary activities rather than on the holding of the county or hundred courts that the Hundred Rolls throw light. Two of the articles of 1274 are connected with the summoning of inquests, and the returns to the comprehensive article, ' qui potestate officii sui aliquos maliciose occasionaverunt ', reveal abuses of power in connexion with the execution of writs and judgements. With regard to the distribution of judicial work between the chief and his subordinates, it would appear from the cases cited below that whilst the sheriff takes judicial fines and amercements in person, or by his most powerful and responsible bailiffs or under-sheriffs,[1] the task of making up panels and taking distresses is as a rule delegated to officials of lower standing.

(a) Fraudulent exemption from jury-service.

De vicecomitibus et ballivis quibuscunque capientibus munera pro recognitoribus removendis de assisis et iuratis.

The evidence under this head is not so voluminous as that concerning the arrest and release of criminals. Only seven hundreds make returns to this article.[2] This may be due to the greater difficulty of getting at the facts ; the Chafford jurors say that the bailiff of Chafford took gifts of many to remove them from juries and assizes, but they know not how much, and the Tendring and Hinckford returns are similar.[3] The vills of Barstable hundred say that the bailiffs allow men to buy themselves off from assizes, and when Elias the bedel went to make up a panel of men he would take 3d. from one and 4d. from another to put less intelligent men in their place.[4] Eleven officials are charged with this offence in Tendring hundred.[5] The amounts taken from individuals

---

[1] e.g. Roger of Kelvedon, under-sheriff, John Baron, Robert de Belencumbre, Roger of Chaudeford—all prominent and powerful hundredors.

[2] Barstable, Hinckford, Chafford, Tendring, Lexden, Thurstable, Freshwell (Ex. R. 4).

[3] p. 156 b, H. Chaforde ; p. 164 a, H. Tendrynges [Ex. R.] ; p. 146 b, Hengford, Felsted.

[4] p. 137 b, Stanford ; p. 138 b, Ramestene Belhus.

[5] p. 141 b, Bures ad Montem.

vary from 3*d*. to 20*s*. In one case we are told that the bailiff
took 30*s*. in five years from six men that they might be
exempt from jury-service, and nevertheless put them on
assizes.[1] Again, Richard le Brun takes 12*d*. from William
Sumner that he may be exempt from a certain assize, and
then amerces him 2*s*. for not coming.[2]

The summoning of a jury without a royal writ seems
hinted at in the statement of the *De Ministris* roll : ' Oliverus
senescallus Roberti de Brus distringit homines de Hatfeld ad
iurandum sine precepto domini Regis contra libertatem
suam.' [3]

De vicecomitibus et aliis ballivis qui amerciaverint illos qui
summoniti fuerint ad inquisitiones factas per preceptum domini
Regis pro defalta cum per eandem summonitionem persone
venerunt sufficientes ad inquisitiones huiusmodi faciendas.

(b) The fining of jurors.

A few returns are made to this article. John Barun of
Hinckford and Roger of Chaudford of Witham hundreds have
been in the habit of summoning more men than were needed
to assizes and inquests, and fining men for not appearing,[4]
and the bailiffs of Rochford, West Uttlesford, and Hinckford
have also fined men unjustly for this reason.[5]

From the fact that no sheriff is accused of the offences
connected with summoning juries, we should naturally infer
that the sheriff as a rule delegated the duty of making up
panels to his subordinate officials.

A great many petty extortions on judicial pretexts are
alleged against the sheriffs and bailiffs. Some of these were
certainly inflicted at the tourn, but the county or the ordinary
hundred may have been the scene of others. The fine *pro*
pulchre placitando—*pro beu pleider*—declared illegal by the
Statute of Marlborough c. xi, is mentioned four times as being
habitually levied [6] at the sheriff's tourn. Possibly the fine
taken by Walter of Essex in Chelmsford hundred from R. de

(c) Unjust fines and amercements.

---

[1] p. 147 b, Beucham de Waus.
[2] 137 a, Parochia Sancti Laurentii.
[3] Ex. R. 4, m. 8, Hatfeld Regis.   [4] pp. 150 b, 151 a.
[5] p. 146 a, Foxherthe ; p. 162 a, Rocheford (Ex. R.) ; p. 163 a, Westho-
delesford (Ex. R.).
[6] p. 136 a, Parva Wodeham, Toleshunte Tregos ; p. 136 b, Toleshunte
Crepinge ; p. 139 a, Wyvenho.

Hayrkesden 'pur ceo ke il neis respundit au primer mot a turn de viscunte' is the same.[1] Again, men are fined for failure to attend the tourn when they owe no suit there,[2] and vills of the liberty of Rayleigh and the honour of Boulogne are forced to attend tourn and hundred in spite of their ancient privilege.[3] Amercements for failure to appear when cited are reported to the discredit of Richard le Brun,[4] but the nature of the injustice is not clear from the scanty report. A general charge of unreasonable fines and amercements is brought against Walter of Essex.[5] There are a few isolated instances of irregular fining. John Barun takes 30s. from a man for failing to appear to make his law.[6] Walter of Essex extorts two marks from a monk on account of a pretended excommunication.[7]

It was part of the sheriff's duty to levy the amercements imposed by the justices in eyre, and there are various instances of the abuses arising from the exercise of this function by himself and his underlings. Two sheriff's clerks, sent by Walter of Essex to execute the commands of Roger de Seyton, justice of the Essex eyre of 1272, to attach three men and bring them before the justices at Colchester, use the opportunity to extort from them meat, corn, wool, and money, and make no restitution after the three prisoners have fully paid the justices' amercement.[8] Two bailiffs of Hinckford hundred, sent to collect the amercement laid by the justices in eyre upon the vill of Stisted, take 60s. in place of the 40s. due.[9] The common amercement of the whole county, to which there are two references,[10] has probably been

---

[1] p. 143 a, Petite Watham. [2] p. 145 b, Chishell Parva.
[3] p. 137 b, Fobbinge, Westorenden ; p. 138 b, Parva Bemflet.
[4] p. 136 a, Toleshunte Tregos.
[5] p. 144 a, Ginge Joyberd and Laundry.
[6] Or possibly, for failing to appear on a certain law-day. The text runs as follows : ' Jon Barun prist de Jurdan le Graunt trente souz pur ceo ke il ne vint mie a une loi certeyn la ou il li aveit dit ke il aveit dit encuntre li ' (p. 143 b, Springfeud).
[7] p. 145 b, Depeden : ' W. de B. cepit monacum . . . et imposuit super eum quod fuit excommunicatus . . . et monacus fecit finem cum W. vicecomite pro ij marcis pro debarracione (?) sua.'
[8] Ex. R. 4, m. 8 (V. Colecestr'). [9] p. 159 a (Ex. R.).
[10] ' W. de E. cepit viijs. pro murdro et pro merciamento comitatus generalis ' (p. 145 a, Stansted. Cf. p. 146 a, Bockynges et Stisted).

imposed by the justices in eyre, and the same may be the case with the *murdrum* fine, which we are told has been irregularly exacted by William of Blumvile (sheriff 1269–70), by Walter of Essex (thrice), by Roger of Kelvedon, and by Robert of Belencumbre.[1] One charge brought against Roger de Chaude-ford is probably connected with the *murdrum* fine. A felon having taken sanctuary in Terling church, the bailiff takes 2s. from the vill, and, on his own authority and without warrant, empowers the felon to abjure the land, himself putting the cross into his hand.[2] Again, John Barun takes a mark ' ad opus suum ' from the vill of Halsted to be quit of an amercement of eight marks, but nevertheless does not acquit the vill.[3] On the other hand, Roger of Kelvedon takes 2s. from a man on the unjust pretext that he had been amerced before the justices.[4]

Of all the offences charged against the local officials, the forcible seizure of beasts is among the most common. Judicial distraint was undoubtedly the pretext in many cases, and it is probable that many of the ' outrageous takings ' which the Hundred Rolls report were made under the colour of execu-tion of the judgements of superior courts, or to initiate pro-ceedings in such courts. As a rule, however, the jurors are not concerned to defend the sheriff or bailiff who seized the goods or lands of their neighbours, and no pretext is given for the seizure. In a few cases it is clear that the seizure is an exercise or abuse of the royal right of prise ;[5] in a few cases we are told that the beasts were taken as a distress. More than a dozen instances of unjust distraint are alleged in the Essex returns. Thomas Sporun, bailiff of Dengie hundred, prolongs the distraint of a horse, of which the distrainee had sought delivery, and rides it himself till it is at the point of death, when he leaves it to die at the house of Sir Roger of Tilbury.[6] Two Barstable bailiffs distrain the

(d) Wrong-ful dis-traints.

---

[1] p. 138 b, Magna Beinflet ; p. 145 a, Parva Berdefeld, Stansted, Magna Samford ; p. 146 a, Pentelawe ; p. 147 b, Stebing ; p. 152 b, Bekentre (Ex. R.). The amounts taken *pro murdro* range from 1s. (Little Bardfield) to 44s. (Stebing).

[2] p. 150 b, H. Witham.

[3] p. 147 b.

[4] p. 146 a, Brudon et Balidon.

[5] See below, iii (*c*).

[6] p. 136 b, Parochia Sancti Laurentii.

cattle of William Cruste for arrears of rent, when no such arrears are owing, and extort 3s. from him to return the distress.[1] Two other bailiffs of the same hundred seize, the one a cow, the other two horses belonging to John Wimbis to compel from him the payment of 5s. which he had already paid twice, and to recover the beasts he is forced to pay seven more shillings.[2] W. Giffard takes a horse and uses it for carting hay for five days, on the false pretext that its owner was a pledge, and thus extorts 18d. for the recovery of the false distress, and half a mark as well from four pledges.[3] Roger de Redleges takes a mare worth 5s. for a *beau pleider* fine, and keeps it till it dies.[4] A constable of Colchester seizes and sells the beasts of a poor man on the pretext of his indictment, whereas he was not the person indicted.[5] John Barun seizes the cow and calf of a man lawfully indicted by the country, but keeps them for his own profit.[6] Richard le Brun takes a distress of four horses from Roger Garpevile 'unde perdidit agriculturam unius saisionis'.[7] The *De Ministris* roll brings a general charge against the officials of Lexden hundred. ' R. de Kelleveden dum fuit clericus vicecomitis, W. de Crepping dum fuit cum constabulo castrae Colecestriensis, et R. de Creting ballivus huius hundredi . . . per falsas occasiones et iniustas et graves districciones extorserunt . . . magnam summam pecunie', and makes the same accusation against the official of Rochford, Tendring, Hinckford, and West Uttlesford hundreds.[8]

Among the earliest legislative results of the inquests of 1274–5, it may be noted, were the new regulations as to distraint which form clause 13 of the statutes of the Exchequer of October 1275.[9] These begin with an allusion to the great damages sustained by the commonalty of the realm by wrongful taking of distresses by sheriffs and other the king's

---

[1] p. 138 a, Estorinndon.   [2] p. 138 a, Leindone.   [3] p. 138 a, Wulgefen.
[4] p. 143 a, Petite Watham.   Note also a distress *pro debito iudeysmy* ; p. 145 a, Dunmauw Magna.
[5] p. 139 a, Holande Parva.   [6] p. 147 a, Gestinthorp.
[7] p. 137 a, Parochia Sancti Laurentii.   Cf. below on the Statutes of the Exchequer.
[8] Ex. R. 4, m. 8, H. H. de Lexinden, Rocheford, Tendryng, Hengeford, Westodelesford.   [9] S. R., i, p. 197 b.

bailiffs, for the king's debts or for any other ones, and provide for the fair treatment of the beasts taken, prohibit their too speedy sale, safeguard the beasts ' that gain a man's land ' (as in the case of Roger Garpevile), and command that all distresses be reasonable and not outrageous. As we have seen, two of the new chapters of the eyre inquired as to the observance of these regulations.[1]

The new *capitulum* of 1279 was to inquire concerning (e) Main-those who bind themselves unjustly by mutual oaths to tenance. uphold the pleas or causes of their friends, by which means the truth of the matter cannot be found. This, like the Trailbaston inquiries[2] later, would seem to suggest a wide prevalence of the practice of maintenance, and it is the more remarkable that, in the long tale of the malicious exercise of official power, so few charges of this kind are reported. 'Willelmus Paxston sustinuit partem in hundredo Hugonis Textoris contra Willelmum Curt ita quod non potuit habere legem ita quod dictus Willelmus amisit v. solidos iniuste.'[3] From the two other references[4] to W. Paxston it is clear that he was an official, but his precise status cannot be determined, so that it remains doubtful whether he was holding the court as hundred bailiff, or whether he came in as a shire official to wrest the course of judgement in favour of his friend. Another case of the abuse of official power in the interests of a friend may be revealed by the charge brought against Walter of Essex of unjustly arresting W. Martel on the petition of Ralph of St. Osyth in connexion with a dispute between them over the making of a pond.[5]

iii. *The Fiscal Functions of the Shire Officials*

Almost every activity of the officials of the shire, it is becoming clear, tended to translate itself into terms of financial extortion. The *certum* paid at the tourn, the fines

[1] See above, Chap. I, p. 37. [2] See above, Chap. I, § 5, i.
[3] p. 147 a, Finchincfeld.
[4] p. 143 a (Chelmsford H.), p. 147 a (Hinckford H.).
[5] p. 141 b, Bures ad Montem.

and amercements levied directly or by means of distress
would alike form part of the monies for which the sheriff
accounted at the Exchequer.[1] On the other hand, there are
certain spheres of the sheriff's activity in which he is pre-
eminently the fiscal agent of the crown. In the collection of
the debts owing to the Exchequer, in the collection of fines
for encroachments or royal privileges, in the prise or purveyance of goods for royal use his functions are firstly and mainly
those of a collector of revenue. Moreover, though the
administration of feudal escheats and the collection of
extraordinary taxation might be assigned to special escheators
and *taxatores*,[2] the co-operation of the sheriff was essential to
their effective action. In collecting the twentieth of 1270,
which, as will be seen, bulks especially large in the Essex
returns, sheriffs and bailiffs, as well as ' collectors ' proper,
were concerned.

(*a*) The
King's
Debts.

Two of the articles of the inquest touch upon the king's
debts, but there are no returns to the inquiry whether officials
have been diverting to their own use money owing to the
king's creditors.[3] On the other hand, there are copious
returns to the article ' qui receperint debita Regis vel partem
debitorum et debitores illos non acquietaverint '. It will be
noted that the question does not refer especially to sheriffs
and bailiffs, as do the articles dealing with police and judicial
business. The evidence of the Sheriffs' Accounts, as of the
Hundred Rolls in general, goes to show that special collectors .
of the king's debts were appointed from time to time,[4] but
it is clear that the sheriffs and their ordinary officials also

---

[1] The Sheriffs' Accounts, preserved at the P. R. O., afford the best
illustrations of the relation between the sheriff's farm and his administrative activities. Many instances from this source are quoted in M. A. Hennings, The Local Administration of the Sheriff in the Thirteenth Century,
a thesis presented in 1916 for the degree of M.A. in the University of London,
which, though unpublished, is accessible at the University Library.

[2] See below, iii (*b*).

[3] See article 23 of the inquest.

[4] e.g. see references to *receptor debitorum d. R.*, R. H., i, p. 130 b (Yorks.) ;
to *receptor Vicecomitis*, R. H., ii, p. 107 a (Salop) (cf. Sheriffs' Accounts
22/2) ; to *collectores debitorum d. R.*, R. H., ii, p. 244 a (Wilts.) ; to
R. de Radenham ad debita D. R. levanda in com. Wyltescire assignatus,
R. H., ii, p. 256 a.

collected debts, and that their status was recognized by the Exchequer.[1]

The Essex returns show us some forty-eight officials concerned with the collection of the king's debts, all of whom we have met in other connexions. Three sheriffs are mentioned; a charge is brought against Ralph of Arden, sheriff 1254–6, of failing to acquit a debtor of 20s.; Matthew de la Mare, sheriff 1261–3, is charged with three similar offences; whilst, as usual, there is a long row of accusations against Walter of Essex. Mention is made also of two under-sheriffs, Roger of Kelvedon and William de la Mare; a sheriff's clerk and a sheriff's serjeant, twenty bailiffs of hundreds, one clerk of the hundred, nine sub-bailiffs or bailiffs' clerks, five seignorial bailiffs, and only seven officials of indeterminate status. Both the *Inquisitiones* and the Extracts are unusually precise in their references to the officials who have been defrauding the king's debtors.

The offences alleged against the collectors are fourfold. In the first place, they have taken payment from the king's debtors and given no receipt. Richard and Geoffrey le Sol, bailiffs of Dunmow, have carried off two quarters and a half, and three bushels of wheat from William de Boscho for the king's debt, and given him no quittance.[2] The bailiffs of the Prior of Canterbury take half a mark from W. Picot for the king's debt and give him no quittance.[3] Ypolitus, sub-bailiff of Dengie hundred, takes 40d. from Stephen Comyng for the king's debt and gives him no tally for it.[4] Walter of Essex takes £20 0s. 2d. from the men of Writtle, and keeps the tallies, so that they have no receipt to show.[5] These are typical examples from a long list of similar charges.

Secondly, the collectors have extorted from the king's debtors sums in excess of those owing to the king. Where only 40s. are due to the Exchequer for amercement, the

---

[1] Note mandate of 9 Ed. I to the sheriff of Salop and Staffordshire which recognizes the payment of royal debts to ' vicecomitibus aut eorum receptoribus seu ballivis ' (Sheriffs' Accounts 41/1, cited Hennings, p. 73).
[2] p. 144 b, Lyndesel.
[3] p. 146 a, Bockynges et Stisted. See also p. 159 b, Daneseye H. (Ex. R.).
[4] p. 159 b [Ex. R.].
[5] p. 143 a, Writel.

bailiffs of the archbishop of Canterbury have collected 60s.[1]
Most often a debt which has been already paid is re-exacted.
John Barun demands half a mark of William Stric, of which
he has already been acquitted, and William is forced to pay
17d. to John Barun, 4d. to his 'garsun', and 10d. to Gilbert
de la Dune on this score.[2] Geoffrey Turpeyl, again, extorts
44s. from Thorold Camerarius, when he has already fully
paid and been quit of the debt.[3] It is, of course, most unlikely
that any of these extra sums ever reached the Exchequer,
but this aspect of the matter does not as a rule interest the
jurors.   One return, however, asserts that Walter of Essex
took from the vill of Hatfield Regis six marks of the king's
debt, of which he kept 4s. for himself.[4]

Thirdly, the collectors have also extorted money, by distraint or by other means, from men who owed the king
nothing. Richard Doreward distrains John Reimund for 40d.
of the king's debt when he owes nothing, and gets 20d. from
him twice over.[5] Sometimes the nature of the pretext is
indicated. Robert of Horkesley is compelled by Roger of
Kelvedon to pay a mark for a scutage which the bishop of
Rochester ought to have paid.[6] William Picot has had a cow
distrained for half a mark claimed by the Exchequer which
William had already paid to the bailiffs of the Abbot of Westminster on whose fief he dwells.[7] Again, a poor man of
Tendring hundred is forced to contribute 2s. towards the
debt of Lexden hundred.[8] Here the bailiff of Lexden would
seem to be aggravating the offence of extortion by going
outside the district within which he had authority to collect
the king's debts. The vill of Little Waltham is forced to pay
first half a mark, then 4s., and then 3s. for the king's debt,
' et tut a tort ke il ne saverent le pur quey '.[9] A long series
of returns state simply that the collector ' imposuit super

---

[1] p. 141 b, Wythermundeford.
[2] p. 144 a, Ginge Joyberd and Laundry.
[3] p. 146 b, Finchincfeld.   [4] p. 154 a, V. Hatfeud (Ex. R.).
[5] p. 138 a, Estorinndon.   [6] p. 140 a, H. Lexeden.
[7] p. 161 b, Wythermundeford.
[8] p. 141 b, Mescinge. For debts incumbent upon a hundred as a whole,
see Pollock and Maitland, i, p. 611.
[9] p. 143 a, Petite Watham.

eum quod fuit in debito d. R. et non fuit '.[1] There are no
allusions to the fraudulent use of green wax in the exaction
of pretended Exchequer debts, a practice to which the
Hundred Rolls for some other counties refer.[2]

Fourthly, the collectors have taken money from men to
gain a respite from the enforcement of payment. This might
seem to be an injury rather to the king than to the countryside, and the returns are correspondingly scantier, but in
some cases at least it looks as if the official has extorted the
bribe ' pro respectu debiti domini Regis ' by threats. Walter
of Essex distrains William of Aumbly for the king's debts,
and takes two and a half marks from him for granting a
respite.[3] Payments of 6d., of 18d., of 2s., 4s., and other
unspecified sums are made to bailiffs and other officials for
respiting such debts.[4] In one case, however, the bailiff distrains
for the king's debt contrary to the royal mandate, by which
a respite had been granted till the time of the sheriff's
account.[5]

' Debita domini Regis ' is a comprehensive term which   (b) The
includes many different kinds of payments owing to the royal   Twentieth of 1270.
Exchequer. Judicial fines and amercements have been
considered elsewhere ; of fines for redisseisin or purprestures
or the concealment of treasure-trove, concerning which
article 21 of the inquest makes inquiry, the Essex returns
give no information. On the other hand, they are exceptionally full in the information they give with regard to the
Twentieth of 1270, an article on which, as we have seen,
formed part of the inquest, certainly, in Lincolnshire,
Northants, and Rutland, and very possibly in some other
counties,[6] and they throw a useful light on that somewhat
involved fiscal transaction.

The writs for the collection of the Twentieth are apparently
lost, and the precise procedure employed must remain con-
jectural. In the last collection of a similar tax for which the
procedure is recorded—the Thirtieth of 1237—four knights

---

[1] e.g. p. 146.   [2] e.g. R. H., i, p. 187 a (Herefordshire).
[3] p. 159 b (Ex. R.).   -
[4] p. 136 b, Parochia Sancti Laurentii ; p. 159 a, Hengeford H. (Ex. R.).
[5] p. 159 b (Ex. R.).   [6] See above, Chap. I, p. 33.

had been appointed in each county to receive the money assessed and collected by freemen of each vill.[1] In the next following collection, the Fifteenth of 1275, the special commissioners themselves collected the tax, at times chosen by themselves.[2] The part played by the sheriff was in each case subordinate. In 1237 he had to call the hundred court at which the assessment was made, and to assist in its collection if necessary. In 1275 he was to assist the commissioners in their collection. In 1270 also special commissioners were appointed, two or three for each county, whose names are to be found on the Pipe Roll for 1272-3.[3] These collectors paid the money over to special treasurers, who accounted for it to the Exchequer. In several cases sheriffs were appointed as collectors in their own counties,[4] but in Essex this was not so ; the names of the collectors are quite unfamiliar. The evidence of the Hundred Rolls is thus, at first sight, surprising. The sheriffs and the ordinary shire officials are represented in them as exacting payments *de vicesima* right and left all over the country. In Kent, where returns *de vicesima* are frequent, the names of the royal collectors, Fulk Peyforer and Henry de Malemeyns, are given,[5] but in the Essex rolls there is throughout no reference to W. de Grantcurt and W. de Ripariis, the collectors of the Twentieth for that shire. On the other hand, the returns for Essex mention *taxatores* and *collectores vicesime*. Under the special heading ' de inquisitionibus vicesime ', the expression recurs several times,[6] and under the vill of Little Holland reference is made to the *taxatores eiusdem ville*,[7] whilst the *taxatores* of Warmingford are mentioned as being despoiled by Roger of Kelvedon.[8] Roger of Kelvedon is accused also of taking half a mark for the Twentieth from two men of Birchanger,[9] and under Waltham hundred the name of one of the *collectores vicesime* is given—John Osegod.[10] From these allusions it

---

[1] Stubbs, Select Charters (8th ed.), p. 366.
[2] Rot. Parl., i, p. 224 ; C. R. C., p. 250 (24 October 1275).
[3] Pipe Roll 1 Ed. I, m. 6.
[4] e.g. in Cambridge, Leicestershire, Kent, Northumberland, Southants.
[5] R. H., i, p. 232 b (V. de Leysnes).
[6] p. 139 a.   [7] p. 139 a, Holande Parva.   [8] p. 140 a.
[9] p. 156 b, Birichang'.   [10] p. 150 a, Nasingg.

seems probable that the work of assessment, and, to some extent, of collection, was performed, as in 1237, by the local unit,[1] and that each vill or hundred had its own *taxatores*, who paid over the sums collected by them to the county collectors. It may be conjectured that the sheriff interpreted a command to assist in the collection [2] as giving himself and his subordinates the right to act as supervisors of the *taxatores ville*, or as intermediaries between them and the royal collectors. One phrase suggests even that the collectors were appointed by the sheriff's staff, but it is ambiguous and capable of another interpretation: ' R. (de Kelvedon) cepit de W. de Large xii*d.* quia imposuit super eum quod fuit collector visesyme et non fuit.' [3] However that may be, the ordinary officials of the county of Essex must have played a prominent part in the collection of the Twentieth.

As with the exaction of other royal debts, officials of all grades have a hand in the collection. Twenty-five names are mentioned in this connexion, the large majority of them being those of hundredors. Three of the servants of Walter of Essex, a constable and a bailiff of Colchester, and an escheator's clerk are also mentioned, and the only unfamiliar figure is that of Simon, the queen's chaplain.[4] Between them these officials extort sums varying from 3*s.* to 40*s.* from a great number of vills and a few persons. There are in all ninety-four references to the tax, and the total of the sums alleged by the jurors to have been taken ' ultra rectam vicesimam ' amounts to £50.[5] The typical entry is half

---

[1] This conjecture is strengthened by a passage in the Lincolnshire rolls (R. H., i, p. 249 a) : ' Dicunt quod Rogerus de Trehamton et socii sui sunt collectores vicesimi denarii de Wapentakio de Asewardthirn. Dicunt et quod homines de Helpringham et Thorp collegerunt inter se vij libros pro denario vicesimo de quibus solverunt v. libros v*s.* 1*d.* et q. et residuum remanet penes Iohannem prepositum de Helpringham, nec habent de solucione facta aliquam talliam.'

[2] The many mandates on the Patent Roll commending the taxers and collectors of the Twentieth not to intermeddle with the religious houses who have made a fine and received quittance from the king, are addressed to the sheriffs as well as the taxers. E.g. P. R. C., p. 467 (October 25, 1270), *et passim.*

[3] p. 147 a, Stevynsted.   [4] p. 138 a, Est Tilleberi.

[5] The symmetry of this total seems remarkable, but is probably no more than a coincidence ; no principle is traceable in the allocation of the various

a mark from the vill; some twenty vills are forced to pay this addition to the lawful tax. There is no great variety in the narration of the exactions; the following examples are characteristic: 'W. de Essex, vicecomes Essexie, cepit de predicta villa xviiij*s.* extra taxacionem vicesime domini Regis.'[1] 'Solvit ad opus vicesime dimidiam marcam ultra certam visesimam.'[2] 'Apres la certeyne paie de lur vintime vint le viscunte e prist de eus quatorse sous e pris cest apres nef souz e pus vj*s.* e quatre deners.'[3] 'Ubi solverunt plenarie visesymam postea venit W. de E. vicecomes et W. de Bradeleye et Digun clericus dicti vicecomitis et ceperunt iiij*s.* et iiij*d.* duobus hominibus iniuste pro visesyma.'[4] 'R. Derbi cepit de Rogero preposito de eadem villata xxvj*s.* pro visesyma ultra taxacionem primo factam.'[5]

The last entry, which has many parallels, suggests that the officials may have had more right behind them than the indignant jurors of the villages imagined; the Patent and Memoranda Rolls show the accounts for the Twentieth of 1270 dragging out over many years,[6] and it may be that the 'first taxation' was incomplete and based upon an unsound assessment. The Patent Rolls record the appointment of an inquisition into the defective collection of the Twentieth in Yorks, Northumberland, Cumberland, Westmoreland, and Lancashire in June 1271, with power to the respective sheriffs to levy the arrears from detainers of the same.[7] A similar inquisition was appointed for Kent, Surrey, and Sussex,[8] and William of Middleton with two others was appointed to collect

items of pence, shillings, half marks, and marks that go to make it up. The amount recorded for Essex on the Pipe Roll is £912 7*s.* 9½*d.* on the first payment and £14 1*s.* 4½*d.* on the second.

[1] p. 139 a, Alesford.   [2] p. 138 b, Dunton.
[3] p. 143 b, Brumfeud.   [4] p. 144 b, Chiken'.
[5] p. 147 a, Gestinthorp. There are also exactions for not paying on the right day (136 b, Tolleshunte Creppinge); for respiting the tax (p. 144 b, Royng Scte Margarete); and for Newport (p. 143 b) the unique entry occurs: *non solverunt visesymam.*
[6] First entry on Rot. Pat. February 27, 1270 (P. R. C., p. 477); last entry July 23, 1276 (P. R. C., p. 154). July 18, 1273 (C. R. C., p. 21), accounts of the Twentieth to be audited. November 6, 1273, W. de Middleton gives over the key of the chest 'de vicesima' to the Barons of the Exchequer (Mem. R. K. R. 48, m. 2 d).
[7] P. R. C., p. 543.
[8] November 7, 1271 (P. R. C., pp. 585–6).

arrears in Suffolk and Norfolk.[1] In Norfolk the sheriff was associated with him in this duty. A reference in the unprinted Extract Roll makes it highly probable that W. de Middleton's activities were extended to Essex also. ' W. de Essex, postquam idem Prior (de Merseye) finem fecerat cum Rege pro vicesima ipsum et villanos suos contingente extorsit ab homagio eiusdem prioris pro eadem vicesima xviij*s*. ix*d*. *ob* et de amerciamento coram W. de Middleton ij marcas.'[2] It is not impossible that some standard assessment of half a mark to the vill was imposed by some authority less arbitrary than the will of Walter of Essex and Roger of Kelvedon. As it stands, however, the evidence is incomplete.

Certain other phrases in relation to the Twentieth are of interest, though again difficult of interpretation. There are, in the first place, various references to the Tower. The vills of Thundersley, West Horndon, and Barons Gifford pay the due Twentieth *ad turrim*.[3] At Ginge Joyberd Landry, Walter of Essex takes one mark for the Twentieth and then another mark ' apres lur certeyne paie a la tur de Lundres '.[4] In other passages the phrase is ' solvit ad scaccarium d. R.',[5] and this would suggest that the Tower was the treasury where the sums collected for the Twentieth were deposited. On the other hand, the Pipe Roll describes the sums paid in for the Twentieth as being received at the New Temple [6] by the three treasurers, who render account of it to the Exchequer.

The other phrase that requires elucidation refers to Colchester. We have seen that two constables and a bailiff of Colchester play some part in the collection of the Twentieth, and there are several allusions suggesting some special due

---

[1] March 6, 1271 (P. R. C., p. 591) ; July 3, 1271 (P. R. C., p. 548).

[2] Ex. R. 4, m. 8 (H. de Wensetre). The Patent Roll under January 20, 1271, notifies the collectors and the Sheriff of Essex that the prior of Mersey has satisfied the king of the Twentieth, for himself and for his villeins, and commands them to make restitution, if they have taken anything on this account (P. R. C., p. 508). The amount of the fine was 5 marks (P. R. C., p. 539).

[3] p. 137 b, Bures, Westorindon, Tundresle.

[4] p. 143 b, Ginge Joyberd e Laundry.

[5] p. 144 a, Scolne, Rothing Alba, Roynch Plumne.

[6] ' Reddunt compotum de dccccxij*l*. vij*s*. ix*d*. et *ob* receptis ad novum templum Lond' de vicesima predicta in comitatu Essex per manus W. de G. et W. de R. collectoribus eiusdem vicesime in eodem comitatu.'

claimed by Colchester Castle in this connexion. 'W. de Essex cepit de eadem (villa) decem solidos *pro dispectu Colecestrie* ultra taxacionem vicesime ubi dicta villa omnino solverit ad scaccarium d. R.'[1] It may be that Colchester Castle, which was as a rule, as we have seen, in the sheriff's custody, and was in that of Walter of Essex from January 1271 to April 1272,[2] served as the sheriff's treasury for the funds of his office, and came to be associated in the shire with shrieval dues. If so, these passages would be the equivalent of the phrase 'ad opus Walteri de Essex', used of the extra taxation taken by the constable of Colchester from the village of Ardleigh.[3] The phrase *pro dispectu*, however, still remains obscure.[4]

(c) Prises.   The abuse of the royal right of prise by the king's bailiffs had been a subject of inquiry under the old chapters of the eyre ever since 1208.[5] A great many of the forcible seizures of beasts reported in the Hundred Rolls had probably this privilege as their pretext, but in comparatively few cases is this stated. When we are told, for instance, that Walter of Tillingham came by the sheriff's command and drove six bullocks and twelve sheep away from the priory of St. Valery's,[6] we cannot tell whether this is a distraint or a prise. In some cases, however, it is clearly stated that the seizure was *ad opus domini Regis*. Richard of Suthcherche's serjeant, for instance, drove off the two cows of Robert of Stanford and never gave a penny for them.[7] Walter of Tillingham took a horse and kept it till it had been redeemed with 22*s.*, and then returned it so worn out that it died next day, and took oxen and sheep 'for the king's use' and kept them till 16*s.* had been paid for their recovery.[8] Richard le Brun seized a quarter of oats in Maldon market for the king's use,

---

[1] p. 144 a, Scolne. See also p. 144 b, Bernaston Pless' (Dunmow H.) ; p. 145 b, Hamborden (Uttlesford H.) ; p. 147 b, Mapelderhested Mangna (Hinckford H.) ; Parochia Sancti Laurentii (Dengie H.).

[2] P. R. C., January 20, 1271, p. 509 ; April 1, 1272, p. 642.

[3] p. 139 a, Ardle.

[4] Note also p. 144 a : 'La Niwelonde dit ke il paerent a W. de E. vicunte caraunte deners pur le despit de Colecestre ou il ne vindrunt point.'

[5] See above, Chap. I, p. 20.   [6] p. 136 a, Bradewell.

[7] p. 136 a, Parva Wodeham.   [8] p. 137 a, Par. S. Laurentii.

and Bartholomew Hangdon took half a load of hay.[1] W. of
Bradeleye took an ox for the king's use and gave neither
penny nor tally for it nor showed warrant for the taking.[2]
W. of Essex received from W. of Blumvile thirteen quarters
of wheat taken for the king's use, and paid no more than 2s.
a quarter for them when the market price was 5s. a quarter,
and kept the sacks into the bargain.[3] Richard of Suthcherche
took much corn at Barling because the king was at Stratford,
and paid nothing for it.[4] An entry on the Memoranda Roll
for 1275 seems to refer to the same incident,[5] and shows that
this unjust prise probably belonged to the period of the war
with the disinherited, May 1267, when Henry III was with
his army for five weeks at Stratford.[6]

To the same period belongs the most picturesque series of
extortions recorded in the Essex returns. Richard of Suthcherche, in preparation for the siege of London, levied
requisitions on the vills of Chafford Hundred ; of oats and
wheat, of bacon, beef, cheese, and pease, ' pur sustenir le
ost au Rey ' ; of chickens to feed the wounded and tow and
eggs to make dressings for their wounds and linen for bandages,
of cord to make ropes for the catapults,[7] of picks and calthrops
and spades to lay low the walls of London, and finally of
cocks, forty and more, to whose feet he declared he would
tie fire, and send them flying into London to burn it down.[8]

---

[1] p. 138 a, Wulgefen ; cf. p. 143 a, Petite Watham ; p. 143 b, Ginge
Joyberd e Laundry.   [2] p. 158 a, Halliggebur'.
[3] p. 145 a, Alta Estern.   [4] p. 138 a, Barlinge.
[5] Mem. R. L. T. R. 48, m. 6 d (*Communia de termino Sancte Trinitatis*)
'Baronibus pro Magistro Thoma de Cantilupo Canonico Sancti Pauli London'.
'Cum Ricardus de Suchirche tempore quo fuit vicecomes domini
Henrici regis in comitatibus Essex et Hertford et tempore quo idem
H. rex fuit cum exercitu suo apud Stratford cepisset blada eiusdem
magistri Thome apud prebendam suam de Barling ad valentiam
xl*li*. iiij*s*. iiij*d*. et idem Ricardus prefato Thome inde adhuc satisfacere
differt asserendo quod blada illa ceperat ad opus eiusdem Henrici Regis
et quod ipse non tenetur eidem Thome inde respondere ; Rex volens
quod hinc inde fiat quod iustum fuerit in hac parte mandat Baronibus
quod vocato coram eis predicto Ricardo et audita querimonia predicti
Magistri Thome in negotio predicto in premissis fieri faciant quod de
iure,' etc.
[6] Wykes (Annales Monastici, R. S., vol. iv), p. 202 (May 10–June 15).
[7] Or crossbows ?
[8] p. 149 a : ' Presente est par les jures des viles du hundred de Chafford
ke Sire Richard de Sutcherche, qant il fut viccunte de Essexe, ke il prist

For these prises Richard claimed an allowance of 200 marks at the Exchequer, but never paid a penny to those from whom the goods were taken.[1] Besides this wholesale commandeering of the goods of the hundred, fifteen cases of unjust prises are recorded in all, the offenders being most of them sheriffs, but also several of the more notorious bailiffs of hundreds.

(d) Customary dues and casual revenues.

As steward of various miscellaneous fiscal rights of the crown, customary and casual, the sheriff had opportunities of petty extortions, and there are a few such instances noted in the Essex Rolls. There are two references to *ward penny*; Peter Bude exacted 12*d.* unjustly on this pretext from a man who never had a horse, and should therefore have been exempt,[2] and William of Haningfield claimed 2*d.* of ward penny from a fief that had never paid it, and eventually took 1*s.* 6*d.* and a load and a half of oats.[3] There is also one reference to the taking of pannage; but as there is very little information about the official inculpated, it is uncertain whether the wrong was done in the king's name or by a seignorial official.[4] There is an allusion to a customary payment of bread, wine, and ale, exploited by the bailiffs of Barstable hundred and the Honour of Rayleigh for the extortion of arbitrary amercements.[5] There is an instance of an abuse of the king's right to 'royal fish'; the bailiffs of Colchester

en la vile de Wokindon la Rokele viij cocs, et dit ke il freit lier fu as pes de cocs e puis le freit voler en Lundres pur arder la vile, et gelines a grant partie, et dit ke les malades del host les mangereient ; et uoif fit il prendre en checune vile quatre cent et plus a fere entretes a gent nafres, et lyn et estupes a fere entretes et plastres a plaies as tut le fil ke ly et sa gent poeynt trover, en eglise ou de hors ; si le fist il prendre et dist ke il en freit fere cordes as arbalestes a en sailer la vile de Lundres, et de checune vile fist il prendre v picoises, et autant de trubles, e autant de besches, et si lur dist ke hom en batereit les murs de Lundres, et sachet ke il ne espervia en mustier ne de hors ke il ne prist qant ke il poeit prendre, ce est a saver, frument, et aveine, et grut, et brays, et qant ke il pout trover, et bacun et char, et dist a tut le pais ke il le prist al hus le Rey et pur sustenir le ost au Rey. Ce maus . . . fist il el tens ke il fust vicecunte de Essexe, ce est a saver ke qant il prist de choses avaunt dites si fist il carier a sa mesun a Sutcherche.' See also the entries on T. de la Neulaunde (p. 148 a) ; ecclesia de Opministre (p. 148 b) ; and see Engl. Hist. Rev., January 1916, The Legend of the Incendiary Birds, p. 98.

[1] p. 149 b.   [2] p. 146 b, Gelham Mangna et Parva.
[3] p. 137 b, Westorendon.
[4] p. 138 a, Dunham. H. de Ginges takes the swine of T. de Chauceus for pannage and kills three of them.   [5] p. 138 b, Horindon.

seized and carried off a great fish, worth 22s., which had been caught by the fishers of East Donyland, although it was not a whale.[1]

The forfeitures to the crown of the property of felons may be included here under the head of casual revenues. There are not many instances of abuses arising under this head. W. of Frowyk claims as felon's goods the beasts of Robert de Cruce, alleging them to be the property of Robert's mother, who had drowned herself in the sea.[2] The seizure and sale of the goods of Robert of Mortimer described by the jurors of Amperden may have been an instance of the confiscation of felon's goods; the facts given leave it an open question whether a distraint, an escheat, or a forfeiture is being described. The grievance of the villagers, however, is interesting; they complain that the beasts were not sold on the spot, but taken to Chelmsford, although they were ready to pay the full price for them. They seem to be claiming the first refusal of the beasts as their customary right.[3]

From the legal point of view, the revenues due to the crown in its feudal capacity should be sharply distinguished from those coming from other sources. In administrative practice, it is possible that the heading 'the king's debts' covers some feudal as well as national obligations. So far, however, as the feudal rights of the crown in the shire are distinguishable, their fiscal aspect will be considered in the following section, where the returns to the articles dealing with the offences of escheators are analysed.

As we have seen, the relations of the escheator to the sheriff are ambiguous, and the organization of the escheator's office was at this date in a state of transition. When the inquest of 1274-5 was being taken, there was still, as there had been through the greater part of the reign of Henry III, only one escheator for all England south of the Trent. The sheriffs were subordinate to his authority, and the county escheators and sub-escheators were dependent upon him and independent of the sheriff, in theory, at any rate. In practice

(e) Escheats: the offences of escheators and sub-escheators.

---

[1] p. 139 a, Estdonilonde.   [2] p. 141 b, Bures ad Montem.
[3] p. 145 b, Hamborden.

the sub-escheators would find the sheriff's co-operation indispensable, if only-for the summoning of inquests,[1] and their relations with the sheriff were probably intimate.

Nine of the articles of the inquest deal with the misconduct of escheators, but the returns to these are slight as compared with those concerning the misdeeds of sheriffs and bailiffs of hundreds. The Extract Rolls supply more information than the *Inquisitiones*. There are twenty entries with regard to the waste of manors seized into the king's hands. Robert of Pereres and Thomas de Cleye, sub-escheators, have sold oaks to the value of £15 and underwood worth £6 8s. in Stansted Park, and taken a large number of deer, goats,[2] and coneys. Roger de Fering and Ralph de Poley take herbage and tallage, fowls and other profits for the manors of Thurrock Gray and Aveley.[3] Roger of Fering, again, destroys the stew of P. Perdyz in Estwode.[4] From Reynham manor Geoffrey de Mores took profits of the court and of the mill, lambs, peacocks, capons, fowls, and cheese, and made waste in the warren to the extent of 100s.[5] Besides this wrong done to the king's interests, the returns report injustices to the tenants of the manors during the time of escheat—the holding of the court of Aveley manor twice on one day so as to extort a mark from the free tenants and villeins,[6] the extortion of five marks for the grinding of corn,[7] the confiscation of a plough team.[8] Finally, Robert of Pereres extorts two marks from Joyce de Munfichet in return for his good offices in securing her her dowry.[9]

There are twelve cases reported of the seizure of lands which ought not to have been taken into the king's hands at all. Roger of Fering seized the lands of W. Fitz-Henry of Halsted which were not of the king's fee, and would not relinquish them till he had received half a mark.[10] Other sub-escheators go to the houses of the newly dead, and seal

---

[1] v. P. R. C., p. 306, December 8, 1268. [2] p. 145 a, Stansted.
[3] p. 156 b, H. Chafforde (Ex. R.).
[4] p. 162 b, H. Rocheford (Ex. R.).
[5] p. 156 b, H. Chafforde (Ex. R.). [6] p. 148 b, H. Chafforde.
[7] p. 156 b, H. Chafforde (Ex. R.).
[8] p. 157 a, H. Wensetre (Ex. R.).
[9] p. 164 a, Tendrynge H. (Ex. R.). [10] p. 147 b, Halsted.

up the doors of the barns till a fee is paid for them to be opened.[1]

The claimant of the lands of Ralph of Foxcot induces Roger of Fering to seize them, as though they had been of the king's fee, and to hand them over to him.[2]

There are three instances of escheators taking fees wrongfully for the exercise of their office.[3] No returns are made to the article which inquires concerning the making of fraudulent extents of lands or the tampering with inquisitions *de aetate heredum* or the appropriation of wardships or marriages to the escheator's own use. There is one case reported, in answer to article 35, of the unlicensed marriage of an heir, owing presumably to the escheator's connivance.[4]

It has already been pointed out that the legislation on distraints in the statutes of the Exchequer refers to the sheriffs' and bailiffs' abuse of their power. It seems probable that the changes in the organization of the escheator's office also owe something to the facts brought to light by the inquest of 1274–5. The remedy provided was to make the sheriffs, in most of the counties of England, escheators in their own shires, to account for the wards and escheats therein to the Exchequer, when they accounted for their counties.[5] Three stewards were appointed for the whole realm to supervise the sheriffs' control of escheats and to keep the king's demesnes throughout the land. It was probably felt that the Exchequer's control of the sheriff was the most effective weapon for safeguarding the king's demesne rights in the county, but to those who have studied the Essex returns it seems dubious whether either the king or his subjects would gain much by the substitution of a Walter of Essex for a Roger de Fering.

iv. *The Administrative Functions of the Shire Officials*

In considering the general administrative functions of the officials of the shire, their relations both to the king and to

---

[1] p. 154 b, Berdestaple H. (Ex. R.). Cf. p. 143 a, Wydeford.
[2] p. 157 a, H. Wensetre.
[3] p. 162 b, H. Rocheford (Ex. R.) : ' De eschaetoribus . . . capientibus munera.'
[4] p. 162 b, H. Rocheford : ' De hiis qui prece, pretio vel favore. . . .'
[5] S. R., i, p. 197 a.

each other have to be considered. The choice of subordinates by the sheriff not only affects the well-being of the whole county, but also brings credit or discredit upon the king's service. The loyalty or disloyalty of the sheriff and his officials is reflected in their execution of royal mandates, their stewardship of castles, which have a military as well as a fiscal importance, and their use or abuse of official power.

(a) Appointment of Hundredors.

De vicecomitibus qui tradiderint ballivis extorsoribus populum gravantibus supra modum hundreda . . . ad altas firmas ut sic suas firmas levarent.

The information already exhibited prepares us for the summary statement of the *De Ministris* Roll, repeated in hundred after hundred, that the bailiffs of the hundred ' per falsas occasiones et gravas et iniustas districciones extor-serunt a quampluribus de patria maximam summam pecunie et alia dampna eis intulerunt, sicut particulatim patet in inquisitione '. The *Inquisitiones* and the printed Extracts give the figures, in many cases, of the amount by which the farms of hundreds have been raised by the extortionate bailiffs. These may be best set forth in tabular form.[1]

Besides these specific charges, Richard of Suthcherche (1265–7), Richard of Harlow (1267–8), and John of Kaumvil (1268–9) are accused of having appointed extortionate and oppressive bailiffs who sorely grieve the people.[2] The reason for these appointments lay in the fact that the farms of the hundreds went to make up the sheriff's farm. An entry for Hinckford hundred makes this clear. ' I. Barun insultavit hundredum de Hengford ad viginti libros plusquam solebant dare, ad dampnum populi, & dictus W. vicecomes Essexie cepit predictam pacationem de predicto Iohanne.' [3] When the sheriffs appointed men to hold the hundreds who, contrary to the Statute of Marlborough, raised the farm of the hundred, they were saving themselves trouble in developing the personal profits of their office.

The sheriffs appear to have had their bailiffs well in hand generally, but there is one isolated case of what appears to

---

[1] See opposite page.   [2] p. 165 a.   [3] p. 148 a, H. Hengford.

RISE IN FARMS OF HUNDREDS OF ESSEX

Name of Bailiff.	By whom Appointed.	Name of Hundred.	Old Farm.	New Farm.	Increase.	Page Reference.
Robert de Smalebrege	Ralph Gernun	Lexden	10 M.	24 M.	14 M.	139 b.
Richard de Cretinge	?	„	„	26 M.	16 M.	„
(1) John de Essex	?	Hinckford	£16 to £20	£42	£22 to £26	159 a [Ex. R.]
(2) Nicholas de Eyvil	?	„	„	„	„	„
(3) Robert de La Launde	?	„	„	„	„	„
(4) Elias de Polheye	?	„	„	„	„	„
(5) John Barun	?	„	„	„	„	„
(6) Robert de Belencumbre	?	„	„	„	„	„
(7) John Barun* (nunc)	Walter of Essex (1270–4)	„	„	£32	20 M.	148 a, 159 a [Ex. R.].
Henry de Codinton *	R. of Suthcherche (1265–7)	Chafford }	100s.	200s.	100s.	148 a.
	?	Witham	„ M.	20 M.	166s. 8d.	148 b.
Roger de Chaudeford *	W. of Essex	Chelmsford	10 M.	20 M.	10 M.	150 b.
William de Haningefeld *	„	„	?	?	£8	153 b [Ex. R.]
John Barun	T. of Sandwich (1274–5)	„	?	?	£6	153 b [Ex. R.]
Richard le Brun	„	„	?	?	£7	153 b [Ex. R.]

Those marked * were holding office in Michaelmas 1272 (A. R. 238, m. 50).

be an attempt of the bailiff to defraud the sheriff. ' Ballivi
retinent viijd. de feodo Avicie de Hedingham ubi deberent
solvere vicecomiti ad turnum suum.' [1] But for the most part
there is no sign of any cleavage of interests between sheriff
and bailiff. The following passage gives an illuminating
instance of official *esprit de corps :* ' W. de Essex cepit de
G. de Impinhull x.s. viijd. quia nescivit dicere quis verbera-
verit I. Barun.' [2] There is some satisfaction in knowing
that a bailiff occasionally got his deserts at the hands of the
men of the hundred.[3] The eyre roll of 1272 also shows that
some of these bailiffs had not escaped the hand of authority
before 1274. In Dengie hundred, Gilbert de la Dune and
Walter of Tillingham had been amerced ' pro pluribus transgressionibus' before the justices,[4] and W. de la Mare had
been sent to gaol for refusing to arrest an indicted felon.[5]
But these are the exceptions ; for the most part the bailiffs
appear to escape with whole skins.

(b) Execu-
tion of
writs.
*Qui . . . non sustinuerunt execucionem mandatorum domini
Regis . . . vel aliquo modo ea fieri impedierint.*

Under this general heading a few sweeping charges are
brought against the royal and seignorial officials in Essex ;
' omnes ballivi quotquot fuerunt minus executi fuerunt
mandata domini Regis quam facere debuerant.' [6] The bailiffs
of the Earl of Cornwall are accused of resisting the king's
escheator in the exercise of his office.[7] More definite charges
are also made with regard to the execution of writs, in the
return to this article and to Article 26: ' Si non fecerint
summonitiones secundum formam brevis domini Regis . . .
sed minus sufficienter executi fuerint precepta regia, prece,
pretio vel favore.' Two of the seneschals of R. de Brus are
charged with ignoring royal writs, the one for restoring
a distress, the other for authorizing an attorney.[8] The
bailiffs of Mary of Symmingham refuse to execute a writ

[1] p. 147 b, Halsted. [2] p. 147 b, Mapelderested Mangna.
[3] Cf. A. R. 238, m. 43, Hundredum de Aungre. Nicholas de Fyfhide,
distraining for debts, is beaten.
[4] A. R. 238, m. 41 d. [5] *Idem,* m. 46.
[6] p. 148 a, H. Chafford.
[7] p. 155 b, H. Lexinden (Ex. R.).
[8] p. 142 b, Writel ; cf. also p. 161 a, Wrytel (Ex. R.).

de aetate probanda.[1]   The bailiff of Rochford hundred takes a bribe not to execute the king's writ according to due form.[2] The serjeant of Newport detains a distress, contrary to the king's mandate.[3]   Richard of Harlow refuses to execute a writ of the king's delivered to him by Richard de Mora, even though he has taken half a mark to do so.[4]   John of Belsted, the constable of Ongar Castle, continues to take toll from the king's tenants in Havering in defiance of a mandate from the king.[5]   Walter of Essex refuses to execute a writ for taking a feudal aid on behalf of Peter de Marnill until Peter has paid half a mark, and John Baron extorts 4s. for himself for the same business.[6]   Henry of Codinton and Nicholas of Staunton go beyond the king's writ in summoning an excessive number of recognitors.[7]   W. de la Mare refuses to execute a writ against John of Staunton in consideration of a mark given to him by John.[8]   Nicholas Trereger and Hugh of Crepping carry about a prisoner from prison to prison and from shire to shire for six months in order to evade the execution of the king's writ for his delivery.[9]

Articles 30 and 31 of the inquest inquire into the conduct (c) Custody of public works by those who have charge of the king's castles of castles. or manors—whether they have abused this position of trust to put money in their own pockets by claiming a larger allowance than they spend, or have diverted to their own use material procured for such works.   There are only three returns to these articles in the Essex Rolls.   The king's carpenter superintending the felling of trees in Kingswood for Dover Castle made a present of two valuable pieces of timber to Roger of Kelvedon and Roger of Gasebek.[10]   The Abbot of St. John's removed a log belonging to the king from the same wood and took it to his abbey;[11] and the marshal, Robert of Sproteshale, also appropriated a piece of

[1] p. 162 b, H. Rocheford (Ex. R.).
[2] p. 162 b, H. Rocheford (Ex. R.).
[3] p. 164 b, H. Westodelesford (Ex. R.).   [4] p. 142 a, Writel.
[5] p. 152 b, H. Bekentre (Ex. R.).
[6] p. 158 b, H. Hengeford (Ex. R.).
[7] p. 156 b, H. Chafford (Ex. R.).
[8] p. 164 a, H. Tendrynges (Ex. R.).
[9] p. 157 a, H. Wensetre (Ex. R.).
[10] p. 163 a, Colecestr' (Ex. E.).   [11] *Idem.*

timber, in spite of the resistance of the bailiffs. There is no reference to the keeping of Colchester Castle, in which Edward might be expected to take a special interest, since it had been granted to his keeping for five years, and committed by him to Walter of Essex in 1271,[1] after the death of William de Charles, his steward, and sheriff of Essex for a few months.

(d) Exaction of fees for the exercise of official functions.

Qui dona vel lucra aliqua receperint pro officiis suis exercendis vel non exercendis vel exequendis.

The sheriffs and bailiffs are charged with exacting fees for taking distresses[2] and executing writs,[3] and, in general terms, for exercising their office.[4] On the other hand, as has been seen above in connexion with their police and judicial duties, they are very ready to take bribes for the evasion of such duties—for delaying to arrest criminals,[5] for releasing men from attendance at an assize,[6] and for other such relaxations of office.

The extortion of money for the performance of official duties was an offence as inevitable among unsalaried officials as the raising of the farms of hundreds. The returns of 1274–5 give examples alike of the exaction of unwarrantable fees and of the acceptance of bribes for the pretermission of official duties. There are a series of presentments against coroners, similar to those evoked later by ' Kirkby's Quest '.[7] Henry of Codham has refused to hold an inquest over a boy drowned at Blunteshal till a fee of 6s. has been paid, and has extorted a gold ring from Agnes of Tolleshunt before consenting to come and view her dead son.[8] Similar charges are brought against the coroners Thomas of Rammesden and Adam of Graveshal of taking fees ranging from 4s. to 8s.[9] Richard le Brun and Walter of Tillingham extort money from vills for compelling the coroners to come and view persons dead by misadventure.[10]

[1] P. R. C., p. 509.   [2] p. 138 a, West Tilleberi.
[3] p. 147 b, Halsted, 157 a H. Wensetre (Ex. R.).
[4] p. 162 b, H. Rocheford (Ex. R.).
[5] p. 137 a, Par. Scti. Laurentii.   [6] *Idem.*
[7] See A. R. 194.   [8] p. 150 b, H. Witham.
[9] p. 152 b, H. Bekentre (Ex. R.) ; p. 164 a, H. Tendrynges (Ex. R.).
[10] p. 160 a, H. Daneseye (Ex. R.) ; p. 164 a, H. Tendrynges (Ex. R.).

Qui potestate officii sui aliquos maliciose occasionaverunt et (e) Mali-
per hoc extorserint terras, redditus aut alias prestaciones. cious exercise of
The unprinted Extracts ' De Ministris ' group under this official
power.
article returns which cover a wide range of activity.   An
attempt has been made to discover, as far as possible, the
grounds on which these extortions were made, and to discuss
each class of exaction in connexion with the corresponding
functions of the sheriff.   There remain, however, a great
number of cases for which no justification, even nominal, is
suggested ; cases that can only be classified according to the
nature of the wrong suffered by the injured party.   The
most circumstantial narrative of this order is given by
Petronilla de Assildeham in her *querela* against Richard le
Brun[1] and Richard le Bel.   ' Petronilla de Assildeham
queritur de Ricardo le Brun et Ricardo le Bel de Haniggefeld
quod idem cum sequela venerunt ad domum predicte P. in
villa de Assildeham de nocte super quadam die Lune post
festam Sancti Martini iij annis elapsis vivente marito dicte
P., intraverunt domum, et dixerunt, " Rustice, ubi sunt
denarii tui ?   Trade nobis vel morieris." Et dixerunt, " Non
habemus denarios."   Tunc ipsi verberaverunt ipsos P. et
maritum et ligaverunt cum cordis ad sanguinis effusionem,
et ipsos depredaverunt

> de j panno xj ulnarum russetti, pretii ulne xd.
> ,, j tunica pretii iij*s*.
> ,, iiij libris lane pretii iiij*s*.
> ,, j tapeto   ,,   ij*s*.
> ,, iij linthiaminibus pretii cuiuslibet viij*d*.
> ,, uno quarterio et dimidio mixtuli.
> ,, vj bussellis pisarum.
> ,, uno quarterio et dimidio avene.
> ,, j porco iacente in sale pretii iiij*s*.
> ,, iij carcoisis multonum   ,,   ij*s*. et vj*d*.
> ,, sepe multonis   ,,   xij*d*.
> ,, caseo   ,,   viij*s*.
> ,, butiro   ,,   xxij*s*.

---

[1] Bailiff of Dengie Hundred, Michaelmas 1272. The date of the offence
is Martinmas 1271.

de j lagena de seima	pretii	xij*d*.
„ v pellibus agnorum courettis	„	ij*s*. et vj*d*.
„ ij capuciis de brunetto novo	„	xij*d*.
„ j lana cerica	„	xij*d*.
„ cera	„	xij*d*.

et de aliis rebus minutis, summa totalis iiij libri, et ea bona asportaverunt et demiserunt ipsos ligatos donec liberati fuerunt per vicinos.'[1] In this narrative the bailiff of the hundred combines housebreaking, extortion of property and personal violence. Other instances may be quoted of all these types of ' malice '. Five other charges of housebreaking are made : W. of Haningfeld entered the house of W. Maunsde, and forcibly excluded him until he had paid a mark.[2] William of Creppinge with other bailiffs went to the house of Stephen Crawe, broke the doors down, broke open a chest in his room, and carried off five shillings in silver.[3] The seneschal of Robert de Brus drove Alexander le Tenturel out of his house and felled trees across the door so that both entry and exit were impossible.[4] A similar charge is brought against Richard Cok, another bailiff of R. de Brus,[5] and Roger of Chaudeford is charged with breaking open a chest in the house of Richard de Redlege and taking thence a book and other chattels, Richard himself being in prison.[6]

The extortion of money and of movable goods is the commonest of the malicious offences charged against the county officials. Some forty-seven charges of taking money unjustly, with no pretext assigned, are made in the inquisitions and the extracts. They range in amount from the 2*d*. which Hugh Mory, sub-bailiff of Hinckford, extorted from Matilda the widow of Henry Miller,[7] to the 15*s*. 6*d*. which Sir Alwulf Senn has to pay to Richard le Brun.[8] The following entries are typical : ' H. de Lawefare ballivus extorsit

---

[1] p. 137 a, Parochia Sancti Laurentii. See also p. 142 b, Assildeham, where the husband of Petronilla is called Reginald le Bat, and the pretext of the bailiffs is given—arrest for a murder of which the country had acquitted the couple.

[2] p. 138 b, Barlinge.   [3] p. 141 a, Bures ad Montem.

[4] p. 142 b, Writel (cf. Ex. R. 4, m. 8 (V. de Writel).

[5] p. 142 b, Writel.   [6] p. 150 b, H. Witham.

[7] p. 147 a, Gelham Mangna et Parva.   [8] p. 136 a, Danseie.

de A. de M. dimidiam marcam per potestatem officii sui.'[1]
' R. le Brun cepit iniuste Avicia Sawall iiij*s*., Ricardo Fullo
vj*d*., a Isabella relicta prepositi de Tollesbiri xvj*d*., a Serlone
le Wole xvj*d*., a Galfrido Anketin ij*s*., de Willelmo le Follur[2]
xij*s*.' There are thirty-seven charges of the seizure of beasts
or other movable property with no alleged cause.   Cows,
sheep, wheat, oats, carts, and horses are all taken from
victims as lowly as the nameless poor woman whose cow was
taken by Hugh Mory, ' e ne sont pur quel achesun ',[3] to
those as lofty as the Abbot of Westminster, from whom
Richard of Suthcherche took eleven loads of wheat and six
of oats.[4] . . . William of Thorp took a horse from the vicar of
Little Hoyland and rode it, keeping it for a whole quarter
at the charges of the countryside.[5]   Sixty-nine sheep were
taken from Alice Cainturel and detained for a year or
more.[6]   Only two instances are given of the seizure of lands.
' R. Pricke, ballivus de Wensetre, per protestatem officii sui extorsit a Simone Preston iij acras terre cum prato in Leyre de qua
terra idem R. refeoffavit ipsum Simonem et cepit ab eo xl*s*.'[7]

A few cases of personal violence are recorded.   A number
of officials of Uttlesford hundred attack John Blunt, beat
him, wound him, rob him of a purse and a silver seal, and
take him to prison at Chesterford.[8]   Two of the Chelmsford
bailiffs bind and ill-treat a woman and take 40*s*. from her.[9]
Henry of Ginges seizes a man with his corn, and forces him
to ransom himself with 10*s*.[10]

In all these cases of extortion, heavy as the cumulative
evidence against the officials appears to be, the inadequacy
of the information given by the juries is liable to mislead us.
A story that looks, in the Extracts, like a case of barefaced

---

[1] p. 142 b, Writel.   [2] p. 136 b, Tolleshunte Creppinge.
[3] p. 144 a, La Niwelonde.   [4] p. 138 b, Magna Bemflet.
[5] p. 141 b, under the article *De vicecomitibus capientibus munera*. . . .
There are other indications that the countryside had to contribute towards
the expenses of the bailiffs' horses. Protests are made against the increase
in the number of the mounted officials (*ballivi et cacherelli equites*) in
Norfolk, in the unprinted Ex. R. 4, m. 3 (H. de Fourhowe), and in Notts.,
R. H., ii, p. 307 a (Wapentake de Bersetlawe).
[6] p. 137 a, Parochia Sancti Laurentii.
[7] Ex. R. 4, m. 8 (H. de Wensetre).   [8] *Idem*, H. de Esthodelesford.
[9] p. 143 b, Ginge Joyberd e Laundry.   [10] p. 138 a, Dunham.

highway robbery by two bailiffs of Brentwood, who rob
a man of four new pairs of shoes, a pair of boots and a new
girdle, turns out, in the *Inquisitiones*, to be a case of connivance at the escape of a felon.[1]   The statistics of official
extortion and maladministration given above must be taken
as rough approximations and no more ; yet even this inadequate analysis throws some light on the nature of local
government in the thirteenth century.

§ 5. Conditions in Essex compared with those in Gloucestershire

To gain any idea as to how far the conditions indicated
above were general, and how far peculiar to Essex, some
examination of the returns for other counties is necessary.
The Gloucestershire returns have been examined from this
point of view, and as a result of the comparison, a few points
of interest have been noted.   The original returns for this
county are, however, very defective, only six hundreds[2]
being represented out of the twenty-four for which Extracts
are extant.[3]   Such records differ so materially in character
from those for Essex that their evidence must be taken as
suggestive rather than conclusive as to the difference of local
conditions in the two counties.

Even allowing for the defects in the original returns, there
are some marked contrasts.   The Essex Extracts occupy
thirteen pages of the Record Commission Edition, whilst
those for Gloucestershire fill eight.   Of the 188 peccant
officials mentioned in the Essex returns, 127 at least are
named in the Extracts ; a list for Gloucestershire, based on
both Extracts and Inquisitions, only includes 30 names.
One of two explanations of this contrast may be offered ;
either the Gloucestershire officials were less extortionate and
oppressive than those of Essex, or else the Gloucestershire
jurors were less frank than those of Essex.

---

[1] Cf. pp. 156 a, 149 a.
[2] An unprinted roll for Cheltenham hundred is extant.   For the other
hundreds see R. H., i, pp. 166–74.
[3] R. H., i, pp. 175–83.   These extracts include returns for six boroughs,
three vills, a manor, and a liberty, as well as the twenty-four hundreds.

Another contrast is in the proportion of seignorial to royal officials in the two counties. In Gloucestershire 11 out of 30, over a third, are seignorial; in Essex 22 out of 188, or less than an eighth. Again, the proportion of returns dealing with royal rights and seignorial encroachments to those covering administrative abuses is far greater in Gloucestershire than in Essex. As we have seen, there is no ' De Ministris ' roll for Gloucestershire, but it is impossible to draw any inference from this fact. Even so, Gloucestershire stands out, as might 'have been expected, as a county of great manors, liberties, and lordships, and the Hundred Rolls suggest forcibly that here the king stood to lose more and the countryside to suffer more at the hands of the great lords than at those of the royal officials. In Essex the seignorial official, as we have seen, plays a very subordinate part in the history of wrongs related by the villagers. The question arises whether the seignorial was not less rapacious and vindictive than the royal official, feeling, perhaps, more awe for a lord who might at any moment descend upon him than the sheriff or bailiff of the hundred felt for the remote Exchequer at Westminster.

The character of the administrative abuses reported by the Gloucestershire juries differs in no general respect from that of the Essex offences. The largest class of abuses is that connected with the police duties of the sheriff and his staff, with the arrest and release of suspects. As in Essex, charges are brought of refusal to arrest indicted felons, of false accusation of the innocent, of sharing the spoil of thieves, of extortion of fees for replevin. Complaints are made that tourns are held too frequently, and that those who are not bound to come are compelled to attend them.[1] Twelve instances are given of abuses in connexion with the making up of inquests.[2] As regards abuses connected with the fiscal business of the shire there is less reference, proportionately, to the collection of royal debts,[3] and more to the maladministration of royal lands and property. There

---

[1] pp. 167 a, 168 a, 170 a, 171 b, 173 b.   [2] pp. 170 a, 171 b, 173 b.
[3] There is no reference to the Twentieth in Gloucestershire.

are comparatively few returns to the article on the malicious exercise of official power.

Scanty and cautious as are the inferences that may be made from a comparison between the returns for these two counties, they suggest forcibly the desirability of carrying such an examination further. The voluminous returns for Lincolnshire and Shropshire, for instance, supply the basis for a far more comprehensive and satisfactory investigation of local variations.

§ 6. GENERAL CONCLUSIONS

In studying the evidence of the Essex Hundred Rolls as to the abuses of local administration we have been compelled throughout to take the standpoint of the jurors of the hundreds—the *patria*. The one-sided character of the information thus obtained was indicated at the outset. Sympathy with the sufferings of the cheated and oppressed countryside cannot blind us to the fact that the sheriffs and bailiffs are left speechless and undefended in these records. But if the point of view of the hardworked and underpaid local official should not be forgotten, that of the central government is at least as important. It is not merely the zeal of the topographer and genealogist, and the lack of interest in the history of administration that has for so long obscured the manifold nature of the inquest of 1274–5, and caused it to figure in history as no more than an inquiry into feudal privilege and usurpation. To the jurors of Essex the feudal rights of the crown might be of far less weight than the personal wrongs of the men of the shire, but it would be a grave mistake to regard the king's object in ordering the inquest as wholly altruistic, and in its judicial consequences the *Quo Warranto* proceedings far outweigh in bulk any known ' De Ministris ' records.[1] Should any trace of an extensive punishment of officials exist, it will probably be found in some Exchequer

---

[1] An exhaustive search of the records has not been possible, but neither the Assize Rolls, the Memoranda Rolls, nor the Coram Rege Rolls have afforded any evidence of judicial action against officials on a large scale, either in Essex or elsewhere. One such case, initiated, however, by the injured party, is cited above, p. 175, note 5.

record.[1] As in the notorious state trials of 1291, the king
may not have been above making monetary profit out of the
misconduct of his servants.

We have seen that the jurors, whilst well informed and
zealous as to their own injuries at the hands of the royal
officials, are apt to be ignorant when it is a question of royal
rights and wrongs. Whilst the local officials' point of view can
only be conjectured, that of the central administration can
sometimes be inferred from the notes made by the justices
in eyre upon the verdicts of the hundreds which they carried
with them on their *iters* in 1278 and the following years. In
the case of Essex, such notes are lacking ; [2] as we have seen,
the original verdicts for the hundreds appear to be lost. From
the rolls of other shires, however, it becomes clear that the
justice demanded by the returns of 1274–5 was often long
deferred ; in many cases it seems unlikely that it was ever
obtained. Not till 1287 did the justices in eyre reach Gloucestershire, and the notes upon the Gloucestershire Hundred Rolls
show how large a proportion of both complainants and accused
were dead before that date. Moreover, they show that to the
justices the officials' offence against the king was more serious
than that against the countryside ; they suggest that the
extortionate bailiff was to be condemned not so much for his
extortion as for the fact that the money or goods taken were
converted to his own use and not to that of the king. To the
statement of the misdeeds of Maurice of Berkeley is appended
the note, ' Nichil hic, quia nemo queritur '.[3] Most significant
is the note on the return of the Wapentake of Hellowe in
Lincolnshire. The jurors of 1275 show to the king that the
bailiffs of the wapentake threaten them with grievous penalties
on account of their verdict, and they supplicate the king and
his council for a remedy and defence against this. Six years
later the justices' note to this appeal is ' Sequantur omnes
quibus huiusmodi transgressio dicta occasione facta est '.[4]

---

[1] According to Britton, the Court of Exchequer was the tribunal for
erring officials (I, p. xxii).

[2] On the roll for the Essex Eyre of 1285 (the first after 1274) there
are only five references to the inquest of 1274–5 (A. R. 242, mm. 77 d,
81 d, 83 d, 85 d, 100).

[3] R. H. i, p. 168 a.   [4] R. H. i, p. 276 b.

On the other hand, the usurpation of royal rights, the loss of royal privileges is closely examined ; the *Quo Warranto* inquiries are piled up in the records of these eyres, and have become famous in history. The case was clearly different when the injured party was the crown and not the subject.

When the long delays of justice are considered, and the condition of the administration revealed by the trials of 1289–93 is remembered, one hesitates whether to regard the administrative articles of the inquest of 1274 as an expression of an unrealized and unrealizable ideal of justice and good government, or as a bid for popularity on the part of a new ruler, who wished to impress his people with the contrast between his own and his father's methods of government, but found himself unable, if he had ever seriously intended, to live up to the standards set by his drastic inquiries into local maladministration. To those countrymen who had welcomed the suspension of the general eyres in 1272, the issue of the inquests of 1274–5 in the proclamation of the eyres of 1278–87 may well have seemed a fiasco, unredeemed by the legislative activity of 1275–8. And when the proceedings of those eyres are examined, the verdict of the Dunstable annalist is explained, if not justified : ' Dominus Rex misit inquisitores ubique ad inquirendum qualiter vicecomites et alii ballivi se habuissent ; *sed nullum commodum inde venit.*' [1]

---

[1] Ann. Dunstapl., p. 263 (Annales Monastici, R. S., vol. iii).

INDEX OF PLACE-NAMES

SUBJECT INDEX

XII

PROCEEDINGS AGAINST THE CROWN
(1216–1377)

BY

LUDWIK EHRLICH, B.Litt., D.Iur.

PREFACE

My thanks are due to the authorities of the Public Record Office, and above all to Mr. Crump, Mr. Hilary Jenkinson, and Mr. Charles Johnson, for their kindly assistance and their inexhaustible patience. The encouragement which they have never failed to give me, and their suggestions, have been most valuable and are sincerely appreciated.

I also wish to thank Dr. A. J. Carlyle for the encouragement which I have received from him, and Mr. P. T. Williams, formerly of the Library of Exeter College, for his kindness and helpfulness.

The debt I owe the Editor of the series can hardly be measured or expressed. It has been accumulating in the course of many years, ever since I came to Oxford for the first time.

L. E.

Exeter College, Oxford.

CONTENTS

CHAPTER II

THE REIGN OF EDWARD I

CHAPTER III

THE REIGNS OF EDWARD II AND EDWARD III

CONTENTS

SOME ABBREVIATIONS

A. PRINTED AUTHORITIES

Adams = G. B. Adams, Origin of the English Constitution.
Anson = Anson, Law and Custom of the Constitution.
Baldwin = Baldwin, King's Council.
Br. = Bracton, De Legibus et Consuetudinibus Angliae.
Bresslau = Bresslau, Handbuch der Urkundenlehre I, 1st ed.
Brook = Brook, La Graunde Abridgement.
C. C. R. = Calendar of Close Rolls.
C. Ch. R. = Calendar of Charter Rolls.
C. I. = Calendar of Inquisitions.
C. P. R. = Calendar of Patent Rolls.
Chron. = Chronicles of the Reigns of Edward I and Edward II, ed. Stubbs. [R. S.]
Cl. R. = Close Rolls of the Reign of Henry III.
Cole = Cole, Documents Illustrative of English History.
Cutbill = Cutbill, Petition of Right.
Dial. de Scac. = Dialogus de Scaccario, ed. Hughes, Crump, and Johnson.
E. H. R. = English Historical Review.
Fitzh. = Fitzherbert, La Graunde Abridgement.
H. E. L. = Pollock and Maitland, History of English Law, 2nd ed.
Holdsworth = Holdsworth, History of English Law (vol. i, 2nd ed., ii, iii).
Langlois = Langlois, Textes relatifs à l'histoire du Parlement . . . jusqu'en 1314.
L. Q. R. = Law Quarterly Review.
M. C. = Magna Carta, 1215.
M. J. = Mirror of Justices, ed. Maitland. [S. S.]
M. P. = Maitland, Memoranda de Parliamento, 1305. [R. S.]
McIlwain = McIlwain, High Court of Parliament.
McKechnie = McKechnie, Magna Carta, 2nd ed.
Madox = Madox, History and Antiquities of the Exchequer.
Maitland = Maitland, Constitutional History of England.
N.-B. = Maitland, Bracton's Note-Book.
P. W. = Parliamentary Writs, vol i.
Pl. Ab. = Placitorum . . . Abbreviatio.
R. Hung. = M. Rogerius Hungarus, Miserabile Carmen, Scriptores Rerum Hungaricarum, i. 292 ff.
R. L. C. = Rotuli Litterarum Clausarum, ed. Hardy.
R. P. = Rotuli Parliamentorum.
R. S. = Rolls Series.
Ryley = Ryley, Placita Parliamentaria.
Rymer = Rymer, Foedera.

S. R.	= Statutes of the Realm, vol. i.
S. S.	= Selden Society.
Stubbs	= Stubbs, Constitutional History of England, 4th ed.
Tangl	= Tangl, Die päpstlichen Kanzleiordnungen von 1200–1500.
Tout	= Tout, History of England . . . (1216–1377) (Political History of England, vol. iii).
Winkelmann	= Winkelmann, Acta Imperii Inedita I.

B. CLASSES OF DOCUMENTS AT THE PUBLIC RECORD OFFICE

d. = dorso.   f. = file.   m. = membrane.   r. = recto.

A. P.	= Ancient Petitions.
C. D. D.	= Chancery Diplomatic Documents.
C. F. N. S.	= Chancery Files, New Series.
C. I. P. M.	= Chancery Inquisitions Post Mortem.
Cl.	= Close Rolls.
C. R.	= Coram Rege Rolls.
L. T. R.	= Exchequer Memoranda, Lord Treasurer's Remembrancer's Rolls.
P. C. P.	= Parliamentary and Council Proceedings, Chancery.
T. S.	= Placita in Cancellaria, Tower Series.

A dagger (†) denotes reference to a document printed wholly or partly in the Appendix.

An asterisk (*) denotes that the word is interlined. In the excerpts from the L. T. R., the marginal notes are in quotation marks.

CHAPTER I

THE REIGN OF HENRY III

INTRODUCTORY

Postulates of legal thought. At the bottom both of the moral and of the legal notions of the thirteenth century, we find a number of what one is tempted to call ' postulates of mediaeval legal thought ' ; they were taken for granted to the extent of being only exceptionally discussed ; they were never expressly disputed.[1] As one such postulate might be mentioned the acceptance of rules governing the Universe, applying to Deity and its position, to nature, to mankind ; [2] as another postulate, the distinction between right and wrong, and the idea that what is wrong ought to be made right.[3] Whatever the origin of such ideas, they can be found in what we know of mediaeval thought, or of thought in the thirteenth century.

Thus, when discussing the position of the king, Bracton was, as we shall see, rather apt to err on the side of exaggerating the king's exemption from human judgement. Yet it was clear to him that the king's mission was to represent God on earth : not to do what was right would be *ex hypothesi* contrary to the very institution of kingship ; [4] it would mean making the institution defeat its very aim.

Another fundamental conception was that of acquired rights or, to use the mediaeval term, the conception of rights (*iura*). Mediaeval jurists knew the distinction between law and rights just as well as that distinction had been known to Roman jurists or as it is known to-day. It is true that the Roman (and modern) distinction between private and public

---

[1] Cf. Dicey, Law and Public Opinion, 20.
[2] Br., fol. 5 b ; H. E. L. i. 182 ; Maitland, 101.
[3] Cf. Vinogradoff, Common-Sense, 19.   Br., fol. 5 b.

law was not very popular with (though known to [1]) mediaeval thinkers. But the conception of rights they applied very extensively.

From the point of view of the Middle Ages we can roughly define a right as the legally recognized possibility of enjoying something and excluding others from enjoying it.[2] Now, that which one had the legally recognized possibility of enjoying might vary in character.[3] It might be the holding of, and the drawing of revenue from, a market; it might be the holding of a court;[4] the cultivation of some land; the services from that land; freedom from a certain interference on the part of other people, especially of the king and his officials.[5]

Among the ways in which rights could be granted, the most important was grant by charter.[6] Kings often broke their charters; and Henry III certainly did so. But, at least in the thirteenth century, with which we are now concerned, it was seldom, if ever, done openly without justification.[7] John was released from the obligations accepted in the Great Charter or, to retain the language adopted by us, that grant or recognition of rights was declared void, as extorted by *vis et metus*.[8] Henry III was advised to protest that his minority had been an obstacle to a lawful grant.[9] The fact that kings had to reissue charters during their lifetime, and to confirm charters of their ancestors,[10] need not detain us. Reissues and confirmations only served to remind the king of what he ought not to infringe. Human psychology was here called to aid instead of abstract legal reasoning. And, according to the individualistic point of view, the new king

---

[1] Br., fol. 3 b.

[2] We thus find the Roman idea of ownership adapted to mediaeval requirements, for the mediaeval conception of rights was coloured by the idea of property.

[3] Br., fol. 56 a.   [4] M. C., c. 34 ; H. E. L. i. 527.

[5] Ibid., ii. 3–4, although the terminology is different. An explanation of the seeming difference between former and present-day thought, Vinogradoff, Common-Sense, 84.

[6] Holdsworth, ii. 15 ff.   [7] Cf. e.g. H. E. L. i. 518.   [8] Rymer, 135–6.

[9] McKechnie, 181 ; cf. H. E. L. i. 523 ; Adams, 280 ; Holdsworth, iii. 356 ; Stubbs, ii. 39.

[10] H. E. L. i. 179 ; Adams, especially 283.

had to confirm the grants of former kings lest, not being a party to them, he should not feel bound by them.[1]

The king and the law. The king's legal position in the time now considered has been characterized by describing ' the king's rights as intensified private rights '.[2] ' If the whole law were written down, we should not be sent to one great chapter of it to learn the law of the kingship ; rather we should see at the end of every proposition of private law or procedural law some note to the effect that this proposition must be modified before it is applied to the king's case. . . . He has hardly a power for which an analogy cannot be found elsewhere '.[3] The way in which we group all legal rules is of course largely a matter of individual choice. With a certain amount of skill and labour, one could probably succeed in writing down a given system of law in several different ways. But the statements just quoted should probably not be taken to imply that the king's rights were only intensified rights of a feudal lord. If a manor was organized as a kingdom in little,[4] it does not follow that the kingdom was a manor in large. Whatever we mean by feudalism, kingship in England was not a product of the feudal system. There had been a time when grants were non-feudal ; politically it may have been necessary for the king to renew the old, and to make new, grants. But this did not change the legal position according to which grants of immunities or ' liberties ' were but the renunciation, on the part of the king, of some of his rights.[5] There would be very little explanation of many well-known phenomena of the thirteenth-century law, were we to disregard the ' national '[6] or public[7] element. Why

---

[1] Fundamental conceptions like those just mentioned were not a peculiarity of the thirteenth, or any other century. They are, in one form or another, necessities of human thought. We must have some ultimate, *a priori* criteria. Generally accepted as they are, disputes will turn on the question, not whether they are true, but whether something is in accordance with them.

[2] H. E. L. i. 512, margin.   [3] Ibid. 512–13.

[4] Holdsworth, iii. 352, reference to Vinogradoff, Villainage, 324–5.

[5] But see Maitland, 24–5.   [6] e.g. Stubbs, ii. 110 ; Holdsworth, iii. 352.

[7] Already in the Dial. de Scac. 125 we read : ' Debetur haec prerogativa dignitatis publicae potestati, ut cuiuscunque sit, cuicunque vir aliquis in regno militet vel ministret, si regi necessarius visus fuerit, libere possit assumi et regiis obsequiis deputari.'

should the king have rights different in degree from the
rights of his lieges? Why should he be considered God's
vicar on earth? Why should debts due to him be preferred
to debts due to his subjects?[1] Why should he have the
right of seizing goods?[2] Why should his vassals' men
fight for him and not for them?[3] The judges were busy
interpreting acts and rules in his favour in so far as logic
allowed. We cannot account for this by pointing out merely
that they were appointed by him. We must add that though
this was undoubtedly the motive of their action, the legal
justification lay in the character of the king as sovereign.

Practice and Bracton. In trying to obtain from the time
of Henry III all the possible light on our subject we shall
first look at the extant monuments of practice, above all at
the plea rolls, from which extracts are best accessible in
Bracton's Note-Book, and at the exchequer rolls. Then we
shall consider some of Bracton's statements with the object
of pointing out what a mediaeval jurist of first-rate importance
thought of the legal problems which we are discussing.

A. Practice

The king and the law. From the study of the original
documents of the time we derive an impression of a legality,
real or pretended, pervading the whole system of relations
between the king and his subjects.

The king's acts judged by the law. The king's claims were,
as a rule, judged according to law. This may be seen in
a number of instances. The king wished to recover an
advowson[4] which, he alleged, was wrongfully held by a prior;
he brought an action[5] and traced his descent back to Henry
the Second who had been seised of that advowson as of fee
and right. The defendant showed that he had the advowson
by some one's gift; the king's attorney replied that the donor
had been only the king's bailiff; the defendant retorted that

---

[1] L. T. R., roll 15 m. 4 d. 'quia nos debemus preferri omnibus aliis
donec debita nostra nobis persoluantur.'

[2] M. C., c. 28; McKechnie, 386.   [3] Maitland, 161–2; Adams, 188–9.

[4] To be quite exact, 'medietatem aduocacionis'.

[5] 'Dominus rex petit uersus priorem de Kenillewurthe.'

he had the land by a fine with the king. These were all but
legal arguments, such as would be used in any private case.[1]
The advowson of a church had been given to an abbey by
the guardian of the last patron and the gift had been confirmed
by that patron ; an assize of darrein presentment was brought
by the king who had become seised of the manor; but
judgement was given for the defendant because the king
could not claim any better right to the advowson than the last
patron, who had confirmed the grant of it.[2] In another case
the jury were expressly asked to say whether certain land
had been given by the king in exchange or of his own will
(*in escambium . . . uel ad uoluntatem suam*); the record was
finally sent to the king, and the clerk remarks that he knows
that the king afterwards gave back the land, but does not
know whether this was done by judgement of the king's court
or of his own will.[3] The king was vouched to warranty, but
would not accede to the voucher ; he said that nobody was
bound to warranty without being called upon by the king's
writ, which, however, did not lie against the king ; but he gave
also legal arguments. The court decided against the defendant,
but they reserved to the defendant the right of recovering
against the king in exchange, unless indeed he preferred to
recover against the plaintiff in the present action, by writ
of right.[4] An abbot, summoned to answer the king in a plea
of *quo warranto*, pleaded that

'cum Iohannes Rex pater Domini Regis terram illam ei
confirmauerit non potest idem Dominus Rex petere contra
confirmacionem patris sui cum non sit alius qui petat nisi
Dominus Rex.'

For this reason, the summons was dismissed.[5] The king owed

---

[1] N.-B., pl. 199, A.D. 1222.

[2] Ibid., pl. 1732, A.D. 1226 'Nec Dominus Rex plus' clamare potest
quam predictus Henricus si uiuus esset, consideratum est quod Dominus
Rex nichil clamare potest, et ideo Abbas habeat seisinam suam.'

[3] Ibid., pl. 565, A.D. 1231 'Recordum missum est Domino Regi et
Dominus Rex reddidit ei seisinam suam, set nescitur utrum per iudicium
curie sue uel per uoluntatem suam.'   [4] Ibid., pl. 1108, A.D. 1234–5.

[5] Ibid., pl. 1274, A.D. 1238–9 'quia habet confirmacionem Iohannis
Regis de terra illa que expressam facit mencionem de terra de Ellefordia
. . . consideratum est coram Domino Rege quod Abbas recedat quietus
cum seisina sua.'

a debt to his serjeant-at-arms (arrears of the latter's stipend).
When the widow of the serjeant asked for payment, a writ
of search was sent to the exchequer and its transcript on the
memoranda roll contains the expression : ' cum eadem Maria
asserat Regem teneri '.[1]

The king's wrongs. The lawyers of the thirteenth century
did not shrink from declaring that the king, either by himself
or through his servants, had committed a wrong. On the
contrary, the wrong which we should consider the one most
corresponding with a modern tort, the wrongful disseisin for
which, as Bracton tells us,[2] punishment was inflicted in the
case of ordinary persons, was recognized, in very many cases,
as the king's act. This is especially worth noticing because
the theory was soon going to develop that the king could not
be a disseisor, and this theory was connected with the modern
interpretation of the maxim, ' The king can do no wrong.' [3]

It hardly needs pointing out that the Great Charter
contained special provisions concerning men who had been
disseised by John, Richard, or Henry II.[4] In a case of the
time of Henry III, the jury found that Henry II had disseised
a man who had refused the king's huntsman his dinner.[5] In
another case the court took into consideration the king's
admission ' quod primo disseisiuit ipsum Eustachium sine
summonicione et iudicio per uoluntatem suam '.[6] Similar
confessions are frequent.[7]

In such cases it was adjudged that disseisin by the king
did not deprive the disseisee of his rights ; the king as

---

[1] L. T. R., roll 45, m. 6 r.   [2] Below, p. 43.
[3] Below, pp. 61–2, 139–40.   [4] M. C., cc. 52, 56, 57.
[5] N.-B., pl. 769, A.D. 1233 ' Tempore Henrici Regis aui Domini Regis
quia predictus H. denegauit cuidam Hospeshort uenatori Domini Regis
dinnerium suum uenit Dominus Rex et disseisiuit H. et terram illam dedit
ipsi Hopeshort.'
[6] Ibid., pl. 1106, A.D. 1234–5.
[7] e.g. ibid., pl. 1133, A.D. 1235–6 ' in quas non habuit ingressum nisi
per disseisinam quam Dominus Rex fecit eidem Iohanni '—this in the statement of claim ; ' postea recordatum est et a Domino Rege et consilio suo
. . . quod Comes Gloucestrie seisinam habuit per ipsum Dominum Regem
sicut ipse Rex cognoscit postquam disseisiuit ipsum Walterum ' ; ibid.,
pl. 1136, eod. anno : ' et quia Dominus Rex cognoscit quod ita fuit
seisitus et per eum disseisitus, consideratum est quod Comes recuperauit
seisinam suam ' ; cf. ibid., pl. 1141, eod. anno. See also Madox, 69, n. d.

disseisor had no more rights than any other disseisor, and, accordingly, his grant would not give any right to the grantee ; here is a beginning of the later doctrine that the king's unlawful orders were no orders at all, and of the proceedings upon *scire facias* to annul letters patent granting, e. g., land to which the king had no right.

It was readily recognized that an act of the king or of the king's officials could result in a wrong, and we frequently find writs, in which a complaint against such an act is recorded and a remedy ordered, with some such addition as ' nolentes eidem in hac parte iniuriari '.[1]

If the king had disseised somebody, or in some other way held land of which somebody else had been disseised, and if then the disseisee was to have back his seisin, in every case a writ with instructions had to be sent to the king's minister who was in charge of the land. During Henry III's reign the formula : ' (plenam) seisinam habere facias' seems to have been used (alongside of the word *restituas* in the latter part of the reign) for such restitutions as well as in cases in which the king's seisin had been lawful.

We find the formula used, on the one hand, in a writ of 1241 ordering the livery of dower assigned to the widow of a tenant in chief,[2] in a writ of 1238 ordering the livery of land granted by the king for the year and the day which the king had in it,[3] in writs of 1247 ordering the livery of land to heirs whose homage the king had taken,[4] in a writ of the same year relating to a wardship granted until the age of the heir,[5] and in a writ of 1238, ordering the restitution to the lady of land which the king had held for the year and day.[6] On the other hand, we find the same formula in the entry of a writ of November 21, 1234, issued in execution of the judgement in favour of Hubert de Burgh : [7]

' Dominus rex reddidit H. de Burgo . . .. manerium de Camel

---

[1] e. g. Cl. 88, m. 5 r.†
[2] Cl. R., 25 Hen. III, 261; as to the later formula, cf. C. C. R., 2 Ed. I, 61.
[3] Cl. R., 22 Hen. III, 66.   [4] Ibid., 31 Hen. III, 540–1.
[5] Ibid., 31 Hen. III, 531.
[6] Ibid., 22 Hen. III, 30 ; as to the later formula cf. C. C. R., 6 Ed. I, 477.   [7] Cl. R., 19 Hen. III, 17.

cum pertinentiis, quod habuit de dono domini J. regis.
Et mandatum est vicecomiti . . . quod de predicto manerio
cum pertinentiis, una cum bladis domini regis, carucis et
instauris que rex ibidem habuit, eidem comiti plenam
seisinam habere faciat,'

in the entry of a writ of February 2, 1235, also for Hubert de
Burgh : [1]

' Rex reddidit . . . manerium de Leylaund cum bladis, carucis
et omnibus aliis instauris que rex in eodem manerio habuit
die Purificationis Beate Marie, anno etc. xix Et mandatum
est . . . escaetoribus regis, quod eidem comiti de . . . manerio
cum bladis . . . sicut predictum est, plenam seisinam habere
faciant,' [2]

in a writ of October 7, 1240 : [3]

' Et quia per eandem inquisitionem accepimus quod W. . . . .
quando habuit custodiam castri nostri de Sauvere, per
voluntatem suam ipsum abbatem iniuste et sine iudicio
disseisivit de una acra et una roda prati . . . et aliter in
manum nostram non devenit, tibi precipimus quod de predicto prato eidem abbati plenam seisinam habere facias,'

and in a writ of 1247 stating that the king had learned by inquisition that what constituted a woman's dower had wrongly
been taken into the king's hand and should be restored.[4]

In spite of a slight differentiation, we find no great change
in terminology in the last years of Henry III.[5]

The order to restore ('predictum molendinum una cum

---

[1] Cl. R., 19 Hen. III, 45.

[2] It will be noted that chattels are being restored only if they were on
the manor on the day of the issue of the writ. Another writ, of November 14,
1234, also for Hubert de Burgh, orders restitution of chattels, ' nisi catalla
illa vendita fuerint per manum ballivorum regis ad opus regis vel data per
preceptum suum ' (Cl. R., 19 Hen. III, 10). What was no more there
could, of course, not be restored ; but we may have here an application
of a principle which was applied later on, namely, that the king was in
the position of a *bonae fidei possessor*, ' qui fructus consumptos (*or* perceptos) suos facit, extantes restituere debet ' (below, p. 139). The writs
ordering restitution of chattels speak of delivering ('liberet', Cl. R.,
19 Hen. III, 2) or causing to be restored ('reddi faciat', ibid., 10), writs
ordering the delivery of chattels granted by the king speak of causing to
have ('habere facias', ibid., 31 Hen. III, 533), and not of letting have
seisin (below, p. 64 n. 2 ; but cf. H. E. L. ii. 32 ; Maitland, L. Q. R. i. 324).

[3] Cl. R., 24 Hen. III, 229.   [4] Cl. R., 31 Hen. III, 508.

[5] Since the close rolls for the years 1248–72 have not yet been published, our investigation had to be based on an inspection of some original
close rolls.

omnibus inde perceptis a tempore capcionis eiusdem in manum nostram . . . restituatis ') was given where an escheator had taken into the king's hands a windmill constructed on the party's soil within the royal demesne, as constructed to the king's *dampnum et nocumentum,* and the king had learned by inquisition that this assumption was incorrect ; [1] the order to deliver (*liberetis*) was given where the king had granted a manor until the age of the heir, [2] and where the king had assigned dower. [3] The order to let have (or let have back) seisin (or plenary seisin) was given where land of a supposed enemy of the king during the Barons' War had been granted to some one else, was taken into the king's hand on the original tenant's assertion that he had been on the king's side, and was restored to the grantee because the assertion was not proved ; [4] also, where the bailiwick of a forest was granted to the son of the late bailiff, [5] where an heir had been found to be of age and had done homage, [6] where the king granted year, day, and waste of the lands, goods, and chattels of a felon, [7] but also, where land had been seised into the king's hand as having been held by a deceased tenant in chief, whereas he had held it in the right of his wife. [8]

The differentiation which we shall observe early in Edward I's reign, [9] had not yet taken place.

The king's privileges. While the king's acts were judged according to the law, the law gave the king a quite special position. It is not our purpose to analyse the position of the king in those days, as a whole. We must remark, however, that quite apart from the question whether the king was, or was not, only a feudal lord, pure and simple, there can be distinguished, in the legal position of the king in that period, two elements. On the one hand, the power of the king was personal : the king died, [10] the king could be under age, [11] the king could sit in his own courts and adjudicate in person. [12]

---

[1] Cl. 88, m. 5 r.†   [2] Ibid., m. 4 r.   [3] Ibid., m. 5 r.

[4] Cl. 89, m. 13 r.†   [5] Ibid., m. 5 d.†   [6] Cl. 88, m. 3 r.

[7] Cl. 89, m. 8 r.   [8] Ibid., m. 9 r.   [9] Below, pp. 62–4.

[10] e.g. H. E. L. i. 521.   [11] Ibid., 522.

[12] Ibid. 515 ; Madox, 553–4 ; N.-B., pl. 1124 (*quod reddat* brought by the king).

On the other hand, there was a growing sense of an institutional, as contrasted with the personal, character of kingship. Since the king 'could be under age', litigation which touched royal rights had to be postponed until the king came of age.[1] But the orders of the regent were given as the king's orders, only with the quaint addition that they had been sealed with the regent's seal because the king had as yet no seal of his own.[2]

The king's actual power.   After all has been said about the king being bound by law, and about the king's wrongs being recognized as such by the law, it still remains true that the king's power was tremendous.   It is well known that he had, in so far as feudal rights were concerned, a better position than other feudal lords,[3] and that apart from strictly feudal rights he claimed for himself, or there were claimed for him, whenever possible, special rights and privileges.[4]   Even where a party might consider himself aggrieved, the king's order would be fulfilled by his officials ; for instance, some one complained that he had been disseised and that somebody else was in possession ; the defendant showed that he had entered by a fine with the king ; then the king ordered that the disseisee should be restored to his land ; this was enough to make him recover.[5]   A certificate by the king, whether by charter or by word of mouth, exceeded every other proof.[6] Where a party had entry through the king, it was enough to show that he had been put into possession by the sheriff on the strength of a royal writ, to abate an assize of novel disseisin.[7]   This last case seems rather extraordinary, because the assize was not stopped provisionally, until the king's pleasure would be known (such a course would, indeed,

---

[1] H. E. L. i. 523.

[2] e.g. L. T. R., roll 1, m. 7 d. 'Et in huius rei testimonium has literas patentes sigillatas sigillo dilecti et fidelis nostri W. marescalli domini penbrocensis rectoris nostri et Regni nostri quia nondum sigillum habuimus eidem Briano fieri fecimus.' Cf. C. P. R. i, *passim.*

[3] H. E. L. i. 512.   [4] e.g. above, p. 11, n. 7.

[5] N.-B., pl. 1059, A.D. 1225 'postea precepit Dominus Rex quod dictus Willelmus . . . talem seisinam haberet de terra de Cotesmora qualem habuit quando terram illam cepit in manum suam. Et ideo habeat seisinam.'

[6] Ibid., pl. 239, A.D. 1224 ; cf. H. E. L. i. 515, n. 5.   [7] N.-B., pl. 401.

have followed logically from a case referred to above),[1] but
the plaintiff was actually put in mercy and the defendant
was acquitted. This proves, not only that ' if there is disseisin
at all, the king is the principal disseisor ; but he cannot be
sued ' ; [2] but that the case was decided for good and all,
and that no way of approaching the king was reserved to
the plaintiff. In other words, the king's act, though wrongful,
was not called in question. We know but few particulars
of the case ; something may have been hidden behind
the facts as recorded. In any case, there is an apparent
discrepancy between the cases quoted above to show that
the king's wrongs were recognized as wrongs, and the present
case ; an explanation may be found in the king's great
power, and in the probable unwillingness of the average
judge to meddle with what was perhaps a personal act of
the king.[3] The peculiar position of the king served as the
legal ground of the judicial decision.

The king's administrative machine. This brings us to an
important point : the king, besides being just a feudal lord,
was the head of a great administrative machine. It is not
advisable to argue about the position of the king by analogy
with the position of the lords.[4] For the lords had their
privileges, at least legally, as grants from the king ; in
organizing their estates they imitated the organization
developed by the king. Now, the king's administrative
machine was used, not only to administer his estates, to
collect his charges or, as they were called, debts, but also,
to carry into execution his orders intended to settle disputes between private parties, and to administer justice
in what are described as pleas of the crown, i. e. criminal
cases. All this may cause us to look at the king's position from
a point of view from which we may perceive origins of later developments, germs of conceptions which were t oprevail later.
Before the date of Henry III's death, there was an administrative machine, not only working in the king's interests, but
also, as becomes a true bureaucracy, anxious to increase the

---

[1] Above, p. 14, n. 6 ; below, p. 23, n. 3.   [2] N.-B. ii. 330, n. 4.
[3] See also N.-B., pl. 1163.   [4] Above, p. 11.

sphere of its own activities and the amount of its fees. For this purpose it was using the king's power. This was done in a characteristic way. There was the institution of a writ ; it could contain the king's order, addressed, for instance, to the sheriff, and directing him to make somebody come to the exchequer and answer the claim of some one else ; [1] now, if the sheriff did not obey the order he would be punished for contempt of an order of the king ; therefore, the sheriff had to abide by the order ; and, again, if the sheriff summoned the party to come to the exchequer and the party did not come, the sheriff would distrain the party who had disobeyed, and until he obeyed, the summons made in the king's name and by the king's order. All this is clear enough, until we hear that the king himself, he who was supposed to have given the order to the sheriff and for whose contempt punishments were threatened, had not given such orders at all ; on the contrary, he wished his exchequer not to trouble about private cases, but to devote its energies solely to the king's affairs ; [2] a wish which, as we know, the exchequer officials were by no means eager to fulfil.[3] From this we learn that the king's sheriffs were bound to obey orders of their superiors, whether such orders did or did not correspond with the instructions which the superiors had, in their turn, received, as long as the orders reaching the sheriffs were formally the king's orders ; and, again, that there could be no disobeying the sheriff merely because one might think that the order executed by the sheriff was contrary to instructions given by the king to the exchequer officials ; and, finally, that there was a presumption in favour of the legality of the acts of the king's officials, and that the presumption could only be defeated by a special procedure.

[1] e.g. L. T. R., roll 45, m. 2 d. : distraint by order of the exchequer, to abide by a recognizance entered into before the barons of the exchequer.

[2] e.g. the writ de placitis scaccarii prohibitis (M., 56 Hen. III), L. T. R., roll 45, m. 1 d. ; Madox, 594–5 s. ; H. E. L. i. 192–3 ; Holdsworth, i. 101, n. 9. The writ speaks only of pleas already pending before the barons, but the margin shows what its meaning was understood to be, and the first part of the writ shows clearly the same tendency. See also Gross, L. Q. R. i. 138 ; but cf. Baldwin, 40.

[3] Holdsworth, i. 101.

Remedies. The great power of the king adds interest to the question, how a man wronged by, or in the name of, or by the order of, the king could get his wrongs redressed ?

No punishment in the ordinary course. We must begin with a negative statement : how these wrongs could *not* be redressed. First of all, in the ordinary course of events it could not be expected that the king would be punished. An excommunication by the pope, or the distress provided for by Magna Carta, c. 61, both had in view compulsion rather than punishment ; the Earl of Chester, who carried the sword of St. Edward at Henry III's coronation, was supposed by Matthew of Paris to have done so in order to show that he had the right to restrain the king if the king acted wrongfully.[1] But this explanation seems one of doubtful value ; [2] even the Articles of the Barons provided for the safety of the king, queen, and their children ; [3] it appears much more probable that the sword, which was one of the insignia of royal power, was carried by the earl as one of the king's household, possibly because Henry, being a child, could not carry it himself. In any case, this theory would have related to extreme cases ; [4] even the barons demanded from the king, in 1215, only that he ' redress ' (*emendare*) [5] his wrongs ; and in everyday practice it would have been unthinkable that the king should, e. g., make a fine with himself for the breach of his own peace.

Remedies and ordinary procedure. If we disregard great constitutional crises, it is still necessary to point out a curious confusion which seems to have arisen out of certain statements of Lord Somers in his judgement in the Bankers' Case.[6] ' I take it to be generally true,' he said, ' that in all cases where the subject is in the nature of a plaintiff, to recover anything from the king, his only remedy at common law

---

[1] H. E. L. i. 182, n. 5.

[2] Matthew of Paris could have borrowed the theory from the German *Rechtsbücher*, but we can hardly say the same of the men who made the arrangements for Henry's coronation, because there is nothing to show that at that time the theory was even in existence in Germany. In practice, it was not applied until 1300.

[3] c. 49.   [4] H. E. L. i. 182.   [5] Articles of the Barons, c. 49.

[6] 14 St. Tr. 1.

is to sue by petition to the person of the king . . . in like manner, in the same book (i. e. Ryley's Placita) . . . several parties sue by petition for money and goods taken for the king's use ; and also for wages due to them ; and for debts owing to them by the king. . . . The parties, in these cases, first go to the king by petition ; it is by him they are sent to the Exchequer ; and it is by a writ under the great seal that the Exchequer is empowered to act. . . . So far was it from being taken to be law at that time, that the barons had any original power of paying the king's debts.' [1] Did this mean that the subject had to bring a petition to ask for a remedy, or was the petition the ordinary course of procedure ? The word *remedy* can, of course, mean different things. If, however, we take a remedy to denote a means of restoring an infringed right, the distinction will be clearer. We may add at once, that so far as the reign of Henry III is concerned, Lord Somers' statement would seem inapplicable because, as will be pointed out later, the petition was not yet in use in England at that time. Apart from that, however, did Lord Somers mean that parties to whom wages were due, or who had sold goods to or for the benefit of the king, or to whom money was otherwise due, could, in the later Middle Ages, get it only by approaching the king ? Or did he imply that this was the case if the other ways of having their claims satisfied had failed ? Lands and tenements, advowsons and rents, which were held of the king in chief, or which the king's officials claimed to be so held, were taken, on different occasions, into the king's hands ; sometimes regularly (e. g. if a tenant had died) and sometimes irregularly (e. g. if the late tenant was erroneously supposed to have held from the king in chief). In either case there might be people who would claim the thing back. If the king's tenant in chief died, his heir within age, the king would have the wardship of the land and of the body of the heir, and the latter's marriage. But when the heir came, or if he was, of age, he had to prove this, to do homage, and to sue out a writ ordering restoration of the land.[2] This was what

---

[1] 14 St. Tr. 83.   [2] e.g. Cl. 88, 55 Hen. III, m. 3 r.

we may call the ordinary course of procedure and it was pure routine business; hence, except in cases in which the king might take special interest—the writs were sued out without the king's interference, save, of course, for the taking of the homage. There were many kindred cases, in which, if the facts were as alleged, the legal position would be quite clear; for instance, if on the tenant's death his widow applied for dower and had it assigned.[1] Here, it seems, the chancery could usually act by itself. It issued orders—hypothetical orders, if necessary—which contained the legal rule to be applied in each particular case; but, both in the case of ordinary application and in quest of remedy, it might be necessary or unnecessary to apply to the king himself.

It must be admitted that in many cases the line of demarcation was not exactly clear. This will appear from a consideration of the ways in which the subject could act, if he wished to have his claims against the king satisfied. We are primarily concerned with remedies; but this difficulty of distinction may compel us to touch upon what we have called the ordinary course.

Coram rege terminari debet placitum quod ipsum tangit.[2] Throughout the reign of Henry III, we see the principle constantly applied that whatever touched the king must be determined before him. Thus, a defendant in a plea *quod reddat* claimed to be seised by special writ of the king whom he vouched to warranty; the case was, accordingly, sent before the king.[3] A grant had been made by King John in exchange, and a fine to that effect had been entered into; in an assize brought by the grantee and touching the subject of the grant the justices sent the record before the king, without whom they would not proceed; the king ordered them to decide the case.[4] The practice was, however, by no means uniform. Where the king's grant extended only to 'sicut ipse unquam melius tenuit', and at the time of the grant the king had not been seised, the justices proceeded

---

[1] e.g. Cl. 88, 55 Hen. III, m. 5 r.   [2] N.-B., pl. 1220.   [3] N.-B., pl. 1183, A.D. 1236–7; cf. pl. 1365.   [4] Ibid., pl. 1236, A.D. 1237–8; cf. pl. 1766.

with the case and the plea of the king's grant was disallowed.[1]
But where a fine had been entered into before Henry II (or
was it in his court only ?) and it was alleged that at that time
one of the parties to the fine had been under age and in the
king's wardship, judgement was postponed ; when the king
would come of age, he would, together with his council, give
orders as to judgement.[2]

Whence was this principle derived? We may allow much
for the subserviency of the king's judges.[3]   But that subserviency by itself could not have given rise to a rule of vital
importance, if such a rule had had no foundation in mediaeval
legal thought.   At the bottom of this principle lay probably
the general idea that one could be judged only by one's own
consent, and that any change in one's position could only
be brought about by one's own will.   This is why seignorial
jurisdiction could develop, in England or elsewhere ; for
the man agreed to be his lord's ' justiciable '.[4]   Again, one
could be distrained and otherwise persecuted for refusing
to attend court in what we may call civil cases ; if, however,
the refusal was persisted in, one could be punished for
disobedience to the king's order, but could not forfeit
one's rights.[5]   We know that even later on consent to
be tried by a jury had to be extorted by threats of
punishment.[6]   Now, the king was not under feudal allegiance
to anybody in his realm.   His judges were appointed by him,
but it was not understood that he thereby submitted to their
jurisdiction.   The king could not logically be expected to
order a sheriff to summon the king before the king : ' Henricus
Dei gratia . . . vicecomiti Middl. salutem.   Praecipe Henrico
Regi Anglie quod iuste et sine dilacione reddat A. B. . . . et
nisi fecerit summone eum quod sit coram me uel iusticiariis
meis . . .' It would be absurd to summon one to appear before
oneself.   Other arguments have been adduced against the

---

[1] N.-B., pl. 164, A.D. 1222 ; this case may have been a foundation for the
enactment referred to by Bractón, below, p. 51.
[2] Ibid., pl. 1639, A.D. 1223.
[3] H. E. L. i. 587 ; cf. above, p. 12.   [4] Ibid. i. 527.
[5] Ibid. i. 595–6 ; even (ibid. 593) in real actions the right was not lost.
[6] e. g. Y. B., 30–31 Ed. I, 531, R. S.

possibility of a writ like that mentioned by Wilby J.[1] Besides, everybody knowing something of diplomatics will agree that the king would not be made to speak of himself in the third person (' praecipe Henrico '). To do that, the mediaeval scribes were too pedantic. Nor, again, could a king be distrained for failing to comply with his own orders and thus showing contempt of himself. This explains why, in 1215, the barons were anxious to get clause 49 of their Articles adopted in the king's charter. For the king would thus agree to the jurisdiction of certain men over his acts. He would submit to the jurisdiction of a body which could not claim that jurisdiction otherwise. And again, this explains why the king's servants, while acting in his interests, enjoyed the privilege of not having their acts questioned without the king's consent ; [2] for otherwise the king's interests might be prejudiced. And, finally, this also explains why, if a king waived this privilege, his escheators could be made defendants in an assize of novel disseisin when they had committed a wrong not otherwise punishable : as soon as the king had waived his right, the king's servants could raise no objections ; for their acts made them responsible and the exemption was only on behalf of the king.[3] The case of vouching to warranty concerned the interest of the king and also that of the party. Bracton reports an attempt to curtail the possibility of abusing the voucher.[4] The Statutum de Bigamis had the same aim. In the later development aid prayer became a uniform institution, used not only in real actions but also in what we may call cases of torts.

This principle, then, that where the king's interests were involved, recourse must be had to him, made ordinary suits against the king impossible. But alongside of it, stood the

---

[1] Y. B., 24 Ed. III, 55 ; cf. H. E. L. i. 516. Stubbs, ii. 250, n. 1, mentions Matthew of Paris as speaking of ' brevia impetrata contra regem ' (Chr. Mai. iv. 367) ; but the passage runs : ' brevia contra regem et consuetudinem regni impetrata penitus revocentur', and *regem* is an obvious mistake of either a copyist or the printer for *legem*.

[2] N.-B., pl. 401 : a sheriff was directed to produce the king's writ ordering what was alleged to have been a disseisin ; on the strength of the writ the action failed, above pp. 18–19.

[3] e.g. Stat. Westm. i, c. 24.

[4] Below, p. 51.

principle that a wrong committed by the king or his servants remained a wrong. Again, if the king had the right not to be judged by anybody in his realm against his will, his subjects had rights too. If the king expected his rights not to be infringed, his subjects expected the same as to their rights. We have seen that the king would seldom openly defy a request for justice simply on the ground that he had the power to do what he pleased.

Neither writ nor petition. There were no writs against the king. We are told so by Bracton.[1] We have a remark to the same effect on the plea rolls;[2] and we have noticed other reasons for rejecting the possibility of such writs.[3]

But it is nearly as certain that in the days of Henry III there was as yet no prescribed way of proceeding against the king by petition presented to the king. We may adduce a good deal of evidence to this effect, though it will be indirect evidence. For as to the use of writs, the contrast between cases in which the king, and those in which other people, were defendants, was quite obvious; let us assume, however, that in the case of a claim against the king the party who considered himself aggrieved could apply in person either to the king or to his council or to the exchequer; we cannot expect a direct statement to the effect that no written petition was necessary; the necessity of a written petition would be a later development and, at least, there would be no reason to affirm that it was unnecessary.

Nor should it deceive us if we read that somebody 'petiit' against the king;[4] for we also read that the king 'petit' against a private person;[5] true, the term 'petere' was also used in connexion with 'a domino Rege' in the sense of 'to ask of';[6] but this does not imply that the request

---

[1] Below, p. 45.   [2] N.-B., pl. 1108; H. E. L. i. 516, n. 7, 8.
[3] Above, pp. 24–5.

[4] N.-B., pl. 1235, A.D. 1237–8 'Willelmus Lungespeye peciit uersus Dominum Regem.'

[5] Ibid., pl. 199, A.D. 1222 'Dominus Rex petit uersus Priorem de Kenillewurthe,' cp. pl. 1220, A.D. 1237–8.

[6] Ibid., pl. 1221, A.D. 1237–8: request in the name of the king of Scotland : '. . . uenerunt ad Dominum Regem et petierunt a Domino Rege quod ipse redderet Regi Scocie . . . comitatum . . .'

was in writing. Again, in a case of a private request the words
' ad petitionem suam ' were used (' Abbas . . . accessit ad Dominum Regem et tantum fecit cum Domino Rege quod inpetrauit
ab eo quod perambulacio fieret inter terram ipsius Nicholai
et boscum Domini Regis qui fuit foresta sua, et ad peticionem
suam facta fuit perambulacio per quam boscus predictus et
pastura remanserunt Domino Regi ').[1] But the whole
context makes it probable that the request was by word of
mouth. Throughout the records, the word 'petere' is used,
in the period under consideration, to signify 'ask for'
(e. g. judgement) or 'sue for' (i. e. sue somebody for something).[2]

One need not assume that in the time of Henry III a
request would in no case be put down in writing. From the
beginning of Henry III's reign dates a document[3] which has
the heading ' Peticiones Philippi de Vlecot ', and contains
seven paragraphs (one of them above the heading), each
beginning with a ' Petit ' or ' Item petit '. As we shall see,
the idea and name of petitions was at that time (1220) well
developed at the Court of Rome;[4] it is conceivable that
Philip made use of it. But the document appears more like
a draft or a memorandum; five of the seven paragraphs
have crosses placed against them, probably to denote that
they have been dealt with; moreover, Philip was just about
to leave for Poitou and Gascony[5] and he probably left a
memorandum to somebody competent to deal with it, in
order to have his (Philip's) affairs looked after during his
absence; in any case, one of the seven requests was, we know,
complied with; we do not know about the others. The document dates from a time when Henry III was as yet a minor.
Finally, we must note the very abrupt formulation of the
requests, quite unlike either contemporary petitions to the
pope or later petitions to the King of England.

We must also mention, in this connexion, another document, supposedly from the time of Henry III.[6] It begins,

---

[1] N.-B., pl. 254, A.D. 1227.　　[2] Ibid., *passim*; cf. Cutbill, 22.
[3] D. D. C., no. 673†; first mentioned by Baldwin, 66.
[4] Below, p. 94.　　[5] Below, p. 232, n. 3.　　[6] P. C. P., f. 44, m. 1 a.

' Sire Adam del noef Marche fu endette en Juwerie ', and
ends, ' Dont il crient merci a nostre seignur le Reis, quil
eit pitie de eus quil puissent auoir e fere coe que a eus apent.
issi que le Reis ne seit perdaunt ne eus desherites.' There
is no endorsement, there is nothing to show that this form
was obligatory, or that it was widely used, even should it
be proved that this document does date from the reign of
Henry III.[1]

Description of remedies. We have seen that the king had
at his disposal a great administrative machine, with a, comparatively speaking, strong organization. That machine was
working continually, and though the king could, and from
time to time did, interfere in person with its working,[2] it
would be all but impossible for him to direct or to supervise
all its activities. The machine was working in the king's name,
and its acts were *prima facie* protected by the king's position ;
how, then, was a subject to get reparation in the case of a
wrong inflicted by a sheriff, or a bailiff, or even the exchequer ?

Complaints. First of all, whoever wished to complain of
a sheriff or a bailiff, could go to the exchequer and obtain
a writ summoning the official complained of to justify his
behaviour, or ordering him to desist from the action which
was held illegal. In this respect, the mediaeval exchequer
has rightly been called an administrative tribunal.[3] Thus the
modern idea that an official who commits a wrong is responsible

---

[1] We are using the term ' petition ' in its technical sense. Bracton did
not, as is suggested by Baldwin, 66, use the term ' petitio ' as equivalent to
' complaint ', but as request for something in the legal sense—a lawsuit
(even by the king, see above, p. 26). In the technical sense, in which we
are using the word, a petition was a petition in writing, and it is the
origin of written petitions that we are trying to explain in the present
section. As late as 1276 the written petition was not the obligatory way
of bringing forward claims against the king (cf. the claim of Gloucester,
below, pp. 82–3). The first group of petitions which is known to us comes
from the year 1278 (R. P. i. 1–14).

[2] Even personal orders to the exchequer are recorded, e.g. Madox, 624 ;
the king sat personally in the exchequer, ibid., 553–4 ; Holdsworth, i. 101.

[3] H. E. L. i. 192. Already in the Dial. de Scac., 66, the upper exchequer or, as we may say, the exchequer proper, appears sitting as
a court which had to consider the king's interests above everything else,
but within the limits of law : ' vnum tamen officium omnium est et
intentio vt regis vtilitati prospiciant, salua tamen equitate, secundum
constitutas leges scaccarii.'

personally was not yet of absolute effect; the king could claim the act as his own. On the other hand, the king's exchequer exercised jurisdiction over acts of the officials, and not only punished them for violating their duties against the king, but also held them responsible for wrongs done to private parties. The individual responsibility of the officials was, moreover, hampered only by the king's privileges. If the king waived his privilege, the official would be made responsible in the ordinary way.[1]

A prior complained that he was being distrained for the whole fine imposed on the hundred of Derhurst by itinerant justices, although he held only one part of the hundred and an abbot held the other part. The abbot pleaded that liberties had been excepted, and that, by the king's charter, he had a liberty excepting him in such cases. The pleadings in the exchequer turned on the question whether the liberty had been waived because the abbot's tenants had paid a fine, and whether the king's charter providing that such waivers on the part of some men should not deprive the abbot of his liberty related only to the future, or also to the past; (as an interpretation of the king's charter was involved, the case was sent 'coram rege').[2]

A sheriff distrained one who was only pledge (surety) for another for a fine, although the principal debtor sufficed for the amount; the exchequer sent a writ to the sheriff directing that if that was so he should leave the complainant alone and distrain the principal debtor.[3] In another case we find a writ ordering the sheriff to summon a former sheriff before the barons, where he should account for money collected from the complainant and would receive punishment

---

[1] Below, p. 111. The exchequer could of course, as a rule, try cases of infringements of their official duties only of officials subordinate to it, such as sheriffs or bailiffs. There is an interesting remark in the record of the case of Hubert de Burgh (below, p. 36) to the effect that after the outlawry had been declared void those inlawed asked that the damage they had suffered before the outlawry should be made good by those on whose advice they had been inflicted. The principle thus relied upon was to become of the utmost importance later on; it is interesting to find it applied at such an early date. But the record contains no mention of the way in which the claim thus raised was treated.

[2] L. T. R., roll 15, m. 1 d.†   [3] Ibid., m. 2 r.†

for failing to acquit the complainant before the exchequer so
that the complainant was now again distrained for money
already paid.[1] A tenant in frankalmoin was distrained for
scutage although the donor sufficed for that gift ; the charter
witnessing the grant was brought before the barons of the
exchequer, and they sent a writ to the sheriff to release the
distress and to distrain the principal debtor.[2]

In all these cases the writs originated in the exchequer.
The enrolment of such writs on the memoranda rolls was
often simplified in the following way : Instead of copying
the whole writ, the clerk would start with the ' Monstravit ',
and had to write ' Regi ' instead of ' nobis ' because it was not
a verbatim copy. The enrolment would conclude ' et ideo
mandatum est ', thus showing what had been done and why.[3]
Such writs were returnable before the barons, and there is
in most cases no mention that the barons had received
orders to issue those particular writs. Thus we may conclude
that even in the writs originating in the exchequer the formula
' monstravit ', ' questus est ' could be used ; this, again,
would show that the proceedings were begun by a party's
application to the exchequer.[4] Such a writ is found in 1255 [5]
with respect to the act of a former sheriff who had unjustly
taken and sold two oxen belonging to the complainant. The
present sheriff was ordered to summon the former sheriff
to come and answer to the party for the said trespass. A writ
closely following [6] speaks of bailiffs of a hundred who would
have to answer to the king for their trespass.[7]

But if the party could get his remedy by applying to the
exchequer, it does not follow that the remedy had to be
restricted to such applications ; above all, there were cases
in which it was precisely of an order of the exchequer that
complaint was made.

Accordingly, we find on the exchequer rolls, besides writs
emanating from the exchequer, also writs which had been sent
to it. These latter could be sent, it seems, either upon

---

[1] L. T. R., roll 15, m. 2 d.†   [2] Ibid., m. 3 r.†   [3] e.g. ibid., roll 30, m. 3 d.†
[4] e.g. ibid., roll 20, m. 5 d.   [5] Ibid., roll 30, m. 11 d.
[6] Ibid., m. 12 d.
[7] Cf. also ibid., m. 12 d., and roll 35, part 1, m. 9 r. and 17 d.

the king's special order, or else as writs of course. We must restrict ourselves to observing that such a distinction can be made. The rôle played by the chancery in this connexion will be discussed in the next chapter.[1]

In 1271, some one (A) complained that the barons of the exchequer distrained him unjustly; he had owed some money to somebody else (B) and had entered before the barons into a recognizance for the sum due. B owed some money to a third party (C). B forfeited his lands and chattels to the king; the king ordered A to pay to C the debt which he owed to B. This was done and nevertheless the barons distrained A. We have here an episode in the fight for jurisdiction, on which the barons were bent. It seems as though they wished to let the debtor under the recognizance pay again because he had not paid directly to the man to whom he had recognized himself to owe the money. This was a good way of getting fees for the writ ordering distress. It was also a means of letting all whom it might concern know what a safe thing a recognizance was; in other words, it was an advertisement for the exchequer. A writ came to the exchequer, stating that the king knew from C's letters patent and from C's admission that the money had been paid, and ordering the barons to leave it alone.[2]

---

[1] In any case, the fact that a writ begins with the words 'monstravit nobis', 'questus est nobis', &c., does not prove that an application had been made to the person of the king, either by (written) petition or otherwise. We have seen examples of this in writs emanating from the exchequer. There were also many writs of course beginning with a 'significavit nobis', 'monstravit nobis', 'questus est nobis', 'indicavit nobis', &c. (Holdsworth, i, App. nos. III, XII A (1), XII B, XVIII); Reg. Omn. Brev., 1531, fol. 92 a, 93 a 'trespass, quaestus est nobis'; ibid., fol. 227 'De ventre inspiciendo, monstravit nobis,' &c. Formulae like 'monstravit nobis', 'significavit nobis', 'ostendit nobis', &c., seem to have been used where the writ had to contain the statement on which it was based; where, however, the addressee had to do something without 'reasoning why', the writ would contain a bare order. In a wider sense applications to the chancery were applications to the king. But this would cover also applications to the chancery for ordinary writs, e.g. for a writ of right. Sir Paul Vinogradoff has suggested that the writ of *Monstraverunt* is 'a variation of the peculiar process employed to insist upon a right against the crown', Villainage, 103, 'connected with petitions to the king against the exactions of his officers', ibid. 104.

[2] L. T. R., roll 45, m. 2 d.† Such cases may serve as a good explanation of the 'persistent recourse to their tribunal of creditors', H. E. L. i. 193; cf. Baldwin, 47, n. 2.

A demesne was being distrained for the aid to make the king's eldest son a knight. A writ was sent to the exchequer ordering the barons to do what was just ; if the allegation was true and if that would be just (i. e. if there were no facts unknown to those by whose order the writ issued, justifying the course adopted by the barons) they were to leave the demesne in peace and to distrain the fees.[1]

Restitution and compensation. The next class of cases calling for our attention comprises those in which restitution or compensation was claimed. One preliminary remark may be allowed. Money was the last thing of which a mediaeval king had too much. In the case of land, which had been wrongfully taken from somebody, it was the rule to restore what had been taken. But where money had to be restored, or compensation paid, the king and his bureaucracy would be willing to give land, advowsons, liberties, rights to hold markets ; in short, anything rather than hard cash. On the other hand, those who were to receive payment probably did not complain much ; in the economic system of the Middle Ages money was not as necessary as it is now ; and the parties might prefer a profitable grant to a sum of money which would not be fixed too generously. Even where payment in money was necessary, the king would assign to a creditor money due to the exchequer from some other person, rather than pay directly out of the exchequer. Moreover, since many people either held from the king in chief or otherwise owed him (as sheriffs, escheators, &c.) frequent payments, a party who had a claim against the king could either set off that claim while accounting at the exchequer, or, if there was no sufficient warrant for the set-off, could get a writ of *allocate* directed to the barons.[2]

Where restitution was due, the king's officials would sometimes make important restrictions. Thus, William le Messor had been given, during the king's minority, certain land which by the law of inheritance one Walter de la

---

[1] L. T. R., roll 30, m. 1 d.

[2] Madox, 673. Instead of a writ the king could send the order by messenger, e.g. L. T. R., roll 20, Communia, m. 1 r. ; above, p. 28, n. 2.

Paude should have obtained in fee : for William had paid
for the land two marks more than had been offered by
Walter. Later, a writ was sent to the barons saying that
if the facts were as stated Walter had been manifestly
wronged. Logically speaking, the grant to William was *ultra
vires* of the king ; in later days, a *scire facias* would issue to
show cause why the land should not be taken back into the
king's hands and restored to Walter. Theoretically the king
should pay back William's expenses, and restore to William the
money paid into the exchequer. On the other hand, Walter
should pay the amount which he had offered (not the amount
paid by William). But the jurisprudence of Henry III's
time was inclined to consider the king's interests above
other things. The barons were ordered to let Walter have his
land ; but Walter must pay to William the money paid by
William to the exchequer, and his reasonable expenses on
the land. In other words, Walter had to pay a larger sum
only because William had paid that larger sum to the king ;
besides, Walter had to restore to William the latter's impensae,
although he himself had been deprived of the use of the land
for some time.[1] Perhaps behind the writ there was a wish,
on the part of the king's officials, to teach people that they
must pay money as demanded from them. In any case, the
wish to shift off money payments is evident.

It is quite possible that some demands for restitution or
compensation could be disposed of without application to
the king. We cannot, however, lay too much stress on the
fact that the king was becoming much more of an institution
than might at first be supposed. We may, indeed, read that
a record was sent to the king (' recordum missum est Domino
Regi et Dominus Rex reddidit ei seisinam suam set nescitur
utrum per iudicium curie sue uel per uoluntatem suam '),[2]
and yet we are unable to say for certain where the king himself
and where his officials were meant.

Applications to the king. Let us suppose that one had been
disseised by the king, or by his orders, or that the king had
in his hands land which a party claimed ; the claimant

---

[1] L. T. R., roll 15, m. 8 r.†   [2] N.-B., pl. 565, A.D. 1231.

could come before the king's council, or perhaps, simply before that part of it which was acting as the 'coram rege' court, and could claim the land. It is possible that, as a matter of internal organization, judges would communicate with the king personally before giving their decision ; or else the party could address the king in person, if he was present in the court, or if the social position of the claimant made it possible for him to communicate directly with the king.

A personal application to the king is often mentioned. In one case the jury found that the claimants had come to the king and had shown him how he had wilfully disseised them of their land. The king, inasmuch as they had told him that, gave them certain lands and tenements in exchange.[1] In another case [2] Eustace of Estuteville came to the king's court in which Walter of Raleigh was acting as justice. The king was present in court. Eustace complained that he had been wilfully disseised by the king's bailiffs, acting under the king's orders. He asked for justice, namely, that seisin be given back to him, whereupon he would be willing to answer anybody's claim. This statement was first made by one Allan of Waxtonesham, apparently a pleader.[3] But Allan was put in mercy, because Eustace disavowed that which Allan had told. Thereupon came two other men, Hugh Wack and William de Mastak, and said that they had come before the king at Northampton and had said that they could not, without their wives, answer for this manor of which they were seised as in the right of their wives (apparently they had been summoned to answer the king's claim) ; they said that the king had afterwards wilfully disseised them ; they therefore asked to be restored to their seisin and they would answer anybody's claim ; they claimed not to know of Eustace's seisin or disseisin. Then the king, 'in whose presence all this had been said' (*sic*) 'came and recorded' (recollected) that he had disseised

---

[1] Above, p. 33, n. 2.   [2] N.-B., pl. 1106, A.D. 1234–5.

[3] '. . . qui narrauit pro Eustachio . . . Eustachius deaduocauit id quod pro eo narrauit.' On pleaders, Holdsworth, ii. 262 ff.

Eustace although Eustace had offered him £1,000 if the king would leave him seised and not let him be disseised except by judgement. The king also admitted that the disseisin had been wilful, without summons or judgement; Eustace now repeated his offer of £1,000; the offer was accepted; the king recollected that after the said disseisin he had given the land to Hugh and William, but then took it back, on the advice of the magnates of his curia, because of waste; now he willed and ordered that in his court judgement be at once given and justice done. The court had no difficulty in deciding that, as appeared from the king's confession, Eustace had first been disseised by the king without summons or judgement; the land was, therefore, restored to Eustace and he was to answer to Hugh and William and their wives according to the law of the land, by an assize of *mort d'ancestor* or by writ of right. In this case there was obviously no petition. The claim of Eustace was put forward by word of mouth, as were also the claims of Hugh and William. Judgement was given by the court as such, and not by the king, though the king ordered judgement to be given. The proceedings were conducted on a legal basis, like other proceedings in the king's bench; this is why they were formally recorded; the record roll is officially called 'roll of pleas which followed our Lord the King before Walter de Raleigh '.[1]

In 1230 the bishop of Norwich asked for the amercements of his tenants in fee throughout his liberty.[2] The king asked him by what warrant he claimed those amercements, and he answered that by charters (or a charter?) of King John. He was asked whether he desired judgement on the charters so that if judgement were against him he might lose the amercements for ever, and if judgement were for him he might have them. He first agreed, but then said that he could not do so without the archbishop and the other bishops and their councils. The position of the bishop seems to have made it easy for him to address the king directly. He applied in the king's curia ('coram rege'), in the presence of

---

[1] N.-B. iii. 123.   [2] Ibid., pl. 391.

the king. Nothing enables us to suppose a written petition.
The whole request was obviously to be decided upon at once ;
only when threatened with a possible loss of his claim, the
bishop thought fit to postpone his request : he expected,
perhaps, to put some pressure on the king afterwards without
risking his right ; for if it were otherwise, why should he lose
then and not lose later ?

In the famous case of Hubert de Burgh and his fellow-
sufferers,[1] those outlawed came before the king at Gloucester and
asked that the king be told by his court whether the outlawry
was just and in accordance with the custom of the realm ;
if it was not, they asked that this be redressed in the
king's court. ' And whereas the king would exhibit justice in
his court to everybody,' he convened the archbishop, bishops,
earls and others, and they decided that the outlawry was
null ; judgement was pronounced by William Raleigh.[2] Here
again no written petition seems to have been presented.

Another case, in which the claimant was William Longsword,[3] is not only characteristic of the proceedings under
Henry III, but throws some light on proceedings in former
days. William claimed the custody of the castle of Salisbury
and (the hereditary shrievalty of) Wiltshire ; he based his
claim on the right of his mother, who had been the daughter
and granddaughter of earls of Salisbury. William's claim was
put forward in 1237–8, in the king's bench, before the king
himself and in the presence of the papal legate (at least, if
there were adjournments, the king and the legate were present
when judgement was given ; if there were no adjournments,
they were present throughout the proceedings). The claim
was recorded like one against any private person.[4] The
king (or perhaps his attorney) answered that during John's
reign a jury had found, between that king and the claimant's
father and mother, that they had no right ; the king put
himself on the record ;[5] the record was looked into and it

---

[1] N.-B. pl. 857.   [2] Ibid. ii. 667, n. 1 ; Holdsworth, ii. 184.
[3] Ibid., pl. 1235, A.D. 1237–8.
[4] ' Willelmus Lungespeye peciit uersus Dominum Regem ' ; cf. above,
p. 26, n. 4.
[5] ' Et inde posuit se Dominus Rex super recordum curie sue.'

was found that by that verdict John had remained in seisin
('per quam iuratam Dominus Iohannes Rex remansit in
seisina'); the proceedings had been 'in curia Domini
Iohannis Regis coram iusticiariis suis'. Therefore it was
finally decided that 'remanet Dominus Rex quiete in
seisina sua'. The way in which the king himself (or his
attorney) answered the claim by calling attention to the
previous verdict, would lead us to suppose that William had
claimed the same rights from Henry III before.[1] We may
observe that the claimant apparently came in person into
court and raised his claim ; the king's answer did not amount
to a plain *nihil*, as, in later days, read the endorsement on
petitions in analogous cases, if the king was sure that the claim
was baseless : here the king raised the *exceptio rei iudicatae*,
but the court verified it by reference to the records and then
gave its formal decision ; stress was laid, not on that case
of the time of Henry III, but on the verdict of the days of
John ; the case in the days of John had been between the
earl and his wife, plaintiffs, and the king, defendant ; otherwise the king could not have, as in the present case, 'remained
seised', but would have to 'recover seisin'; stress was laid,
not on the judgement following the verdict, but on the
verdict itself.[2]

In two cases Hubert de Burgh claimed manors from which
the king had wilfully disseised him, giving them to their
present tenants. The king was vouched to warranty, but
claimed judgement that he was not bound to warranty ;
for the present tenants and others had (falsely) suggested
to him that Hugh was outlawed so that the king could
dispose of his lands ; and now the outlawry had been
adjudged null.[3] In each case the plaintiff recovered, and
a day was given the defendant against the king ' whether the

---

[1] ' Et Dominus Rex nunc sicut alias ei respondit quod tempore Johannis
Regis patris sui . . .'

[2] ' Per quam iuratam . . . remansit in seisina ; . . . consideratum est . . .
quod carta illa non est contraria predicte iurate capte in curia Johannis
Regis.' (This is an interesting illustration of how in later days the verdict
of a jury could come to be understood as the ' iudicium parium ' of M. C.
c. 39.)

[3] Above, p. 36.

king ought to warrant him '.[1] In neither case was there
a written petition to the king ; the proceedings against the
king arose out of proceedings between private parties, and
nevertheless the day ' against the king ' was given simultaneously.[2]

In 1255, while the king was present at the exchequer, an
official of the bishop of Norwich came to claim a monstrous
fish which, he alleged, belonged to the bishop. The king
argued for a time, and finally showed to the bishop's representative that the fish was really the king's or, at least,
that the claim as it had been put forward by the bishop was
untenable. The king ' wished to consider the matter at some
other time ', and the claimant got an adjournment into
a parliament.[3]

A writ of November 1, 1271,[4] states that land of Matthew
of Knelle had, because of Matthew's alleged part in the
Barons' War, been assigned to Robert of Cokefende ;
Matthew came in person to the king's court and maintained [5]
that he had been on the king's side with Gilbert of Clare.
The latter was summoned before the king and his council [6]
and could not remember whether Matthew had been with
him, but undertook to find it out. Matthew was given a day
in court (*coram nobis*) and was to bring word from the earl.
Since he failed to appear, it was decided [7] to let Robert have
seisin of the land in question, saving the right of Matthew.
In this case there seems again to have been a personal application to the king in his court, without a written petition.[8]

---

[1] N.-B., pl. 1141 and 1136, A. D. 1235–6.
[2] It may be interesting to compare the legal institutions just described,
with those of France. We find there some institutions closely resembling,
at least in theory, those which existed in England. See Appendix, pp. 201–2.
[3] L. T. R., roll 30, m. 9 d.†; cp. R. L. C. I. Introd. p. xxxviii.
[4] Cl. 89, m. 13 r.†
[5] ' Nuper ad curiam nostram veniens nobis intimasset . . .'
[6] ' Prefatum comitem venire fecimus coram nobis, qui in presencia
nostra et consilii nostri constitutus . . .'
[7] ' De consilio nostro iam prouidimus . . .'
[8] A writ of the same year mentions a personal application to the king
and his council for the bailiwick of a forest which had been held by the
applicant's father (' ad nos et consilium nostrum accessisset et nos
rogasset '), Cl. 89 m. 5 d.† Another writ of the same year mentions what was apparently a personal application for dower (' ad nos

B. Bracton

General. Bracton's task in dealing with the law of kingship was not easy. He had to face those great inherent
difficulties which are well known to every student of political
science and constitutional law : doubts were arising in the
segregation of legal from non-legal elements ; it was difficult
to define clearly what was actually in a state of fluctuation.[1]
Some of Bracton's statements may seem to us not quite
clear, or even inconsistent ; but the questions discussed by
him were by no means settled and could be argued from
different points of view.

Besides, Bracton had to concern himself with mediaeval
interpretations of old Roman theories.[2] Thus, when declaring
that the king's power extends only so far as the law gives it
to him, Bracton considers it necessary to add that this is
not inconsistent with the principle, ' Quod principi placuit,
legis habet vigorem '.[3]

Furthermore, one could find, in Bracton's days in England
itself, two tendencies, which were not confined to politics
but could be found in legal theory : the royalistic tendency
and that other one, of which a prominent exponent was
Simon de Montfort.[4] To bring such contradictory contentions to a satisfactory compromise was by no means easy.
Here one had to deal not only with law, but also with political
tendencies, not only with what was, but also with what

venit et nos instanter rogauit ') ; ibid., m. 13 r.† We assume that there
was, in the days of Henry III, no necessity for written petitions. But
there was no possibility of writs against the king ; the examples adduced
above fully justify the pope's mention of suits against the king (Stubbs,
ii. 250) ; but that the suits were commenced by writ would be an unwarranted inference.

[1] H. E. L. i. 526.   [2] Cf. Holdsworth, ii. 211 ff., especially 214–15.

[3] Br., fol. 107. It would seem that the difficulty alluded to by McIlwain,
High Court of Parliament, 102, does not necessarily arise. Bracton may
have quoted only the first part of the sentence, expecting his readers to
know the whole of it, or, more likely, he may have given his quotation,
not as a sentence in itself, but only because the words, ' lege regia quae
de imperio eius lata est ', seemed to him to correspond with, and to cor-
roborate, his view that ' lex facit regem ' (fol. 5 b, &c.) ; while the *cum*
was meant to show that the principle, ' quod principi placuit legis habet
vigorem ', was especially founded on the act of conferring power.

[4] The clash of these two tendencies has been pointed out by Vinogradoff,
L. Q. R., I. 188.

people wanted and, as a means to their end, asserted, to be law.

Bracton's treatise begins with a full acceptance of the theory of two swords.[1] But Bracton gave the theory an explanation suitable to English conditions. The jurisdiction on earth [2] is divided between the two vicars of God, namely, the Pope and the temporal ruler. The temporal ruler is, of course, able to communicate with God without the interference of any other ruler, especially of the emperor.[3] The Pope as well as the temporal ruler have ordinary jurisdiction ; all the others are only their delegates.[4]

The jurisdiction could in either case be exercised only if accompanied by the means of enforcing judgements ; the spiritual courts could enforce judgements *in spiritualibus*, the temporal *in temporalibus*. Jurisdiction without the means of enforcing judgements would be a delusion.[5]

The king and the law: the king's position. Bracton characterizes the position of the king as that of vicar of God *in temporalibus.* An early theory of the divine right of kingship was thus proclaimed. The divine right was, however, divine both ways : it gave an exalted position but implied clear duties : the king had only such powers as were conferred on him by the law ; for it was the law that gave him his position ; the same law by which even Christ, and His Mother, did abide ; had they not done so, it would have simply meant that they employed might instead of destroying the devil's power by their justice ; so also the king, if he should use merely his might instead of limiting himself to the exercise of rights attributed to him by law, would be playing not God's, but the devil's game.[6]

The king's privileges. The king was, indeed, as much under

---

[1] Br., fol. 5 b, 55 b, 107 b, 400 b, 412 a.

[2] Ibid., fol. 1 b ' Iudicia enim non sunt hominis sed dei ' ; fol. 2 a ' author Iustitiae est deus, secundum quod iustitia est in creatore '.

[3] The emperor is not mentioned as the king's superior. This is a disregard of his claims or, strictly speaking, pretences, common in all self-respecting countries in the Middle Ages.

[4] See also Br., fol. 108 a.

[5] Ibid., fol. 106 b, 107 a, 175 a. Bracton accepts here the claims of Henry III as against those of ecclesiastical judges ; cf. Stubbs, ii. 66.

[6] Br., fol. 5 b ; cf. 107 b.

the law as any other monarch in any legal system. But the king had a number of peculiar rights. According to Bracton all secular jurisdiction was, so far as human beings were concerned, in the king : it could be in others only by delegation.[1] Whether this theory was sufficient to explain the facts, we may leave, for the present, undecided. At any rate, Bracton proclaimed it.

Then, among the attributes which were peculiar to the king, we can distinguish two groups : the first group consisted of rights which could be granted by him to private persons ; these were, for instance, rights to things which, as Bracton puts it, ' de iure naturali esse deberent inventoris ', which, however, in the Middle Ages were usually claimed by the kings (' habet . . . de iure gentium ' [2]). But there was a second class of royal prerogatives : ' ea . . . quae iurisdictionis sunt et pacis, et ea quae sunt iustitiae et paci annexa, ad nullum pertinent, nisi ad coronam et dignitatem regiam, nec a corona separari poterunt cum faciant ipsam coronam . . . Huiusmodi . . . iura sive iurisdictiones ad personas vel tenementa transferri non poterunt, nec a privata persona possideri, nec usus nec executio iuris, nisi hoc datum fuerit ei de super.' [3] The residuary power was here clearly claimed : ' sicut iurisdictio delegata non delegari poterit, quin ordinaria remaneat cum ipso Rege.'

The king had not yet a number of prerogatives which would be attributed to him later on. For instance, the principle, ' Nullum tempus occurrit regi ', was in force only as to claims of which the objects were transferable royal privileges : thus, the right of wreck obviously belonged to the king. The king could part with such privileges only by special grant [4] ; his action or, to use Bracton's expression, his *petitio*, was not lost by the lapse of time, because the burden of proof rested, in view of the peculiarity of the thing, on the defendant. But wherever the king must supply proof, he would lose his action by the lapse of time just as anybody else would.[5]

[1] Br., fol. 108 a.   [2] Ibid., fol. 55 b ; cf. 120 a.
[3] Ibid., fol. 55 b.   [4] Ibid., fol. 55 b.
[5] Ibid., fol. 56 a ' In aliis vero ubi probatio necessaria fuerit, currit tempus contra ipsum sicut contra quoscunque alios '.

The king can do no wrong. From this whole legal position
it follows that the king, if he wished to use his power
as vicar of God, was bound not to do wrong. A wrong would
consist in the violation of any right. For if a right was
violated, it remained violated even if it was the king and not
somebody else that had violated it. In other words, there
was the principle, 'The king can do no wrong'.[1] But it meant,
that the king must not, was not allowed, not entitled, to do
wrong; his acts, if against the law, were not legal acts, but
iniuriae, wrongs. There was, in this respect, no difference
between the king and others—no difference in theory, at
least. The king's wrong, his wrongful act, his disseisin for
instance, would be spoken of as if done by anybody else.[2]
This similarity of treatment culminates in the statement that
it must be found out, ' *quis sit ille qui deiicit, princeps scilicet*
ex potentia [3] vel aliquis pro eo vel nomine suo, vel iudex . . .
vel *privata persona* '.[4]

Bracton made the above distinction only to distinguish the
remedies which would serve the disseisee; he did not admit
for a moment that a ' wrong ' should not be attributed to
the king simply because of his royal position; the king was
not allowed to dispose of rights which did not belong to him,
even if they had originally been his but were granted away; [5]
and, where he was bound to warrant, or to compensate, his
obligation did not, in its nature, differ at all from the obliga-

[1] ' Nihil enim aliud potest rex in terris . . . nisi id solum quod de iure
potest ' ; Br., fol. 107 a.

[2] As to the king : ' Quod factum suum corrigat et emendet (fol. 5 b) ;
iniuriatur et detrahit libertati prius concessae . . . sine iuris iniuria resu-
mere non poterit . . . quod factum suum, quod magis voluntarium est
quam iustum, revocet et emendet . . . (fol. 56 b) ; ut factum suum corrigat
et emendet . . . sed si alius ex facto et disseisina principis . . . quod factum
suum emendet vel in personam suam redundabit iniuria manifeste . . .
quod sine principe (qui fecit iniuriam) per se vel suos respondere non
debet, quia ipse princeps per se fecit iniuriam . . . factum suum emendare
quasi a lege compulsus et quasi in persona sua, cum sit ei submissus,
debet firmiter observare ' (fol. 171 b ; cf. Cutbill, 15–16), &c. As to
private persons : ' Item incidit in assisam . . . etiam ille cuius nomine fit,
dum tamen factum suorum et iniuriam advocaverit ' (fol. 171 a) ; ' Si
autem deadvocaverit et iniuriam suorum emendaverit ' (fol. 171 b).

[3] i.e. pure might ; cf. about Christ : ' non virtute uteretur potentiae '
(fol. 5 b).

[4] Br., fol. 171 b.   [5] Ibid., fol. 56 b.

tion of a private person.[1] The person vouching the king would, indeed, have to use, 'cum quadam curialitate', a phrase to the effect that he could not answer without the king; but Bracton is anxious to add that 'nihil aliud est dicere, non possum sine rege respondere, quam vocare ipsum ad warrantum licet per alia verba'. To Bracton's mind the king was bound not to infringe rights; it was the king's duty to redress wrongs done by himself or on his behalf; and it was the king's duty to discharge all other obligations arising for him as they would arise for a private person. In other words, the private person who would have a claim against another would have the like claim against the king; there is nothing to suggest that such a claim would be different in its nature because it was directed against the king.

Let us suppose that the king was willing to redress his or his servants' wrong; what should the reparation consist in?[2]

Bracton does not give us a direct answer; but as the king's wrong did not differ from that of a private person, we may infer that the redress should also not be different. We must add, however, an important modification.

The king was only bound to redress the injury done. This means that he should, if possible, bring the infringed right back to the state in which it had been before the infringement. The punishment of the wrong-doer, however, did not find an analogy in the case of the king. Bracton does not say this, because to him it must have seemed obvious. He tells us repeatedly that the purpose of an assize of novel disseisin was to recover the thing and to get the adversary punished;[3] the punishment in the case of such an assize would be threefold, namely, corporal punishment, punishment in money, and damages. Besides, an ox had to be given by the defendant to the sheriff.[4] Nobody will suppose that the king had to

---

[1] Br., fol. 382 b 'Quaero an ille teneatur ad warrantiam cum ad warrantum vocetur, et videtur quod sic, quia res cum homine transit ad quemcunque'.

[2] This is the question which lies at the bottom of the controversy about the modern scope of the petition of right. The king is willing to do right; and we are to find out what he must do in order that right may be said to have been done.

[3] Br., fol. 161 b, 164 b.   [4] Ibid., fol. 161 b.

give an ox to his sheriff, or that, he would condemn himself to corporal punishment, or make a fine with himself
propter spoliationem pacis[1]; as to damages, Bracton does not
say why they should not be paid by the king; but he treats
them distinctly as a punishment. On the other hand, he says
that the assize did not necessarily lie for punishment, for it
might be confined to exacting punishment from one and
restitution from another party.[2] Then, again, he asserts that
he who was guilty, not of disseisin, but only of unjust detention or he who was not guilty at all, would only have to
make restitution, 'immunis enim esse debet a poena qui
immunis erat a culpa, quamvis quis teneatur ad restitutionem,
licet non ad poenam, nisi pro iniusta detentione. . . . Item
non tenetur aliquis heres de facto, scilicet de disseisina antecessoris sui quoad poenam disseisinae, licet teneatur ad restitutionem '.[3] Thus we come to the conclusion that the payment
of damages, bearing a distinctly penal character, would not
be required in the case of the king, in so far, at least, as the
emendatio of his wrongful disseisin was concerned; but the
restitution of the thing would certainly be required.

On the other hand, restitution in such a case related, not
only to the thing itself, but also to all the issues received in
the meantime.[4] This was obviously not punishment but
restitution, a part of the *emendatio*, and there is no reason to
believe that this duty did not extend to the king. Yet this
rule was soon to be subjected to an important limitation.[5]

Remedies. But to have a claim is one thing; to enforce it, is
another. Was there any remedy against the king? Could it
be used against the king's will? The modern petition of right
has for its legal basis in the courts of law, the consent of the
king that the court decide what is law on that particular
question. The sovereign is *ex hypothesi* willing to do what
justice requires. Such questions did not present to Bracton's
mind any difficulty. He was, however, considering a further

---

[1] Br., fol. 161 b.   [2] Ibid., fol. 164 b; but cf. fol. 172 a.
[3] Ibid., fol. 172 a.
[4] Ibid., fol. 165 a: 'Acquiritur vero per assisam istam non solum ipsa
res spoliata corporalis, verum etiam omnes fructus medio tempore percepti cui competit querela.'   [5] Below, pp. 63 f., 137 ff.

question : what if the king refused to redress a wrong
admittedly done ?

There is in Bracton's work some uncertainty about the
matter. Bracton does not mention a petition as the means
of proceeding against the king; he says that the person
wronged had but one remedy : ' locus erit supplicationi quod
(ut) factum suum corrigat et emendet.' [1] But this *supplicatio*
must not be identified with the later *petitio*. First of all,
Bracton used *petitio* in an entirely different sense, namely,
that of an action, even of an action brought by the king ; [2]
secondly, if there had been a formal requirement of such
a petition, we may assume that Bracton would have alluded
to it or even described the procedure ; thirdly, this *supplicatio* to the king reminds us very closely of that other step
which the wronged man was sometimes required to take :
a man disseised by another in the name of third persons
should, if possible, approach those third persons, so that it
might be known whether when they learned of the injury
they would be willing to redress it. [3] With this should be
compared the statement about the *supplicatio* to the king
in the analogous case of disseisin in the king's name : ' locus
erit supplicationi, ut factum suum corrigat et emendet ' [4] ; and
also the other statement : ' absque eo quod hoc prius domino
regi ostenderit, quod factum suum . . . revocet et mendet ' [5].

---

[1] Br., fol. 5 b, 171 b.

[2] We shall try to show in the next chapter that the word *petitio* was
the technical name, adopted from abroad, for petitions to the king ;
but *petitio* in the sense of suit, demand, &c., was used in England very
early, and the superimposed meaning did not do away altogether with
that originally prevailing. The word supplication was used in Bracton's
days and, indeed, throughout the thirteenth century, to denote the act
of supplicating ; the written instrument was called petition. This was
true abroad ; it was also true in England under Edward I, when the
petition became so widely used (below, pp. 85–6); if in Bracton's days
petitio was the technical term, why did he not use that term if he
wished it to denote written petitions ? If it was not, if the technical term
was *supplicatio*, how could it have changed so suddenly that under
Edward I the name *supplicatio* was no more used for the document itself ?
and why should the term be different in England from what it was elsewhere, considering that it was the same Latin language ?

[3] Br., fol. 172 b ' si autem adire possint de facili, adeundi sunt, ut
sciatur utrum iniuriam emendare voluerint vel non, cum de iniuria eis
constiterit '.   [4] Above, p. 42, n. 2

[5] Br., fol. 56 b.

What should happen if the king refused to redress his wrong? We find in Bracton traces of two theories,[1] both starting from the same point of view, but different in effect. There was no doubt that a king who had done wrong ought to redress it : Bracton is as emphatic on this point as on any; nor, indeed, could it be otherwise if we take into account all that he says about the mission of the king and about the king's legal position. Then, again, a king who did not redress his wrongs was using his power in a way directly contrary to his mission.[2] Furthermore, if the king refused, he ought to be *punished* : the expression *poena* is used twice, and the phrases are almost identical.[3]

But who was to inflict such a punishment? or, at least, who might compel the king to redress his wrongs? Hardly any of Bracton's statements are better known than those in which he advised the man who had suffered wrong from the king and had not received reparation : ' satis sufficiat ei ad poenam quod dominum expectet ultorem. Nemo quidem de factis (regis) praesumat disputare, multo fortius contra factum suum venire.' [4] To assure the king that he was acting as the vicar of the devil, and not of God, was in Bracton's days certainly very impressive. If a pope proceeded to excommunicate a ruler, and absolve the latter's subjects from their allegiance, this could in theory be done only because the ruler had acted in a way which would promote the devil's' rather than God's cause. Such excommunications could be more or less effective according to the actual conditions of the time, but they were not, for any king, a pleasant thing to be reminded of. Whether Bracton was thinking of them at all is a different question : he was, in any case, very far from preaching the doctrine of passive obedience. If we carry the most royalistic of his statements to their logical conclusions, we can only say that, while the king was not allowed to do any wrong, yet there was, within his realm, no tribunal, legally organized, competent to judge him. The statement, ' Rex non debet esse sub homine, sed sub Deo et sub lege ',[5]

---

[1] Above, p. 39.   [2] Above, p. 9.   [3] Br., fol. 5 b, 171 b.
[4] Ibid., fol. 5 b, 6 a.   [5] Ibid., fol. 5 b.

does not necessárily imply that he 'could not be judged, for example, by the pope or the council [1] : shortly before Bracton had said : ' Parem autem non habet *in regno suo* . . . item nec multo fortius superiorem nec potentiorem habere debet, quia sic esset inferior *sibi subiectis.*' Thus, what Bracton had in mind was by no means *all* tribunals composed of human beings.

In any case, Bracton obviously meant only a legal impossibility of compelling the king to redress his wrongs. But he saw another possible course of human events :

' Item cum non semper oporteat regem esse armatum armis sed legibus, addiscat rex sapientiam, et conservet iustitiam . . . cum sit honor et gloria in sermone sensati, et lingua imprudentis subvərsio ipsius, et principatus senſati stabilis, et rex sapiens iudicabit populum suum. Si autem fuerit insipiens, perdet illum, quia a capite corrupto descendit corruptio membrorum, et si sensus et vires non vigeant in capite, sequitur quod caetera membra suum non poterunt officium exercere.' [2]

If the king's behaviour became rotten, the whole body politic would be affected by the rot. This organic theory of society seems to imply clearly that the subjects had the most undoubted and lawful interest in their king's behaviour, for they could be doomed because of it. We find here a distinct justification of an action of self-preservation, not quite legal, but, should the need arise, permissible.

Moreover, Bracton recognized also an opposite theory, which was well known and not at all unanimously rejected in the thirteenth century ; namely, that there was, within the realm, a body legally able to judge the king. This did not mean the king's judges. To Bracton they were, as we have seen, only the king's delegates ; [3] they acted only where the king himself could not dispose of the judicial business.[4] Bracton did not even allow them to judge men accused of high treason, for their lives, limbs, and estates : for the king's judges only represented the person of the king, and the king could not be judge in his own case (he was prosecutor,

---

[1] Cf. Stubbs, ii. 12, on the ' great international tribunal at Rome '.
[2] Br., fol. 107 b.   [3] Above, p. 41.   [4] Br., fol. 108 a.

or, at least, offended).[1] But there was the curia, the earls,
and the barons. That they tried hard to obtain rights of
compulsion against the king, we know well.[2] Bracton did
not accept their claims wholesale. He seems to have inclined
to the view that they had not, or should not have, such
a power. But his statements are by no means so final and
conclusive as they might seem at first. Some of those in which
he formulated the royalistic theory took the form of postulates
or suggestions (*debet*) : ' Item nec multo fortius superiorem,
nec potentiorem habere debet, quia sic esset inferior sibi subiectis. . . . Ipse autem rex non debet esse sub homine, sed
sub deo et sub lege.'[3] This statement seems curiously
modified by the following phrase, which makes the former
meaning still less definite :
' Sic ergo rex, ne potestas sua maneat infrenata, igitur non
debet esse maior eo in regno suo in exhibitione iuris, minimus
autem esse debet vel quasi in iudicio suscipiendo si petat.'[4]

The following statement presents an analogy ; it is contradictory in itself, unless Bracton was putting down the views
of the king's party just in order to explain them in his own
way, or even politely, *cum quadam curialitate*, to contradict
them,[5]

' Potentia vero omnes sibi subditos debet praecellere.
Parem autem habere non debet, nec multo fortius superiorem,
maxime in iustitia exhibenda, ut dicatur vere de eo, magnus
dominus noster, et magna virtus eius etc. Licet in iustitia
recipienda, minimo de regno suo comparetur.'[6]

And, finally, there is that well-known passage :

' Sufficiat ei pro poena quod dominum expectet ultorem
qui dicit : mihi vindictam et ego retribuam, nisi sit qui dicat
quod universitas regni et baronagium suum hoc facere debeat
et possit in curia ipsius regis.'[7]

Here the two views were very explicitly contrasted ; and
' under this *nisi sit qui dicat*, Bracton may well be stating
his own opinion '.[8] The case of the trial for high treason [9]

---

[1] Br., fol. 119.
[2] M. C., c. 61 ; Provisions of Oxford ; Stubbs, ii. 78.
[3] Br., fol. 5 b.   [4] Ibid., fol. 5 b.   [5] N.-B. i. 31.
[6] Br., fol. 107 a ; as to Lewis IX, see Appendix pp. 201–2.
[7] Br., fol. 171 b.   [8] Above, n. 5.   [9] Above, pp. 47–8.

affords an analogy : who should judge in such a case ? [1] Not
the king. Not his judges.

' Videtur, sine praeiudicio melioris sententiae, quod curia
et pares iudicabunt, ne maleficia remaneant impunita, et maxime ubi periculum vitae fuerit, et membrorum vel exhaere-
dationis, cum ipse Rex pars actrix esse debeat in iudicio.' [2]

Here, then, those judging would derive their power, not
from the king, but from the general principle that justice
must be done by somebody, and that it was obviously a case
in which otherwise justice would not be done. Bracton
accepts here the claims of the barons as put forward in 1233.[3]
It would seem, then, that Bracton did not consider the application of the same principle to proceedings against the king
absolutely unthinkable.[4]

The king and his justices. Among the pleas which ought
to be determined before the king or his justices,[5] Bracton
mentions cases arising out of fines made in the king's court
and not carried into effect : ' quia nemo potest finem inter-
pretari, nisi ipse rex, in cuius curia fines fiunt.' Here,

[1] An inconsistency has crept in here ; if the king could not be judge in
his own case, namely, where he was prosecutor or otherwise interested,
why should this rule be applied to treason only ? A plausible answer
seems to be, that Bracton was trying to fit the then clause 29 (formerly
39) of Magna Carta into his reasoning. Apart from that, this statement
of Bracton's is a direct confirmation of the claims of the barons, put
forward in 1233 in connexion with the proceedings (Stubbs, ii. 48–9)
against the Earl of Pembroke. It is, in the same degree, a flat repudiation
of the claim of the royalists. This, by the way, bears out Dr. Holdsworth's
suggestion (ii. 187), that Bracton's sympathies were perhaps with the
baronial party.

[2] Br., fol. 119.   [3] Above, n. 1.

[4] We have so far refrained from quoting the disputed passage on
fol. 34. The passage, however, should not be questioned as to its authen-
ticity. Its words resemble those which Bracton used elsewhere. There
is, in the disputed passage itself, an expression of the two points of view
which can be found also in other parts of Bracton's work. The fact
that it supplements the idea expressed in an undisputed passage (namely,
that the king's charters should not only not be interpreted, but also not
be avoided), speaks for its logical connexion with the text. But the fact
that it stands only in some manuscripts, and that even in these its place
varies, makes its character of an afterthought almost certain. And the
fact that in those manuscripts in which it can be found it stands always
as a whole, and that the two parts (' Item . . . irritetur ' and the rest)
are always found together, indicates that this was one addition and not
two separate additions. Appendix, pp. 202–5.,

[5] Br., fol. 105 b, 106 a.

therefore, the king acts as an arbitrator, and his justices
seem to represent him fully.   But in the undisputed part of
the passage De Chartis on fol. 34 it is said, that neither the
justices, nor private persons, should or could dispute or
interpret royal charters ; in cases of doubt the king's interpretation and pleasure were to be awaited.   Even where the
king's charter was falsified or unauthentic, it would be better
and safer that judgement were given 'coram ipso rege'.
Here is a new departure from the principle that the justices
represented the king : they were really contrasted with him ;
we may assume that this statement, inconsistent with what
Bracton says elsewhere, was only made because such was
the actual practice.   In any case we have here the (more or
less subconscious) formulation of the idea that, for practical
purposes at least, the justices should not necessarily be
identified with the king.   But such a theory was not yet
quite recognized by Bracton.   He repudiated it expressly as
to proceedings for high treason against the king's subjects ; [1]
and even where he speaks of the king's 'receiving justice',
he only means the king's suits. [2]

The king's servants.   Where a bailiff or a servant of the king
disseised some one in the king's name, the assize should be
taken but judgement should not be given before the king's
will was known. [3] This relates apparently to cases where the
bailiff or servant claimed to act in the king's name, but
where the king's interference was not yet proved.   For though
in Bracton's time the king himself used occasionally to disseise a man, there is no reason to suppose that he did it
otherwise than by an order to his own servants.   The presumption was that the act had been done by the king's order,
and though the fact of the disseisin was clear (as the assize
had been taken) judgement could not be given unless the king
allowed it, i.e. disclaimed the act.   This presents an interesting
analogy with the treatment of private defendants and their
alleged principals : ' si . . . falsus fuerit procurator qui deiecit,
non mecum erit agendum sed cum eo, nisi cum suum factum

[1] Above, pp. 47-9.
[2] e.g. Br., fol. 5 b 'Minimus autem esse debet vel quasi in iudicio
suscipiendo si petat'.   [3] Ibid., fol. 171 b, 172 a.

ratum habuero, quia ratihabitio in hoc casu comparatur mandato.'[1] The presumption in favour of the king's order and,
accordingly, the inadmissibility of a judgement by justices
was, we may add, soon abolished by the Statute of Westminster I (c. 24) : while the possibility of redress by the king
de son office was preserved, a writ of novel disseisin was given
against the aggressor.[2]

Vouching the king to warranty. In connexion with vouching
the king to warranty Bracton notes that, according to
a recent enactment,[3] the king should be vouched to warranty
or, in other words, proceedings should be discontinued until
the king's pleasure was known (' ut litem protraheret ') only if
the king was bound to exchange (' nisi ita sit quod rex teneatur
ad escambium '). This principle was to be confirmed soon
by the so-called Statutum de Bigamis.

[1] Br., fol. 171 b.   [2] Above, p. 25.   [3] Br., fol. 382 b.

CHAPTER II

THE REIGN OF EDWARD I

INTRODUCTORY

Old and new law. In dealing with the time of Edward I, we shall have more than once to repeat remarks made about the time of Henry III, partly in order to utilize new evidence of the same conditions and partly to bring out the changes of which in the time of the English Justinian there occurred so many.

Postulates of legal thought. We find the same postulates of legal thought. Prominent among them was the distinction between right and wrong. Stress is laid upon it in numerous documents. For instance, in the oath of the king's councillors, as preserved in a formula of 1307,[1] we read, among other stipulations :

' E qe vous ne lerrez pur nully, . . . qe vous ne facez faire a chescun, de quel estat ou condicion quil soit, droiture et reson solunc votre poair et a votre escient, e qe de nully rien ne prendrez pur tort faire ne droit delaier. . . .'

There was, too, the idea that every wrong ought to be redressed. Thus, the widow of Edmund of Cornwall had brought a writ of dower ; the king was Edmund's heir ; as Edmund by his charters had promised warranty on behalf of his heirs, the justices would not go on with the case because the king's interests would be affected. A petition was presented, and the endorsement ordered the justices to meet and to do right, ' ita quod pretextu regis non fiat iniuria '.[2] An escheator asked for a remedy, because he had been ordered, in an assize of novel disseisin, to pay damages : actually he had delivered the land to a bishop by virtue of the king's writ. He had been convicted together with the bishop's executors ; but the damages were exacted from him alone.

[1] Ryley, 514 ; cf. Baldwin, 348.
[2] A. P. E. 62.†

We read in the record that although the bishop could not be convicted of his wrong because he was dead, still the wrong and sin were not repaired or abolished ; nor could they be repaired until what had been taken away should be restored. It was, therefore, decided by consent of the bishop's executors, that they should indemnify the escheator.[1] In a document of the same year (21 Ed. I) we read : ' Dominus Rex, in quantum poterit, volens quod unicuique de regno suo de Iniuria sibi facta celeris fiat iusticia. . . .' [2]

Closely connected with this was another idea : that evil-doers must be punished. To select again only one statement, from the same year :

' Si iudicium predictum suo robore staret, remaneret transgressio cognita et confessa in Curia Regis inpunita, quod esset inconveniens.' [3]

There is hardly a point requiring less proof than that the notion of acquired rights, whatever their object, was generally accepted, and that those rights were thought of as inviolable.

A very instructive list of the infringements apparently most complained of can be found in the first chapter of the Statute of Westminster I. In the third chapter of the Statute of Westminster II we read about a husband losing a tenement which was the right of his wife. We have perhaps no better monument of the idea of rights and of their sacredness than the so-called Statutum de Tallagio non concedendo.[4] It not only safeguarded rights relating to material things, but contained also a promise that all clerks and laymen of the realm would have all their rights, liberties, and free customs, as freely and wholly as they used to have them best and most fully at any time. All statutes issued by the king or his ancestors, and all customs introduced in their time, which would withstand those rights, liberties, and free customs, should be null and void. These were obviously ideas connected with the not very much later notion of the birthrights of Englishmen.

---

[1] R. P. i. 117.   [2] Ibid., 99 b.   [3] Ibid., 110 a.
[4] Its value for the history of legal thought of the time is not destroyed by its being ' (historically) apocryphal ' (Holdsworth, ii. 245).

THE KING AND THE LAW

The king's legal position. ' In old times, every writ, as well of right, as of possession, would well lie against the king, of which nothing is changed now, but that much that he willeth that one sue against him by bill where before one sued by writ.' [1] This is a well-known passage ; and it truly deserves considerable attention. Its historical part was, indeed, wrong ; no writ could have issued against the king.[2] But the statement shows what legal ideas were current at the time when it was made. If this were legal heresy, a pleader would not have dared utter it in court. The contention as to the actual state of the law was clearly that the king could not, was not allowed to, interfere with anybody's property or possession. In other words, at least in this respect, legal thought did not distinguish, *in abstracto*, between the king and other persons.

In the writ proclaiming Edward's peace after Henry III's death, we read that the king is under an obligation to all and every one of his realm, to exhibit justice and to preserve peace.[3] In the case of Gloucester and Hereford the king's council declared that the king ' est omnibus et singulis de regno suo iusticie debitor '.[4]

It might be said that the justice mentioned here related to private disputes. Such a limitation would not be justified. As a general rule, the king was bound to do right where his own interests were concerned, just as he was in adjusting differences between his subjects. The record of proceedings following upon a writ of *Diem clausit extremum* states that ' Dominus Rex unicuique, prout tenetur, iusticiam facere voluit '.[5] And, as we shall see, the endorsement, *fiat iustitia,* was applied to petitions relating to private actions as well as to those which complained of the king's officials and to those which asked for remedies against what were legally the king's own acts.

The king's debts were clearly called so. In innumerable

---

[1] Y. B., 33–5 Ed. I, 471, R. S.
[2] Above, p. 26 ; cf. H. E. L. i. 516–17.
[3] Rymer, ii. 497 (Nov. 23, 1272).
[4] R. P. i. 74 b.   [5] Ibid. i. 129 b.

cases it was said that the king was bound in debts, and that they should be paid according to law.

For instance, in 1290, Paul de Pagrave complained that the late sheriff of Norfolk had taken, in the presence of the supervisor of the king's works, some of Paul's goods and chattels, to be used for the repair of the king's castle. He (Paul) had not yet been paid for them. A hypothetical writ was sent to the exchequer : the king willed the payment to be made if, as was alleged, he was bound to make it ; if, therefore, the barons (and chamberlains ?) of the exchequer should find that the allegation was true, let them cause payment of the debt to be made to Paul, ' prout de iure et secundum legem et consuetudinem scaccarii fuerit faciendum '.[1]

The wrongs, the *iniuriae* done by the king's officers, on the king's service, were, without any hesitation, admitted to be wrongs. We have many writs to the exchequer, stating, for instance, that a demand was being unjustly made on the king's behalf, and ordering redress because the king did not wish the complainant to be wronged.

Such was the writ on behalf of Samuel Lowon, with the clause ' nolentes ei iniuriam fieri '.[2] Such was, again, the writ on behalf of Robert de Ros ; Robert claimed to be entitled to amercements ; he and others were, however, unjustly distrained by the exchequer, with a view to his paying the amercements into the exchequer. The enrolment of the writ in the exchequer contains the following passage :

' et quia Rex non vult eis in hac parte iniuriari, mandat Baronibus quod inquisita inde plenius veritate quod iustum fuerit secundum legem et consuetudinem regni inde fieri faciant.' [3]

In 1290, Theobald de Verdun complained that the barons of the exchequer, without the king's order or any other reasonable cause, ordered him to be distrained for a relief of £100, although he was holding of the king in chief by one knight's fee only. The distress was contrary to the Great Charter according to which he ought to pay 100s. only.

[1] L. T. R., roll 61, m. 7 d.†   [2] Ibid., roll 49, m. 8 d.   [3] Ibid.

A writ was sent to the barons, stating that the king did not wish Theobald to be wronged in this respect; the barons were ordered to search the rolls of the exchequer; should they find that Theobald held and ought to hold his lands by one knight's service only, they were not to distrain him or cause him to be distrained for more than those 100s.[1]

The king's privileges. But while legally the king was expected to act according to law, and while the acts of his officers were judged by the law, it is true that the law gave to the king a peculiar position. That position is summed up, as we know, in the word ' prerogative '.[2] The king had special privileges like those which we have observed in the former reign. For instance, from 34 Ed. I comes the mention (by Bereford C. J.) that what was attested by the king's charter could not be denied.[3] But we observe also the growth of new royal privileges. Roughly speaking, we can distinguish those directly established, and those logically derived from the king's position.

To this latter group belongs the differential treatment brought about by the Statute of Gloucester (1278). That statute gave, as we know, damages in an assize of novel disseisin, against those into whose hands the tenements had

---

[1] L. T. R., roll 61, m. 10 r.†

[2] There was compiled, in the time of Edward I, a series of rules defining special privileges of the king. For a time, it was supposed to be a statute, issued in the seventeenth year of Edward II; but we know now that it dates from the time of that king's father (Maitland, E. H. R. v. 753); already to Cutbill, 13 n., it was ' plain that the statute was promulgated early in Edward I's reign '. Internal evidence has been known for centuries to prove that it was not a statute but a private (or semi-official) compilation, below, p. 132, n. 2. It contains only a partial enumeration of the king's rights in regard to feudal tenures. But at this incompleteness we should not wonder. The subject was already far too complicated to be exhausted in a limited number of sentences. In those days, as to-day, no list can exhaust the position of a ruler, for that position is determined necessarily, not only by legal considerations, but also, e.g., by political facts. In the text itself the word ' prerogative ' does not occur. But it was being used at that time as a noun (Pl. Ab. 192, rot. 45; Fleta, ed. Selden, 68; R. P. i. 97, no. 10, 116–17, no. 24; as to the Dial. de Scac. above, p. 11, n. 7. Otherwise H. E. L. i. 512).

[3] Y. B., 33–5 Ed. I, 185, R. S. Bereford C. J.: ' Veistes le plee entre le Roy de Escoce e un B, ou une chartre ne poeit estre dedit pur ceo qe la chartre le Roi fust mis avant en testmoignance de ceo fet, auxi com ore ? '

come (and not only against the original disseisors). The chapter in question (1) was not understood to apply to the king. The explanation is, perhaps, that according to the individualistic point of view the king would have had to ' grant ' to his subjects such a right against himself, or else he could not be bound by the statute. In any case, there arose a new and a very important difference between the king and his subjects. The same chapter gave the recovering party the right to costs, as a part of damages. Here, too, and for the same reason, the king could not feel bound by the statute ; this is why in later proceedings against the king (until the Petitions of Right Act, 1860) costs were not given against the king.[1]

An illustration is provided by a case to which we shall refer as the Hautboys case.[2] Bartholomew de Redham had been disseised by Robert Baynard and another. He recovered seisin in an assize of novel disseisin. In their turn, however, Bartholomew with another, who was Queen Eleanor's bailiff, entered upon tenements belonging to Robert, other than those which Bartholomew had recovered. Robert brought an assize of novel disseisin ; but, to quote the writ, they held the tenements in the hands of the queen.[3] *Therefore*, the assize could not be taken.[4] Robert petitioned the king, who, with the queen's consent, assigned commissioners to inquire from what lands and tenements the complainants had been ejected, by whom, when, how, and what damages and hardships they had suffered on that occasion ; furthermore, to hear and determine the case according to the law and custom of the realm. The commission remained unexecuted. The queen died. Another commission, and still another, were sued out. Finally, in 1301, one more commission issued to inquire and to certify the king. An inquisition was taken, and at last orders issued to the keeper of the king's manor not to intermeddle with the tenements any more, but to restore them to Robert's heir.[5]

---

[1] 3 Comm., 400 (ed. 1770) ; Robertson, Civil Proceedings, 397–8, 613.
[2] T. S., f. 1, m. 1–2.†   [3] Ibid., m. 1–2–7.†   [4] Ibid., m. 1–2–2.†
[5] C. C. R., 1301, 415–16, 425.

The disseisin complained of occurred about three years after the Statute of Gloucester; proceedings were taken against the queen and, after her death, against her heir, the king. The king paid no damages. The conclusion is simple : the first chapter of the statute of Gloucester did not apply to the king.

Apart from these royal prerogatives, arising simply from the non-application of new rules to the king, we know of other cases where new privileges were claimed for the king and—what is more important—gained recognition.

As Bracton put it, the principle 'nullum tempus occurrit regi' ought to be applied only in cases in which a special royal right had been appropriated by a private person.[1] An early case in the time of Edward I shows that the principle was already appealed to in cases not covered by Bracton's statement. The king brought a *quare impedit* against the Earl of Gloucester (Gilbert de Clare). Gilbert's title was based on an old fine ; the royal attorney alleged that it had been made without the king's consent. The' earl contended that in any case it had been made long ago. 'Ad quod dicit attornatus Quod nullum tempus occurrit Regi unde petit iudicium curie.'[2] We have later pronouncements to the same effect.[3]

We have seen, too, that, at least in the earlier part of Henry III's reign, the king was often vouched to warranty.[4] Bracton required the warrantee to say, 'cum quadam curialitate', that he could not answer without the king, but even in Bracton's opinion this was nothing short of vouching to warranty.[5] Under Edward I, there was no more vouching. We only hear that one could not answer without the king, and in one of the earliest year-books preserved, the reporter remarks, 'Nota per hoc quod Rex non potest vocari ad warrantiam.'[6] It was even disputed whether the king was legally bound to warrant. Thus in a later case Brumpton J. asserted, for the purpose of an argument, 'qe sy le Rey vus

---

[1] Above, p. 41.   [2] Pl. Ab. 196, rot. 30.
[3] Y. B., 20–1 Ed. I, 69, R. S. : 'Le Roy est prerogatif ; par quey nul prescripcion de tens ne court encontre ly' ; cf. ibid., 113.
[4] e.g. above, p. 37.   [5] Above, pp. 42–3.
[6] Y. B., 21–2 Ed. I, 287, R. S.

graunte e conferme une tere, si serra il lye a la garantie par cel graunt.' Counsel retorted : ' Ce est especialte en le R qil ne se lye a garantie a nuly.'[1]

Let us note the case between the earls of Gloucester and Hereford.[2] A number of statements in that case seem expressions of the tendency which was to result in the absolutism of the Tudors and in the claims of James I. The king, by letters patent, had ordered his justices to take an inquisition by the oath of magnates as well as of other honest and lawful men of Wales, Gloucestershire, and Herefordshire. None should be excepted, because the affair touched the king, his crown, and dignity. Magnates were assembled ; they were required to promise, with their hands on the Book, to do what they should be ordered on the king's behalf. They protested that this was unheard of, and that never had such an order come to their March except in affairs touching it. Thereupon they were told that the king, for purposes of common utility, was through his prerogative in many cases above the laws and customs of his realm (' pro communi utilitate, per prerogativam suam in multis casibus est supra leges et consuetudines in regno suo usitatas ').[3] This assertion of the king's special rights is characteristic, although, after all, the magnates did not take the oath. But the words used here do not mean that the king was considered *legibus solutus* in the later wide sense. The interpretation arose out of the mediaeval point of view : the king was in many cases above the laws and customs of his realm. The inference is that other laws and customs bound him. It is also interesting that the prerogative was regarded as based on considerations of common utility.

When the case came before the king's council, the Earl of Gloucester had many objections to the course of procedure as it had been adopted. The council overruled them. A rumour, they said, had reached the king, of an enormous offence perpetrated against his injunction : it was incumbent on the king, for the preservation of his peace, and for the

[1] Y. B., 30–1 Ed. I, 99, R. S.
[2] R. P. i. 70–7.   [3] Ibid., 71 b.

salvation of the people committed to his care, to order an inquisition to be taken immediately, by all means available without a violation of the law. The earl had asserted that the writ of *scire facias* ought to issue only out of a record and process, like a writ judicial; but the council declared that the king, from whom all the ministers (servants subject to him) had their records, was the superlative and highest record and excelled all his ministers, processes, and records of rolls.[1] The council also decided that if the king recollected and recorded that a plea was pending in his court before himself, he might, and ought to, order a *scire facias* to issue because it proceeded in such a case from a record as solemn as was his own.[2]

In the time of Henry III we often heard that the king had disseised a man. Under Edward, there are no more mentions of disseisin by the king. In later years, a theory was developed that if judgement was given to remove the king's hands, the king was *ipso facto* out of possession.[3] That theory was based on certain dicta coming from the fourteenth century.[4] It would be wrong, however, to assume that as a result of such a judgement the demandant could enter, if the claim was directed against the king, any more than he could where it was directed against a private person.[5]

We have numerous writs to escheators, sheriffs, and other royal ministers ordering them to remove the king's hands : if the king were *ipso facto* out of possession, the party who had been given restitution would but have to enter—and why should he pay for the writ?

In the Hautboys case,[6] we have two such writs for the one, and one writ for the other party. Another writ to the like effect (namely, to let the petitioner have his tithe of rabbits) resulted from one of the endorsements mentioned above and from an inquisition taken on the strength of it.[7] Many other

---

[1] This contrasts very curiously with Coke's comment on the first Statute of Westminster (2 Inst. 186): the king being a body politic cannot command but by matter of record.   [2] R. P. i. 74-7.
[3] Staunford, fol. 78 a ; Finch, Law, 459 ; 3 Comm. 257 (ed. 1770).
[4] Below, p. 135, n. 2.   [5] H. E. L. ii. 103.
[6] Appendix, pp. 240-1, n. 1 ; above, p. 57.   [7] Below, p. 110, n. 3.

writs to the same effect can be quoted,[1] but this is unnecessary as we have at least two pronouncements which clearly state the legal position. One is contained in a judgement of 1293 : [2]

' Nec licet alicui Escaetori terras seu tenementa aliqua, postquam in manum Domini Regis ea seysierit, reddere quoquomodo alicui heredi seu alii sine precepto Domini Regis.'

The other pronouncement dates from 1301.[3] We learn that at an earlier date the king had ordered that no lands and tenements taken into his hands by his ministers were to be delivered at all except *per ipsum dominum regem* (by the king's own order). A statute (made at Lincoln) ordered that in certain cases a writ of *amoveas manus* should issue out of the chancery ; this, needless to add, is conclusive evidence that at least the latter writ was necessary.

Yet, there was a grain of truth in the theory. If the king had seised some land, he had, or ought to have, done so on a legal basis; for instance, by virtue of an inquisition which informed the king of his right. If the king (or, what amounted to the same thing, a royal official authorized to take the proper steps) saw from the same inquisition, or from a new one, that the king had in reality no such title as he had been supposed to have, the legal foundation fell away. The king could indeed, by virtue of his power, remain seised, and then deliver the seisin to the man who had a better title than the king. That would mean, however, that the king was seised, knowing that he had no right to be seised, from the moment when he had come to know that his title was not good enough, until the moment when seisin was actually restored to the party. To use the terminology of Roman law, during that time the king would be a *malae fidei* possessor. Therefore, a new theory seems to have been acted on : while the actual relation between the official and the land, the *corpus*, as the Romans might say, remained unchanged, the king had lost the *animus possidendi*.[4] If we accept this theory, a fundamental principle will become clear : the king was assumed

---

[1] e.g. C. C. R., 33 Ed. I, 278–9. [2] R. P. i. 91, no. 1. [3] Ibid. 145.
[4] Some of the chancery officials, who were clerks, might have introduced this distinction which was well known at that time (H. E. L. ii. 50, 54).

to be always a *bonae fidei* possessor.   His possession ceased
at the moment when he lost his bona fides.   It might cease
of his own free will, because he *wished* to abide by the law.
But in any case it ceased.   If it did not, his power would be
used to do what no one else was allowed to do : to retain
a thing to which he had no right.   That would be wrong.
And the king was bound not to do wrong.

Our theory is borne out by the study of the writs which
had to be sent out in any case, whether the king's title was
good or not, before the party could have seisin.   During
Edward's reign we find a variety of writs serving different
purposes, and from that time on we can study the differences
between cases in which different writs were used.   There
might be an order to deliver (' liberes '), to restore (' restituas '), not to intermeddle further (' te de cetero non inter-
mittas '), to cause to have seisin (' habere facias seisinam ').
Obviously, each writ must have been devised to serve in
a certain group of cases, but in some doubtful cases different
writs may at different times have been used for purposes
which really could be served by one and the same writ.   What
concerns us here is the form used in cases in which the king
had no right to take seisin, but we must give a few examples of the use of the different writs.   Thus, where the
king had assigned dower to the widow of a tenant in chief,
the order would be ' to deliver ' [1].   Where a clerk had been
charged with a felony and had purged his innocence in the
canonical way, the order would be ' to restore '.[2]   A similar
writ would issue where a tenant in chief and his wife had been
jointly enfeoffed by a third person to hold of the king by the
service of (part of) a knight's fee and the king, after the
husband's death, had taken the tenements into his hands and
had taken the homage of the widow.[3]   But where the king
had clearly no right, the proper writ was ' not to intermeddle
further '.   Such was the writ, almost immediately following
Edward's accession,[4] ordering the escheator ' to permit Bartholomew . . . son of Herbert . . . to have his father's lands

---

[1] e.g. C. C. R., 2 Ed. I, 61.   [2] Ibid., 18 Ed. I, 59.
[3] Ibid., 23 Ed. I, 422.   [4] Ibid., 1 Ed. I, 4–5, December 18, 1272.

and not to intermeddle further with them, as the king learns by inquisition . . . that Herbert at his death held nothing of the king in chief by reason whereof the custody of his lands might or ought to pertain to the king, and that Bartholomew is his next heir '.[1] The formula appears to have been soon simplified by omitting the order to cause to have seisin. For instance, in 1275 we find an order to the escheator not to intermeddle further with certain lands on account of the king's order to take the lands into the king's hands, as the king had learned by inquisition taken by the escheator that the late tenant at his death had held his lands of the king in chief by socage and not by any service whereby the custody of his lands might or ought to pertain to the king.[2] A writ issued two days later added to the order ' not to intermeddle ' with certain lands in any wise, the direction ' so that Laurence . . . or others wishing to claim right therein might not have what pertained to them '.[3]

A clause was added ordering the restitution of issues (thus a writ of December 2, 1289, contains an order to the escheator not to intermeddle in any way with the lands specified in the writ, which the escheator had taken into the king's hands by reason of the death of the tenant in chief, and to restore the issues thereof, as the king had learned by an inquisition taken by the escheator that the man and his wife had been jointly enfeoffed of the lands by others than the king).[4] But as the restitution of issues was apparently not generally awarded, where the king had seised without having a right to the lands, and had therefore afterwards removed his hands, the *Articuli super Cartas* (1300) made the restitution of the issues compulsory (c. 19). The king's unlawful seisin would be no seisin at all, but only an encroachment, although one protected by the full force of the royal administrative machine. That was different from the days when an escheator had to cause one disseised by the

---

[1] The writ directing the inquisition had issued on September 7, 1272, and the inquisitions were taken on various days between September 13 and November 20 ; C. I. i. 284–5, no. 822.

[2] C. C. R., 3 Ed. I, 164, May 4, 1275.   [3] Ibid.

[4] Ibid., 18 Ed. I, 59 ; cf. 6 Ed. I, 468 ; 7 Ed. I, 526, &c.

king to have full seisin of the land. It was a new application of the principle that the king was not allowed to do wrong.[1]

But all this did not relate to chattels. Issues, as we have seen, had to be ' restored '. Of land you could be seised, or you could intermeddle with it by virtue of the royal power. But goods and chattels you either had or you did not have.[2]

The king's actual power. The king's legal position gave him great actual power. To describe it would mean to write a history of his reign. Hence, only a few facts shall be mentioned.

The king not only appointed the judges, but could also remove them. Edward I, it is true, exercised this right in order to do away with corruption and, like the great states-man he was, refrained from exercising it personally : for instance, in 1290, he ordered the treasurer and barons to judge three justices accused of bribery.[3] Yet it is he that was their supreme lord ; as the formula of 1290 of their oath has it, every judge had to denounce the wrongs of his fellow-judges first to the king's council, and, if that was without the expected result, to the king.[4] The justices, being the king's officials, were bound to give special attention to the rights of the king and of his wards.[5] In the formula of 1307

---

[1] After the lack of title had come to the knowledge of the king or of those acting for him, the king was no more seised ; his official was only intermeddling.

[2] By a writ of 1281 (C. C. R., 8 Ed. I, 78) the sheriff is ordered, not to intermeddle further with a certain manor, and to deliver the custody of it to one Robert de Staundon, retaining in the king's hands the lands which John de Chetewynd had held at his death of a tenant in chief, a minor in the king's wardship ; for the king had learned by an inquisition taken by the sheriff that Chetewynd had held nothing of the king in chief as of the crown, but that he had held the manor in question of Staundon by the service of one small knight's fee. The formula used here is explained by the fact that wardship was a chattel (H. E. L. ii. 116), hence the custody of the manor had to be ' delivered ' (cf. above, p. 16, n. 2).

[3] L. T. R., roll 61, m. 14 r.; cf. e.g. Holdsworth, ii. 240.

[4] L. T. R., roll 61, m. 10 r.†

[5] R. P. i. 92, no. 1 ' Cum potius pertineat ministris domini regis, et maxime Justiciariis suis statum Domini Regis et iura heredum in custodia ipsius Regis existentium manutenere, quam in aliquo infringere ', we read in a record. This was to safeguard the preservation of the legal *status quo* ; but stress was laid on the position of the justices as the king's servants.

of the oath, to be taken, among other king's councillors, by the judges, the point about the king's rights is stressed even more :

' E qe votre peyne, eide, e consail, a tot votre poair dorrez e metterez as droitures le Roy et de la Corone garder et maintenir, sauver et repeller, par la ou vous porrez, santz tort faire. E la ou vous saverez les choses de la Corone et les droitz le Roy concelez, ou a tort alienez, ou sustretz qe vous le frez saver au Roy. *E qe la Corone acrestrez a votre poair e en loiale manere.*' [1]

We have seen the actual amount of royal power in the case of Gloucester and Hereford.[2] The statute of Westm. I (c. 15) tells us that in four cases people were not replevisable by the common writ ; one of these was, if the arrest had been made by the king's command.

Where the ' right ' of an individual had been violated (for instance, if some one's land remained unduly in the king's hand), the king would usually restore the land or otherwise ' do right '. But where, in the eyes of mediaeval men, there was no such violation of a right, where, for instance, the king owed a debt for money borrowed, or for expenses incurred, the case was not always easy. If the king delayed payment, if he paid only a part, or if he refused to pay debts of his father though he had inherited his assets—there was no obvious way of compelling him to change his decision.

In 1290 we find a petition for 80 marks, in consideration of the payment of which the petitioners would acquit the king of 700 marks due to them. The petition was granted.[3] In 1278, a petition for money due from Henry III was answered as follows : ' Nondum est ordinatum de debitis Regis patris acquietandis ; et cum ordinatum fuerit, prosequatur.' [4] In 1290, a petition to the same effect was refused : ' Rex non habet Consilium reddendi debita patris

---

[1] S. R. i. 248.
[2] Above, p. 59.
[3] R. P. i. 53, no. 85. Idem : ' petunt quod Rex solvat eis iiii marcas pro quibus parati sunt remittere Regi DCC marcas quas Rex eis debet de arreragiis feodi sui ad Scaccarium. Responsio : Rex precipit Thesaurario quod satisfaciat eis de iiii marcis et recipiat quietanciam de . . . DCC marcis.' [4] Ibid., 1, no. 3.

sui.'[1]   A petition (coming from the last years of Edward I
or the first years of Edward II) for a salary due to a late
servant of the king received an endorsement ordering the
petitioners (executors) to wait for an improvement in the
king's financial position.[2]   And, apart from cases of refusal or
delay, we again see the tendency, observed in the former
reign,[3] to avoid, as far as possible, payments in money; but
the petitioners themselves sometimes preferred, it seems,
a certain grant, for instance of a custom, or of land, to
cash payment, if indeed they did not despair of the latter.
In a petition brought probably in the reign of Edward I or
soon afterwards,[4] one Arnaud de Poilland asked for his wages
and the payment of his men who had served the king in
Gascony; he asked that the little custom ' de Roian ' of
Bordeaux might be granted to him, until the king's debt
should be paid (out of it).   The endorsement directed that
the king be certified about the manner of Arnaud's service
and about the way in which the king could satisfy his debt
to Arnaud.

But even where ' rights ' had been infringed, they might
remain unrestored for a long time.   The king might interfere
now and again, to accelerate the administration of justice,
and yet the formalism of the king's ministers, who were
bound to safeguard the king's interests, might cause long
delays.

There is a characteristic entry on the parliament roll of
1307:

' Concordatum est per Consilium, quod ista Inquisicio tradatur Cancellario, ut scrutatis Rotulis Cancellarie de feodis
que fuerunt . . . Avelyne . . . de hiis que ibi invenientur
tangentibus feodum petitum certificet Thesaurarium et
Barones per breve Regis de Cancellaria et mittatur dicta
Inquisicio eisdem Thesaurario et Baronibus sub pede Sigilli
Regis Cancellarie.   Et mandetur dictis Thesaurario et Baronibus per breve de Cancellaria quod scrutatis Rotulis et Memorandis de feodis supradictis, et visis tam illis Memorandis
quam evidenciis Cancellarie, si compertum fuerit quod dicta

---

[1] R. P. i. 59, no. 164.   [2] A. P. E. 609.†   [3] Above, pp. 32–3.
[4] A. P. 14605.†

Avelyna et antecessores sui tenuerunt dictum feodum de dicto Archiepiscopo et predecessoribus suis, tunc Thesaurarius et Barones, vocatis Iusticiariis et aliis de Consilio, faciant eidem Archiepiscopo debitam recompensationem de feodo predicto, vel ipsum et successores *de feodis que de Rege tenet pro rata portionis exonerent.*' [1]

' Compensation ' is only one alternative. The other one is allowance in such payments as the petitioner, the king's tenant in chief, is, or as his successors will be, obliged to make. This latter method might or might not be convenient to the archbishop : it was convenient to the king. One had to go a long way before one's claim against the king was satisfied. A writ from the chancery to the exchequer enclosing the inquisition, and another writ notifying them of the result of the chancery search ; a meeting of justices and others at the exchequer ; all this seems logical enough, but it would take probably much more time than would have been necessary to obtain a satisfactory result in an ordinary lawsuit. In another case,[2] in 1305, the petitioner's land should have remained in the king's hand for a year and a day only ; after many years, however, the petitioner had not yet recovered it ; when he petitioned the king, some doubts arose whether, without reasonable cause, the king would have held the land so long ; there followed a search for a title which the king might have ; finally, the king ordered by word of mouth that justice be done.[3]

Germs of later developments. We have, so far, considered the position of the king as the individual ruler. In later years, English law came to give the king a political, as distinguished from his natural, capacity. Was there anything, in the period now under consideration, to indicate the approaching centralization of ' public authority ', its exercise ' in the public interest ', the development of an administrative

---

[1] R. P. i. 210, no. 91.   [2] Ibid. i. 184–7.

[3] From the powerful position of the king resulted privileges for the queen. It was human that the queen should be treated by the king's servants with special consideration, even if legal logic could not have justified this. Hence the queen could not be sued by writ, hence also the king's administrative machine was used to enforce the queen's claims. See Appendix, pp. 206–10.

machine working in the name of the king, instead of a number of officials appointed by the king to assist him in the management of his affairs?

In legal theory, all feudal grants proceeded ultimately from the king; in legal theory, therefore, all the jurisdictional powers of the lords were delegated to them by the king.[1] This principle, expounded before Edward I's time by Bracton, was now being asserted and applied in a way of which we have at least one remarkable instance; this was a case against the bishop of Durham; he had accepted the responsibility for an act of his men, consisting in the imprisonment of certain persons carrying the king's writs into the bishop's liberty. The court declared that the bishop's liberty was derived from, and depending on, the crown; that the bishop had it by the king's deed; they declared, therefore, that in so far as the exercise and maintenance of the king's privileges (*regale*) within that liberty was concerned, the bishop was the king's servant (minister); and that the king's power extended throughout the realm, within as well as without the liberties.[2]

The administrative machine was, in the first instance, the king's. Hence the king's personal orders could and would be taken and obeyed. Moreover, '... the doctrine that the king's will can only be expressed by formal documents, sealed, or signed and countersigned, does not belong to the twelfth or thirteenth centuries. On the contrary, the king's will expressed by word of mouth is more potent than any writ '.[3]

---

[1] Otherwise H. E. L. i. 528–9. Although (above, p. 24) seignorial jurisdiction could develop in England because the man agreed to be his lord's 'justiciable' and, so far as the individual man was concerned, the lord could exercise jurisdiction over him only after he had become his 'justiciable', yet to exercise jurisdiction at all, the lord had to secure a grant from the king.

[2] Pl. Ab. 257, rot. 101 'Et libertas dicti episcopi Dunelmensis capitur in manum Regis in hec verba. . . . Et quia . . . episcopus cum libertatem predictam a corona exeuntem et dependentem habet per factum Regis in hoc minister ipsius Regis est ad ea que ad regale pertinent infra eandem libertatem loco ipsius Regis modo debito conservanda et exequenda'.

[3] H. E. L. i. 515. The king used to send by word of mouth orders to the exchequer (e.g. L. T. R., roll 48, m. 6. r.; roll 49, m. 3 r.; roll 52, m. 5 r.). In one case the king *ore suo proprio* ordered justice to be done (above, p. 67). Indeed, the case of Gloucester and Hereford suggests that the king's order would be valued, in its oral form, higher than in that of a plain chancery writ based on a judicial record, in other words, higher

But the institutional character of this administrative machine was growing. We find an assertion of the doctrine that any wrong done to the king's officials while they were carrying out their official duties was a wrong done to the king himself. In an attachment for taking away writs and panels carried by a coroner's clerk, the defendant took exception to a suit instituted by the king and not by the party; the king's attorney replied that this was a contempt of the king because the man was the king's servant.[1]

Mention must be made here of the institution of writs. The history of the writ presents the first instance of treating what was formally the king's order, not according to its face value, but as an order that might be disregarded. This was to lead, first, to the avoidance of royal charters and letters patent; then, to the declaration that the king's unlawful orders could, and had to, be disregarded.[2]

Another conception which was gaining in prominence at the time now discussed was that of public utility : it was to help effectively in developing the ideas of the body politic and of the state. In the great case between the earls of Gloucester and Hereford a somewhat unusual procedure was justified by the king's council on the ground that the sooner a transgressor (of the king's injunction) could be convicted, ' tanto honorabilius est Regie Maiestati, et Regno et Populo utilius et magis necessarium '. The first statute of Westminster had a number of references to the profit of the realm and of the people.[3] In a letter to the pope, the king speaks of a parliament which he had held [4] : he had ordered in it many things which concerned the better position of the English Church and the reformation of the realm, and

than what Coke would call ' the king's command by matter of record ' (2 Inst. 186). Cf. below, p. 142.

[1] Pl. Ab. 284 rot. 46 ' Et Reginaldus dicit quod non debet ad hoc breve respondere quia dicit quod Dominus Rex motu suo proprio de huiusmodi iniuriis privatis personis illatis sectam habere non debet ex quo aliena accio sibi competere non potest. . . . Et Iohannes . . . qui sequitur pro Rege dicit quod quelibet iniuria ministris Regis licet minimis illata vertitur in dedecus ipsius Regis '.

[2] Above, p. 15.

[3] Especially preamble and Chap. 50.

[4] Meaning the parliament in which Stat. Westm. I was enacted.

which thus meant an increase of the common profit of the people.[1]

Legality. Having attempted to view the position of the king in its various aspects, let us come back to the fundamental principle : despite all his power, the king was bound to observe the law, which had made him king. This was true not only of the king ; it was not only a moral or, let us say, a political obligation. We find it emphasized in the very oath of the king's councillors to which we have alluded before ;[2] they had to take pains, to help, to give advice, and to use all their power to guard and maintain the right of the king and the crown, to save and to defend (?) them wherever they could do so without doing wrong ('par la ou vous porrez, santz tort faire '). Here, too, was one of the ideas which were to result in the modern interpretation of the principle, ' The king can do no wrong '.

REMEDIES

Remedies and ordinary procedure. The question is again before us, what, if the king or his officers did wrong a subject ? Before trying to describe the remedies, we must refer once more [3] to the difference between a remedy and ordinary procedure.

That difference is illustrated by the following case which occurred in Edward I's time : certain building operations for the enlargement of the Tower of London had made necessary the use of some adjoining land. For this purpose was taken, among others, land belonging to the hospital of St. Catherine. The tenants of the land were indemnified, according to an estimate of the mayor and aldermen of London and of other men selected for the purpose ; on the other hand, the hospital, of which the land had been taken, received, in compensation, no lump sum : there was to remain on the land an annual charge amounting to what had been the annual

[1] P. W. 381–2 'Ibique multa statuisse . . . que melioracionem status ecclesie Anglicane reformacionem regni eiusdem respiciunt et communis profectus populi sapiunt incrementa '.

[2] Above, pp. 52, 65. [3] Above, pp. 21, 23.

rent.[1] The warden did not take out the king's letters patent promising annual payment. Giles de Audenarde, the constable, who was in charge of the operations, afterwards paid the money year by year to the hospital, and had an allowance of these payments in his account in the exchequer. On the strength of the rolls of his account, and also on his personal testimony, the hospital obtained a writ of *liberate* in the first year after Giles had retired ; it is not clear whether such *liberates* issued afterwards. Finally, however, the friars were told that no more *liberates* would be issued without the king's letters patent. The friars brought a petition to the king in parliament. Giles was called before the council and gave evidence. It was ordered that the chancery rolls be searched for the *liberate* and that the case be brought again before the king and council.[2] It seems clear that the rent was paid here, originally, without an application, on the part of the payees, either to the king, or to the exchequer, or to the chancery ; later a *liberate* was granted, without reference to the king ; and only afterwards, the issue of a new *liberate* having been refused, a petition was brought to the king in parliament. Thus the petition or the proceedings upon it may be said to have been the remedial course, while suing for payment to the constable, or even for a *liberate* to the chancery, was the ordinary course of business.

If we see that petitions were presented to the king on some subject, we need not suppose that the matter was outside the jurisdiction of the lower authorities. For instance, we know a number of cases in which the barons of the exchequer gave respite to some of the king's debtors.[3] And still, we know that in very many cases petitions were presented to the king asking for respite[4] ; in other cases writs of respite issued from the chancery to the exchequer, although we do not know whether a petition had been presented to the king.

---

[1] 'Remansit fundus pro domino rege ut supradictum est necessario occupatus, obligatus hospitali beate Katerine predicte in lxxiii s. v d. annuatim percipiendis a Domino Rege pro fundo Hospitalis predicti occupato.'   [2] R. P. i. 156, no. 11.

[3] e.g. L. T. R., roll 62, m. 11 r.†; K. R., roll 47, m. 5 d.

[4] e.g. M. P., nos. 178, 185.

Coram rege terminari debet placitum quod ipsum tangit. The principle which we have seen applied in Bracton's days, and before then, ' coram rege terminari debet placitum quod ipsum tangit ', continued in force.   In 1290, the bishop of Carlisle petitioned ' quod Dominus Rex . . . ei remedium facere velit, et gratiam, cum nemini liceat Cartas regias nisi ipsis Regibus iudicare '.[1] The same principle was given prominence in the following decision [2] :

' Et quia videtur Curie quod Inquisitio ista Domino Rege inconsulto, tam propter Cartam ipsius Domini Regis porrectam, quam nemo per Inquisitionem patrie vel alio modo iudicare debet nisi solus Dominus Rex, quam ratione Ballive predicte que est ipsius Domini Regis, et ad quam predictus Henricus dicit predictam Libertatem pertinere, Dictum est partibus, quod sequantur versus Dominum Regem, quod precipiat procedere ad predictam Inquisitionem capiendam si voluerit, vel quod alio modo faciat voluntatem suam in loquela predicta.'

As is known from the so-called Statutum de Bigamis, the justices were agreed that one could not see how a case might be proceeded with, if the defendant claimed that he could not answer without the king, and if his claim was based on such a charter that a private person would have been bound to warranty.   Cases might arise, however, in which the king's charter contained no promise of warranty, or by which he had only granted as much as was in him, or had but confirmed or ratified a private deed :   even in such cases, the justices were bound, not indeed to supersede the proceedings, but, *after* the case had been shown to the king, to proceed without delay.   This latter clause brought about some difficulty of interpretation.   Its meaning seems to have been this : in the first group of cases, the proceedings had to stop, *until* a *procedendo* came ;   in the second group, they had to be adjourned for a definite time, and in the meantime ' the king ' had to be notified ;   on the appointed day the case would be proceeded with, *unless* a writ *ne procedatur rege inconsulto* was brought.   Later practice seems to have been in accordance with this interpretation.

[1] R. P. i. 23, no. 13.   [2] Ibid. 26, no. 16.

But doubts often arose whether in a particular case the proceedings should be superseded or not; and the fear of the judges, lest they should act against the king's interests, must sometimes have prompted them to take what for them, at all events, would be the safer course. Thus in a case of dower the defendant pleaded that his lands were in the king's hands; the court resolved that, as this was only by way of distress, judgement could be given for the plaintiff; but execution was stayed until she should have sued to the king.[1] In the case of a writ of right, the defendant pleaded that his lands were seised by the king; the plaintiff answered that the freehold was still in the defendant. 'It would be reasonable that he should answer,' said Brumpton J., 'but as we cannot hold the plea while the tenements are seised, I advise that you who have to plead against them send to court and purchase permission; for we shall hold no such plea before we have an order.'[2] There is no doubt that what was meant here by suing to the king, or by purchasing 'permission', was not an application to the court *coram rege*, the king's bench. Indeed, in later days the king's bench used to grant aid from the king, just as any other court. It seems very likely that in the days of Edward I a permission to proceed was already applied for, as a rule, at the chancery; and the expression 'purchase grace', used by Brumpton J., seems to point in the same direction. But in some cases the permission was, or even had to be, petitioned for.[3] We must again note the curious discrepancy between theory and practice: for in theory, all the courts in which the royal justices adjudicated were the king's courts.[4]

It was, of course, impossible for the king to dispose of all the business himself. He had, as we have seen, a great machine to work for him. Our consideration of the ways in which claims against the king were satisfied or, failing satisfaction, remedies were asked for, will fall into two parts: first, we shall give a sketch of such procedure as did not, and, secondly, of that which did, involve an application to the

[1] Y. B., 22 Ed. I, 407, R. S.   [2] Ibid., 30–1 Ed. I, 173, R. S
[3] e. g. R. P. i. 49, no. 46.   [4] Above, pp. 41, 47, 50.

king or his council.   Now and again we may have to mention
ordinary steps as well as remedies.

Procedure without application to the head.   Fleta tells us
that it was the office of the clerks of chancery ' supplicationes
et querelas conquerentium audire et examinare, et eis super
qualitatibus iniuriarum ostensarum debitum remedium exhi-
bere per brevia Regis ' [1] ; we cannot help thinking that this
related, not only to wrongs done by private individuals, but
also to complaints of parties claiming to be aggrieved by
royal officials.   It must be admitted that by no means were
all cases fixed in which the chancery could interfere on its
own responsibility.   If we went by the wording of Statute
of Westminster II, we should find nothing to indicate that
the writ ' in consimili casu cadente sub eodem iure ' was to
relate only to private cases.   Complaints against royal officials
might be thought of as falling under the same rule, if the
legal position was quite clear.   In any case the procedure, being
of vital importance, was changed as often as seemed expedient.

Thus, Edward I ordered that lands and tenements taken
into the king's hands should not be delivered without the
king's own command.   This apparently proved inconvenient
to the king, or injurious to his people, or both.   Hence, in
the twenty-first year, a statute, made at Lincoln, provided
that, notwithstanding that former enactment, a new procedure should be adopted by the chancery.   Where the
escheator, upon inquisition, had taken lands and tenements
into the king's hands, by virtue of a *diem clausit extremum*,
and it appeared, after the inquisition had been returned into
chancery, that nothing was held from the king in chief,
a writ should at once be sent from the chancery to the
escheator, ordering him to remove the king's hands from
the lands and tenements, and to restore the issues to the
party.[2]   This procedure was most similar to what was known

---

[1] Fleta, book ii, ch. 13, s. 1.

[2] R. P. i. 145.   Based on Coke's information (4 Inst. 79), the opinion
is prevalent now that no juries appeared in the chancery (e.g. Baldwin
240).   This was true later, but not in Edward I's time.   Indeed, juries
continued to be summoned to chancery up to the fifth year of Edward III
(below, p. 173).   In 1305 we read in a writ to the sheriff of Oxfordshire :

afterwards as the *monstrance de droit*; it was simply an application for a writ which would have been due had not the king forbidden the granting of such writs. It seems clear that even this writ to the escheator, to remove the king's hands, would not issue unless the party sued for it. In any case, we have here an illustration of a later statement, that traverse was introduced by statute, but monstrance lay at common law : *it did*, was abolished, and now was restored.

Exchequer. The collection of the king's revenue was bringing the king's interests into constant contact with those of his subjects. There were, at the exchequer, lists of men, in the several parts of the realm, who owed to the king rents, services, or money lent to them. The king's ministers had to collect these debts and to account for them at the exchequer. If somebody was distrained unduly, for instance, for a debt which had already been paid, he had, it seems, to go to the exchequer and to prove that the distress was un-justified. This, at least, would be the *argumentum a contrario* which is suggested by one of the Ordinances of 1311[1]: the people felt much aggrieved, because different debts were de-manded by summonses of the exchequer, although in some cases the summonees had tallies and writs of acquittance to show that the debts were paid, and in other cases they were actually exempted by their franchises; the king ordered, there-fore, that in the accounts of sheriffs and other ministers there should thenceforth be allowed such tallies, writs, and fran-chises, as were allowable, if they were shown to the court. In other words, the minister had to leave the supposed debtor alone, despite the summons from the exchequer, and take from him only the document, in order to explain at the exchequer why the summons had been disobeyed. It may be that before that statute a minister who had received such a sum-mons was helpless, even if he knew that the party had paid the debt. On the other hand, the statute may have been

'Tibi precipimus quod venire facias coram nobis in Cancellaria nostra tot probos et legales homines de Comitatibus predictis per quos rei veritas inde melius sciri poterit ad reddendum nos super premissis plenius certiores' (C. F. N. S., f. 691, no. 119; C. C. R. 33 Ed. I, 3 44).
[1] R. P. i. 284, no. 24.

merely a reminder to the exchequer, upon popular complaint, that their formalism should not be pressed too far. The word *desoremes* seems to point to the conclusion that the power now given to the ministers was new. But we must not be too prompt in drawing such inferences from mediaeval legal language.

' In the exchequer,' says Fleta, ' the barons will be entitled to hear and determine complaints ('querelas conquerentium ') against actual sheriffs, escheators, bailiffs, and other royal ministers, of personal wrongs, except of false judgements.' [1]

In 1274, a writ from the exchequer to the sheriff of Devonshire states the complaint of Walter of Bath, who was distrained for the whole of a debt due to the king, while he ought to answer for a part only. The sheriff was ordered, if that was so, to distrain Walter for his part only, and the other debtors for the balance.[2]

The barons of the exchequer formed, as we know, a court. ' Quia in Curia Regis coram Baronibus de Scaccario suo consideratum est . . . ' we read in an early exchequer record.[3] The exchequer received the accounts of the king's ministers ; this, however, meant not only the mechanical duty of adding and subtracting, and of viewing the writs which were offered to justify claims of allowances ; the exchequer allowed claims also where there were no writs to serve as warrants.

Thus, in 1279, the king ordered the barons to certify him at his next parliament of all the allowances to his sheriffs

---

[1] Fleta, bk. ii, ch. 27.

[2] L. T. R., roll 47, m. 8 r.† The marginal note is ' Deuon' pro Waltero de Bathon' '. There is no mention that this was a writ addressed to the barons by the king. The entry begins, ' Monstrauit Regi '; this may denote a transcript either of the writ emanating from the exchequer, or of the order sent by the king to the exchequer. But in this latter case we should expect a passage ' et ideo Rex mandat baronibus ' (or ' eisdem '). Furthermore, we read : ' Ita quod habeat omnes denarios ad scaccarium in quindena sancti Iohannis Baptiste Regi solvendos et breve.' There was, therefore, a writ ; it was addressed to the sheriff (' non distringas ') ; and as the writ would be in the king's name, and in the first person (even if it had issued from the exchequer), the words ' Et Rex precipit ' could not stand in it. The conclusion is, that the writ was sent directly from the exchequer, without their having received an order from outside ; in short, the complaint, too, had been made directly to the exchequer.

[3] Ibid., roll 50, m. 1 r.

and bailiffs, which were claimed from the barons, whether by writs or not.[1] This writ does not contravene our contention, but shows that the king ordered all the claims, which ordinarily ought to have (and actually had) been brought before the barons, to be brought before himself. It was a removal of records into a higher court, although the lower court had the right to adjudicate.

If there was a difficulty, the exchequer could send the accountants ' elsewhere ' to get a formal allowance. Thus, in 1279, Walter de Grauntturt, collector of the fifteenth in the counties of Norfolk and Suffolk, owed to the king, upon account in the exchequer, £16 odd : respite was granted to him until the next parliament so that in the meantime he might seek an allowance of the sum or else pay it at that date.[2]

Chancery. If the collection of the king's revenue caused grievances which were not redressed by the local officials or in the exchequer, the next step was to go to the chancery. We have seen Fleta's statement about the writs framed by the clerks of chancery, upon the ' supplications and complaints of complainants '.[3] We know that one who claimed an allowance could go to the chancery and get a writ of *allocate*. Such writs might be hypothetical, i. e. conditional on the truth of the allegations. But whether, granted the truth of the facts, allowance in a given case should be made, was often decided by the writ itself.[4] Hence the complaint that, at the suggestion of bailiffs, the king's writs were made, to the king's grave detriment, in the case of various allowances.[5]

In all such cases the application to the chancery might be, not an application for a remedy, but a step in the ordinary course of business. But apart from writs of *allocate*, there were cases in which the action of the exchequer was *complained of* in the chancery. For instance, the king had granted to the men of his manor of Edenstowe and of Camberton certain tenements for 20 marks yearly, at his will ; afterwards the king granted part of these tenements

---

[1] L. T. R., roll 52, m. 3 d.†   [2] Ibid., roll 53, m. 3 d.†
[3] Above, p. 74.
[4] But see Appendix, pp. 211-13, on the difference between hypothetical orders and writs of warrant.   [5] Ryley, 446, and above, pp. 76-7.

to a convent; the men still had to pay the whole rent, although their revenue was diminished by the grant to the abbot. We have their petition, addressed to the chancellor, and formally endorsed; as a result, a writ issued to him who supplied the place of the treasurer and to the barons of the exchequer.[1] The endorsement was, ' Habeant breve Thesaurario et Baronibus de Scaccario quod exonerentur. Teste Magistro Willelmo de Blida.' The writ contains many details which cannot be found in the petition (for instance, the names of those to be discharged). Apparently the petition was presented for the purpose of having the writ ordered in principle; then the petitioners communicated with a clerk about the details. We have other writs by which the king orders the exchequer to redress some grievance as to the collection of the king's revenue; those writs issued obviously on a mere application to the chancery, and we have no trace of the proceedings which had led to their issue. Thus, in the first term of Edward I's reign, a writ was sent to the barons on behalf of Reynald de Grey, sheriff of Nottingham-shire and Derbyshire, and son and heir of John, late sheriff of those counties. The barons were ordered to discharge Reynald of money which he and John ought to have received but which had been remitted to the debtors.[2] At the time when the writ issued Edward was not yet in England. Another case was that of Theobald de Verdun who was distrained for higher relief than he ought to pay.[3]

Daily needs. There was another group of cases which to us may seem negligible, but which must have been very important for men of that time. The king's household was expensive; many articles of daily use had to be provided; the king's politics required the keeping of soldiers, quite apart from the feudal services.[4] How were those needs satisfied? Were the things simply taken and the owners then compelled in each case to sue for payment to the king by petition? Or were the king's officials to buy goods and then to sue to the

---

[1] A. P. 14808†; C. C. R., 31 Ed. I, 27.   [2] L. T. R., roll 47, m. 1 r.†
[3] Ibid., roll 61, m. 10 r.†; above, pp. 55–6.
[4] See, e.g., the two petitions in the parliament of 1305, M. P., nos. 272, 274.

king, by petition, for allowance of each particular expense? Or did they account to the king, by way of petitions, so that what remained for the barons of the exchequer was a comparison of figures and the enrolment of writs of *allocate*?

First of all, the king had his purveyors and was entitled to have certain goods commandeered for his use.[1] Where there was no right to a prise (without payment), enactments were repeatedly made to ensure regular payment. Thus, the first statute of Westminster ordered that payment or agreement should be made within forty days. It is mentioned that purveyors often took goods for the account of the king or his garrisons, and then appropriated the money received from the exchequer, the wardrobe, or some other source, instead of paying it to the creditors.[2] According to the *Articuli Super Chartas*,[3] the purveyors must either pay, or make their agreements. In this way, and in so far as these enactments were obeyed (they often were not [4]), many claims of the king's creditors were satisfied by payments made through the purveyors. If cash payment was made, there was again no need of going to the king. Fleta describes [5] the daily expenditure by the wardrobe and the clerks of the several household offices. It was the duty of the clerk of the kitchen, ' denarios recipere de garderoba pro officiis Emptoris, Poletae, Salsariae, Aulae, et Camerae, et Scutelriae, et creditoribus satisfacere competenter '. The clerk of the marshalsy of the horse should ' emere foenum, avenam, literam et ferramenta, et inde recepta pecunia in garderoba, satisfacere creditoribus '. The keeper of the wardrobe was to receive daily accounts of the expenses made by the several offices, and was, in his turn, to render a yearly account at the exchequer. In these cases the wardrobe, and other subordinate offices of the royal household, paid directly. In other cases the wardrobe, or individual officials, whether of the household or not, gave bills which served as warrants for writs of *liberate* to be sent to the exchequer. We know of a number of writs issued *per*

---

[1] See e.g. Stat. Westm. I, c. 7.
[2] Ibid., c. 32.
[3] Art. Sup. Chart., c. 2.
[4] Cf. Stubbs, ii. 423–4.
[5] Fleta, book ii, chs. 14, 18, 20.

billam de garderoba.[1] In all such cases there was no application to the king, but the whole thing was transacted as
a matter of course.

In the case of St. Catherine's hospital [2] money was paid at
first directly by the constable of the Tower of London, to
whom the sums thus paid were afterwards allowed in his
account at the exchequer; later on, his testimony and the
rolls of his accounts served as warrant for a writ of *liberate.*

It is also probable that hypothetical writs could issue to the
exchequer from the chancery upon mere statements made by
the parties in chancery.[3]

Lack of uniformity. To find a uniform way of proceeding
in cases of the same or of similar character might be impossible. In issuing writs, in giving warrants for them, in
allowing claims, in paying cash for goods, the departments to
which these duties belonged exercised apparently a certain
amount of discretion. We can, therefore, find precedents for
opposite contentions.

Thus, the Ordinances of 1311 [4] ordered the exchequer to
allow tallies, writs, and franchises, which were pleaded in
discharge of debts due to the king. These allowances were
to be made

' sur l'acounte de chescun Viscounte et d'autres Ministres
le Roi qi acounte devient rendre a l'Escheqier . . . si les dites
acquitaunces soient monstreez a la Court; Issint qe mes ne
courgent en demaunde par defaute de allouance. Et si le
Tresorer e les Barons de l'Escheqier ne le facent en la fourme
avantdite, eient les Pleintifs leur recoverier par petitions en
Parlement '.

The sheriffs and other officials had, therefore, to take the
acquittances to the exchequer and to ask for allowances; if
the treasurer and barons refused, the parties had to petition
the king in parliament. Thus, the barons could either allow
or disallow the plea of acquittance. An annuity was granted
to a lady by the king's letters patent, as compensation for

---

[1] e.g. L. T. R., roll 62, m. 10 r.;   C. C. R., 29 Ed. I, 444 ;   31 Ed. I,
25 ;   34 Ed. I, 361 ;   35 Ed. I, 509.
[2] Above, pp. 70-1.   [3] e.g. L. T. R., roll 61, m. 7 d.† ; above, p. 55. .
[4] Above, p. 75.

a manor. The letters patent were duly enrolled at the exchequer. We do not know whether, on the strength of them, she was ever paid; but in 6 Edward I [1] she brought a petition complaining that she had asked the chancellor and the treasurer to pay her the amount due for the current term, and they had answered that they would pay her no money without the king. The endorsement was, ' Fiat per illos de Scaccario iuxta tenorem litterarum quas inde habet '. There was no mention that a writ was to be sent as a warrant. Nor would the endorsement of the petition serve as a warrant ; for we have many endorsements ordering writs to be sent to the exchequer, so that apparently the mere endorsement would not be enough.

On the other hand, in the case of St. Catherine's hospital,[2] a *liberate* issued on the mere testimony of the constable of the Tower, accompanied by a search of the rolls of his account ; and allowance had been made to him for annuities paid, without either writ or letters patent. Afterwards the chancery refused to give a new *liberate* without the king's letters patent as a warrant : it follows, that letters patent would be a sufficient warrant for a *liberate*.

Henry III had granted to William de la Cornere, a justice of oyer and terminer, out of the fines and amercements made before William and his fellow-justices, £30 for his expenses. In 1275 William came before the barons and proffered Henry's letters patent. These are set out in full in the record, which then states that out of that sum William had received £29 : ' et sic restant reddendi eidem magistro xx solidi.' [3] William had taken the money on the strength of the letters patent ; there was no close writ to serve as a warrant for the barons to enrol the letters ; nevertheless, the barons took it as a matter of course that William had taken the money, and that 20s. were still due to him. Yet we know of cases in which, in addition to letters patent, close writs were presented to the barons in order to get an allowance. For instance, a close writ current of 1279 [4] orders the barons to

---

[1] R. P. i. 12, no. 56.　　　[2] Ibid., 156, no. 11 ; cf. above, pp. 70-1.
[3] L. T. R., roll 48, m. 4 d.†　　[4] Ibid., roll 52, m. 5 r.†

allow every year to the takers of wine at Southampton a certain amount of wine : for the king, in compliance with a charter of Henry III, had granted to an abbot and convent that they would receive the said wine every year, without any further letter or mandate from the king to the barons.

Applications to the king. We come to cases of applications to the head; that is, to the king and his council.

Personal application. Many applications, prayers for grace, or complaints against the king's officials, were made to the king by word of mouth. The king was a man, like others, he talked to his fellow-men, he had servants, friends, courtiers ; we cannot suppose that in every case in which he was asked to use his power in somebody's favour, that person presented the king with a written instrument. In 1290 a petition was brought for manors for which the petitioners had made fines. The answer was : ' Responsum est per Regem per se absque petitione '.[1] In the first few years of Edward I, the application, we have reasons to believe, was frequently by word of mouth. Thus, in 1274, a writ was sent to the exchequer concerning the debts of two late sheriffs. The claimants, the writ states, ' dicunt se non debere . . . plene respondere ' ; if the writ contained nothing else, we might suppose that it was issued by the chancery, on a complaint made there. But the writ orders the barons to communicate to the king the result of their inquisition, ' ut quod iustum fuerit in hac parte Rex fieri faciat '.[2] This shows that the writ issued on the king's initiative; the *dicunt* is, therefore, significant. At the very same time,[3] we read that master Robert de Beuerlaco 'ad Regem accedens asserit' that he had made certain expenses in connexion with the king's coronation, and had not yet been reimbursed. The barons were ordered to hear Robert's account and to notify the king, so that the king might cause Robert's claim to be satisfied, either by writ of *liberate* or otherwise.

A case of 1276 seems to show that even proceedings against the king were not yet necessarily originated by petition. The record of pleas before the king in Michaelmas term,

---

[1] R. P. i. 51, no. 68.   [2] L. T. R., roll 48, m. 1 d.   [3] Ibid., m. 2 d.

1276, contains a case in which Gilbert de Clare, earl of Gloucester and Hertford, ' *petiit versus Dominum Edwardum Regem* Castrum et Burgum Bristollie cum pertinenciis ', with certain exceptions.[1] The case was adjourned, and was afterwards heard in the full council, before the king, the archbishop of Canterbury, two bishops, and many other magnates. It was decided that the claim should be refused, because the king and his ancestors had been seised for a long time, and the earl himself was telling of seisin in the time of Henry II.[2] Here again a list of those present was appended, much larger than the preceding one. It seems, therefore, that judgement was given at another meeting. There is no mention of a petition, or a *supplicatio*. The offer to prove is expressed as it would be in private suits (' paratus est verificare prout Curia Domini Regis consideraverit '). The application seems to have been made in the king's bench and adjourned before the full council. The words, ' petiit versus dominum . . . regem ' made the case look similar to that of William Longsword in the former reign.[3] True, Gilbert was a powerful man. But in later years we see his petitions[4]; we have petitions of the queen,[5] of the king's brother,[6] of the widow of the king's first cousin.[7] In later years, therefore, the earl would have been expected to adopt a similar course. And, though later many acts of government would be done by the king's word of mouth, and on oral application, yet such orders to the exchequer as those quoted above[8] would issue probably upon petitions.

Petition: Origin. ' In old times, every writ, as well of right as of possession, would well lie against the king, of which nothing is changed now, but that much that he willeth that one sue against him by bill where before one sued by petition.'[9]

---

[1] P. W. 6; cf. Cutbill, 13, 18; Stubbs, ii. 275.
[2] ' Quia predictus Comes narrat de seisina antecessoris sui, . . . Videtur Curie et dictum est predicto Comiti quod predictus Dominus Rex nunc non debet . . . de tam longinqua seysina . . . antecessorum suorum . . . eidem Comiti . . . respondere.' [3] Above, pp. 36–7.
[4] R. P. i. 8, no. 33 (A.D. 1278); ibid., 69, no. 5 (A.D. 1291).
[5] Ibid., 192, no. 4. [6] Ibid., 7, no. 29. [7] A. P. E., 62.
[8] Above, pp. 81–2. [9] Y. B., 33–5 Ed. I, 471, R. S.; cf. above, p. 54.

In the time of Edward I, as witnesses the passage just quoted, no writ could be brought against the king. We have a statement to the same effect in a petition of 1278 ; [1] and for reasons which have been stated in the chapter on Henry III, [2] it is quite safe to assume that since writs began to issue, there never was a possibility of writs against the king.

But the same passage proves that, at least in the later years of Edward I, a petition (bill) was necessary to prosecute claims against the king in cases in which, against private persons, writs of right or possessory writs would be used ; while in the days of Henry III we have seen no mention of the necessity of any such petition.

In 6 Edward I, from which we have the first large group of petitions, they presented a most varying aspect ; about the end of Edward's reign the form of petitions had become almost rigidly fixed.

The petitions printed in the Parliament Rolls, [3] as presented in a parliament of the sixth year, are sixty-one in number. Of these, forty are in French and twenty-one in Latin. The first words of the petitions are :

Ceo monstre (nos. 1, 3, 19, 41), Ce vu muster (no. 30), A. B. mostre (no. 58), Monstrant a nostre Seignur le Roy (no. 9), La mustrance (no. 44), Chier Sire Roy, ce vous monstre (no. 34), A. B. prie (nos. 6, 10, 15, 16, 24, 31, 37, 43, 56–7), A. B. vos requert (no. 52), La hautesce nostre Seignur le Roy requiert (no. 38), Ces sunt les peticions (no. 29), Ce est la pleynt (no. 23), A. B. . . . se playnent (nos. 48, 50), Cest est la requeste (no. 7), A vostre hautesse (no. 8), A nostre seignur le Roy (nos. 12, 17, 22, 25, 27, 40, 45), Ce est le droit (no. 5), A. B. porta bref (no. 64), A. B. morust, sun fiz (no. 18), A. B. tient (no. 28), Come nostre Seigneur (no. 33), Cum entre (no. 51), Petitio A. B., significat idem (no. 21), Petit A. B. (no. 59), Petitio A. B. (no. 39), A. B. queritur (no. 62), Supplicant regie maiestati (no. 49), Significat Regie Maiestati (no. 54), Monstrat Domino Regi (no. 35), Significat vobis (no. 26), Monstrat vobis (nos. 13, 47), Magnificentie Regis monstrant (no. 4), A. B. petit (nos. 11, 55, 60–1), Querela hominum (no. 14), Dicit A. B. (no. 20), A. B. pro servicio suo magno (no. 42), Memorandum (nos. 46, 63, 65).

[1] R. P. i. 7, no. 31.   [2] Above, pp. 24–6.
[3] R. P. i. 1–14.

On the other hand, of the whole number of petitions which have been published by Maitland as corresponding to the mentions on the parliament roll of Lent 1305,[1] two are in Latin, the rest are in French; ten are continuations of petitions brought at the same time; one hundred and twenty begin ' A nostre segnur le Roy '; and thirteen begin in a different way; even here, however, the difference consists mostly in the fact that the name of the petitioner, or the ' prie ', is put before ' a nostre '.

The petitions of 1278 had in common a positive feature : they were endorsed. There has not yet been found a petition from Henry III's time which would have an endorsement. In the reign of his son, whether the endorsement contained a plain refusal, or an order that a writ should issue, or a hint that some other procedure should be adopted, an endorsement there was, in almost all cases.

The petitions were, in the official language, always referred to by that name. Two verbs were in use : *petere*, and *supplicare*. *Supplicare* was used to describe the act of ' humbly praying ', as would be said afterwards. *Petere* had, obviously,[2] first of all the old meaning, ' to ask for something legally ', ' to sue ' (*petere versus*) ; in this sense, or in a closely allied one, even later records would read : ' et hoc petit ut inquiratur per patriam.' The other sense was new, and was suggested by the noun *petitio* (for instance, in the formula mentioned above, ' petit A. B.'). The formula adopted in writs issuing upon petitions was ' supplicavit nobis . . . per petitionem suam ' or ' monstravit nobis . . . per petitionem suam '.[3] This use corresponds exactly with what we find in formularies of the court of Rome : the documents were referred to as *petitiones*, while they used to begin with *monstrat, supplicat*, or other verbs.[4]

Fleta says[5] that the clerks of chancery had to hear and examine ' supplicationes et querelas conquerentium '. He was probably making a distinction between applications in the

[1] M. P.
[3] e.g. M. P., nos. 32, 166, 168, 178, 212.
[5] Fleta, Book ii, Ch. 13, s. 1.
[2] Above, pp. 26, 45.
[4] Below, p. 94.

ordinary course (e. g. for a ' diem clausit extremum', or livery), and complaints (requests for remedies).[1]

The official rolls of parliament, containing the ' business-like Latin' statement of the substance of the petitions,[2] have, as a rule, the words : 'Ad petitionem A. B. petentis. . . .'[3] On the roll of the parliament of Carlisle, 1307,[4] we read in one case [5] : 'Memorandum quod ad supplicacionem . . . emanavit breve Regis de Cancellaria in hec verba : Edwardus. . . . Supplicavit Nobis per suam peticionem. . . .' In another case [6] the entry begins : 'Dominus Rex, ad supplicationem Thome . . .'; but then we read : 'tenuit tenementa in peticione contenta.'

Beginning in 21 Edward I,[7] we find on the rolls of close writs entries showing where the warrant consisted in the endorsement of a petition ('per petitionem de consilio', or 'per petitionem'). In such entries, the word 'petition' was used practically always [8], and the word 'supplicatio' never.[9]

Next, let us note a tradition that it was Edward I who introduced petitions in England. A statement to this effect was usually combined with an assertion that in earlier days writs could be used against the king. Because this latter assertion was not true, being ' an old fable ',[10] ' a pious legend of Westminster Hall ',[11] the whole tradition has fallen into discredit. The tradition as to Edward's innovation was perhaps connected with the other statement in order to

---

[1] Stubbs, ii. 282, n. 1, seems to assume that these *supplicationes* (*et querelae*) were petitions in the technical sense, and even that they corresponded with the later petitions to the chancellor for equitable relief. Fleta, however, means only requests for established remedies, while doubtful cases were dealt with, as he says elsewhere, in the king's court in parliament. Above, pp. 74, 76.   [2] M. P., p. lv.

[3] Ibid., nearly all the entries on pp. 5–232 and 301–13. The roll of Irish petitions (ibid., 232–54) has in most cases the formula : 'ad petitionem . . . qui petit.'

[4] R. P. i. 192–215.   [5] Ibid., 204, no. 75.   [6] Ibid., 210, no. 92.

[7] The first instance seems to be C. C. R., 21 Ed. I, 287.

[8] In two cases (ibid., 27 Ed. I, 240) the words ' per billam ' (by bill of council) were used, though this may relate to a written note (like ' bill of the exchequer ').

[9] e.g. Ibid., 21 Ed. I, 291 ; 23 Ed. I, 424 ; 25 Ed. I, 49, 115 ; 33 Ed. I, 221.

[10] H. E. L. i. 517.   [11] Ibid., 516.

explain how people used to proceed before his time.[1] Even the words : ' de quei nest ore rens raunge me qe tant qil voet qe home siwe ver luy par bille . . .'[2] appear, in view of the fact that ' the king could die ',[3] to refer to the king who was then ruling. If that was so, and if we assume that Edward I introduced the petition and that that fact was generally known, we can understand why the statement was not more explicit. On the other hand, those who discussed the same subject in the time of later kings,[4] would naturally mention Edward I by name.

There appears to have been a particular connexion between petitions and the council. Many petitions were addressed either to the king and council, or only to the council. Of the petitions preserved from a parliament of 6 Edward I[5] (sixty-one in number), forty-three were addressed to the king; seven had no address; six were addressed to the king and his council; three to the council only; two to the king's court. But of the not quite one hundred and fifty petitions printed by Maitland as connected with the Lenten parliament, 1305,[6] no less than eighty were addressed to the council. Nor should this be regarded as a meaningless detail. The notes of warrant on the rolls of writs, beginning in 21 Edward I,[7] show at first always that the petitions had been sent from the council.[8] It is only late

[1] The story of the writ may have been derived by the lawyer, who, to our knowledge, was the first to propound it in court, from an ambiguous statement in M. J. 7.
[2] Y. B., 33–5 Ed. I, R. S. 471 ; above, pp. 54, 83.
[3] H. E. L. i. 521.   [4] e. g. Ibid., 516, n. 5.
[5] R. P. i. 1–14 ; above, p. 84.   [6] M. P. ; cf. above, p. 85.
[7] e. g. C. C. R., 21 Ed. I, 287.
[8] e. g. By petition of council, C. C. R., 21 Ed. I, 287 ; 23 Ed. I, 424 ; 25 Ed. I, 49, 115 ; 26 Ed. I, 182, 185–6 ; 27 Ed. I, 238–41, 246 ; 28 Ed. I, 346–7, 350 ; 29 Ed. I, 420–1, 427–33, 467, 480 ; 30 Ed. I, 541–2, 545–8, 550, 551, 563, 599 ; 31 Ed. I, 44 ; 32 Ed. I, 184–6, 218 ; 33 Ed. I, 243–7, 254–8, 266, 277, 280, 284, 294–301, 304, 306 ; 35 Ed. I, 483–5, 487–91, 495–6, 498–9, 501, 505–6, 518–19, 528–9, 531 ; cf. C. P. R., 21 Ed. I, 21–3, &c.; by bill of council, C. C. R., 27 Ed. I, 240 ; cf. above, p. 86, n. 8; by council and petition, C. C. R., 31 Ed. I, 6 ; by the king by petition of council, ibid., 21 Ed. I, 291 ; by petition returned from the council, ibid., 27 Ed. I, 238, 242 ; 34 Ed. I, 416 ; 35 Ed. I, 488 ; by the king and petition of council, ibid., 21 Ed. I, 291–2 ; 27 Ed. I, 240–1, 253 ; 33 Ed. I, 249, 293, 295, 297, 324 ; by petition and inquisition

in Edward's reign that we have mentions of such petitions serving as warrants, without reference to their having been sent from the council.[1]

We know of two ordinances which provided that in certain cases the parties should proceed by petition : in both it is said that the petition was to be presented in parliament.

One is the ordinance or enactment (20 Edward I) which prescribed that no writs of inquisition *ad quod damnum* should issue from the chancery in the case of monks wishing to acquire property, ' nisi per petitiones in pleno parliamento porrectas '.[2] The other ordinance, made in 1311,[3] concerns allowances of tallies, writs, and franchises : if the treasurer and barons did not allow such tallies and other warrants, 'eient les Pleintifs leur recoverier par petitions en Parlement'.

We also have two proclamations, made in 1305, on the occasion of the two parliaments of that year, and concerning the delivery of petitions [4] : in either case those who wished to deliver their petitions at the parliament in question should do so from a certain day to another certain day, and not later. In both cases there were men specially appointed to receive the petitions. If the petitions, instead of being brought before the king's council in parliament, could be brought at other times, why should special days be appointed for petitions to be presented in parliament ? In every such case a man who was late presenting his petition in parliament would have been able to present it to the king at some other time.

returned from council, ibid., 29 Ed. I, 425–6; in two cases (ibid., 27 Ed. I, 240) we have ' by bill of council ', perhaps denoting a written note, like ' bill of the exchequer ' ; cf. above, p. 86, n. 8.

[1] e. g. By petition, ibid., 30 Ed. I, 515–17 ; by king and petition, ibid., 30 Ed. I, 553 ; by petition under the privy seal, ibid., 30 Ed. I, 515–19 ; by privy seal and by petition sent from the king, ibid., 32 Ed. I, 168–9 ; by petition before the king, ibid., 30 Ed. I, 547 ; 33 Ed. I, 297 ; by petition sent from the king from Scotland, ibid., 33 Ed. I, 260 ; by petition of parliament at Lincoln, ibid., 33 Ed. I, 281. The warrant ' by petition of council ' was the endorsement of petitions brought in what was called a parliament, see e.g. M. P., nos. 5, 12, 32, 52, 53–7, 84, 100, 117 : in all these cases the petitions are presented in the parliament and enrolled on its roll, and the writs are the result of the endorsement.   [2] R. P. i. 78, no. 4.

[3] Ibid., 284, no. 24 ; above, pp. 75, 80.   [4] M. P. 3 ; R. P. i. 182.

There were complaints, in Edward I's time, of a multitude of petitions which were brought before the king, creating a grievance on the part of the men who were attending the king's parliaments.[1] Hence, in the eighth year of Edward's reign, it was ordered that petitions which touched the seal should first come before the chancellor, those touching the exchequer should first come to the exchequer, &c. ; if the affairs could not be disposed of without the king, then those chief officers would themselves carry the petitions before the king ; no petition was thenceforth to come before the king and his council except through the hands of the said officers. If this order had had the meaning attributed to it by Lord Somers in the Bankers' Case,[2] it would have done away with parliamentary petitions altogether :

' This law being made,' he said, ' there is reason to conclude that all petitions brought before the king in parliament after this time, and answered there, were brought according to the method of this law ; and were of the nature of such petitions as ought to be brought to the person of the king.'

The enactment contained no mention that the petitions were to be addressed to the chief officers. It only said that the king and his council should not be bothered with such petitions as could be expedited by those officers. On the other hand, the enactment emphatically directed that no petition should be brought before the king and council except by the officers ; it follows that it lay with them to decide whether they should take a petition to the king, or decide it themselves. Either, therefore, no petitions should be addressed to the king at all, but petitions addressed to the different departments should be brought by the king's officers before the king ; or, the petitions were presented formally to the king, but they were collected by some person or body of persons, assigned by them to the different officers and, if necessary, brought by the latter before the king. The first inference is absurd ; for the ordinance speaks obviously of petitions presented in parliament, and does not mention that

---

[1] Ryley, 442 ; not quite exact, therefore see Appendix, p. 235.
[2] 14 St. Tr. i, on p. 82.

henceforth they should not be presented in parliament; besides, we know that petitions continued to be presented, and were dealt with, in the way indicated as the second alternative. In any case, there were changes of procedure; from the twenty-first year we have another enactment.[1] Petitions delivered in the parliaments should, first of all, be well examined; those which touched the chancery, the exchequer, or the justices respectively, should be bound in separate bundles; those which were to be sent before the king and council in still another bundle, just as those which had been answered before. Here, then, is an express mention that petitions which were assigned to the several departments had been presented formally to the king, in his parliament. It will be noted that the procedure was different from that prescribed in the eighth year: for the petitions to be sent to the several departments were at once separated from those to be sent before the king and his council. Moreover, the arrangements made as to all petitions would have to be reported to the king before the work of delivering (i. e. the expedition[2]) of the petitions would begin.[3]

Both ordinances referred to petitions presented in parliaments. The complaint mentioned in the first ordinance was of a multitude of petitions brought in the king's parliaments. If they could have been presented elsewhere, why should people present such floods of them in parliaments, where they would be regarded as a sort of public nuisance? Why not present them outside the parliament, for instance in the chancery?

[1] Ryley, 459.   [2] M. P., p. lvii.

[3] We translate ' il les commence ' ' they would begin (to deliver) them '. Stubbs, ii. 276, translates ' before he (the king) proceeded to transact business'. The difficulty consists in the fact that ' il commence ' is in the singular; we may assume that a single receiver was meant, and this would explain the construction; or else we may assume that the ordinance was dictated, for instance, at a meeting of the council, and by mistake the singular ' il commence ' was taken down instead of the plural ' ils commencent ' (cf. the ordinance of the eighth year which has ' il porterunt ') ; it will be noticed that ' il commence ' and ' ils commencent ' would be pronounced in the same way. The hastiness of form of both ordinances (the former contains what was obviously an afterthought) might explain much. In any case, ' il les commence a deliverer ' can hardly have meant ' before he proceeded to transact business '.

But what was meant by those parliaments ? Fleta says :

'Habet . . . Rex curiam suam in consilio suo, in parliamentis suis . . . ubi terminate sunt dubitationes iudiciorum, et novis iniuriis emersis nova constituuntur remedia, et unicuique iusticia, prout meruerit, retribuetur ibidem.'[1]

A parliament has been defined as 'an assembly regularly meeting at stated periods, and acting generally as the King's ordinary council, or as a court of justice '.[2] Edward I, on the morrow of the close of Easter, 1275, held, what the preamble of the first statute of Westminster describes as his first parliament general : from that time onwards, we can make out a (perhaps not quite complete) list of the parliaments which were, during his reign, alluded to in writs and other documents as held or as intended to be held. Such a list [3] would mention parliaments, from 1275 until 1282, about every Easter and about every Michaelmas.[4] We know of a parliament after Michaelmas only, in 1283 and 1284 [5], Easter and Michaelmas parliaments in 1285,[6] an Easter parliament in 1286,[7] then three parliaments in 1289.[8] Hilary, Easter, July, and Michaelmas parliaments were held in 1290,[9] one

[1] Fleta, Book ii, Ch. 2, s. 1. We are quoting this passage from the manuscript in the British Museum, because ' Fleta Seldeni ' contains one or two small misprints. Baldwin, 66, observes ' the emphasis which is placed upon the remedies which are provided not by general rule but for individual instances.' The emphasis, however, is due to the fact that in his translation he omits *constituuntur*.

[2] Report from the Lords' Committees on the Dignity of a Peer, i. 169.

[3] From ' The " Placita " in Parliament of the eighteenth and of some succeeding years ' it is inferred (ibid.), ' that Edward, in the early part of his reign, frequently held four Parliaments every year ' (cf. Stubbs, ii. 275). Our evidence does not bear out this statement, least of all for the period 1275-89.

[4] P. W. 381 ; C. C. R., 3 Ed. I, 229 ; C. P. R., 3 Ed. I, 120 ; C. C. R., 3 Ed. I, 167, 200 ; ibid., 4 Ed. I, 338 ; ibid., 305 ; ibid., 5 Ed. I, 372 ; ibid., 380 ; L. T. R., roll 52, m. 3 d., C. P. R., 6 Ed. I, 275 ; C. C. R., 6 Ed. I, 465, 470, 505 ; ibid., 7 Ed. I, 521 ; ibid., 582 ; ibid., 8 Ed. I, 9, 11, 15 ; ibid., 23, 30-1 ; ibid., 9 Ed. I, 75, 91 ; ibid., 84, 88, 92 ; ibid. 91, 105 ; ibid., 10 Ed. I, 153.

[5] Ibid., 11 Ed. I, 216, 218 ; ibid., 12 Ed. I, 274.

[6] Ibid., 13 Ed. I, 331, 365, 367 ; ibid., 335.

[7] Ibid., 14 Ed. I, 388.

[8] Stubbs, ii. 125 ; C. C. R., 17 Ed. I, 6 ; ibid., 51.

[9] R. P. i. 15 ; C. C. R., 18 Ed. I, 132 ; Stubbs, ii. 126 ; R. P. i. 46.

only in 1291,[1] three in 1292,[2] two in 1293,[3] three in 1294,[4] and in 1295,[5] two at least in 1296[6]; in 1297, one early in the year, one after Easter, and one, held by the king's son, in the autumn.[7] An Easter parliament was held in 1298,[8] Lenten and Easter parliaments in 1299 and 1300[9], a Lenten parliament in 1301,[10] a summer and an autumn parliament in 1302,[11] a Lenten parliament in 1304,[12] a Lenten and a September parliament in 1305,[13] an Easter parliament, 1306,[14] and a Lenten parliament in 1307.[15]

It was at these periodical meetings that the so-called petitions in parliament were presented.

If, as in the ' Model Parliament ', the king assembled men other than those who had attended on former occasions, that did not change the character of the *curia regis in parliamento*, in so far as it was a meeting at which petitions of the king's subjects were presented and dealt with.

Let us look to other European countries : will the history of·their institutions in the thirteenth century not give us some useful hints ?

Our first reference will be to Hungary. A chronicler tells us of the causes of the hatred which existed between King Bela IV (1235–70) and his subjects.[16] The nobles, he says, among other things, often complained that the king had, contrary to the custom of the realm, and in order to oppress them, ordered that noblemen of whatever eminence could not move affairs in his court, or talk to him personally, but had to present *supplicationes* to the chancellors, and thereafter

---

[1] R. P. i. 66.   [2] Ibid., 70, 87–8, 107.
[3] C. C. R., 21 Ed. I, 278–9, 314, 321 ; R. P. i. 125 ; C. C. R., 21 Ed. I, 303.
[4] Ibid., 22 Ed. I, 384–5 ; Stubbs, ii. 130 ; C. C. R., 22 Ed. I, 395–6.
[5] Ibid., 23 Ed. I, 424 ; R. P. i. 132 ; C. C. R., 23 Ed. I, 459–61, 463.
[6] Ibid., 24 Ed. I, 489 ; P. W. 26–7.
[7] C. C. R., 24 Ed. I, 492 ; P. W., 27–8 ; C. C. R., 25 Ed. I, 4, 21 ; P. W. 29 ; C. C. R., 25 Ed. I, 67.   [8] R. P. 143 ; P. W. 38.
[9] C. C. R., 27 Ed. I, 294 ; P. W. 41–2 ; C. C. R., 28 Ed. I, 373 ; P. W. 131, no. 63.   [10] C. C. R., 28 Ed. I, 406, 408–11.
[11] Ibid., 30 Ed. I, 531, 583 ; ibid., 31 Ed. I, 100 ; ibid., 30 Ed. I, 559, 598.
[12] Ibid., 32 Ed. I, 225.
[13] Above, p. 88.   [14] Stubbs, ii. 165.
[15] R. P. i. 216. Note the mistake of Coke, 2 Inst. 408.
[16] R. Hung., cf. Bresslau, 681.

await the end of the business. Many went away without
having their business expedited, because the chancellors
humbled some of them and raised others at will ; and only
through the chancellors could the king be approached.[1]
Those who were in favour of the king tried to justify his
actions, and were giving the following answer to such complaints [2] : since the king had to attend with all his power to
the reformation of the whole realm of Hungary, he could not
give to everybody a benevolent hearing ; he therefore ordered,
on prudent consideration, that the affairs of his subjects
should, *following the example of the court of Rome*, be expedited
by petitions ; he ordered his chancellors to dispose as speedily
as possible of the easy and simple affairs, bringing before him
those that were difficult and important. This was done in
order that affairs should speedily come to their due end.
Yet men of ill intentions misrepresented what had been
thought out to make things easier for the oppressed.[3] It
may be observed that the written request was first called
supplicatio and then *petitio*. The writer obviously wished
to state the case of both sides with equal fairness. The
magnates complained that instead of approaching the king
and talking with him, they had to supplicate ; the word is
used with an angry emphasis. The king's defenders averred,
that it was only a petition, such as was used in the pope's
court : it was to be handed in at the chancery in order to
leave to the king more time for important business.

In Sicily we find, in the years 1242–68, a series of ordinances
minutely regulating the procedure on petitions.[4] In one of
these ordinances we find a clear threefold division : petitions
of justice between private parties, petitions of justice against
the king in connexion with fiscal affairs, petitions of grace.
We may add that, throughout the ordinances, to denote the
document presented, the word *petitio* is used always, and the
word *supplicatio* never.

In the court of Rome petitions were very frequently used,
and there were minute arrangements for dealing with them.

[1] R. Hung., c. 6.   [2] Ibid., c. 8.
[3] Ibid., c. 11.   [4] Appendix, pp. 213–14.

An early formulary (officially rewarded by the university of Bologna in 1215)[1] contains a special chapter de peticionibus.[2] We read there[3]: ' Forma componendi peticiones que imperatori et regibus porriguntur sumi possunt (sic) de forma peticionum summi pontificis per industriam prouidi oratoris. Nam ubi dicitur uestre significat sanctitati, dicatur imperiali uel regali maiestati, uel celsitudini seu clementie.'[4] Another formulary, composed by the cardinal Guala Bichieri in 1226 or 1227,[5] uses the word petitio throughout, as do the other thirteenth-century formularies. It contains, however, the following statement[6]: ' In petitionibus omnibus igitur recte formandis, hiis quinque principalibus utimur verbis : supplicat, insinuat, petit, significat et conqueritur, secundum diversas causas diversimode procedentes.' In the ordinances of the papal chancery[7] we find the word petitio used throughout the thirteenth century and the first quarter of the fourteenth century.[8] We have even, somewhere between 1254 and 1256, a mention of peticionarii.[9] It was not till in the fourteenth century that the word supplicationes was adopted in the papal chancery[10] : the word petitiones was still used in a constitution of John XXII, of 1331.[11]

On the other hand, petitions were not used in all European countries.[12] What was said above seems to show that the institution of petitions was organized, at least in Hungary and in Sicily, either in direct imitation of, or in close

---

[1] Its author was Buoncampagni of Florence ; it has been published by Rockinger, Briefsteller und Formelbücher, Quellen und Erörterungen zur Bayer. und Deutsch. Gesch., ix.

[2] Ibid. 151 ff.   [3] Ibid. 154.

[4] Cf. some of the formulae of the petitions presented in 6 Ed. I, above, p. 84.

[5] Auvray, Note sur un traité des requêtes en cour de Rome, Mélanges d'archéologie et d'histoire, x. 112–17. It was, in a sense, official, having been approved by the pope.

[6] Ibid. 116.   [7] Published by Tangl.

[8] Tangl, especially 43–5, 54, 58, 61, 65, 98, 114–15.

[9] See Appendix, p. 213, about the peticionarius in Sicily.

[10] Tangl, Introd. xxv ; cf. Simonsfeld, Neue Beiträge zum päpstl. Urkundenwesen, Abh. der Bayr. Akad. der Wissensch., Hist. Kl., xxi. 333 ff., especially 383, n. 1.

[11] Tangl, 115, paragr. 20 ; cf. Teige, Beiträge zum päpstl. Kanzleiwesen, Mitteilungen des Instituts für Oesterr. Geschichtsforsch., xvii. 408–40.

[12] Bresslau, 687–8.

connexion with, the order adopted by the court of the pope.

We may now presume to offer, as to the way in which the petition came to be used in England, a conjecture which would do justice to all the facts set out above.

On returning to England, after his father's death, Edward intended to hold a meeting of his prelates and magnates, called parliament, at least once or twice a year.[1] He wished to give everybody an opportunity of approaching him; therefore, he ordered that those who had complaints or requests to make should come when that parliament was taking place. If the requests were brought before the full meeting by word of mouth, many things which could have been disposed of in a routine way occupied too much of the meeting's time. If the purely oral requests were first heard by officials assigned to hear them, it might be difficult to establish whether those officials had exercised their discretion in the right way. Following an institution which was in use at the court of Rome, and was imitated by some secular rulers, Edward ordered (at some time in the period 1275–8) that the requests should be presented in writing. He was broad-minded enough not to insist on the adoption of a rigid formula : hence the variety of types presented by the petitions of the sixth year.[2] The more the institution became known and used, the more did it tend towards uniformity. The name of the petition, together with its idea, was adopted from foreign countries. In every case an answer had to be written on the petition ; this was new, too, and was borrowed from abroad. The application was one to a court, unless it related to a matter of pure grace ; but even in the latter case the king would discuss the matter with the council. What was asked for, was ordinarily some order by the king, either a writ to the escheator to restore land, or a *procedendo*, or a writ to the exchequer. The request for such an order would of course be either expressed or only implied.[3]

---

[1] P. W. 381.   [2] Above, p. 84.
[3] There is an interesting analogy with the royal letters which were issuing in Sicily as a result of the endorsement, Appendix, pp. 213–14.

The peculiar position of the king of England accounts for the fact that so many petitions were addressed to him and his council. The petitions were presented on the occasion of the meetings of the council in parliament. Had a form been prescribed at once, it would probably have been the form of an application to the king only, just as writs issued in his name and not in that of his council, and just as elsewhere petitions were addressed to popes and to kings. The character of the petition as application to a court suggested to many petitioners the advisability of adding the council, or of addressing the king's court or council only. As time went by, a compromise was effected, not by order, but by usage : and the petitions came to be addressed, in so many cases : 'a nostre seignur le roi et a son conseil.'

We assume, then, that the petition was originally the way of approaching the king's parliaments, whatever was the composition of those assemblies. In later days the same way of proceeding by petition may have been adopted, apart from parliaments, where a large class of cases had to be dealt with under one and the same principle, so that the party had only to prove the facts : for instance, the king went to Scotland on an expedition, and for political reasons decided that those who had behaved in a certain way were to be rewarded at once. He might order those concerned to present their claims in writing ; the royal officials would examine the facts and writs would issue ' by petition sent from the king '.[1] But this does not do away with our theory as to how the petition came to be used in England.

Classification. We turn to the consideration of the legal character of those petitions which we know to have been presented in Edward I's time.

We can distinguish petitions of grace, and petitions asking, not for grace, but for justice, for right ; in this latter group, there might be disputes relating to private parties only ; or the king might be interested in the result. Again, all petitions belonging to this group (asking for right) could be subdivided into such as could be brought to an end without the king's

---

[1] Above, p. 88, no. 1.

interference (for instance, a party instead of taking out a writ against another party, petitioned the king) ; [1] such as ordinarily could be terminated without the king's interference, but that the party complained of the course adopted by royal officials ; [2] and those in which a party had a claim against another party but was compelled to ask for a new kind of writ.[3] Likewise, where the king's interests were concerned, in some cases the complaint could have been made elsewhere ; [4] in other cases there was a complaint about the course adopted by the departments concerned.[5] In some cases it was impossible to proceed without the king.[6]

If this classification is accepted, we shall have a clue to the development of the petition of right. In Edward's time, every petition based on positive law was a petition of right. The phrase *fiat iustitia* or *soit fait droit* is found in endorsements on petitions relating to private disputes, as well as on

[1] e.g. M. P., no. 172.   [2] e.g. ibid., no. 420.
[3] e.g. ibid., no. 251.
[4] e.g. ibid., no. 137 : the community of Cumberland complained, that having sold goods to the sheriff for the use of the king's army, they had obtained no payment although the money had been allowed to the sheriff in his account. The endorsement directed the petitioners to approach the exchequer, and if their allegation be true, ' vicecomes puniatur per poenam constitutam . . .' Apparently punishment could have been exacted even without the petition.
[5] e.g. ibid., no. 249 : charged twice for the same thing.
[6] e.g. requests for a *procedendo*. Maitland, ibid. 353–5, has classified the petitions brought in that parliament of 1305 of which he has published the records. There may be some discussion as to the correctness of the distribution in the several groups (e.g. the case in no. 41 was one essentially touching the king ; cases of request for a set-off of debts, e.g. that in no. 88, were as much requests for legal relief in matters touching the king, as prayers for the payment of debts). But the principle of Maitland's classification will be found to correspond best with the facts. Apart from ' petitions of a general character by the estates of the realm ', he distinguishes petitions for legal relief in cases in which the king was concerned ; petitions for favour to be granted by the king ; and petitions relating to private wrongs. Putting on one side the request for favours (i.e. petitions of grace), we have the rest consisting of claims for legal redress, either where the king was concerned, or as to private wrongs. It will be seen that I have ventured to change this arrangement still further, by placing in one class the cases in which the party wanted only justice against his private opponent ; in the other class cases where either something was claimed from the king (land, payment, a *procedendo*), or complaint was made of the king's officials. Cf. also the division of petitions in Sicily, Appendix, pp. 213–14.

those which set forth claims against the king. The following examples may suffice :

In 1278. On petitions relating to private disputes : ' Fiat breve Thesaurario et Baronibus de Scaccario quod audiant loquelam inter ipsos Abbatem et Conventum, et dictos Mer-catores, et faciant Iusticiam.[1] Scribatur Iusticiario Hibernie quod faciat iusticiam.[2] Videatur carta in Chancellaria, et certificetur Curia per factum (?) et rotulos Iusticiarii foreste, et fiat iusticia.'[3] On a petition claiming dower from the king : ' Videant I. de Kirkeby et Narratores Regis raciones si quas Rex habet pro se ; et (sic) nullum habeat dicta Defen' (sic) fiat statim Iusticia petenti.'[4]

In 1290. On a petition complaining against a justice : ' Veneant (sic) partes ad placita coram Rege, Et viso Recordo fiat Iusticia ex officio Iusticiariorum.'[5]

In 1305. On a petition relating to private wrongs : ' Scri-batur Senescallo de Burdeaus quod, vocatis partibus, faciat ei iustitiam, etc.'[6] On a petition complaining of distraint for tallage which was not due : ' Habeat breve de Cancellaria Thesaurario et Baronibus de Scaccario quod visa carta, etc., faciant iustitiam.'[7] The wardship of a manor had been seised into the king's hands ; a private party claimed it, and had it provisionally delivered to him, pending final discussion ; he petitioned for a final settlement of the dispute ; the endorsement runs : ' Habeat breve de Cancellaria Thesau-rario et Baronibus quod visis inquisitionibus retornatis in Cancellaria et scrutatis memorandis eiusdem Scaccarii tan-gentibus idem negotium, si quae sint, faciant inde iusti-tiam, etc.'[8]

In 1306. On a petition complaining of undue exactions by summons of the exchequer : ' Mandetur per breve de Cancel-laria Thesaurario et Baronibus quod inquirant, si sit, Et si invenerint per Inquisicionem quod ita fuerit, ut suggeritur, fiat ei Iusticia.'[9]

From the reign of Edward I we have very few French endorsements. For instance, the sixty-one petitions of the sixth year printed in the Parliament Rolls [10] all have Latin endorsements ; so have the over twelve-score petitions of

---

[1] R. P. i. 2, no. 4. [2] Ibid. 10, no. 42. [3] Ibid., no. 41.
[4] Ibid. 7, no. 31. [5] Ibid. 56, no. 131. [6] M. P., no. 410.
[7] Ibid., no. 190. [8] Ibid., no. 182.
[9] R. P. i. 196, no. 30.
[10] Ibid. i. 1–14 ; above, p. 84.

the Michaelmas parliament, 1290.[1] Among the nineteen petitions of 1302 printed in the Parliament Rolls from Ryley's Placita [2] only one has a French answer which runs as follows : ' Le Roi ne entendi unkes de granter letres a defendre qe dreit fu fait, e pur ceo seit mande letre as lieutenanz le Rey, quil ly facent dreit.' [3] In 1290 we find on an Irish petition an endorsement of which the last words are : ' facent dreit as parties '.[4]

Procedure on petitions. In order to obtain an idea of the way in which petitions were dealt with in Edward I's parliaments, we must begin with the process of ' receiving ' petitions ; it will be convenient to discuss first the Lenten parliament, 1305, of the documents of which we have, thanks to Maitland, an elaborately edited collection. Our conclusions will then be viewed in the light of earlier and later sources.

The parliament just mentioned met (or began) on February 28.[5] On February 5 the king had addressed a writ of the privy seal to the chancellor,[6] commanding him :

1. To cause, together with the treasurer, a proclamation to be made that all those who wished to present petitions to the king and his council at his forthcoming parliament, should deliver them to men assigned to receive petitions, between then and the 7th day of March at the latest ;

2. to include in the proclamation the names of those who were assigned to receive the petitions ;

3. to cause the proclamation to be made in the great hall at Westminster, at the chancery, before the justices of the bench, at the exchequer, in the Guildhall, in Westcheap, and in all other places where the chancellor might think fit ;

4. to deliver, together with others of the king's council in London, before the king came, as many of those petitions as possible, so that no petitions should come before the king himself except those which could nowise be delivered without the king ;

5. to have these latter petitions well tried and examined and set in good order ;

6. to inform the king without delay how the order had been carried out, what arrangements had been made, and,

---

[1] R. P. i. 46–65.   [2] Ibid. 154–8.   [3] Ibid. 154, no. 2.   [4] Cole, 81.
[5] M. P. lvii.   [6] Ibid. lvi f. The translation is not quite exact.

in particular, whom he (the chancellor) had assigned to receive the petitions.

This writ is not copied on the parliament roll, but the roll contains the proclamation made in pursuance of the order, and adds that (as is also stated in the proclamation itself) the petitions were to be delivered to Sir Gilbert de Roubury, Master John de Caen, Sir John de Kirkby, and Master John Bush. The record says that the king afterwards assigned five other men (whose names are set out) ' to receive all the petitions which touched the realm of Scotland '. Then other men are enumerated as assigned ' to receive and answer all such petitions put forward by people from Gascony as could be answered without the king '. The king also assigned five other men ' to receive all the petitions of those from Ireland and from the isle of Guernsey, and to answer those which they could answer without the king. And all the petitions which touched the said countries of Scotland, Gascony, Ireland, and Guernsey were at once delivered, to those assigned for this purpose, by the said Gilbert ' and the others.[1]

We assume that the four original receivers were not only to receive the petitions from the public and to make them into bundles ; but that, together with the chancellor, the treasurer, and others, if the latter would help them, they were to answer all those petitions which could be answered without the king. Because the number of petitions appeared too large, and the king was told, on his arrival, that many petitions which could be disposed of without him, were still ' undelivered ', or perhaps because it appeared advisable to let the petitions from parts other than England be handled by specially selected committees, such additional committees were constituted.

The business of every one of the committees (including, therefore, the English committee) was [2] to examine and even to answer petitions. Maitland says this of the committee to be called into existence by the king's writ to his chancellor. The same, however, seems true of all the committees. They would, first, endorse petitions which ought not to have come

[1] M. P. 3–4.   [2] Ibid. lvii.

before parliament as petitions, because they related to affairs forming properly the subject-matter of common pleas ; such petitions would be endorsed, e.g., ' Sequatur in Cancellaria iuxta legem et consuetudinem regni,[1] Sequatur per breve de transgressione in Cancellaria,[2] Si intendat habere ius, adeat Cancellariam et ibi impetret,'[3] etc.[4] Secondly, the committees would dispose of petitions which touched the interests of the king, but ought to be dealt with by the exchequer, or the chancery, or other offices, and not by the heavy machine of parliament. We find, for instance, a complaint that the king's bailiffs had been ill-treated while discharging their duties ; the answer was that in each case the treasurer should be notified and he would grant a remedy.[5] There might be cases where the petition was obviously not clear enough : ' Ostendat quid pro se habet et inquiratur de statu antecessorum . . .,'[6] etc.[7]

In support of the above hypothesis[8] it may first be remarked, that, as we learn from the roll, the Scots, Gascon, Irish, and Guernsey petitions were delivered by the four original receivers to the newly appointed committees. But there is no entry as to the delivery of English petitions to any new committee.

Now, those who had originally been appointed were (so we read in the writ to the chancellor) ' assigned to receive the petitions '. This concerned the public and was repeated in the proclamation. But ' assigned to receive the petitions ' were also (as we know from the record) the members of the committee for Scotland. ' . . . as it seems plain that in the first instance all petitions are to pass through the hands of Roubury, Caen, Kirkby, and Bush, we may perhaps believe that the committee for Scotland had the same power that

[1] M. P., nos. 28, 115. [2] Ibid., no. 30. [3] Ibid., no. 120.
[4] Cf., in the sixth year, R. P. i. 1–14, nos. 8, 16, 22, 28, 49, 50.
[5] M. P., no. 144. [6] Ibid., no. 124.
[7] Cf., in the sixth year, R. P. i. 2, no. 5.
[8] Our interpretation of the word ' receiving ' implies that it was a technical term, and that those appointed to ' receive ' petitions understood its technical meaning. This solution appears more probable if we consider that there was not yet in use a designation corresponding to the later one, ' auditors of petitions ' ; hence the members of the non-English committees were also called ' receivers '.

was given to the committees for Gascony and for Ireland, that it consisted not merely of receivers and sorters of petitions, but of triers and auditors.' [1] This is quite plausible ; it applies also to the four men originally appointed, in regard to English petitions.

It is true that the writ to the chancellor ordered him and others of the council (and not specifically those assigned as receivers) to deliver petitions before the king came. But out of the four original receivers three were members of the council,[2] and the fourth was, like one of the three just mentioned, a master of chancery and notary of the Holy See. Nor were all the members of the other committees members of the council.[3] As to the chancellor, it seems that it was incumbent on him to supervise the whole preliminary stage. Two of the receivers were masters of chancery, and therefore his subordinates. Another receiver was remembrancer of the exchequer, and thus the treasurer would be his superior. If the treasurer and chancellor would help, their help would of course be accepted by the receivers.

We must for a moment leave the petitions in the hands of the receivers, and compare our results with what is suggested by documents from other years of Edward I's reign.

In a parliament of 6 Edward I, a petition was presented by the prior and friars of the hospital of St. John of Brackley.[4] It complained that the sheriff of Northampton, by summons of the exchequer, was exacting an unjust charge. After a statement of the facts and the request, the petition proceeds :

' Ceste peticion fut autre fet baille a mestre Roberd de Scardeburgh, e a misire Nichole de Stapleton, ke dunks furent assignes a receivre peticions ; e respondu fut por meme ceus kem alast al Eschequere, et kem mustrast ilekes les avaunt-dites chartres le Roy, e ke ees serroient alloees.   Le Atturny le Priur issi le fist, e respondu li fut par les Baruns del Esche-kere ke nule chartre ne alloereyent saunz especiel comaunde-ment nostre Seignur le Roy.   E pur ceo, prient il pur deu akun remedie del avaunt demaunde ke le Viscunt lur de-maunde.'

[1] M. P. lx.   [2] Ibid. cviii.
[3] Ibid. cviii f.   [4] R. P. i. 9–10, no. 41.

It is not said that the petition had been presented in a parliament. But there had been men specially appointed to receive and answer petitions. When their answer proved insufficient, neither they nor another committee like themselves were approached, but a like petition was presented in what we know to have been a parliament. This points to the conclusion that the former petition had also been brought in a parliament. Besides, we assume that in those early years the very aim of a petition in England was to bring a complaint before a parliament. Sir Robert de Scardeburg was a clerk of the chancery in 6 Edward I,[1] while Nicolas de Stapleton was a justice in eyre in the third year,[2] and a commissioner of oyer and terminer in many cases of that time.[3] He was a justice of the king's bench in the sixth year,[4] if not before. Those two, then, had been appointed to receive petitions, to expedite the simple ones and—we may safely add—to put the more difficult ones before the king and his council.

We come to the well-known ordinance of 8 Edward I.[5] It was an administrative ordinance ; it was to be known to those concerned, namely, to the receivers of petitions and to the government departments. It directed that the receivers, instead of (answering some and) sending (other ?) petitions to the king, were to cause all the (other ?) petitions to come to the departments concerned, and that only if the officials considered it necessary, should they (the officials) themselves bring the petitions before the king. This seems to have been a desperate remedy : if consistently applied, it would have destroyed the possibility of a direct communication between the king and his wronged subjects. Exactly the same state of affairs had brought about quarrels between the king of Hungary and his subjects : [6] the new arrangement was not practical and cannot have remained in force for long. At any rate, in the twenty-first year we find a

---

[1] C. C. R., 6 Ed. I, 501.   [2] C. P. R., 3 Ed. I, 89.
[3] Ibid. 115, 177, 239.   [4] C. C. R., 6 Ed. I, 503.
[5] Above, pp. 89–90.   This ordinance was in no sense a statute. In form, it is a schedule affixed to the close roll. It is not enrolled otherwise.
[6] Above, pp. 92–3.

distinctly different procedure :[1] not only does there reappear a group of petitions which were to be sent by the receivers directly to the king and his council, but even the other petitions would not be delivered before a report had been made to the king; this was apparently to prevent the sending away of petitions which ought to come before the king and council.

We do not know whether the ordinance of the twenty-first year was allowed to fall into disuse, or was expressly changed. In any case, the procedure which was adopted in the Lenten parliament, 1305, was not in accordance with it : the chancellor was then told that as many petitions as possible should be answered (delivered [2]) before the king came.[3]

From the record of another parliament held in 1305 (it began on September 15) it appears that the king sent to John Kirkby and the three other original receivers of the Lenten parliament, close writs under the great seal notifying them that the king had appointed them to receive all the petitions which should be presented in the parliament ; the receivers were therefore ordered to come to London as speedily as possible, and to receive all petitions from their arrival (*extunc*) every day until a certain day after Michaelmas.[4] The record states that on September 27 a proclamation was made to the effect that all those who wished to hand in their petitions at that parliament were to deliver them to the four men who had been assigned, between then and the next Sunday, and not later. We find no mention of any other committees. Moreover, the proclamation was not made until about a fortnight after the parliament had begun ; it was about the same length of time before it began that the men appointed to be receivers were ordered to come, as soon as possible, to London. The proclamation which was finally made, directed that petitions should be handed in to the same men. We may assume, therefore, that the proclamation was made as soon as they came to London. If the work of the receivers had been purely clerical, then, if they were late,

[1] Above, p. 90.
[3] Above, p. 99.
[2] M. P. lvii.
[4] R. P. i. 182.

some other men would have been assigned to collect and sort the petitions. If, however, we suppose that a certain experience was required in order to expedite those petitions which could be disposed of during the preliminary stage, this would explain the delay; apparently the receivers (or a sufficient number of them) were not there; therefore, even if the petitions had been collected, they would not be dealt with.[1]

What was done with petitions once they were in the hands of the receivers? The answers of the receivers consisted of endorsements, given perhaps, if necessary, after hearing the parties; some petitions were refused *prima facie* because they did not contain anything to support the claim, or else because no wrong had been done as yet: ' Nondum iniuriatum est, conqueratur post iniuriam.'[2] In the case of the hospital of St. John of Brackley[3] we were told that the receivers had ordered the petitioners to go to the exchequer, and to show their charters there: the charters, it was said, would be allowed. It should be noted that no writ was either ordered or sued for. The prior's attorney went to the exchequer and was told that no charter would be allowed without the king's special order. We know of many endorsements of a similar character, that is, with directions to the petitioners

---

[1] According to our theory, these four receivers were not only to collect petitions, but also to answer those which could be answered without approaching the king. They would, therefore, endorse petitions which *prima facie* should not have been brought at all, e.g. petitions instead of which writs at common law should have been substituted (M. P., no. 267); they would also refer to the several government departments such petitions as could be expedited in the ordinary course or by remedies obtainable without approaching the king. The enactments of the eighth and twenty-first years mention no special committees of auditors; had such committees been introduced, both enactments would probably have been unnecessary. It might be said that since, in the parliaments of Edward II and his successors the triers were persons of distinction, therefore, a committee consisting of two masters of chancery, one justice, and one exchequer remembrancer, would seem not exalted enough. But in one of the first years of Edward I a petition had been answered by two men assigned to receive petitions, one of whom was a justice and the other a clerk of chancery (above, pp. 102–3). The same reasons which allowed the function to be entrusted to this first committee in the seventies of the thirteenth century could dictate the appointment of the second group in 1305.

[2] R. P. i. 46, no. 13.   [3] Above, pp. 102–3.

to go to some department where justice would be done to them.[1] In such cases there was, legally speaking, no order to the exchequer, but advice to the petitioners, and a bare promise or direction, 'fiet (or *fiat*) ei iustitia', just as there had been a bare promise in the case of the hospital of St. John of Brackley. The following endorsements may be quoted as examples :

From 1278 : ' Eat ad Cancellariam,[2] Sequatur in Curia Cancellarie,[3] Audiatur in Cancellaria, et fiat ei iusticia,[4] Sequatur per breve de Cancellaria,[5] Sequatur, et fiet ei iusticia, si sequi voluerit,[6] Prosequatur•coram Iusticiariis Regis ad placita Regis,[7] Si concordia facta fuerit in Curia coram Iusticiariis, prosequatur ibi ; si extra Curiam, non pertinet ad Regem ;[8] Sequatur versus Iusticiarios, et audiatur, et fiat ei Iusticia,[9] Eat coram Iusticiarios de Banco.'[10]

From 1290 : ' In Cancellaria.[11] An Irish petition[12] has the endorsement : Ceste chose ne fu unkes mostre a la justice e pur ceo ne serra rien fet si la ke la justice ly faille de dreit. E si lur est dit kil mostrent ceste chose a la justice. E si il ne voeillent remedie purver veignent al procheyn parlement e le Rey purverra remedie.'

From 1305 : ' Sequatur in Cancellaria,[13] Sequatur in Cancellaria iuxta legem et consuetudinem regni,[14] Perquirat sibi per communem legem si voluerit.'[15]

In some cases the parties were sent to the wardrobe.[16]

The petitions which had not been answered by the receivers, were sent before the council, the king, or both. We are unable to discuss here the relations between the king and his council. If we find endorsements like ' Concessum est per Regem '[17] on one hand, and ' Concessum est per Consilium, quod sic fiat, et Baronibus de Scaccario mandetur in forma predicta '[18] on the other hand, the difference must

---

[1] e.g. A. P., E 10, E 12, E 20, E 117, E 145, E 205, E 462, E 732, E 920.
[2] R. P. i. 12, no. 55.   [3] Ibid. 10, no. 48.   [4] Ibid. 10, no. 44.
[5] Ibid. 6, no. 28.   [6] Ibid. 10, no. 45.   [7] Ibid. 11, no. 50.
[8] Ibid. 14, no. 64.   [9] Ibid. 3, no. 12.   [10] Ibid. 9, no. 39.
[11] Ibid. 57, no. 136.   [12] Cole, 70.   [13] M. P., nos. 18, 104.
[14] Ibid., nos. 28, 115 ; cf. above, p. 101.   [15] M. P., no. 172.
[16] e.g. ibid. 324, no. 6 : ' Voise en garderobe pur aconter ove Sire Johan de Drok(enesford) e il li paiera.'
[17] R. P. i. 54, no. 106.   [18] Ibid. 50, no. 52.

remain unexplained, so far as the present investigation is concerned.[1]

Of the petitions which were not answered by the receivers, some were tried and decided before the council. In other cases the council gave a hypothetical decision and left departments (the chancery, the exchequer, or even subordinate officials) to ascertain the truth; in a third group of cases decisions were postponed, and it was ordered that in the meantime the council should be better informed, e. g. by a search for documents, by inquisitions, &c.; in the last group, the cases would be sent to the chancellor, or the exchequer, or the king's bench, or some individual commissioners, with the order to do right.

Of cases tried and decided before the council we have many examples. What is said to have been a petition in 8 Edward I[2] had the endorsement: 'Iudicium redditum contra ipsam, concordatum est per consilium et omnes Iusticiarios. et Ideo ipsa eat sine die. et rex retineat custodiam,' etc. To mention at random a few other cases, an inquisition was endorsed in 1290: 'Deliberatum est per Consilium quod Rex tenetur reddere ei Ballivam si placet'; the king acceded to the decision, and the endorsement goes on: 'Rex redd(it) ei ballivam de gratia.'[3] On a petition brought in the same parliament we read: 'Concessum est per Consilium quod inde habeat Breve in Cancellaria.'[4]

The council could of course hear evidence.[5] Even juries were summoned before the council.[6] It goes without saying that the decision, even if it went the whole length of the request made in the petition, might sometimes result only in an intermediary step, e. g. the grant of a *procedendo*,[7] or the order that the petitioner's account should be heard in some office. Thus, in one of the last years of Edward I a petition in parliament had been endorsed: 'Adeat garderobam et

---

[1] But see below, pp. 139–62, 191–2.　　[2] P. C. P., f. 1, m. 14.†
[3] R. P. i. 62, no. 203.　　[4] Ibid. 59, no. 167.
[5] e.g. M. P., no. 257 'Escaetor recordatur coram consilio quod mandavit subescaetori suo quod faceret extentas, etc, et quod idem subescaetor est in faciendo easdem et quod nullus impedit. Ideo. . . .'
[6] P. C. P., f. 44, m. 20.　　[7] e.g. M. P., nos. 77, 141.

computet ibidem, et de eo quod dominus Rex sibi teneatur Thesaurarius Garderobe assignabit ei certum terminum solutionis.' The petitioner took the petition to the wardrobe, but the treasurer of the wardrobe refused to intermeddle with the account. Thereupon in the next parliament a similar petition was presented, asking for the assignment of a place where the account could be rendered, the gages allowed, and so on. Here the answer was : ' Habeat Breve Thesaurario et Baronibus de Scaccario, quod audiant compotum suum.'[1]

If the examination of a petition resulted in a refusal,[2] no further steps were necessary. Otherwise, either a writ would be ordered, or directions would be given in some other way. The following examples are taken from the last year of Edward I : ' Quia testatum est per Thesaurarium coram Consilio quod fecit plenarium servicium suum annis xxviii et xxxi ; Concordatum est, quod habeat breve de Cancellaria pro Scutagio suo levando, et quod ipse sit quietus de Scutagio ab eo exacto pro exercitibus predictis.'[3] In the case of inquisitions *ad quod damnum* for alienating lands into mortmain, a writ of inquisition had to be petitioned for in each case :[4] this explains the number of writs endorsed, e.g., ' Habeat inquisicionem secundum novam formam.'[5] But without giving writs, a petition could be favourably answered and the officials concerned could receive oral orders :

' Preceptum est Thesaurario,[6] Preceptum est Cancellario quod provideat de idoneo Custode,[7] Dictum est Iusticiariis quod procedant, et quod Gustos respondeat.[8] Rex ordinavit inde voluntatem suam,[9] Rex dixit voluntatem suam Thesaurario et Rogero de Brabanzon et sociis ipsius Rogeri assignatis ad negotia illa audienda et terminanda,' etc.[10]

Secondly, a hypothetical decision might be given and the department concerned or the individual officer would have to ascertain the truth.

---

[1] P. C. P., f. 44, m. 22.†
[2] e.g. R. P. i. 55, nos. 120, 121 : ' nichil fiet '.   [3] Ibid. 194, no. 19.
[4] Above, p. 88.
[5] R. P. i. 63–5, nos. 212, 215–8, 220–2, 228, 234–5, 242–3, 249.
[6] Ibid. 49, no. 43.   [7] Ibid.   [8] Ibid., no. 46.
[9] M. P., no. 351.   [10] Ibid., no. 64.

Thus, in 1290 : 'Inquiratur in Cancellaria de dono facto Ingelarmo. Et si sic inveniatur, fiat ei aquietantia de L. marcis ;[1] Si ita sit, habeat Breve quod procedatur in placito ;[2] Scribatur Vicecomiti et Escaetori quod fiat inde Inquisitio ; Et, si ita sit, dotetur.'[3]

In 1305 : 'Coram Iustitiariis de utroque Banco et vocetur Hugo le Despenser. Si tenementa in villa illa sint legabilia et testator legare potuit secundum consuetudinem burgi Oxoniae, fiat breve de Cancellaria Maiori et Ballivis Oxoniae in forma usitata de huiusmodi legatis.'[4]

In 1307 : 'Mandetur Thesaurario et Baronibus de Scaccario, quod, auditis rationibus suis, si ostendere poterit quod non teneat nisi pro uno feodo, et inde fecerit servitium, de residuo sit quietus.'[5]

Thirdly, cases could be sent to boards, individual officers, or special commissioners to inquire and to certify the king, or the council.

Thus, in 1305 : ' Breve fiat Thesaurario et Baronibus quod videatur scriptum et examinetur plenius negotium et certificetur Rex ;[6] Inquiratur per tenentem locum Regis in Scotia et Camerarium per quod ius Iohannes de Soules habuit dictum manerium, et certificent Regem ad proximum parliamentum ;[7] Adeat in Cancellariam et habeat breve ad escaetorem quod inquirat in propria persona in praesentia conquerentis si interesse voluerit super contentis in petitione et certificet Regem.'[8]

In 1307 : ' Fiat breve de Cancellaria Iohanni de Drokenesford, Custodi Garderobe Regis, quod computet cum executoribus de contentis in petitione et faciat eis billam de debitis que debentur per dictum Computum, ut Rex tunc super hoc dicat voluntatem suam.[9] '

Lastly, cases could be sent for trial and decision before the government departments, or individual officers.

Thus, in 1278 : ' Tradatur R. de Hengham, et ipse et ipsi de consilio audiant eos.'[10]

In 1290 : ' Comes Gloucestrie clamat custodiam de feodo et Maritagio et ponatur ad Scaccarium, et ibi fiat Iusticia.[11]

---

[1] R. P. i. 57, no. 143. [2] Ibid. 47, no. 15. [3] Ibid. 58, no. 153.
[4] M. P., no. 256. [5] R. P. i. 197, no. 41. [6] M. P., no. 207.
[7] Ibid., no. 293 ; cf. nos. 390–2, 394. [8] Ibid., no. 219.
[9] R. P. i. 199, no. 51. [10] Ibid. 3, no. 11. [11] Ibid. 47, no. 22.

Audiatur coram Cancellario et Iusticiariis ad placita Regis de peticione sua ; [1] Cancellarius vocat(is) Iusticiariis provideat eis remedium et aliis in hoc casu perpetuo duraturum.' [2]

In 1305 : ' Fiat breve Cancellariae Thesaurario et Baronibus quod videant cartam et inquirere faciant de seisina, et ulterius faciant quod iustum fuerit.[3] Veniant ad Scaccarium tam senescallus quam querens, et ostendat querens quid habet de aquietantia, et super hoc fiat iustitia et mandetur breve de Cancellaria.[4] Tradatur Cancellario et fiat ei iustitia.[5] Adeat Thesaurarium et Iohannem de Drokenesford et Rex habebit ratum quod ipsi facient, etc.[6] Ita responsum est ad istas duas petitiones. Sequantur coram Rogero le Brabanzon et sociis suis, et illi faciant quod iustum fuerit, per consilium Thesaurarii et Cancellarii et aliorum de Consilio si necesse fuerit.' [7]

In the Hautboys' case [8] we have at once examples of different ways of dealing with petitions : upon a petition presented to the king, complaining of wrongful disseisin by the queen's bailiffs, there were first assigned, by the queen's consent and will, two commissioners to inquire, and to hear and determine. Afterwards other commissioners were appointed (as the former had done nothing) to inquire and to do speedy justice to the parties ; the queen having died in the meantime, the king was now one of the parties. As this commission also had no positive result, the king, upon renewed petition, assigned another set of men to take the inquisition and to send it to the king. This resulted in an inquisition being taken, and the lands and tenements were restored to the petitioner. Thereupon another party petitioned as to other tenements, an inquisition was taken and returned to chancery. Upon a still further petition, the inquisition was viewed (or the inquisitions were viewed) and orders were given to restore the tenements.[9]

Personal responsibility of officials. In the time of Henry III

---

[1] R. P. i. 58, no. 158.　　　　　　[2] Ibid. 60, no. 176.

[3] M. P., no. 4. As a result of this writ, an inquisition was taken by the constable of the castle and keeper of the manor. By another writ (C. C. R., 34 Ed. I, 388, dated May 30, 1306) the constable and keeper was ordered to let the petitioner have his tithe of rabbits.

[4] M. P., no. 19 ; cf. nos. 21–2, &c.　　[5] Ibid., no. 34.

[6] Ibid., no. 58.　　　[7] R. P. i. 183.　　[8] T. S., f. 1, m. 1–1–2.†

[9] Another way, not of proceeding against the king, but of complaining against his servants, was to approach the auditors of complaints (' auditores

the king's servants, if their acts which they claimed to be official were complained of, could not be proceeded against in the ordinary way, except by the king's permission (special or general).[1] For, right or wrong, their acts were the king's acts, and as such could be complained of within the realm only to the king or to bodies appointed by him for this purpose. This general position was not changed under Edward I.[2] But (apart from the fact that the king's lower officials could be complained of to the exchequer,[3] and all of them to the king) the king was gradually waiving his privilege with regard to the lower officials.

The first Statute of Westminster (c. 24) gave an assize of novel disseisin against any escheator, sheriff, or other bailiff of the king who, without warrant or order or authority certain, inherent in his office, should disseise somebody of a freehold or of anything belonging to a freehold. It was left to the party whether he would not, instead of bringing the assize, prefer to leave to the king *de son office* the punishment of the offender. The second statute of Westminster provided (c. 13) that persons illegally imprisoned by sheriffs should have their action by a writ of false imprisonment against the sheriffs, as they would have it against any other person. The same was to apply to actions against bailiffs of franchises (ibid.). The *Articuli super Chartas* (c. 18) gave a writ of waste against the escheator or his subescheator, as it had been given by the Statute of Gloucester for private cases.[4]

querelarum '). Fleta regards them as sitting as court (Book II, Chap. 2, sect. 4 ' Habet etiam curiam suam coram Auditoribus specialiter a latere Regis destinatis, quorum officium non extenditur nisi ad iusticiarios et ministros regis, et quibus non conceditur potestas audita terminare, sed regi deferre, ut per ipsum adhibeantur pene secundum meritorum qualitates '. (This passage is quoted from the manuscript at the British Museum.) Apparently they were appointed merely to hear complaints and report them to the king. (Cf. R. P. i. 25, no. 16 ' Domino Regi et eius Consilio Iohannes . . . alias coram Auditoribus Querelarum monstravit, supplicando.')   [1] Above, pp. 25, 51.

[2] In the Hautboys' case (above, pp. 57, 110) an assize could not be taken where the queen's officials had taken land into the queen's hands.

[3] The officials were, of course, responsible to the king ; the disciplinary proceedings could result, not only in punishment for the guilty official, but also in reparation for the wronged party.

[4] See also Stat. Westm. I, cc. 1, 19, 26, 30, 32 ; Stat. Westm. II, cc. 38, 39, 44 ; Art. Sup. Chart., cc. 2, 9. As to the financial standing required of certain officials, see Appendix, pp. 214-15.

CHAPTER III

THE REIGNS OF EDWARD II AND EDWARD III

INTRODUCTORY

New and old law. In the fourteenth century, legal principles were developed more by political events and by judicial decisions and discussions than by an ambitious jurist or a conscious legislator. In 'the history of the common law during the fourteenth and fifteenth centuries there is no such rapid expansion as marked the twelfth and thirteenth centuries. Rather we see an elaboration of the machinery of process and of the rules of pleading, and a detailed working out of principles already established in the thirteenth century.'[1] We can trace practically every new development to ideas which had existed in the former reign. And yet, taken all together, the new developments are striking. In many a domain we see a real change. In some respects there was at least a struggle of ideas. The king's prerogative, for instance, had not yet assumed the forms in which it was attributed to the Stuarts by some of their more obsequious judges. But expression was already being given to all the principles which were to be so hotly contested in the seventeenth century. Both James I and Coke might have found all the arguments needed to support their respective contentions in the historical sources of the years 1307–77.

Postulates of legal thought. We start with the distinction between right and wrong. It occurs, for instance, in the frequent *dicta* that if the king was seised, whether rightly or wrongly, one must sue against him by petition.[2] This

---

[1] Holdsworth, ii. 338.

[2] e.g. Y. B., 17 Ed. III, 10 : ' Le quel le Roy avoit droit ou tort, home suera le chose hors de sa main . . . par peticion ' ; Y. B., 24 Ed. III, 55 : ' Quant le Roy est seisi, etc. soit ceo a droit, soit ceo a tort, home suera devers luy par peticion.' Cf. also e.g. Y. B., 17 Ed. III, 10–11 : ' . . . si le Roy fuist seisi de l'avowson, fuit ceo a droit ou a tort, il averoit le presentement . . .' ; 22 l. ass. pl. 28 : ' . . . quant il seisist, tout soit il a droit ou a tort, il commit pur certein terme.'

distinction was closely connected with the conception of law. In the period now considered, by ' law ' could be meant, either what might be called justice, or else positive law. Yet we should not press the distinction too far. In some cases it was, no doubt, clear. In other cases it was quite difficult to trace.

Henry III granted to the men of St. Albans that they should not implead or be impleaded by a royal writ of attaint with regard to any freehold in their town. The charter was confirmed by Edward II and Edward III. There arose a case in which the charter was pleaded and allowed. Thereupon issued a *scire facias*, ordering the men and community of St. Albans to show cause in chancery why the clause which had been made to the prejudice of the common law and of the commonwealth should not be revoked. The king's attorney demanded the revocation of the charter, because the common law, by which all those of the realm should be governed, was restrained by the king's charter from taking its right course in the administration of justice. Thus, he argued, the charter had been made in perturbation of justice and common law (*in perturbacionem iuris et legis communis*), and such a thing the king could not do. Therefore the charter, being contrary to common law, ought to be revoked and annulled (' et sic eadem carta ut legi communi contraria revocabilis et adnullabilis existat '). The court held that the charter was contrary to the common law, and, if charters of that kind were to be granted and to remain in force, then complainants would be deprived of their legal remedy, and that would turn into the disinheritance of the whole community of the realm. Therefore the charter was revoked and annulled.

The law which was declared to have been infringed by the charter was more than what we should call pure morality : for its infringement caused the revocation of the charter. Yet the law was not strong enough to make the charter which was infringing it *ipso facto* void : the charter had to be annulled. The proceedings were not in error ; the judgement of the royal justices who had allowed the charter was not complained of. It was the charter itself that was complained of, and was annulled.[1]

[1] T. S., f. 2, m. 23.† The record is specially interesting because of its

A statute of 1321 granted a pardon to those who had prosecuted the Despensers.[1] But in a parliament held in the following reign

'it was found that the said statute, ordinance, provision, and acquittance had been made in violation of reason and common right ("contre reson et commune droit"), of the king's oath made at his coronation, and of the tenor of the Great Charter of the liberties of England, which is fortified (sanctioned) by a sentence of excommunication,[2] and wherein it is contained that the king shall not deny or delay unto any man right or justice ; and that the said acquittance was made more for the emboldening and favouring of malefactors and disturbers of the peace to commit felonies, trespasses, and crimes, than for remedy and redress of wrong : Wherefore our Lord the King, having regard to the matters aforesaid, and to this . . . that he could not at that time withstand the said force upon the sudden, to do right as it behoved him ; that the suit of another he ought not, neither could he, release or pardon, without doing wrong ; and also considering the counsel and the request of the said prelates, earls, barons, knights of shires, and the commonalty of the realm, in that behalf made, for the salvation of his soul and of their souls . . . the said statute, ordinance, provision, and all the acquittances to whomsoever made by the said statute, ordinance, and provision, accord and assent, did repeal and annull for ever, as a thing done against reason, law, and the custom of his realm, and in prejudice of him and his Crown and of his royal dignity.' This was done 'in his . . . full parliament at York, of his royal power, with the advice and consent of the prelates, earls, barons, knights of shires, and the commonalty of the realm, there assembled by his command '.[3]

We know what political events had led to this act.[4] But a modern Act of parliament can always be repealed by a later Act, without any justification. Apparently, therefore,

wealth of detail, but the case was not the only one of its kind that arose during this period. There are petitions to the king asking for remedies where some people had privileges (by royal charters) of answering or not answering in certain courts ; the results are complained of as contrary to right and reason. The answer is that those who feel themselves aggrieved should sue at common law, e.g. R. P. i. 414, no. 157, A.D. 1321–2. ; ibid. ii. 37, no. 32, A.D. 1330.

[1] Stubbs, ii. 365.

[2] Above, p. 46.

[3] S. R. 187–8.

[4] Stubbs, ii. 365–7.

in those days there was a higher law, by which even Acts of parliament had to abide.[1]

Similarly, in 1341, the chancellor, treasurér, and others, when sworn to observe certain newly made statutes, pro-tested that

'they could not keep them in case those statutes were con-trary to the laws and customs of the realm, which they had sworn to keep '.[2]

In a petition of the commons of 1352, after a mention of the king's obligation according to the Great Charter, reference is made to his (the king's) law, 'which law is the sovereign (highest) right of his realm and of his crown.' [3]

It was a fundamental postulate that right should be done to all.   More particularly, this phrase seems to suggest the administration of what we might call positive law.   Thus we read in the record of a parliament held in 1330 :

'Item, Pur ce qe nostre Seignur le Roi voet qe les Leis de sa terre soient meintenues, et qe droit soit fait as touz, auxibien as poures come as riches, Si ad nostre Seignur le Roi comande, qe ses Justices . . . pur Brief du Grant Seal, ne Lettre de la targe, ne autre Lettre ou mandement que-cumqe, ne pur priere de nully, n'esparnient ne lessent a faire Droit a touz, solonc la Lei et la custume du Roialme.' [4]

Among the legal conceptions which were dependent for their protection on what we should call positive law was the notion of acquired rights.

Its strongest expression was the doctrine, already familiar

---

[1] On this 'fundamental law ' see McIlwain, chap. ii.

[2] R. P. ii. 131, no. 42. Soon afterwards the king himself repudiated the statutes, asserting that his consent had not been genuine (Stubbs, ii. 411 ; S. R. 297 ; cf. R. P. ii. 140, no. 4).

[3] Ibid. ii. 241, no. 40 : ' Item prie la Commune, qe come contenu soit en la Grande Chartre, " Qe nostre Seignur le Roi ne vendra ne deleiera droit a nulli " : Et ceux qi vodroient purchacer Briefs en la Chauncellerie, queux Briefs sont la primere partie de sa Leie, quele Leie est soverein Droit de son Roialme et de sa Corone, ne poent aver Briefs sanz Fyn faire . . . Prie la dite Commune qe lui plese, pur Dieu et pur Droit . . .'

[4] Ibid. 60, no. 23. Law and reason regulated also the relations of men and the Church ; ibid. 338, no. 98 : '. . . Item fait a penser, coment ley et reson et bone foy volent, qe ceo q'est done a Seinte Esglise par devotion soit despendu a l'Honour de Dieu, solonc la devotion et l'entent de donour, et non pas hors de Roialme sur noz Enemyes.'

to us,[1] that one could be deprived of one's rights, judged, made to pay, only by one's own consent. An assertion of the doctrine of individual consent will be found in the case against Sir William de Thorpe, sometime Chief Justice. The record and process of the case were read in parliament before the lords (1350–1) and the king asked for the latter's opinion. They answered that the judgement was reasonable, because Sir William had himself by his oath made himself amenable to such a penalty, and had then confessed to receiving bribes.[2] In 1366, on considering King John's deed to the pope promising homage for England and Ireland, the lords and commons declared that neither King John nor anybody else could place his realm or his people in such a subjection without their assent.[3]

THE KING AND THE LAW

The king's legal position   The king's power was given him by the law, the king's position was determined by the law. Hence, the king was bound to observe the law. In his coronation oath the king was made, as is well known, ' to grant, to keep, and . . . to confirm to the people of England the laws and customs that had been granted them by the ancient righteous and godly kings of England . . .; to cause to be done in all his judgements equal and right justice and discretion, in mercy and truth, . . . to keep and to defend the righteous laws and customs, which the community of the realm would establish, and to enforce them . . . according to his power '.[4]   Thus the laws were considered as already in existence, as already granted; the people were already enjoying them. The king had to obey these laws, and to enforce them. The Ordinances of 1311 stipulated that no felony should be protected by the king's charter of pardon,

---

[1] Above, p. 24.
[2] R. P. ii. 227, no. 10.   [3] Ibid. 290, nos. 7–8.
[4] S. R. 168 ; Stubbs, ii. 331 f ; Maitland, 99 f. The position did not depend on the king's good will. The king was made to ' grant and promise ', so that the subjects should have, not only their rights as of old, but also a claim against the king, based on his own grant. The repetition of promises on the part of the king was due to the mediaeval (and not only mediaeval) idea that two promises are better than one.

or in any other way, except where the king could, according to his oath, exercise grace, ' and that by process of the law and the custom of the Realm '.[1] The king's writs would repeat that he was bound by his oath to preserve as best he could the peace and quietness of his people.[2] A petition asking the king to influence the course of proceedings in a court was expressly answered to the effect that the king could send ' curteise lettres ' under his privy seal, that the petitioner be helped so far as that could be done without offending the law, ' mes la Ley ne put il desturber '.[3] In 1376–7 the king, in reply to a petition of the commons, pointed out that he had no power of repealing a statute without the consent of parliament.[4] ' Owele et dreyt justice et discrecioun, en misericorde et verite ', according to the king's oath, were expected, not only in cases in which differences between subjects were to be determined, but also in disputes in which something was claimed by or from the king. The law decided the subject-matter of the controversy, and the law prescribed the procedure to be adopted.

Occasionally the king, or his representatives, would be reminded of the king's obligations. The defendant's pleader in a *quare impedit* brought by the king boldly stated (in 1312) :

' We want this (to go) as to the demonstrance of the king, because we understand that he wants to be guided, in his own court, by right and by reason, as the others will.'[5]

In 1340, Sir Geoffrey de Staunton petitioned the king in parliament and wound up his petition with the statement that by enacted statutes right was to be done to all, according to the king's obligation accepted by his oath.[6]

[1] R. P. i. 285, no. 28.   [2] Ibid. 355 b.
[3] Ibid. 477, no. 101, and cf. ii. 83, no. 45.
[4] Ibid. ii. 368, no. 44, cf. below, p. 129, n. 1.
[5] Y. B., M. 6 Ed. II, S. S. 74.
[6] R. P. ii. 123 a : ' Eantz regard as Estatutz faitz, Qe nul commune Lei soit delaie, ne les Juggementz purloignies par difficulte ou oppinions, einz droit fet as touz, come nostre Seignur le Roi est tenuz par son Serement.' See also the exceptions in S. R. 280–1, no. iv, indicating that doubts might arise had the ' kings, queens, and their children ' not been specially exempted.

In the king's suits, or in suits against him, the king was considered just a party. Thus, in a petition of 1324–5 the bishop of Exeter complained that for more than eight years a plea had been pending between the king and the bishop, ' et chescune partie ad dit pur lui ses resons '.[1] In 1310, the king sent to the exchequer a writ directing the barons to cause the examination of a case, which was pending before them, by petition, between the king and Sir Henry FitzHugh, as to a wardship and marriage. The barons were to cause to ' faire a lune partie et a lautre hastiue acomplissement de droit selonc ley et reson et lusage de nostre royalme '.[2]

The king's claims against his subjects had to be based on the law. Thus, in the time of Edward III, the earl of Warwick, whose tenant had died, seised the lands and the body of the heir. Afterwards the child inherited other tenements from one who held from the king in chief. The king, ' par resoun de sa prerogative ', challenged the earl's right to retain the custody of lands and body. But because the earl had seised them at a time when only he and nobody else had the right to seise them, it was adjudged by the whole council that the king should not have the custody of either lands or the body of the heir.[3]

In a case of 1342–3 the chancellor held that since the king's title was based on the rights of an abbot, and the abbot could not have had a *quare impedit*, consequently the king could not have one. It was contended for the king that when the escheator seised the advowson into the king's hand, this by itself could give the king a title even if the king had not presented, and until the advowson was sued out of his hand by petition. But the chancellor held that this was so only in cases of a special command, and was not true in cases of a general command.[4] In 1369 a *quare impedit* was brought by the king. The question was whether a certain grant

---

[1] R. P. i. 421, no. 18. The petition reminded the king that he ' deit voler et veust qe droit ne soit delaye ne denie a nulli encontre la Grant Chartre '.

[2] L. T. R., r. 80 ; Brevia directa Baronibus, T. m. 1 d.†

[3] Y. B., 20 Ed. III, pt. II, 139–41, R. S.

[4] Ibid., 17 Ed. III, 179–81, R. S.

by King Henry could be said to relate, by implication, to an advowson. The court held that since 'the statute' *Praerogativa Regis* had been made in the days of Edward I, therefore before that statute such a grant by implication was possible, just as it could have been made by any other man.[1]

In another *quare impedit* brought by the king in the same year, counsel for the defendant pointed out that the plea of plenarty against the king was taken away by statute, where the king claimed as in the right of some one else ; where, however, he claimed in his own right, 'il n'ad pas pluis avantage, que n'ad auter person.'[2] In another case the tenements of a prior had been seised into the king's hand on the supposition that he was an alien enemy, but on his suit to the king it was proved that he had been born in Gascony, within the king's allegiance. Restitution was granted to him, and the king sent a writ to the escheator stating that by his special grace he had granted the prior restitution. The escheator was ordered to remove the king's hands, but no mention was made of a certain advowson. Later on, the king brought against the prior a *quare impedit* in respect of the church to which the advowson related. The opinion of the justices of the bench was demanded on the point. They decided that the writ had divested the king of everything, for the seisure had been general and the restitution had also been general ; although the writ purported to have issued by the king's grace, yet it was proved that the king had no right to seise ; therefore, they concluded, the king had no right. The prior's presentee obtained the church.[3] Where the

[1] Y. B., 43 Ed. III, 21–2.

[2] Ibid. 14.

[3] 27 l. ass. pl. 48 : ' . . . Pur que il avoit restitucion etc. Pur que le Roy per son brief reherse, etc. (et ?) Mande a l'Eschetor que de sa grace especial il avoit grant que il avera restitucion, et luy command d'ouster la maine sans parler d'avowson, puis quel livery et restitucion le Roy port Quare Impedit vers le Prior d'un voidance puis la restitucion etc. Sur quoi le Conte d'Arundel et Sir Guy de B. . . . demanderent des Justices lour oppinions ; queux disoient que depuis que le seiser le Roy fuit general, et la restitucion general, coment que en le brief fuit reherse qe il se fist de sa grace ; uncore al' matere prove que le Roy n'avoit droit a seiser : pur que coment ne fist le brief le Roy mention de avowson, uncore tout devest de le Roy. Pur que de lour avise le Roy n'avoit pas droit ; per que le Roll fist ratif(ication) ale presentee le Prior.'

king, having corrody and patronage, had granted away the patronage and claimed to have the corrody, it was held in chancery, in 1352, by all the justices, that he had implicitly given up his corrody, which, it was said, could not have remained to the king even if it were expressly reserved.[1]

So far as claims against the king were concerned, they, too, were decided according to the law. That means that, unless there was a special rule to the contrary, the law applied was the same as between subject and subject. It is perhaps superfluous to point out that feudal tenures were based on conditions which equally bound both contracting parties. ' Le Roy est tenus de faire restitution a son heire ' is the characteristic expression used in a case relating to the royal prerogative,[2] and many similar expressions might be quoted.

We hear much of the king's debts, and of his obligation to pay them. Thus, in 1319, the king sent a writ to the exchequer stating that the king owed (*tenetur*) to one Andrew de Arcla a sum of money, and that, wishing to satisfy the said Andrew, as he (the king) was bound to do, he had granted him the ferm of the city of Carlisle; since Andrew complained that he was not paid, the king ordered the barons to hear Andrew's complaint, to call the bailiffs whose duty it was to pay, and to cause ' eidem Andree super premissis fieri . . . debitum et festinum iusticie complementum '.[3]

In one of the first years of Edward III the executor of the king's victualler petitioned for a payment, or assignment in lieu, of a debt which was due from Edward II to the deceased. The endorsement directed the exchequer to see whether the debt was clearly still due and whether the petitioner was executor, and if so, to make payment, allowance, or assignment.[4] A similar petition based on a bill of the wardrobe was sent to the exchequer with the simple direction to do (what) reason (required).[5]

A petition of 1330 alleged that, in consideration of a certain

---

[1] 26 l. ass. pl. 53.   [2] 18 Ed. III, Fitzh. Sci., fa. 10.
[3] L. T. R., r. 90 ; Brevia directa Baronibus, M., m. 139 r.
[4] A. P. 1784.
[5] Ibid. 1786† ; cf. ibid. 1785† ; cf. R. P. i. 302–3, no. 57 ; 308, no. 80.

grant to be made by a convent to King Edward II, that king had entered into an agreement (covenaunt) with the convent to take steps that the latter be allowed to incorporate (appropriate) certain churches. The agreement had been kept by the convent, but not by the king. The endorsement of the petition directed that the petition be sent to the chancery ; the chancellor was to examine those who had been in the king's suite at the time of the alleged compact ; if it were found ' qe le covenauntz soient tielx ' and that it had not been performed, then ' it seems to the council, if it pleases the king, that the king owes to the petitioners ('qe le Roi lour doit faire ') restitution, or other satisfaction' ('ou autrement lour gree ').[1] At the bottom of the decision was the principle that the king should no more than anybody else receive the benefit of a compact without at the same time performing what he had undertaken.

In another case Maventus Fraunceys, a merchant, had contracted to supply Edward II, at Newcastle-on-Tyne, with 800 quarters of wheat. He bought the wheat in France, but during the passage the wheat was carried away by Flemish pirates. The merchant petitioned Edward III, in a parliament of 1328, for payment of the money. It seems that the petition was hypothetically decided in his favour. Commissioners were appointed on August 26, 1328,[2] to inquire whether the alleged robbery had been committed. The inquisition [3] was taken in 1329, and was returned into the chancery. In 1330 Fraunceys brought another petition in parliament, complaining that although the king had sent to the exchequer his writ of the great seal and three writs of the privy seal to let the petitioner have payment or assignment, nothing had been done in the matter by the barons.[4] The petition was endorsed to the effect that it be sent to the treasurer and barons, that they consider the petition, inquisition, the king's orders, and all the other evidence mentioned in the petition, and make payment of the debt, so that Fraunceys be reasonably satisfied without delay and that no

[1] R. P. ii. 31, no. 1.   [2] A. P. 10542.†   [3] Ibid. 10543.
[4] Ibid. 10541† ; R. P. ii. 32, no. 9.

more complaint might reach the king.[1] A writ to that effect, dated December 8, 1330, was sent to the exchequer. At the exchequer, after an inspection of the documents sent with the petition,[2] Fraunceys was ordered to produce the deed of the transaction. He produced an indenture, and the case was adjourned. Fraunceys obtained another writ of the great seal and asked for payment. Finally, the court gave judgement against the petitioner because the indenture showed that the wheat was to be delivered at Newcastle-on-Tyne ; in other words, according to the agreement Fraunceys was to take the risk connected with the delivery. The court considered that the sum was not to be paid, unless the king wished to pay as a matter of grace. Such an answer was returned in 1333. When, in 1336, another writ was sent to the exchequer to make payment or to send the documents of the case to the king, the reply was to the same effect.[3]

The claim in this case was not for restitution, although the petition presented in 1330 ended as follows :

‘ Endroit de ses pertes qe amontent a cynk centz livres et plus, il se mette en vostre grace, et le Roi gaigne de cele purveance plus de mille marcs.’ [4]

From the record of the case it would follow that the king was not bound to pay, although the transaction had been

---

[1] ‘ Soit ceste Peticion, ensemblement od l’enqueste, mande as Tresorer et Barouns et chamberleins de l’Escheqer, qe eux, regardez la Peticion, l’enquest, et les mandements, et totes autres evidences dont la Peticion fait mencion, lui facent fair paiement de la dette, issint q’il soit resonablement servy saunz delay, qe pleint mes n’aveigne au Roi par cel encheson.’
[2] These included a ‘ probatio ’ offered before the commissioners at Dover, in accordance with the king’s order, by four seafaring merchants, whose evidence did not, however, relate to the mercantile customs but to the facts concerning the purchase, the loading, and carrying off of the wheat, as well as to the fact that one of those merchants, acting in Fraunceys’ name, had attempted to induce the Flemings to restore the wheat. It was mentioned that the refusal of the Flemings was a result of the fact that the king’s writing found on board proved the destination of the wheat for the king’s purveyance. Was this an attempt to show that the king should bear the risk ? In any case, Fraunceys himself does not seem to have insisted on this point.
[3] ‘ Pro eo quod absque Waranto sufficienti huiusmodi satisfaccionem facere non valemus, remittimus vobis . . . peticionem et Inquisicionem, L. T. R. roll 103 Communia, Recorda, m. 18† ; A. P. 10540–4†.
[4] R. P. ii. 32, no. 9.

profitable to him and detrimental to the petitioner. The proceedings in the exchequer were conducted on a strictly legal basis. The exchequer would only make an award against the king if the petitioner had a legal claim. This is proved by the wording of their decision. If Fraunceys had not accepted the risk, if his claim would have been tenable against a private individual, it would have been allowed against the king too. As it was, the claim was rejected on a strictly legal ground, one which might have served successfully in the case of any other defendant.[1]

In the celebrated case of Robert de Clifton an inquisition, taken by commissioners appointed upon his complaint ('querela'), not upon any petition, but on application to the chancery ('par commissioun de la Chancellerie'), established that the keepers of the royal castle of Nottingham, beginning with Robert of Tiptoft, had cut Robert's meadows by trenches and dikes, and had, by constructing weirs and continuing some other works, caused him damage to the amount of £15, in addition to which they were by continuing their works inflicting damage to the annual amount of £10, whereas by the same works the king's estate, through the increased value of certain mills, had been bringing profits which were higher by £20 a year. Robert brought a petition in parliament (18 Ed. II), stating his case, enclosing a transcript of the commission and inquisition, and asking that the king, in compensation, grant him the bailiwick of the honour of Peverell. The endorsement points out that, while the affair touches the king very closely ('si hautement'), yet the inquisition is only *de office* (which probably means that the commission had been issued as a matter of course on application to the chancery), and directs the appointment of certain lords of the council ('asquns Grantz du Conseil le Roi') 'de surver, enquere, et certifier le Roi'.[2] From a later reference we know that this second commission was appointed on December 12, 18 Edward II; who were the commissioners,

---

[1] The later stage of the case has no legal meaning so far as our problem is concerned; the king's action may be considered to have aimed at extending grace to Fraunceys.   [2] R. P. i. 416–17, no. 3.

or when the inquisition was taken, we do not know. The
result must, however, have been identical with that of the
first inquisition, because in 1 Edward III (March 10, 1327),
a writ to the exchequer, setting out Robert's claim as presented in his petition and established by this latter inquisition, ordered the sum of £35 to be allowed in the debts due
to the king from Robert and his ancestors. We learn from the
writ that Robert had brought another petition in 1 Edward II.[1]
Since the writ was sent two years after the first inquisition
and petition, it will be seen that the whole sum petitioned for,
including the damage during the two intervening years, was
granted.   The claim was treated as a matter of right and not
of grace, and the letters patent appointing the commissioners
state as their purpose ' ut in premissis quod iustum est fieri
faciamus '.   We may conclude that at any rate where an
action taken on the king's behalf had resulted in the king's
profit to the detriment of the subject, the king was bound to
indemnify the subject, though we do not know whether the
amount of compensation could legally be made to exceed
the amount of profit accruing to the king.   The fact that
Robert asked for a bailiwick does not weaken the certainty
of the fact that the claim was obviously a legal one, because
the financial difficulties of the king would naturally make
him willing to make grants rather than to pay cash, and the
subject may have expected higher profits from such a grant
than from a carefully measured sum of money.[2]

Robert died a few months after the writ had been sent to
the exchequer, and his heir was his son Gervase, then a boy
of fourteen.[3]   Twenty years later, upon Gervase's *gravis
querela*, by letters patent worded, *mutatis mutandis*, entirely

---

[1] Cl. 145 (1 Ed. III), m. 1 r 'Cum Robertus de Clifton . . . patri
nostro suggesserit . . . et dictus pater noster volens cerciorari . . . assigna-
uerit quosdam fideles suos per breue suum sub data duodecimi diei
Decembris anno regni sui decimo octauo . . . ac per inquisicionem inde . . .
captam et in Cancellaria ipsius patris nostri retornatam, compertum sit,
quod villa . . . Et predictus Robertus iam nobis per peticionem suam
coram nobis et consilio nostro in parliamento nostro exhibitam supplicauerit : vt sibi remedium in premissis fieri faceamus (*sic*).   Nos quod
iustum fuerit fieri volentes in hac parte, vobis mandamus, quod eidem
Roberto . . . allocetis. . . .'   Cf. C. C. R., 1 Ed. III, 83–4.
[2] Above, pp. 32, 66; below, p. 144.   [3] C. I. vii, no. 30.

like those for Robert, commissioners were appointed to inquire into the damage which Gervase claimed to have suffered during the twenty years from the same cause. The inquisition, returned by the commissioners, is again, *mutatis mutandis*, worded just like that originally found for Robert, but Gervase's damages were assessed at £5 a year, and the profits accruing to the king at 20 marks a year. Gervase brought in parliament a petition which, with the obviously necessary changes, was undoubtedly copied from that of Robert.[1] In conclusion, however, apparently relying on the precedent established in his father's case, he asked to have £52 7s. 1¾d. set off against debts due from him since the time when he had been sheriff of Nottinghamshire and Derbyshire ; as to the remaining £47 12s. 10¼d., he asked for ' payment or convenient assignment '. The endorsement directed the petition to be sent, with the inquisition, to the king's bench, where the king's serjeants and the constable of the castle should be called ; then ' soit fait dreit a la partie '. A writ which purports to have the petition and inquisition as enclosures, was sent to the justices (' faciatis quod de iure fuerit faciendum ') and a copy of the writ, of the petition, of its endorsement, of the letters patent appointing the commissioners, and of the inquisition, is entered on the record roll. The constable was summoned but did not appear, the usual order for distraint was given—and here the record ends.[2] The Year Book [3] tells that Gervase had sued to the king by petition, and as a result had obtained the order for the appointment of a commission, and that then he presented another petition as a result of which the case was sent to the king's bench. The keepers (*sic*) came. ' Th.', apparently Thorpe C. J., said that whereas the endorsement ordered the verdict itself to be sent, actually only the ' tenor ' of the verdict had been sent, wherefore the court ordered the ' pl '(aintiff) to cause the verdict itself to come, if he so desired, and sent the keepers away without a day.

---

[1] We do not know Robert's second petition ; but we can suppose that it was a copy of the first and that that of Gervase was modelled on one of them.
[2] C. R. 351, m. 45.†   [3] Y. B., 22 Ed. III, 5.

The writ says, ' inquisicionem . . . vobis mittimus sub pede sigilli nostri '. The record speaks of the tenor of the inquisition, but does not mention that the keeper came or that any decision was reached. The point mentioned in the Year Book appears very technical, but there is no reason why it should not have been entered on the roll. The Year Book report does not seem quite exact ; for instance, it mentions two petitions, whereas it seems that there was only one, after the inquisition. It should be noted that the letters patent were not issued upon petition and make no mention of any petition,[1] and the petition which we know does not mention any preceding petition. On the other hand, the report says that this (as it says) second petition asked for restitution ' de ses damages et que ce soit redresse '. This is an interesting contemporary formulation of the legal character of the claim. In any case it seems clear that the petition was one of right, that it was based on undoubted precedent or, what is more, that it was based on absolutely the same facts as those which had led to a decision in favour of the petitioner's father ; the claim was taken to be a legal one, and both the commission and the order to the justices were made in clear connexion with the former case. The fact that the record is unfinished is no evidence that the claim was unfounded. We have innumerable records which do not show the end of cases, for instance, because the parties came to terms. Finally, if the report in the Year Book be correct, we must assume that a further part of the proceedings was not recorded ; why not assume that later on the irregularity was remedied and a record entered elsewhere ? It could easily be remedied since we know that the inquisition had been returned into the chancery. But, even assuming that the petition of Gervase was not decided upon, this would in no way impair the strength of the precedent established in the case of Robert.[2]

---

[1] Cf. the first inquisition in Robert's case, also upon his ' querela ', and described as *de office* upon a ' commissioun de Chancellerie ', above, p. 123.

[2] Gervase asked only for what was due to him for the time of his own tenancy. Of the few months intervening between the writ to the exchequer in favour of Robert, and Robert's death, there is no mention. Was this a kind of *actio personalis* ? Edward III had ordered an allowance to be made for the damage done in the time of his father, above, p. 124.

The king can do no wrong. We must now face the following questions : Could something that had been done against the law, whether by the king himself or on his behalf, be attributed to the king? If so, was such a forbidden act *ipso facto* void, or had special steps to be taken to redress the wrong done?

We shall find that the first question must be answered in the affirmative. Things were granted by the king which the king had no right to grant ; lands were seised into the king's hand which the king had no right to seise ; charges were imposed which the king had no right to levy. In all such cases, the presumption was not that the act was not the king's act, but that it was the king's act. In some cases, as we shall see, the presumption was defeated in favour of a personal responsibility of the royal officials. Where it was not, we have full statements to the effect that something was being done wrongfully, that some one was being wronged, and, alongside of these, the statements that the king could not behave in that way, that he was not allowed to do wrong. This, as in Bracton, was the meaning of the rule which may be expressed in the well-known words, ' The king can do no wrong.' As yet, it was far from referring to ' torts ', and from excluding their imputation to the king. If the king, or anybody else, said that the king ' could not ' do something, that meant, not that the act would not, if done, be attributed to the king, but that the king was no more allowed to do it, than a subject was allowed to commit a trespass or a felony.[1]

The bill containing the doctrine which was ascribed both to the prosecutors of Gaveston and to Despenser [2] discussed

---

[1] Stubbs, ii. 41, and Anson, ii. 13, 16, trace the principle, the king can do no wrong, in its modern meaning of non-responsibility, to the minority of Henry III. See below, p. 131.

[2] As we know, this doctrine was considered a justification for compelling the king to do away with Gaveston (Chron. i. 153–4, and Intr. li ff.), but it is also recorded as part of the indictment of the Despensers (S. R. 182). We need not investigate here which version was true, i. e. whether the doctrine had been set up at the time of Gaveston's fall, or during the period of the Despensers' influence, or perhaps was used both on the former occasion and during the latter period. In any case it was a doctrine advanced by powerful men, and not merely by occasional speculators.

the remedial course to be adopted ' if the king happened not to be guided by reason ' (' si le Roi par cas ne se meigne par resoun, en droit de la Corone '). The case was put mildly, but the subsequent threat of pure violence shows that the case under discussion was that of the king ' doing wrong '. We need not investigate whether the opinion proclaimed in the bill did or did not represent an official statement of the law. It is obvious that in contemporary thought the wrongs of the subjects were traced directly to their source, and if that source happened to be an act of the king people would say so. Edward II was told so, and however broken he might have been by his defeats,[1] the fate with which he met was, after all, the application of a doctrine.

A proclamation made in the parliament of 1341 announced that every one who felt aggrieved *by the king* or by his ministers or by others should put forward a petition and he would have his remedy.[2] In 1359 a charter which had been granted by Henry III to the men of St. Albans was annulled because it was considered that the grant had been unlawful. The king's attorney stated expressly that the charter had been made against the law, and this the king ' could not do ' (' in perturbacionem iuris et legis (communis, quod) Rex facere non potuit, facta erat '). The ' could not ' obviously means ' was not allowed to '.[3]

In 1340 it was said during argument that in a certain case the king ' could not ' enter.[4] The terms *peot* and *deit* were used interchangeably ; ' could not ' meant ' must not ' ; we are told by Thorpe J. in 1343 that if the king be seised, whether he be right or wrong, the thing must be sued out of his hand,[5] and Wilby J. says in 1350 that if the king be seised, rightly or wrongly, one will sue against him by petition.[6]

---

[1] Tout, iii. 301–2.

[2] R. P. ii. 127, no. 5 *in fine* : ' Et auxint fu dit overtement a touz qe chescun qi se sent grevez par le Roi, ou par ses Ministres, ou autres, q'ils mettroient Petition avant, et ils averont bon et covenable remede.'

[3] Above, p. 113

[4] Y. B., 14–15 Ed. III, 345, R. S. ; Hill : ' Sil ne teigne du Roi, tout soit il fermer au Roi, le Roi ne deit pas entrer sur salienacion ; qar si le Roi doune t rre a moi, qest tenu de vous, rendant a lui certein rente, tout aliene jeo, le Roi ne peot entrer.'

[5] Above, p. 112, n. 2.   [6] Above, p. 112, n. 2.

It was argued in the chancery, late in the reign of Edward III, that the king could not ('ne purra my') without the assent of parliament grant by charter to the commonalty of London the right of changing the law of inheritance or of making tenements devisable by charter.[1] From 50 Edward III comes the pronouncement that the king 'could' grant tolls to be levied in fair and market, but not through-tolls, i.e. tolls for passing over highways.[2]

The acts of the royal officials were, as a rule, attributed to the king. On the other hand, if the king had ordered an official to do wrong, the official could plead the royal order.

Thus, in a case of false imprisonment the defendant said that he had acted under a royal commission. Although the commission was against the law, yet the plea was allowed.[3]

We come now to our second question. If the king did, or if on his behalf was done, an act which the law forbade, was such an act *ipso facto* void, or had special steps to be taken in order to avoid it? In some cases the mere operation of the law would justify the disregard of a royal order. Such cases, however, were not numerous. We can say that each one of them was the result of an exception, which had to be proved. As a general rule, if the king wronged one, one had to petition the king for a remedy, or to adopt some other course prescribed by the law. The king's order, even if unlawful, was the king's order. Acts of the royal officials, if done by them in their official capacity, were the king's acts; the king was supposed to derive profits from them, if any profits there were. Conversely, therefore, such officials were protected by the king's position. Redress could be had, against them too, only in the special way prescribed by the law, unless the law or the king's special orders had deprived them of the privileged position, which they enjoyed as the king's servants.

[1] 49 l. ass. pl. 8; cf. Y. B., 49 Ed. III, 4. Cf. above, p. 117, n. 4.

[2] Brook, Prerog. 112: 'Vide tit. tolle in Fitzh. 2 que le roy poet graunter tolle deste pris in faire et market sed nemy de prender pur passage in le haute chemin, s. through-toll, car ceo ne poet este pris nisi per praescriptionem . . . .' Cf. R. P. ii. 41, no. 52.

[3] Brook, Faux Imprisonment, 9, reference to '24 Ed. III, 9': '. . . et admittitur bon iustificacion coment qe le commission soyt contra legem.'

Thus in an assize of novel disseisin a royal commission
was pleaded, and it was shown that it had been directed to
the escheator and to others. The court elicited the fact that
the commission had not been strictly obeyed, inasmuch as
seisin had been taken but the inquisition directed by the
commission had not been taken. Thereupon the justice
suggested that the taking of seisin before an inquisition
had been without warrant. Counsel submitted that the man
who had thus acted ' was the king's minister by force of the
commission, and whether he had seised rightly or wrongly
the assize would not be taken ' ; for, he argued, if an escheator
had testified the fact of seisin into the king's hand, whether
with cause or without cause, the court would supersede the
proceedings. The court, however, held that whereas the
escheator was the king's servant, and could (?) seise by one
reason or another, the special commissioner had no cause
to seise if an inquisition had not been taken as directed.[1]
This seems to mean that the court would have considered
the commission a sufficient warrant to grant aid, if the terms
of the commission had been complied with. Moreover,
counsel and court seemed agreed that if the escheator had
seised, although the king had no right, the assize could not
be taken.

There might be cases in which royal writs could be
disobeyed. That was the dawn of new ideas. From our
present period we have some notable examples of the way
in which these new ideas were put into practice. In the
Ordinances of 1311 it was laid down that nothing should
be done in the king's courts by virtue of the king's letters
under his privy seal, contrary to right or the law of the

---

[1] 30 l. ass. pl. 5 : ' . . . Shard(eshull) : Aves pris la Enquest come la commission voyle ? Que dit que non, causa ut supra. Shard. : Vous n'aves
pas garrantie a prendre, etc. forsque apres l'Enquest pris ; et si vous avez
pris devant ceo, est sans garrantie.—Fich. Il est ministre le Roy par force
de la commission, et tout seisist il a droit ou a tort, vous ne prendres pas
l'Assise car si l'Eschetor ust tesmoigne la seisin, le quel que ceo fuit
par cause ou sans cause, vous successeres.—Sh. L'Eschetor est ministre le
Roy, que fuit (puit ?) seisir auxy bien sur une cause, come sur autre, et
est charge des issues de tout temps puis le seisir, mes J. B. n'ad cause de
seisir, s'il n'est enquis come la commission voet. Pourquoi repondes.'

land ('encountre droiture ou lei de terre').[1] In 1346 Edward III instructed his justices that they should not, on account of any letters or other orders which might come to them from the king, omit to do right ; if such letters or orders came, they should not be considered any more than if they had not come at all.[2] A proviso to the same effect was inserted in the oath of the justices.[3]

In 1340 it was enacted that charters of pardon made in a certain objectionable way (i.e. if certain statutes were thereby infringed) should be held null.[4]

An enactment is said to have been made at the coronation of Edward III, to the effect that during his minority every officer of his entourage would alone be responsible for acts done in his office : such an assertion was made in a petition of 1330,[5] but the statement itself shows the exceptional character of the enactment. The rule was to a different effect.

The king's privileges. While the king's position was determined by law, it remained privileged in many respects. As before, the privileges had either existed of old, or they were being worked out anew. In the latter case, if there was a special enactment, as for instance in the case of the Statute of Treasons,[6] it was in the nature more of an explanation or definition, than of an entirely new creation. More numerous were new prerogative rights, worked out either by courts of justice or else by administrative officers who were in charge of the king's affairs. The rules thus laid down would for the most part be based on other well-known and generally

---

[1] R. P. i. 285, no. 32.   [2] S. R. 303–4, no. 1.

[3] Ibid. 306 : ' Et qe vous ne delairez a nulli commun droit, pur lettres du Roi ne de nul autre . . . et en cas qe ascunes lettres vous veignent contraires a la ley, qe vous ne ferrez rien par tieles lettres, einz certifierez de ceo le Roi, et irrez avant de faire la ley nient contresteantes meismes les lettres.' Cf. R. P. ii. 390, no. 68.

[4] S. R. 286, c. 15 ; cf. Y. B., 19 Ed. III, 189–91, R. S.

[5] R. P. ii. 46 a : ' . . . Et sembla au dit Geffrei, qe tout ensi nostre Seigneur le Roi commande son Chaunceller faire chose prejudiciale a la Corone, ou contre le commune Ley ; nepurquant son Chaunceller se deut aviser dait executer tiel comandement, sicome ordeine feut a Westmonstre, au Parlement et au Coronement du Roi illoeqes, Qe chescun Officer d'entour le Roi respondroit de son office a son peril durant le nonage de nostre Seignur avantdit.' Above, p. 127, n. 1.

[6] S. R. 319–20 ; cf. M. J. 15.

recognized principles, but would form an important addition to the garland of the king's peculiar rights.

We hear again and again that such special privileges are exceptions, and that apart from them the ordinary rules apply to the king.[1]

Of the king's special privileges we may mention some that seem to throw light on our subject.[2]

The king's seisin was specially protected.

Thus, in 1352 it was asserted by counsel and granted by the court that if the king seised a wardship to which (not he, but) somebody else was entitled, the heir after attaining his full age could not enter without first suing to the king.[3]

In a note in the Year Book of 1370 [4] we read :

‘ In the chancery they hold it for law that if the heir sue livery of lands out of the king's hands, which lands had been seised by reason of his minority, and if he (the heir) sue inquisitions in some one county, but not in all counties in which the lands lie, then if by reason of the inquisitions thus sued he has livery of lands in the county in which he has sued, and if without inquisition or livery he enter the lands in another county, then the king will be able to reseise all his lands, by reason of his abatement upon the king's possession in part (“ en parcel ”) ; he will be charged in respect of the issues of the meantime.’

This rule was obviously an application of the more general rule that no one could enter upon the king, and that, in particular, lands seised into the king's hands by reason of the heir's minority had to be sued out of the king's hands. But the extensive interpretation applied to the principle

---

[1] e.g. Y. B., 43 Ed. III, 21–2 ; R. P. ii. 265, no. 18.

[2] The *Praerogativa Regis* (above, p. 56, n. 2) was declared not to be a statute in 18 Ed. III (Fitzh. Sci., fa. 10). In 29 Ed. III (R. P. ii. 265) and 43 Ed. III (Y. B., 43 Ed. III, 21–2) it was referred to as (a statute) made in the reign of Edward I.

[3] 26 l.·ass. pl. 57 : ‘ Par Thorp, si le Roy saisi un deins aage ou attient a autre, etc, l'heir ne peut entrer a son plein aage sans suire au Roy.’ Brook, Peticion, 40, says that this Thorpe was justice ; but it probably was R. Thorpe, and not W. Thorpe, the justice. Brook adds : ‘ quere si cel suit sera par peticion ou par monstrance de droit ’ (below, p. 176, n. 2).

[4] Y. B., 44 Ed. III, 12. It is added that Lord Percy (‘ le Seigniour de Percy ’) had been in such a case, but put himself on the mercy of the king and made a fine. Brook (Resseiser, 4) mentions another such case of the same year.

in this connexion shows the way in which the king's privileges were enlarged.

A writ to the escheator, or to the sheriff, or to whosoever was holding tenements in the name of the king, was necessary, as it had been under Henry III and Edward I alike, if the king was restoring what he had no right to hold. We have innumerable writs to escheators or other ministers, ordering them, during the earlier part of our period, ' not to inter-meddle further, restoring the issues ',[1] or, during Edward III's reign, also ' to remove the king's hands and not to inter-meddle further, restoring (or delivering) the issues '; until the later years of Edward III's reign the former, shorter, and the latter, longer, formulae are used concurrently,[2] but toward the end of the reign the longer formula seems to have been more generally adopted.[3] Sometimes, before the intro-duction of the traverse,[4] the order was, to remove the king's hand and not to intermeddle further, delivering the issues, if the facts be found by the exchequer or by the minister to be as alleged by the claimants.[5] Sometimes the escheator was ordered to remove the king's hand without delay,[6] and we may infer that in cases of delay the tenements could not be entered by the claimant. There is no reason why such an order should be given if without it the party could have entered.

The formula used in the earlier writs had been based on the theory that the king's seisin terminated when he (or the proper officials) received notice of the illegality of the seisin ;[7] yet there was a long way from the acceptance of that theory to allowing the successful claimant to enter. At the same time, a difference in legal consequences must have existed

[1] e.g. C. C. R., Ed. II, 289.

[2] e.g. to remove the king's hand and not to intermeddle further, restoring the issues, ibid., 15 Ed. III, 320 ; 17 Ed. III, 203 ; 22 Ed. III, 429 ; 34 Ed. III, 38 ; 37 Ed. III, 495 ; not to intermeddle, restoring (or delivering) the issues, ibid., 15 Ed. III, 152–3 ; 17 Ed. III, 13, 193 ; 22 Ed. III, 434 ; 34 Ed. III, 38 ; 35 Ed. III, 226 ; 44 Ed. III, 126.

[3] e.g. 46 Ed. III, 379 ; 47 Ed. III, 500 ; 50 Ed. III, 293–4.

[4] Below, pp. 175–6.

[5] e.g. the treasurer and barons, C. C. R., 31 Ed. III, 385 ; the escheator, ibid., 35 Ed. III, 303 (upon petition).

[6] e.g. ibid., 8 Ed. III, 290.   [7] Above, pp. 61–2.

between the writs now discussed, and those of ‘ delivery ’ of dower,[1] or those ordering the escheator ‘ to cause ’ the heir who was of age and whose fealty and homage had been taken, ‘ to have seisin ’.[2] The difference was probably, first of all, in the amount of the fees. Besides, Coke says that ‘ upon every livery the kinge hath the value of the land for halfe a yeare, but upon an ouster le mayne the kings hands be amoved without any profit ’, &c.[3]

It should be noted that the judgement, given either in the chancery or in the king’s bench,[4] would run ‘ quod manus domini regis amoveantur et (the tenements in question) restituantur una cum exitibus medio tempore perceptis ’. Hence, people used to say that the king had removed his hand in chancery, or in the king’s bench, or that the king’s hands had been removed by judgement.[5] The addition, during our period, in the writ, of the order ‘ to remove the king’s hand ’[6] seems to prove that that language was inexact ; the addition itself may well have been devised to obviate the inferences apparently drawn from the short formula of Edward I and Edward II, as will be seen from the following case of Edward III’s tenth year :[7]

In an assize of novel disseisin, the defendants asserted that the king had seised the tenements after the tenant’s death, that the plaintiff had then entered, together with other men, and that the sheriff, obeying a writ which he received, had taken the *posse comitatus* and had ejected the plaintiff. The king having afterwards ‘ ousted his hands ’ in chancery, a writ of *amoveas manus* was brought to the escheator and the defendants then entered. The plaintiff contended that he had entered after judgement had been given in chancery. The following dialogue took place in court :

Hillary (for the plaintiff) : As to what you say that we abated on the possession of the king, we say that the king

---

[1] Above, p. 62, and during the present period, Dec. 2, 1359, C. C. R., 33 Ed. III, 604.

[2] Above, pp. 15–17, and during the present period, e.g. Sept. 19, 1356, ibid., 30 Ed. III, 279.

[3] 2 Inst. 693.　　　　[4] Below, p. 173.　　　　[5] Above, p. 60.

[6] Above, p. 133.　　　　[7] Y. B., 10 Ed. III, 2.

sent his writ to the escheator to oust his hand, and after-wards Walter and E(ustace) entered . . . and, Sir, I say that all the time is the king's hand ousted in the chancery, and after the king has ousted his hand in the chancery, I can advocate the entry into the tenements even without suing a writ to him who has the custody by the king's commission : for the king's hand is ousted all the time by the judgement in the chancery.

Shardeshull J. : That is not so : for the keeper by commission will all the time be charged for the issues, until a writ comes to him to oust the hand.

Hillary : Certainly, he will be charged for all the time after the king had removed his hand in the chancery.

The judge then suggested that if the plaintiff thought he had a right to enter, he might admit that his ancestors had entered after judgement in chancery but before the keeper had received the order ; then, the plaintiff might await the judgement of the court. Or else, he might say that his ancestors had entered after the keeper had received the writ, and then the assize would decide. Counsel for the plaintiff would not withdraw his statement of the law, but demanded certain admissions from the defendants, and finally the court ordered him to say something else if he wanted to have the assize. Issue was then joined, not on the question whether the defendants had disseised the plaintiff, but on the question who had a right to the reversion.[1] Counsel's statement that after judgement in chancery one could enter upon the king without suing a writ to him who kept the land in the king's name was promptly denied by the judge, and yet it may have been made in good faith,[2] as a result of a misconception.

[1] Cf. H. E. L. ii. 49.

[2] Though believing himself right, counsel may have been afraid to jeopardize his client's case by demanding judgement on a point which the court would be anxious not to decide in a way prejudicial to the king's interests. A decision in accordance with counsel's contention might have necessitated many administrative changes (in the practice of issuing writs ordering not to intermeddle, in the routine of accounting at the exchequer, &c.). At all events, this case does not seem to offer sufficient justification for the later theory (above, p. 60) that ' the party for whom judgement was given might enter forthwith into the lands, and should be said no disseisor ' (Staunford, 78 a). Cf. Finch, 459 : ' Upon judgement against the king in a petition, he is presently out of possession, and therefore every judgement is in itself a moveas (sic) manu (sic) or an ouster re (sic)

to obviate which the order ' to remove the king's hands ' was adopted in later writs.[1]

Later on in the reign of Edward III the courts continued to take it for granted, that a writ of *amoveas manus* was necessary. At first, the writ seems even to have received a strict interpretation.

Thus, in, 1350, the king brought a *quare impedit*; the defendant contended that he had sued to the king and had proved his right, ' par qe le Roy ousta sa main, et commanda a deliverer a nous les issues ', etc.[2] Counsel for the defendant observed that his claim was based, not on the act of the escheator, but on the judgement given in the chancery. (Skip : ' Per la livere fait par l'Eschetor jeo ne suy pas a claimer, mes per Jugement rendu in la Chancery que le Roy ousta sa main, etc.') The judges, however, insisted that the king's writ apparently related only to the rents and tenements, but not to the right of presentation.

Shardeshull J. said : ' Quand le Roy comanda de l'Eschetor d'ouster sa main del' presentement etc. . . . . nous veioms nulle part que le Roy ousta sa maine del' presentement mes de rente, et ceux issues : pur que il semble qe ceo luy demurre.'

Finally, judgement was given for the king :

Wilby : ' Pur ceo que le Roy ne ceo pas ad ouste del presentement sans ceo q'il ust ouste sa main especialment, et il presenta *ut supra*, durant sa seisin, et n'est pur cel presentement repelle : par qe sues brief al' Evesqe pur le Roy.' [3]

In other words, the court utterly disagreed with the opinion that judgement in chancery was by itself enough to make the defendant's presentation valid.

But somewhat later,[4] following the advice of the justices of the bench, it was laid down that the writ to the escheator was issued as a matter of right, and not of grace, and that

maine.' This latter statement is explained by Blackstone, 3 Comm. 257 (ed. 1770), as follows : ' And by such judgement the crown is instantly out of possession ; so that there needs not the indecent interposition of his own officers to transfer the seisin from the king to the party aggrieved.'

[1] Above, pp. 133-4.   [2] Y. B., 24 Ed. III, 28-9, 59-60.
[3] Ibid. 28-9 ; cf. Stoner J. : ' Pur ceo qe nous ne veioms pas qe le Roy se ousta del presentement.'   [4] 27 l. ass. pl. 48 ; above, p. 119, n. 3.

therefore the writ should be interpreted extensively, and not restrictively.

The fees, possessions, and advowson of a prior had been taken into the king's hands because the prior was supposed to be an alien enemy. He proved to be the king's subject, born in Gascony, ' pur que il avoit restitucion '. The king sent to the escheator a writ setting out the affair and telling him that of his special grace he had granted restitution.[1] The writ ordered the escheator to remove the king's hand, but did not mention the advowson.[2] Afterwards the king brought a *quare impedit* against the prior. The justices of the bench were consulted and declared that the king's seisin had been general, and the restitution had been general; therefore, although the writ mentioned that the king had done it of his grace, yet it was proved that the king had no right to be seised ('uncore al' metere prove que le Roy n'avoit droit a seiser '). Hence, although the writ did not mention the advowson, yet the king had been divested of everything ('tout devest de le Roy'). Thus, the whole question turned on the interpretation of the writ : for it is in the writ that the mention of grace was contained.[3]

Where the king had no right to be seised he would restore the issues. Thus, Wilby J. is reported as saying :

' Si le roy seisi ce qu'il nad mye droit a seisier, il la fra liuerer ou les issues.' [4]

The rule applied, not only if the king had seised because of a mistake (e. g. on the basis of an erroneous inquisition), but also if the king, while not entitled to the tenements, was entitled to seisin until the party claiming the tenements should prove the title. Thus, in a case of 1344, counsel alleged that since the king had delivered the issues, that

---

[1] ' Pur que le Roy per son brief reherse etc. (et ?) Mande a l'Eschetor que de sa grace especial il avoit grant que il avera restitution.'

[2] ' Et lui command d'ouster la maine sans parler d'avowson.'

[3] This judgement certainly does not warrant the conclusion that, even in the absence of a writ to the escheator, the king would have had to suffer entry by the prior. Brooke, Traverse d'office, 49, observes in the conclusion of his summary of this case : ' . . . et sic videtur que lexecucion de chescun trauerse est ouster le maine, car home ne poit entrer sur le Roy.'   [4] Fitzh., Prerogative. 19, 27 Ed. III.

proved that the king's seisin had been null.[1] Counsel for
the king pointed out (arguendo) that where the tenant and his
wife hold jointly of the king, in the case which was mentioned
above, the wife would have a writ of *amoveas manus*, including
an order to deliver the issues, although the king was entitled
to seise.

But the rule as to the restitution of issues was subject to
an important limitation : the king would not restore issues
of which he had been ' servi ',[2] in other words, those, for which
the official, whether sheriff, escheator, or bailiff, had answered
at the exchequer. We have an endorsement to that effect
from, it seems, 1326,[3] and writs to the same effect from 1328.[4]
The same rule is reported as obtaining later on. Thus, in
a case just mentioned,[5] Shardeshull J. said that the escheator
could only deliver those issues which remained with him,
i. e. those which he had raised and for which he had not yet
answered at the exchequer. The interpretation of this rule
seems to have been liberal. In 1350 we are told by the
court that livery of issues extends to rents and things which
the escheator can levy, even after he had accounted for them,
as long as he had not actually paid them in. But, it was
added, money in the king's coffers would not be restored :

' Et non allocatur, per Curiam. Que dit, que le livere des
issues sera solement entendue de rents et choses leviable par
l'Escheator, queux seront liveres ; mesqe l'Eschetor eit accompt de eux, et non pas paies. Mes dit fuit que les deniers
in cofres le Roy ne seront pas liveres.' [6]

---

[1] Y. B., 18 Ed. III, 171–87, R. S. : ' Grene . . . le Roi nous ad livere
les issues, quele prove la seisine le Roy nulle, qar en tiel cas il ne dust pas
seisir.'   [2] R. P. ii. 5.

[3] A. P. 8084 † : writ of 1 Ed. I as to the restitution to the followers of
Lancaster ; the judgements against them having been annulled, restitution
was to relate to the tenements ' una cum exitibus et arreragiis . . . de quibus
dicto patri nostro non est responsum ' ; R. P. ii. 421 b. In consequence
we find the following endorsement, A. P. 14665 † : ' Seit ceste peticion
maunde en Chauncellerie e le Chaunceller se auise de la cause de la prise
des terres e tenementz contenuz en ceste peticion en la meyn le Roi, e sils
furent prises en la meyn le Roi par cause de la quele ele etc e ne mye par
autre seient les terres et tenementz restituz oue les issues e arrerages etc
dount le Roi nest my seruy.'

[4] R. P. ii. 420, nos. 1–3 ; 425, no. 10.

[5] Y. B., 18 Ed. III, 171–87, R. S.   [6] Y. B., 24 Ed. III, 28–9.

When the case was continued, counsel said that he knew well that after the money was in the king's coffers he could not have it back, but that that was at least against the law : [1]

Skip : '. . . si rent fuit leve par l'Eschetor, mesqe il avoit de ceo accompt, par le Ley jeo reavera cel rent apres tiel Jugement etc. Mes jeo say bien que apres les deniers sont in les coffres le Roy jeo ne les puis pas reaver, et a le meins cest encontre la Ley.' [2]

The rule did not seem quite intelligible in the days of Edward III, since counsel declared it to be ' contrary to the law '. But if we assume that the king had to be considered as either a *bonae fidei* possessor or not having seisin at all (because he did not have the *animus possidendi* if he did not have the *bona fides*), then another rule of Roman law will serve as an explanation : *bonae fidei possessor fructus consumptos* (or *perceptos*) *suos facit, extantes restituere debet.*[3] As long as the issues were in the hands of the escheators, or sheriffs, or bailiffs, they were *extantes*. Once the money had been paid into the exchequer, the *fructus* had become *percepti.*[4]

To mention another privilege, the king, in seising the chattels of felons and traitors, considered himself free from any obligation to repay their debts. An endorsement to that effect is

---

[1] Y. B., 24 Ed. III, 59–60.
[2] Coke mentions this rule as still in force at his time, 2 Inst. 572.
[3] Inst. 2. 1. 35 ; Inst. 4. 17. 2 ; D. 10. 1. 4. 2 ; D. 41. 1. 40 ; cf. C. 3. 32. 22 ' Certum est mala fide possessores omnes fructus solere cum ipsa re praestare, bona fide vero extantes, post litis autem contestationem universos .' This was, of course, a rule of Justinian, and not of classical Roman law ; cf. Girard, Manuel élém. de droit rom., 4th, ed. 321–3.
[4] The rule that the king was always to be considered a *bonae fidei* possessor and, consequently, never a disseisor, led in 1485 to the unanimous conclusion of all the justices and serjeants assembled in the chancery, that ' the king could not be said to have committed a " tort " ' ; ' for if one wants to disseise another for the benefit of the king, where the king has no right, the king cannot be said to be disseisor ' (Y. B., 1 Ed. V. 8 : ' Nota que fuit dit a mesme le iour en le Chauncerie, et agree par toutz les iuges et serieantz la esteantz, que le roy ne poet este dit vn que fist tort : quar si vn voet disseisir un autre al opez le roy, ou le roy nad dreit, le roy ne poet este dit disseisor. Quod nota.'). A quarter of a century earlier, it had been argued, for the king, that ' le roy puit faire tort a un home sibien come un autre person puit faire, et envers luy jauray remedy par voie de peticion, come jauray envers un autre persone par voie d'accion ' ; but the other side argued that ' le roy ne puit estre disseisor ' (Ibid 35 Hen VI, 61).

found on a petition asking for the payment of debts incurred by Roger de Mortimer through prizes made for him.[1] The king had a number of privileges as to procedure. In a case of 1338-9 a *scire facias* had issued at the suggestion of a party. It was pleaded that a statute had forbidden the king to record, except by due process of law, and that the writ in question was issued, not upon the record of a process, but upon suggestion. To this Willoughby C. J. answered emphatically that ' if the king recorded something of his own view such a record would never be annulled ' (' qant le Roi recorde ascune chose de sa vewe demene cel record ne sera jammes anienti ').[2]

In the same year, Stonore stated that if something was alleged on the king's behalf, it must, for the king's advantage, be held as not denied, until it was traversed.[3] The judges, in accordance with their oath,[4] had to watch *ex officio* that the king's interests be not infringed. In 1352 it was held that if a party alleged that the land in dispute was in the king's hand the justices would inquire into the truth of the statement.[5]

A writ of right was brought for an advowson which Edward II had given to a prior and his successor in frankalmoin. The defendant prayed aid of the king ; the plaintiff pointed out that the king's charter did not contain a clause of warranty. Aid was granted nevertheless, apparently because the king had masses and prayers which he would lose if the defendant lost his advowson.[6]

In a later case a writ came to the justices directing that if they found the lands in question to be identical with certain lands named in the writ they should not proceed without

[1] R. P. ii. 51, no. 82, 4 Ed. III : 'Le Roy tient les chateaux des treitres et felons si franchement, q'il n'est mye tenuz a acquiter lour dettes.' Cp. Les Olim., i. 602 (1265), which seems to explain this rule : the king seised ' tamquam principalis dominus, non tamquam successor ipsius '.

[2] Y. B., 12-13 Ed. III, 97–101, R. S. It is an idea practically identical with that expressed in the case of Gloucester and Hereford (above, p. 60).

[3] Y. B., 13-14 Ed. III, 115-17, R. S. [4] Above, pp. 64-5.

[5] 26 L. ass. pl. 10. As to other royal privileges, see e.g. Y. B., 20 Ed. III, 505–21, R. S. (king allowed to change his count) ; Y.B., 43 Ed. III, 14 (two titles alleged in the king's count, objection overruled) ; ibid. 20 Ed. III, pt. i, 339–43, R. S. ; and ibid. 521-3 (no final judgement against the king ; cf. ibid. 417–69). [6] Y. B., 6 Ed. III, 25.

consulting the king. The justices decided that they could not go on with the case without a writ *de procedendo*, although the assize said that the lands were different from those mentioned in the writ.[1]

The king's actual power. Certain facts of the reign of Edward II and the first years of his son show beyond doubt the great power wielded by the king. Lancaster was put to death, however illegally, when Edward II ' recorded ' his treasons and other crimes, which, it was contended, were ' notorious and manifest ' to the magnates and his people.[2]

We may also mention the case against Roger de Mortimer in 1330. It is enough to glance at the indictment, to appreciate how tremendous was that royal power which Roger was charged with having ' a lui accroche '.

In some cases the king's power would by itself serve as an excuse. Thus, in a case of false imprisonment the defendant pleaded a royal commission to take all those who notoriously were felons or trespassers, although they had not been indicted. That was admittedly contrary to the law, yet the defendant had only to show that the plaintiff had caused the death of some one ; this, together with the commission, was held a sufficient justification. It seems that the defendant

---

[1] 40 l. ass. pl. 14. In a case against a prior who was a French subject, the defendant brought a writ of *circumspecte agatis* (so that no damage should result to the king), because the possessions of the prior were seised into the king's hands. Although the king's writ did not order the justices to supersede the case, the court would not even take an inquisition, because from the king's writ it appeared that the tenements were in the king's hands, and according to the order they were not to do anything that might turn to the prejudice of the king (Y. B., 21 Ed. III, 24–5). A year later, the defendant in a suit brought the king's writ to a like effect ; the king, however, had no right to seise. Nevertheless the justices superseded the proceedings until the plaintiff brought a *procedendo in loquela*. It contained the usual clause that they should not proceed to judgement *nobis inconsultis*, and the case was adjourned until the plaintiff brought a *procedendo ad iudicium*. The reporter of the case notes the fact that the king had no right to seise. ' But when he has seised, be it rightly or wrongly, (and) commits for a certain term, the justices will supersede ' (22 l. ass. pl. 28) ; cf. Y. B., 10 Ed. III, 26 ; 43 l. ass. 13 (Brook, Aide del roy, 90) ; R. P. ii. 70, no. 2.

[2] Ibid. ii. 3 ; cf. Vinogradoff, Magna Carta, c. 39, 94. The fact that Lancaster had not been arraigned, put to his answer, and convicted, according to the law and custom of the realm, was asserted to be one of the chief errors in the judgement, which was reversed, on account of the political events, in 1 Ed. III (R. P. ii. 4, 5).

was not even one of the commissioners, but had acted under their authority.[1]

The king's orders need not be given by ' matter of record '.[2] In a *scire facias* (in chancery) the summonee obtained aid from the king; the chancellor received the king's oral order to proceed in the case, and, apparently upon his request for a written warrant, the king said that his word (*dictum*) ' plus sufficere debet pro warranto ' than a writ under the privy seal.[3] In another *scire facias* the defendant claimed that aid from the king had been granted and that no writ ordering the justices to proceed was recorded. Wilby, who was of counsel, answered that the record had a mention that there had been a conversation with the king and that the justices had been told to go on. This, he contended meant that they had been so told by the king, and such an order was as strong as if a writ had been sent. After further discussion (it was alleged that there had been a writ but that it was at the treasury) the justices decided to proceed.[4] In 1357, in a case in the chancery, begun by a *scire facias*, the chancellor, by the king's order, had to take the advice of all justices and then certify the king. The justices were unanimously of the opinion that as the defendant was seised by the king's grant as of his freehold, the manors in dispute between plaintiff and defendant could not be answered for by the

[1] Brook, Faux imprisonment, 9, said to be 24 Ed. III, 9: ' Faux imprisonment, le defendant dit que le commission le roy tali die fuit direct a luy, et auters pur prender ceux qe fuerunt notorious eslaunder pur felonies ou transgressions, non obstante qe ils ne fuerunt endicts, et hoc est contra legem, et qe le plaintif aueit naufre J. N. al mort par qe ils eux prist etc. et admittitur bon iustificacion coment qe le commission soyt contra legem quod nota, et un homme a qe les commissioners direct lour precept de prendre le plaintif fist cest iustificacion sur le matter, et nemy les commissioners mesme ' ; above, p. 129, n. 3.

[2] As was asserted, later on, by Coke, 2 Inst. 186. In a case in which, obeying a royal writ, the justices had superseded, Hillary C. J. C. P. afterwards said that the king had now ordered them by his writ and by word of mouth, to go on with the case (Y. B., 15 Ed. III, 139–45, R. S.: ' qant al Roi, il nous ad mande par bref et par sa bouche nous dit qe nous ailloms avant.') Cf. the angry order of Edward I, related, not as in any way irregular, by Bereford C. J. C. P., ibid. 3 Ed. II, S. S. 196; Vinogradoff, Magna Carta, c. 39, 95.

[3] C. R., roll 351, m. 131†, below, pp. 156–7.

[4] Y. B., 29 Ed. III, 34–5.

defendant except upon original writ at common law. The
chancellor reported this opinion to the king, who ordered
the chancellor to proceed in the business (apparently in
order to decree that the chancery was not the proper court).
Thereupon the plaintiff was non-suited. Thus, despite the
unanimous opinion of the judges, the chancellor was compelled, according to the king's order, to report the case to
king and to take his orders.[1]

[1] T. S., f. 2, m. 16–2, proceedings upon a *scire facias* to show cause why
certain tenements should not be reseised into the king's hand and delivered
to the heir, and why the defendant should not account to the king and to
the heir. The defendant stated his reasons, and Johannes de Gaunt ' qui
sequitur pro domino rege ' replied. Then, ' dominus Rex precepit Cancellario suo ut omnes Iusticiarios congregari faceret et quod ipsi exposito eis
toto processu predicto se inde plenius informarent et quod dictus Cancellarius de informacione et auisamento dictorum Iusticiariorum in hac
parte prefatum dominum Regem certificaret qui quidem Iusticiarii sic
congregati viso et examinato toto processu predicto unanimiter concordarunt et dixerunt quod ex quo predictus Iohannes de vfford tenet predicta maneria per cartam domini Regis ad terminum vite sue absque
aliquo reddendo, reuersione eorundem maneriorum ad eundem dominum
Regem post mortem eiusdem Iohannis de vfford spectante et idem
Iohannes virtute eiusdem carte de eisdem maneriis cum pertinenciis vt
de libero tenemento suo est seisitus predictus Iohannes de vfford non
tenetur predicto domino Regi de firmis et exitibus maneriorum predictorum
. . . nec sine breui originali ad communem legem de maneriis predictis
prefato Comiti respondere, et dictus dominus Rex sibi relacione per
Cancellarium suum predictum de deliberacione et auisamento Iusticiariorum predictorum sic super hoc habitis precepit eidem Cancellario vt
ad discussionem negocii predicti procederet et super hoc predictus comes
in Cancellaria Regis predicta solemniter vocatus non venit ideo consideratum est quod predictus Iohannes de vfford eat sine die.' The king
could facilitate litigation by ordering that the issue of writs be less expensive (e.g. R. P. ii. 241, no. 40 ; cf. 261, no. 39). Where one could obtain
no justice against a powerful opponent, the king's intervention might
turn the scale. In 1355 a woman petitioned the king in parliament for
a remedy in her case against the bishop of Ely, who had been strong
enough to frustrate all her attempts at obtaining justice. If no other
remedy could be successful, the petitioner asked that the king might
take the case into his own hand. The king declared that he would do so,
ibid. 267, no. 30 : ' Par quoi ele requert humblement a nostre Seignur
le Roi et a tut son bon Conseil, q'ils voillent sur ceste chose ordiner qe ele
puisse vivre en pees, et les soens, qar ils sont grantement manacez de
jour en autre. Par quoi jeo requer a Monseignur le Roi, qe s'il ne puisse
deliverer bonement a cest foitz, q'il voille prendre entierment la Querele
en sa tres graciouse main tant qe il soit de leisir de trier, et qe ele ne soit
mye trie hors de sa presence . . . Quelle Petition entendue, nostre Seignur
le Roi ottrohi a la darreine clause de sa Petition, et dist overtement, Jeo
prenk la querele en ma main.' The king could also give special facilities
for the trial of cases ; he could give, for instance, the privilege of pleading
at the exchequer in cases which ordinarily would have to be pleaded

In such a state of affairs we need not be surprised to find that occasionally there happened what we might term a shortage of justice. Thus in one of the later parliaments of Edward II wine merchants of Gascony complained that some time before an assignment had been made to them in respect of money which the king owed them, but that afterwards the assignment was changed and that in the later letters patent a sum of 300 marks which had been granted them in compensation for the delay was withheld. The answer was : ' Ex precepto Regis subtracte sunt, ideo nichil.' [1] But even where a remedy could finally be had, the king's power enabled his officials to do a good many wrongs which it was difficult to redress.[2]

Now, as before,[3] those who claimed against the king, however clear their case might be from the point of view of law, would leave the king a certain choice of ways in which the king would acquit himself of his obligation. Thus, in the reign of Edward II a lady complained that the king by his grant had deprived her of her part of the county of Kildare, and asked that he compensate her to the value of that part in England, in land or otherwise.[4]

If the king. owed money, his creditors might be glad to have the debts allowed in their accounts at the exchequer. For instance, from 5 Edward III we have a number of writs, upon petition in parliament, ordering the treasurer and barons to allow certain sums, which the king owed, in the customs duties due from the petitioners who were exporting wool.[5]

That new privileges were being established for the king, and that the king's interests were safeguarded so carefully, is

elsewhere. Thus, Edward II sent a writ to the exchequer in 1310 directing them to retain the pleas of certain merchants relating to recovery of debts and other subjects, because the merchants had well deserved of the king (L. T., R., roll 80, Brevia dir. Baronibus, T., m. 7 r.).

[1] R. P. i. 406, no. 108.

[2] The grievances against purveyors were so general that their very title became unpopular and it was desired to change it to that of buyers (S. R. 371). All enactments intended to obviate abuses on account of purveyance were, however, carefully preserving the royal privilege itself. For some complaints, see, e.g., R. P. ii. 269–70, nos. 10–19.

[3] Above, pp. 32, 66, cp. 124.   [4] A. P. 40.†   [5] R. P. ii. 444, no. 96.

explained partly by the dependence on the king of his officials. During our period the dependence was as clear as ever. Thus, in 1327, in an assize of novel disseisin relating to the common of a moor, the defendants contended that the moor formed parcel of a manor which had been granted by the king to some one, with the remainder to Hugh Despenser, and that through Hugh's forfeiture the reversion belonged to the king. The assize was taken, because the tort complained of was one of the defendants, and the charter seems not to have related to the subject-matter of the claim ; but the case was adjourned, in order to ' speak to the king '. Stonore (C.) J. recalled how certain justices assigned had been in great danger, and one of them had been suspended from office because without consulting the king a judgement was given which affected the course of water supplying the king's mills.[1] It is true that the action taken by the justices in the case thus related had been quite irregular,[2] but the severity with which the irregularity was punished would probably not have been matched had the case affected only the interests of private parties. The exemplary punishment seems in any case to have had its effect upon the minds of judges.

Origins of a body politic. It is only by the king's personal power, and not by deductions from theory, that we can explain the privileges attributed to, or at least enjoyed by, the queen (not only the queen-consort, but also the queen-dowager)[3] and the royal princes.[4]

But the king's position, and above all the growth of the king's power, must not be considered merely results of the king's hold on his subordinates. At the bottom of the development was a series of ideas, which we can characterize as beginnings of the conception of the ' body politic '.

National consciousness was growing ;[5] the ' commonalty

[1] 1 l. ass. pl. 1.
[2] Although we do not know when the case here reported actually occurred, we may note a consideration which admittedly influenced at least some, and probably all, of the justices. In this light, Coke's quarrel with James I appears all the more important.
[3] Appendix, pp. 206–10.   [4] Appendix, pp. 210–11.
[5] R. P. i. 420, no. 14, complaint of English Cistercians that the abbots of Ireland refuse to receive any of those belonging to the ' nacioune

of the realm of England ' [1] was something distinct from the other groups in Christendom ; the importance of the language as a national characteristic was being emphasized ; [2] the conception of common utility, ' the common profit of the realm ' [3] was spreading. In concrete form, it meant that there were things in which everybody, or at least many people were interested ; hence many regulations affecting everyday life ; [4] hence the justification of oppressive legislation by the assertion that it concerned *commodum Reipublicae*.[5]

The king was urged that he desired, or ought to desire, above everything else, the good government of his commonalty.[6] That brings us nearer the assumption, not yet that the king existed only for the commonwealth, but that the king's power was limited so as not to enable him to do things prejudicial to the good of the commonwealth.

The limitation was not often applied in ordinary litigation, but there is at least one curious expression of it during the reign of Edward III. The limitation is laid down in a writ issued *per consilium*, and seems thus to be emphasized as a legal rule. The case in question is that of St. Albans,[7] in which a writ of *scire facias* issued to show cause

' quare . . . carta sic in preiudicium legis communis et rei publice facta quod ad illam clausulam revocari non debeat '.

d'Engleterre', whereas they ' de commune dreyt devyent resceivre gentz de chescune nacioune ', in despite of the king and of his people of his land of England ; cf. the endorsement ordering a remedy ' pur commune profit ' ; the grant of a ninth in 1340 is enrolled as made in consideration of the mischiefs and dangers on the one hand, the honour, profit, and quiet on the other hand, which would accrue to the king, ' and to the whole nation of England ' (' au dit nostre Seignur le Roi, et a tote la Nation d'Engleterre ') according to whether the king would or would not receive that aid (R. P. ii. 112, no. 6).

   [1] R. P. i. 128, no. 9, and many other instances ; cf. S. R. 292.
   [2] Stressed particularly in the king's appeals for help against his adversary of France, who was threatening la Lange Engleys, la Lange d'Engleterre, Lingue Anglicane deletio(nem), ibid. 300, 302 ; R. P. ii. 362, no. 12 ; 453–4, nos. 119–20. Cf. Tout, 420.
   [3] e.g. R. P. i. 351 b, 453, no. 29.
   [4] S. R. 280–1, 353–6, 378–81 ; R. P. ii. 278–82, 318, no. 15.
   [5] Ibid. 458, no. 127 ; cf. also ibid. 319–20, no. 28.
   [6] In a petition of the commons (1355) it is said : ' nostre Seignur le Roi, (qi) sovereinement desire le bon governail de sa commune, et nome ment de les povres,' ibid. 266, no. 28.
   [7] Above, p. 113 ; Appendix, pp. 243–6.

A charter was a sacred thing, and it was necessary to give ample justification if one wanted to take away a privilege which had been granted by a king and confirmed by his successors during a century. New ideas must indeed be dawning if one could obtain the repeal of an old privilege because the privilege clashed with the requirements of the common law ; the common law had come to be looked upon as a common inheritance of all men of the realm :

' Carta predicta est legi communi contraria et si huiusmodi carte concederentur et in suo robore starent, conquerentes a remedio iuris excluderentur quod in exheredacionem totius communitatis regni cederet.'

The consolidation of the nation was likely to obliterate too strict boundaries between the feudally separated parts of the realm. When the Bishop of Durham complained that the royal power properly belonging to him within his domain was infringed by royal officials, he had to apply again and again that a royal decision be given in his favour. The case was investigated like other cases between private parties and the king.[1]

Two other ideas, although perhaps not new, throw some light on the interdependence of the different tendencies which we are considering.

In 1376–7 the commons petitioned that no charges be imposed without the common assent of the lords and commons. The answer was, that the king would not impose them, except in cases of grave necessity, for the defence of the realm, and where he would be able to do so reasonably.[2]

The other idea was also based on the assumption that royal power might, at least in some cases, be exercised for the profit of the commonwealth as much as, or more than, for that of the king. An enactment of 1323–4 relating to Irish affairs prescribes that neither the justice of Ireland, nor any other royal officer in that country should exercise the

[1] R. P. i. 362–4, no. 9. In the middle of Edward III's reign the Statute of Treasons made it absolute treason to levy war against the king in his realm ; S. R. 319–20 ; R. P. ii. 239, no. 17 ; cf. M. J. 15, above, p. 131, n. 5.

[2] ' Le Roy n'est mye en volentee de le faire, sanz grande necessite, et pur la defense du Roialme, et la ou il le purra faire par reson, R. P. ii. 366, no. 25.

right of purveyance, except in times of necessity, for the common profit of the realm.[1]

Kingship was steadily tending to assume an impersonal character. This is shown, for instance, by the doctrine [2] that homage and the oath of allegiance were 'rather by reason of the crown than by reason of the person of the king'; that, indeed, before the estate of allegiance had descended no allegiance was due to the person.

The administrative machine of the king, while retaining the purpose of serving the king's interests,[3] was also increasing its institutional character. Similarly, the development of the writ was tending ultimately to make the king's order a symbol.[4]

REMEDIES

Revolution. Under Edward I it had, broadly speaking, been understood that a remedy, whenever due, would be applied. But just as in the reigns of John and Henry III, so under Edward II [5] people were compelled to formulate their views on what should happen if the king refused to apply remedies where remedies were obviously due. The views now expressed—and acted upon—do not seem to differ very materially from those which had been held by Bracton.

We have referred to the characteristic doctrine, expressed early in Edward II's reign,[6] that homage and oath were due to the crown rather than to the person of the king. Therefore, if the king happened not to be guided by reason in the exercise of his royal power ('si le roi en cas ne se demeyne mye par reson en droit de lestat de la corone') his subjects were bound by their oath to lead the king back to the proper exercise of his royal power, for otherwise they would not act according to their oath ('si ligez sontz liez par lur serment fait a la corone de remener le roy en lestat de la corone par reson et autre-

---

[1] S. R. 193.   [2] Above, p. 127, n. 2.

[3] Apart from what was said above (pp. 131–41) it is only necessary to remember the favourites of Edward II and the predominance of Isabella and Mortimer in the first few years of Edward III, in order to realize the importance of the personal element.

[4] Appendix, pp. 211–13.   [5] Chron. ii, Introd. li.

[6] Above, p. 127, n. 2.

ment ne serroit point lur serment tenuz '). This theory corresponds closely to Bracton's theories.[1] But the formula which we now consider went further than the formula of Bracton. The question was asked, in what way the guidance of the subjects should be forced on the king. Reference to royal judges was repudiated here as by Bracton,[2] but so was that to the curia, which, according to Bracton,[3] might be called upon to impose reins upon the king. The ' universitas regni et baronagium ', which might, according to Bracton,[4] do so ' in curia ipsius regis ', are now, as ' the king's lieges ', charged with the same duty, without reference to the king's court, but with a clearer mention of the means that might be used ; for we have a special mention of violence (' Dont il convient par le serement savoir qe quant le roi ne vult la chose redrescer ne ouster qest pur le commun people malveise et damaiouse pur la corone en le people ajugez qe la chose soit oustie par asparte '). To demonstrate the legality of such violence the formula was wound up with what is really a repetition of Bracton's statements in different words : the king is bound by his oath to govern his people, and his lieges are bound to govern together with him in aid of him (' qar il est liez par seon serement de gouerner seon people et les ligez loiez de governer oueqe lui en aide de lui ').[5]

[1] According to Bracton (above, pp. 47–8), if the king were *insipiens*, he would bring the doom upon the heads of his subjects (' si . . . fuerit insipiens, perdet illum ') ; and it might be said (' nisi sit qui dicat ') that ' universitas regni et baronagium suum hoc facere debeat et possit in curia ipsius regis '. The argument of duty was now explicitly stated in Despenser's formula. They would be doomed if they disobeyed their oath.

[2] Above, pp. 47–50.   [3] Below, p. 204.   [4] Above, p. 48.

[5] This is, *mutatis mutandis*, like Bracton's, ' comites dicunt quasi socii regis (fol. 34), comites . . . quia a comitate sive a societate nomen sumpserunt, qui etiam dici possunt a consulendo : reges enim tales sibi associant *ad consulendum et regendum populum Dei* (fol. 5 b), si rex fuerit sine fraeno, id est sine lege, debent ei fraenum apponere, *nisi ipsimet fuerint cum rege sine fraeno* ' (fol. 34). It is true that all that was asked for at the time of Edward II was the banishment of Gaveston. Yet the principle was to remain in human minds long after Gaveston's death. Although later on Despenser was charged with having formulated this theory, as with something very wicked, the fact remains that it contained, after all, nothing new, except for the express introduction of the principle of violence. The principle of compulsion against the king must have been well before men's minds, if not by the memory of the struggles under John and Henry, at least by the study of Bracton or, more probably, by the study of an

The principle of violence was not defined as to its object.
' The thing ' to be removed was not necessarily the person of
the king.   Yet the treatment extended to Edward II, although
by that time both Despensers had found themselves united in
his suite, was little short of the application of the same
principle.   And although his enemies and murderers were
not able to act more publicly on the same principle, that
might be ascribed rather to a desire of working things smoothly
so far as possible, than to the conviction that they were
acting, from beginning to end, without any legal justification
whatever.

Ordinary remedies and the ordinary course.   We shall now
consider those institutions which were devised to serve in ordinary conditions, i.e. the remedies against illegal acts of the
royal administrative machine where the king did not refuse
to do right, and where complaints brought in a prescribed
way were dealt with without the necessity of applying extraordinary sanctions.   The distinction between remedies and
steps necessary in the ordinary course of business [1] can always
be traced, although at times great caution is required.

Coram   rege   terminari   debet   placitum   quod   ipsum   tangit.
The wealth of sources for this period enables us to consider
the fundamental principle ' coram rege terminari debet
placitum quod ipsum tangit ',[2] in its different aspects, and
to distinguish clearly three meanings.

The first meaning was, that apart from cases of violence
no one who was not appointed by, and therefore a representative of, the king was competent to give decisions which
would affect the rights of the king.   In this sense the justices,
in contrast, for instance, to the courts of feudal lords, were
the king's officers as much as were sheriffs or the barons of
the exchequer.[3]

abridgement such as Fleta, which (below p. 203, n. 2) took over the
now disputed passage of Bracton, on fol. 34.
   [1] Above, pp. 21–3, 70–71.   [2] Above, pp. 23, 72–4.
   [3] Bracton (above, pp. 47–8) refused to the royal justices the right to try
men charged with treason, for that would make the king a judge in his
own case; the formula of Despenser (above, pp. 148–50) maintained that one
could not redress the king's wrongs by suit at law, because in that case
the only judges would be those appointed by the king, and thus if what

In 1348, a petition presented in parliament complained of error in a judgement given in the king's bench for the king against a private party. The king assigned certain earls and barons and some of the justices to determine the affair. Before anything was done, the parliament came to an end, and the king left. The commissioners ('les deputies') remained, however, and began the consideration of the case. An objection to further proceedings was taken, apparently on behalf of the king; it was said that the judgement of the king's bench could not be reversed except in parliament; that the parliament was ended, and that therefore 'ulterius nihil agendum est' in the case; for the king was making the laws by assent of the peers and the commons, and not by the peers and commons. The king had no peer in his own land and could not be judged 'by them'. It was true that in the time of King Henry, and before, the king would be impleaded 'like other men from the people'. But King Edward his son had ordered that one should sue to the king by petition; and kings would never be judged except by themselves and by their justices.[1] The objection seems to have proceeded from the king's attorney, or, at any rate, from a person acting on behalf of the king. We do not know what decision was given, but the objection seems well-founded: the petition had been brought in a parliament, and as the commissioners were a sort of committee of the parliament, it follows that their powers had lapsed as the parliament ended.

had been done by the king's will were not according to reason, the same error would be maintained and confirmed (Chron. 153: 'Outre ceo donqes fait a demander coment hom doit donqes mener le roi, ou par suite de lei, ou par asperte; par suite de lei ne poet hom pas le redrescer, qar il ni avoira pas juges si ceo ne faist de par le roi, en quel cas qe se soit si la volunte le roi ne soit acordant a la reson et ensi il ni averoit mie fors qe error meintenuz e confermez').

[1] Y. B., 22 Ed. III, 3: 'Et les deputies demeurreint, mes le Roy meme fut ale; devant queux allege fut qe le Jugement ne peut estre revers, si non en Parliament. Et depuis qe ceo est finy, ulterius en cest besoing nihil agendum est. Et fut dit, qe le Roy fit les Leys par assent(e) des Pers et de la Comune, et non par les Pers et la Comune. Et qe n'avoit nul Per en sa terre demen : et qe le Roy par eux ne doit estre adjuge : Et qe en temps le Roy H. et devant le Roy fut emplede come seroit autre home de people. Mes Ed. Roy son fils ordonna, qe home suiroit vers Roy par peticion ; mes onques Rois ne seront adjuge si non par eux memes et leur Justices.'

They could, indeed, maintain their competence only on the supposition of an inherent right which they would have as peers of the realm, in the sense in which Bracton had thought it possible, ' sine preiudicio melioris sententie, quod curia et pares iudicabunt ' in the case of men charged with high treason. It is against this implication that the pleading was directed. Whether a petition was or was not necessary, in any case only the king and his justices could judge the king.[1]

Secondly, the principle that ' coram rege terminari debet placitum quod ipsum tangit ' granted, that it was for the king's organized government machinery to adjudicate wherever his interests were concerned, might mean that a distinction must be made between the different organs. In a way curiously anticipating the idea of a separation of powers in its modern French interpretation, this second meaning of our principle was directed against the very same royal justices who, according to the first meaning, were within the principle. Where the king's interests were concerned, the royal justices could do nothing, unless they had a special order from the king. That meant, broadly speaking, two things :

First, no plea which would incidentally concern the king's interests, even by involving the interpretation of his charter, could be proceeded with by the justices without the king's order ; [2] of course, no action against the king could be enter-

[1] The version of the history of petitions as stated apparently *on behalf of the king*, squares with the hypothesis which we have ventured to formulate (above, pp. 95–6). As to the time of Henry III, it was said only that he was impleaded like a subject, and (it seems) was judged by his justices. This can be taken to mean, solely that no petition was necessary, but that one might come *coram rege* and state one's claim. No mention is made of a writ against the king.

[2] ' We show that this is the king's right, and therefore this will not be tried without consulting him,' said counsel in one case (Y. B., 5 Ed. III, 65). ' The king's right will not be put into pleadings (ne serra my mis en plee) without consulting him,' we hear soon afterwards (ibid., 7 Ed. III, 30). In a writ of right relating to an advowson, the defendant prior pleaded frankalmoin by the former king's gift, and, despite the plaintiff's protests, despite the lack of a clause of warranty, aid was granted. ' The king would have masses and prayers and would not lose them without being made a party ' (ibid., 6 Ed. III, 25, above, p. 140). A defendant pleaded that he was parson by the king's presentation, and that the lands in question were part of the endowment of his church (' parcelles de glebe de sa Eglise '). Aid was prayed and granted, although the king had only the right of presenting (43 l. ass. pl. 13 ; cf. Brook, Aide del Roy,

tained, in our period, without his permission, special, as in the case of an endorsement on a petition, or general, as in the case of certain proceedings ordained by statute.[1]

Secondly, the king's officials could not, except by the king's permission, special or general, be made responsible before the ordinary courts ; on the other hand, those who actually were, or for special purposes were considered to be, the king's officials, could be brought to answer before a court, though not before the ordinary law courts. In other words, members of the royal administrative machine were responsible, as a rule, not before an ordinary court, but before a court appointed by the king *ad hoc*, or else before the exchequer. Although for a party aid from the king was a good means of delaying the proceedings and perhaps defeating the action altogether, yet the underlying idea was that of protecting the interests, not of the party, but of the king. Where the king's interests could not possibly be affected aid would not be granted. Thus the king had granted some lands and the grantee had enfeoffed another, who afterwards was arraigned by assize of novel disseisin. He prayed aid from the king, but it was not granted because he was a stranger to the king's charter so that the warranty could not extend to him.[2] In a later case, aid from the king was refused because the charges in question were based on the defendant's own deed and covenant which would cause no damage to the king.[3]

But the limits of aid-prayer were not rigidly fixed. In cases of doubt, the justices preferred to be on the safe side. In one case,[4] the defendants in an assize of novel disseisin obtained aid from the king although the tort was supposed in their persons. Where aid from the king had been granted, the plaintiff brought, first a writ *de procedendo in loquela*,

---

90). 'While the tenements are in the king's hand, we shall not hear the plea without the king's special order,' said Hillary C. J. C. P. in 1341, when a writ of entry was brought against a minor in the king's wardship (Y. B., 15 Ed. III, 279–81, R. S.). Aid was granted because eight marks were reserved to the queen, and if the land were recovered by the plaintiff the king would lose by that much (Y. B., 10 Ed. III, 17).

[1] Below, pp. 175–6.
[2] Fitzh., Aide del Roy, 1 (A.D. 1358).   [3] Y. B., 48 Ed. III, 18.
[4] Above, p. 141, n. 1.

and then a writ *de procedendo ad iudicium*; afterwards, on the basis of the judgement, a *scire facias* was sued; aid was again prayed and obtained because the defendant was a dean, against whose predecessor the original judgement had been obtained, so that he was considered a different person; apart from that, the king might have something of a later date in discharge.[1] The justices would supersede proceedings where the king had sent them an order, not, indeed, to supersede, but to act cautiously so as not to affect his interests because the tenements were in his hands.[2]   A writ came to the justices ordèring them not to take the assize without consulting the king.   The plaintiff contended that the writ had issued at the mere suggestion of the defendant, and that the lands in question were really different from those referred to in the writ.   The court decided that they would have to supersede the proceedings even if the king had wilfully usurped the possession ('jeo pose que le Roy ust accroche ceux terres . . . et le Roy averoit possession') of the lands in question.   *A fortiori* they must supersede when the king told them, whether rightly or wrongly, that the lands to which he referred were those in dispute between the parties.

The justices were unwilling to interpret royal charters even if according to the Statutum de Bigamis[3] they might have done so.   A defendant pleaded a grant by the king's grandmother, confirmed by the present king.   In vain did the plaintiff invoke the Statutum de Bigamis, pointing out that there was no clause of warranty.   Aid from the king was granted.   Stonore J. said that 'whether the king wished to grant him the tenements or not, no one must judge, except the king himself, for no one should interpret the king's charter'.[4]   It was successfully urged in court that one would have aid from the king although the king's charter did not

---

[1] Y. B., 17 Ed. III, 56.
[2] Y. B., 21 Ed. III, 24–5; cf. e.g. 22 l. ass. pl. 24; Y. B., 22 Ed. III, 6; ibid., 24 Ed. III, 23; 38 l. ass. pl. 16.   [3] Above, p ; 2.
[4] Y. B., 9 Ed. III, 32–3: 'Car a charte le Roy nul home doit enterpreter.'   That seems almost like a translation of Bracton's 'De cartis vero regiis nulli licet nisi ipsis regibus iudicare' (fol. 34).

contain a clause of warranty.[1] ' It is for the king alone and for no one else to judge his deed, and the deeds of his ancestors,' we hear again in 1352.[2]

We have been contrasting the king with the justices. But what was meant by 'the king'? In some cases, as we shall see, the word was taken in its literal meaning. Generally speaking, however, if aid from the king was granted, the plaintiff had to apply to the chancery for a writ *de procedendo*.[3] Before such a writ was granted, the officials would have to find out whether the king's interests were not affected. If they were, then the merits of the case would be tried at least so far as to ascertain that there was no collusion. If the king's interests were not affected, then a writ *de procedendo* would be granted.

Thus, in a case of 1364 the defendant successfully prayed aid from the king. In due course a writ came to the court ordering them to supersede the proceedings altogether. For upon application to the chancery for a *procedendo* the case had been tried and it had been found that the demandant had no right to recover. The court dismissed the case (' comanda le tenant aller a Dieu '), and the judge said that when one prayed aid of the king and had (a claim of) warranty against the king, the parties would come to the chancery and there the warranty would be tried between them : and after the warranty had been tried they would plead to the action in the chancery : for otherwise, by collusion between the demand-ant and the tenant, the king might be put to loss by force of the warranty, although perhaps the demandant would have no right to recover. If, however, the case had been tried so far that the parties put themselves on the country, then the proceedings in the chancery would end, and a writ would be sent to the justices ordering them to take the verdict.[4]

---

[1] Y. B., 10 Ed. III, 26 : 'Et Court granta l'eid. Et dit fuit, mesque le Roy donna en fee simple a tenir de chief Seigniors, home avera eyd, mesque la charte ne voit pas garrantie.'

[2] 25 l. ass. pl. 8. As to late aid-prayer, Y. B., 22 Ed. III, 6 ; Fitzh., Aide del Roy, 69 (A.D. 1358) ; as to aid granted twice in the same case, on different grounds, Y. B., 29 Ed. III, 17. [3] R. P. ii. 23, no. 29.

[4] Y. B., 38 Ed. III, 14 : 'Et in cas quils pledont a Pais, donqe ils surseront in Chancery ; et le Roy nous mandra brief aller avant a prendre l'Enquest,' etc. ; cf. below, p. 171.

In another case the same judge stated the distinction between cases in which the right would, and those in which it would not, be tried in chancery. If a reversion were reserved to the king, then the case would be tried in the chancery. In other cases a writ would be sent to the justices to proceed.[1]

We may conclude, that upon aid from the king being granted the plaintiff had to apply, in the first instance, to the chancery. There it would be found out whether the king's interests would be affected by judgement for the plaintiff.[2] If they would, then either the case would be tried on its merits and ultimately the court below would be directed to dismiss the case (that would happen if the plaintiff had clearly no right) ; or, the case would be tried in chancery up to the point of issue joined, and the case would then be sent back to the justices to take the issue.[3] In some difficult cases even the chancery proceedings would be superseded, and thus no *procedendo* granted to the plaintiff, until he sued to the king by petition.

We have seen that the justices would not allow themselves to judge royal charters. The king himself was to judge his charters. It follows that it was for the king to declare his charters void. Yet it is the chancery that declared the king's charters void, or repealed. We have seen an example of that jurisdiction in the case of St. Albans. In another case [4] the earl of Kent ' petitioned ' [5] the king for the repeal of a charter by which the king had granted away a rent belonging to the earl's inheritance. The ' petition ' was endorsed to the effect that the archbishop and others of the council should call those from the chancery and should do what ought to be done according to law and reason. A *scire facias* issued calling upon the king's grantee to come into chancery and show cause why the charter should not be

---

[1] Y. B., 38 Ed. III, 18–19 : ' Coment qu'il avera l'aide, il ne sera pas trie en ceo cas en la Chancerie ; car il n'est my en ceo cas come si la reuersion fuit au Roy : car en ceo cas le Roy nous mandra brief d'aler auant.'   [2] Above, p. 155, n. 4.   [3] Above, p. 156.
[4] Y. B., 21 Ed. III, 47 ; C. R., roll 352, m. 131.†
[5] Below, p. 181.

repealed, as based on an untrue suggestion. He came and took objection to the action which, being taken to deprive him of his freehold, should therefore have been taken at common law. The objection was overruled because the suit was taken in order to repeal a royal charter, and that could not be done elsewhere but only in the chancery.[1] The defendant objected further to the composition of the court, as not based on the endorsement of the petition. This objection, too, was overruled, and the Year Book says that that was because by law the suit must be tried in the chancery.[2]

Where acts of royal officials were complained of, it was not for the ordinary courts to decide whether the acts had been legal or otherwise. The acts had been done on the king's behalf, and had to be investigated, either by the exchequer, as more especially representing the king, or else by the king's special commissioners.

In 1314–15 a party complained that a former sheriff had refused to return a petty *cape* which had been awarded by the justices of the bench. The petition was endorsed, ' per commune Consilium : Sequatur ad Scaccarium versus predictum Iohannem, qui tunc fuit Vicecomes ; et ibi fiat sibi iustitia.'[3]   A statute of 1320 regulates the proceedings at the exchequer against sheriffs and other ministers who, having collected the king's debts, and having given tallies or other acquittances to the debtors, failed to acquit the latter at the exchequer. Among other things, it was provided that in certain cases the defendants (i.e. the ministers) should not

---

[1] According to the record, Sir John pleaded that by virtue of the Great Charter he ought not to lose his freehold except upon action brought in the *placea* delegated to hear common pleas, whereas the chancery was but a *placea officii*. The record, however, consistently speaks of ' the court '. According to the Year Book, this objection of Sir John ' non allocatur, eo qe cel suite est a repeller le chartre du Roy, qel ne peut ailleurs estre fait qu'en le Chancerie.' The record does not give any such reason, and only states that John was told to answer over.

[2] ' Et puys ils diseint Sir, c'est en suit commence par petition q'est endosse qe l'Archevesqe et autres etc. Per qe n'entendons pas qe devant autres qe eux devons estre mis a respondre. Et non allocatur ; eo qe par la Ley ce sera al' Chancerie.' The record gives an entirely different reason, namely, the king's personal order given orally to the chancellor who had purposely gone to the king to ascertain his pleasure.

[3] R. P. i. 331, no. 214.

only be condemned in the principal debt, but also in damages to the plaintiffs (i.e. to the parties complaining, who had been compelled to pay again). The statute contained a proviso that it was not intended to affect the existing right of private parties to complain at the exchequer against sheriffs or other ministers, as that right had reasonably been used before then.[1]

In 1330 ' it was agreed by the king and his council, that all the sheriffs of England be removed without being put into their places again, and that other fit (covenables) men be put into their places; and that good men conversant with the law be assigned throughout England to inquire into, hear, and determine, at the suit either of the king or of private parties, all cases of abuse of power (conspiracies, oppressions, grevances, fausines, duretes, et trespas) committed by sheriffs, coroners, undersheriffs, underescheators, constables, bailiffs, hundreders, and other such ministers, and also by others, since the accession of Edward II.[2] Endorsements on petitions of the same year complaining, for instance, of exactions and abuses by the bailiff of certain royal manors of ancient demesne, and of exactions by the sheriff of Somersetshire and Dorsetshire, directed the petitioners to sue before the committee thus appointed.[3]

The king could waive his privilege, for a group of cases, and then the officials complained against would be treated like private individuals. Thus, in the case of certain abuses, purveyors had to be treated like private evildoers, and in 1354, upon petition of the commons, the king ' granted ' that the purveyors be not allowed to seek special protection behind letters of the privy seal.[4] On the other hand, where the defendants could be included in the category of the king's ministers, the king's privilege might be available for

---

[1] S. R. 180 : ' Et nest mie lentencion de nostre Seignur le Roi, ne de son counseil, qe par cest estatut, seit nul homme forclos, qil ne se puisse pleindre sur Viscounte, et autre Ministre, qant il sera trove al Escheker ; et qil respoignent illoeqes, auxi come ad este use renablement devant ceo temps.'

[2] R. P. ii. 60, no. 21.   [3] Ibid. 38, no. 37 ; 40, no. 47.

[4] Ibid. 260, no. 34.

private parties in order to ensure trial at the exchequer with some advantages to the complainant.

Thus a petition complained during Edward III's reign of waste done in the tenements of the petitioner while he had been a minor in the king's wardship. The council directed the justices and the clerks of chancery to ordain a remedy for such cases. Finally it was ordered that a writ be sent to the treasurer and barons of the exchequer, to summon those who had by royal commission held the lands of the petitioner, because by reason of the wardship they were royal officials ('tamquam ministros Regis racione custodie quam habuerunt '), to hear the reasons and to do justice.[1]

The principle, 'coram rege terminari debet placitum quod ipsum tangit ', had a third, a still more restricted, meaning. It might mean a reference to the king himself, as distinguished even from the chancery, the exchequer, or the council in parliament.[2]

Although, as a rule, a *procedendo* in private lawsuits might be obtained at the chancery, yet there were cases in which application was made to the king by petition. The Ordinances of 1311 provided that a parliament be held once or twice a year,[3] and as justification of this enactment served, apart from the necessity of redressing grievances against royal officials, the fact that in many cases defendants in the king's courts alleged that they ought not to answer without the king.[4] Perhaps those cases could be legally determined

---

[1] A. P. 8352†. Of course, if wrongs inflicted by private mal-feasants were falsely stated to be done on the king's service, the protection ordinarily enjoyed by the king's officials would not apply. Thus in 1321–2 a petition complained of two men who with twenty-eight others had killed a man, beaten the petitioner and taken away his goods, purporting 'to be with the king ' ('mesme seux diseient q'y il esteient ov le Roi ') wherefore no attachment was brought against them ('par qei nul atachement ne se (?) fist sur eux '). This latter was, indeed, due also to the fact that they were afterwards with a powerful magnate. The endorsement sent the petitioner to the common law ('sequatur ad communem legem ubi voluerit ', R. P. i. 412, no. 148).

[2] After all, the chancery and the exchequer were offshoots of the council (as were, for that matter, the law courts). The committees appointed to hear petitions in parliament (below, pp. 188 ff.) were also committees of the council. There might be cases, in which reference had to be made to the king in person. [3] Stubbs, ii. 346. [4] R. P. i. 285, no. 29.

without the king ; still, the possibility of a direct application to the king was taken for granted.

In 1315 the community of Bristol were summoned before the king's council because of certain complaints made against them by the constable of the castle and the keeper (*custos*) of the city. The council, after the jury had given their verdict, decided to communicate with the king because the affair specially concerned him and involved a prejudice to his crown.[1] A petition of Walter de Stapledon, bishop of Exeter, was endorsed in 1324–5 as follows :

'Coram Rege, quia tangit ipsum ; videtur tamen Consilio, quod ista Peticio mittenda est cum Brevi Regis Iusticiariis Domini Regis ad Placita sua tenenda assignatis, coram quibus processus inde pendit, eis mandando quod ipsi procedant ad Iusticiam faciendam similiter videtur (this is apparently an endorsement on behalf of the king, and before *similiter* a full-stop may be supplied). Ideo fiat Breve ut supra.'[2]

About 1315, a prior presented a petition showing his right to the advowson of a church. The petition was sent to the king's bench with an order to discuss the matter, but not to proceed to judgement without certifying the king. In 1324 the prior brought another petition, which was endorsed by the council as follows :

'Videtur Consilio quod id quod petitur est concedendum verumptamen quia tangit Dominum Regem, coram Domino Rege.'

In a parliament of 1325 the prior complained by another petition that, having obtained the endorsement in 1324, he had sued ever afterwards before the king and his council for a *procedendo ad iudicium* but had failed to obtain one. The petition was again endorsed *coram rege*, but after that the king ordered a writ *de procedendo ad iudicium* to be issued.[3]

Actions to repeal royal charters or, in general, royal grants, had to be brought in the chancery[4], because these affairs touched

---

[1] R. P. i. 361 b 'Et ideo ad iudicium. Set quia premissa tangunt Dominum Regem et preiudicium Corone sue, ideo loquendum est cum Rege.'   [2] Ibid. i. 421, no. 18.
[3] Ibid. i. 439, no. 38.   [4] Above, pp. 156–7.

the king too closely to be left to the ordinary courts; but even the court of chancery was not allowed to proceed where the king's interests would be specially affected and aid from the king might be granted.[1] Just as a *procedendo* in a case before the ordinary courts would issue from the chancery, and would be in Latin, so where a case was being tried in chancery, a *procedendo* might have to come from an officer who was in closer contact with the person of the king: it would come under the privy seal, and would be in French. In *Kent* v. *Molyns* a royal charter contained a clause promising compensation should the grantee lose the rent granted by the charter. Upon *scire facias* issued in order to repeal the charter, the grantee prayed and obtained aid from the king; afterwards the king by word of mouth ordered the chancellor to proceed.[2]

In two later cases (1366), during proceedings in chancery following a *scire facias* to show cause why certain lands should not be restored to a private party, the defendants prayed and obtained aid.[3] In a still later case (1375), following a *scire facias* to show cause why certain tenements should not be taken into the king's hand and restored to the plaintiff, the defendant first obtained aid, and the case was adjourned; a writ *de procedendo in loquela* (in French) was duly brought and the case was proceeded with. Later on, the plaintiff was ordered to bring on a certain day a writ *de procedendo ad iudicium*. After he had brought that writ (again in French) judgement was given for the plaintiff.[4]

On the other hand, there is at least one case showing that if a court had been specially ordered to deal with a given case, it would not declare itself not competent because the defendant alleged that the case touched the king too closely to be proceeded with in that court.

Following upon a petition, a writ under the privy seal was sent to the chancellor, and in accordance with the writ a *scire facias* issued. The summonee urged that no one except

---

[1] 33 l. ass. pl. 10.
[2] C. R., roll 352, m. 131†; above, pp. 156–7. In Y. B., 21 Ed. III, 47, it is said 'Et puis brief vient *de procedendo*'. That is not true; above, p. 157, n. 2.
[3] T. S., f. 4, m. 10 and 19–2.† [4] Ibid., f. 7, m. 22.

the king himself could judge the manner of his purchase. The chancellor answered that the king had sent the petition to the court of chancery ('le roy nous ad mande la petition . . .'), meaning probably that that gave them authority to decide the case.[1]

Exchequer. During the period now considered, the procedure of the exchequer was made the subject of minute regulations, particularly towards the end of Edward II's reign.[2]

The court of exchequer was receiving applications, which either were made in the ordinary course of business (e.g. requests for allowances in connexion with expenditure by the king's ministers), or amounted to complaints. In any case the application would be followed by judicial proceedings, including, if necessary, not only legal argument but also collection of evidence, and by a judicial decision.

If we look at the memoranda rolls of the exchequer, we cannot fail to be impressed by the changes which had come about since Henry III's days. Where, for instance, formerly we should have found a short note to the effect that the king (by his writ) had ordered a certain allowance to be made, there is now, apart from the enrolment of the writ, a record of the proceedings and of the decision similar to the records of the king's bench or common bench.

Thus, during the minority of Edward II, Thomas of Swansea petitioned the treasurer and the council for an allowance, in view of his faithful services to Edward I. Upon discussion of the matter in the presence of the earl of Lincoln, the allowance was granted.[3]

In the very frequent case of debts exacted on behalf of the king, where it was alleged that such debts were not due, the procedure came to be settled as follows: The party would

---

[1] Y. B., 17 Ed. III, 59 'R. Th(orpe) . . . vous voyez bien que par cest suit est suppose que le Roy sera restraint de purchase in sa terre demesne : ovesqe ceo nul home puit juger forsqe le Roy mesme de la manere de sa purchase. Sh. Chaunc. le Roy nous ad mande la petition l'Evesque etc. Per qe nous agardoms la terre soit seisie in la main le Roy et la charte repelle.'

[2] Red Book of the Exchequer, Intr. cccxliiii, R. S.

[3] L. T. R., roll 80, **Communia Recorda**, Hil., m. 3 r.

come to the exchequer, and traverse the king's claim, in a way which, as to form, hardly differed from the traverse used in the chancery later on.[1] The court would order jurors to come to the exchequer, or else would depute one or several of its members to take an inquisition. Or else, the party would come to the exchequer and would show on the basis of the material already at the disposal of the court that the claim was unjustified. This procedure corresponded to the monstrance in chancery.[2] Finally, judgement would be given for or against the party.

Thus, in 1356, we find an inquisition according to which two men were responsible to the king for certain chattels. The inquisition was traversed, juries were summoned into the exchequer, but as they did not come the chancellor of the exchequer and the clerk of the pleas were assigned to take the inquisition. They sent in the inquisitions, which were in favour of both traversants, and judgement was given that the traversants go without day.[3] In another case of the same year the sheriff of Hertford and Roger de Roleye had been assigned to inquire as to the goods and chattels of outlaws. By an inquisition taken before them it was found that certain goods were forfeited, and the vill of Sabritcheworth was attached to be at the exchequer and answer to the king for the value of the goods. At first they denied that they had ever had the goods, therefore the sheriff was ordered to send a jury to the exchequer. The jury did not come at the appointed date, nor after further adjournments, and to obviate more delay the clerk of the pleas was deputed to take the inquisition. Before, however, he had done so, the men came to the exchequer and confessed that they owed the sum, and therefore it was ordered that they be charged.[4] In 1369 (43 Ed. III) we find again, to name just one or two examples, the case of a clerk who had received an advance at the exchequer on account of the freight of victuals to be sent to Calais. After his death the exchequer roll reminded the officials that the money had not been accounted for. The

---

[1] Below, p. 175-9.   [2] Below, pp. 175.
[3] L. T. R., roll 128, Com. Rec., Hil., m. 5.†   [4] Ibid., m. 4 d.

sheriff of Kent was ordered to inquire what goods, chattels, lands, and tenements the late clerk had left, and to take some of them into the king's hands on account of the said debt. The inquisition was duly returned, and there came the executor of the late clerk complaining that he was unjustly distrained, because he had completed the administration of all the goods and chattels long before he knew of the debt. He offered to aver his statement, and a jury was summoned to the exchequer to find whether it was true.[1]   It was found by an inquisition that a rent had been alienated, although the manor from which it was issuing was held from the king in chief. The rent was, therefore, seised into the king's hand. The party concerned came into the exchequer and showed that the seizure was unlawful. The court having come to the same conclusion ('visis et auditis premissis per barones liquet evidenter quod dictus redditus . . . minus iuste seisitus fuit in manum regis') the party was sent away without day, and the court decided that the king's hands be removed. The escheator was ordered to remove the king's hands, if the seisure had been made for that reason and for no other.[2]   In another case, an inquisition taken by an escheator showed that an abbot had acquired a piece of meadow, and the escheator, considering this an infringement of the statute of mortmain, seised the tenement into the king's hand. The abbot's attorney came into the exchequer and asserted that the acquisition had taken place before the statute was published. An averment was offered, and a jury was summoned. As it did not come, however, despite several orders to the sheriff, an inquisition was taken by commissioners, and the court decided that the king's hands be removed.[3]

---

[1] L. T..R., roll 141, Comm. Rec., Mich., m. 1 d.
[2] Ibid., Trin., m. 5 r.
[3] Ibid., m. 9 d.† In some cases the party appeared as a defendant in proceedings which were meant to correspond with an action of account. Thus in a case of 18 Ed. II a woman was attached to answer to the king for the relief due from some lands. She pleaded non-tenure, and a jury was summoned (ibid., roll 95, Comm. Rec., Pas., m. 3 r.; cf. the case, mentioned in n. 1, ibid., roll 141 Mich., m. 1 d.). Sometimes a *scire facias* would issue from the exchequer, to show cause why lands acquired by the dead hand should not be seised into the king's hands (e.g. ibid., Hilary term, *passim*).

Sheriffs when accounting, and also other parties, would apply at the exchequer for allowances. Allowances were, in effect, a means of satisfying claims against the king, just as were cash payments. Allowances were obtained at the exchequer, as a rule, in the ordinary course of procedure, though in cases of doubt there were awards by the barons, often with the result that a bill of the exchequer was sent to the chancery directing the issue of a writ as warrant.[1] In 18 Edward II Robert of Bures, keeper of forfeited lands in Norfolk and Suffolk, came to the exchequer and prayed to be discharged (' peciit exonerari ') of a certain sum, because owing to an inundation the hay which was supposed to have yielded that sum had been carried away. The board decided to inquire whether the hay had perished through the fault or negligence of the keeper, or otherwise. By letters patent of the exchequer special commissioners were assigned, and the inquisition taken before them served as the basis of an award by the board that the keeper be discharged.[2] In the same year Gilbert Talbot, while accounting at the exchequer, prayed an allowance, but as the barons did not know whether the expenses had been necessary, or for the king's greater profit, they decided upon an inquisition and assigned commissioners. Upon their report it was awarded that the allowance be made.[3]

[1] Examples of such writs by bill of the exchequer ('per billam de scaccario'), L. T. R., roll 80, Breuia Pas., m. 4 r., 6 r.

[2] Ibid., roll 95, Comm. Rec., Hil., m. 5 d.†

[3] Ibid., Pas., m. 9 d.† Cf. R. P. ii. 33, no. 11, a sheriff complains by petition in parliament (4 Ed. III) that no allowance was made to him at the exchequer for nine hundreds which, though originally in the king's hand, had been granted away. The endorsement directs the petition to be sent to the treasurer and barons, who should hear the complaint and do right thereupon, having regard to the Statute of Northampton. The complaint seems to show that an allowance should have been made by the treasurer and barons, and that the petition was presented by way of remedy. In the same year, a former sheriff petitioned the king complaining that the barons of the exchequer had refused to allow him money spent on purveyance for two royal castles, because they thought that the warrant was insufficient and because he could show no indentures to prove the delivery of the goods. They had ordered him to sue to the king for a better warrant, and to get indentures from those to whom he had delivered the goods. This latter was impossible as the men could not be found. The petitioner prayed that the treasurer and barons be ordered to assign men who would take an inquisition. The endorsement directed the petition to

The proceedings of the court of exchequer were based upon the principle of inquisition *ex officio*, that is, the court (on its behalf the treasurer, or some barons) appeared not only as judges, but at the same time as examiners of the party whose conduct was to be judged.

Thus, in 1325, the archbishop of Dublin, formerly treasurer of Ireland, was accounting at the exchequer for the expenditure of the Irish treasury. He asked for the allowance of £1,931 which he had paid by order of Gaveston to different magnates in connexion with a military expedition. William of Everden and William of Fullburn, the two barons of the exchequer who acted as auditors of the archbishop's account refused to allow the sum because the archbishop could not show any warrant from the king but only an order from the king's deputy. The archbishop, who pleaded that the king had ordered him to obey Gaveston, appealed to the treasurer and barons. The treasurer and barons, after a consultation, decided to put the case before the king, and the king ordered the allowance to be made.[1]

We find no mentions of the king's attorney. It seems right to assume that the court itself examined the party. Sometimes [2] we read ' dictum est pro Rege ', ' petitur pro domino Rege quod inquiratur ', or some similar phrase, but the very fact that no attorney is mentioned (in the chancery, or in other courts we usually find his name with the addition ' qui pro domino rege sequitur ') points to the conclusion that it is a member of the court that made the statements for the king. Of course, the ' petitur ' seems an obstacle to this interpretation. But we may take it as a motion on the part of one of the barons.

If the exchequer failed to do right, one could apply at the chancery for a hypothetical writ directing the exchequer to do right. We might quote, as examples, two cases from 4 Edward III. In one case, the late keeper of the castle and honour of Pontefract had shown to the

be sent to the treasurer and barons, who should see the petition, hear the petitioner's reasons, and do right to him (R. P. ii. 34, no. 18). This was clearly the remedial course, and ordinarily the barons could have ordered the inquisition to be taken.

[1] L. T. R., roll 95, Comm. Rec., Hil., m. 7 r.†   [2] Ibid., Pas., m. 9 d.†

king—these are the words of a writ which came to the exchequer—that the barons had disallowed expenses which he had incurred upon oral orders of Edward II. The writ contained a schedule with particulars which the late keeper had shown before the king ('quas quidem particulas sic deallocatas idem Thomas coram nobis exhibuit'). The order was hypothetical, to allow the expenses if the barons could see that they had been made for the king's profit. An inquisition was taken as to some of them; as to the others, Thomas was allowed to make a statement on oath. The writ seems to have issued upon application, not to the king in person, but to the chancery. One argument against this inference is that the writ mentions the particulars as shown 'before us'. This, however, may be understood as meaning the king as represented by the board authorized to issue the writ. On the other hand, the schedule has the rubric 'Peticiones Thome . . . de diuersis particulis super compotum suum coram Baronibus . . . deallocatis et eciam de diuersis particulis in compoto suo non annotatis . . .', and begins 'Idem Thomas petit sibi allocari . . .', and there follow almost twenty items. This schedule, then, which reminds us of the supposed 'petition' of a century before,[1] is very far from the usual form of a petition, and the writ does not mention a petition at all. It does not seem likely that, if Thomas had approached the king, and if he wanted to present a written document, he would not have adopted the usual style. When, however, he was applying to the chancery, his 'petitions' were simply a schedule of items, and there was no need to adopt the form usual in petitions to the king.[2] Another example out of many is presented by the case of the prior of St. Helen, Isle of Wight ; we find a hypothetical writ, beginning 'Monstrauit nobis', and containing no mention of a petition.[3]

In some cases writs from the chancery might have to be sued for in the ordinary course of business.

A petition of uncertain date brought under Edward III prayed for an order to the exchequer to make an allowance although the petitioner had lost the two writs ordering him

[1] Above, p. 27.
[2] L. T. R. roll 102, Comm. Rec., Mich., m. 30.†   [3] Ibid., m. 13 r.

to expend some money. The petition mentioned that writs of *allocate* had been sued out before (' siwy Brefs de allocate '), but they contained directions to the exchequer to collect the writs ordering the expenses.[1] The endorsement seems to contain a mistake, for the petitioner is sent to the chancery, and if it were found there that such writs of *allocate* were issued before, he was to have similar writs again. In fact, it was not the *allocate* but the writs ordering the petitioner to pay that were missing. In any case, the writs of *allocate* had originally issued without the king's special order, and only upon application to the chancery. Otherwise we should find a mention, either of a petition to the king or else of the king's former order that the writs of *allocate* should issue.[2] We may call attention to the writs issuing by bill of the exchequer. Here, too, there was no application to the head, although the exchequer had to receive a warrant from the chancery, while they in turn supplied the chancery with a warrant in the form of a bill.[3]

Chancery. During the period now considered the chancery became a distinct court, although it was derived from the council. It might be the king's council in chancery, and yet it was a court by itself. A petition presented in 1328 was endorsed as follows : ' Et soit la certificacion retourne en Chauncellerie, et le Chaunceller apelle a luy ceux qi son de Conseil le Roi, et face droit.' [4] Another petition, presented in 1347, complained that the petitioners had ' sued to the king's council, in the chancery and elsewhere . . . , yet the chancellors for the time being, and others of the council, had wilfully delayed them . . . '. The endorsement states that

---

[1] R. P. ii. 394, no. 94.

[2] In 1315 the master and friars of the hospital of St. Lazarus of Jerusalem in England complained that since the transfer of the exchequer from London to York, under Edward I, they had not received an annual subsidy (granted to them by King Henry) for the hospital of St. Giles outside London. The endorsement ordered the petitioners to show the charter at the exchequer and to give information, whether the subsidy had been paid upon writs of *liberate*. As such writs do not seem to have been mentioned in the petition (of which we have only a Latin enrolment) it seems to follow that what was meant was writs, obtained not upon the king's special order, but as a matter of course upon showing the charter (R. P. i. 344, no. 24).   [3] Above, p. 165, and below pp. 212–13.

[4] R. P. ii. 23, no. 29.

' this affair was before now, at the suit of the heirs, sent (? manye) into the chancery and before the council ; and since nothing was shown or said at that time why the king should remove (his) hand, it was agreed by the council that the manor should remain in the king's hand until something else would be shown in evidence of their right. And in case anything has been found since, to declare their right, it seems to the council that the record and process made previously in the chancery and before the council, as is said above, be made to come before the council in parliament. . . .' [1]

In a case which was tried late in the reign of Edward III (1367–9) one party complained that the consideration of the case was unlawfully transferred from parliament into the chancery. The other party answered that the documents in the case

' visa fuerunt coram Cancellario et aliis de consilio Regis in parliamento iuxta indorsamentum eiusdem peticionis et abinde de assensu Cancellarii et aliorum consiliariorum predictorum per manus Cancellarii prout moris est ad faciendum partibus iuxta formam peticionis predicte iusticiam delata et ibidem visa et examinata et errores inde assignati et sic processus inde in Cancellaria factus per Warantum fiebat. . . .' [2]

The, at first uncertain, character of the chancery as a separate court is well illustrated by a secondary detail— the headings of chancery records. At first they varied. We find : Placita coram cancellario,[3] Placita apud London in capella Noui Templi London, coram domini Regis Cancellario,[4] Placita in Cancellaria Regis coram Cancellario suo,[5] Placita in Cancellaria domini Regis,[6] Placita coram rege in Cancellaria sua apud Westmonasterium,[7] Placita in cancellaria Regis apud Westmonasterium,[8] Placita in Cancellaria domini Regis apud

---

[1] R. P. ii. 197, no. 85.
[2] T. S., f. 5, m. 19, 41–3 Ed. III.
[3] Ibid., f. 1, m. 2–1, 33 Ed. I.
[4] Ibid., f. 1, m. 5–1 a, 10 Ed. III ; cf. m. 5–2 a, 10 Ed. III (slightly different).
[5] Ibid., f. 1, m. 22, 19 Ed. III.
[6] Ibid., f. 2, m. 7–7, 28 Ed. III.
[7] Ibid., f. 1, m. 13–8, 15 Ed. III ; m. 21–2, 19 Ed. III ; and 25–4, 22 Ed. III.
[8] Ibid., f. 2, m. 5 and 6–4, 28 Ed. III ; m. 12–7, 29 Ed. III ; m. 21–4, 32 Ed. III ; m. 24–2, 33 Ed. III.

Westmonasterium,[1] Placita in Cancellaria coram Rege et consilio suo.[2] The heading 'Placita coram domino Rege in cancellaria sua apud Westmonasterium ',[3] in its abbreviated form 'Placita coram rege in Cancellaria ',[4] finally superseded all the others.[5]

The chancery remained the office meting out remedies to all who felt aggrieved. There was, in fact, a standing formula which we see endorsed on many parliamentary petitions: ' Let every one who ₊feels aggrieved come to the chancery and right will be done to him.' [6]

One applied to the chancery, as a rule,[7] for a writ. Unless it was a writ of course, the court had to decide whether a writ should be awarded. In one case, for instance, some one applied at the chancery for a writ to have a manor out of the king's hands, by virtue of an inquisition of office. For the king, however, an averment was tendered that the inquisition was not true. Thereupon commissioners were assigned to take a new inquisition, and finally the case was sent to the

---

[1] T. S, f. 2, m. 13, 29 Ed. III.

[2] Ibid., f. 2, m. 17, 30 Ed. III.

[3] e.g. ibid., f. 4, m. 1–3, 5–9, 11, 13, 15, 17, 21–6, 40–1 Ed. III.

[4] sua, e.g. ibid., f. 2, m. 18–7, 36 Ed. III.   [5] 4 Inst. 79.

[6] A petition known as A. P. 181, identical in its text with that printed in R. P. i. 383–4, no. 114, has the endorsement : ' Cch(acun) qe se sent grèue veigne en Chancellerie et li seit fait remedie sur les choses contenues etc. Irr. Coram Rege.' It is a petition of prelates, lords, and others, against undue levying of scutage. The printed petition dates from 14 Ed. II ; its Latin endorsement is much longer, and is different in effect. In 18 Ed. II a petition of the Channel Islands against a royal minister was answered thus : ' Chescun qe se sente greve veigne en Chancelerie, et il avera Bref en son cas, de venir les errours devaunt le Roi, a redrescer les illoeqes ' (ibid. i. 416, no. 1). The chancery was considered the proper place to apply for remedies if any one had to complain of a miscarriage of justice. An enactment of the second year of Edward II promised to obviate a number of grievances, and those who would complain to the chancellor that any one had contravened one of the points then enacted; should have, by a writ of the great seal, such remedy as the chancellor would deem reasonable (ibid. i. 445, no. 4, ' a ceux qe se voudront pleinder a Chauncellier, qe nul hom soit venuz encontre aucun des ditz pointz, le Chancellier, par Bref du Grant Seal, en face tele remedie come il verra que face a fere par reson '). Cf. ibid. ii. 91, no. 8, 9 Ed. III, ' Celi qi se sente greve veigne en Chancellerie et monstre sa grevance, et il auera sur ce remedie et droit ' ; and ibid. 318, no. 19, ' Viegne celui qe se sentra grevez en Chauncellerie, et il avera remedie par la commune Loy.' Cf. ibid. 250, no. 25 ; 271, no. 24; 372, no. 74.

[7] As to proceedings upon scire facias, see below, pp. 171 ff.

king's bench.[1] In another case, an application was made for
a *procedendo* because aid from the king had been granted
on account of a reversion reserved to the king and his
heirs. The result of the application was, however, a *supersedeas*. It was said in the king's bench that in such cases
the chancery had to entertain the plea as to the action
itself, and would send the case, with a *procedendo*, to the
king's bench only if the trial in chancery had resulted in
a joinder of issue ; otherwise, by collusion between demandant and tenant, the king might be compelled, by virtue
of his warranty, to restore the value, although the demandant
had no right to recover.[2] A woman applied for livery ; the
case seemed difficult ; all the justices of both benches were
summoned to the chancery to discuss it.[3] In yet another
case it was said that if in an action of dower aid from the
king was granted, the whole case would be discussed in the
chancery before a writ of *procedendo* would be sent to the
justices.[4] If a party was entitled to have land restored to
him according to the Statute of Lincoln,[5] or to have dower
from lands held by the king, a writ had also to be awarded.[6]
The court must decide whether such writs were due. Sometimes the case was sent to the parliament.[7]

It is probably as the office issuing the king's charters and
letters patent that the chancery became the court competent
to pronounce upon their validity, and to repeal them ; [8]
here, too, would take place proceedings upon *scire facias* to
show cause why tenements should not be taken into the
king's hands [9] and restored to the demandants.

[1] 29 l. ass. pl. 43 ; cf. the query of Brook, Trav. de office, 20.
[2] Y. B., 38 Ed. III, 14 ; cf. ibid. 18–19, above, pp. 155–6.
[3] Ibid. 44 Ed. III, 45,
[4] Ibid. 46 Ed. III, 19–20.   [5] Above, pp. 74–5; cf. 21 l. ass. 15.
[6] e.g. Y. B., 21 Ed. III, 1–2 ' La feme T. suist in la Chancery, issint que
la terce part de mesmes les tenements furent a luy assignes a tenir in nosm
de dower.'
[7] e.g. R. P. i. 419 b, ' E issint ad le dit Robert suy en Chauncellerye
en priaunt remedie taunt qe ore a la Pentecouste qe le Chaunceller luy ad
ajournee en Parlement.' This was in accordance with Stat. Westm. ii,
c. 24.
[8] e.g. Fitzh. Peticion, 19, 46 Ed. III ; also case of St. Albans, above
p. 113.
[9] e.g. T. S., f. 1, m. 5–1 a.

The procedure in chancery became settled, and instead of the frequent endorsement of petitions with a specific direction, the general endorsement, that the chancellor do right and reason, was held to be a sufficient warrant to adopt the ordinary chancery procedure.[1]

There was an important limitation on the jurisdiction of the chancery: that court would award no damages. In a case of 1369 we are told that the chancery awarded that the land be reseised and dower delivered to the woman; ' but nothing of damages, because damages are not awarded in the chancery '.[2]

In the consideration of cases before the court of chancery, the king's interests were safeguarded in a way different from that used in the exchequer. In actions, whether between the king and a private party, or between two private parties, the king was represented by an attorney (' qui pro domino rege sequitur '), or by his (the king's) serjeants, or by a party whose interest coincided with that of the king— and not by the president of the court. Thus, in 1315, a party applied ' in Cancellaria Regis apud Westmonasterium, et postmodum coram Consilio Domini Regis ibidem ', for the livery of certain tenements. Gilbert Toudeby and Geffrey Scrope, whom we know to have been pleaders,[3] opposed the application on the king's behalf.[4] From Edward III's reign we may mention, by way of example, ' Iohannes de Cloue qui sequitur pro Rege '.[5] In another case the king's interests were represented by an escheator.[6] The king's attorney

---

[1] Y. B., 24 Ed. III, 64–5.
[2] ' Mes rien de damages, pur ceo qe damages ne sont my agarde en Chancerie ', i, 43 l. ass. pl. 32.   [3] e.g. Y. B., 6 Ed. II, S. S. Intr. liii.
[4] R. P. i. 353 b.   [5] T. S., f. 1, m. 13–8, 15 Ed. III.
[6] ' Et predictus escaetor qui sequitur pro Rege ', ibid., f. 3, m. 1, 34 Ed. III ; ibid., f. 4, m. 11, 40 Ed. III, a case of contempt by intruding into certain manors after they had been seised into the king's hands, ' Iohannes de Holand qui sequitur pro Rege.' In at least one case there is no mention of any one appearing for the king, ibid., f. 5, m. 4, 41 Ed. III. But in the preceding records of a similar character (traverses of inquisitions) there appears Michael Skillyng (ibid., m. 1–3), and as he will be found also in the cases immediately following, some of which are upon scire facias (ibid., m. 5), while others are traverses, ibid., m. 10–17, &c., it is a reasonable inference that the lack of a mention in this case was accidental.

became, in fact, a standing figure in the chancery.[1] The same person would retain that office for years.[2] The legal aspect of each case which came up in the chancery would be discussed there. That might furnish a sufficient basis for judgement.[3] If it did not, and issue was joined, the jury could at first be summoned into the chancery.[4] That practice continued certainly until 5 Edward III (1331).[5] But even before it was discontinued, cases were already sent to the king's bench after issue had been joined in the chancery, and, beginning at the latest in 1336, this latter practice became the unbroken rule.[6]

[1] Above, p. 172, as to John de Cloue ; T. S., f. 2, m. 12–7, as to John de Gaunt.

[2] Michael Skillyng begins to appear in that capacity at the latest in 38 Ed. III (ibid., f. 3, m. 16–2) and continues until the end of the reign of Edward III (ibid., f. 9, m. 6), and later.

[3] e.g. 43 l. ass. pl. 20, application for pardon and livery ; T. S., f. 4, m. 4, 40 Ed. III, *scire facias* for the king against the prior of the hospital of St. Mary without Bishopsgate, the prior proffered a charter, ' qua carta visa consideratum est quod predictus Prior eat inde sine die ' ; m. 5, eod. anno, *scire facias* upon petition in parliament, the defendant vouched the rolls of the chancery and, after they had been searched, the plaintiff's case failed ; cf. m. 6 and 15, eod. anno ; f. 5, m. 20, 43 Ed. III, 43 l. ass. pl. 21, petition by the warden and scholars of the Hall of Valence Mary, Cambridge, for the repeal of a presentation made by the king in violation of the petitioners' rights ; since the presentee could show no sufficient cause, and no averment that the petitioners' allegations were false was offered for the king, it was considered ' quod predicta presentacio . . . per dictum dominum Regem sic facta reuocetur ' ; T. S. f. 5, m. 24–5, 44 Ed. III, upon traverse of inquisition, following ' divers inquisitions ' and a certificate, it was considered that the king's hands be removed and that the manor together with the issues be restored to the traversant.

[4] Above, p. 74, n. 2.

[5] There is a writ of 19 Ed. II saying : ' Preter illos venire facias coram nobis in eadem Cancellaria tunc ibidem xii probos et legales viros tam milites quam alios de hundredo de Suthwalsham et preter illos de quolibet trium hundredorum eidem hundredo proxime adiacencium xii probos et legales homines tam milites quam alios . . . ad recognoscendum super sacramentum suum. . . .' T. S., f. 1, m. 2–3 a ; cf. another one from 5 Ed. III (' quod venire facias coram nobis in cancellaria nostra . . . viginti et quatuor . . . ad recognoscendum super sacramentum suum . . .', ibid., f. 1, m. 4–1 a and the inquisition actually taken, ibid., m. 4–1 c. ' Inquisicio capta in cancellaria Regis apud sanctum Edmundum.').

[6] e.g. T. S., f. 1, m. 5–1 b, 10 Ed. III ; cf. 4 Inst. 80. The *venire facias* was sometimes (e.g. T. S., f. 2, m. 14–5), but not always (e.g. ibid., f. 6, m. 1, 3) sent from the chancery immediately upon joinder of issue. The record of the proceedings in the chancery (or, more probably a transcript) was either sent to the king's bench in a writ (C. R., roll 352, m. 131 †) or delivered by the chancellor in person (ibid., roll 351, m. 45 †).

During Edward III's reign certain enactments and ordinances enabled the chancery to entertain practically all complaints which formerly had to be made to the king. Only in exceptional cases would there remain the necessity of applying to the person of the king, by petition.

A most important writ, dated January 23, 1349,[1] addressed to the sheriffs of London, ordered the proclamation of an ordinance to the following effect : since the king was very busy, he directed that all those who had to pursue with him affairs touching the common law of England pursue them with the chancellor, the archbishop-elect of Canterbury ; those who had affairs touching the king's special grace should pursue them with the said chancellor, or with the keeper of the privy seal. These two dignitaries were to expedite such affairs as they could, and if they could not expedite any affair without the king, they should send the petitions of the parties, together with their own advice, to the king ('ita quod ipsi, vel eorum alter petitiones negotiorum, quae per eos, nobis inconsultis, expediri non poterunt, una cum avisamentis suis inde ad nos transmittant vel transmittat, absque alia prosecutione penes nos inde facienda, ut hiis inspectis ulterius praefato Cancellario, seu custodi inde significemus velle nostrum ') ; no one else should henceforth pursue such affairs with the king ('et quod nullus alius huiusmodi negotia penes nosmetipsos de caetero prosequatur ').

We shall deal afterwards with the proceedings upon the petition.[2] For the present we note that all affairs touching the common law should be presented to the chancellor. That meant, even cases in which[3] a claim against the king (e.g. for dower), was based on the common law.[4] Generally speaking,

[1] Rymer, iii. 181 ; R. L. C. i, Gener. Intr. xxviii (wrong date !) ; C. C. R., 22 Ed. III, 615 ; Baildon, Select Pleas in Chancery, xvii–xviii.
[2] Below, pp. 179 ff.   [3] Below, pp. 186 ff.
[4] Stubbs, ii. 282, says : ' When early in the reign of Edward III, the Chancellor ceased to be a part of the king's personal retinue and to follow the court, his tribunal acquired a more distinct and substantive character, . . . petitions for grace and favour began to be addressed primarily to him, instead of being simply referred to him by the king, or passed on through his hands. In the 22nd year of that king such transactions are recognised as the proper province of the Chancellor.' I have found no reference to prove the contention that from the beginning of the reign of Edward III

all claims against the king, unless specially reserved for the king's decision, were to belong to the chancellor's domain. That, of course, did not comprise claims which *prima facie* should have been settled elsewhere : by payment through subordinate officials, or by application in the wardrobe, or in the exchequer. Such cases would come before the chancellor only if the party applied for a *mandamus*, because right had been withheld.

But certain cases were reserved for the king. Edward I had ordered all land once taken into his hands to be kept until he would order restitution.[1] That rule had been relaxed by the statute of 1301,[2] which allowed a sort of monstrance : a party could come into the chancery and sue a writ of *amoveas manus*. He must show that the inquisition on which the king's claim was based in reality gave no right to the king. This, however, was a very partial remedy : an inquisition might be erroneous, or else land might be in the king's hand without any proper inquisition. That the remedy was of no far-reaching consequences will be seen from the fact that as late as in 1341 counsel could assert that ' when the king is seised, there is no remedy or recovery by law, save by petition '.[3] The statement was, of course, too general, and counsel may have made it just for the sake of argument. Yet he probably would not have made a statement which was not, at least to a certain extent, based on what might be called a justifiable generalization.

The grievance caused by false inquisitions was partly remedied by a statute of 1360–1 ; we say partly, because the new remedy was available only, where lands or tenements were seised into the king's hand upon inquisition taken by the escheator, indicating that the king's tenant had alienated

petitions for grace and favour began to be addressed primarily to the chancellor. Cf. Anson, ii. 151 : ' . . . In the twenty-second year of Edward III matters which were of grace were definitely committed to the Chancellor for decision.' This seems to be a misunderstanding. What was defined in 1349 as the ' proper province of the chancellor ' was petitions touching the common law. Petitions of grace were to be submitted either to him or to the keeper of the privy seal.

[1] Above, p. 74.   [2] Above, pp. 74 f.
[3] Y. B., 15 Ed. III, 139–45, R. S., per Thorpe.

them without the king's licence, or that the king's tenant by knight's service had died seised in his demesne as of fee, and that his heir was within age. In those cases he who claimed the land might come into the chancery and traverse the inquisition ('et voet tranverser loffice qe fut primes pris par mandement du Roi . . . soit il a ceo receu '). The issue would then be tried in the king's bench, and 'right further done ' ('et soit le proces mande en Banc le Roi a trier, et outre faire droit ').[1]

This remedy seems to have applied only if an inquisition had been taken by the king's order. A statute of 1362[2] gave a similar traverse in cases where land had been seised into the king's hands, not by virtue of an inquisition taken by the king's order,[3] but by virtue of an inquisition ex officio.[4] The escheator was bound to send his inquisition to the chancery within a month after he had seised the land. If he did not, the party could sue a writ of certiorari to him. Instead of sending the inquisition, the escheator might at times send simply a certificate, i.e. a reply to the effect that he had seised the land because he had found by inquisition what seemed to him a justification of the seisure. He would of course specify the grounds.

[1] S. R., 368, 34 Ed. III, c. 14. An early traverse by virtue of this statute is found in Wythyngton v. Rex, T. S., f. 3, m. 1, Pas. 34 Ed. III: 'PLACITA IN CANCELLARIA REGIS APUD WESTMONASTERIUM . . . Accedens ad Cancellariam domini Regis Iohannes . . . grauiter conquerendo monstrauit ' : he offered to aver that an inquisition taken by the escheator was untrue ; the escheator maintained that it was not, and the case was sent to the king's bench. (Before the inquisition now traversed there had been one against and one for John.)

[2] S. R., 374–5, 36 Ed. III, c. 13.

[3] The order would be a writ from the chancery, e.g. a diem clausit extremum ; the latter would be sued by the heir who wanted to get his ancestor's tenements ; for, if the tenements were held from the king in chief, one could not enter without having obtained a writ to him who held the tenements on the king's behalf, and such a writ would not be granted by the chancery before an inquisition had been taken and had established the applicant's right.

[4] 'des autres terres seisiez en la mein le Roi par enqueste doffice (i.e. not such as were in the king's hands by reason of wardship) . . . sil eit nul homme qe mette chalenge ou claym as terres issint seisiez, qe leschetour mande lenqueste en la Chancellerie, deinz le mois apres les terres issint seisies, et (perhaps ou) qe brief lui soit livere de certifier la cause de sa seisine en Chancellerie, et illeoqes soit oie sanz delay de traverser loffice, ou autrement monstrer son droit, et dilleoqes mande devant le Roi, affaire finale discussion sanz attendre autre mandement.'

There are in existence very many inquisitions sent to the chancery by the escheators, either upon, or without, special writs of *certiorari*, and traverses upon such inquisitions or certificates.[1] Generally speaking (though there might be slight differences in individual cases), the record of a traverse or monstrance would begin, 'Dominus Rex (nuper) volens certiorari super causa captionis . . ., mandavit . . .',[2] or 'Compertum est per inquisicionem per . . . ex officio suo [3] (or 'de mandato Regis ',[4] as the case might be) captam et in Cancellaria sua retornatam (or 'missam', or 'per certificationem ').' After the purport of the inquisition, there follows the statement that one (the complainant) came into the chancery and complained that the land &c. had been seised unjustly into the king's hands, stating in what points he considered himself aggrieved: it might be either because the statements of the inquisition were untrue (that was a real traverse), or because the party could 'otherwise show his right ', i.e. establish his right without denying the truth of the inquisition (that was a monstrance). Thus, in a case of 44 Edward III, upon several inquisitions taken by the king's order and returned into the chancery, the party asked for restitution. The king's attorney objected, but upon full deliberation with the whole council it appeared to the court that nothing had been alleged for the king that would justify the retention of the manor and forest in question in the king's hands.[5]

The idea of the traverse was not new. In 17 Edward III Thorpe J. had said that where the king was seised in another's right, so that, if he were not king, there would be no need of a *precipe quod reddat*, neither would a petition be necessary because it takes the place of an original against other persons ; therefore, he said, it was enough to traverse the office

[1] e.g. T. S., f. 4, m. 1, 8, 17.
[2] e.g. ibid., f. 8, m. 4.   [3] e.g. ibid., m. 6.   [4] e.g. ibid., m. 14.
[5] 'Et super hiis et aliis allegatis ex parte domini Regis habita plena deliberacione cum toto consilio domini Regis videtur Curie quod nichil allegatum est pro parte domini Regis quare dicta (*sic*) in manu domini Regis remanere deberent. Ideo consideratum est quod dominus Rex manum suam amoveat et tenementa predicta deliberentur predicto Henrico ' (ibid., f. 5, m. 22).

that had been found for the king.[1]   In a much earlier case
(16 Ed. II), a petition complaining that a false inquisition had
been returned into the chancery added that the petitioner
had come to the chancery and had there shown her right
and her charters, 'annihilating' the false suggestion.[2]   In
29 Edward III a *certificacio* of an escheator, sent to
the chancery by the king's order (i.e. upon *certiorari*) was
traversed, issue thereupon was joined, and the case was sent
to the king's bench.[3]

Finally, certain proceedings in the exchequer, where
parties complained, e. g., of wrongful distress, were, in their
fundamental idea, very similar, though the procedure was
different, in so far as juries would even later on be summoned
to the exchequer, and as there was, as a rule, no special
attorney of the king.[4]   The monstrance was, after all, only an
application for a writ, based on a matter of record.   If an
heir in the king's wardship had attained full age and sued
livery, or if a man applied for an *amoveas manus* according
to the Statute of 1301,[5] that was a monstrance.   After the
two enactments mentioned above the cases in which an
application to the king was necessary became exceptional.

Were the traverse and monstrance in the chancery
suits by the king, or against him?   It seems that the king
was defendant.   He held the land in his hands, whether for
a time (where he claimed wardship, or so) or for ever (where
he claimed escheat).   Unless the party took the necessary
steps, the land remained with the king according to his claim.
He was taking the issues, unless judgement was given for
the claimant.   He might indeed, pending judgement, let the
party have the land if the party found sureties.   The act
by which the king let the party thus provisionally have the
land was described as 'lesse et baille les terres issint en debat
au tenant, rendant ent au Roi la value, si au Roi appartient'.[6]

---

[1] Y. B., 17 Ed. III, 187–9, R. S.: 'Quant le Roi est seisi forsqe en
autri dreit, de quel tenaunce, tout fut il autre persone, Praecipe quod
reddat ne girreit pas vers luy, homme suyra pas par Peticion, qest en lieu
doriginal vers autre persone, mes suffit de traverser office qe trove est
pur luy.'   [2] A. P. 190.†   [3] T. S., f. 2, m. 12–7.
    [4] Above, pp. 162–7.   [5] Above, pp. 74 f.
    [6] 'Issint qil face seurete qil ne fra wast ne destruccion tanqe il soit
ajugge,' S. R. 375, in the above-mentioned statute of 1362.

All this seems to prove that the king was like a man who had entered. Anybody who claimed against him had to take action, or the king would remain seised. In a word, the king was (despite the description of the applicant as ' tenant ') in the better position of a tenant, who was sued, and not in that of a plaintiff, who had to sue, for land. It was different in the exchequer, where traverses of inquisitions were intended to bring about the release of distress of which the object was to compel payment of a debt to the king.

Petitions. As a rule, the king had to be approached by petition ; even a queen [1] or a high dignitary [2] would present petitions. Of course, where a matter of pure grace was concerned, those around the king were in a better position than other subjects of the king.[3] The king might order an act of grace, for instance a payment by way of gift, upon the oral request of one of his high officials, or courtiers. But the rule for all cases of legal claims, and also for appeals to the royal grace, except very few cases, seems to have been to approach the king by petition.

In parliament. Until the ordinance of 1349 [4] a petition should, as a rule, be brought in parliament. There is much evidence to support this contention. First of all, we read in very many petitions that petitions in the same matter had already been presented in a former parliament, or in former parliaments.[5] Provision was made again and again for the

---

[1] e.g. R. P. i. 302, no. 54 (8 Ed. II), petitions of Queen Margaret, addressed, one to the king, the other to the king's council.

[2] A. P. 14671, bishop of Ely ; cf. R. P. i. 428, no. 47 ; ibid. 314, no. 105, bishop of Lincoln.

[3] Cp. the report on the requests to Edward III, in his last years, through Alice Perriers, ibid. iii. 13, 14.   [4] Above, p. 174.

[5] Thus A. P. 10549† ' Le dit Rogier son age auoit accompli et eit suwi en chauncellerie et par peticion en plusours parlements dauoir plener restitucion ', in the time of Edward III, for cf. R. P. ii. 48, no. 70 ; A. P. 14720 b,† early in the reign of Edward III, ' Qe come le dit Johan en le primer parlement nostre seignur le Roi qore est auoit mys sa bille ' ; R. P. i. 294, no. 26, 8 Ed. II, ' Robert . . . ad suy de temps en temps, et de Parlement en Parlement ' ; ibid. 418, no. 8, 18 Ed. II, petition by the bishop of Durham, ' Qe come autrefoitz il livra ses Peticiouns en Parlement,' he prays that the petitions be answered. Endorsement : ' Au procheine parlement ' ; cf. ibid. ii. 13, no. 4 ; 17, no. 14 ; 25, no. 33 ; 80, no. 33, 8 Ed. III, the abbot of St. Albans, ' Com il ad suy par Peticions en divers Parlementz ' ; ibid. 82, no. 42 ; 88, no. 63, ' Come il eit sue en

delivery of petitions, and at times it was emphasized that many grievances could only be remedied upon petitions in parliament.

The Ordinances of 1311 point out that in many pleas the defendants allege that they cannot answer without the king, and that in many cases people are aggrieved by royal officials, and of all these grievances there can be no remedy without a common parliament.[1] In a parliament held in 1332 it was announced that as petitions from the people had not been received or answered at the parliament, the king would hold another parliament ;[2] in 1330 a proclamation was made that all those who wished to complain of wrongs done by royal officials, by councillors, and other magnates, should come to Westminster, to the next parliament, and there and then state to the king their complaints.[3]

A petitioner under Edward II or, more probably, in the first part of the reign of Edward III, complained that a manor which he held for life had been taken from him and then given to the king, and that because of this he ' could not by the law of the land have a recovery without this common parliament '.[4] In 1327, a petition of the commons relating to assarts was answered to the effect that every one who felt aggrieved should bring his petition containing details (' en especial ') in parliament, and right would be done to him.[5]

From all this we are allowed to infer that if petitions could have been brought with equal ease in parliament and outside it, there would be no reason why people should wait so long.[6]

Outside parliament. But in some exceptional cases petitions to the king could, even before 1349, be presented, although no parliament was assembled.

A petition of 1318, presented by Lucas Periers, formerly

plusours Parlements pur le Manoir de Oneston ' ; ibid. 93, no. 19 ; 97, no. 2, 12 Ed. III, the burgesses of Scarborough complain, ' Come devant ses heures en diversez Parlementz s'en sount pleint ' ; R .P. ii. 98, no. 4 ; 100, no. 9 ; 122, no. 31 ; 180, no. 22 ; 208, no. 15 ; 409, no. 176.

[1] R. P. i. 285, cl. 29 ; this may, of course, have related, not only to a legal, but also to a practical impossibility.

[2] Ibid. ii. 65, no. 11.   [3] Ibid. 443, no. 93 ; cf. 67, 201.

[4] A. P. 2390.†   [5] ' Et il aura droit,' R. P. ii. 11, no. 3.

[6] Cf. Y. B., 12–13 Ed. III, 243, R. S. ; ibid., 18 Ed. III, 157–69, R. S. ; ibid., 24 Ed. III, 64–5 ; also possible inference from ibid., 16 Ed. III, pt. I, 109–21, R. S.

physician to Queen Margaret, bears the somewhat unusual endorsement, that ' my lord wishes that you (Master Thomas of Charleton) make hastily letters to the chancellor to inquire of the right to the church in question according to the purport of this bill '.[1] The petition seems endorsed by the king's private order, and there is nothing to suggest that it had been brought in a parliament or in a formal meeting of the council. In 7 Edward III the abbot of Stanley stated in his petition in parliament that he had ' siwy . . . par plusoures Billes en Parlementz et hors de Parlementz ' ;[2] but to whomsoever his petitions outside parliament had been addressed and presented, it seems clear that he had ultimately to come to parliament. On the other hand, the fact that he could claim to have brought petitions outside parliament shows clearly that there was some possibility of adopting the latter procedure.

In the same year, a ' bill ', in fact a memorandum, by, or on behalf of, the young earl of Kent (then in the king's wardship) was sent to the chancery under the privy seal, enrolled as ' billa ' (though referred to as petition) and served as basis of the *scire facias* against Sir John Molyns.[3] In 1347 the abbot and convent of Quarrera, in the Isle of Wight, brought a petition in parliament complaining that they had often sued by petition to the king and his council, ' en diverses conseilleis et Parlements '[4]. The petitions mentioned as presented in the king's council were apparently a reminiscence of the time when a parliament was a meeting of the king's council.[5] Thus even under Edward III there was a possibility of petitioning the king, not in a parliament, but at a meeting of his council, which had come to be different from a ' parliament '.

In yet another case, in 1334, the villains of the king's manor of Penrose petitioned the king in parliament, mentioning that at one time they had handed a petition to the king and his council ' en privete a Keniton ',[6] whereupon the council had ordered certain steps to be taken on their behalf.

[1] A. P. 12025.†   [2] R. P. ii. 70, no. 2.   [3] Above, pp. 156-7.
[4] R. P. ii. 188, no. 53.   [5] Above, pp. 87-92, 95-6.
[6] R. P. i. 308, no. 83.

This shows that at that date the handing of a petition to the king and his council might be considered a 'private' way, while the public or ordinary way would be, it seems, to present a petition in parliament. But in exceptional cases petitions could be brought outside parliament.

We assume that the rule was to present petitions in parliament. This rule was changed when, in 1349, the chancellor and the keeper of the privy seal were directed to send to the king the petitions touching affairs which they could not expedite *rege inconsulto*. No other steps should be taken by private parties to approach the king. The ordinance was intended to ease the king ('Quia circa diversa negotia nos et statum regni nostri Angliae concernentia sumus in dies multipliciter occupati'). We may assume that the parties would present petitions addressed sometimes to the king, at other times to the chancellor. The ordinance says, 'ipsi vel eorum alter petitiones negotiorum quae per eos . . . expediri non poterunt . . . ad nos transmittant'; the *quae* may refer either to *negotia* or to *petitiones*. The meaning probably was, 'those petitions which relate to such affairs as . . .'; all this related, of course, only to affairs which previously were usually brought before the king by petition, and not to cases in which, for instance, the chancellor had to be approached beforehand as well.

On the other hand, it seems that no stringent formalities were to be observed. One would probably be allowed to present at the chancery a petition addressed either to the king or to the chancellor. Petitions addressed to the chancellor are found both before and after 1349.[1]

The Ordinance of 1349 enabled everybody to petition the

---

[1] e.g. A. P. 14764, the endorsement mentions that 'il est tesmoigne deuant le conseil'; ibid. 14789, the endorsement begins 'Il semble an conseil'; A. P. 14791; ibid. 14792,† 4–6 Ep. III; most of ibid. f. 297, ibid. E 280, endorsed 'coram rege et magno consilio,' ibid. 15574† (48 Ed. III, by the countess of Hereford; cf. C. C. R., 48 Ed. III, 28); T. S., f. 1, m. 14–3, by Richard, earl of Arundel. A petition addressed to the chancellor, or, for instance, to the treasurer and barons of the exchequer, was in practice, in many cases, only a form of statement in writing, the obvious idea being that the party's allegations could afterwards easily be checked. For an example of a bill (called in Latin *peticio*) to the exchequer, see e.g. L. T. R., roll 80, Com. Rec., Mich., 3 Ed. II, m. 3 (case of Nicolas of Kirkeham).

king (though indirectly) at any time. For both before and after that ordinance receivers and triers of petitions were appointed in practically every parliament ; if the ordinance had meant that all petitions had to be presented to the chancellor or the keeper of the privy seal, and that they would, as a rule, be decided by these two officials, there would be no reason to appoint receivers and triers ; if, on the other hand, the ordinance had meant that the petitions were to be presented in parliament and delivered by the receivers to the chancellor and the keeper, there would be no reason to appoint special triers of the petitions. Thus it seems that the new rule did not extend to parliaments. Moreover, we know that the ordinances of the eighth and the twenty-first years of Edward I, which regulated the procedure on petitions in parliament,[1] were enrolled in the chancery only, and there is no trace of their having been made publicly known by proclamation. That was because they merely contained directions for the receivers and for royal officials, and did not alter the way in which the public were to present the petitions. In 1349 a different procedure was adopted because every one who wanted to petition the king might be affected.

The Ordinance of 1349 was made in exceptional circumstances, during the Black Death. The chancellor himself, one of the two officials appointed to receive the petitions, died soon. The fact that an individual chancellor was named in the ordinance would perhaps mean that the ordinance was not to continue in force after another chancellor had been appointed. It may have been an emergency measure, intended to alleviate the consequences of the fact that for the time being no parliament could be convened. Yet the change proved permanent.[2] This is what probably happened : Since a proclamation had been made that people should present their petitions to the chancellor or the keeper of the privy seal, after the demise of either, or both, of these officials

---

[1] Above, pp. 89–90.

[2] For an example of a ‘ bill ’ presented to the chamberlain, towards the end of Edward III's reign, to be laid before the king, and for the story of the chamberlain's hesitation and of Alice Perriers' influence brought to bear in connexion with the acceptance of this ‘ bill ’, which Edward III declared to be reasonable, see R. P. III. 13–14, above, p. 179 n. 3.

their successors probably continued to give redress in the way once adopted ; but no more proclamations were made, for no one who would come, e.g., before the new chancellor would meet with a refusal or be ordered to await a parliament. In this way the practice probably established itself.

This does not mean that no more petitions should be, or were, brought in parliament. On the contrary, apart from the fact that receivers and triers of petitions continued to be appointed, we may point out that as early as 1351, what we might call a speech from the throne expressly invited the king's subjects who had common or individual complaints to put forward their petitions in parliament.[1] Invitations to the same effect were repeated in later parliaments, but there was, as a rule, the limitation that in parliament should be presented petitions touching such subjects as could not be settled elsewhere.[2]

The number of petitions presented in parliament by individuals decreased rapidly after 1349. The rolls of parliaments after 1349, so far as printed, contain very few such petitions.[3] We find mostly petitions of the commons, or

[1] R. P. ii. 225, no. 4.

[2] e.g. ibid. 254, no. 3, 28 Ed. III, one of the reasons why the parliament was summoned was, ' Qe ceux qi avoient Petitions a mettre en Parlement des Grevances ou d'autres busoignes qe ne purroient estre esploite hors du Parlement, les livereient as Clercs souz nomez, de les mettre en Parlement ; et le Roi assignera certeins Prelatz et autres Grantz de les respondre, et ent faire droit ' ; cf. 46 Ed. III, ibid. 309, no. 2, ' Qe touz ceux qe se sentont grevez en ascun point qe ne poet estre amende ne redresce en nul des Places le Roi mes en Parlement, q'ils meissent avant lour Petitions ' ; see also ibid. 318, no. 14, 47 Ed. III, in a petition of the commons, ' Les Petitions de chescuny Droit dont remedie ne peot estre suy en nul autere Court mes en Parlement, q'elles soient ore en ceste present Parlement acceptez ' ; compare with this the general form of the statement in 15 Ed. III, ibid. 127, no. 5, ' Chescun qi se sent grevez par le Roi, ou par ses Ministres, ou autres, q'ils mettroient Petition avant, et ils averont bon et covenable remede.'

[3] e.g. ibid. 226, nos. 8–9 ; 243, nos. 54–6 ; 255, no. 8 ; 256, no. 13 ; 263, nos. 1–2 ; 267, nos. 29–30 ; 274, nos. 1–3 ; 297, no. 21 ; 353, no. 179 ; 372, nos. 76–7 ; 374–5, nos. 93–4 ; 459, nos. 129–30 ; 461, no. 134 ; there are some petitions of London, of other cities, of counties, &c., e.g. ibid. 314–15, nos. 46–9 ; 343–9, nos. 130–53 , 352–3, nos. 167–78 ; 354, no. 178, &c. Among petitions by individuals may be mentioned a petition by the prince of Wales, ibid. 371, no. 65, 51 Ed. III ; for examples of other petitions presented in parliament by individuals see 33 l. ass. pl. 10 ; Fitz. Peticion, 18, 46 Ed. III ; moreover, it seems that now and again a petition would, as in former days (above, p. 181) be decided by the council, outside

petitions of all estates. These latter petitions had already obtained a legal standing quite different from that of petitions presented by individuals.[1]

It is true that some of the petitions presented after 1349 may have been lost, and others omitted from the printed edition by mistake. The fact remains that immediately after the Ordinance of 1349 the number of private petitions brought in parliament decreased very considerably. The order was made to ease the king. But the result probably was to ease the parties as much, if not more.

But why did parliaments accept private petitions at all? First, there still were cases which could only be decided in parliament. No doubt is left about this in the proclamations which invite petitioners to come forward, if their grievances cannot be remedied elsewhere. Apart from that, the king could not have debarred private parties from presenting petitions in parliament. The Ordinance of 1349 was made by the king alone, and it seems more than doubtful whether Edward III could by such an ordinance have changed the law, of which the right to petition the king in parliament had come to form an important part. Already the Ordainers of 1311 had laid down that the ' delivery of bills ' was one of the chief purposes for which parliaments had to meet.[2] But after 1349 private petitions were presented in parliament[3] probably because the petitioners would not trust the royal officials,[4] or because they hoped to obtain the support of the lords or the commons.[5]

Classification. As under Edward I,[6] some petitions were

parliament. A petitioner's statement in 1354 (R. P. ii. 263 a, 28 Ed. III) that he had often shown his grievances ' in the last parliament, and also in several councils ' may be taken to mean that the suit before the council was by direction of the chancellor. Perhaps his petition, handed to the chancellor, had been sent before the council.

[1] For instance, during a parliament held in 20 Ed. III, petitions of individuals were accepted only during the first three days (R. P. ii. 157, no. 2), while the commons were invited (ibid. 160, no. 11) to bring, after that time, any petitions (i.e. bills) which might turn to their profit ' and ease '. [2] Ibid. i. 285, no. 29, above, p. 159.
[3] e.g. T. S., f. 4, m. 5 ; f. 5, m. 19. [4] A. P. 10505.†
[5] See the general request of the commons in 45 Ed. III that private petitions then presented be heard and acted upon, R. P. ii. 304, no. 16.
[6] Above, pp. 96–9.

of grace and some of right. Of grace were, of course, not only those which asked for a gift, e.g. for the remission of a rent due to the king,[1] but also petitions the matter of which lay properly within what we may call the domain of administrative discretion, or of high policy (such as complaints against suits to the court of Rome).[2] Those petitions which were of right related either to disputes between private parties, or to claims against the king. In the former case they would contain either complaints against judges, juries, &c.,[3] or they would ask that a step necessary on behalf of the king be taken, e. g. a *procedendo* issued,[4] or they would constitute 'informations', i.e. the party, while believing or pretending to believe that he had a legitimate interest in a certain step, asked the king to take that step in the king's own interests.[5] If the petitions related to claims against the king, they would be either complaints against the king's officials, such as bailiffs,[6] sheriffs,[7] the treasurer, the chancellor,[8] or against the exchequer or the chancery;[9] or they would be petitions for restitution (of a wood,[10] of lands and tenements [11]), or for payment or assignment,[12] including claims for damages,[13] or for allowances.[14]

---

[1] e.g. R. P. ii. 188, no. 54.   [2] Ibid. 184, no. 40.
[3] e.g. Y. B., 24 Ed. III, 24, one Thomas Hubert complains of the release of jurors, the petition is sent to the justices with a writ ordering them to do 'droit et raison'.   [4] e.g. P. C. P., f. 45, m. 30 a† ; A. P. 9990.†
[5] e.g. A. P. 6841.†   [6] e.g. R. P. ii. 13, no. 3.   [7] e.g. A. P. 1770.†
[8] e.g. R. P. ii. 378, no. 2.
[9] e.g. ibid. i. 318, no. 125, 8 Ed. II, complaint by a late sheriff that the exchequer has refused him an allowance ; the endorsement directs that an order be sent ('mandetur') to the exchequer to do what would be just ; ibid. 346, no. 36, complaint of unjust distraint by the exchequer, with a similar endorsement ; ibid. ii. 23, no. 29, 2 Ed. III, complaint that the petitioner, although he had shown his right in the chancery, could have there no remedy ; the endorsement orders the chancellor to summon those of the king's council, and to do right ; A. P. 10549,† early in the reign of Edward III, a complaint that no livery had yet been granted although the petitioner, who was in the king's wardship, had come of age.   [10] A. P. 15555.†
[11] e.g. Y. B., 13 Ed. III, 239–41, R. S. ; 43 l. ass. 29.
[12] e.g. A. P. 1784,† temp. Ed. III, by the executor of a late royal victualler for payment, or, if there be no ready money at the exchequer, for a proper (covenable) assignment so that he might readily get the sum due to him ; the endorsement is in the terms of the petition ; ibid. 1785,† a similar petition with an endorsement ordering the petitioner to sue to the king ; ibid. 1786,† a similar petition with two endorsements ; first, *coram rege* ; second, directing the issue of an order that the exchequer see the petition

Our distinction is confirmed by the Ordinance of 1349 ; there we find ' negotia communem legem regni nostri Anglie concernentia ' contrasted with ' negotia gratiam nostram specialem tangentia '.[15] The former should be brought before the chancellor, the latter before the chancellor or the keeper of the privy seal. The affairs touching the common law must necessarily have comprised claims against the king. A writ of the privy seal to· the treasurer and barons of the exchequer and to the justices of the king's bench, dated May 21, 1329, mentions that a certain man is suing before them by petition against the king, to oust the king of the wardship of certain lands and tenements. A writ addressed to the same on the following day refers to the cause which was pending before them by petition, ' between us and ' the petitioner for the wardship and for the marriage. The king ordered that the case be well and diligently examined, and that to one party and to the other right be quickly done

and do what is reasonable ; ibid. 10540–4,† the case of Maventus Fraunceys (above, pp. 121–3) ; R. P. ii. 33, no. 14, 4 Ed. III, for payment of goods taken for the king's use ; the endorsement orders the petitioners to go to the wardrobe, and to account there, and they are to be paid ; ibid. i. 416–18, the case of Robert Clifton (above, pp. 123–4), with a request that, in compensation for the damage sustained, a certain bailiwick be granted him ; Y. B., 22 Ed. III, 5, C. R. R., 351, m. 45,† the case of Gervais Clifton (above, pp. 124–6).

[13] See preceding note *in fine*.

[14] e.g. R. P. i. 320, no. 143 ; 394, no. 94, an allowance could not be made because the writs of *allocate* which had been obtained, apparently without an application to the king, contained the formula that the writs commanding the alleged expenditure should be collected, and the petitioner had lost the said writs. The endorsement contains an hypothetical order to the chancery to issue similar writs, above p. 168.

[15] The term ' by the king's special grace ' was sometimes applied to such cases, but we are told that that was wrong (above, pp. 136–7). If even the restitution of land which had been wrongfully seised into the king's hands were a matter of grace, how much more so would be the issue of an order to justices to proceed in a private case ! In other words, what petition would not be a petition of grace ? Clode, Petition of Right, 16–17, suggests that petitions of right in the modern sense of the word were petitions of grace, cf. Anson, ii. 152. The petition of right had nothing to do with matters of grace, in fact the name of petition of right implies a contrast with a petition of grace. So far as the administration of justice was concerned, petitions of right were dealt with on the Latin, i.e. Common Law, side of the chancery, and their records are still preserved among the *Placita in Cancellaria*, which include such other proceedings at common law as *scire facias*, proceedings upon recognizances, monstrances, traverses, &c. See also 4 Inst. 79, where the difference is very strongly emphasized.

('enfacez faire a Lune partie et a lautre hastiue acomplissement de droit') according to law and reason and the usage
of the realm ('selonc ley et reson et lusage de nostre
Royalme').[1]

But in thinking of the petition we must keep in view two
different principles, which are in force to-day as much as
they were at that time : first,[2] according to law the king
might be bound to make restitution, to pay, &c. ; secondly,
although he who had a claim against the king had also
a remedy by petition, the king could legally refuse a petition
of right ; this was a consequence of the nature of a petition.
In a sense, that would be a wrong—and the king was not
allowed to do a wrong ; it would be, in other words, an
infringement of a right which the party had, while at the
same time it would be the exercise of a right which the king
had.   But this contrast is more apparent than real.   In
ordinary circumstances [3] there was no legal way of compelling the king to accept the position of the defendant.
The wrong remained a wrong ; in practice this consideration usually outweighed all the others, and ordinarily
a petition of right would not be *prima facie* refused without
some legal justification in substance.

Procedure upon (private) petitions in parliament.[4]   The
petitions which were presented in parliament would be
received, exceptionally by the chancellor,[5] as a rule, however,
by receivers, who were appointed ordinarily at the beginning
of every parliament.[6]   The practice continued throughout

---

[1] L. T. R., roll 80, Brevia dir. Baron., Trin., m. 1 d.†

[2] Above, pp. 120 ff.

[3] See also Y. B., 19 Ed. III, 189–91, R. S., for a discussion whether the
king was allowed, by waiving in proceedings upon a petition of right
a privilege which he would enjoy if he were defendant in an ordinary suit,
to affect the rights of other parties who might insist that the petition was
abated as a writ would be.

[4] We refrain, of course, from discussing 'public' bills, Stubbs, ii.
602 ff.

[5] R. P. ii. 201, no. 4, 22 Ed. III : 'Et puis fu dit as dites Communes,
qe touz les singulers persones qe vourroient liverer Petitions en ce Parlement les ferroient liverer au Chanceller.   Et qe les Petitions touchantes
les Communes ferroient liverer au Clerc du Parlement.'

[6] In 3 Ed. II it is complained that the knights, citizens, burgesses, and
others who had come to the king's parliament by his order, and wished to
deliver petitions as to wrongs and grievances which could not be redressed

the period now under discussion.[1] The time-limit for presenting private petitions was, as a rule, rigidly fixed.[2] Early
in the reign of Edward II there set in the practice of appointing
committees, different from receivers, to try the petitions.
The first mention of such auditors or triers seems to be found
in the endorsement of a (parliamentary) petition of 1308: 'Videtur auditoribus . . . propter quod ordinatum est per consilium'; [3]
we have similar mentions from 1314.[4] The record of a
parliament of 1315 contains [5] the following statement :

'Eodem die concordatum fuit, quod Petitiones reciperentur
et expedirentur, prout ad alia Parliamenta prius fieri con-
suevit. . . . Et nominati fuerunt pro petitionibus Angliam
tangentibus recipiendis . . . et inde Proclamatio facta fuit. . . .
Die Iovis sequenti concordatum fuit quod super Peticionibus
procederetur . . . et nominati fuerunt pro Petitionibus Angliam
tangentibus audiendis et expediendis.'

This does not mean that the practice was not recent. If it
had been a well-established custom, the triers would perhaps
have been appointed at the same time as the receivers (this
was the later practice).

The new procedure differed from that of Edward I's
time ; [6] on the other hand, it was henceforth to remain the

by the common law or in any other way without a special warrant, did
not find any one to receive their petitions according to the usage of the
parliament(s) of Edward I (R. P. i. 444).

[1] e.g. ibid. i. 350 ; ii. 68, no. 1 ; 112, no. 3 ; 126, no. 3 ; 135, no. 5 ;
146, no. 3 ; 164, nos. 2–3 ; 225, no. 3 ; 236, no. 2 ; 254, nos. 4–5 ; 264,
nos. 2–3 ; 268, nos. 2–3 ; 275, nos. 2–4 ; 283, nos. 2–4 ; 289, nos. 1–4 ;
294, nos. 2–4 ; 299, nos. 3–5 ; 303, nos. 1–3 ; 309, nos. 3–4 ; 316, nos. 7–9 ;
321, nos. 3–5 ; 363, nos. 13–15).

[2] e.g. ibid. 157, no. 2 ; cf. 160, no. 11.

[3] Ibid. i. 276, no. 18.

[4] Ibid. 292, no. 15 ' Videtur auditoribus peticionum '; and see ibid. 314,
rubric, ' Responsiones Petitionum Anglie per Auditores earundem facte
in Parliamento Regis.' In 9 Ed. II the appointment of such a committee was decided upon and there is on the roll an allusion to precedent
(ibid. 350).

[5] Ibid. i. 350.

[6] Instead of the royal proclamation and the king's writ to the chancellor
and treasurer, which we have seen in the first parliament of 1305, and
instead of a writ to the receiver which we have seen later on in the same
year (above, pp. 99 ff., 104–5), it was ' agreed ', while the parliament of
1315 was already assembled, that petitions should be received and tried,
and the receivers were appointed (R. P. i. 350 ' Eodem die concordatum
fuit . . . Et nominati fuerunt ').

same, in this respect, not only throughout our period [1] but until the last quarter of the nineteenth century.[2] The auditors endorsed those petitions which ought not to have been presented in parliament, and probably a number of others which could receive *prima facie* decisions. Thus a petition of 14 Edward II [3] is endorsed as follows :

'Veniant Senescallus Hospicii Regis, et Custos Garderobe, etc. Et exponatur eis negocium contentum in Peticione, ut ipsi in hac parte tale apponant remedium quale decet et expedit pro Querentibus.'

Then the endorsement goes on :

'Postea exposito facto predicto ipsi Regi, Magister Robertus de Baldok nunciavit Auditoribus Peticionum ex parte eiusdem, quod placet eidem Regi quod iste Peticiones, et alie consimiles, liberentur Roberto de Northburgh, ut, vocatis partibus coram Senescallo Hospicii et ipso, fieri faciat tale remedium in hac parte quale de iure fuerit faciendum,' etc.

It seems that the first part of the endorsement, which simply directed that the proper officers should remedy a grievance, was decided upon by the auditors. Afterwards, doubts having apparently arisen, the affair was reported to the king, who decided that the auditors should send that petition and similar petitions before the proper officials, instead of summoning the officials (' Veniant '). Thus the endorsement by the auditors, though afterwards overruled, was originally put down by the auditors themselves.

The procedure which the auditors were to follow in 1332 was as follows : The petition which the auditors had tried and determined should be sent, under the seal of at least one of them, to the chancery (apparently in order to have writs issued) ; those petitions which were not yet determined should remain until the following day in the custody of the

---

[1] R. P. i. 365 a. (Cf. 377, no. 54; ii. 45 b ; 68, nos. 2–3 ; 113, no. 21 ; 114, nos. 28–9 ; 126, no. 3 ; 135, no. 5 ; 146–7, no. 3 ; 157, nos. 2–3 ; 164, nos. 2–3 ; 226, no. 5 ; 236, nos. 3–4 ; 254, nos. 6–7 ; 268, nos. 4–5 ; 275, nos. 5–6 ; 283, nos. 5–6 ; 289, nos. 5–6 ; 294, nos. 5–6 ; 299, nos. 6–7 ; 303, nos. 4–5 ; 309, nos. 5–6 ; 317, nos. 10–11 ; 321–2, nos. 6–7 ; 363, nos. 16–17).   [2] Anson, i. 369–70.   [3] R. P. i. 377, no. 54.

clerks, under the seals of the auditors, and thus from day to
day until they were determined. Those petitions which
ought to be tried and determined before the king should be
sent before him, and he would summon those whom he wished
to summon. Before these latter petitions were reported
on to the king, they too should remain under the seals of
the auditors.[1] Details of the procedure might, of course,
vary from time to time.

The petitions not disposed of by the auditors would be
sent before the council as a whole[2] or even before the king.[3]

[1] R. P. ii. 68, no. 3 : ' Item est acorde, qe les. Petitions qe triez serront
et terminez par les ditz Prelatz, Barons, et Justices, issint ordinez Triours,
soient mandez en Chauncellerie, souz lour Sealx, ou de deux, ou de un
de eux au meins : Et qe le remenant des Petitions demoergent souz les
Sealx des Triours en la garde des Clercs, tant qe a lendemain ; et issint de
jour en jour : Et qe les Petitions qe sont a trier et a terminer devant le
Roi, soient triez devant lui, appellez a lui tielx come il voudra. Et qe
meismes les Petitions demoergent desouz les Sealx des Auditours, ou d'ascun de eux, tant qe ils soient reportez devant le Roi.'
[2] e.g. ibid. i. 297, no. 34, 8 Ed. II, ' Videtur Consilio . . . Unde consulendum est super hoc cum Domino Rege.' Thus the case first came
before the council, and was then to be reported to the king ; ibid. 298,
'no. 38, eod. anno, ' Videbatur Consilio ' ; ibid. 304, no. 64, eod. anno,
Responsum est : Videtur Consilio . . . Postea petitione ista coram Magno
Consilio audita et intellecta . . . non est visum Consilio ' ; ibid. ii. 14,
no. 4, 2 Ed. III, a complaint that a parliamentary petition which had
been endorsed and handed in to an official who was to have brought it
to the chancery, was not as yet executed ; the endorsement is, first,
' Veigne la Bille devant le Conseil ' ; and then, ' Portet coram Consilio
Cartas et Munimenta sua ' ; ibid. 391, no. 73, in the reign of Edward III,
' Quia istud negocium videtur arduum, terminetur coram magno Consilio.'
[3] e.g. A. P. 190,† 16 Ed. II, the petition was first endorsed, ' Quia testatum est per W. de Airemynne quod terre tenementa et libertatas capta
sunt in manum Regis per speciale preceptum Regis ideo coram Rege et
magno consilio.' Then came an endorsement beginning, ' Il semble
a grant conseil nostre seigneur le Roi.' A petition in the same affair,
Chancery Inq. Post Mortem, Ed. II, file 87, m. 9–5,† is endorsed, first,
' coram Rege', with the addition ' Veniat inquisicio cum peticione et
ostendatur carta coram consilio ', then ' Porceo qe la chartre . . . est vewe
. . . auis est au conseil qe le Roi deit ouster la main sil plest a lui et pur
ce deuant le Roi '. Then comes the sentence ' Il semble lour auis couenable
sil plest au Roy '. The affair was not decided ; in the next parliament
another petition was presented, the council repeated its advice and sent
the petition ' deuant le Roi', the advice was approved by ' ces qe sunt
deputez en especial par le Roi', and the king accepted the advice and
ordered the petitioner to sue livery in chancery (ibid. m. 9–9†).
A. P. 8057, temp. Ed. III, is endorsed first, ' coram Rege', then ' Adeant
Cancellarium, Dominus enim Rex dixit ei voluntatem suam super contentis in petitione ' ; in R. P. i. 393, no. 34, 15–16 Ed. III, one of the
endorsements runs, ' Videtur Consilio quod est faciendum set tamen
coram Rege'. Cf. ibid. 436, nos. 21, 23 ; 437, no. 29 ; 439, nos. 36, 38 ;
440, no. 42. '

In such cases there is an endorsement *coram rege*, in addition to a decision *in merito*. The latter usually precedes the former, but we may well assume that it was endorsed first, and that the decision in substance was endorsed later on. Sometimes an endorsement is accompanied by the condition *s'il plest au roi*;[1] now and again we find a further endorsement stating that the king agreed.[2] We hear that certain petitions were read before the king in the parliament,[3] or before the king, prelates, earls, barons, and other magnates.[4] In 1334 we read on a petition:

' Suent devers le Roi, qar le Roi ad reserve la chose dont la Peticion fait mencion a luy mesmes.'[5]

On a petition of 1348 we read:

' Il semble au Conseil q'il fait a otroier a ceste requeste, s'il plese a nostre Seignour le Roi. Puis la Peticioun monstre au Roi, le Roi le ottreia.'[6]

It seems clear that in all such cases the auditors sent the petition either directly *coram rege*, or before the council who then decided to report the case to the king. We may assume that even cases purporting to be sent directly before the king were at first dealt with by a person, or persons, whose duty it was to prepare the case for the royal decision. In 1322 it was ordered that such petitions ' should be tried and determined before the king, after those whom the king wished to summon had been summoned '.[7] In 1340 we read of a special committee assigned to sit ' on ' the petitions endorsed *coram rege*.[8] Sometimes the first endorsement of the petition would already point to a difference between petitions which should be decided *coram rege*,[9] and those *coram rege et magno consilio*.[10]

[1] R. P. ii. 31, no. 1 ; 36, nos. 26, 28 ; 38, no. 39 ; 39, no. 40.
[2] Ibid. 41, no. 50.   [3] Ibid. 54, no. 10.   [4] Ibid. 55, nos. 12–13.
[5] Ibid. 78, no. 25.   [6] Ibid. 222, no. 66. Cf. also ibid. 217, no. 45.
[7] Ibid. 68, no. 3.
[8] ' Sont assignez de seer sur les Petitions coram Rege ' (ibid. 114, no. 29). In any case the decision seems to have been only provisional, ' if it pleased the king ' (above, n. 1, 2).
[9] e.g. ibid. 188, nos. 50, 54.
[10] e.g. ibid. 189–90, nos. 56–63, above, pp. 106–7, 159–62.

If the auditors, instead of deciding a petition, sent it before the king, or before the king and the great council, that meant delay. And this explains why in 1362 the commons complained that those assigned to hear petitions would, if anything touched the king, endorse the petitions *coram rege,* 'and thus nothing is done, nor the mischiefs and grievances redressed '. It was prayed, therefore, and the king agreed, that such petitions should be seen by the triers and answered by them on the advice of the chancellor, treasurer, and others of the council, and endorsed according to law and reason.[1]

The petitions which did not meet with *prima facie* rejection were determined in one of the four ways which we observed under Edward I.[2]

First, then, the case might be tried and decided, either before the council[3] or before the full parliament.[4]

Secondly, the petition might be decided upon hypothetically (whether by the auditors, or the council, or the king himself), and the chancery, or the exchequer, or an official, or special commissioners might be ordered to find whether the facts were as alleged.

Thus on a petition of Edward II's time we read :

' Assignentur fideles in Cancellaria ad inquirendum in presencia Custodum Episcopatus de contentis in peticione veritatem et retornetur inquisicio, et si per inquisicionem comperiatur quod peticio supponit, mandetur Custodibus quod amoueant manus etc. et exitus illi etc.'[5]

On a petition of the beginning of Edward III's reign we read :

---

[1] R. P. ii. 272, no. 31 ; the petition related only to the parliament in which it had been presented.   [2] Above, pp. 107 ff..

[3] e.g. P. C. P., f. 45, m. 30 a† ; A. P. 190† : ' Il semble a grant conseil nostre seigneur le Roy qe la dame deist estre restitute a les tenementz . . . pur ceo qe ele ad monstre chartres '; A. P. 4975, 'Pur ceo qe tesmoigne est deuant le conseil . . . sue . . . a la commune lei.'

[4] e.g. A. P. 556 a, temp. Ed. III. The endorsement begins : ' Ceste peticion fu lu par comandement nostre seignur le Roi en plein parlement deuant Prelatz Barons et touz autrez et respondue par assent et acord de touz en la manere desouth escript.' There follows a refusal of the request.

[5] A. P. 3781 ; an inquisition having confirmed the petitioners' allegations, a writ orders the keepers not to intermeddle further, and to restore the issues (the petition was the warrant for the issue of the writ), C. C. R., 17 Ed. II, 94.

'Soit ceste peticion mande en Chancellerie et le Chanceller pris a lui les Justiz et autres sages du conseil ordeinent
remedie en ce cas.'[1]

On another petition of Edward III's time we read :

'Seit ceste peticion maunde en Chauncellerie et le Chauncellier se auise de la cause de la prise . . . en la main le Roi
et si ele fut prise en la main le Roi par cause . . . et nemy
par autre seit la baillie restitute oue issues et arrerages dount
le Roi nest my seruy.'[2]

On still another :

'Soit ceste Peticion, ensemblement od l'enqueste, mande
as Tresorer et Barouns de l'Escheqer ; qe eux, regardez la
Peticion, l'enquest, et les mandements, et totes autres
evidences dont la Peticion fait mencion, lui facent fair paiement de la dette, issint q'il soit resonablement servy saunz
delay, qe pleint mes n'aveigne au Roi par cel encheson.'[3]

On a petition of 1314 :

'Responsum est per Consilium : Liberetur Petitio Thesaurario de Garderoba, et audito compoto ipsius Iohannis de
debitis in quibus Regi tenetur, et in quibus similiter Rex
tenetur eidem, de hiis que clara inventa fuerint fiat ei alloca-
tio.'[4]

Thirdly, the case might be adjourned in order to let courts
or officials supply the king or the council with evidence or
with records. Thus, an endorsement of 1322–3 runs :

'Ostendat cartam Regis in Cancellaria, qua ibidem visa

---

[1] A. P. 8074 † ; cf. A. P. 10549 † (eod. temp.).
[2] A. P. 1755 (eod. temp.) ; cf. A. P. 8084† ; R. P. ii. 399, no. 118 ;
Y. B., 12–13 Ed. III, 243, R. S.: upon petition in parliament, 'le Roy maunda
al Chaunceler qe il ferroit venir les parties, et qe il veist lour chartres, et,
sil yavoit rien en la dreyn chartre en damage de la primere, qe la chartre
en cel point fut repelle.'
[3] R. P. ii. 32, no. 9, 4 Ed. III. Endorsements with hypothetical
decisions, directing the exchequer to find out the truth, are also found in
A. P. 1784†, in the case of Maventus Fraunceys (A. P. 10540–4 ; above,
pp. 121–3) ; in A. P. 2351, 'Soit mande as Tresorer Barons et Chamberleins
del Escheker qe vewes les billes sil troessent qe la dette soit uncore due
qil lour facent paiement ou assignement Receiuantz les billes et chargeantz etc.' ; R. P. i. 372, no. 9 'Ita responsum est : Mandetur per Breve
de Magno Sigillo Thesaurario et Baronibus de Scaccario, quod contineat
effectum Petitionis, quod, visa Inquisitione capta . . . et aliis Memorandis
dictum negocium tangentibus ; Et si compertum fuerit . . . tunc ipsum
Radulphum faciant inde exonerari de xx.s. predictis sic ab eo iniuste
levatis.'   [4] Ibid. 314, no. 104.

assignentur fideles ibidem ad inquirendum de contentis in peticione et aliis etc. veritatem . . . et si per inquisicionem comperiatur quod peticio supponit . . . certioretur inde Rex.' [1]

Another one from Edward III's time :

' Avis est au Conseil, qe pur ce qe le Parlement est ore ajourne etc., q'il eit un Supersedeas tan qe au Parlement par Surte etc. et auxint Bref a Sire Will. de Claydon, de certefier sur la cause de l'amerciment ' etc. [2]

Fourthly, the petition might be sent to the king's bench, or to the chancery, or to the exchequer, or to an official, or to commissioners, with the order to do right.

Thus on a petition presented early in the reign of Edward III we find the following endorsement, referring the case to the king's bench :

' Soit cette peticion mande deuant le Roi et illoeqes apellez les serjauntz le Roi et oiez les resons pur le Roi et pur le partie, soit fait droit.' [3]

On a petition of the reign of Edward III we read :

' Soit mande Bref comprenant l'effect de ceste Peticion a les Justices en Bank le Roi, qe veue la Charte . . . et apelez devant eux la persone . . . et oiez les resones etc. facent droit.' [4]

On another petition of Edward III's reign we read :

' Soit ceste peticion maunde en Chauncellerie et illeoqes appelle le Counsail la Roigne et oiez les resones dune part et dautre soit ent outre fait droit.' [5]

On a petition of 1330 :

' Soit ceste Peticion mande en Chauncellerie, et outre soit mande a l'Escheqer, de certefier. . . . Et la Chaunceller ent certifie, soient appellez les Sages du Conseil, si mest(ier) soit, et eu lour avis outre soit fait droit.' [6]

---

[1] A. P. 4735.†
[2] R. P. ii. 409, no. 176 ; cf. i. 334–6 (8–9 Ed. II) ; 419 b ' Mittatur ista Petitio in Cancellariam, et ibidem, visis certificatione et inquisitione de quibus Peticio facit mencionem, si certificacio et inquisicio concordent transcriptis consutis huic Petitioni, remittatur Peticio cum transcriptis coram Rege et Magno Consilio.' [3] A. P. 14720 b.†
[4] R. P. ii. 378, no. 2. [5] A. P. 8051.† [6] R. P. ii. 47–8, no. 67.

On another :

' Assignentur fideles in Cancellaria, ad inquirendum . . . et retornata ibidem Inquisicione, fiat Iusticia.' [1] In the same parliament : ' Soit ceste Peticion mande as Tresorier et Barons de l'Escheker, qe eux appellez qe sont appeller, et oiez les resons, facent droit.' [2]

On a petition of the reign of Edward II :

' Mandetur Thesaurario et Baronibus quod si eis constare poterit quod responsum erat Regi de bladis quod faciant sibi inde habere solutionem et si inde non respondebatur Regi faciant venire coram eis captores bladorum et ulterius fiat iusticia.' [3]

An example of the assignment of special commissioners to hear and determine a petition will be found in 1330 :

' Assignentur certi fideles ad inquirendum super contentis in Peticione, et ad audiendum compotum eorum, et ad faciendum ulterius quod iusticia suadebit ' (not 'sua dabit ').[4]

In the same year it was decided [5] to appoint justices who would hear and determine complaints against sheriffs, coroners, undersheriffs, and others,[6] and it is to them that certain petitions were again referred with the promise that they would do right.[7]

The directions to the king's courts, or to officials or commissioners, were sometimes quite detailed. Examples, apart from those already cited, may be found in the following endorsements. In 1354 or before :

' Soient certeins gentz en queux le Roy saffie assignez denquere des articles et circumstances de ceste peticion en presence du gardeyn du dit maneret sil vorra estre come il

---

[1] R. P. ii. 49, no. 73.   [2] Ibid. 46, no. 63.
[3] A. P. 172 ; cf. A. P. E 153† ; cf. R. P. i. 292, no. 14, with reference to the justices assigned to hear and determine complaints against bailiffs and other subordinate officials in ibid. 282–3, no. 18. Another petition was endorsed in 1314 as follows : ' Responsum est per Consilium : Mittatur ista Petitio Custodi Quinque Portuum, Et mandetur ei, quod audita querela ipsius Roberti super contentis, tunc faciat sibi iustitiam, secundum Legem et Consuetudinem Portuum predictorum ' (ibid. 316, no. 115) ; still another petition of the same year : ' Responsum est per Consilium : Mandetur Senescallo quod, vocato predicto Ricardo, faciat predicte Dionisie iustitiam super contentis in Petitione ' (ibid. 320, no. 142). Cf. the endorsement in C. R., roll 351, m. 45† ; Y. B., 22 Ed. III, 3, above, p. 151.
[4] R. P. ii. 32, no. 5.   [5] Above, p. 158.   [6] R. P. ii. 60, no. 21.
[7] Ibid. 38, no. 37 ; cf. 37, no. 30, and 40, no. 45.

sera garny, et ceo qe serra troue soit returne en Chauncellerie et outre ent fait droit illeoqes, ou en autre place ou la busoigne purra estre termine par la ley.'[1]

In or before 1366 :

'Soit ceste peticion mande en Chauncellerie et illoeques veues les enquestes dount ceste peticion fait mencion et appelez les parties et oiez lour resons outre soit fait droit.'[2]

But at least in some cases the fact of an endorsement in a certain sense would take the place of a repetition of rules of procedure which everybody knew. Thus, where restitution of land had been made to a party after proceedings which had originated with a petition, the judgement given for the party against the king was afterwards challenged because the petition had prayed that the king do right and reason, and not specifically that he restore. It was held, however, that the judgement was good in law.[3] That was the first step to a recognition that an endorsement ' Let right be done ', as it came to be used later on, would be a sufficient warrant for a royal court to entertain proceedings against the king.

It seems that petitions had to be supported personally by the petitioners or their representatives. Hence, in 1340, we hear :

' Et qe ceux qe voudrent suyre lour Petitions, qe ne sont pas unqore responduz en certeyn, y soient au dit jour, et ils y serront oietz et duement responduz.'[4]

After a petition had been endorsed, it would, as a rule, be sent to the chancery.[5]

---

[1] T. S., f. 2, m. 14-1.† After the inquisition had been taken by the commissioners (appointed by letters patent m. 14-3†) and returned (m. 14-4†), the king's attorney traversed the inquisition on behalf of the king, issue was joined and the case was sent to the king's bench (m. 14-5†).
[2] Ibid., f. 5, m. 6.   [3] Y. B., 24 Ed. III, 64–5, above, p. 172.
[4] R. P. ii. 114, no. 28, 14 Ed. III.
[5] Ibid. 68, no. 3, 6 Ed. III, above, p. 191, n. 1. It seems that this record states a decision which was new, if at all, only in so far as it related to the number of seals ; that the petitions should be sent to the chancery seems to have been implied as a matter of course. In the case of the Pembroke estate (T. S. 5, m. 19–4, 41–3 Ed. III, above, p. 169, n. 2), one of the parties complained, *inter alia*, that certain proceedings in the chancery had been based on no warrant. The other party answered, ' quod omnes propartes inquisiciones processus predicti una cum recordo de assisa predicta visa fuerunt coram Cancellario et aliis de consilio Regis in parliamento iuxta indorsamentum eiusdem peticionis et abinde de assensu

Procedure on petitions outside parliament. By inference from the Ordinance of 1349[1] we assume that a petition outside parliament should be presented at the chancery,[2] or to the keeper of the privy seal; if the petition could not be decided upon without the king, the chancellor or the keeper of the privy seal would send the petition to the king together with his advice (which, however, need not be endorsed on the petition: ' una cum avisamentis suis '). The king would then signify his will to the chancellor or the keeper of the privy seal (' ut hiis inspectis ulterius prefato Cancellario seu custodi inde significemus velle nostrum '). There is no mention that this royal pleasure would be signified by way of endorsement, but we may suppose that this frequently was the way of recording the king's decision. We know of one petition which the chamberlain hesitated to accept, but, under the influence of Alice Perriers, Edward III intervened in person and declared the petition reasonable.[3]

After the king has signified his will, the petition would come back, either to the keeper of the privy seal (who would in appropriate cases send a writ of privy seal commanding e.g. the chancellor, or some other official, to execute what the king had decided), or to the chancery.[4]

If the chancery had received an endorsed petition, whether the petition had been presented in parliament or outside parliament, the proceedings would be regulated by the endorsement. In some cases all that had to be done was to send a writ to a person or an office, whether enclosing the petition[5] or rehearsing its contents.[6]

In other cases the proceedings were to take place in chancery, either at once[7] or after an inquisition had been

Cancellarii et aliorum consiliariorum predictorum per manus Cancellarii prout moris est ad faciendum partibus iuxta formam peticionis predicte iusticiam delata . . . et sic processus inde in Cancellaria factus per Warantum fiebat.'   [1] Above, p. 174.
 [2] e.g. 37 l. ass. 11, ' E. de F. que fuit ouste vient en la Chancery et monstra coment il fust ouste de la terre et pria par peticion que droit a luy fuit fait ; et sur ceo son petition fuit endorse et mande en Chauncerie.'
 [3] R. P. iii. 13, above, pp. 179, n. 3, 183, n. 2.
 [4] See note 2.   [5] e.g. R. P. ii. 32, no. 9, above, p. 194, n. 3.
 [6] e.g. R. P. i. 372, no. 9, above, p. 194, n. 3.
 [7] e.g. R. P. ii. 212, no. 27, ' Soit ceste Peticion livere en Chancellarie,

taken.[1] If in the chancery issue was joined the case would, after the first few years of Edward III, be sent to the king's bench and the issue would be tried there.[2]

Such a procedure (petition, endorsement, commission, inquisition, trial in chancery and, if necessary, in the king's bench) would hardly differ from that which was still in use in Coke's days.[3] But an inquisition was of course not necessary in every case in which a petition had been sent to the chancery with the direction to determine the case. Thus in 1366, upon petition in parliament, a *scire facias* was sent to a tenant directing him to come to the chancery and show cause why lands and tenements which he held should not be held of the petitioners, instead of the king. In the course of the proceedings the rolls of the chancery were vouched, and after they had been seen judgement was given for the king (i.e. against the petitioners).[4] Similarly, in 1369 the warden and scholars of the Hall of Valence Mary, Cambridge, petitioned the king, complaining that the king had presented to a church of which they claimed the advowson. The king delivered the petition to the chancellor : ' precipiens ei quod vocatis (partibus) predictis 'necnon iusticiariis de utroque banco et aliis de consilio domini regis ac servientibus ipsius Regis eisdem partibus plenam iusticiam fieri faciat.' On the appointed day there came the chief justices of the king's and the common bench, also other justices, the king's serjeants, and others of the king's council. The summonee knew no

et soit fait venir le dit Phelip par Brief a respoundre en Chancellerie s'il sache rien dire par quei sa Chartre de mesme l'office ne doit estre repelle, et oiez les resons des parties, soit fait droit.'
   [1] R. P. ii. 213, no. 31 : ' Soient bones gentz assignez d'enquerre sur les choses contenuz en ceste Peticion, et l'enqueste ent prise retourne en la Chauncellarie, soit fait droit.'
   [2] e.g. T. S., f. 2, m. 14–5, 29 Ed. III, above, p. 197, n. 1.
   [3] Coke, Book of Entries, 419 b–433 b.†
   [4] T. S., f. 4, m. 5 'Et super hoc rotulos Cancellarie predicte vocant ad Warantum, per quod dictum est Custodi rotulorum Cancellarie . . . quod venire faciat hic in Curia rotulos predictos. Et quia visis rotulis illis sic in Curia ostensis (follows the result of their inspection, and lack of denial on the part of the demandants), consideratum est quod seruicia penes nos (*sic*) et heredes nostros remaneant . . . et quod iidem Iohannes de Middelton et Cristiana nichil capiant per peticionem et breue sua supradicta,' above, p. 173, n. 3.

sufficient reason why the presentation should not be repealed, and the king's serjeants did not traverse the petitioners' statements. Therefore the presentation was repealed.[1]

Personal responsibility of officials. The rule remained in force [2] that acts of royal officials had to be answered for at the exchequer, because they concerned the king. An endorsement of 1314 runs :

'Responsum est : De vastis et destructionibus factis in Hospitalibus per custodes positos per Regem tempore vacacionis eorundem, sequatur versus huiusmodi custodes ad Scaccarium. De vastis et destructionibus factis per custodes positos per alios Dominos quam per Regem, sequatur versus eos per communem Legem, etc.' [3]

On the other hand, the king's order would be considered a good justification of an otherwise unlawful act.[4]

It was, of course, possible to complain by petition.[5]

But the privilege that the king's officials should not, for their official acts, be sued at common law was a privilege belonging to the king and not to the officials. If the king waived it, the officials were responsible before the ordinary courts just as other people were. The king's privilege had been waived, before the present period, in the case of sheriffs, escheators, and purveyors.[6] During the present period, a number of enactments put special stress on the responsibility of the latter.[7]

---

[1] T. S., f. 5, m. 20 ; 43 l. ass. 21; Brook, Peticion, 18 ; above, p. 173, n. 3.

[2] Above, pp. 110–11, 153.

[3] R. P. i. 303, no. 59, 8 Ed. II ; cf. ibid. 321, no. 150 ; 330–1, no. 214 : complaint against a sheriff who would not return a petty *cape* issued from the bench : 'Responsum est per commune Consilium : Sequatur ad Scaccarium versus predictum Iohannem, qui tunc fuit Vicecomes ; et ibi fiat sibi iusticia ' ; A. P. 1770†, 'Sue vers les viscontes al Eschequer ' ; cf. A. P. 8352† ; above, p. 159.

[4] Brook, Faux imprisonment, 9 ; above, pp. 129, 142.

[5] e.g. R. P. ii. 10, no. 33 ; 12, no. 33.   [6] Above, p. 111.

[7] e.g. R. P. ii. 161, no. 23 ; 241, no. 41 ; 260, no. 34 ; 342, no. 126 ; as to the required financial standing of sheriffs and other ministers, Appendix, pp. 214–15.

APPENDIX A: NOTES

I. Proceedings against the King in France in the Thirteenth Century [1]

Louis IX, in his 'Enseignements à son fils', mentions that complaints against the king are judged by his council, and advises his son to tell the judges that they should not support him more than anybody else; for then they will more boldly judge according to right and truth.[2] Records show that such suits against the king were commenced by word of mouth, and that they were discussed and decided on strictly legal grounds. There are two cases which forcibly remind us of the case of William Longsword.[3] In one of them, decided in 1260,[4] 'dominus Johannes de Valeriaco petebat a domino Rege, quod sibi restitueret seu redderet castrum Montis Regalis ... Dominus Julianus de Perona, miles, et magister Johannes de Ulliaco, responderunt e contrario, pro domino Rege, quod idem Johannes non debebat super hoc audiri, cum alias, quando eandem terram petebat a domino Rege, racione donacionis sibi facte ... racionibus suis ac racionibus domini Regis plenius intellectis, per ius dictum fuit et responsum eidem Johanni de Valeriaco quod Rex non tenebatur eidem super hoc respondere, et cecidit a petitione sua. Dominus Johannes dixit e contrario quod audiri debebat, non obstantibus premissis, secundum iura scripta, cum eciam semper fuerit protestatus quod in verbo suo posset emendare, nec de prima peticione sua subisset iudicium. . . . Tandem partes pecierunt ius super hoc sibi fieri. Quia, secundum consuetudinem Francie, ex quo aliquis cadit a peticione sua secundum unum modum petendi, postmodum, per alium modum petendi, nisi de novo emerserit, non debet audiri, iudicatum fuit concorditer ab omnibus . . . non debet super hoc audiri, nec tenetur dominus Rex eidem Johanni super hoc respondere.' It will be seen that the word *petitio* was used in the sense of an action pure and simple.[5] Moreover,

---

[1] Above, p. 38, n. 2.

[2] c. 19: 'Se aucuns a entrepris querele contre toi (por aucune injure ou por aucun tort qu'il lui soit avis que tu lui faces—this passage contained in one MS. only) soies toz jors por lui et contre toi devant ton conseil, sanz mostrer que tu aimes trop ta querele, tant que l'an sache la vérité; car cil dou conseil en porroient doter à parler contre toi, ce que tu ne dois voloir. et commande à tes juges que tu ne soies de rien sostenuz plus que uns autres, car ainsi jugeront ti conseillier plus hardiement selonc droiture et selonc verité,' Bibl. de l'Ecole des Chartres, xxxiii, 431–2.

[3] Above, pp. 36–7.   [4] Les Olim, i. 469–70.

[5] In the same sense the word was used, e.g., in a note of the acts of a parlement of 1269, ibid. 773 'Nota quod in peticione mobilium,

the king as well as the claimant asked for judgement ('partes pecierunt'). Instead of an arbitrary refusal on the part of the king to hear the application, the *exceptio rei iudicatae* was formally raised and insisted on. The court had to decide whether the king ' was bound to answer ' or not. The other case,[1] decided by the parlement in 1261, was that of the bishop of Mende. The bishop had previously asked for the restitution of certain castles. An inquisition had been taken, but it was not found ('per inquestam inde factam') that the castles belonged, as the bishop had alleged, to another castle which had been restored to the bishop as having been only allowed ('racione comodati seu precarie' —*not* preterie) to the king. Upon this inquisition, judgement had been given against the bishop and his suit had been dismissed ('iudicatum fuisset contra ipsum episcopum, nec admissa fuisset eius peticio'). In the present parliament the bishop again claimed the castles from the king ('idem episcopus, in hoc parlamento, iterum peteret a domino Rege castra predicta'). The king's 'men' asked that his suit be not admitted, since judgement had already been given against him. They would not answer further unless ordered by the court to do so. After further discussion of strictly legal points, judgement was given against the bishop.[2]

II. The Disputed Passage in Bracton, fol. 34 [3]

Woodbine's edition of Bracton [4] has established, by a comparison of nearly all the extant manuscripts, that the disputed passage can only be found, as Professor Vinogradoff had pointed out, in some manuscripts, and not necessarily the best ones. This by itself would prove

---

facta peticione in curia contra partem presentem, non recipitur rei contramandacio. Hoc dictum fuit inter Johannem de Mauquinchy, militem, et Guillotum, nepotem suum.'   [1] Les Olim, i. 507–8.
    [2] ' Gentes domini Regis dixerunt quod idem episcopus non debebat ad hec petenda admitti, secundum usus et consuetudines huius curie, cum alias eadem castra, ex eadem causa pecierit, et contrariam sentenciam reportaverit ; propter quod aliud eidem respondere nolebant nisi de iure; episcopus ad hoc respondit quod alias pecierat hec castra, ex eadem causa, set tanquam pertinencias castri Gresie, modo ea petit, racione comodati ; propter que vult ea sibi restitui, vel ius (i.e. or judgement). Tandem, partibus petentibus super hoc ius sibi reddi, quia idem episcopus eadem castra pecierat, tanquam pertinencias castri Gresie, quod quidem castrum Gresie cum pertinenciis pecierat, ratione conmodati facti domino regi Ludovico, et nunc eadem ratione commodati repetit, que causa est eadem, iudicatum fuit contra ipsum episcopum, quod non erat in peticione huiusmodi audiendus.'
    [3] Above, p. 49, n. 4, Cutbill ; 15, n. 2, 'it may be doubted whether the original text stood thus ' ; Vinogradoff, L. Q. R. i. 188 ; N. B. i. 29–33 ; cf. Bracton and Azo, 65, S. S.   [4] Woodbine, 252, 332–3.

that the passage was a marginal addition which afterwards found its way into the text. Besides, some manuscripts give the passage after what is called section 2, others after what is called section 3.[1] That the passage was written in the thirteenth century is not disputed ;[2] but doubts are continually expressed whether Bracton was its author.[3] Yet internal evidence supports the conclusion that the passage was an afterthought of the author of the whole work, or, at any rate, that both the ideas and the wording correspond with what we find elsewhere in the work.

First, as to the ideas. The passage in dispute occurs in the sixteenth chapter of the second book. The section in which it is commonly found consists of two parts. The first part, ' De chartis . . . ad iudicium', is considered authentic. We are primarily concerned with the second part, ' Item . . . stridor dentium '. This passage consists again of two parts, namely, the first part saying that nobody can be a judge concerning the king's deeds or charters,[4] and the second part from ' Sed dicere ' to the end. The sentence ' item . . . irritetur ' only continues or supplements the idea expressed in the foregoing section, namely, that if there arises a dispute as to the meaning of a charter, the king ought to be approached for his decision. This is a *maius*, necessary if we are to admit the logical justification of the *minus* contained in s. 2. Thus, the disputed passage itself contains the statement, not of one view, but of two views, each one logically excluding the other and each one expressed with emphasis. The second part, i.e. the remainder of the disputed passage, is obviously a remark on a preceding statement. What does ' sed ' mean ? If we translate it ' but ', then the whole passage right to the end would be an admission that a counter-argument was possible ; since, however, the passage begins ' sed dicere poterit ', we should be entitled to expect an answer to such an argument. Either, therefore, the whole passage is quite unfinished, or else we must take ' sed ' to mean ' although '. In this sense it would correspond with ' nisi sit qui dicat ' on fol. 171 b, to which expression attention has already been called in this connexion by Maitland.[5]

[1] Woodbine, 124, n.
[2] It can be found in Fleta ; Cutbill, 15, n. 2 ; Holdsworth, ii. 200.
[3] e.g. Woodbine, 333.
[4] The meaning appears to be ' nobody '. For, though Woodbine's edition proves that the *nec* after *item* was arbitrarily added in the three texts hitherto printed, the second *nec* can be found in almost all manuscripts which contain the passage at all, and also the subsequent *sed* points to a negative rather than a positive sentence.   [5] N.-B. i. 33.

The meaning of the passage beginning with ' sed ' is this : it could be said that, once the king's acts are considered lawful, i.e. judged and found lawful, they could as well, should occasion arise, be considered unlawful ; now, the king has superiors, namely, God and the law, and also his curia. The curia consists of his counts and barons, who are his socii, and he who has a socius has a magister ; therefore, should the king go without reins, it is their duty to impose reins on him, lest they, together with him, be without reins : for in this latter case, the subjects would complain to God, and God's punishment would come over them. In other words, if the curia did not prevent or redress the king's misdeeds, they would be responsible for such misdeeds. Therefore, it is their duty (for it is the duty of everybody to avoid deserving God's punishment) to correct the king's act, This idea was not at all unpalatable to Bracton, as witness other passages of his book ; apart from fol. 171 b,[1] it occurs on fol. 107 b [2] in the phrase beginning ' si autem fuerit insipiens, *perdet illum* '. Hence, on fol. 171 b we read ' nisi sit qui dicat quod universitas regni et baronagium suum hoc facere debeat et possit ' : the argument was obviously one of duty (' debeat '), for everybody ought to try to escape his own *corruptio* [3] and God's consequent punishment.

Secondly, as to the words of the disputed passage. The ' autem ' after ' rex ' occurs, as Woodbine's investigations [4] have shown, only in one out of all the manuscripts compared ; this makes the whole reasoning look much more like a series of arguments which ' could ' be brought forward. As to the words used in the last part of the disputed passage (' sed dicere . . . dentium '), we can once more distinguish two parts, namely, one to the effect that the curia could restrain the king, and the other, the threat of God's punishment if they did not. We shall call the second part the biblical, the first the non-biblical part. In the non-biblical part there are several expressions which Bracton used elsewhere. ' Imponere ei quod iniuriam emendet ' resembles the numerous mentions of ' emendare iniuriam, emendare factum ', e.g. on fol. 5 b, 56 b, 171 b, 172 a. That the king has God and the law as his superiors is recognized on fol. 5 b. To match the expression ' comites dicuntur quasi socii regis ', fol. 5 b has ' Comites videlicet quia a comitate sive a *societate* nomen sumpserunt, qui etiam dici possunt consules a consulendo : reges enim tales sibi *associant* ad consulendum et regendum populum dei.' These last words remind

---

[1] Above, p. 48.   [2] Above, p. 47.   [3] Br., fol. 107 b.
[4] Woodbine, 124.

us of the statement that ' qui socium habet, habet magistrum '. As to ' et ideo si rex fuerit sine fraeno, id est sine lege, debent ei fraenum apponere, nisi ipsimet fuerint cum rege sine fraeno ', the expression *fraenum* is used, in connexion with the king, in other passages of the treatise : ' Sic ergo rex ne potestas sua maneat infraenata ',[1] ' licet omnes potentia praecellat, tamen . . . ne sit ineffraenata, fraenum apponat temperantiae, et lora moderantiae, ne cum ineffraenata sit, trahatur ad iniuriam '.[2]

The biblical part is a remarkable combination of phrases : the prayer (' in chamo . . . constringe ') is taken from Ps. xxxii. 9 ; God's answer (' Vocabo . . . ignorabunt ') is a free adaptation (probably a quotation from memory) of Jer. v. 15.[3] The further words of God's threat (' quae destruet eos et evellet radices eorum de terra ') may perhaps be traced, at least partly, to Ezek. xvii. 9 (' Nonne radices eorum evellet ? ') ; and the last words of God's threat (' et a talibus iudicabuntur, quia subditos noluerunt iuste iudicare ') is probably a reminiscence of Matt. vii. 2 ' In quo iudicio iudicaveritis iudicabimini '. The final sentence, in which Bracton himself says what God would do to them (' et in fine, ligatis manibus et pedibus eorum, mittet eos in caminum ignis, et tenebras exteriores, ubi erit fletus et stridor dentium ') is composed of two passages taken from Matthew, namely, xxii. 13 ' Ligatis manibus et pedibus eius mittite eum in tenebras exteriores ', and xiii. 42 ' et mittet eos in caminum ignis. Ibi erit fletus et stridor dentium.'

The biblical passage does not stand alone in Bracton's treatise. We find a similar one, for instance, on fol. 2 a, dealing with punishment for unjust judges. Bracton considered judging to be primarily the king's business. Except for the passage on fol. 119 b, this was his view throughout.[4] The words of the passage on fol. 2 a do not point out clearly who would be punished. But the reference to kings and princes, and the statements on fol. 1 b, point to the conclusion that the king, too, though not he alone, was included in the threat : everybody who did not fulfil well his judicial duties was meant to fall under it. ' Caveat igitur quilibet.' We have here again the ' mittent eos in caminum ignis, ubi erit fletus et stridor dentium ', among a number of other biblical or quasi-biblical phrases.[5]

---

[1] Br., fol. 5 b.
[2] Ibid., fol. 107 a.
[3] Pointed out by Maitland, N.-B., i. 30.
[4] Above, pp. 48 ff.
[5] Cf. fol. 106 b, 108 a ; Holdsworth, ii. 183.

III. Proceedings against Queens and Royal Princes

The queen had had of old a privileged position. She had the right to ' the queen's gold ',[1] she had officials and a council of her own ;[2] she had certain privileges concerning purveyance, distinct from those enjoyed by the king.[3] Her privileges were, first, those of the king's wife or mother, but such as no other wife could have. She could bring an action ;[4] we find a query whether time runs against her ;[5] she could make grants, and these, once confirmed by the king, were considered, for purposes of aid to be granted from the king, the king's grants, even if the confirmation contained no clause of warranty ;[6] this might be justified on the ground that a financial loss sustained by the queen would affect the king's interests ; but then, why was the queen allowed to make grants ? Indeed, we are told that the queen's deeds were really the king's,[7] but if that was so, why were some of them confirmed by the king while others were not ?

If the queen could sue at common law, as no other feme covert could, it might be logical to allow actions against her. And there would certainly be little logical justification for not allowing actions against a queen-dowager.

Yet it is certain that at least in the period 1272-1377 the queen could not be sued by writ. In the Hautboys case,[8] in the time of Edward I, an assize of novel disseisin brought against two men who, it turned out, had committed the act in the queen's name, could not be taken, and one of the writs says that that was because the tenements were in the queen's hands and the defendants were not. *inde tenentes*.[9] The king, by consent of the queen, assigned commissioners.

We have a number of petitions against the queen or, rather, a number of complaints to the king of wrongs done by the queen's officials. The usual answer is, that the officials, or the whole council of the queen, should be called before the council of the king.

The citizens of Winchester complained that the queen's ministers did not allow them, in their account, alms paid by the city to certain

---

1 Madox, 240 ; R. P. i. 299, no. 42 ; ii. 133, no. 60.
2 Below, pp. 207–9.
3 e.g. R. P. ii. 228, no. 20 ; S. R. 365.
4 Y. B., 18 Ed. III, 1–2 ; cf. Brook, Patentes, 41.
5 Ibid., by the reporter.
6 Ibid., 9 Ed. III, 32–3 ; Fitzh., Aide del Roy, 66.
7 Y. B., 9 Ed. III, 32–3.   8 Above, p. 57.
9 T. S., f. 1, m. 1–2–2†, below, p. 239.

religious houses, although formerly those alms had been allowed from the rent paid to the king. The endorsement directs the extent which was in the wardrobe to be looked up and the queen's council to be called before that of the king.[1] In another case [2] distress by the queen's officials was complained of ; the answer was, ' Due petitiones audiantur coram toto consilio et vocentur clerici et attornati domine Regine ad ostendendum rationes suas.' A petition of the clergy and laity of the land asks the king *and queen* for remedy against unjust distress by the queen's men ; the petition has, first, an endorsement directing it to be sent to the council ; then comes the order to call Master Robert, who was in charge of the ' queen's gold ', before the council ; finally, there is the general promise that if those who feel aggrieved come they will be heard and justice done to them.[3] We may conclude that those were no cases for ordinary courts, because, though the council could decide in any case, there would have been some mention of the ordinary course.[4]

In 1336 a writ of dower was brought against the queen-dowager (Isabel). Counsel for her demurred on the ground that she was ' a person of dignity and excellence, so that she would not have to answer to a writ but suit by petition would be made to her '. The plaintiff asked for an adjournment in order that the council of the queen could ' be talked to ' in the meantime. The request was refused, probably because that would create a sort of precedent in favour of giving the plaintiff the right to be answered.[5]

Many petitions to the king, containing complaints against the queen, were sent before the queen's council ; we have many others, complaining that the queen or her council had failed to do right. In 1320 a petition was brought in parliament complaining of one who had taken, on behalf of the queen, a fish worth 13*s.* and had neither paid, nor issued a tally. The endorsement was, that the petitioners should sue before the steward and treasurer of the queen.[6] In 1334

---

[1] A. P., E 85.   [2] Ibid., E 104 ; cf. E 102, E 103.   [3] Ibid., E 158.
[4] In the time of Henry IV a judge expressed (real or feigned) astonishment at the suggestion that the queen should not be sued by a writ (Y. B., 11 Hen. IV, 67). ' Gascoigne : Ou veistes vnques le Roygne auer tiel prerogative que suit par peticion serra fait a luy ? Norton : Jeo ne parle a tiel entent que le suit serra fait al Roygne, mes al Roy. Thirning : Tout temps ad Praecipe quod reddat gise vers le Roygne, et auters maners des briefs, car el est person exempt, nient obstant le couerture. Gascoigne : Quant al brief respoygnes.'
[5] Y. B., 10 Ed. III, 26.
[6] R. P. i. 382, no. 103 ' Sequatur (*sic*) coram Senescallo et Thesaurario Domine Regine.'

tenants of an ancient demesne, then in the queen's hands, complained of distraint by an official of the queen for a rent which was
charged only by a clerical mistake. The petition is addressed to the
king and his council, but it contains an offer to prove the petitioners'
case ' par qant qe le Conseil nostre dit Dame vodra agarder '. The
petitioners were directed to sue before the queen's council for discharge.[1] In 1347 one Robert Bertrem complained that the manor of
Burton Leonard which he held from Queen Philippa in his demesne
as of fee was wrongfully taken into the queen's hands by her steward.
Robert sued by petition before the queen's council, showing his right
and praying restitution of the manor, but his right had been delayed
for three years, and still was being delayed. He prayed, therefore,
that law and reason be done him (' De quoi il prie qe Ley et reson
luy soient faites '). The answer was, that the petition be sent to the
chancery, that the queen's council be called there, and that after
hearing the reasons for both sides right be done.[2] In 1335 the men of
the forest of Macclesfield petitioned the king in parliament against the
wasteful and destructive administration of that forest, which was
held by the queen-dowager, on the part of the bailiff of Macclesfield.
The complaint included cases of interference with the administration
of justice (the bailiff would not let juries indict men before justices
in eyre). The answer was, that the petition be shown to the queen
so that she could take the advice of her council.[3] A rent was due
from one of the king's manors and had been paid always until
Edward III granted the manor to his queen Philippa : by order of
one of her councillors the rent was then withheld and when it was sued
for before the queen's council, they answered that they could not try
those things ('cestes choses') without the king. Thereupon a petition was
brought to the king, and endorsed as follows : ' Soit le Conseil Madame
la Roine apelle devant le Conseil le Roi, issint qe droit soit fait de chose
contenue en ceste Peticion.'[4] Conversely, a petition for the restitution
of church property which had been taken by Hugh Despenser the father,
had been endorsed in parliament to the effect that an inquisition be
taken and returned into the chancery, and that right be done. Yet because the manor was in the hands of the queen-dowager ' home n'ad
volu rin en frere ' (sic). Another petition was brought in parliament
and it was ordered that the inquisition come before the chancellor.[5]

---

[1] R. P. ii. 81, no. 35 : ' Seyent devers le Consail la Royne q'ils soient
deschargez.'   [2] Ibid. 192, no. 70 (i.e. A. P. 8051†).
[3] R. P. ii. 95, no. 22.   [4] Ibid. 395, no. 99.   [5] Ibid. 25, no. 33.

In some cases a complaint might, it seems, be made directly to the king, without first approaching the queen. Thus in 1321–2 men from Pevensey, within the Cinque Ports, brought a petition to the king in parliament complaining that the queen's treasurer and steward caused wrongfully the levy of tallage from which they should be free. ' And we cannot, dearest Lord, have a release of the said distraints unless we yield (' fesoms gree ') to their demands.' They asked for a remedy. The endorsement directed them to show the charters in the chancery : ' et habeant Breve Ballivis Regine super contentis in Peticione in forma debita.' [1] In a case in which apparently aid had been prayed from the queen, the king ordered the chancellor to see the records of the case, to summon the council of the queen, and if they could not show cause why judgement should be further delayed, to send to the justices a writ *de procedendo ad iudicium*. The petitioner ' ad longement suy et prie au dit Counsail la dite Roigne, de venir en la Chancellarie s'il sache rien dire pur la dite Roigne . . . Lequele Counsail n'ad mie volu faire, ne unqore ne voet . . .' ; the petitioner therefore brought another petition in 1347–8. This was sent to the chancellor with the instruction to summon the queen's council, the king's serjeants, and some of the justices, and, if nothing could be shown reasonably to prevent the judgement, or if the queen's council would not come, to send the writ *de procedendo ad iudicium*.[2]

Where a claim was raised against the queen's executors (who represented the queen [3]), because the queen had by deed promised for herself and her assignees to acquit her lessor of certain services due in respect of a manor which had been let to her, the lessor had to petition the king for a remedy against the executors. The endorsement is as follows :

' Responsum est per Consilium : Veniant querentes in Cancellariam et habeant Breve ibidem executoribus Regine ; et mittatur Petitio in Brevi ; et mandetur eisdem executoribus, quod ipsis informatis super contentis in Petitione veniant in Cancellariam et ibidem examinetur negotium : Et si inveniatur quod Regina tenetur in arreragiis contentis, referatur Regi, et Rex faciet iusticiam.' [4]

To sum up, the queen-consort as well as the queen-dowager could have, and dispose of, property separate from that of the king ; she could sue, but suit against her was possible only by petition to her or to the king. As a rule, no action at common law lay against her

---

[1] R. P. i. 405, no. 100.
[3] Holdsworth, iii. 453.
[2] Ibid. ii. 206–7, no. 7.
[4] R. P. i. 312, no. 94.

ministers for their actions undertaken on her service. If judgement in a case between private parties might affect her interests, aid would be granted from the king, who after all was her heir-prospective. And where the king had confirmed her grant, the justices would strain as far as possible their power of granting aid, by holding that the king's confirmation of the queen's gift made it the king's own gift.

It seems that at least some royal princes also enjoyed the privilege of being petitioned, and not sued at common law. Thus in 1314–15 Robert de Monhaut complained that his father had been disseised of a manor in the reign of Edward I by the justice of Chester, and that despite suits ' de temps en temps, et de Parlement en Parlement ' neither the petitioner's father nor he himself could recover his right. The endorsement (' responsum est per Consilium sic ') points out that the tenements are now by the king's gift in the hands of the king's son, Edward, earl of Chester (afterwards Edward III). Therefore the king willed (' Rex vult ') that the earl or his justice of Chester be ordered (' mandetur ') to summon those of the earl's council in those parts, and also the late justice of Chester who had committed the disseisin; all possible information as to the rights of the king and the petitioner should be collected and then a report made to the king so that the king might better and more safely answer the petition.[1] It might be argued that the case concerned the king as donor. But it is safe to assume that if the donee had been a private person, either the endorsement would have sent the petitioner ' ad communem legem ', which would enable the defendant to pray aid of the king and compel the plaintiff to sue for a *procedendo*—or else a *scire facias* might perhaps be granted to the petitioner calling upon the donee to show cause why the lands should not be seised into the king's hand and restored to the petitioner.

From the reign of Edward III we have a clearer case. The earl of Hereford and Essex petitioned the Prince of Wales for the restitution of a certain castle and lands which belonged to the heir's inheritance but were in the prince's hands. To that petition the prince answered that he held the things asked for by a gift of the king, with a clause of warranty, therefore without the king he could not answer to the petition. The earl sued to the king, who ordered the chancellor to assemble his justices and serjeants, and also other experts of the king's council, as well as of the council of the prince, to try the affair. Before them the earl showed his right to the castle and lands, in accordance with the petition, and, as he maintained,

---

[1] R. P. i. 294, no. 26.

after a due discussion ('pleynement debatue') nothing was found to bar the earl's right. Yet the earl was compelled to present another petition to the king in parliament (1347) complaining that the justices and others who were there would not do anything for him. He therefore petitioned that 'ley et resoun' be done to him. The endorsement directed the petition before the king and the Great Council.[1]

The petition to the prince obviously took the place of a suit at common law. It is true that the castle and land were situated in Wales. But it seems that, ordinarily, after the prince had failed to do right, a *scire facias* or even a suit at common law would have been admissible. Political considerations were allowed to influence the order of obtaining justice.

IV. Hypothetical Orders and Writs of Warrant

The writ was, on its face, usually a royal order. It was either hypothetical or absolute (a precept). Writs (apart from judicial writs) issued from the wardrobe, from the chancery, from the exchequer. Thus far we may say that a writ was a royal order, issued in the king's name by his ' agents ', because the king could not himself do all the work. But the writ came to be more than that. In some cases it was in fact not an order, not even a hypothetical order, but a warrant ; the officer concerned could use it, or he could leave it unused. Thus, in 1279, a writ of the great seal came to the exchequer, ordering the barons to allow in the account of a former sheriff of Cumberland, for the custody of Carlisle castle, a sum of money equal to that which used to be allowed to former sheriffs. The barons found that that allowance had amounted to £30 a year ; they considered, however, that this allowance would be too high because in peace time the sheriff could make good use of the castle and had but little work in *custodiendum* ; they postponed their decision ; afterwards they communicated with the chancellor and an allowance was made of only £10 a year.[2] The chancellor was the chief of the office which had issued the writ. But theoretically the writ had issued as the king's order, and there was no other royal order to countermand it. Later on, in the reign of Edward II and his son, it frequently happened that a writ ordered the exchequer to discharge some one, either directly, or on ascertaining the truth of certain allegations, and yet the exchequer would include in their investigation questions not mentioned in the writ.

In 1324, a writ of the great seal came to the exchequer stating that

[1] R. P. ii. 185, no. 44.   [2] L. T. R., roll 52, Communia, m. 1 d.

whereas the master of the hospital of Ospring held some land by grant of Henry III in frankalmoin, the sheriff by summons of the exchequer exacted in respect of that land an aid for the marriage of the king's eldest daughter. The charter of Henry III had been shown to the king, or, more probably, to his official in chancery ('quam inspeximus'). There was no order to investigate the case further. Since the king did not wish the master to be wronged in that respect, he ordered the treasurer and barons to let the master be quit of the aid from that land. The master came to the exchequer and, putting forward the charter of Henry III, prayed to be discharged according to the order. A search of the exchequer rolls showed that the aid was exacted in respect of the land in question. Nevertheless, the court decided upon an investigation whether the master or his predecessors did not, at the time when the aid was granted and levied, hold tenements other than those contained in the king's writ and in the charter. Eighteen men were summoned to come before the court, or else before one of the barons if he happened to come out into the county at an earlier date. The jury did not come, and there was some delay, but finally the baron sent the inquisition. On its basis it was decided ('consideratum est') that the master be discharged and go quit of the sum with which he was charged.[1] In this case the royal order was obeyed only with a modification, namely, after an additional trial of the case. Here is an example of institutionalism, so far as the issue of orders in the king's name was concerned. For the writ was probably not the king's order at all, but an act of his agents, or servants.[2]

A royal ordinance of 1274[3] directed that allowances should henceforth be viewed at the exchequer, and the treasurer and barons should then inform the chancellor of the allowances which ought to be made ('de debitis allocacionibus faciendis'); and thereupon writs of *allocate* should be made according to such certificates. Thus, the exchequer bill was to be the warrant for the chancellor, the writ a warrant for the exchequer. We find, therefore, many writs of *allocate*, directed to the exchequer, but issued at the exchequer's order. In 1291, there is an entry on the memoranda roll that the treasurer and the barons sent a 'bill' to the chancellor to let a writ of *allocate* be made for the guardian of the bishopric of Ely.[4] On the very same

---

[1] L. T. R., roll 95, Communia Recorda, Mich., m. 61 r.
[2] In some cases, at least, the order to investigate was explicitly made.
[3] Ryley, 446–7.　　　　　[4] L. T. R., roll 62, Communia, m. 8 d.†

day the writ issued, and was enrolled soon afterwards as the king's order to the barons.[1] Writs of *allocate* issued *per billam de scaccario* are found throughout our period.[2]

V. Procedure on Petitions in Sicily about the Middle of the Thirteenth Century

An ordinance of Frederick II, issued between 1242 and 1246,[3] contains minute regulations as to the way in which petitions ought to be dealt with. All petitions had to be delivered to one of the king's officials, either very early in the day, or in the evening. For this purpose he had to attend, at those times of the day, before the chancery building. Three days were assigned every week for the reading of the petitions : this should be done by the emperor's chaplain, before one or two masters assigned for this purpose, in a room from which all others had been removed. After having been read, some petitions were kept by the official in charge, while others were distributed among the notaries. An answer was written at the back of each petition. If for answering a petition the emperor's ' conscience was required ', the official in charge of the petitions was to put it in council at the feet of the imperial throne ; if the petition specially concerned the emperor, or some one of his court, then the communication was to be made to the emperor alone. His order would be communicated by the intervening official to the notaries, so that they should expedite the business. The notaries were not allowed to deal with private affairs except on having received petitions in the prescribed manner ; every notary had to swear that, as a rule, he would expedite each petition within two days after receiving it.

A somewhat later ordinance (perhaps from Manfred's reign, 1258–66 [4]) contains the rule that the *peticionarius* should receive petitions and bring them to the chancery. Those containing legal claims against the king should be dealt with by a body consisting of councillors appointed by the king, and of some (or one) of the masters of accounts (*magistri racionales*), who knew the fiscal laws, and could therefore defend and declare them. The petitions which were to be expedited *de mera conscientia regis*, were reported, in the presence of the chancellor, by the logotheta ; the same applied to all petitions referred to the king. In fine, petitions of simple justice between private men should be

---

[1] L. T. R., roll 62, Communia, m. 10 r.†
[2] e.g. ibid., roll 80, Brevia, P., m. 4 r., 6 r.
[3] Winkelmann, 736 cf. 734), no. 988, ii.   [4] Ibid. 739, no. 989.

expedited by the justiciar and the judges of the great court. We see here, in the ordinance probably issued in what were the last years of Henry III in England, a clear threefold division : petitions of justice between private parties, petitions of justice against the king, and petitions of grace. After having been read in the chancery and 'approved' (i.e. after an answer had been given in accordance with the request), the petitions were handed over to the prothonotary, who distributed them among the notaries. Then, according to the answer which had been written on the back of each petition, the notaries had to write out the letters which the endorsement ordered.

A still later ordinance (1268)[1] directs the prothonotary to receive all petitions ; those which related to justice already done ('que sapiunt expeditam iusticiam') or to the ordinary business of his office he had to decide upon himself, ordering letters to be made. Those relating to other departments he was to send to these latter. The remainder should be read on Sundays in the chancellor's house, or on Mondays or Wednesdays at the king's residence ('in hospicio regis') ; the reading should be attended by the chancellor, the prothonotary, the justiciar or his lieutenant, together with the judges, proctors, and fiscal patrons, the notary of acts, the masters of accounts, and those notaries of the chancery and of accounts who could be spared from other work ; there should also attend those others of the king's council who could come. During the reading a further distribution of petitions took place, and on the back of each petition was written the office to which the petition related. In cases of urgency, or if it seemed expedient, the chancellor or the prothonotary or others could go before the king and ask for his orders. One official was specially assigned to receive from the chancellor the petitions of grace, and to write a summary account of them in French on one roll : that roll would be read to the king in private every Friday, in the presence of those whom the king might summon.

VI. Financial Standing of Certain Ministers

The holders of certain offices were required to have a certain financial standing, or they would be disqualified. The same rule applied to jurors because, by a false verdict, they could cause much damage.

The Provisions of Oxford stipulated that sheriffs should be 'substantial men, and holders of land'.[2] In 9 Edward II it was enacted that no one should be sheriff who had not enough land in the

---

[1] Winkelmann, 740, no. 990.   Stubbs, Select Charters, 9th ed., 386.

county of his shrievalty to answer to the king and to the people, and that the hundreds should be in the charge of people who had enough land at least within the same county.[1] This latter enactment was confirmed repeatedly, e.g. in 1 Edward III,[2] 20 Edward III,[3] 21 Edward III,[4] and later on.[5] If a coroner had not enough land in the county, his office was considered vacant and a new election could be ordered.[6]

APPENDIX B :

EXTRACTS FROM DOCUMENTS AT THE PUBLIC RECORD OFFICE

An asterisk (*) means that the word is interlined.

I. From the Exchequer Memoranda, L. T. R.

The marginal notes are in quotation marks.

Roll 15 (28 Hen. III), Communia, M., m. 1 d. ' Glouc.' Prior de Derhurst venit et conqueritur quod cum Hundredum de Derhurst esset amerciatum ad quinque marcas exceptis libertatibus coram Iusticiariis ultimo Itinerantibus apud Gloucestriam, vicecomes distringit eum pro toto murdro cum ipse nichil teneat nisi medietatem ipsius Hundredi et Abbas Westmonasterii aliam medietatem. Vnde petit quod Abbas distringatur pro sua medietate desicut ipse soluit suam medietatem. quia idem Abbas ut dicit semper consueuit participare de eadem medietate in merciamento pro murdro. Et Abbas venit et dicit quod non videtur ei quod debeat. quia patet per rotulum Iusticiariorum quod totum Hundredum fuit amerciatum exceptis libertatibus et ipse habet quietanciam de murdris in eodem Hundredo per libertatem carte domini Regis. Et Prior respondit quod istud non debet ei nocere. quia licet Abbas habet quietanciam per cartas domini Regis tenentes sui de predicto Hundredo, scilicet Philippus de Coleuille et socii sui de eodem Hundredo tenentes de medietate ipsius Abbatis soluerunt xvi *sol.* viii *d.* de fine facto ante iudicium pro hoc eodem murdro sicut continetur in M. xxv in Glouc. Et Abbas dicit quod licet ille Philippus et socii sui soluerunt illam medietatem dicti murdri, hoc non fuit per ipsum Abbatem et hoc non debet ei nocere

---

[1] R. P. i. 343, no. 23 (stat. of Lincoln); 353, no. 5 ; cf. Art. Sup. Chart., c. 9.   [2] R. P. ii. 8, no. 15, and 11, no. 15.   [3] Ibid. 161, no. 22.
[4] Ibid. 168, no. 30.   [5] e.g. ibid. 238, no. 15.
[6] e.g. C. C. R., 15 Ed. I, 447 ; 19 Ed. I, 159.

quod venerunt contra libertatem carte sue eo quod habet carte (*sic*) domini Regis in qua continetur quod licet aliquis usus non fuerit ista libertate ea tamen de cetero utatur. Et Prior dicit quod carta illa non debet ei nocere in illo articulo quia ille articulus non respicit tempus preteritum set tempus futurum. Et quia istud negocium tangit cartam domini Regis, datus est dies utrique parti coram Rege apud Westmonasterium a die sancti Michaelis in i. mensem. Et Prior ponit loco suo Iohannem de Welleford et quisitum est ab Abbate si ipse petit amerciament(um) dicti murdri ad opus suum. uel ad opus hominum suorum et datus est eidem dies ad respondendum ad eundem diem.

m. 2 r. ' Norff. et Suff.' Rex vicecomiti. Monstrauit nobis Herbertus de Alenzon quod cum esset plegium Radulphi carettarii et sociotum suorum de xxx *s.* pro placito apello, tu distringis predictum Herbertum ad reddendum nobis predictos xxx *sol.* desicut predictus Radulphus et socii sui satis sufficiunt ad solucionem predictorum denariorum. Et ideo tibi precipimus quod si ita est de demanda quam facis predicto Herberto de predictis denariis ei pacem habere permittas. Et aueria etc. Et distringas predictos Radulphum et socios suos ad reddendum nobis predictos denarios. Teste ut supra (i.e. J. Francis', October 11).

m. 2 d. ' Buk. et Bed.' Mandatum est vicecomiti quod venire faciat coram Baronibus in crastino sancti Andree Saerum de Wahull ad ostendendum de quo teneat medietatem uille de Rauenestone et utrum de nobis in capite quare debeat habere scutagium suum sicut ei scutagia sua Rex concesserat an de alio de quo Rex debeat habere scutag(ium) cui non concessit scutagia sua. Et habeat ibi tunc hoc breve. Teste A. Thesaurario Sancti Pauli London. xvii die Octobris. (Follow several writs, Teste ut supra. Among them the following :)

' Somerset et Dorset.' Rex vicecomiti. Monstrauit nobis Reginaldus de Moun quod Thomas de Cirencestr. tempore quo fuit vicecomes noster in Comitatibus tuis leuauit scutagium nostrum de Kery de feodis ipsius Reginaldi. Et quia tu exigis ab eo (*sic*) Reginaldo xl *s.* de eodem scutagio, tibi precipimus quod venire facias coram predictis Baronibus in crastino sancti Martini predictum Thomam ad respondendum nobis de predictis xl *s.* et audiendum iudicium suum de hoc quod non acquietauit predictum Reginaldum ad scaccarium de predictis denariis. Et interim pacem habere permittas eidem Reginaldo de predictis xl *s.* Et aueria etc. Et habeat tunc hoc breue. Teste ut supra.

m. 3 r. ' Essex.'   Rex vicecomiti. Monstrauit nobis Abbas de Stratfford quod cum teneat in liberam et puram elemosynam terram quam Galfredus Buquent tenuit in Gingel Landr' et terram que vocatur terra Mich(aelis) et viiito acras terre cum pertinenciis in eadem villa de dono Willelmi de Ferar cuius cartam protulit coram Baronibus tu inde exigis ab eo scutagium Wasconie. Et quia iniustum est quod elemosyna distringatur cum predictus Willelmus habeat unde ei warantizet predictum donum, tibi precipimus, quod eidem Abbati de scutagio eodem pacem habere permittas. Et distringas predictum Willelmum ad reddendum nobis scutagium predictum per alias terras.   Teste ut supra (i.e. A. Thes. sancti Pauli London') . . . London, III die Nouembris).

H., m. 8 r. ' Baronibus pro Waltero filio Radulfi de la Paude.' Rex eisdem. Monstrauit nobis Walterus filius et heres Radulfi de la Paude, quod cum idem Radulfus tenuisset unam virgatam terre cum pertinenciis in . . . Walterus de Burgo tempore quo habuit custodiam dominicorum nostrorum terram illam post mortem predicti Radulphi dimisit Willelmo le Messor eo quod idem Willelmus dedit nobis ii marcas plusquam idem Walterus nobis dare uoluit. Et quia si ita est manifeste iniuriatum est eidem Waltero. vobis mandamus quod eidem Waltero de predicta virgata terre cum pertinenciis seisinam habere faciatis, dum tamen idem Walterus satisfaciat predicto Willelmo de pecunia. quam nobis dedit pro seisina predicte terra habenda et de custu suo in terra predicta rationabiliter apposito. breve est in forulo marescalli. et mandatum est vicecomiti (Hereford ').

Roll 20 (32 Hen. III), Communia, M., m. 1 r. ' De Allocacione vadii Ade Cok.' Edwardus de Westmonasterio venit coram Baronibus et precepit ex parte domini Regis alloc(are) Ade Coke singulis Annis vnam libram pro custodia foreste et domorum R. de Clarendon' quamdiu eorum custos fuerit sicut Allocatum fuit in compoto suo Anno xxx per breve regis.

m. 1 d. ' Pro eodem Iohanne.' Monstrauit Regi Iohannes de Curtenay quod dominica baronie que fuit Iohannis de Neuill cuius custodiam habet distringuntur pro feudis que tenentur de eadem Baronia. de quibus exigitur auxilium ad primogenitum filium Regis militem faciendum.   Et Ideo mandat Rex Baronibus quod si ita est et iustum sit quod predictum auxilium de feudis predictis per legem regni debeatur, tunc ipsi feoda distringi faciant pro eodem auxilio et ipsa dominica in pace dimittant.   Breve est in forulo marescalli.

Roll 30 (39 Hen. III), Communia, M., m. 3 d. ' Cantebr.' Monstrauit

Regi Radulphus de Litlinton' quod cum ipse nichil regi debeat nec aliquid veniat nomine eiusdem Radulphi in s(eruicium) regis ut dicit, Willelmus Louell' et Willelmus Wardeben' balliui vicecomitis Cantebrigiensis iniuste ab eo exigunt dimidiam marcam pro h(uius-modi). . . . Et Ideo mandatum est eidem vicecomiti quod venire faciat etc. in octabis sancti Martini predictos Willelmum et Willelmum ad ostendendum quo Ŵarranto ipsi exigunt ab eo predictos denarios. Et habeat breue.

H., m. 9 d. ' Memorandum de pisce monstruoso.' Sedente domino Rege in scaccario venit Willelmus de Dabenham senescallus episcopi Norwicensis et petiit quendam piscem magnum monstruosum captum in terra cuiusdam pueri qui est in custodia ipsius episcopi cuius antecessores semper consueverunt habere Wreckum ut dicebat, sicut liquet per inquisicionem quam dominus Rex inde fieri fecit. Et responsum fuit ei per dominum Regem quod ostenderet cartas si quas haberet per quas clamaret talem libertatem alioquin per inqui-sicionem predictam in quam Rex se non posuit nichil caperet. maxime cum nullus habeat wreckum nisi per dominum regem in terra sua. Et tunc quesitum fuit a predicto Willelmo utrum predictus piscis captus fuit super terram uel in mari, respondit quod in mari non longe a terra et quod captus fuit viuus its quod circiter sex batelli submersi fuerunt antequam posset capi. Et tunc respondit ei dominus Rex quod desicut ipse cognouit quod piscis captus fuit in mari et viuus, non* potuit* esse* wreckum* et* uoluit alias super hoc habere consideracionem. Et datus est ei dies in parliamento.

Roll 45 (56 Hen. III), Communia, M., m. 2 d. ' Baronibus pro Gode-fredo de Beumund.' Monstrauit Regi idem Godefredus de Beumund quod cum dudum teneretur Roberto de Ferrar' in centum marcis et recognicionem inde coram eisdem Baronibus fecisset et dictus Robertus teneretur Stephano de Eddeworth in quinquaginta libris per finem inde factum de quibusdam dampnis et iniuriis sibi per ipsum illatis et Rex postmodum cum terras et tenementa ac alia bona et catalla dicti Roberti per forisfacturam suam de quo nondum satisfecit cepisset in manum suam, volens indempnitati dicti Stephani prospicere mandasset predicto Godefredo quod de Centum marcis predictis quibus prefato Roberto tenebatur, solueret predicto Stephano L libras predictas sicut per litteras ipsius Regis patentes quas inde habet et quas Rex inspexit apparet. iidem Barones nichilominus ad instantiam dicti Roberti racione recognicionis predicte coram eis acte distringunt predictum Godefredum ad soluendum prefato

Roberto L libras predictas in dampnum ipsius Godefredi non modicum et grauamen. Unde cum constat Regi per litteras dicti Stephani patentes quas Rex inspexit et per confessionem eiusdem, quod predictus Godefredus soluit sibi illas L libras et omnia bona ipsius Roberti sunt adhuc in forisfactura Regis Rex mandat quod predictum Godefredum de predictis L libris pacem habere et quietum esse faciant. Et districcionem siquam eidem Godefredo fecerint relaxent. Teste etc.

Roll 47 (1 Ed. I), Communia, M., m. 1 r. ' Baronibus pro Reginaldo de Grey.' Monstrauit Regi idem Reginaldus filius et heres Iohannis de Grey quod cum dudum Rex commisisset prefato Iohanni quondam patri suo et postmodum sibi Comitatus Notingham et Derby cum pertinenciis custudiendos quamdiu Regi placuerit reddendo inde per annum ad scaccarium tantum quantum Simon de Heden' quondam vicecomes Regis eorundem comitatuum inde prius ibidem reddere consueuit, et prefatus Simon toto tempore quo habuit custodiam predictorum Comitatuum percipere consueuerit singulis annis de Communitate ville Notingham c s. et de communitate ville Derby c s. de auxilio vic(ecomitis) sicut alii vicecomites ibidem prius eos percipere consueuerunt et Rex ante commissionem suam prefatis Iohanni et Reginaldo factam de comitatibus predictis remiserit et perdonaverit hominibus villarum predictarum predictas decem libras annuas inperpetuum Ita quod prefati Iohannes et Reginaldus nichil inde receperunt tempore predicto, iidem Barones nichilominus ipsum Reginaldum de predictis decem libris annuis tam de tempore suo quam de tempore patris sui onerant in compoto suo ad scaccarium predictum Rex nolens ipsum Reginaldum in hac parte indebite onerari, mandat quod si constare poterit prefatum Simonem dictas decem libras annuas recepisse et Rex eas ante commissionem prefatis Iohanni et Reginaldo factam de Comitatibus predictis communitati villarum predictarum remisisse et predictos Iohannem et Reginaldum nichil inde tempore suo recepisse tunc ipsum Reginaldum de predictis decem libris annuis de tempore suo exonerent prout de iure fuerit faciendum.

(2 Ed. I), P., m. 8 r. ' Deuon. pro Waltero de Bathon'.' Monstrauit Regi Walterus filius et heres Walteri de Bathon' qui tenet quandam partem terrarum que fuerunt Reginaldi de Valle Torta et Radulphi de Valle Torta quod cum plures sint tenentes de eisdem terris, tu distringis ipsum ad reddendum nobis ccccxxx libras que nobis debentur de debitis eorundem Reginaldi et Radulphi. ac si non essent alii tenentes nisi ipse solus. Et Rex precipit quod si ita est tunc non distring(as) ipsum Walterum nisi pro porcione ipsum contingente de predictis denariis. Et distringas alios tenentes de eisdem terris ad reddendum Regi porcionem ipsos contingente (sic) de predictis debitis. Ita quod habeat* (sic) omnes denarios ad scaccarium in quindena sancti Iohannis Baptiste Regi soluendos et breue.

Roll 48 (3 Ed. I), Communia, H., m. 4 d. ' Memorandum de quibusdam finibus et amerciamentis concessis Magistro Willelmo de la Cornere per dominum Henricum regem.' Memorandum quod die Lune proxima post festum conuersionis sancti Pauli venit coram Baronibus de Scaccario apud Westmonasterium magister Willelmus de la Cornere et protulit coram eisdem litteras patentes domini Regis Henrici in hec verba. Henricus . . . omnibus ad quos presentes litere peruenerint salutem. Sciatis quod de finibus et amerciamentis factis coram dilecto et fideli nostro magistro Willelmo de la Cornere et sociis suis ad negoci(um) mercatorum Anglie contra Flandrenses audiendum et terminandum assignatis concessimus prefato Magistro Willelmo xxxta libras ad expensas suas quas fecit circa negocium predictum exequendum inde acquietandas de gracia nostra speciali. In cuius rei testimonium has literas nostras fieri fecimus patentes. Teste me ipso apud Messenden' xviii die Iulii anno regni nostri lvi. De quibus idem Magister recepit xxix *li.* de subscriptis videlicet de hominibus de Iernem' xx *li.* a Roberto de Basing' ciue Londoniensi iiii *li.* a Ranulpho Ricardi Londoniensi c *sol.* et sic restant reddendi eidem magistro xx *sol.*

Roll 52 (7 Ed. I), Communia, H., m. 3 d. ' Baronibus de allocacionibus vicecomitibus faciendis.' Rex mandat Baronibus quod de omnibus allocacionibus vicecomitum et aliorum ballivorum suorum quas sibi ex quacumque causa fieri petunt a predictis Baronibus per breuia regia vel sine breuibus et de omnibus causis circumstanciis et calumpniis suis, certificent ipsum dominum Regem in proximo* parliamento suo quod erit in quindena Pasche proximo futura vt tunc inde fieri faciat quod de iure fuerit faciendum. Teste . . . .

P., m. 5 r. ' Baronibus pro Abbate et conuentu de bello loco.' Rex mandat eisdem quod cum celebris memorie dominus Henricus Rex pater suus per cartam suam quam inspexit concesserit pro se et heredibus suis dilectis sibi Abbati et conuentui de bello loco Regis vnum dolium vini de recta prisa percipiendum singulis annis de dono suo et heredum suorum infra Natiuitatem domini et Purificacionem beate marie ad missas celebrandas in ecclesia sua de bello loco. Idem Rex qui nunc est ad instanciam venerabilis patris R bathonensis Wellensis episcopi Cancellarii sui concessionem predictam acceptans, et predictis Abbati et conuentui graciam uberiorem in hac parte facere volens, concessit predictis Abbati et conuentui quod decetero percipiant et habeant predictum dolium vini de recta prisa sua de anno in annum per captores vinorum suorum Suhamptone sine speciali littera uel mandato aliquo alio a se super hoc impetrando. per quod mandauit Michaeli de Columbar' captori vinorum suorum apud Suhampton. et omnibus aliis qui pro tempore fuerint captores vinorum suorum ibidem singulis annis (*sic*) habere faciant prefatis Abbati et conuentui vnum dolium vini de recta prisa sua inter vina sua de recta prisa acquietata ad celebracionem diuinorum in ecclesia sua predicta.   Et ideo mandat eisdem Baronibus quod predicto Michaeli et aliis captoribus vinorum suorum qui pro tempore fuerint ibidem et qui litteras patentes dictorum Abbatis et conuentus recepcionem predicti dolii vini testificantes sibi detulerint, debitam eisdem captoribus inde allocacionem per testimonium litterarum patencium predictorum Abbatis et conuentus singulis annis habere faciant, absque aliqua alia littera uel mandato suo eisdem Baronibus super hoc dirigendis.   Teste etc. vii die Februarii etc.

Roll 53 (7–8 Ed. I) Communia, M., m. 3 d. ' De die dato Waltero de Grauntturt.' Audito compoto Walteri de Grauntturt collectoris quintedecime tam de Comitatu Norff' quam Suff', debet xvi *li.* xiiii *s.* ii *d.* De quibus habet diem vsque ad proximum parliamentum post Pascham ut interim sibi querat allocacionem uel quod tunc soluat denarios.

Roll 61 (18 Ed. I), Communia, H., m. 7 d. ' Baronibus et Camerariis pro Paulo de Pagraue.' Monstrauit Regi Paulus de Pagraue grauiter conquerendo quod Willelmus de Raching' nuper vicecomes Norff. defunctus quedam bona et catalla ipsius Pauli ad valenciam xix marcarum apud Norwicum pro reparacione et emendacione castri Regis ibidem faciendis in presencia superuisorum operum Regis ibidem ad opus Regis cepit, nec sibi in aliquo satisfecit, Rex igitur solucionem predictam si ad hoc vt dicitur teneatur fieri volens, mandat Baronibus quod si ei (*sic*) constiterit ita esse tunc eidem Paulo solucionem debiti sui predicti fieri* faciant* prout de iure et secundum legem et consuetudinem scaccarii fuerit faciendum. Teste Rege apud Westmonasterium xxv die Ianuarii anno xviii.

m. 10 r. ' Baronibus pro Theobaldo de Verdun.' Monstrauit Regi Theobaldus de Verdun quod cum ipse omnes terras et tenementa sua in Anglia de quibus Iohannes de Verdun pater suus cuius heres ipse est fuit seisitus in dominico suo vt de feodo die quo obiit teneat et tenere clamet de Rege in capite per seruicium feodi vnius militis tantum pro omni seruicio : Barones absque mandato Regis vel alia causa rationabili ipsum distringi faciunt ad reddendum Regi pro releuio suo c *li*. pro terris et tenementis suis predictis in ipsius Theobaldi exheredacionis periculum et contra tenorem magne carte de libertatibus Anglie, in qua continetur quod Comes pro Comitatu integro c *li*. Baro pro baronia integra c marcas miles pro feodo militari integro c *s*. dent pro releuio suo. Et quia Rex non wlt quod eidem Theobaldo iniurietur in hac parte, mandat Baronibus quod scrutatis rotulis scaccarii de releuiis predicti Iohannis de Verdun et aliorum antecessorum predicti Theobaldi si inuenerint quod idem Theobaldus terras et tenementa sua cum pertinenciis in Anglia que sunt de hereditate paterna per seruicium feodi vnius militis tantum de Rege teneat in capite et tenere debeat, tunc ipsum Theobaldum ad plus Regi reddendum pro releuio suo predicto quam c *s*. non distringant vel distringi faciant, et demandam occasione vlterioris releuii ei factam relaxent eidem. Teste Rege apud Westmonasterium viii die Februarii anno xviii°.

(**Ibid.**) 'Sacramentum Iusticiariorum.' Le serement des Justices est, ke ben e lealment seruirunt le Rey en office de la Justecerie e dreiture a lur poer frunt a tuz ausibien a poures cum a riches . e ke pur hautesce, ne pur richesce, ne pur faur, ne pur haur, ne pur estat de nuly persone, ne pur ben fet, dun, ne promesse de nuly ke fet lur seit ou lur purra estre fet, autri dreiture ne desturberunt, ne respiterunt cuntre resun, e cuntre les leys de la tere. mes saunz regard de nuli estat ne de persone, lealment frunt fere dreiture a chescun sulunc les leys vsees e ke ren ne prendrunt de nuly saunz cunge le Rey. E puys graunta le Rey ke puissent prendre manger et beiure kaunt a la Jurnee. Item puys aiusta le Rey cest poinz al serment coe est asauer ke il iurrunt ke a nule malice de nul de lur cumpaynuns ne assenterunt, mes cele desturberunt en kaunt ke il purrunt. e si il ne la poent fere il le mustrunt a ceus del cunseil le Rey. e si il ne le amendent, il le mustrunt al Rey mesmes.

Roll 62 (19 Ed. I), Communia, H., m. 8 d. Memorandum quod die Lune proxima post festum Purificacionis beate Marie anno predicto Thesaurarius et Barones mandauerunt Cancellario domini Regis billam scriptam sub hac forma : Fiat breue de Allocate Nicholao Frenebaud custodi Episcopatus Eliensis de nouem libris decem et nouem solidis sex denariis pro expensis suis tempore vacacionis episcopatus predicti (follows the enumeration of other sums).

m. 10 r. 'Baronibus pro Nicholao Fermbaud.' Rex mandat Baronibus quod allocent eidem Nicholao (follows enumeration of the sums stated in the bill on m. 8 d.). Teste Rege apud Euesham iii die Februarii anno etc. xix. per billam de scaccario.

m. 11 r. 'Pro Margeria La Russe.' Concessum est Margerie La Russe quod reddat Regi xii *s.* qui Regi aretro sunt de viii *li.* i marca de quibus atterminata fuit, ad scaccarium sancti Michaelis proximo futurum.

Roll 80 (3 Ed. II), Brevia directa Baronibus, T., m. 1 d. 'Baronibus pro Henrico filio Hugonis.' Edward par la grace de dieu etc. au Tresorer et as Barons de nostre Escheker et as Justices de nostre Baunk saluz. Nous vous mandoms qe le bosoigne qe pent deuant vous par peticion entre nous et mons(ieur) Henri le fiz Hugh' sur la garde des terres et tenemenz qe furent a Jsabell de Ryhull qe tynt de nous en chief, et sur le mariage le heyr meisme cele Isabell facez bien et diligeaument examiner, et enfacez faire a Lune partie et a lautre hastiue acomplissement de droit selonc ley et reson et lusage de nostre Royalme. Done souz nostre priue seal a Kenyntone le xxii iour de May Lan de nostre regne tierz. 'Baronibus per Regem.' Edward par la grace de dieu etc. au Tresorer et as Barons de nostre Escheker et as Justices de nostre Baunk saluz. Nous auoms entenduz qe mons(ieur) Henri le fuiz Hughe suit deuaunt vous par peticion vers nous pur nous ouster de la garde des terres et tenemenz qe furent a Isabell de Ryhull qe est a die comaunde et qe tient de nous en chief et du mariage del heir meisme cele Isabell les queus garde et mariage ount este en les meynz nos Auncestres totes les foitz qe les heirs de meismes les terres et tenemenz ount este de meindre age apres la mort lour auncestres a ce qe nous auoms entenduz. Par quoy nous vous mandoms qe vous soiez tendres de nostre droit en cele partie, et facez si bien et si diligeaument examiner cele bosoigne, qe nous n'y perdoms nostre droit par defaute de bon examinement. Done souz nostre priue seal a Kenynton le xxi iour de May Lan de nostre regne tierz.

Roll 95 (18 Ed. II), Communia, Recorda, H., m. 5 d. 'Essex. De Roberto de Bures exonerando.' Robertus de Bures nuper custos terrarum forisfactarum in Comitatibus Norffolk, Suffolk et Essex venit hic modo et peciit exonerari de c *sol.* vi *d.* de quibus dicit se oneratum esse infra quandam summam* xi *li.* iii *s.* ii *d.* De quibus oneratur ut asserit super compotum suum redditum hic de exitibus manerii de Thakstede in Comitatu Essex de anno xvi Regis nunc de precio feni crescentis super lxxvii acris et tribus rodis prati in eodem manerio de Thakstede . . . asserendo totum fenum quod creuit eodem anno xvi super xxxiii acris de predictis lxxvii acris et tribus rodis per inundacionem et cretinam aquarum absque culpa seu negligencia ipsius Roberti asportatum fuisse et demersum. Ita quod nichil inde recepit eodem anno nec ob causam predictam recepisse potuit etc. Et visis compoto et particulis compoti ipsius Roberti de exitibus manerii predicti de eodem anno, compertum est quod oneratur de xl *li.* iii *s.* ii *d.* de feno lxxvii acrarum et trium rodarum prati particulariter et per diuersa precia venditi etc. Et quia non constat si fenum perueniens de predictis xxxiii acris . . . asportatum fuit per inundacionem et cretinam aquarum vt dicit, nec eciam si predictum fenum perditum fuit per culpam seu negligenciam ipsius Roberti nec ne, concordatum est quod inquiratur inde. Et Iohannes . . ., Iohannes . . ., et Simon . . . vel duo eorum assignantur ad inquirendum super premissis per litteras patentes huius scaccarii datas xv die Februarii hoc anno xviii. Et iidem Iohannes et Iohannes liberarunt hic inquisicionem coram eis super premissis captam apud Balidon' in Comitatu Essex die . . . que est inter Brevia executa pro Rege eodem anno xviii per quam compertum est (in accordance with his statements, without fault or negligence on his part) Ita quod idem Robertus nec aliquis per ipsum aliquid inde percepit seu percipere potuit occasione predicte inundacionis. Et Ideo consideratum est quod predictus Robertus exoneretur in compotum (*sic*) suo de exitibus terrarum predictarum de predictis c *s.* vi *d.* et inde quietus existat.

    m. 7 r. ' Hibernia. De prestitis allocatis Alexandro de Bykenore nuper Thesaurario Hibernie.' Memorandum quod cum Alexander de Bykenore Archiepiscopus Dublinensis nuper Thesaurarius Hibernie computasset hic modo de exitibus Thesaur(arie) predicte . . . et petiuisset allocacionem de (sums spent by order of Gaveston), Willelmus de Euerden et Willelmus de Fulburn' Barones huius scaccarii auditores compoti predicti etc. huiusmodi prestita prefato Archiepiscopo in compoto suo pro eo quod nullum Warantum a domino Rege ad hoc faciendum ostend(it), nisi tantum preceptum dicti Petri etc. penitus deallocarunt. Et super hoc prefatus Archiepiscopus peciit quod Thesaurarius et Barones desicut habuit in mandatis a domino Rege quod prefato Petro in omnibus pareret et intenderet cuius preceptis resistere non audebat, quod habita ad premissa consideracione debita, sibi prestita predicta velint allocare etc. Et deliberato inde inter Thesaurarium et Barones, videtur eis quod expedit loqui inde cum

Rege antequam fiat allocacio etc. Et facta inde domino Regi relacione per W. Exon. Episcopum Thesaurarium etc. Idem Thesaurarius presens hic modo (date) nunciauit Baronibus hic ex parte Regis quod prestita predicta allocentur prefato Alexandro in compoto suo non obstante quod non ostend(it) Warantum aliquod, nisi quod allegat preceptum dicti Petri de huiusmodi prestitis faciendis etc. Et pretextu dicti precepti Regis prestita predicta allocantur eidem Alexandro in compoto suo predicto etc.-

P., m. 9 d. ' Glouc. De quibusdam allocacionibus faciendis Gilberto Talbot custodi castri ville et Bercone Glouc.' Computante hic modo . . . Gilberto Talbot . . . idem Gilbertus peciit sibi allocari . . . Et deliberato per Barones quia non constat Curie si necessario oportebat Regem retinere ibidem unum tascatorem ad vadia Regis (and whether other things had been ad maius commodum Regis, or necessary, &c.) concordatum est quod inquiratur inde antequam fiat allocacio in premissis (two commissioners are appointed, they return an inquisition, whereupon) consideratum est quod predicte summe . . . allocentur eidem Gilberto in compoto suo predicto, pretextu Inquisicionis predicte.

Roll 102 (4 Ed. III), Communia, Recorda, M., m. 30. ' Ebor. De quibusdam allocacionibus faciendis Thome Deyuill' nuper custodi Castri et honoris de Pontefracto.' Dominus Rex mandauit hic breue suum de magno sigillo suo quod est inter Communia de anno tercio huius Regis in hec verba. Edwardus . . . Thesaurario et Baronibus suis de scaccario salutem. Monstrauit nobis dilectus nobis Thomas Deyuill, quod cum ipse tempore quo fuit custos Castri et honoris de Pontefracto ex commissione domini Edwardi nuper Regis Anglie patris nostri per preceptum eiusdem patris nostri oretenus sibi factum aliquas fecisset misas et expensas et aliquas alias pro vtilitate patris nostri pro melioracione rerum in custodia sua existencium fecisset et apposuisset, auditores tamen compoti sui ad dictum scaccarium nuper redditi de tempore predicto, dictas misas et expensas ei deallocarunt, pro eo quod speciale Warantum non habuit de eisdem quas quidem particulas sic deallocatas idem Thomas coram nobis exhibuit, supplicando vt eius indempnitati in hac parte graciose prospicere dignaremur. Nos prefatum Thomam nolentes indebite pregrauari, quandam cedulam dictas particulas deallocatas continentem vobis mittimus presentibus interclusam, mandantes, quod visis et diligenter examinatis parcellis illis, eidem Thome de misis et expensis per ipsum sic per preceptum patris nostri oretenus appositis, quatenus inde vobis constare poterit, ac eciam de aliis parcellis quas inueneritis ipsum Thomam vtiliter pro melioracione rerum in custodia sua existencium pro commodo ipsius patris nostri apposuisse sicut predictum est, debitam allocacionem fieri, necnon de parcellis illis vnde minus racionabiliter vltra id quod recipere potuit oneratus existit, exonerari faciatis prout iuxta discreciones vestras racionabiliter fore videritis faciendum. Teste me ipso apud Ebor. viii⁰ die Augusti anno regni nostri secundo. Et tenor cedule de qua fit mencio superius in breui et* que* consuitur* eidem* breui* sequitur in hec verba.

Peticiones Thome Deyuill nuper Custodis castri et honoris Pontisfracti de diuersis particulis super compotum suum coram Baronibus de scaccario domini Regis deallocatis, et eciam de diuersis particulis in compoto suo non annotatis quas posuit in expensis necessariis et. . . .

Idem Thomas petit sibi allocari xx s. deallocatos eidem super compotum suum de anno xv⁰ quos dicit se soluisse octo hominibus in circuitu parci de Rochewell per diuersa loca vigilantibus tam per noctem quam per diem, dum Rex traxit moram ibidem per xv dies, ne aliquis intraret in eundem, quolibet capiente per diem ii d. per preceptum Regis oretenus (follow many other items).

Et super hoc videlicet ad quindenam sancti Michaelis hoc anno venit hic predictus Thomas Deyuill et peciit allocacionem sibi fieri super premissis iuxta tenorem mandati Regis supradicti. Et inspectis brevi et particulis in dicta cedula contentis visum est Curie quod quoad summas in eadem cedula contentas quas dictus Thomas asserit se soluisse (follow some of the items) expediens est et necesse pro domino Rege quod inquiratur inde, et quod de aliis particulis in eadem cedula contentis habeatur deliberacio inter Thesaurarium et Barones antequam vlterius etc. Et Simon de Ba(ld)reston assignatur per litteras patentes huius scaccarii ad inquirendum super premissis (and to return the inquisition on a certain day ; the same day is given to Thomas ; the inquisition is returned). Et super hoc venit hic predictus Thomas et petit consideracionem Curie super premissis etc. Et quoad particulas in dicta cedula contentas de quibus non est inquisitum, prestitit sacramentum quod eedem particule bene et fideliter posite fuerunt per tempus predictum in melioracione rerum in custodia sua tunc existencium et alias pro commodo Regis eodem videlicet modo quo superius particulariter annotantur in processu predicto.

Et recitato coram Thesaurario et Baronibus toto processu illo, concordatum est vnanimiter quoad particulas illas de quibus non est inquisitum vt permittatur quod stetur sacramento predicti Thome in hac parte. Et consideratum est quod tam eedem particule vnde non est inquisitum que se extendunt ad xi *li*. xvii *s*. v *d*. quam alie particule in dicta Inquisicione annotate per eundem Thomam solute (follows a repetition) . . . allocentur eidem Thome in compoto suo predicto, et quod idem Thomas de aliis summis de quibus superoneratus fuit in eodem compoto suo de firmis (follow details) exoneretur et quietus existat pretextu breuis Regis, cedule, Inquisicionis, sacramenti et scrutinii predictorum.

Roll 103 (5 Ed. III), Communia, Recorda, M., m. 18. ' De Mauento Francisci de solucione sibi facienda pro bladis per ipsum prouisis ad opus Regis Edwardi patris.' Dominus Rex mandauit hic breue suum de magno sigillo quod est inter Communia de anno ivto in hec verba : Edwardus . . . Thesaurario et Baronibus ac Camerariis suis de scaccario salutem. Quandam peticionem coram nobis et consilio nostro exhibitam per Mauentum Fraunceys Mercatorem per quam idem Mauentus nobis supplicauit solucionem ei fieri de eo quod sibi debetur racione cuiusdam prouidencie in partibus Francie ad opus celebris memorie domini Edwardi . . . patris nostri facte videlicet pro octingentis quartariis frumenti de quibus extra mare extitit depredatus una cum quadam inquisicione super hoc de mandato nostro capta quam coram nobis et eodem consilio nostro venire fecimus vobis mittimus presentibus interclusam. Mandantes quod inspectis peticione, inquisicione et mandatis et aliis euidenciis de quibus peticio illa facit mencionem, vos prefate Thesaurari et Camerarii eidem Mauento celerem solucionem de eo quod sibi debetur pro bladis predictis, vel vos Thesaurari et Barones prefato Mauento competentem assignacionem de debito predicto in certo loco ubi satisfieri possit fieri faciatis. Ita quod racionabiliter sibi deseruiatur de eodem debito indilate. et quod de (*sic*) querela ad nos amplius non eueniat occasione supradicta. Teste me ipso apud Westmonasterium viii die Decembris anno regni nostri quarto. (Follows the petition and endorsement A. P. 10541, below, p. 256). Inquisicio vero super premissis et probacio dicti Mauenti inde capte fuerunt prout inseritur in eisdem apud Douorr die veneris proxima post festum sancti Matthei apostoli anno secundo Regis huius coram Willelmo de Stothon et Thoma de Fauersham assignatis per litteras Regis patentes de magno sigillo suo datas apud Notyngham xxvii die Augusti dicto anno secundo ad recipiendam probacionem dicti Mauenti tam per sacramentum proborum et legalium mercatorum mare excercencium, quam aliorum proborum et legalium hominum de libertate quinque portuum plenius veritatem, super suggestione facta domino Regi nunc (follows the petitioner's statement) in quibus quidem probacione et inquisicione continetur quod Petrus Byne mercator de societate Bardorum de Florencia, Bernardus Pouche, Stephanus Bek et Bercaldus Valent' mercatores mare excercentes venerunt coram prefatis Willelmo de Stothon et Thoma de Fauersham apud Douorr' die et anno supradictis et optulerunt se nomine dicti Mauenti omnia et singula premissa probaturos quiquidem Petrus et alii super premissis Iurati et singillatim examinati fuerunt, et dictus Petrus dicit super sacramentum suum quod cum dictus Mauentus mense Iulii ... ex certa conuencione ... per seruientes suos apud villam de sancto Waler' onerasset quandam nauem vocatam la graunde neef' de seint Walery de octingentis quartariis frumenti pro prouidencia dicti Regis Edwardi patris pro guerra sua Scocie precium cuiuslibet quartarii ibidem empti xi *s.* quam quidem nauem iidem seruientes et Nauti eiusdem nauis versus partes scocie simul cum aliis nauibus de huiusmodi prouidenciis oneratis duxisse voluissent, quidam Scacinus de Neuenpott' Flandr' vna cum aliis malefactoribus Flandr' vi armata mense et anno predictis, in costera maris iuxta Douorr' dictam nauem depredauerunt ceperunt et eandem cum predictis octingentis quartariis frumenti inuitis marenariis et seruientibus dicti Mauenti vsque Neuenpott' in Flandria abduxerunt et inde voluntatem suam fecerunt, et quod statim postmodum dictam nauem apud Neuenpott' in Flandria inuenit et peciit nomine dicti Mauenti dictum frumentum sibi liberari et quod predictus Scacinus et ceteri complices sui dictum bladum pro eo quod quandam litteram dicti Regis Edwardi patris magno sigillo suo signatam et dictam prouidenciam vt predictum est testificantem in naui predicta inuenerunt, eidem Petro liberare omnino recusarunt, set dictum bladum penes se hucusque detinet (*sic*) iniuste qui quidem omnia et singula vidit et personaliter prosecutus fuit Et quod prefati Bernardus ... Stephanus ... et Bercaldus ... super premissis separatim examinati cum predicto Petro concordant in omnibus. Et quod ad huius rei veritatem plenius scrutandam, predicti ... simul inquisierunt per sacramentum (of the jurors, who said) quod predicta nauis cum predicto blado cartata vt predictum est in eundo versus predictas partes scocie in costera maris iuxta Douorr' ... per predictum Stacinum et alios complices suos Flandr' vi armata depredata fuit et de dicta costera maris vsque Neuenport' in Flandr' abducta fuit cum octingentis quartariis frumenti precium cuiuslibet quartarii xi *s.* vt predictum est per violenciam et maliciam dictorum malefactorum et absque necligencia predictorum marinariorum seu seruiencium dicti Mauenti. ... (Follow three writs of the privy seal (in French), one of 1 Edward III and two of 2 Edward III, addressed to the treasurer and barons, directing them to finish the case. One of them culminates in the following order :) aillez auant a finale discussion faire de la busoigne solonc droit et bone equite et solonc les ditz maundemenz, et si trouez soit qe rien lui soit duz par reson de la dite purueance, adonqes de ceo qe lui sera ensi dutz lui facez auer couenable assignement. (The court asks Mauentus to show a deed as to the purveyance ; he produces a part of an indenture written in French. Thereupon) videtur Curie non esse procedendum in premissis absque maiori auisamento inde habendo, etc. (The case is again adjourned, Maventus brings a further writ of the great seal to make payment or assignment or to certify the king.) Et petit idem Mauentus quod solucio vel assignacio sibi fiat in hac parte secundum tenorem mandatorum Regis predictorum. Et inspecto processu predicto, quia in dicta Indentura continetur quod prefatus Mauentus assumpsit super se ad faciendum prouidenciam predictam et ad liberanda blada predicta apud Nouum castrum super Tynam pro certo precio in eadem Indentura contento : visum est curie quod pretextu premissorum non potest rite procedi ad huiusmodi solucionem vel assignacionem petitas faciendas. nisi Rex prefato Mauento graciam facere uoluerit specialem in hac parte. Postea fit certificacio domino Regi super premissis ex communi consilio et assensu Thesaurarii Baronum Iusticiariorum de vtroque Banco et aliorum de consilio Regis eis assidencium sicut continetur (on the Memoranda Rolls, Records, P., 6 Ed. III). Postea peticio et Inquisicio predicte remittuntur Regi in Cancellaria sua pretextu breuis de magno sigillo inter Communia (reference to Memoranda Rolls, T., 9 Ed. III).

Roll 128 (30 Ed. III), Communia, Recorda, H., m. 5. ' Suff. De Iohanne filio Edmundi de Shardelowe attachiato pro xx *li.* que fuerunt Rogeri Brom vtlagati.' Presentatum fuit per quandam Inquisicionem captam apud Hallestede in Comitatu Essex in Octabis sancti Iohannis Baptiste anno xxvii Regis nunc coram Iohanne de Coggesale tunc vicecomite Essex' et Petro Perpount quos Rex prius . . . assignauerat . . . ad omnia bona et catalla pro feloniis vtlagatorum, seu in exigendo positorum etc. in manum Regis seisienda et saluo custodienda quousque Rex aliud etc. . . . quod Rogerus Brom vtlagatus pro felonia habuit xx *li.* argenti in denariis numeratis, et quod Willelmus Blaby . . .

dictas xx *li.* cepit apud Alfhamstoun et illas abstulit de garcione dicti
Rogeri, easque misit Iohanni filio Edmundi de Shardelowe qui manet
in Comitatu Suffolk' qui iuste debet inde domino Regi respondere, per
quod idem Iohannes filius Edmundi attachiatus fuit essendi hic modo
in Crastino sancti Hillarii, ad respondendum et satisfaciendum Regi
de predictis xx *li.* (He does not come then, but comes by his attorney
on February 9) et dicit quod de predictis xx *li.* vel aliqua parte inde
versus Regem onerari non debet, dicit enim quod xx *li.* vel aliqua alia
bona seu catalla que fuerunt dicti Rogeri Brom . . . ad manus ipsius
Iohannis filii Edmundi nunquam deuenerunt. Et hoc pretendit
verificare prout Curia etc. Super quo videtur Curie expediens esse
quod prefatus Willelmus de Blaby veniat antequam vlterius, etc.
(After several adjournments William comes in person, John comes by
his attorney. John repeats his statement and his offer to aver.) Et
predictus Willelmus . . . dicit pro se quod de predictis xx *li.* vel aliqua
parte inde versus Regem onerari non debet, Dicit enim quod non cepit
apud Alfhamstoun xx *li.* de denariis prefati Rogeri Brom, nec eas
abstulit de garcione ipsius Rogeri Brom, neque eas misit prefato
Iohanni . . . prout ei imponitur, nec xx *li.* vel aliqua alia bona seu
catalla que fuerunt dicti Rogeri . . . ad manus ipsius Willelmi . . .
deuenerunt. Et hoc pretendit verificare prout Curia etc. Ideo
inquiratur super premissis, videlicet in dicto Comitatu Suff' inter
Regem et dictum Iohannem . . . et in dicto Comitatu Essex inter
Regem et dictum Willelmum. . . . Et preceptum est vicecomitibus
Suff' et Essex per duo breuia separatim quod vterque eorum venire
faciat hic (date) xviii etc. de villa . . . quorum quilibet etc. et qui
nulla affinitate etc. ad recognoscendum etc. (The same day given to
John and William ; they came and the sheriffs returned the writs
and the panels, but the jurors did not come.) Et concordatum est
quod Willelmus de Stowe Cancellarius et Robertus de Charwelton'
clericus placitorum huius scaccarii assignentur per duas commis-
siones sub sigillo huius scaccarii ad inquirendum separatim super
premissis (one in each county ; their commissions are made and they
are to return the inquisitions on a certain date ; to each sheriff is
sent an order to distrain the jurors ; on the given day John and
William came by their attorneys, Robert had returned an inquisition
taken in the presence of John, the jurors in which say that none of the
money had ever been had or received by John). Requisiti vlterius pro
Rege si predictus Rogerus die quo vtlagatus fuit habuit huiusmodi
xx *li.* vel aliqua bona seu catalla : dicunt quod non. (William de

Stowe has also returned an inquisition, taken in the presence of William of Blaby, the jurors in which say that William did not take, carry off, or have the money.) Ideo predicti Iohannes filius Edmundi de Shardlowe et Willelmus de Blaby quoad premissa sine die. . . . **Roll 141 (43 Ed. III) Communia, Recorda, T., m. 9 d.** ' Somerset De exonerando Abbatem sancti Augustini Bristoll' de vna parcella prati vocati . . . acquisita sine licencia Regis.' Presentatum fuit per quandam Inquisicionem captam . . . coram . . . Escaetore domini Regis . . . quod Abbas sancti Augustini Bristoll' appropriauit sibi unam parcellam prati . . . Et modo . . . venit hic prefatus Abbas per . . . attornatum suum Et dicit quod predictus Escaetor pratum predictum virtute Inquisicionis predicte cepit in manum domini Regis. Et hoc minus iuste. Quia dicit quod predecessores sui . . . ante publicacionem statuti de terris et tenementis ad manum mortuam non ponendis editi tenuerunt pratum predictum Et hoc pretendit verificare etc. per quod petit quod manus Regis inde ammoueantur et pratum illud sibi restitui etc. Ad quod dictum est pro Rege quod idem Abbas appropriauit sibi pratum illud diu post statutum predictum sine licencia domini Regis etc. Et hoc petitur pro domino Rege quod inquiratur etc. Et predictus Abbas dicit vt prius Et petit similiter Ideo fiat inde Inquisicio. Et preceptum est vicecomiti. (There come manucaptores, therefore) pretextu manucapcionis illius mandatum est Escaetori . . . quod manum Regis inde ammoueat et illud pratum Abbati liberet habendum in forma predicta. (After several adjournments due to absence of jurors, commissioners are appointed and an inquisition is taken before them, and returned.) Ideo consideratum est quod manus Regis de prato predicto ammoveantur Et quod non fiat execucio versus predictum Abbatem pro exitibus prati illius pretextu premissorum. Salua semper accione Regis si alias inde loqui voluerit.

II. From the Chancery Diplomatic Documents

No. 673. Peticiones Philippi de Vlecot.

[1] Petit quod habeat literas vicecomiti Notingham quod liberet eidem Philippo filiam que fuit Galfredi Luterell.[1]

[2] Petit ut Dominus Rex scribat Domino Dunelmensi Episcopo quod

---

[1] This part is written above the heading ' Peticiones . . .' on the right half of the membrane. It is in two lines, the second of which is a prolongation of the heading.   [2] Here a cross has been made.

non trahat eum In causam coram Decano, Preceptore, et Magistro
Godardo Canonico Eboracensibus pro exitibus Iudiciorum* Epi-
scopatus Dunelmensis de* tempore Custodie sue. quam diu fuerit
In seruicio domini Regis In Pictauia per preceptum domini Regis.

¹ Item petit ut scribat eisdem Iudicibus ne procedant In causam
predictam quamdiu etc.

¹ Item petit ut scribat eidem domino Dunelmensi quod non molestet
coram predictis Iudicibus Rogerum de Berneuat clericum fr' Ecclesia
de Witebernia contra rationabile donum Domini Iohannis bone
memorie quondam Regis quam diu idem Rogerus fuerit In seruicium
ipsius philippi agentis In partibus Pictauie pro expedicione negociorum
domini Regis.

¹ Item petit ut scribat (supradictis) Iudicibus quod non procedatur
In causam predictam contra eundem Rogerum quamdiu ut supra.

¹ Item petit ut conferantur sibi littere domini Regis quod In prima
Eskaeta perficiatur ei excambium terre que fuit E. de vesci ad valorem
(se)scentarum librarum per annum. Pro . . . Regis quas idem philippus
modo habet In excambium predictum.

Item petit ut dominus Rex per litteras suas seueraliter* capiat
In proteccionem omnes terras, wardas, Res et possessiones eiusdem
Phillippi (*sic*) et suorum . . . quamdiu fuerit in seruicio domini Regis.²

III. From the Close Rolls

Cl. 88 (55 Hen. III), m. 5 r. Rex . . . Iohanni de Reygate Eschaetori
suo vltra Trentam salutem. Cum Alanus filius Bartholomei de
Wymtona quoddam molendinum ad ventum in solo suo proprio
infra dominicum nostrum de Ragenhil leuari fecisset, et vos perpen-
dentes idem molendinum ad dampnum et ad nocumentum nostrum
ibidem esse constructum molendinum illud in manum nostram
cepissetis, et nos super premissis certiorari et prefato Alano iusticiam
facere volentes : vobis mandassemus quod diligenter inquireretis
vtrum molendinum predictum ad dampnum seu ad nocumentum
nostrum ibidem esset constructum necne (and if so, what was the
damage, &c.), ac vos inquisicionem illam feceritis per quam accepimus

---

¹ Here a cross has been made.
² Letters patent of September 16, 1220, announcing the appointment
of Philip to be steward of Poitou and Gascony, C. P. R., 4 Hen. III, 249.
Letters of protection, addressed to the sheriffs of Essex, Kent, Nottingham,
Warwick, Leicester, Lincoln, and York, ibid. 252.

quod dictum molendinum constructum est in proprio solo ipsius Alani et infra dominicum nostrum predictum et quod non est ad dampnum et nocumentum nostrum (follow details). nos eidem Alano in hac parte iniuriari nolentes. vobis mandamus quod predictum molendinum vna cum omnibus inde perceptis a tempore capcionis eiusdem in manum nostram : prefato Alano restituatis. Tenendum eodem modo quo illud tenuit ante capcionem eiusdem in manum nostram. Teste Rege apud Westmonasterium iiii^to die Iunii. . . .

Cl. 89 (56 Hen. III), m. 5 d. Rex Galfredo de Neyuille Iusticiario forreste sue vltra Trentam salutem. Cum dilectus et fidelis noster Willelmus de Leyburne filius et heres Rogeri de Leyburne dudum defuncto eodem Rogero ad nos et consilium nostrum accessisset et nos rogasset vt de balliua forreste nostre de Inglewode de qua predictus Rogerus fuit seisitus vt de feodo die quo obiit plenariam seisinam habere faceremus, et nos eandem seisinam eidem Willelmo concessissemus et vobis pluries mandeuerimus quod eidem Willelmo seisinam illam sine dilacione habere faceretis Ita tamen quod si aliquis versus eum de eadem balliua loqui voluerit stet inde recto in curia nostra secundum legem et consuetudinem regni nostri (and he had not obeyed the order, de quo miramur quam plurimum et mouemur—he is directed to carry out the former orders). Teste Rege apud sanctum Edmundum ii die Septembris.

m. 13 r. Rex . . . Ricardo de Cliff' Eschaetori suo citra Trentam salutem. Cum Rogerus de Leyburn, qui de nobis tenuit in capite diem clauserit extremum propter quod Alyanora de vallibus Comitissa Winton' que fuit vxor prefati Rogeri ad nos venit et nos instanter rogauit vt dotem suam ipsam contingentem de terris et tenementis que fuerunt predicti Rogeri quondam viri sui sibi assignari faceremus secundum legem et consuetudinem regni nostri, volentes quod dos illa sibi per nos assignetur : vobis mandamus (to make without delay an extent of all lands and tenements of which Roger had died seised, &c.) et extentam illam inde distincte et aperte factam nobis sub sigillo vestro et sigillis eorum per quos facta fuerit sine dilacione mittatis et hoc breue. Ceterum, cum prefata Comitissa nobis intimauerit, quod vos tam terras et tenementa que ipsa tenuit de hereditate sua propria et in dotem de terris et tenementis que fuerunt R. de Quency quondam Comitis Winton' et Willelmi de vallibus quondam virorum suorum quam terras et tenementa illa de quibus prefatus Rogerus quondam vir suus et ipsa coniunctim feoffati fuerunt, cepistis in manum nostram et ea sibi detinetis, Nolentes eidem Comi-

tisse in hac parte iniuriari : vobis mandamus quod omnes terras et
tenementa que sunt de hereditate prefate Comitisse, et eciam de dote
sua de hereditate predictorum Comitis et Willelmi quondam virorum
suorum sibi sine dilacione restituatis. Ceterum, quia predicta Comitissa
dicit, quod predictus Rogerus et ipsa coniunctim feoffati fuerunt (of
certain manors and lands) prout in cartis inde confectis plenius continetur, volentes super hoc adplenum certiorari vobis mandamus,
quod executoribus prefati Rogeri scire faciatis ex parte nostra quod
inspeccionem cartarum predictarum et transcriptum earundem vobis
habere faciant, et vos nichilominus per sacramentum proborum et
legalium hominum de balliua vestra per quos etc. veritatem premissorum plenius inquiratis. Et inquisicionem illam et transcriptum
cartarum illarum nobis habere faciatis sub sigillo vestro. Ita quod
sibi in hac parte fieri faciamus quod de iure fuerit faciendum. Prouiso
quod omnia bona et catalla in terris et tenementis predictis existencia
salus custodiantur in manu nostra quousque executores predicti ad
nos venerint et securitatem nobis fecerint de debitis que idem Rogerus
nobis debuit reddendis ad scaccarium nostrum. Teste Rege apud
Westmonasterium secundo die Nouembris. . . .

(**Ibid.**) Rex vicecomiti Sussex. salutem. Monstrauit nobis Robertus
de Cokefende quod cum occasione transgressionum impositarum
Matheo de Knelle tempore turbacionis habite in regno nostro dedis-
semus et concessissemus prefato Roberto viginti libratar' (*sic*) terre
de terris et tenementis ipsius Mathei in Comitatu Sussexe habend(as)
in forma dicti de Kenilleworth, et idem Robertus seisinam predictarum
viginti libratarum terre habuisset in forma eiusdem dicti ex assignacione dilecti et fidelis nostri Simonis de Kreye et sociorum suorum
Iusticiariorum ad placita predicta assignatorum, ac idem Matheus
nuper ad Curiam nostram veniens nobis intimasset, quod paratus fuit
ostendere, quod toto tempore turbacionis predicte fuit in seruicio
dilecti et fidelis nostri G. de Clare Comitis Glouc. et Hertf. et sibi
in adiutorium ad deliberacionem Edwardi primogeniti nostri, et quod
fidei nostre et ipsius filii nostri toto tempore turbacionis predicte
constanter adhesit, propter quod prefatum Comitem venire fecimus
coram nobis, qui in presencia nostra et consilii nostri constitutus,
dixit, quod non constabat ei certitudinaliter, si prefatus Matheus
secum uel sibi in adiutorium in premissis extitisset, et quod veritatem
premissorum per balliuos et fideles suos ad plenum inquireret, et nos
super hoc per prefatum Matheum per litteras suas patentes redderet
cerciores, ob quod prefato Matheo diem prefiximus coram nobis in

octabis sancti Michaelis proximo preteritis, ita quod tunc haberet Warantum suum a prefato Comite coram nobis, si illud a prefato Comite infra diem illum perquirere posset, Idem Matheus nec ad diem illum venit, nec Warantum suum habuit ad diem supradictum, propter quod de consilio nostro iam prouidimus, quod prefatus Robertus eandem seisinam de predictis viginti libratis terre habeat, quam prius inde habuit ex assignacione Iusticiariorum predictorum in forma predicta.   Ita tamen quod predictus Robertus non faciat vastum vendicionem uel exilium de domibus boscis ad terras et tenementa illa spectantibus, saluo iure predicti Mathei in forma dicti predicti cum inde loqui voluerit Et ideo tibi precipimus, quod prefato Roberto de predictis viginti libratis terre seisinam suam rehabere facias et ipsum in seisina illa manuteneatis (sic), protegas et defendas. Teste Rege apud Westmonasterium primo die Nouembris.

Cl. 97 (8 Ed. I), m. 6 d. in cedula. Pur ceo ke la gent / ke venent al parlement le Rey sunt souent deslaez e desturbez a grant greuance de eus e de la curt. par la multitudine des peticions ke sunt botez de vant le Rey de queus le* plus porreient estre espleytez par Chanceler e par Justices : purveu est ke tutes les peticions ke tuchent le sel veynent primes al chanceler / e ceus ke tuchent le escheker / veynent al escheker. e ceus ke tuchent Justices v ley de terre / veinent a Justises e ceus ke tuchent Juerie veynent a Justices de la Juerie.   E si les bosoings seent si granz. vsi de grace' ke le Chanceler e s[1] ces autres ne le pussent fere sanz le Rey ꞓ dunkes il les porterunt par lur mein demeine de vant le Rey. pur sauer ent sa volente.   [2]Ensi qe nule peticion ne li[3] veigne deuaunt le roi e son conseil, si* fors par les mains des auauntdiz chaunceller e les autres chef ministres.[2] Ensi ke le Rey e sun consail pussent sanz charge de autre bosoingnes entendre a grosses bosoingnes de sun reaume e de ses foreines terres.

IV. From the Parliamentary and Council Proceedings, Chancery

f. 1, m. 14 (marked ' 8 Ed. I ') (?). Auis est a Crestiene des Marreis, ke ele ne deit perdre le fe ne* la* garde* de la moite de Hasteldone dont Gileberd le Franceis morut vestu et seisi. et son heir de denz age, tut ne vst ele homage ne seruice del auantdit Gileberd ne son lessur auant de li.   Pur ce ke Gileberd fu feffe de vn Richard de

---

[1] This is struck out.
[2] This is not a part of the original text, but is written below the whole text and is referred to by insertion marks //.
[3] This is struck out, and directly before *li* is a blot.

vernon, ne pas demy au deuant sa mort. Le quel Richard tynt lauantdite meite de Hasteldene de Peres de Anesi ky heir feffa Crestiene des Marreis del autre meite. k' est chef de Hasteldene od tutes les apurtenances. Fesant le seruice de vn cheualer et rendant quatre mars par an pur tut le maner, a sire Willam de Fiennes, et sire Willam, ket le seruice al Rey.

(Below). Iudicium redditum contra ipsam, concordatum est per consilium et omnes Iusticiarios. et Ideo ipsa eat sine die. et rex retineat custodiam etc.

f. 44, m. 1 (marked ' temp. Hen. III ') (?). Sire Adam del noef Marche fu endette en Juwerie a Londres pur la quel dette il engaia sun manoir de Carleton' el conte de Nichole. E la moite del manoir de Benetle el conte de Euerwik. E puis vint sire Adam e feoffa Johan lefferon de Londres del vn manoir e del autre tut vtre forspris Les auoisons des Eglises, par bone chartre si com il piert par le transescrit del vne chartre que ci est atachee. que parelt de Carleton', e autre tele est cele de La moite de Benetle. Des quels manoirs Johan recut seisine pleinere, e fist coe que a seignur append. remua baillifs, e autres i mist. prist feutes e homages. plez e purchaz. e tint sa seysine bone e entiere. de La chandeillur desques a La seint Johan. e en cele seysine morut. vient nostre seignur le Roys e troue Johan endetee en Juwerie. e cels meismes manoirs obligez a la dette en sun nun par chartres que sont trouees en wiche de Juwerie e entre en La terre com en sun gage. e tient e prent les espleiz. vint sire Adam e fet entendant al conseil nostre seignur le Reis e aillure par la ou il uolu que Johan ni out onques fie ne franc tenement ne dreit. e si nul out, quil lui rendi sus en sa vie e riens nad . . . Johan . . . valoir lui peusse fors sun simple dit. e sur ceo procura un equeste deuant les Barons del eschekere e La fist venir . . . com il voleit pur engetir le Reis de sun gaie e esloigner les heirs de lur dreit. mes cele enqueste ne passa mie. Car les . . . tuz Jurs e chalengerent lestat le Reis e le Lur. E Ja le plus tart si ont les Barons donee la seisine a sire Adam . . . manoirs. mes les heire ne seuent si come est de par le Reys ou nun. Dont il crient merci a nostre seignur le Reis, quil eit pitie de eus quil puissent auoir e fere coe que a eus apent. issi que le Reis ne seit perdaunt ne eus desherites.

m. 22 (between 1300 and 1307). Item idem Iohannes de* Sheffeld* recepit de denariis domini Regis C Libras et* amplius* de quibus compotum suum nondum reddidit pro prouidenciis faciendis versus . . . domini Regis tempore quo dominus Iohannes de Warenna

comes Surr' locum domini Regis in Scocia tenebat domino Rege in
Flandria tunc existente unde petit idem Iohannes quod per consilium
ordinetur ubi compotus ille reddi debeat, quia sepius optulit se reddere
compotum predictum in Garderoba et Scaccario et semper recusant
admittere et ignorant ubi compotus ille reddi debeat. Et in vltimo
parliamento Westmonasterii consimilem petitionem liberauit idem
Iohannes domini Regis consilio. et sic erat ei responsum. Adeat
garderobam et computet ibidem, et de eo quod dominus Rex sibi
teneatur Thesaurarius garderobe assignabit ei certum terminum
solucionis. qui quidem Iohannes ad Thesaurarium garderobe cum
petitione sua accessit prout per consilium erat ordinatum et predictus
Thesaurarius recusavit et ad huc recusat recipere compotum predictum. et dicit quod de compoto predicto non vult se intromittere.
Vnde petit dictus Iohannes quod ad huc distincte per consilium ordinetur ubi compotus ille reddi debeat. et quod vadia sua sibi allocentur.
cum misis rationabilibus et . . . predictum compotum tangentibus.
Cxviii Libre xiii solidi iiii denarii. Peticio Iohannis de Sheffeld clerici.
    (Endorsement) Habeat breve Thesaurario et Baronibus de Scaccario,
quod audiant compotum suum.

f. 45, m. 30 a. A nostre seignur le Roi et son conseille prie William
de Bayouse qe come il ad suwy par peticion en parlement de xii mees.
xxiiii . . . de terre et xxiiii acres de pree od les appurtenaunces en
Helperby en le Counte Deuerwyk queux Thomas de Bayouse dona
a J . . . Bavour . . . et a Johanne sa femme et a les heirs de lour corps
issantz, et qex apres la mort mesme ceux Johan et Johanne a . . . com
fitz et heir les ditz Johan et Johanne deueraient descender, et queux
tenementz apres la mort le dit Johan furent pris en . . . le Roi come
forfaitz par tant qil fu dit qe une Begon de Bayouse son frere fuist
arette del aherdaunce Roger de Morti[1] . . . de la Meer, et qe le dit
William nauereit accioun viuant le dit Begon', Ou le dit William ad
proue suffisamment en Banc le Roi par agard de la Court qe le dit
Begon' morust a Rome et feust enterre en lieu certeyn, et ia soit ceo
qe nulle rene poet estre troue ne par enquestes prises deuant Leschetour, ne par enquestes prises en Bank le Roi ne par serche feit . . .
Chauncellerie nen Lescheqer, pur le Roi a forbarrer le dit William de
sa accion et qe le droit le dit William . . . et duement soit troue come
apiert plus playnement par le tenour de record et procees de tote la
bosoigne cosue . . . peticioun nepurquant les Justices du dite Banke
le Roi delayent daler au jugement pur le dit William a son graunt . . .

----

[1] This helps in establishing the time.

et desheritesoun dount il prie pur dieu remedie et brief as Justices
daler au iugement solonc lay et custume du r. . . .
(Endorsement) Coram Rege et Magno consilio.

Pur ceo qe le tenour del record et proces du plee dont mencion
est faite en ceste peticion ad este vewe et examine deuant le conseil
et auis est au conseil qe la mort le dit Begon est sufficiamment prove :
soit mande a les Justices assignez a tenir les plees le Roi qils aillent
au jugement en le dit plee nient contreesteant qe les tenementz sont
en la main le Roi (and notwithstanding the preceding writ).

V. From the Placita in Cancellaria, Tower Series

f. 1, m. 1-2-9. Writ of novel disseisin (dated December 18, 1273)
for Bartholomew de Redham against Robert Baynard and others.

m. 1-2-8. Assize taken between the same at Aylesham, January 2,
1281.

m. 1-2-7. Writ (dated July 16, 1293) directed to the treasurer
and chamberlains, returnable before Hugh de Cressingham and
William de Carleton who are assigned ' ad inquirendum per sacramentum proborum et legalium hominum . . . eiectionis predicte
veritatem et ad plenam et celerem iusticiam predictis Roberto et
Willelmo inde secundum legem et consuetudinem regni nostri faciendam '. The facts will appear from the writ on m. 2.

m. 1-2-2. Writ (dated March 26, 1300) per peticionem de Consilio
to the sheriff of Norfolk. ' Monstrauit nobis Robertus filius Roberti
Baynard quod cum Bartholomeus de Redham dudum in Curia nostra
coram nobis apud Aylesham recuperasset seisinam suam versus pre--
dictum Robertus Baynard patrem predicti Roberti filii Roberti cuius
heres ipse est de quodam tenemento in magna Hauboys per recognicionem assise nove disseisine, ibi inde inter eos capte. quod quidem tenementum ad manus Alianore quondam regine Anglie consortis nostre
ex dimissione predicti Bartholomei postmodum deuenit, idem Bartholomeus et Walterus Buckeskyn tunc balliuus eiusdem regine et
ministri sui prefatum Robertum Baynard de decem mesuagiis, septem
cotagiis, quadraginta et sex acris terre, tribus acris prati, quatuor
acris alneti, tribus solidatis redditus, et tercia parte vnius mesuagii
cum pertinenciis in Magna Hauboys simul cum quindecim villanis et
catallis et sequelis suis et cum libera piscaria in (aq)ua de Magna
Hauboys, et tribus mesuagiis, triginta acris terre et quinque solidatis
redditus cum pertinenciis in Scothowe que villa in breui nostro
originali non continebatur, ultra recognicionem Iuratorum assise

predicte, pretextu iudicii redditi in assisa predicta eiecerunt et ea in manu prefate regine tenuerunt ; Et insuper iidem Bartholomeus et Walterus Willelmum Baynard, de vno mesuagio, quater viginti acris terre, decem acris prati et sex solidatis redditus cum pertinenciis in magna Hauboys pretextu iudicii predicti, licet in hac parte non disseisitorem nec in assisa predicta tanquam disseisitor nominatus extiterit, similiter eiecerunt et ea in manibus predicte Regine tenuerunt, propter quod iidem Robertus et Willelmus quasdam assisas noue disseisine . . . per breuia nostra versus prefatos Bartholomeum et Walterum de predictis tenementis de quibus fuerunt sic eiecti arrainiauerunt, ad quarum assisarum capcionem procedi non potuit, pro eo quod tenementa illa fuerunt in manu prefate Regine, et predicti Bartholomeus et Walterus inde* tenentes non fuerunt, per quod de assensu et voluntate predicte Regine assignauimus [1] Iohannem de Luuetot, et Willelmum de Sancto Claro, ad inquirendum ˙per sacramentum proborum et legalium hominum de comitatu Norff. tam illorum videlicet qui in assisis predictis Iuratores fuerunt, quam aliorum proborum et legalium hominum de eodem comitatu neutri parcium suspectorum, per quos rei veritas melius sciri posset, de quibus terris et tenementis, post iudicium in assisa noue disseisine coram nobis apud Aylesham vt predictum est redditum tam predictus Robertus quam prefatus Willelmus taliter eiecti fuerunt, et in quibus villis, et per quos et a quo tempore, et in cuius vel quorum manibus terre vel tenementa illa existerent, et qualiter, et quo modo, et que dampna et iacturas iidem Robertus et Willelmus occasione eieccionis huiusmodi sustinuerunt, et ad loquelam illam audiendam et terminandam, secundum legem et consuetudinem regni nostri ; super quo nichil adhuc actum est. ac postmodum loco predictorum Iohannis et Willelmi assignauimus Willelmum de Syselham, Hugonem de Cressingham et . . . Willelmum de Carleton', ad inquirendum per sacramentum proborum et legalium hominum de Comitatu predicto (follows repetition of the formula), super premissis omnibus plenius veritatem, et ad plenam et celerem iusticiam inde partibus predictis faciendam, secundum legem et consuetudinem regni nostri, super quo similiter nichil adhuc actum est, in ipsorum Roberti et Willelmi dispendium non modicum et grauamen et exheredacionis periculum manifestum. Nos igitur super premissis cerciorari et partibus predictis plenam et celerem iusticiam fieri volentes in hac parte assignauimus (follows a mention of the assignment of commissioners—see m. 1–2–6—and

[1] C. P. R., 13 Ed. I, 207.

the order to send jurors before the commissioners and to notify the heirs of Bartholomew).

m. 1-2-6. Letters patent, C. P. R., 28 Ed. I, 547 (March 26, 1300) per peticionem de Consilio, directing John de Butteturte, William de Carleton and William Haward quod ad certos diem et locum quos vos omnes, vel duo vestrum ad hoc prouideritis, quam uis terre ille et tenementa post mortem predicte consortis nostre in manu nostra existunt, non omittatis quin inquisicionem predictam faciatis, et eam distincte et aperte factam nobis sub sigillis vestris necnon sub sigillis eorum per quos facta fuerit distincte et aperte sine dilacione mittatis et hoc breue. The facts are as stated on m. 1-2-2.

m. 1-2-1. Writ of privy seal (dated August 25, 1300) to the chancellor. Nous vous mandoms que endroit de Lenqueste que touche Robert le fuiz Robert Baygnard, et que est retornee en nostre Chauncellerie, a ce que nous auoms entendu tot touche il nous ou autre, faciez faire execucion pur le dit Robert endue manere, et sicomme vous verrez que reison soit selonc le purport de meisme Le enqueste. Done souz nostre priue seal a Douzquer le xxv. iour daugst . Lan de nostre regne vint et oytisme.

m. 1-2-5. A nostre seynur le Rey e a sun conseyl prient les heirs sire Bertelmeu de Redham ke a ou la . . . Reyne la companye ke mort est auoyt ocupe par ses balifs x. li. de terre en Hautboys del heritage les auantdiz heirs e le Rey de sa grace granta al dereyn parlement a Westm. a les heirs avantdiz e a Robert Banyard ke en mesme la manere se pleynt de partie de terre de sun heritage coupe en la vile auantdite . Bref de enqueste deuant sire Johan Butteturte e sire Williame Howard ke lendemeyn de cluse Pasche dereyn passe pristrent le auantdit enqueste a Leu en le Conte de Norff. et trouerent lur sugestion vereye e pus retornerent le enqueste en chauncelerie . par quey les heirs auantdiz prient la grace nostre seynur le Rey ke il pur le alme la Reyne lur face restitucion des avantdiz x. li. de terre. Norff.[1]

---

[1] The writ here asked for issued on February 13, 1301 (C. C. R., 29 Ed. I, 425–6), by petition and inquisition returned from the council. It was directed to the keeper of the manor of Aylesham and ordered him to deliver a messuage, 130 acres of land, 20 acres of meadow and pasture, and 5s. of rent, to the heirs of Bartholomew de Redham, because the king had learned by inquisition that bailiffs of the late queen had ejected Bartholomew from the premises.

In favour of Robert, son of Robert Baynard, there is one writ dated January 14, 1301 (ibid. 415–16), issued by privy seal (probably that on m. 1-2-1) to the keeper of the king's manor of Burgh, to restore

(Endorsement) tradatur [1] cancellario [1] videantur inquisiciones.

Quibus visis et examinatis compertum est quod tenementa in Inquisicione contenta occupabantur super patrem heredum querencium. Ideo tenementa illa restituantur eisdem heredibus.

f. 2, m. 14–1. A nostre seignur le Roi et a son conseil monstre Isabelle qe fust la femme Godefray de Hunstone qe come mons. Johan de Glammorgand pier meisme ceste Isabelle dona et lessa le maneret de Broke en lisle de Wyght oue les appurtenantz qest de petite value, a les auantditz Godefray et Isabelle a auoir et tenir a terme de lour deux vies, la reuersioun regardaunt a lauandit mons. Johan et a ses heirs. Et puis lauandit Godefray par sa faite aliena lauandit maneret oue les appurtenantz a Johan de Stopham et a Johan atte Felde en fee, par quele feffement ils furent seisitz. sur queux Thomas haket a qi nostre seignur le Roi auoit done et graunte la garde et le mariage Nichol fitz et heir le dit mons. Johan de Glammorgand. aparceyuant ceste alienacioun estre faite a la deseritisaunz le dit Nichol, come en le droit Nichol le dit Thomas entra et ousta es auanditz Johan de Stopham et Johan atte Felde. Et puis nostre seignur le Roi et son conseil furent apris qe le dit Nichol fust soot et Idiot par la Idiocie de qi nostre seignur le Roi seisit mesme le maneret oue les appurtenantz, et issint par la cause auandit vncore est seisi. Prie la dite Isabelle a la treshaut excellencee nostre seignur le Roi qe lui pleise de sa grace en oeure de charite graunter a faire restitucioun du dit maneret a lauandite Isabelle a tenir a terme de sa vie, de puis qe la dite alienacioun ce fist en temps qele esteit couert de Baroun sauntz son assent.

(Endorsement) Soient certeins gentz en queux le Roi saffie assignez denquere des articles et circumstances de ceste peticion en presence du gardeyn du dit maneret sil vorra estre come il sera garny, et ceo qe sera troue soit returne en Chauncellerie et outre ent fait droit illeoqes, ou en autre place ou la busoigne purra estre termine par la ley.

m. 14–3. Letters patent, dated July 18, 1354, per peticionem de parliamento, to William de Shareshulle, John de Stonford, and Richard de Birtone. Supplicauit nobis Isabella que fuit vxor Gode-

to Robert the lands which had been taken into the king's hands by reason of the queen's death and which had been appropriated to the use of the queen after Robert had been ejected from them beyond the recognition of the original assise ; and there is another writ to the same keeper, dated February 13, 1301 (C. C. R., 29 Ed. I, 425), by petition and inquisition returned from the council, ordering him not to intermeddle further with other tenements which had been occupied in the same way.

[1] This is struck out.

fredi de Hunstone per peticionem suam coram nobis et consilio nostro
in vltimo parliamento nostro apud Westmonasterium tento exhibitam
(follows the statement of the contents of the petition on m. 14–1).
Nos volentes tam pro nobis quam pro prefata Isabella in hac parte
fieri quod est iustum, assignauimus vos et duos vestrum ad inquirendum per sacramentum (follows the usual formula, and then a repetition
of the allegations), et si (the manor) in manu nostra ea de causa adhuc
existat, an alia, et si alia tunc qua, quo titulo qualiter et quo modo
et si prefata Isabella ius quod habuit in manerio predicto alicui concesserit, remiserit aut relaxauerit, seu statum suum inde in aliquo
mutuauerit (sic) necne, et si sic tunc cui vel quibus quo tempore
qualiter et quo modo, et si manerium predictum teneatur de nobis in
capite, an de alio (and as to the form of tenure) et de omnibus aliis
articulis et circumstanciis premissa tangentibus. plenius veritatem.
They are ordered to take the inquisition, et eam distincte et aperte
factam nobis in Cancellaria nostra sub sigillis vestris vel duorum
vestrum et sigillis eorum per quos facta fuerit sine dilacione mittatis.

m. 14–4. The inquisition confirming the statements contained in
the petition ; the petitioner has not alienated the manor, granted,
released, or changed her estate. The inquisition is endorsed : Istud
negocium mittitur coram Rege pro alia inquisicione inde capienda
prout patet in Recordo huic inquisicioni consuto.

m. 14–5. Placita in Cancellaria domini Regis de Crastino
Ascensionis domini anno regni eiusdem domini Regis videlicet
Anglie xxix et Francie xvi⁰. Compertum est per inquisicionem
per Iohannem de Stonford et Ricardum de Birtone de mandato Regis
captam et in Cancellaria sua retornatam quod (follow the contents
of the inquisition as on m. 14–4) per quod prefata Isabella petit
manerium predictum extra manus nostras sibi liberari tenendum ad
terminum vite sue iuxta formam doni sibi et prefato Godefredo (follow
details) inde facti.

Et Iohannes de Gaunt, qui sequitur pro domino Rege dicit quod
predictus Iohannes de Glamorgan fuit seisitus in dominico suo vt de
feodo die quo obiit de manerio supradicto, absque eo quod idem
Iohannes manerium predictum in* vita* sua* prefatis Godefredo et
Isabelle in forma predicta dedit et concessit. Et hoc petit quod*
inquiratur pro domino Rege per patriam. Et predicta Isabella dicit
quod predictus Iohannes manerium predictum cum* pertinenciis*
per quatuordecim annos ante mortem suam dedit et concessit prefatis
Godefredo et Isabelle ad terminum vite eorundem sicut predictum

est. et quod ipsi virtute doni predicti inde seisiti fuerunt in forma
supradicta, et hoc pretendit verificare per patriam. Et super hoc
datus est dies prefate Isabelle coram Rege in xva sancte Trinitatis
vbicumque etc. ad faciendum et recipiendum quod iustum fuerit in
premissis. Et preceptum est vicecomiti . . . quod venire faciat coram
Rege ad diem predictum (twenty-four jurors).

f. 2, m. 23–2. PLACITA IN CANCELLARIA REGIS APUD WESTMONASTE-
RIUM IN OCTABIS SANCTE TRINITATIS ANNO REGNI REGIS EDWARDI
TERCII POST CONQUESTUM TRICESIMO SECUNDO ET FRANCIE XIX^{no}.
Dominus Rex mandauit breve suum in hec verba : Edwardus . . . vicecomiti Hertf. salutem. Ex parte Iohannis Else nobis est ostensum quod
cum ipse arrainiauerit coram nobis quandam iuratam viginti et quatuor
militum ad conuincendum iuratores assise noue disseisine que inter
ipsum Iohannem et quosdam alios in brevi nostro originali contentos
summonita fuit et capta apud villam de sancto Albano de tenementis
in eadem villa, et pro eo quod dicti iuratores qui de dicta villa fuerunt,
protulerunt coram nobis ad diem ad iuratam illam capiendam ordinatum quandam cartam domini Henrici quondam Regis Anglie proaui
nostri per quam concessum est hominibus dicte ville quod ipsi non
implacitent nec implacitentur per breue nostrum de attincta de
aliquo libero tenemento in eadem villa Iusticiarii nostri ad placita
coram nobis tenenda assignati, dictam cartam allocauerint et vlterius
ad dictam iuratam capiendam procedere distulerunt, dictique iuratores
postmodum vt predictus Iohannes magis grauaretur, ipsum de re-
disseisina maliciose conuinci et carcerali custodie in villa predicta
mancipari fecerint, in ipsius Iohannis dampnum non modicum et
exheredacionem manifestam, super quo nobis supplicauit vt cum dicta
concessio sit legi communi regni nostri Anglie expresse contraria et in
preiudicium rei publice facta. ipseque virtute allocacionis eiusdem carte
sic facte, ab execucione iuris in hac parte preter (sui) defectum abiudi-
catus existat, velimus sibi super hoc de remedio prouideri. Nos
volentes singulis de dicto regno nostro fieri quod est iustum, tibi
precipimus quod scire facias probis hominibus et communitati ville
predicte quod ipsi per duos vel tres de probioribus et discrecioribus
hominibus eiusdem ville sint coram nobis et consilio nostro in Cancellaria nostra apud Westmonasterium in Octabis sancte Trinitatis
proxime futuris cum carta predicta ostensuri si quid pro se habeant
vel dicere sciant, quare dicta carta sic in preiudicium legis communis
et rei publice facta quo ad illam clausulam reuocari non debeat et
ad faciendum vlterius et recipiendum quod considerari contigerit in

hac parte, et quod prefatum Iohannem habeant tunc ibidem ad informandum nos super negocio predicto. Et habeas ibi nomina illorum per quos eis scire feceris et hoc breve. Teste me ipso apud Westmonasterium quarto die Maii Anno regni nostri Anglie tricesimo secundo. . . .[1] (Follows the sheriff's return.) Et ad eundem diem comparentes in Cancellaria predicta pro predictis hominibus et communitate dicte ville de Sancto Albano, Willelmus Atte Halle, Philippus de Westwyk, Willelmus Hostiller et Iohannes Atte Grene de eadem villa de Sancto Albano dicunt, quod dicti homines et communitas de sancto Albano non habent nec habere possunt corpus predicti Iohannis Else eo quod ipse non fuit nec est in custodia sua (nec) per eos captus aut detentus, sed quod Abbas de Sancto Albano habet custodiam gaole in villa predicta, in qua dictus Iohannes detentus existit, vnde non intendunt quod ipsi de corpore eiusdem Iohannis habendo hic ad presens non (sic) debent onerari. et quoad cartam dicti Regis Henrici proferunt hic eandem cartam, asserentes, quod quodlibet breue de Scire facias de sui natura de aliquo recordo warantizari debet et exquo non constat Curie, nec de recordo et processu habitis in Banco domini Regis de quibus in dicto breui fit mencio, nec de aliquo alio recordo vnde breve istud emana(uit) non habent necesse ad istud breve respondere et petunt iudicium de breui et si Curia considerauerit parati sunt respondere. Et dictum est eis quod respondeant. qui dicunt quod (tempore dicti) domini Henrici Regis nullum breue de attincta nisi solummodo super Iurata assise noue disseisine, et hoc de gracia Regis speciali, et non de iure communi currebat, nec quod dictus rex Henricus tempore suo (quando breuia de) attinctis denegasset, contra ius commune et legem terre tunc currentem fecisset, eo quod breuia huiusmodi postmodum per diuersa statuta tam tempore domini Edwardi Regis aui quam tempore domini (Edwardi Regis patris Regis) nunc et hoc semper de gracia Regis concessa fuerunt, et quod ea racione qua dicta brevia de attincta negare, eadem racione ne currerent concedere potuit, nec per aliquod statutum libertates ante (hec) tempora per Reges concesse reuocantur, immo tam in magna carta quam in singulis aliis statutis omnes libertates expresse et precipue Ciuitatibus et Burgis saluantur ; et ex quo dictus dominus Henricus Rex tempore suo huiusmodi libertates et maxime ville Burgo et Ciuitati concedere posset, quod non potest esse vel dici preiudiciale communitati regni nec alicui alii nisi solummodo Burgo ville aut

---

[1] Supplemented from m. 23–1, which adds, ' per consilium '.

Ciuitati cui talis libertas cum volenti non fit iniuria concessa fuerit, que quidem concessio sic per dictum Dominum Henricum regem facta per cartas domini Edwardi aui et domini Edwardi patris domini (nostri) Regis (et eciam per cartam) eiusdem Regis nunc quam hic ostendunt approbate sunt et confirmate, et eciam dicta libertas per iudicium in Banco domini Regis redditum, eis adiudicatur et allocatur prout per dictum Breve de scire facias supponitur, non intendunt quod dicta carta dicti Henrici* Regis eis sic facta debeat reuocari. Et Iohannes Gaunt qui sequitur pro domino Rege dicit quod cum per cartam dicti Regis Henrici prefatis hominibus dicte ville de sancto Albano sit concessum, quod ipsi non implacitent nec implacitentur per brevia de attincta de aliquo libero tenemento in eadem villa, supponitur manifeste quod communis lex tunc et antea fuit in regno Anglie, quia aliter concessio illa nullius fuisset effectus, et dicit quod tempore dicti Regis Henrici ante confeccionem carte predicte et post attincte iuratarum de gracia regis tam in breuibus assise nove disseisine quam in aliis breuibus concesse fuerunt, Et licet in diuersis statutis postmodum editis contineatur quod attincte de gracia Regis concedi debent, per hoc non probatur quod antea non fuit communis lex in Anglia, set quod huiusmodi attincte ex maiori gracia Regis fuerunt concedende, et cum communis lex per quam singuli de regno regi debent, per cartam dicti regis Henrici restringatur, quominus rectum cursum suum in iusticia facienda habere valeat, euidenter apparet, quod carta illa in perturbacionem iuris et legis communis, (quod) Rex facere non potuit, facta erat, et sic eadem carta, vt legi communi contraria reuocabilis et adnullabilis existat, et ex quo carta illa ea de causa nullius posset esse vigoris confirmaciones predicte super hoc facte stare non possunt, nec effectum capere aliqualem, et eciam in diuersis statutis in parliamentis postmodum tentis de assensu tam baronum comitum (ciuitatum) et villarum quam aliorum de communitate regni Anglie contineatur, quod attincte de gracia Regis generaliter absque excepcione loci concedantur et sic per homines ville de sancto Albano inter alios de regno affirmatur, breuia de attincta per totum regnum tam in vno loco quam in alio iacere et esse concedenda, per quod petit pro domino Rege quod carta illa revocetur et adnulletur. Et quia (manifeste) apparet quod carta predicta est legi communi contraria et si huiusmodi carte concederentur et in suo robore starent, conquerentes a remedio iuris excluderentur, quod in exheredacionem totius communitatis regni cederet : videtur Iusticiariis et aliis peritis de consilio Regis quod carta predicta est omnino

reuocanda et adnullanda, per quod consideratum est quod carta illa*
revocetur et adnulletur (Et in) Cancellaria cancelletur et dampnetur
et perdat vim et vigorem imperpetuum.

m. 23-3. Letters patent of Henry III (C. P. R., 37 Hen. III, 195)
with a note that they are cancelled : Concessimus pro nobis et heredibus nostris probis hominibus ville Sancti Albani quod decetero non
implacitent uel implacitentur per breue nostrum de Attincta de
aliquo tenemento in predicta villa. Nec quod huiusmodi breue currat
decetero in predicta villa de aliquo tenemento eiusdem ville : sicut
nec in aliis Burgis regni nostri. For the confirmations see C. P. R.,
9 Ed. II, 454, and ibid., 1 Ed. III, 94 ; for the exemplification, ibid.,
29 Ed. III, 174.

f. 4, m. 19-1. Writ of *scire facias*, dated August 1, 1366. Certain
lands and tenements have been taken into the king's hands by virtue
of an inquisition taken *ex officio* by an escheator and showing alienation into mortmain, and the king has granted them to William of
Debenham for the term of William's life. The writ directs a notifica-
tion to the escheator and William to come to the chancery on October 6
to show cause ' quare manum nostram de terris et tenementis predictis
sic in manum nostram ex causa predicta captis et eidem Willelmo de*
Debenham* concessis amouere et ea prefatis Simoni Ricardo et Ricardo
restituere non debeamus, et ad faciendum vlterius et recipiendum
quod Curia nostra considerauerit in premissis '.

m. 19-2 (no heading). Ad quem diem partes predicte venerunt et
predictus Willelmus dicit quod ipse tenet tenementa predicta ad
terminum vite sue ex concessione domini Regis reuersione inde post
mortem ipsius Willelmi ad prefatum dominum Regem et heredes
suos spectante sine quo idem Willelmus in placito illo (non) potest
respondere et profert hic in Curia litteras domini Regis patentes hoc
testificantes petendo auxilium de domino Rege quod ei concessum est.
Et (super) hoc datus est dies partibus predictis in Octabis sancti
Martini in eodem statu quo nunc est. Et interim loquendum est
cum domino Rege. Ad quem diem predicti Simon Ricardus et
Ricardus non prosequebantur breue suum predictum.

VI. From the Ancient Petitions

A. P. 40. A nostre seignur le Roi et a son consail monstre Cecille
de Beauchamp, come ele esteit seisie de sa purpartie del Counte de
Kyldar en Irlaunde et res . . . les issues et profitz a ly afferauntz du

dit Counte a lescheker de Duuelyn, quele purpartie nostre seignur le Rey ad done a sire Thomas le fitz Johan[1] Counte de Kyldar ensemblement oue tut le Counte auauntdit. Le quel sire Thomas la dite purpartie tient deuers ly par la reison del doun auantdit, nyent suffraunt la dite Cecille ne ses atturnez rien prendre ne auer a grant damage et desheritaunce de ly. Dount ele prie a nostre seignur le Rey qe luy pleise pur deu la regarder de la value en Engleterre si luy plest, en terre ou en autre chose issi qil ne seit encheison de sa desheritaunce que deu defende. Et amounte par an la dite purpartie par estente sicome Roulle de Chauncelerie tesmoigne : vi. *li*. iii *s*. vii *d*. o͞b. q̄ᵃ.

(Endorsement) Soit mostree a sir Roger de Mortemer et il charge de feire ent dreit.

A. P. 190. A nostre seignur le Roi et a son conseil monstre Isabel qe fuit la femme Hugh Bardolf, qe come ele, a la suyte Robert Lewer, seit ouste de son franc tenement en Empnesworth et Warbleyton, dont lui son piere et son Aiel ount este seisziz peisiblement par les chartres le Roi Henri et le Roi Eduard piere nostre seignur le Roi qore est, par colour dune enqueste en la chauncellerie retourne qe Leschetour de cea Trente fist par un bref qe le dit Robert purchacea en la chauncellerie par fausse suggestion, nouncontrestant qe la dite Isabel vint en la dite Chauncellerie et son droit et ses chartres auantdites illoeqes demoustra en anientissant la dite fause suggestion enpriant qele ne fuit point oustee de son dit franc tenement, par vertue de la dite enqueste issi prise volentriement au nient sachant contre forme de droit et les usages du Roialme, par qei la dite Court apres ses resons monstreez illoeqes entenduz, de la ousteer de son dit franc tenement de tout sursist iesqes tant qe le dit Robert suy un bref de souz le priue seal le Roi as gardeins de son grant seal qem la feist ousteer et seisir les ditz tenementz en la mein nostre seignur le Roi nouncontrestant les chartres des Rois et les resons la dite Isabel auantdites : parmi quele lettre du dit priue seal, issi bref hors de la dite chauncellerie a leschetour pur prendre les ditz tenementz en la mein le Roi contre la fourme de la grant chartre des fraunchises qe contient qe le Roi ne nul de ses ministres nen ouste nul home de son franc tenement, saunz resnable Jugement e ensement contre la forme des ordenances qe le Roi ad accepte qe voillent qe commun dreit ne seit point defait ne delaye par lettre du dit priue seal e que si riens soit par la dite lettre contre dreiture et commune ley de terre fait :

---

[1] John the son of Thomas was second earl of Kildare from 1316 till 1328.

et qe riens ne vaille et qe pur nul soit eu. Et ia soit ceo qe la dite Isabel eit touz jours puis siue en la dite chauncellerie e a drein parlement,[1] enrequeraunt qe sur ceo dreit lui feust fait, et uncore nul dreit ne lui est point sur ceo fait. Si prie el derechief a nostre seignur le Roi et a son conseil qe lui plese commander qe droit et reson sur ceo lui soit fait, issi qe ele soit resaise solom les leys et les usages du Roialme et le tort a lui fait redrescie solom la tenour de la grant Chartre et des ordenances auantdites.[2]

(Endorsement) Il semble a grant conseil nostre seigneur le Roy qe la dame deist estre restitute a les tenementz contenuz en la peticioun. sauff toutz iours a nostre seigneur le Rey son dreit qant il enuodra parler. pur ceo qe ele ad monstre chartres des ancestres nostre seigneur le Roy de mesmes les tenementz donez a les ancestres la dite dame, par les queles chartres luy et ses ancestres ont este seisi des ditz tenementz, e ne mie par purprise.

(Below) Quia testatum est per W. de Airemynne quod terre, tenementa et libertates capta sunt in manum Regis per speciale preceptum Regis ideo coram Rege et magno consilio.

A. P. 1770. A nostre seignur le Roy mustrent ses liges gentz de Brideport qe Johan Erlegh viconte de Dorsete ensemblement oue toutz les autres vicontes qe ont este en Dorsete pus la mort la Reyne Margarete lour vnt denee pleyn retourn de bref parūt qe unke pus qe la seygnerie acrust a nostre seignur le Roy apres la mort la dite Reyne pleyn retorn de bref ne purreint auer come auaunt dont eus prient remedie.[3]

(Endorsement) Sue vers les viscontes al Escheqer.

A. P. 1784. A nostre seignur le Roi et a son Consail prie Richard de Bromlegh executour Gilbert de Bromlegh nadguers vitailler de Cardoyl. qe come nostre seignur le Roi piere nostre seignur le Roi qe or est soit tenuz a dit Gilbert en quatre vintz et xi *li.* xvi *s.* xi *d.* ob. sicome il piert par une bille de la Garderobe qe le dit executour poet monstrer. pleise a vostre seignurie comaunder bref de la chauncelrie a Tressorer

---

[1] R. P. i. 388, no. 6 (15–16 Ed. II).

[2] The present petition was probably brought in a parliament of 16 Ed. II. After Isabel's death (16 Ed. II) the case was taken up by her son Thomas ; the king's final order in C. C. R., 19 Ed. II, 436. The petitions of Thomas, A. P. 4735, below, pp. 250–1, and C. I. P. M., Ed. II, f. 87, no. 9, below, pp. 263–4.

[3] Queen Margaret died in 1318 ; John de Erleye is described in the first year of Edward III as ' late sheriff ' of Somerset and Dorset (C. C. R. 1 Ed. III, 22). The petition must, therefore, have been presented to Edward II.

et as Chaumberleynz de lescheker de auer payement del dit argent,
Et si ensi soit qe le Tressorer et les Chaumberleyns ne ont mye argent
prest pur ly payer. Pleise a vostre seignurie comaunder a Tressorer et
as Barouns de lescheker pur ly faire couenable assignement la ou il
poet prestement estre paye de la dite summe.

(Endorsement) Soit mande as Tresorer Barouns et Chaumberleins
de lescheker qils veue la bille dount la peticioun fait mencioun sils
troessent qe la dette soit unqore due de cler et qe le dit Richard est
executour du dist testament, adonqes facent paiement allouaunce ou
assignement a plustost qils purrent bonement resceiuantz etc. et
chargeantz etc.[1] Irr(otulatur).

A. P. 1785. A nostre seignur le Roy et a soun counseil mostre
Hugh de Bromshulf executour del testament sire James de Balileye
qe come nostre seignur le roy soun Aile, quy dieux assoile soit tenuz
al dit sire James en C iiii x li. ii s. iii d. qadr. del an trentisme secund'
si come piert par bille de Garderobe . prie le dit Hugh, a nostre seignur
le Roy et a soun conseil, qe lour pleise comander al Tresorer Barouns
et as Chamberleyns del Eschecker, quils ly facent paiement, ou couenable assignement de la dite dette, pur dieu et pur le alme soun piere.[2]

(Endorsement) Sue deuers le Roi.

A. P. 1786. A nostre seygnur le Roy et a son conseil mostre Hugh
de Bromshulf executour sire James de Balileye[3] qe come le Roy
Edward son piere ky alme deux assoille, fust tenuz al dit sire James
en cc.lxiii li. x s. vi d. lan de son Regne primer, si come piert par une
bille de Garderobe, par quey le dit executour prie pur dieu quy il
volent de ceo ordiner lour volunte. ensi qe le dit executour purra
estre paie ou par assignement ou en autre manere.

(Endorsement) Coram Rege.

Seit mande a lescheqer qe vewe la bille facent reson.

A. P. 2390. A nostre seignur le Roi et a son conseil monstre William
Giffard chiualer come Thomas fitz au noble Roi Dengleterre Counte

---

[1] The writ in C. C. R., 5 Ed. III, 231 ; it speaks only of £23 16s. It
mentions that the petition was presented before the king and his council
in parliament.

[2] Cf. A. P. 1784, above, and 1786, below.

[3] In C. C. R., 3 Ed. III, 581, Hugh de Bromshulf appears as executor of
the will of James of Dalileye. It follows that A. P. 1785, above, which
mentions the thirty-second year of the reign of the king's grandfather,
refers to Edward I and was brought in the reign of Edward III. It would
seem probable, though not certain, that the present petition was also
brought in that reign, though it may have been brought in the reign of
Edward II.

Marschal[1] dona le manoir de Hasle oue les appurtenaunz en le Counte
Doxenford a mesme celui William a terme de sa vie pur son seruice
a lui fe, et continua sa seisine par quatre aunz et plus, mesme celui
Thomas ad rendu en la mayn le Roi le manoir auantdit ensemblement
od autres terres, et nostre dit seignur le Roi ad done le manoir auantdit
a monsieur William Bonn a lui et a ses heires de son corps engendrez
ensi est il ouste del manoir auantdit du fraunk tenement qil auoit
par quoi il pri remedie desicome il ne poet par ley de terre auoir
recouerer saunce commune parlement pur le rendre au dit nostre
seignur le Roi.

(Endorsement) Pur ce q'il est suppose par la peticion qe le manoir
est en autri mein qe en la meyn le Roi, sue a la commune ley.

A. P. 4735. A noster seignour le Roi e a soun conseil monstre
Thomas Bardolf qe come noster seignour le roi Edward Piere noster
dit seignour par sa chartre[2] eust graunte a Isabele qe fuist la femme
Hughe Bardolf piere lauant dit Thomas qi heir il est le manoir de
Emelesworthe oue les apurtenaunces en le counte de Suthampton
atenir a la dite Isabele toute sa vie issint qe apres sa mort le dit manoir
demoreit a William le fuiz meisme cele Isabele A avoir e tenir alui
e ases heires de soun corps engendres et sil deuia saunz heir de soun
corps engendre qe le dit manoir oue les apurtenaunces reuertereit
a les dreiz heirs la dite Isabel la quele Isabele est morte[3] et le dit
William est mort saunz heir de soun corps engendre . . . quey le dit
manoir deit reuertir au dit Thomas come fuiz et heir la dite Isabele
par la fourme du graunt auantdit. De quoel manoir Robert Lewer
deseysi[4] la dite Isabele par quey la dite Isabele eut briefe de nouele
disseysine devers le dit Robert. quel brief lui fuist graunte par peticion
en parlement pendant quel brief le dit Robert morust apres qi mort
le Gardeyn de . . . en le dit Counte seysit le dit manoir en la meyn
noster seignur le Roy par quey le dit Thomas prie a noster seignur le
Roy qil plese a sa seignurie comaunder qe la verite de ceste chose
seit enqere[5] et qe droit lui soit fait.

(Endorsement) Ostendat cartam Regis in Cancellaria, qua ibidem
visa assignentur fideles ibidem ad inquirendum de contentis in peticione

---

[1] Thomas, son of Edward I and half-brother of Edward II, lived
1300–38, and was created earl-marshal in 1315. The petition must therefore have been brought either under Edward II or (more probably) under
Edward III.
[2] C. Ch. R. iii. 48, 33 Ed. I (November 28).
[3] In 16 Ed. II ; see C. I. vi. 272, no. 454.
[4] In 15 Ed. II, ibid. 352–3, no. 543.
[5] Above, n. 3, and below, pp. 263–4.

et aliis etc. veritatem. et si Isabella vel prefatus Thomas statum suum inde etc. et retornetur inquisicio. et si per inquisicionem comperiatur quod peticio supponit et alia que requiruntur etc. cercioretur inde Rex etc. et fiat inquisicio in presencia custodis. Irr(otulatur).

A. P. 6841. A nostre seignur le Roi monstre Johan de Roos qe come le dit nostre seignur le Roi luy granta le manoir de Turnamehalle le quel fust en sa maine par le forfoture sire Hugh Despenser en le quel le dit sire Hugh purchasa en fee de monsieur Peres de Manle par chater (sic) et par fine leve en la court le Roi et ore le dit Johan de Roos est enplede par sire Johan de Manle soposant qe le dit monsieur Hugh entra par deseisine sauns autre titil auoir et sure ceo ad enfourme certens du paise de fere le dit Johan perdre le manoir auantdit la quele perde serroit au Roi auxibien come a luy pur ceo qe le Roi est tenu de ferre au dit Johan la valu sil perdit. Pri le dit Johan bref* au Tresorer et au chaumburlaines de quer les moniments le dit monsieur Peres fetes au dit Hugh le Despenser qe sount en le Tresori, par les queux le dit manoir pust estre defendu et saufe et bref au les Justices deuant les quex le plee est desurser' du dit plee tanqe les monimentz soient enquisis et mandez.[1]

(Endorsement) Mandetur Iusticiariis ad assisas assignatis quod cum nuper mandatum fuerit eis quod ad assisam capiendam procederent non obstante carta Ita quod ad iudicium inde reddendum non procederent Rege inconsulto nichilominus mandetur eisdem Iusticiariis quod adeo circumspecte in negocio illo se habeant quod preiudicium Regi seu eidem Iohanni non eueniat. Et mandetur Thesaurario et Camerariis quod scrutatis cartis et munimentis que fuerunt Hugonis le Despenser in Thesauraria existentibus quod certificent Regem de eo quod invenerint.

A. P. 8051. A nostre seignur le Roi et son consail monstre son lige Bacheler Robert Bertrem qe come il fuist seisi du manoir de (Burton) Leonard en le Counte de Euerwyk en son demeyne come de fee par les faites et le feffement Johan Bekard et cel estat continua tote la vie le dit Johan le quel manoir est tenuz de ma Dame la Reyne Philip'[2] come de son chastell de Knaresburgh et monsieur Hugh de Hastyng

---

The petition must have been brought between the first year of Edward III (when the manor was granted to John de Roos, C. C. R , 1 Ed. III, 197), and the twelfth year of that king (when John was dead, ibid., 12 Ed. III, 603).

[2] Philippa was the queen of Edward III and died in 1369. The words in brackets are suggested, since the text in those places is completely destroyed.

adonqes Seneschal ma dite Dame fit seiser le manoir de Burton'
auauntdit par resoun del noun age un Johan fitz Roger Maudut cosyn
et heir lauantdit Johan Bekard (come si le) dit Johan de ceo eust
deuie seisi en ostaunt le dit Robert de son fraunk tenement par quoi
il ad suy par p(eticion devant) le consail ma dite dame la Reyne
monstraunt son droit et priaunt restitucion de son manoir auauntdit
et (ad este) delaye de son droit par treys aunz passes et uncore est
et ne peot de son dit manoir nule resti(tucion auer par) quoi il prie
qe ley et reson luy soient faites.

(Endorsement) Soit ceste peticion maunde en Chauncellerie et
illeoqes appelle le Counsail la Roigne et oiez les resones dune part et
dautre soit ent outre fait droit.

A. P. 8074.   A nostre seignur le Roi et son consail monstre Robert
de Veer Counte Doxenford qe comme le Roi Henri le veil progenitour
nostre seignur le Roi qe ore est graunta par sa chartre a Aubric de
Veer auncestre le dit Counte qe li et ses heirs fussent as touz jours
les chiefs Chaumberleyns des Rois Dengleterre prenauntz les fees et
les profitz qe al dit office apendent, et de ceo auoit confirmementz des
progenitours nostre dit seignur le Roi, de quel office li et ses heirs
furent seisis et continuerent lur seisine de cel temps taunqe le Roi
Henry le tiers Besaiel [1] nostre seignur le Roi qe ore est par volentee
sauntz agard et Jugement ousta Robert de Veer counte Doxenford
piere le Counte qe ore est et le dit Counte ad suy de parlement en parlement pur remedie auoir, et uncore prie le dit Counte qe nostre seignur
le Roi et son consail voillent si lur plest regarder ses chartres et
munementz quil ad de cel office, et sur ceo li faire remedie par reson.

(Endorsement) Vigne deuant le conseil et monstre ses faitz et ses
munimentz.

Et puis il monstra deuant le conseil une charte le Roi Henri le
transescript de quel est cosu a ceste peticion et pur ce qe ceste chose
touche especialement le Roi, soit ceste bosoigne (*sic*) deuant le Roi et
son grant conseil.

Soit ceste peticion mande en Chancellerie et le Chanceller pris a lui
les Justiz et autres sages du conseil ordeinent remedie en ce cas.

A. P. 8084.   A nostre seignur le Roi et a son conseil mostre Nichol
de la Beche qe come il ad este tenu en prisone a poi quatre aunz par
le faux procurement Hugh le Despenser et Robert de Baldok et le
surmistrent qil compassa lour mort et autre cause nauoient (pur le

---

[1] This shows that the petition was brought under Edward III, perhaps
in 4 Ed. III (R. P. ii. 397, no. 109) ; the petitioner died in 1331.

mettre) en prisone par quei ses terres et tenementz bienz et chateux furent seisitz en la mayn nostre dit seignur le Roi et ensi uncore (demeure)nt, dount il prie liueree de ses ditz terres et tenementz od les issues du men temps et restitucion de ses biens et chateux auantditz.

(Endorsement) Soit ceste peticion mande en Chauncellerie et* la* cause* vewe* et si les terres soient prises en la mein le Roi sanz cause expresse . . . soit restitut a les (terres) oue les issues et arrerages etc. dont le Roi nest mie serui.[1]

A. P. 8352. A nostre seignur le Roi et a son conseil monstre Johan Paynel[2] qe come il ad este en sa garde graunt temps et ceux qe ount eu et tenu la garde eyent fait Waste et destruccion de ses terres et maisons dount le Roi nad pris nules amendes et il en ad resceu graunt damage e nul remedy ne poet auoir en la Chauncelrie, par qoi il prie au conseil nostre seignur le Roi quil voilent ordeyner coment il puys recouerir ses damages del Waste et la destruccion qe lui ad este faite taunt come il ad este deinz age.

(Endorsement) Videtur consilio quod faciendum est remedium pro heredibus in hoc casu. Ideo tradatur Iusticiariis ut per eos et per clericos de Cancellaria ordinetur remedium prout melius viderint faciendum.

Irr(otulatur)

Postmodum peticione ista Iusticiariis liberata, vocatis coram eis seruientibus Regis et aliis etc. concordarunt in hunc modum :

Mandetur Thesaurario et Baronibus de Scaccario, quod venire faciant coram eis ipsos qui custodiam terrarum habuerunt ex commissione Regis, tamquam ministros Regis racione custodie quam habuerunt et auditis racionibus hincinde fieri faciant eidem Iohanni de vastis quos fecerunt tempore custodie predicte, debitum et festinum iusticie complementum.[3] Irr(otulatur).

A. P. 9990. A nostre seignur le Roi et a son conseil monstre Johan de Seint Loo et Johanne sa femme fuille et heire sir Alisaundre de Cheuerel qe comme le dit sire Alisaundre morust seisi del maner de Wynfred Egle od les apertenaunces en son demeigne comme de fie le

---

[1] Writ to the exchequer (C. C. R., 20 Ed. II, 622) ordering that five manors with other lands in Sussex be restored to Nicholas, if it were found that they belonged to him and that they had been taken into the king's hands without reasonable cause, as Nicholas complained. If there were any reason why that could not be done, then the king was to be certified. Restitution was finally made in 1 Ed. III, R. P. ii. 420, no. 3.
[2] John's father was tenant in chief of Edward II (e.g. C. C. R., 8 Ed. III, 221).   [3] There follows ' Coram magno cons.' cancelled.

quel maner le Roi seisi en sa meyne aprest la mort sire Alisaundre [1] et
le lessa a sire Richard Louel, si prient les auanditz Johan et Johanne
a nostre seignur le Roi qil vousist reprendre meisme le manor en sa
mayne et liuerer a les auanditz Johan et Johanne comme leritage
Johanne selonc le purport de la chartre le Roi faite al auandit sire
Alisandre, ou qe comune droite lor puisse seruir issi qe eux soient
responduz al assise de Mordantcestre qil portent de meisme le maner
vers le dit sire Richard en le Conte de Dorset deuant sire Johan de
Foxle [2] et ses compaignouns Justices assignez en mesme le Conte, et
qe les auanditz Justices puissent aler a lassise prendre et ley et reson
faire ne mye contresteaunt le fet qe le dit Richard ad del doun nostre
seignur le Roi.

(Endorsement) Mandetur Iusticiariis quod non obstante carta
Regis procedant ad assisam capiendam secundum legem et consuetudinem regni Anglie, et quod antequam procedant ad iudicium super
recognicione assise predicte certificent inde Regem ut Rex inde faciat
quod de iure fuerit faciendum..

Super ista peticione nondum emanauit breue, quia nondum est
aliquis prosecutus pro Iohanne de sancto Laudo pro breui habendo.

A. P. 10505. A nostre seignur le Roi et soun counseil monstre
William Elys de Graunt Jernemuth qe par la ou il estoit seisi del
manoir de Blonorton en soun demesne com de fee en la countee de
Norffolk et de mesme le manoir estoit ouste par force dune enqueste
doffice pris deuant leschetour de mesme le Counte par quele trove
fuit qe Rogier de Brom et Robert de Brom deuierount seisi en lour
demesne com de fee del manoir auauntdit et mesme le manoir tendrount
par certein seruice de un William fitz et heir Johan Bernak deinz age
et en la garde nostre seignur le Roi estaunt et nostre seignur le Roi
par sa patente le dit manoir a graunte a un Johan de Olneye sur qei
le dit William Elys vient en la Chauncellerie nostre dit seignur le Roi
com lestatut' voet [3] et monstre ouertement par record de mesme la
Chauncellerie qe William fitz Johan Bernak qe fuist en la gard nostre
dit seignur le Roi morust trois quarters del an et ces terres et tenementz oue toux les apportenaunces plenerment deliueres hors du meyn

The inquisition in Dorset after the death of Alexander Cheverel was
taken in 4 Ed. II, upon a writ of Nov. 17, 1310 (C. I. v, no. 267). The
manor of Wynfred Egle was retained in the king's hand after 1310 (C. C. R.,
4 Ed. II, 295).

[2] John de Foxle was justice of assize in Dorset (among other counties)
in 1311 (Dudgale, Orig. Iuridic. (1671), Chr. Ser. 35). The petition seems
to have been brought in 1311.

[3] This helps in establishing the time.

nostre dit seignur le Roi a Rauf de Crombewell Chiualer et a maude sa femme com de droit la dite Maude et le dit Rauf fist homage a nostre dit seignur le Roi pur ceo qe lauoit issue entre eux pur les terres et tenementz auauntditz et ceo un demy an entier auaunt ceo qe les ditz Rogier de Brom et Robert de Brom deuierount quel chose apiert ouertement par record en la Chancellerie nostre dit seignur le Roi Et outre ceo il apiert par record en Comune Bank nostre dit Seignur le Roi qe Johan Barnak piere le dit William Barnak qe fuist en la garde nostre dit Seignur le Roi soi demyst par fyn a Robert Barnak frere le dit Johan de sa purpartie qil auoit del heritage de Tateshale quele Eue de Tateshale tient a terme deuie de soun heritage en le Counte auauntdit, auoir et tenir a dit Robert et a ses heirs mals de son corps engendres com apiert plenerment par la fyn auantdit qe se leua en le Bank auauntdit, lan nostre dit seignur le Roi quinsime et puis apres desses la dite Eue et pur ceo qe Johan de Orby un des heirs del heritage auauntdit morust et un Johan fils et heir mesme cesty Johan . . . deinz age et en la garde nostre seignur le Roi estaunt, et apres par entre Adam de Clifton chiualer et autres des heirs del heritage auauntdit et lauauntdit Robert Barnak a qy Johan Barnak autres des heirs del heritage auauntdit sa purpartie auoit graunte par fyn com auaunt est dit purpartie saffist en la Chauncellerie des toux les fees et auoisons del heritage auauntdit et le fee par quel le manoir de Blonortone est tenuz fuist alote a la purpartie le dit Robert, com pluis pleinement apiert par record en la Chauncellerie lan Trentesme [1] qi plese au dit nostre seignur le Roi de maunder a soun Chaunceller appeles ses Justices qil aylount al fynal descussion des dites besoignes, selonc ceo qe ley et resoun demaunde.

(Endorsement) Viegne en la Chancellerie et illoeqes droit lui serra fait.

A. P. 10540. (The treasurer, barons, and chamberlains, report to the king that they have received his writ of the great seal, dated at Carlisle, July 6, in the ninth year, setting out the purport of the petition mentioned in the writ mentioned above, and the contents of the writ, which says :) de quo idem Mauentus [2] effectum aliquem nondum vt asserit est assecutus. Nos volentes sibi satisfieri de eo quod sibi debetur ex hac causa, vobis mandamus quod ad satisfaccionem dicto Mauento in premissis faciendam per modum solucionis vel assignacionis procedatis iuxta formam mandatorum nostrorum vobis super hoc directorum. Et si forsitan illud absque alio Waranto a nobis inde habendo non poteritis adimplere, tunc prefatas peticionem et

---

[1] This helps in establishing the time.   [2] Above, pp. 227–9.

Inquisicionem quas vobis sic misimus nobis in Cancellaria nostra sub sigillo dicti scaccarii sine dilacione aliqua remittatis. vt inde faciamus quod pro dicto Mauento fore viderimus faciendum. . . .

Super quo scire velit vestra dominacio regia, quod ad satisfaccionem prefato Mauento faciendam in premissis, non proceditur ex causa annotata in quodam processu inde habito ad scaccarium vestrum cuius transcriptum pro informacione inde habenda pro indempnitate vestra vobis mittimus sub sigillo scaccarii vestri presentibus tachiatum. Et sic pro eo quod absque Waranto sufficienti huiusmodi satisfaccionem facere non valemus, remittimus vobis presentibus similiter tachiatas peticionem et Inquisicionem de quibus superius fit mencio in mandato vestro predicto, quas nobis nuper misistis vna cum brevi vestro regio quod penes nos in scaccario predicto retinemus, eo quod Warantum non habemus ad illud vobis remittendum. Valeat dominacio vestra regia per tempora diuturna. Scriptum apud Eboracum xviii die Iulii.

A. P. 10541, printed in R. P. ii. 32 b, with mistakes and omissions, e.g. the endorsement has ' et chamberleins ' interlined after ' barons '.

Below the endorsement, as printed, is written in another ink : Visum est Thesaurario et Baronibus de scaccario, quod rite procedi non potest ad solucionem vel assignacionem faciendam Mauento Fraunceys iuxta formam istius peticionis, pro eo quod idem Mauentus assumpsit super se ad faciendum prouidenciam bladorum in ista peticione contentorum, et ad liberanda blada predicta apud Novum castrum super Tynam pro certo precio in quadam Indentura inter dominum Edwardum nuper Regem Anglie patrem Regis huius et ipsum Mauentum inde confecta, contento cuius quidem Indenture tenor inseritur in quodam processu inde habito ad scaccarium et cuius processus transcriptum presentibus tachiatur, nisi Rex prefato Mauento graciam facere voluerit specialem in hac parte.[1]

A. P. 10549. A nostre seignur le Roi et a soen counsail, monstre Rogier Husee . qe come le corps le dit Rogier et ses terres, par resoun de son nounage apres le deces Johan . . . heir il est, qi du Roi tint en chief, eussount esteez en la garde le Roi Edward pere nostre seignur le Roi qore est par dixsept auns et en le temps nostre . . . soun regne primer le dit Rogier son age auoit accompli et eit suwi en chauncellerie et par peticion en plousours parlements dauoir plener restitucion . . . dit Johan soen auncestre morut seisi, en son demeisne come de fee, et tout eit estee respoundu a ses peticions qeles fussent maundees en chauncellerie e . . . del diem clausit extremum si troue feusse par les

[1] Other transcripts in the case of Fraunceys in A. P. 10542–4.

dites Enqestes qe launcestre morrut seisi qaydonqes les terres feussent reprises en la main le Roi et liuerez.[1] . . . en chauncellerie feusse serchee et troue par Enqeste qe le dit Johan soen auncestre morrut seisi del manoir de Treuqoer oue les membres de Falington . . . auoweson del Eglise de Farlington en Countee de Suth(amp)t(on). Les dites terres a la main le Roi ne sount pas reprises ne au dit Rogier liuerez dount il prie remedie.

Suth(amp)t(on).

(Endorsement) Pur ce qe la partie qe se pleint est de pleine age soient cerchez les enquestes retournez en Chauncellarie dont les peticions font mencion et si troue soit par les enquestes qe son ancestre morust seisi des manors contenuz en les dites peticions adonqes eit bref de garnir ceux qi sont tenantz des ditz manoirs qils soient en Chancellarie a certein iour a mostrer sil saueront rien dire pur qoi les ditz manoirs ne serront pris en la main le Roi et liuerez a la partie et sils ne viegnent point au iour soient les manoirs pris en la main le Roi et liuerez a la partie et sils viegnent soient les resons del une part et dautre oiez et outre soit droit fait.

A. P. 12025.[2] A nostre seignur le Roy supplie et Recquiert Lucas de Periers Jadiz fisicient la Reyne Marguerite,[3] Come il lait presente de sa grace a leglise de Creckelade, dont lauoyson de droit appartient a lui, par le forfait de Adam de Stratoune qui la dite auoyson auoit pourchacie deuant son forfait, Et le dit presentement est empeechie par maistre Richard de Abyndone qui se fait patron de la dite eglise par cause de heritage, que il voille mander au chancelier ou a son lieutenant, que il face querre et Regarder sans delay les chartres et munimens qui furent au dit Adam de stratoune, Et enquerre especiau- ment du droit de la dite auoyson, pu quoi le droit puist estre trye hastiuement, Et que ce que il auera fait de ceste besoigne, li certifie par le porteur de ces lettres.

(Endorsement) A maistre Thomas de Charleton.[4]

par William de Montagu.[5]

Mon seignur voet qe vous facez hastiuement lettres au Chancellier qil enquerge du dreit del Eglise de Crekkelade solonc le purport de ceste bille.

[1] C. C. R., I Ed. III, 127, 130 ; cf. also C. I. v. 218, vi. 126 ; R. P. ii. 48, no. 70.
[2] Classified as brought in II Ed. II.   [3] Queen Margaret died in 1318.
[4] Thomas de Charleton was at that time keeper of the privy seal (e.g. C. C. R., 10 Ed. II, 440, and see D. N. B., s.v. Charlton.
[5] William de Montagu was at that time steward of the king's house- hold ; see ibid., s.v. Montacute.

A. P. 14605. A nostre seignur le Roi supplie vostre humble vadlet Arnaud de Poilland[1] que come il ad demoere en vostre seruice en diuerses lieux en les par . . . Gascoigne et lui sunt duez de ses gages pur lui et ses gentz darmes et seriauntz apee ii^{M} lxvii livres x s. de chipoteu' sicom plus pleinement piert par bille enseale du seal le conestable de Burdeux et sicom piert par vostre papyre de conestable de Burdeux Pleise a vostre haute seignorie, que de vostre grace lui voilletz granter de tenir la petite coustume de Roian que vostre conestable prent de vostre chastel de Burdeux et qil la puisse tenir par lui ou par son attorne tauntqil soit purpaye de la dite somme.

(Endorsement) Soit escrit as seneschal de Gascoigne et Conestable de Burdeaux, que eux certifient nostre seignur le Roy de la manere de son seruice et en quele manere le Roi purra bonement faire satisfaction a li de les deniers que le Roy lui deit.

A. P. 14665. A nostre seignur le Roi et a son counsail monstre William le Baud Chiualer qe kom* ses terres et ses tenementz furunt seisie en la mayn le Roi purceo qil estoit de la querele le Counte de Lancastre cest a sauoir le maner de Coryngham oue les purtenaunces ouec lauoeson de . . . le maner Et le maner de Dungeseles oue les apurtenaunces en le Counte de Essex Et les maners Petit Hadham . . . Et une charue de terre oue les apurtenaunces en Staundon'. Et une carue de terre oue les apurtenaunces en graunt Hadham . . . chapele de Pelham' en le counte de Hertford, Et le maner de Lobenham oue les apurtenaunces et lauoueson de la Eglise . . . en le Counte de Leycestre et son corps enprisone et les chateux qe estoient en les dites maners seisis en la mayn le Roy et un . . . Dount il prie qe restitucion li soit fet des terres et tenementz et auouesouns auaundites oue les apurtenaunces et des chat . . . maners estoient et des issues des dites maners en le mene temps.

(Endorsement). Seit ceste peticion maunde en Chauncellerie e le Chaunceller se auise de la cause de la prise des terres e tenemenz contenuz en ceste peticion en la meyn le Roi, e sils furent prises en la meyn le Roi par cause de la quele etc. et ne mye par autre seient les terres et tenemenz restituz oue les issues et arrerages etc. dount le Roi nest my seruy.[2]

A. P. 14720 b. A nostre seignur le Roi et a son consail monstre Edward fuiz et heir Johan fuiz Osebern Giffard qe come le dit Johan

[1] C. C. R., 27 Ed. I, 244. Arnald de Poillou of Bayonne, formerl of London, is mentioned as having committed a murder ; his father is guiltless, having been in parts beyond the sea.

[2] Restitution in 1 Ed. III, R. P. ii. 421 b, and C. C. R., 1 Ed. III, 21–2.

en le primer parlement nostre seignur le Roi qore est auoit mys sa
bille de ceo qe il meismes par fyn leue auoit graunte et rendu le manoir
de Wynterburne Houton' oue les apurtenances en le Countee de
Dorsete a mons. Osbern Giffard a tenir a tute sa vie . et que apres
son deces le dit manoir retourneroit au dit Johan et a ses heirs le quel
Osebern le dit manoir bailla a Hughe le Despenser Counte de Wyn-
cestre qi le tynt a tute sa vie, apres qi mort nostre seignur le Roi
seisi le dit manoir. Par quei comaunde feut a Tresorier et as Chaumberleins de maunder en la Chauncelerie tenour de meismes le fyn les
queux ensi firent. Et sur ceo commission estoit fait denquerer si le
dit Counte nul estat auoit del dit Johan et dautres pointz selonq
lendossement de de (*sic*) la dite bille pendant quele sute le dit Johan
morust par quei rin de ceo ne estoit fait. Le quel manoir apres fut
done a mons. Johan Mantrauers le puisne a terme de sa vie et ore
est seisi en la mayn le Roi prie le dit Edward qe plese a nostre seignur
le Roi qe sur ceo droit lui soit fait eiaunt regard de la dite fyn etc. qe
le dit Johan ne fut pas ne le dit Edward nest heir du saunk au dit
mons. Osbern.

(Endorsement) Soit cette peticion mande deuant le Roi et illoeqes
apellez les serjauntz le Roi et oiez les resons pur le Roi et pur le partie
soit fait droit.

Irrotulatur in rotulo cxxxviii . . . anno regni Regis Edwardi tercii
a conquestu quinto.[1]

A. P. 14792. Au Chanceler nostre seignur le Roi prient William
Shouuyn de Brantingby del Counte de Leycestre et Anneyse sa femme
qi de sa grace lour voyle graunter bref al Eschetour de cea Trente,
qil ouste sa meyn dun mees et vne verge de terre oue les appurtenaunces
en Brantingby, et les queux terre, et mees, le dist William aueyt
lesse a ferme terme dun An . a sire Simond de Bereford,[2] denz quel terme

[1] C. R. 284 (P., 5 Ed. III), m. 138 r. Close writ of April 28, 1331,
to the king's bench, with this petition, ' coram nobis et consilio nostro in
parliamento nostro apud Westmonasterium vltimo conuocato . . .
exhibita ', with an order according to this endorsement, ending
' faciatis quod de iure fuerit faciendum '. Follows the tenor, of the
petition and the endorsement. ' Et super hoc venit predictus Edwardus
et petit Iusticiam sibi fieri in premissis. Et quia predicti Iohannes
. . . vel Edwardus Ius suum quod habuerunt in manerio predicto
domino Regi nunc vel patri ipsius Regis Iohanni Mantrauers seu dicto
Comiti vel predicto Osberto remisisse quietumclamasse seu aliud factum
inde fecisse per quod Ius dicti Regis manuteneri poterit in premissis,
super quod Curia hic vult certiorari antequam vlterius procedatur '
(omi. ed, ' fecisse potuerunt '), a writ of search is sent to the treasurer
and chamberlains, and the case is adjourned until June 25. The rest of
the membrane is left blank.
[2] Executed in 4 Ed. III (R. P. ii. 53, no. 2).

le dist Simond fust atteynt de diuers felounies, par quei toux ses terres et tenementz ensemblementes oue toux les terres et mees de lesauandits William et Anneyse furent seysis en la meyn nostre seignur le Roy et unqore sount en sa meyn. Et qe eaux puissent aver lour dites terres pur dieu.

(Endorsement) Soit mande brief al eschetour denquere sur les choses contenues en la peticion et lenquest retourne en Chancellerie, soit outre fait droit. Irr(otulatur).[1]

A. P. 14808. Au Chaunceler' nostre Seygnur le Rey, pryent les bones genz de Carberton' et de Edenstowe, qil voyle fere grace et remedie a eus de lour Commission de coe qe le Abbe de Wollebek ad pris de eus le storth, qe soleyt rendre xx s. Et le Roy ad grante al dist Abbe par sa chartre levantdist storth hors de lour Commission E de coe il prieunt grace et remedie.

(Endorsement) Habeant breve Thesaurario et Baronibus de Scaccario quod exonerentur. Teste Magistro Willelmo de Blida.[2]

A. P. 15555. A nostre seignur le Roi et a son Conseil monstre Margarete qe feut la femme Johan Gyffard de Brymmeffeld qe come ele e Johan Gyffard son fitz purchacerent iointement a eux et a les heirs meisme celui Johan la reuersion du manoir de Walles en le Countee de Gloucester et puis apres recouerirent en la Court le Roi par brief de Wast deus centz acres de bois purtenantes a meisme le manoir et par graunt et lassent la dit Margarete le dit Johan feut en tenance du dit bois tantqe le Roi lui tint son enemy et rebeal pur la querele des grantz contre les Despensers [3] par qoi meisme le boys feut pris en la main le Roi et ad este puis en cea, dount ele prie pur dieu grace et remedie.

(Endorsement) Assignentur sufficientes persone in Cancellaria ad inquirendum in presencia Custodis manerii predicti qualem statum dicti Iohannes et Margareta habuerunt in bosco infrascripto, et qualiter dictus Iohannes solus boscum predictum tenuerit utrum videlicet dicta Margareta remisit et quietum clamavit prefato Iohanni boscum illum, seu ei fecit statum inde ad terminum vite tantum, vel ipse Iohannes boscum illum tenuit ex permissione prefate Margarete, et omnibus aliis circumstanciis negotium illud necessario contingentibus, et retornata inquisicione inde in Cancellaria, fiat vlterius iusticia.[4]

---

[1] C. C. R., 10 Ed. III, 720–1, *procedendo ad iudicium*, the petition is mentioned as presented before the king and council in parliament.

[2] An account of the writ (April 21, 1303) will full particulars of the case, C. C. R., 31 Ed. I, 27.   [3] This helps in establishing the date.

[4] On the basis of that inquisition, writ to deliver, May 4, 1327, C. C. R., 1 Ed. III, 122. See also R. P. ii. 433 b, and C. C. R., 1 Ed. III, 122–3.

A. P. 15574. Plese a Chanceller nostre Seignur le Roy comander lyuere de Dowere a la Contesse de Hereford del manoire Wascote oue les appurtenauncz en le Countee Doxon'. Purceo qe son trescher seignur le Counte de Hereford [1] qe darrein morust qe Dieu assoille nadgairs seignur du dit manoir par decent de heritage apres la mort son piere Comte de Norhampton que dieux assoille dys aunz apres lour esposaus graunta le dit Manoir oue les appurtenauntz a Mons. Gilbert Giffard son bachelor atenir a terme de la vie le dit Mons. Gilbert issint qe le dit Manoir oue les appurtenauntz apres la decees le dit Mons. Gilbert retourneroit al dit Counte de Hereford ou a ses heirs a touz iours. le quele mons. Gilbert morust le primer iour de Decembre lan xlvii et le Eschetour nostre dit Seignour le Roy celles parties ent unqore prent les proffitz.

(Endorsement) Fiat breue de inquirendo de materia infracontenta etc.[2]

A. P. E 62. A nostre seignur le Rei si ly plest prie Margarete, qe fu la femme Edmond jadis Cunte de Cornewall,[3] qe par la ou ele demaunde son deweyre, vers plusour gentz, par bref en la Court nostre seignur le Rei, il ont respundu quil sunt feffez par lauaundit Cunte, et de ceo metterent auaunt ses chartres, qe lyent luy et ses heirs a la garauntye, et dient outre qe nostre seignur le Rei est heir lauaundit Cunte, saunz qi il ne deyuent respundre, et ses Justices par cestes resons, surseent de ren fere taunt qe nostre seignur le Rei voille dire de ceste choses sa volunte, de quele chose la dite Margarete prie, qe grace et remedie luy seit fet.

(Endorsement) Conueniant Iusticiarii et faciant iusticiam ita quod pretextu Regis non fiat iniuria. Et si quid sit in dubio, certificent inde Regem.

Postea certis ex causis concordatum est, quod istud negocium adiornetur usque ad proximum parliamentum etc. Et mandetur O. de Aylesbury et certis executoribus Comitis Cornubie quod portent Londonias omnes cartas scripta et munimenta, que fuerunt dicti Comitis, et ill(is) transcript(is) in quodam libro re(maneant) carte in Thes(aurario) etc. et lib(er) in scaccario etc.

Coram Rege.

altera petitio consimilis mittitur Cancellario.

---

[1] Humphrey de Bohun, seventh earl of Hereford (in succession to his uncle Humphrey, sixth earl), and earl of Northampton (in succession to his father.) He succeeded in 1361 and died in 1372.

[2] Upon that inquisition, writ to assign dower, C. C. R., 48 Ed. III, 28 (June 2, 1374).   [3] Edmund died in 1300.

A. P. E 153. A nostre seignur le rei et a son conseil monstre Williame de Toluse[1] son seriaunt qe come il lui ad apreste cciiii^{xx} ix libres et* xii *d.* a sa graunt bosoigne, Dount il az bones lettres et reconisance del Eschekere . Estre ceo il ad perdu en seruice le Rei une bone nefe nouele qe dunke valust cc Marks, et plus, la quele nefe le Roi lui ad souent promis (b)eaument restorer, deuaunt frere Water et deuant son conseil. Et a la requeste et a la bele promes le Rei, ala la auauntdit Williame condure la vitaile le Rei en Gascoine a graunt meschef et a graunt peril, pur quelz trauals et seruices le Rei lui promist noble auauncement. Dount il prie au Rei pur dieu et en alowance de sa dette, et de sa nefe, et pur son seruice auantdite, quil Lui voile graunter la ville de Purstoke en le Counte de Dorsete, pur la extente taunt qe la dette seit leue. E nest extendu, qe xviii Libres par an.

(Endorsement) Coram Rege Inter alias peticiones de vlt. . . .

Veniat ad scaccarium et computet de bladis et* aliis* bonis* Regis per ipsum ductis in Vasconiam vnde oneratur et computato cum ipso Thesaurarius et Barones facient ei vlterius quod fuerit faciendum de iure.

A. P. E 609. A nostre seignur le Rey e a son consayl. Helewys ke fu femme Richard de Bret . . . ll' et executrix, et les autrez executurs de meme cely Richard priunt remedie e grace de ceo ke ly auaundit Richard fut en le seruice nostre seignur le Rey et son attorne de toute ples deuaunt sire Roger le Brabanzon[2] et se compagnouns tenaunt le Lu nostre seignur le Rey. pur x livres par An dunt arere ly est . lv livres de v ance et demi An Lez queus . lv livres sunt diuisez en le testament. et lez auanditz exsecuturs scharges par quey Le testament ne punt estre par feiz . ne lez dettes payez si il ne heyent remedie e grace de lez auandiz deners le queus Ly furunt assignez pur son graunt trauayl(e) par quey li priunt pur lez aumez lez auncestrez* nostre seignur le Rey. ke remedie et grace lur seit fete issi ke pur la noun pay le alme ne chece en peril.

(Endorsement) Expectent quousque Rex fuerit in meliori statu ad debita sua soluenda. et tunc veniant et fiet eis . . .

---

[1] William de Tholosa (Tholouse) was often sent abroad, on the king's service, in the first years of Edward II (e.g. C. P. R., 7 Ed. II, 102, 117 ; cf. C. C. R., 5 Ed. II, 412, a writ to the collectors of certain customs in the port of London to pay him £184 5s. 2d., being the money which he had paid by the king's orders, and for the expenses on the king's horses in his custody, as appeared by a bill of wardrobe.

[2] Brabazon was chief justice of the king's bench 1295–1316.

VII. From the Chancery Inquisitions Post Mortem

Ed. II, f. 87, m. 9–5. A nostre seignur le Roi prie le soen lige Thomas Bardolf qe come le Roi Edward piere nostre seignur le Roi qore est, granta a Isabelle qe fust la femme Hugh Bardolf mere meisme cesty Thomas qi heir il est le manoir de Emelesworth od les apurtenaunces en le Counte de Suth(am)t(on) a avoir et tenir a tote la vie la dite Isabelle issi qe apres le deces la dite Isabelle, le dit manoir demorast a William fitz meismes ceste Isabelle et a les heirs de son corps engendrez. Et si meismes cesty Williame deuyast sauntz heir de son corps engendre, qe le dit manoir reuertist a les droitz heirs meisme ceste Isabelle, par reson de quele grant lauantdite Isabelle fust seisie, du temps meismes cel grant tantqe Robert Ewer lan quinzysme la disseisit atort par quoi la dite Isabelle suy, deuant nostre seignur le Roi en son parlement pur remedie auoir de cel tort, ou respondu ly fust, qele suysist a la commune ley, vers meisme cely Robert, par quoi ele purchacea son bref de nouele disseisine, en le dit Counte, vers le dit Robert, pendant quel play, le dit Robert morust enemy et rebel nostre seignur le Roi par quoi le dit manoir deuynt en la meyn nostre seignur le Roi, et unqore demoert entre les autres forfetures, et purceo qe la dite Isabelle est morte et lauantdit Williame, sanz heir de son corps issaunt soit deuye, a la suyte le dit Thomas enqueste sur ceo par peticion de parlement soit prise et retourne en Chauncellerye, la copie de quele enqueste est cusu a ceste peticion : prie le dit Thomas qe veue la dite enqueste ley et reson ly soit fait.[1]

(Endorsement) Porceo qe la chartre le Roi quele la peticioune suppose est vewe et est acordaunt a mesme la peticione, et aussint troue* est* par* Lenqueste de ce prise par peticione en parlement en presence de Gardeyn ce qe la peticione contient: auis est au conseil qe le Roi deit ouster la mein, sil plest a lui, et pur ce deuant le Roi.

Il semble lour auis couenable sil plest au Roy.

coram Rege.

Veniat inquisicio cum peticione et ostendatur carta coram consilio.

m. 9–9. A nostre seygnur le Roy prie le soen lige Thomas Bardolf (follows the statement of his case as in m. 9–5) et en le darrain parlement feut mys auant la dite enqueste od la peticion et vewe et examine, fut respondu en la manere qe sensuit (follows the endorsement of m. 9–5 beginning with 'Pur ce' and ending with 'deit ouster la meyn

---

[1] A. P. 190 and 4735, above, pp. 247–8, 250–51.

sil plest aluy. Et pur ce deuant le Roy '). Prie le dit Thomas a nostre seygnur le Roy de sa grace qe loy et reson luy soient faitz.[1]

(Endorsement) Vncore est auis au conseil come deuant qe le Roi doit ouster la mein sil plest a li . et pur ce deuant le Roi.

Vncore semble a ces qe sunt deputez en especial par le Roi qil est a fere sil plest au Roi, et qe le Roi deit hoster sa mayn sauf a chescuny son droit.

Il plest au Roi et pur ceo sue en Chancelrie, et eyt sa deliuerance.[2]

VIII. From the Coram Rege Rolls

Roll 351 (H., 22 Ed. III), m. 45.   Dominus Rex misit quoddam breue suum clausum Iusticiariis suis hic in hec verba. Edwardus . . . Iusticiariis ad placita coram nobis tenenda assignatis . . . Quandam Inquisicionem nuper ad querelam . . . Geruasii de Clifton' de mandato nostro captam et in Cancellaria nostra retornatam, nec non quandam peticionem inde coram nobis et consilio nostro in parliamento nostro exhibitam et ibidem de auisamento eiusdem consilii indorsatam vobis mittimus sub pede sigilli nostri, Mandantes quod visis inquisicione peticione et indorsamento eiusdem peticionis et vocatis coram vobis tam seruientibus nostris quam Constabulario Castri Notingham vlterius prefato Geruasio super petitis in dicta peticione faciatis quod de iure fuerit faciendum (January 24, 21 Ed. III). Tenor comissionis . . . talis est (November 14, 21 Ed. III, C. P. R., 21 Ed. III, 464) . . . Ex graui querela . . . [This commission is, *mutatis mutandis*, very similar to that in R. P. i. 417 for Robert (Gervase's father, and cousin and heir of a former Gervase), the latter has ' ex querela', it has once 'circumiacentes' for 'circumadiacentes', 'ei' for 'sibi', 'eveniunt' for ' euenerunt ', and there are a few other differences due probably to one or the other copyist. The record in C. R., roll 351, proceeds :] 'Tenor vero inquisicionis predicte talis est' (again, apart from the names of the commissioners, the date, &c., the tenor is similar, but the verdict begins, ' Qui dicunt quod due trenchee seu fossata', and then it contains the passage per custodes castri predicti et quator gurgites in diuersis iocis vltra aquam de Trenta leuate sunt in soleo predicti Geruasii de Clifton ex vtraque parte . . .' Part of this passage is omitted in the R. P., probably by mistake. Moreover, the damages are assessed in 21 Ed. III (for Gervase) at £100, ' videlicet per viginti annos in quibus predictus Geruasius extitit tenens predicte ville de Wilford videlicet

---

[1] A. P. 190, 4735, and above, m. 9–5.
[2] The writ in C. C. R., 19 Ed. II, 436.

annuatim Centum solidos . . .,' and the king's profit at 20 marks a year. Other details are similar in both inquisitions.) Peticio inde domino Regi et consilio suo exhibita talis est. (The form of the petition is similar to that in R. P. i. 417, with minor and, of course, the necessary differences. The alleged damage amounts to £100, i.e. £5 a year during the time of his tenancy, and the king's yearly profit is alleged to be 20 marks. The petition ends:) ' sount retornez en la Chauncellerie (no mention of their ' tenor ' being attached) qil plese a nostre dit seignur le Roi et soun counseil en compensacion de la dite perte : maunder brief as Tresorier et Barons et chamberleins del Escheqer˙ de allouer au dit Gerueis lii *li*. vii *s*. i *d*. o' q^a qe sount demandez de lui par somounse du dit escheqer des diuerses dettes du temps qil ad este viscounte des Countez de Notingham et Derby et de lui faire paiement ou couenable assignement du remanant de la dite perte cest assauoir xlvii *li*. xii *s*. x *d*. q^a. Indorsamentum peticionis predicte tale est : Soit ceste peticion et lenquest prise par les enquerours. mandetz deuant le Roi et illoqes appellez les seriauntz le Roi et le Constable du dit Chastel soit fait dreit a la partie.' (Follows appointment of attorneys, and Gervase) ' petit breue de venire faciendo Stephanum* Rommilow* Constabularium Castri predicti coram domino Rege in octabis Purificacionis beate Marie vbicunque etc. Ad informandum dominum Regem super premissis etc. Et habet etc.' (On that day Gervase came, the sheriff had returned the writ, but Stephen did not come. The summoners are amerced and the sheriff is ordered to distrain Stephen to come on the quindene of Easter. The rest of the membrane is left blank.)

Roll 352 (P., 22 Ed. III), m. 131. Iohannes de Vfford Cancellarius domini Regis venit hic in Curia etc. et per manum suam propriam liberauit Willelmo de Thorpe capitali Iusticiario etc. quoddam Recordum quod irrotulatur in hec verba. Edwardus . . . vic. Buk. . . . Cum inter cetera (the king had granted to Edmund earl of Kent a rent), Iamque dilectus consanguineus noster Iohannes filius et heres predicti Comitis nobis supplicauerit vt (since the rent has been granted by the king to John de Molyns upon an untrue suggestion made to the king by John de Molyns) velimus concessionem nostram predictam reuocari (and restore it to the heir on his coming of age), Nos indempnitati nostre prospicere ac exheredacioni prefati heredis precauere volentes vt tenemur (*scire facias* to John de Molyns to appear in the chancery on November 3 to show cause why the grant should not be revoked). Teste Leonello filio nostro carissimo custode

Anglie apud Thame (October 7, 1347), per breue de priuato sigillo. (Follows the sheriff's return, as endorsed on the writ, and the appointment of attorneys.) Quadam (*sic*) billa missa in Cancellariam Regis clausa in quodam breui sub priuato sigillo sequitur in hec verba. Johan de Molyns tient lx *li*. de Rente de graunt le Roi a lui et a ses heires a toutz Jours del heritage Johan fitz . . . nadgers Counte de Kente . . . par suggestion faite en Court noun verreye fesaunt entendre au Roi et a son Counseil qe mesme la Rente feut a Robert . . . et la dit Rente est compris en la chartre de Edmund . . . Indorsamentum cuius bille tale est. Qant a ceste article plest au Roi qe Lerceuesqe et le conseil le Roi facent venir deuant eux si bien leir et la Countesse sa miere come le dit mons. Johan et oient lour resouns et sils troessent qe la busoigne seit en la manere susdit, et le dit Johan ne sache autre chose monstrere pur lui qe adonqes la Rente soit seise en la main le Roi et soit dreit fait au Roi des issues de temps qil ad tenu par tiel suggestioun nient verraie. Recordum et processus in Cancellaria Regis inde habita sequitur (*sic*) in hec verba. Placita coram Rege in Cancellaria sua in Crastino animarum anno regni sui Anglie vicesimo primo et Francie octavo. Buk. Preceptum fuit vicecomiti (follows the writ of *scire facias* set out above). Ad quem diem venit tam Iohannes de Cloue qui sequitur pro domino Rege (and the heir by his guardian, as John of Molyns by his attorney) Et predictus Iohannes de Molyns dicit quod per breue predictum satis liquere potest Curie quod heres predictus (wishes to recover by that writ a freehold) et omne placitum liberum tenementum tangens est placitum commune quod alibi quam in placea ad huiusmodi communia placita tenenda deputata secundum tenorem magne carte de libertatibus Anglie in qua placea quilibet tenens huiusmodi liberum tenementum sic implacitatus habere potest warantiam suam per vocacionem waranti siue per breue de Warntia (*sic*) carte de iure communi deduci non debet secundum legem Anglie per quod non intendit quod Curia ista que est placea officii et non ad communia placita tenenda ordinata velit aut debeat cognoscere in placito supradicto Et dictum est eidem Iohanni de Molyns per Curiam quod vlterius respondeat etc. (The court overrules an objection to the writ as not mentioning ·a vill or a hamlet ; the further objection ' quod istud breue de scire facias de sua natura warantizari debet de aliquo recordo precedenti siue officio siue de peticione ad sectam partis domini Regi porrecta et petit auditum hic in Curia de recordo siue officio siue peticione* vnde illud idem breue warantizatur ', is also overruled.) Et idem Iohannes de Molyns dicit quod quedam peticio alias per prefatum heredem domino Regi exhibita sub certa forma extitit indorsata videlicet quod venerabilis pater Iohannes Archiepiscopus Cantuariensis et Consilium domini Regis venire facerent (follows the purport of the endorsement) : et ita dicit quod prefatus Archiepiscopus qui Iudex esse deberet in causa predicta secundum vim et effectum indorsamenti predicti non est presens hic in Curia. per quod non intendit quod hic in Curia in absencia prefati Archiepiscopi respondere debeat aut de iure teneatur.   Et quia dominus Rex oretenus Cancellario suo qui ea de causa adiuit dominum Regem ad sciendam voluntatem domini Regis quid in isto negocio fieri deberet, precepit quod non obstante forma peticionis vel indorsamenti eiusdem nec expectata presencia dicti Archiepiscopi ad plenariam discussionem negocii predicti secundum legem et consuetudinem Anglie procederet, dictum est eidem Iohanni de Molyns per Curiam quod respondeat etc. (John, saving the said exceptions, pleads that he holds the rent by the king's grant confirmed by charters,) sine quo de eodem redditu respondere non potest Et petit auxilium de domino Rege etc. (Both the king's attorney and the heir answer that the grant was made upon false suggestion, and that the king is a party to this suit.) Et super hiis et aliis negocium predictum tangentibus habito cum omnibus Iusticiariis de vtroque Banco et aliis peritis de consilio domini Regis tractatu et auisamento diligenti visum est eis quod auxilium de domino Rege prefato Iohanni de Molyns in hoc casu concedendum est.   Ideo idem Iohannes de Molyns habeat auxilium de domino Rege etc. (a day is given them) Et interim loquendum est cum domino Rege. Ad quem diem venerunt . . . Et quia cancellarius occupatus fuit circa alia negocia domini Regis, dictum est partibus quod sint hic in Curia de die in diem etc. (Finally, on the following Monday, in the presence of the parties) Cancellarius recitauit totum negocium predictum et dixit quod die dominica proximo precedenti dominus Rex oretenus distincte precepit eidem Cancellario quod in negocio predicto procederet et partibus predictis iusticiam faceret ; non expectato aliquo Waranto sub priuato sigillo ipsius domini Regis. et idem dominus Rex adiecit quod dictum suum plus sufficere debet pro Waranto quam breue sub priuato sigillo suo. per quod dictum est eidem Iohanni de Molyns quod respondeat etc. (He says that a day had been given) vt interim dominus Rex super hiis consuleretur et ex quo ante diem illum dictus dominus Rex non fuit consultus nec predictus heres fuit prosecutus versus ipsum dominum Regem in* negocio* predicto* de habendo Warantum sub magno sigillo vel priuato sigillo Regis de procedendo etc., (he understands that the parties) sunt sine die . . . Et Cancellarius dicit (that they were adjourned from day to day ; he is ordered to answer over.   After more adjournments one of them,) 'quia Cancellarius occupatus fuit circa negocia Regis in parliamento suo apud Westmonasterium ad eundem diem conuocato', issue is joined and the case is sent to the king's bench, where, finally, the charter is revoked.[1]

---

[1] At the end of m. 131 11 d. is the remark : ' plus de isto placito in quodam rotulo sequenti' and below is the following very unusual note : 'Set in Anno domini 1604 cum hoc Recordum abbreviaui non patet vbi hic Rotulus est nec aliquod signum vbi consui deberet de quo miror multum. Arth. Agarde.'

INDEX

The Appendix of Documents is not included in this Index